Prehistory of Australia

Prehistory of Australia

John Mulvaney &
Johan Kamminga

SMITHSONIAN INSTITUTION PRESS
WASHINGTON AND LONDON

Published in 1999 in the United States of America
by the Smithsonian Institution Press
in association with Allen & Unwin Pty Ltd
9 Atchison Street, St Leonards NSW 1590 Australia

Library of Congress Cataloging-in-Publication Data
Mulvaney, Derek John.

Prehistory of Australia / John Mulvaney & Johan Kamminga.

p.   cm.

Includes bibliographical references.

ISBN 1-56098-804-5 (alk. paper)

1. Australian aborigines—Antiquities. 2. Australia—Antiquities. I.
Kamminga, Johan. II. Title.

GN875.A8M85   1999

994.01—dc21   99-21564

National Library of Australia Cataloguing-in-Publication Data available

Set in 10.75/13 pt Adobe Caslon by Bookhouse, Sydney
Printed by South Wind Productions, Singapore
Manufactured in Australia, not at government expense

06 05 04 03 02 01 00 99   5 4 3 2 1

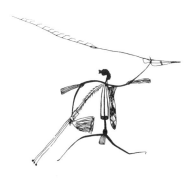

Contents

Figures and illustrations

COLOUR PLATES

Maps

Preface

When Mulvaney's *The prehistory of Australia* first appeared in 1969, so little was known about Aboriginal origins and cultural development that accounts were necessarily sketchy and focused on stone tools. By the time the second edition appeared in 1975, several PhD theses on Australian prehistory had been completed at three universities and recent graduates were publishing their findings internationally. The pace of discovery was such that a short addendum had to be included after the manuscript was with the publisher. We accept that our interpretations may be rejected by other archaeologists, or made erroneous by the passage of time. That reflects the nature of this stimulating discipline, when fieldwork may suddenly change explanations of the past.

This book was written chiefly during 1995–97. While we have made substantial changes in content, we decided to maintain the orientation and much of the structure of the earlier books written by Mulvaney as sole author. The hazards of publishing a review of a rapidly expanding subject are manifest. To update descriptive content after two decades is a large but relatively straightforward task, but to give an adequate coverage of the alternative perspectives and debates is far more difficult. Indeed, our book is a personal appraisal of Australian prehistory because there can be no single version. In particular, views differ widely about when people first arrived on the continent, and about the nature and timing of social and cultural changes.

While many issues currently debated in Australian archaeology are the same as those of twenty years ago—the timing of first human settlement, colonisation of the arid zone, megafauna extinctions, human biology—the discipline has expanded and diversified practically beyond recognition. The book does not stand alone as an introduction to Australian prehistory—it remains primarily a descriptive account of archaeological discoveries, though we deal also with relevant evidence from other disciplines bearing upon the reconstruction of Australian prehistory. Because of the vast dimensions of space and time involved, in future years it is likely that detailed regional studies will replace continental syntheses. Our discussions about chronometric dating methods and the dates of archaeological sites and artefacts are technical but, as the recent controversy about the dating of Jinmium and claims respecting early arrival of people in Australia have shown, reliable dates are crucial for constructing a credible prehistory.

We do not dwell on methods in Australian archaeology, nor explore in detail the important role of theory in interpreting archaeological data. Post-modernism in the humanities has given birth to 'post-processual archaeology', which encourages a diversity of viewpoints where truth is either relative or subject to abstract theorising. Other current perspectives include 'post-colonial archaeology' and 'feminist archaeology'. There is also a growing interest in the politics of archaeology and prehistoric inference. For readers interested in knowing more about the applications of method and theory in Australian archaeology, we recommend the books *Remains to be seen* by David Frankel and *Continent of hunter-gatherers* by Harry Lourandos. The latter examines the evidence for widespread social and economic changes during the last few thousand years based on the theoretical concept of 'intensification'. Forthcoming are *Australian archaeology: an introduction* by Claire Smith, and *Archaeology, indigenous peoples and cultural heritage* by Sarah Colley, both to be published by Allen & Unwin. Readers who wish to know more about indigenous Australian culture and society should refer to the *Encyclopaedia of Aboriginal Australia* edited by David Horton.

STRUCTURE OF THIS BOOK

We briefly describe present and past environmental contexts, and aspects of Aboriginal culture pertinent to the interpretation of the archaeological record. We also maintain a partly historical approach in presenting ideas and interpretations that have not stood the test of time but are still accepted by some readers as current or are essential as background context. Discussions about archaeological sites in Mulvaney's earlier editions are broadened into regional prehistories, though they remain outlines. We look at the prehistory of New Guinea until the time of its physical separation from the Australian continent about 8000–9000 years ago. Because of their potential as a bridge or barrier to contacts, the Torres Strait islands have been given more space, though little demonstrated prehistory exists. Rock art research has flourished over the past two decades, reflected in the influential specialist journal *Australian Rock Art Research (AURA)* edited by Robert Bednarik.

TERMINOLOGY

Mulvaney's earlier editions were intended for a wide range of readers, both in Australia and overseas. We assume that the current readership is even more varied, and as far as possible have avoided the use of specialist scientific language.

The book presents 'prehistory' in the sense that it concerns events and societies before records were written down. This is a convention worldwide, and it does not imply that societies without writing were inferior. Oral traditions are referred to where possible. A person who undertakes field surveys or excavations and writes reports on them is known as an archaeologist, but this book is not only an archaeology of Australia. The most famous synthesiser of the European past was an Australian, V. Gordon Childe, who wrote prehistory: that is, he synthesised the evidence for European societies during times before writing. This is the sense in which we are writing prehistory, not archaeology.

The title of our book may attract criticism as implying that the Aboriginal past is somehow marginal to 'real' history. In 1988 a meeting of the Australian Institute of Aboriginal Studies resolved that it would use the term 'history' in referring to the Aboriginal past before written records. Despite this, the term 'prehistory' is embedded in archaeological writings in Australia and overseas, though it is being displaced by the more general (and less accurate) terms 'archaeology' and, less commonly, 'pre-contact archaeology'. We understand the study of history to rely substantially on documentary (and recorded oral) evidence of events, and prehistory to be reconstruction from many kinds of evidence, especially archaeological data. While these two scholarly disciplines are closely linked, their methodologies are quite different, and their accounts of the human past are framed within vastly different time-scales and levels of resolution—most events in a history are not in focus in a prehistory.

Neither author has indigenous Australian ancestry and our approach to Australian prehistory is based on the tenets and practice of Western science and philosophy. There is the potential conflict between the pragmatism of Western science and the timeless concept of the Dreaming, between human evolutionary theory and belief in a multitude of indigenous creations. Traditionally oriented Aboriginal people believe that their founding ancestors did not come to Australia from Southeast Asia, but were created by supernatural beings within the land itself, and that existing natural features in the landscape testify to Dreaming creations. Paraphrasing the Gospel of St John, the first Australians may point to such sites as symbolising 'before the white man was I am'. These different intellectual viewpoints are crucial elements in contemporary life, but they should not prevent the sincere and documented presentation of one of these explanations of the past.

Throughout we have referred to prehistoric Australians as Aborigines, always capitalised. The term 'Aboriginal people' or 'indigenous people' is used frequently today in reference to contemporary communities, including people of variously mixed ancestry. For the 500 or more tribal groupings and the hundreds of human generations existing before 1788 it is not appropriate to apply the names preferred by different contemporary regional populations, such as Kooris, Murrays, Nyungars, and so on. Such names are meaningful to those regional groupings, but they refer to populations formed since 1788, and they also mean less to people in more traditionally oriented regions. The spellings of names of Aboriginal tribes are adopted from the *Encyclopaedia of Aboriginal Australia*. References to Macassans are about the men of the trepanging fleets which came mainly from southern Sulawesi. Many of them belonged to the Bugis ethnic group.

SOURCES

Although the number of references cited in this book exceeds the bibliography of Mulvaney's previous editions, it is not exhaustive. Except when there is a need to refer to a specific work or author, we list those recent sources which provide more complete bibliographic guidance or critical evaluation.

ACKNOWLEDGMENTS

John Iremonger, then the director of Melbourne University Press, convinced John Mulvaney of the need for a new book, and facilitated partnership with Jo Kamminga with whom Mulvaney first collaborated in 1973, during the Alligator Rivers Region Environmental Fact-Finding Study. We are indebted to friends and colleagues who read sections of drafts and offered critical comment: included are Adi Taha, Harry Allen, Jim Allen, Jim Bowler, Richard Cosgrove, Bruno David, Bob Dixon, Tamsin Donaldson, Mike Barbetti, John Clegg, Noelene Cole, Sarah Colley, Joe Dortch, Neale Draper, Judy Furby, Mick Fleming, David Frankel, Stephanie Garling, Denise Gaughwin, Beth Gott, Colin Groves, Peter Harris, Lesley Head, Geoff Hope, David Horton, Bernard Huchet, Ian Keen, Bob Kirk, Jo McDonald, Jeff Marck, Lys Marck, John Marshall, Kerry Navin, Alan Newsome, Sue O'Connor, Kelvin Officer, Colin Pardoe, Mike Rowland, Robin Sim, Nigel Spooner, Glenn Summerhayes, Paul Taçon, Nick Thieberger, Grahame Walsh, Ian Walters, Alan Watchman, Elizabeth Williams and Richard Wright. Many of them also provided us with their unpublished data. Our debt is considerable to those who provided us with valuable information or assisted in other ways in preparing this or earlier editions of the book. We thank Jon Altman, Paul Augustinus, Peter Bindon, Paul Black, Wilma Blom, John Calaby, George Chaloupka, John Chappell, Peter Clark, Barry Cundy, Bruno David, Peter Dowling, Robert Edwards, Nicholas Evans, Richard Fullagar, Stephanie Garling, Jack Golson, Beth Gott, Mervyn Griffiths, John Head, Peter Hiscock, Rhys Jones, Brian Lees, Isabel McBryde, Campbell Macknight, Vincent Megaw, Mike Morwood, Mary-Jane Mountain, Ken Mulvaney, Henry Nix, Robert Paton, Graeme Pretty, Peter Roy, Moya Smith, Penny Taylor, Jerry Van Tets and Graeme Ward. We alone are responsible for errors of fact and interpretation and deficiencies in scope or emphasis.

The Institute of Aboriginal and Torres Strait Islander Studies provided Jo Kamminga with the facilities to work on this revision. John Mulvaney is grateful to the Australian Academy of the Humanities for its facilities and the assistance of Yvonne Gentry, Caren Florence and Amanda Jacobsen. The Department of

Geography, the Faculties, Australian National University, prepared many of the line drawings, for which we particularly acknowledge the co-operation and artistry of Kevin Cowan and Val Lyon.

JOHN MULVANEY & JO KAMMINGA
JULY 1998

Note: The images that appear in the margins throughout the book represent a small sample of the richness and variety of Aboriginal rock art.

The past uncovered and its ownership

1

Australia became an island continent when it separated from the southern super-continent of Gondwanaland, some 80 million years before the emergence of humanity. The first Australians must have arrived by sea. They almost certainly came from Sundaland, the Pleistocene (Ice Age) subcontinent of Southeast Asia, via the islands in between the two great landmasses. The only terrestrial placental mammals to precede humans were bats and rodents, the latter presumably clinging to floating vegetation or logs. The epic journey to Australia stands as the earliest evidence of sea voyaging by modern humans.

The discovery of Australia's remote human past has proved one of the most exciting and challenging episodes in unveiling global prehistory. Challenging, because discoveries have followed so rapidly, yet the time-scale revealed for continental colonisation is so immense. During the 1950s it was suspected that people occupied Australia earlier than 10,000 years ago, during the last Ice Age—but it was only in 1962 that radiocarbon dates from a Queensland excavation exceeded 10,000 years, the conventional terminal date then accepted for the commencement of the Holocene (post-glacial) period.

The pace of the discovery, excavation and dating of sites accelerated. The earliest known occupation exceeded 20,000 years ago by 1965; in 1969 it approximated 30,000 years, and in 1973 it had stretched to 40,000 years. Such antiquity then exceeded the colonisation of the American continents (as shown by dated occupation) by at least twenty millennia.

Imagine the exhilarating impact upon the comprehension of Australia's human past! Until then, four centuries sufficed for the European contact period, recorded in fragmentary written records until Sydney's settlement in 1788. Given even 40,000 years of human existence, time since 1788 only amounts to 0.5 per cent of that period. Today the proportion may have dwindled further, because new dating techniques hint at 60,000 years or more since people first stepped ashore; but they remain hints yet to be authenticated.

Our chief concern is to sketch the evidence for Australia's story before Europeans, so our sources are essentially archaeological and draw upon many scientific disciplines. Nowhere in the world do written records exceed some 5000 years (one-eighth of our period), and the first fleeting written observations relating to Australia's inhabitants were made in AD 1606. For Aboriginal people, their story is contained in oral traditions handed on by their elders, they believe, since Dreaming times. Each clan has its traditions, and within recent years numbers of them have been written down and published. We emphasise that those traditions are not necessarily in contradiction with our story, yet they relate to a different intellectual tradition, where time and concepts of evidence are so different that, as explained in the preface, we make no attempt to reconcile these two approaches to the past.

The divergence between these two intellectual approaches may not be as great as some Aboriginal people believe, however. This conclusion emerges from the implications of many Dreaming creation activities. The network of Dreaming tracks which criss-cross this continent records the travels of ancestral beings, yet no single significant ceremonial place existed in isolation. On northern shores, even the direction from which powerful Dreaming beings travelled is revealing, because some came from across the sea to Arnhem Land, or arrived in Cape York from the north. In other words, these ancestral beings travelled from beyond the shores and followed the Dreaming pathways to distant creation places. That is, in essence, what archaeologists claim—the Aboriginal past was not static, there are links overseas, and traditions changed across time and place. Archaeologists provide a chronology and a record of Aboriginal settlement which has been cited in contemporary land rights claims.

Our synthesis is constructed from the findings of archaeology and many other academic or scientific fields: prehistoric archaeology, which is about the era prior to British colonisation; and historical archaeology, a fast-growing field concerned with the colonial era and its relics and places, including Aboriginal settlements. Australian archaeologists collaborate with specialists in many other fields, such as ecology, earth sciences, human biology, anthropology and linguistics. They employ a wide variety of scientific methods to analyse the results of surveys and excavations. With the growth of prehistoric archaeology, more highly specialised interdisciplinary fields have developed, such as ethnoarchaeology, the study of contemporary activities and behaviour to help interpret archaeological finds, and taphonomy, which investigates how archaeological sites and relics are formed and preserved.

ETHNOGRAPHIC ANALOGY

A major asset for reconstructing Australia's human past is the relative wealth of the historical and ethnographic records, including written and oral accounts of traditional society and items of material culture held by museums. Although many of these records provide only a sketch of Aboriginal society and culture in particular regions, some rank among the world's more illuminating accounts of the ways in which hunter-gatherer societies organised their lives. British settlers' reminiscences, explorers' journals, and even personal letters are vital primary sources of information, but such records are difficult to interpret and they are not always accurate. The deserts and Arnhem Land experienced colonial control later, so the impact on traditional culture was more gradual; traditional social and economic ways continue. Indeed, some groups of people in the Western Desert lived entirely traditional lives until the 1960s. Not surprisingly, archaeologists tend to rely on the more detailed ethnography from these regions, which may bias interpretations of economic and social features towards those of the arid region, while societies in the temperate southeastern region are underestimated. Despite the catastrophic impact of British colonisation, contemporary Aboriginal oral histories and the rich holdings of museums and art galleries are invaluable records.

Archaeologists often use historical records as a starting-point in interpreting their findings. Recent prehistoric artefacts and archaeological patterns identified by the historical method called the 'Direct Historical Approach' often provide convincing comparisons or explanations. For example, the fishing spear used by Aborigines of the Sydney region at the time of British settlement had three or four small bone prongs, and two of these spears have been preserved in museum collections. Comparable bone points have been recovered from shell and other occupation debris (called middens) dating to within the last 2000 years and are widely recognised as prehistoric examples of spear prongs. The same applies to a stone adze (chisel) flake widely used in the arid zone until the present century, which has a similar antiquity. Since the Direct Historical Approach deals with observations made about the direct descendants of the people whose archaeological remains are being interpreted, its application is limited in time and space.

Although many interpretations based on analogy with historical observations are plausible and constructive, we cannot assume stable continuity in lifestyle between recent prehistoric times and the 'ethnographic present'. Such an assumption can constrain or mislead. The problem is not that the historical picture is irrelevant—clearly it is fundamental—but that the principles for evaluating historical sources are sometimes not adequately applied. In some regions British colonial influences changed aspects of Aboriginal culture and lifestyles even before explorers or settlers arrived. For instance, over most of southeastern Australia all historical observations were made on the survivors of Aboriginal populations that had already been decimated by smallpox. The archaeological record itself reveals change, and the documentary record of Aboriginal Australia recorded during the last 200 years cannot simply be projected back uncritically into remote prehistory. Environmental and other circumstances in the past also differed from those in early colonial times, while social customs and behaviour may also have been different. Consequently, to argue that evidence from AD 1800 applies equally in 1800 BC requires caution. However, the choices available to hunting, gathering and collecting societies display certain similarities, so it is not unreasonable to cautiously take the 'ethnographic present' as a guide to interpreting the past.

HERITAGE PRESERVATION

A growing national maturity led to movements during the 1960s to preserve Australia's heritage across a wide spectrum. In 1965 the Australian Conservation Foundation was established, while in the same year the Australian Council of National Trusts adopted a collaborative approach to preserving the built heritage. This was also the year in which the first state legislation (South Australia) was passed to protect Aboriginal places. Although state laws were seldom fully implemented and most instrumentalities were poorly staffed, by 1975 each state had passed legislation to protect Aboriginal sites.

The landmark event was the 1973–75 Hope Inquiry into the National Estate, which resulted in the creation of the Australian Heritage Commission in 1976. It has compiled a Register of the National Estate with the objective of coordinating and inculcating better conservation practices. Many hundreds of places on the Register are Aboriginal. It is significant that three of the registered properties have been classified as possessing World Heritage status, partly for their global archaeological importance. These are Kakadu, Southwest Tasmania and the Willandra Lakes region. Archaeological research has played a prominent role in these developments. Uluru is another World Heritage place with deep Aboriginal significance.

The move to protect archaeological sites by law came at a time when environmental activists were making similar gains. Trained archaeologists were recruited into government service to administer the new heritage laws. While museums and universities have experi-enced growth, it is the applied field of cultural heritage management, and what is loosely termed 'consulting archaeology', that provides the first employment for many graduates choosing to continue profes-sionally. Consulting archaeology had its beginnings in the large-area field projects of the early 1970s, such as the survey by F. L. Virili of rock engravings at Dampier on the Pilbara coast, and the Alligator Rivers Survey in which both authors were involved. From the 1980s a variety of state and federal legislation requires environmental impact statements for all proposed large development projects and also many small ones. Such assessments usually include field surveys for Abor-iginal sites. Many consultant archaeologists now belong to the Australian Association of Consulting Archaeologists (ACCA) and others are involved on a professional basis as members of Australia ICOMOS, the local affiliate of the International Council of Monu-ments and Sites, a body given responsibility by the World Heritage Convention (1972) for giving arm's length advice to the World Her-itage Committee on the inscription of Australian sites. Australia ICOMOS has developed a widely respected code of cultural conser-vation practice, The Burra Charter. The Australian Archaeological Association (AAA) was founded in 1975 and its journal *Australian*

Archaeology now informs some hundreds of members. Both the ACCA and AAA have codes of ethics to which members subscribe.

There is a continuing debate among archaeologists about the academic research value of fieldwork conducted for environmental impact assessments and cultural conservation studies, and the relatively few publications to result from well financed projects. Nonetheless, some magnificent field opportunities are generated by consulting projects. Whereas the duration of research excavations in Australia has diminished over the years, the amount of field survey work has risen dramatically. Nowadays, many more archaeologists are working as consultants on environmental and heritage issues than are employed in universities and museums. Consultant archaeologists often undertake intensive field surveys of small areas subject to planned development. While much of this work is routine, sometimes there is an unexpected discovery. With each consultancy report, the amount of information about a region's prehistory accumulates and it is this growth that should provide much of the information for future researchers. However, consultancy reports frequently remain unpublished and access is limited. This trend underlines the importance of Site Registers held by state authorities as sources of basic data.

INDIGENOUS PEOPLE AND ARCHAEOLOGY

Aboriginal involvement and control over archaeological fieldwork began in the early 1970s with demands that excavation be approved by traditional landowners. This was a time of drastic reappraisal of government policy towards Aborigines, with the dawn of an assertive Aboriginal nationalism, and with the struggle for legislative recognition of Aboriginal land rights that continues to the present day. Aboriginal people moved into fields of higher education and public administration. Previously, many sites were excavated in ignorance of Aboriginal wishes, and museums displayed artefacts never intended by their owners for public gaze. When Mulvaney began fieldwork, no state permits were needed, and there was no obligation to deposit finds in a public repository. In certain regions, including Arnhem Land, permission to enter an area was first obtained from a local mission; only then was a permit provided by the government administration. Local Aboriginal communities were never consulted.

Archaeologists played a leading role in campaigning for legislation to protect Aboriginal places and material relics. Also, archaeology has given material and scientific support for Aboriginal claims of deep

Members of the northern Queensland Djungan community visiting the Ngarrabull-gan excavation in 1993 during a Ranger training programme coordinated by the Kuku Djungan Aboriginal Corporation: From left, Ross Craig, Malcolm Grainer, John B. Grainer Jnr and archæologist Roger Cribb. (Bruno David)

antiquity, and to a people claiming a share in the land it seems relevant that British occupation of the continent since Captain Cook is less than one per cent of the total period of known human settlement. Aboriginal people assert that both their land and the interpretation of their culture and history have been appropriated by white Australians. They see Australian prehistory as their past, their heritage, and therefore theirs to do with as they wish, and to share with others only on their own terms.

The wheel has turned, and Aboriginal Australians today exert greater control over their archaeological heritage than Native Americans hold over theirs. Federal and all state heritage organisations currently have a policy of consultation with Aboriginal communities about indigenous heritage issues. While there are still instances of mutual resentment and distrust as Aboriginal people gain effective control over their history and heritage, there is also increasing collaboration with archaeologists and movement towards greater mutual understanding. An unfortunate outcome to a significant archaeological project in southwestern Tasmania, when the law was used to recover prematurely archaeological materials under investigation, represents an incalculable cultural catastrophe, leaving both archaeologists and Aboriginal people the losers.

It was during the early 1970s that Aboriginal people first participated in archaeological fieldwork, in a region now the heartland of Kakadu National Park. The need to provide archaeological training for indigenous people was first argued by Harry Allen, now teaching at Auckland University, who incorporated training in the excavation of a large rockshelter in Kakadu. Such involvement in survey and excavation is now the norm. A code of ethics acknowledging Aboriginal ownership of their prehistoric heritage was adopted by the Australian Archaeological Association and each year Aboriginal delegates attend its conferences. Not only are indigenous communities involved in archaeological fieldwork and vigilant in protecting prehistoric sites, but a number of Aboriginal people now practise as professional archaeologists.

RETURN OF HUMAN REMAINS

The evolving struggle for Aboriginal control of their heritage in the 1980s found its sharpest focus on the issue of ownership and disposal of human remains held in museum collections. Archaeologists gave early support to the policy of repatriation to Aboriginal communities of remains of people who lived only a few generations ago. We believe that the first repatriation of human remains was in 1973 when the Northern Territory Museum reinterred a bundle burial taken from its ossuary in rugged country now within Kakadu National Park.

Human bones are a fundamental part of humanity's biological and archaeological record, and some scientists reacted strongly to the potential loss of very ancient human remains, including those of Pleistocene age. The public debate that ensued in Australia and overseas has not been entirely harmonious. The unconditional repatriation of remains hundreds of generations old raises conflicting issues for

Aboriginal people, such as concepts of common humanity and the obligation this imposes, and also the needs of future indigenous generations to know their remote past.

The case for free scientific inquiry has been put by Mulvaney. He argues that the claim of ownership and control is a form of reverse cultural imperialism; that it threatens the preservation of finite sources of information about Australia before 1788; that it places free intellectual inquiry in jeopardy, now and in the future; and that, most importantly, future Aboriginal societies will be deprived of crucial genetic and cultural information. Essentially, Mulvaney fears the emergence in Australia of a brand of intellectual totalitarianism to replace the equally deplorable previous assumptions of white supremacy. Rather than destruction of the potential cultural and scientific data through reburial, he urges custodianship in well-constructed keeping-places, controlled by relevant Aboriginal communities. Another perspective within the profession is offered by the palaeoanthropologist Colin Pardoe, who accepts Aboriginal ownership of their ancestors' remains and whose fieldwork is collaborative and often requested by local Aboriginal communities. Facilitating reburial is now part of Pardoe's research practice, though he mourns the loss of data, research potential, and the scientific standard of replicability of results by restudy of the original material.

Though the wisdom of this decision for all future Australians worries some people, the members of the Australian Archaeological Association have judged that the ethical considerations as presented by Aboriginal people far outweigh actual and potential losses of scientific values. There are now policies in all public museums in Australia governing the acquisition, curation, and return to Aboriginal communities of prehistoric human remains. Three notable collections returned are the Crowther Collection formerly held in the Museum of Tasmania; the Murray Black Collection, curated initially by the Department of Anatomy, University of Melbourne and later by the Museum of Victoria; and the Kow Swamp human remains, also held by that museum. Although the circumstances in which the Tasmanian burials were disinterred was an appalling episode in 'scientific' history and has never been defended, the reinterment of the Murray Black and Kow Swamp collections (see Chapter 10) was preceded by appeals for special consideration, which proved unsuccessful. George Murray Black was a Gippsland grazier who from the 1930s to 1951 acquired more than 800 skeletons, mostly incomplete, from sites between Renmark and Swan Hill on the Murray River.

A proportion of the remains dated to at least 10,000 years ago, and various studies of the collection had already made major contributions to the understanding of human biological evolution, disease, diet and cultural practices during ancient times. The loss of the Kow Swamp remains, in particular, is profound. Not all circumstances are the same, and some Aboriginal communities, while retaining control, have decided prudently that human remains from their regions should be lodged in temporary keeping-places within museums or other public facilities.

It needs to be understood that natural processes of erosion or industrial and housing 'development', rather than archaeologists, cause most disturbance to prehistoric human remains. It is now usual for archaeologists to be commissioned at the request of a community to salvage and rebury these exposed remains. The extent and significance of Aboriginal cemeteries at Robinvale and Lake Benanee, on the Murray River (see Chapter 10), were recognised only after professional fieldwork was requested and supported by the Murray Valley Aboriginal Co-operative to assess disturbance caused by sand quarrying. It is emphasised that, although consultation and interaction by archaeologists with local communities is essential, it would prove unfortunate if field research was restricted to projects requested by such communities. Many significant issues involve research across different regions and their concepts and data collection in the long term benefit Aboriginal society and non-Aboriginal understanding, but in the short term many mean little to an individual community.

The Aboriginal concept of the timeless creations of the Dreaming poses no barrier to the acceptance of archaeological calendars stretching through remote antiquity. In this it differs from Christian fundamentalist belief, which challenges early dates and dismisses archaeology as tainted with 'evolution'. Consequently, radiocarbon dates for archaeological sites, particularly at Lake Mungo, immediately became incorporated into Aboriginal concepts of history. The statement that 'Aborigines have lived in this land for X thousand years' became part of Aboriginal protest. However, Aboriginal creation beliefs assume a virtual biological stability for people, plants and animals, conflicting with Western biological evolutionary theory and environmental evidence. This surely affects Aboriginal attitudes to archaeological explanation of human origins on this continent. Recent archaeological discoveries also coincide with the vogue for New Age dogmas and Christian fundamentalism, so that such beliefs possibly reinforce community opposition to evolutionary biology and research on human remains.

AUSTRALIAN ARCHAEOLOGY

Australian 'dirt archaeology' is as old as British settlement: indeed, Governor Phillip was its first antiquarian excavator. One of the earliest British colonists to identify the stratified depositional sequence at an Aboriginal site was the pastoralist James Dawson, who dug into a Victorian midden. The honour of writing the first realistic excavation reports belongs to Robert Etheridge, who had dug a rockshelter near Sydney in 1891. At about the same time, E. J. Statham, a local historian at Ballina, New South Wales, cut a section through a shell mound in the Ballina estuary. Statham drew upon descriptions of middens excavated in Denmark, calculating that the Ballina mound contained almost 12,000 cubic metres of oyster shell, which he estimated had required 1800 years to accumulate. The British archaeologist Geoff Bailey determined a similar age for a midden he excavated at Ballina in the 1970s.

The full potential of controlled excavation was first demonstrated in 1929, when Herbert Hale, later director of the South Australia Museum, and Norman B. Tindale, its curator of anthropology, excavated at Devon Downs Rockshelter, in the limestone cliffs of South Australia's lower Murray River. Hale and Tindale completed Australia's classic excavation by promptly publishing a systematic report, which utilised the research of scientists in other fields, envisaged the possibility of environmental changes since the arrival of humans, and introduced the concept of archaeological 'culture' to Australian prehistoric studies. Devon Downs was a few kilometres downstream from Moorunde, where Edward J. Eyre served as magistrate and Aboriginal Protector between 1841 and 1844. Eyre's detailed account of the Aboriginal inhabitants provided these and all subsequent excavators with a basic regional ethnology.

Australian prehistorians are indebted to Tindale for demonstrating the reality of ecological and cultural changes within Australia. The thinking of that day was tinged with an isolationist dogmatism, and Tindale's initiative provided new perspectives for local scholarship and an impetus for further research on Australian prehistory. Not many of Tindale's contemporaries appreciated these new possibilities. Most of them would have applauded the sentiments expressed by

R. W. Pulleine in 1928, only a year before the Devon Downs expedition. 'In all our stations', he pronounced with assurance in his presidential address on the Tasmanians to an anthropological congress, 'there is a uniformity of culture only modified by the availability of different materials for manufacture...It is to be feared that excavation would be in vain, as everything points to the conclusion that they were an unchanging people, living in an unchanging environment.' Even in 1949, the prominent Melbourne stone tool collector, S. R. Mitchell, dismissed the Devon Downs results in two sentences in his authoritative book *Stone-Age craftsmen*. Mitchell asserted that prehistoric Australian stone tools represented a single industry and that all the different tool types were in use up to the time of British occupation. Such doctrines rendered fieldwork futile because many shared the opinion that the Aborigines were relatively recent arrivals within Australia, so collectors neither anticipated nor searched for stratified deposits.

It is not surprising that the first to publicise the Devon Downs discoveries overseas was an outsider—the American anthropologist D. S. Davidson. He had dug a site in the Northern Territory, and he realised that the Murray River excavation was 'proof that archaeology in Australia holds tremendous possibilities for future research'. Davidson's 1935 prediction has been shown correct. Yet it was not until the 1960s that any Australian museum or university appointed a staff member whose official designation was archaeologist or prehistorian.

Perhaps the greatest discouragement to the integration of archaeology or material culture studies in Australian tertiary education was A. R. Radcliffe-Brown's tenure of the Sydney University Chair of Anthropology (1926–31), synchronous with the fieldwork of D. S. Davidson, and Hale and Tindale. The Great Depression ended all hopes that further departments of anthropology would be established in Australian universities. Radcliffe-Brown laid some of the foundations for the study of social structure, and his work is a landmark in the history of social anthropology. Yet he promoted doctrines which negated prehistory as a fruitful field of academic study. In a scathing review of one of Davidson's more important works, Radcliffe-Brown asserted in 1930 that anthropology 'will make little progress until we abandon these attempts at conjectural reconstructions of a past about which we can obtain no direct knowledge in favour of a systematic study of the culture as it exists in the present'. It was 30 years before his former department appointed its first lecturer in prehistory.

F. D. McCarthy, one of the pioneers of prehistoric research in Australia, studying rock engravings at Mount Cameron West, Tasmania, 1968. (Robert Edwards)

In 1957 Tindale published his personal appraisal of Australian pre-history. It drew upon a lifetime of knowledge of Aboriginal culture, one major and several minor excavations, and four radiocarbon dates. A year later F. D. McCarthy, a curator at the Australian Museum in Sydney, produced a conflicting synthesis based upon his museum studies of stone artefacts and his fieldwork, chiefly in New South Wales. In Victoria, the pioneer geomorphologist Edmund Gill had written a series of papers which introduced geomorphological and environmental elements into the human past, particularly in his study of traces of early human occupation in the Keilor region, just outside Melbourne. By 1957, Gill also had four radiocarbon dates upon which to hinge his arguments. However, his claims for Pleistocene evidence of human presence then lacked the definitive stratigraphic and cul-tural associations. Tindale, McCarthy and Gill were the outstanding pioneers of prehistoric research in Australia, setting the stage for subsequent professionalism based on university research and teaching. All were museum staff but none was formally a curator of archaeology, and all were inadequately funded for their research. Mulvaney commenced archaeological fieldwork in 1956, and as a lecturer in history at the University of Melbourne introduced a history honours option in 1957. This course was the only prehistory of the Pacific region taught in Australian universities.

WIDENING HORIZONS

The 1960s represent a watershed in Australian prehistoric research. The first generation of professional archaeologists was appointed to Australian universities in the first half of the 1960s, at the beginning of rapid expansion in academia. At that time Australia did not have an established profession of archaeology and there was only one museum curator in 1961 who had formal training as an archaeologist. As Cambridge University was one of the few at that period concerned with regions beyond Europe and Africa, most of these new appointees were from Cambridge. They established a Cambridge intellectual imperium that even to this day is the prime mover of Australian prehistoric archaeology. This imperium has been known by other names—the 'Cambridge connection', 'Cambridge in the bush' and, darkly, the 'Cambridge mafia'. However we judge this era, now drawing to a close, whether as academic colonialism and professional inbreeding or the transplant to the Antipodes of a vigorous intellectual tradition, the substantial contribution these scholars have made cannot be belittled. Other orientations were injected into this intellectual mainstream by the American scholars Richard Gould and Brian Hayden, who independently undertook ethnoarchaeological research in the Western Desert. Meanwhile, outside the system was Alexander Gallus, an émigré from Hungary with a considerable reputation in Central European archaeology. His recognition of art and archaeology at Koonalda Cave and his work at Keilor were early catalysts for research.

So little Australian prehistory was known in the 1960s that the predominant research strategy was to select sites in different regions that had deep cultural deposits to provide stratigraphic sequences and radiocarbon dates; the main analytical method was detailed study of stone artefacts. These were times unconstrained by government regulation or consultation with Aboriginal people—the object of fieldwork was to fill blank areas on the archaeological map, which was for the most part profoundly empty. The main theme of Cambridge prehistoric studies was 'man and environment', nurtured by the teachings of Grahame Clark and Eric Higgs; in keeping with the times, this is now called environmental archaeology or prehistoric human ecology. This direction has held firm, and since the 1960s there has been continuing reliance on ecological concepts in framing prehistory, but a marked decline of interest in stone artefacts.

By the mid-1960s the first graduates in prehistoric archaeology from the University of Sydney were engaged in doctoral research at the Australian National University in Canberra, and some museums had appointed staff archaeologists. As an outcome of a conference held in 1961, the Australian government created the Australian Institute of Aboriginal Studies (the name now recast, with the acronym AIATSIS, to identify the Torres Strait islands as a separate entity), which supported much of the field research in the 1960s and 1970s. By 1975 there were perhaps 50 or so trained prehistorians in the country and the subject was being taught at several universities. Whereas in 1961 Mulvaney could assemble only seventeen radiocarbon dates for his review of Australian prehistory, by 1975 there were more than 150. The broad-brush field projects born in that era provided enough data for the first edition of *The prehistory of Australia* to be written in 1969; results were coming so fast that there had to be an addendum summarising the latest discoveries. When the second edition was prepared during 1973, it required a complete recasting of the book to take new discoveries and ideas into account.

AUSTRALIAN ARCHAEOLOGY IN THE 1990S

Events since the 1960s have set in train fundamental changes in the profession of archaeology and in the structure of the discipline. Numerous universities now teach Australian prehistory or some aspect of it, and a large body of graduate students ensures diversity of research interests. While there is no single direction in contemporary research, many of the issues that engendered debate among prehistorians during the 1960s are still on the agenda, for there have been no easy answers. One is the timing of the first arrival of humans on the continent. Other major themes concern human impacts on the environment, the extinction of many large species of marsupials, and the antiquity and interpretation of art. Because of its interdisciplinary nature and its interpretations of changing data, prehistory is an attractive and exciting study for undergraduates.

Advances have occurred in methodology, with the advent of new techniques for analysing excavated materials. One such development has been the identification of microscopic use-wear and residues, which has added a new dimension to technological studies and reconstruction of prehistoric activities; its full potential has yet to be realised. Rock art is the subject of intensive study by specialists, offering insight into indigenous creativity and cognition. In the area of archaeological theory, the concept of 'intensification', promoted by Harry Lourandos as an explanation for the emergence of the complex hunter-gatherer societies observed ethnographically in Australia, produced prolonged debate. In a neo-Marxist frame Lourandos argued that socio-economic factors—rather than environmental or ecological factors—underlie an increase in economic or subsistence productivity and efficiency over the last 4000–5000 years, and that this phenomenon is apparent in the archaeological record. The impact of his formulation on archaeological interpretation and research directions has been considerable, though opinion remains sharply divided. There is now a considerable amount of written discussion about 'intensification' and the concept remains topical.

Studies on gender in the archaeological record and feminist approaches to prehistory have provoked interest, following four 'Women in Archaeology' conferences since the late 1980s. Some studies identify women's activities represented in the archaeological record, mostly using ethnographic accounts of male and female roles in traditional Aboriginal society. Changes in the pre-colonial-era archaeological record have been interpreted in terms of gender relations. The classic case is Sandra Bowdler's explanation for the appearance of shell fish-hooks and changes in the shellfish composition in the Bass Point shell midden, both reflecting women's activities. Other prehistorians have identified and questioned the explanatory value of androcentric archaeology and ethnography. For example, Caroline Bird has challenged the widespread assumption that stone tool manufacture was an exclusively male activity. Such assumptions have been used to argue that women are 'less visible' in the archaeological record than men, because evidence of women's activities (such as plant collecting) is less likely to survive archaeologically than that of men's manufacture and use of stone tools. Bird cites numerous ethnographic examples of women both making and using stone tools across Australia and New Guinea which question the value of much previous archaeological explanation. Betty Meehan's insightful research on women's food collecting in Arnhem Land provides a significant ethnographic study, also with implications for interpreting shellfish middens.

The teaching of prehistory has emerged as an important educational discipline since the publication in 1961 of the first book (by Grahame Clark) with the title *World Prehistory*. It offers students a useful introduction to disciplines in the humanities, social sciences and science, with tuition in the interdisciplinary nature of an objective approach to reconstructing past environmental, biological, technological and humanistic contexts of human societies. In Australia, however, it offers a further educational benefit. From learning about the life of Australians before European colonisation, it allows students to perceive the nature of Aboriginal societies and their responses to environmental challenges; prehistoric art contains a vast corpus of cognitive resources. It is through such education and a more balanced understanding of the nature of traditional indigenous society that new generations, both white and black, may achieve the mutual understanding which brings reconciliation.

2 The diversity of surviving traces

Consider the consequences for archaeology of an average population, for example, of 50,000 people occupying this continent for 40,000 years. Assuming 2000 generations with a cohort of 50,000 suggests a minimal estimate of 100 million indigenous people—with the actual figure likely to be two or three times greater. So it is not surprising that there should be widespread material testimony to their presence, both above and below ground. Aboriginal sites and other traces are ubiquitous, though many are obvious only to those trained in searching for them but virtually invisible to others. The vast majority are open-air camping places, marked only by discarded pieces of stone, or sometimes an old fireplace containing shells and animal bones. People walking along beach dunes may pass within a few metres of a prehistoric camp with scattered shell refuse and stone artefacts, oblivious to that reality. Cultural features disappear with time through the normal processes of erosion and decay, and often the remnants are not even obvious to the archaeologist. The broadest of these are environments changed by human burning practices. Another, about which too little is known, are Aboriginal trails, tracks and pathways. These were well marked in southeast Tasmania, traversing rugged country but leading to the best river crossings, to naturally sheltered camping sites, and to valleys with food resources. One major Aboriginal pathway where Sydney now stands led from Port Jackson to Botany Bay via inner suburban Maroubra Beach.

There are potentially vast numbers of archaeological sites submerged by shallow seas along Australia's continental shelf, including once spiritually important places with art, stone quarries, and formerly inhabited caves and rockshelters—all of them older than 6000 years. Intriguing they may be, but none so far has been explored.

SURFACE ARTEFACTS

Stone artefacts (called lithics) are found almost everywhere because stone is such durable material. When they lie scattered on the ground the site is identified as a 'lithic scatter'. This is the most common type of prehistoric site encountered by archaeologists; in regions where there are no habitable rockshelters or caves it is often the only type recorded. Lithic scatters may signify quite different human activities but many are open-air camp sites, some of which were large base camps located near water where people returned regularly for extended periods. The stone contents of lithic scatters often comprise debris from toolmaking. Often there is only a small number of finished stone implements, usually lost or discarded items: most finished tools were carried elsewhere. Lithic scatters are often the eroded surfaces of buried deposits of stone artefacts, sometimes also with organic refuse and hearths.

SHELL MIDDENS

Shell middens (from the Danish word for kitchen refuse) are conspicuous around the coast and along inland waterways. They represent mostly the food remains of women's gathering activities and, being so visible in the landscape, are often quarried for landfill and lime-burning. They contain considerable archaeological evidence. Typically, middens are located on headlands, coastal estuaries, and sand dunes along the coastal fringe, and inland on former river banks and lake margins. Sometimes a midden deposit is barely discernible because the layer of shell is thin; this is common for spreads of mussel shells near inland lakes or riversides. In other instances middens are massive in size—one of a cluster at Ballina on the Richmond River in northern New South Wales was estimated to be 33,000 cubic metres in volume (or 23,000 tonnes of shell, providing more than 4600 tonnes of mollusc meat). Many more along the southeast coast of

Lithic scatter—a site containing stone artefacts scattered on the ground—on a wind deflated sand dune, South Keppel Island. (Mike Rowland)

Australia were much larger. One variety of shell midden is represented by the enormous shell mounds around Milingimbi and near the Blyth River in eastern Arnhem Land, and along Cape York—on its eastern coast at Princess Charlotte Bay, and along the western coast at the Love River north of Cape Keeweer, and further north around the Embley and Hay Rivers near Weipa. Along these last two rivers there are at least 500 mounds, ranging from a metre high to veritable hillocks up to thirteen metres high, the largest containing over 200,000 tonnes of shells (chiefly cockles). These mounds began to form 1000 to 1200 years ago and were still being added to when Dutch explorers arrived on the coast. Not surprisingly, they include some of the world's largest surviving shell middens, and a number are listed on the Register of the National Estate.

Concentrated shell preserves well because it creates its own alkaline environment that resists any acidity in the surrounding sediment. Thus middens and their carbonaceous contents of shells, animal and human

Coastal midden deposits, eastern Tasmania, showing successive layers of occupation by Aboriginal peoples. Such scatters usually comprise many activity events from different periods and may include much waste from flaking stone and some complete or broken tools. (Robert Edwards)

Cockle shell mounds at Weipa, Cape York. Note the height above the plain—this provided dry camping during the wet season and a breeze to minimise insects. (D. J. Mulvaney collection)

bones may be preserved for millennia. Most coastal middens are less than 6000 years old, because they fringe the present-day seashore which had stabilised at about that time. In southeastern Australia and Tasmania some middens are 8000–9000 years old, but much older ones have been investigated recently on the Kimberley coast.

Even archaeologists at times have difficulty in distinguishing middens from natural features, such as shelly storm deposits on a beach or a scrub fowl mound. Sometimes a midden may be identified simply by its location inland, where it cannot be a natural formation. One commonly agreed criterion for the identification of Aboriginal midden deposits is a demonstrable selection of edible, mature shellfish species. This is usually restricted to one or two species, such as oyster, Anadara, whelk and turbo shells, although around Sydney Harbour more than 70 shellfish species occur in foreshore middens. This concentration of predominantly edible sized shells contrasts with shell accumulations caused naturally by wave action, which are likely to contain random species and size samples. Other evidence includes layers indicating cultural rather than natural deposition, including the presence of stone and bone artefacts, and manuports (natural stone brought by humans, often as cooking stones); and the presence of various remains of crustaceans, fish, birds and mammals which would be unusual under natural conditions.

In her ethnoarchaeological work among the Anbarra people of Arnhem Land, Betty Meehan identified two kinds of shell middens—'base camps', which were occupied continuously for long periods; and 'dinnertime camps', representing ephemeral camp sites. These ethnographic categories are not a rule-of-thumb guide for interpreting prehistoric middens on the basis of size alone. Despite the importance of middens for archaeology and the impressive size of many of them, shellfish usually provided only a small part of the Aboriginal subsistence base. It has been estimated that one large midden at Ballina, which accumulated over the last 2000 years, contributed less than twenty per cent of the diet of the local people. This accords with Meehan's field research, where shellfish were a staple food but contributed no more than one-tenth of dietary needs, though they were a more significant resource during lean times. Other littoral and marine resources were important to coastal people, as were the plant foods and game obtained from wetlands and adjacent forest environments.

Along most of Australia's southern coastline and southwest coasts, shell middens are scarce because the inhabitants were not interested in shellfish as food. Sometimes access to the seafront or to worth-while collecting areas was difficult, as was the case for much of the Nullarbor coast, but shellfish was ignored for other reasons as well, such as its low food value compared to available terrestrial food resources. However, along the eastern seaboard every coastal dunefield seems to contain middens and shelly lenses marking former encampments and stopover places. It is estimated that there are thousands of middens around Brisbane alone, and this is probably also the case for the Sydney region.

CAVES AND ROCKSHELTERS

True caves, created by water action and dissolution, are commonly found in limestone country, and large ones occur along the southern coast from Victoria to southwest Western Australia, and others in Cape York Peninsula and southern Tasmania. Rockshelters are the result of cavernous weathering of sandstone or quartzite formations by wind and water, or of large rocks broken from a cliff face which lean over and serve to shelter or shade the ground. One example of magnificent rockshelter country is the Hawkesbury sandstone around Sydney, stretching from Wollongong to Newcastle and inland across the Blue Mountains, where there are thousands of shelters with prehistoric occupation, many of them unrecorded.

There is a common misconception about prehistoric cave occupancy. As a general rule, Aborigines did not live in the deep and dark recesses of caves, but camped at the entrance and only ventured into the passages for special reasons. While rockshelters offer a bonanza for archaeologists, they were not necessarily commonly used camp sites. In some desert areas rockshelters were normally used only during rain or dust storms, and over a period of thousands of years visited only occasionally. The reason archaeologists concentrate on such places is that, however little they were occupied, an accumulation of stratified and datable deposits containing stone artefacts and other camp wastes are confined in a limited area, sometimes sparse, at other times packed solid. The alkaline soils in limestone sites may preserve organic materials, while even acidic sandstone may contain stratified stone artefacts and ochre pellets.

These relics of past activities—food debris of animal bones and shells, plant materials or microscopic pollen and phytoliths (plant silica) mixed with ash, the waste from flaking stone, other discarded

Kutikina limestone cave in the Franklin valley, southwest Tasmania. The discovery of Pleistocene occupation in 1981 helped prevent the construction of the Franklin hydroelectric dam which would have drowned the valley. On the left there is two metres of archaeological deposit, while a channel has eroded the area on the right. The cave was abandoned about 14,000 years ago when the rainforest encroached. (D. J. Mulvaney)

The Ngarrabullgan rockshelter on top of Mount Mulligan contains stratified deposits, showing occupation took place by 37,000 years BP until about 900 years BP. Local traditions claim the area is sacred, which may explain its abandonment. (Bruno David)

stone artefacts, and occasionally human bone remains, together with art preserved on rear walls or on roofs—provide a record of natural events and human activities. While most shelters contain shallow deposits, some excavated trenches have penetrated through five metres or more of occupation layers.

EARTH MOUNDS

In areas of poorly drained soils 'oven mounds' are found. They occur mostly in the Murray River Valley, but also along the Murrumbidgee River and in the Macquarie Marshes in southwestern New South Wales. Others are in the coastal wetlands of Van Diemen's Gulf, including Kakadu National Park. Such mounds are roughly circular or oval, mostly covering less than 200 square metres. They may contain masses of charcoal and burnt clay, or pebble heat retainers (cooking stone) used in earth ovens, along with shells and flaked stone artefacts. Along the Murray River, some are crammed with burials. Mounds are usually identified as dry-ground camp sites in seasonally resource-rich but waterlogged areas, but archaeologists Jane Balme and Wendy Beck have speculated that they may have also served as gardens. David Frankel and colleagues from La Trobe University excavated a number of surviving earth mounds in the Murray River Valley, the oldest of which they reliably dated to about 3000 years.

CEREMONIAL MOUNDS AND ROCK ARRANGEMENTS

Ceremonial rock arrangements and earthworks are found in many parts of Australia, but historical records and field surveys indicate that they occur commonly in parts of eastern Australia. Over 1000 are known from New South Wales and Queensland alone.

They are always low constructions, usually less than a metre high, but they have various patterns. It is reasonable to presume that the function of many earthworks and stone arrangements was comparable: their owners viewed them as personifying totemic beings who participated in creation dramas. In other cases, the constructions demarcated areas where ceremonial activities occurred. This function possibly explains the many linear or circular arrangements of stones enclosing a clear area ranging from a few square metres to hectares in area. Many features of earth or piled stones are identified as bora

Portion of extensive stone arrangements on a ceremonial ground near Carisbrook, Victoria. (D. A. Casey)

rings because of historical accounts of 'bora' ceremonies (initiation of boys) at such sites. Sixty-two bora rings have been identified in the region around Brisbane alone, and many others are found widely in eastern New South Wales. Victoria has a few examples, one of which, an earth ring at Sunbury near Melbourne, was excavated by David Frankel. This site had the remains of a small stone cairn at its centre, and a scatter of stone flaking debris, possibly from a ceremonial activity such as cutting hair.

Stone-lined paths and concentric rings of earth or stones required considerable labour to construct. In some places a pair of circles, one larger than the other, are linked by linear earthworks or pathways. For instance, at Tuntable Falls in dense rainforest in New England a 60-metre-long stone-lined track, more than a metre wide, provides access across a steep ridge. Near Sleisbeck, in southern Kakadu National Park, there is a similar ceremonial pathway marked by stones for 1200 metres; it winds its way up a hill, down a valley, to a painted rockshelter.

In northeastern Arnhem Land there are unique stone arrangements, which are more appropriately described as 'pictures'. These consist of small stones that form simple outlines of objects, most of which became familiar to Aborigines only through their contacts with Macassan fishermen seeking trepang and their experiences of their return voyages to Macassar. Motifs include praus, houses, and hearths for boiling trepang. Elsewhere, there are many examples of cairns, or large, single standing stones. Boulders and upright slabs of ironstone in the Hamersley Range in Western Australia are said to be metamorphosed pelican eggs and snake eggs respectively.

The simpler the construction or feature, the greater the difficulty in identifying it as an Aboriginal relic. Some have no distinctive attributes and, without confirmation from informants, would be unrecognised as Aboriginal or even cultural features. The location and survey of stone arrangements, ranging from simple cairns to elaborate ground designs, are a continuing goal of fieldwork.

STONE AND OCHRE QUARRIES

Throughout Australia, various stone and mineral substances were collected, and sometimes quarried, and used to make stone implements and for pigment. Sandstone also was quarried in large slabs for use as grindstones in milling seeds for flour. In the Northern Territory, people still visit certain quarries to collect stone implements for ceremonies or formal exchange and also now for the tourist trade. Pebble beds in watercourses were ideal places to collect stone. They provided a selection of different types, sizes and shapes, pre-sorted for toughness by water transport. In areas where pebbles were collected, there often occur rejected pieces of flaked stone and other debris left after stones had been roughly shaped before they were taken elsewhere for final preparation. In places where particularly desirable stone was exposed over only a small area, the flaking debris may number more than a thousand items per square metre. Some larger stone-collecting localities in the arid interior occur on extensive rock formations, and the flaking debris is scattered over the ground for kilometres. Some collecting sites in the interior have quarry pits and shafts following a seam of high-quality stone or ochre. Adjacent may lie stone debris on knapping floors or 'stone reduction sites' where the early stages of manufacture occurred.

Certain Aboriginal quarries and mines possessed significance that transcended material needs. People did not always prefer the closest source: they exchanged valuable goods, or travelled through arid country to a more distant source, for stone they believed was imbued with spiritual power. The higher repute of the stone, the greater its exchange value; and for some quarries there was inherited custodial ownership. Two quarries, which symbolise the attainments of human perseverance, deserve more fame than the better-known ones such as the Mount William greenstone quarry in Victoria, discussed later. Koonalda Cave, prominent in Australian prehistory for other reasons, served as a stone source on the Nullarbor Plain well over 20,000 years ago, when people first gouged flint nodules from its limestone walls.

Western Australia boasts the immense ochre mine at Wilgie Mia in the Weld Range where the hillside has a cavity 30 metres wide

Koonalda Cave, a sinkhole in the karst limestone of the Nullarbor Plain, a Pleistocene source of flint and water, and a place of ritual wall markings. (D. J. Mulvaney)

Grindstone quarry at Helen Springs (Kurutiti), north of Tennant Creek, Northern Territory. Sandstone blocks were split along bedding planes, after pits were pecked in parallel lines between two to seven centimetres apart and up to two centimetres deep. Impact using pebbles and chisels presumably separated a slab along the mechanically weakened planes. After trimming, these heavy slabs were exchanged over long distances. (Ken Mulvaney)

Wilgie Mia red ochre quarry in the Murchison region of Western Australia. This posed photo was taken in the early 1900s by which time thousands of tonnes of red ochre had been quarried using stone mauls and wooden wedges to prise ochre from thick seams. (Western Australian Museum)

and twenty metres in depth, with shafts following thick red or yellow ochre seams. The quarry represents the removal of many thousands of tonnes of rock. There is evidence that wooden scaffolds were propped against the rock face to provide access to some of the ochre seams. The floor of the main pit is stratified in places to a depth of almost six metres, with quarrying tools preserved throughout the deposit. Heavy stones were used like mauls to batter the rock, and fire-hardened wooden wedges, about half a metre long, prised out the ochre. Wilgie Mia ochre represented the blood of a Dreaming kangaroo creation being; it was extensively traded throughout Western Australia and possibly even as far as Queensland. Although Wilgie Mia may have been mined for thousands of years, it was not exhausted when Aboriginal visits ended, because an ochre-mining company extracted much of the remainder.

That such tonnage extraction of ochre was not exceptional is indicated by other evidence. Excavations in 1958 at Yarar rockshelter in the Northern Territory recovered 20,000 pieces of ochre, weighing 183 kilograms, from 25 cubic metres of deposit. Dieri people from Cooper Creek are known to have travelled up to 500 kilometres annually to collect ochre from the Bookartoo (Parachilna) quarry in the northern Flinders Ranges. In these annual expeditions more than 70 men each returned with 30-kilogram loads of ochre.

ROCK ART SITES

Hundreds of thousands of rock art motifs survive throughout Australia as paintings, drawings, and pecked and abraded 'engravings', on open and sheltered rock surfaces. Rock art is a unique component of the archaeological record because it is the result of past systems of communication, ritual and encoded knowledge. Such motifs may remain significant to Aboriginal groups long after their makers have gone, and positively signify for their viewers Dreaming ancestors and sacred values. The evidence for the antiquity of rock art, the material culture it depicts, and the inferred processes of Aboriginal ritual, aesthetics and communication are so significant that Chapters 20 to 22 are dedicated to this subject.

STONE HUNTING-HIDES AND BIRD TRAPS

Aborigines in certain desert regions constructed hunting-hides of stone in order to prey on birds and animals attracted to food or water. Such structures were hugely successful in tricking raptors such as hawks and eagles seeking easy prey; relics still exist in the Victoria River District. Originally the hides were somewhat like miniature stone huts with a roof of grass on a frame of sticks, but all that remains now are the stone foundations or walls.

CARVED TREES

Field relics that are very vulnerable are carved trees. They occur in eastern and central New South Wales and eastern Queensland, and are particularly concentrated in the Darling River Basin. Upwards of 1000 carved trees are documented, though only about 300 still survive; most are in river corridors not cleared by pastoralists. Usually the bark was removed and then cuts were made on the trunk in patterns of circles, spirals, concentric diamonds and lozenges. Like Old World megalithic monuments, whose art form they recall, these trees marked ceremonial grounds and burial places. While a mass of 120 carved trees around one bora ground has been reported, they frequently occur in small numbers and often singly. The antiquity of the tradition is not known because bushfires consume the dead trees. Many of those recorded, however, were made with steel hatchets in the early nineteenth century.

SCARRED TREES

When Abel Janszoon Tasman stepped ashore in southeast Tasmania, he encountered a sight which no doubt disconcerted his men—massive trees bore notches more than a metre and a half apart, 'forming a kind of steps to enable persons to get up the trees and rob the birds' nests'. Surely, Tasman thought, here live very tall people. Throughout Australia, decaying old eucalypts survive with similar rude footholds cut by Aborigines hunting for possum, or collecting nuts or honey. Others bear long scars where bark sheets were removed to make canoes or shields. The bark was prised off with the aid of wood or stone wedges, and a stone hatchet or rough stone chopper. Various barks were used; river red gum, stringybark and paperbark were especially useful for making receptacles, huts and watercraft. Inevitably, the number of scarred trees has diminished rapidly as they die from natural causes, pastoral activities and bushfires, but they are still being recorded.

HATCHET-HEAD GRINDING LOCALITIES

One of the most important Aboriginal implements was the ground-stone hatchet, more commonly, but less correctly, known as the 'edge-ground axe'. The processes of fashioning and resharpening these tools included the grinding of their surfaces, particularly the cutting edge, on an abrasive stone. Grinding places, where grooves are worn into sandstone bedrock, are usually found near water and close to

One of five carved trees surrounding the grave of Yuranigh, who was buried in 1850 at Molong, New South Wales. Not all the trees have survived, and the carved surface on this tree has been partly covered by regrowth. (D. J. Mulvaney)

camp sites. These sites do not usually convey much new information to archaeologists, but they are an important heritage for Aboriginal people.

FISH TRAPS

Tidal fish traps were one category of field construction that provided Aborigines with a regular bounty. There were many designs. Historical records reveal that traps could provide more than 1.5 kilograms of fish per person a day. They were made of rocks, branches or wickerwork, but those that have survived as field relics are of stone. Perhaps the remains of thousands of traps lie buried beneath alluvial sediments in estuaries and along coasts and former river channels. Hundreds of fish traps are known from the Gulf of Carpentaria and they are also prolific along the Kimberley and Dampierland coasts where tidal ranges are as great as ten metres.

Aboriginal fish traps may be difficult to distinguish from European constructions or natural features. They are notoriously difficult to date, but sediments immediately underlying the few that have been studied are very recent in age. This is logical, considering these relatively fragile structures are designed to filter tidal flow but not the storms to which they are subjected. Whatever their construction, they required periodic maintenance for effective service.

The best-known example of freshwater traps lined the Darling River at Brewarrina. It comprised a convoluted series of stone weirs and pens some 400 metres long, constructed from river cobbles. The enclosures were of different shapes and sizes, and of various heights, to accommodate changes in the level of the river. In Victoria's Western District a series of basalt traps at Lake Condah also catered for varying lake levels.

In the same region eels were caught in enormous quantities by using long basket traps and wickerwork weirs. Much of the evidence for this specialised technology has vanished, but it has been reconstructed from the journal notes of G. A. Robinson who visited the Aborigines near Mount William, and through excavations by Harry Lourandos at Toolondo. At these locations narrow trenches and wider channels, sometimes straight but more often convoluted, had been dug so that eels would migrate from swamps into the traps. Conceivably these earthworks were carried out over many years, or even centuries, by re-digging old channels and adding new ones. Near

Fish trap in the Darling River at Brewarrina, northwestern New South Wales, which yielded catches when the river level fell after periodic rain. (Museum of Applied Arts and Sciences, Sydney)

Mount William this eventually translated into a maze of channels covering more than five hectares.

HUMAN BURIALS

Most people assume that archaeologists excavate burials only to study human anatomy. This certainly is a vital field for biological anthropologists, who may derive information concerning nutrition, diseases, extent and nature of injuries, or apply the recently developed techniques for DNA testing. Such matters are relevant to reconstructing past lifestyles and intermarriage between regional groups of people or their migrations.

However, archaeologists are particularly interested in the evidence which burials provide concerning cultural practices and belief systems

35

of past generations, aspects of significance to contemporary Aboriginal people. Grave goods may provide insight into clothing, ornaments and decoration, receptacles, weapons and food for the deceased. The following examples indicate the importance of burials for providing clues to ancient cultural beliefs.

Historical evidence compiled by Betty Meehan indicates an enormous diversity in Aboriginal mortuary practice throughout the continent in early historic times. In some regions the body was dried and partly dismembered or ritually consumed. Cremation was practised in other regions; or bodies were wrapped in soft bark, skin or matting and buried in a shallow grave, or cached within a hollow tree trunk or ossuary in rock crevices. Erosion of pastoral lands and the banks along watercourses continues to expose prehistoric human remains, but relatively few are encountered during archaeological excavations. The majority of recorded burials belong to the last few thousand years, but some are very ancient. Isolated human burials have been excavated from shell accumulations at coastal camp sites and from the sands of lake-bordering dunes in southeastern Australia. Large cemeteries occur along the Murray River, many of which had been used for thousands of years. The only Aboriginal cemetery encountered outside this river corridor was at Broadbeach, south of Brisbane.

Sometimes personal items and offerings of various kinds accompanied an interment, but as they were usually perishable materials, most known prehistoric human remains lacked surviving material relics. Fibre, skin and wooden artefacts were the first to disintegrate. In one instance, the remains of a coolamon was indicated only by a black stain in the sand. Interestingly, indirect evidence from the high incidence of arthritis of the jaw and unusual wear of the teeth reveal that bulrush fibre was chewed, probably to make large hunting and fishing nets, along the central Murray River. Cultural items most likely to survive are of stone, bone, teeth or shell, such as pellets and powdered ochre, stone tools, bone fish-hooks, kopi widow's caps, necklaces of teeth, and bone pins and points.

At the riverside cemetery of Roonka, up to 30 per cent of the burials had ornaments. Grave 108, dating to some time in the last 5500 years, was distinguished by the sumptuous personal gear, though only bones, teeth and other small fragments were left. The archaeologist Graeme Pretty reconstructed the clothing and ornaments. The grave was a deep vertical shaft containing the skeleton of a young man in a half-sitting position and, resting on his side, that of a child about seven years old. Around the body of the man had been a long garment, almost certainly a skin cloak, held fast at the left shoulder by a bone pin. A series of bone pins for the garment ran down the front of the body, and over the left shoulder were found the remains of animal paws which probably dangled as tassels. Feather trimming, revealed by fragments of quills, ran along the left side of the garment. These scraps of material evidence suggest the existence of a far more elaborate skin cloak than any recorded after British colonisation. Two strings of notched wallaby teeth, comprising 75 matched pairs, had encircled the man's forehead. The child's remains bore traces of red ochre and were accompanied by elaborate body ornaments. A coiled bead necklace of snake vertebrae, strung in opposing groups, had been laid on the small body; a single-strand headband of animal teeth had formerly encircled the child's head, but had become dislodged and was found resting on the man's arm. On the child's chest was the skull of a brolga; presumably it had been a pendant dangling from a string.

Another notable burial was discovered in 1969 on the shore of Lake Nitchie in western New South Wales by the geomorphologist Jim Bowler, and formally described by the anatomist N. W. G. Macintosh. This was a very large man (about 182 centimetres tall), whose body had been crammed into a pit dug into hard calcareous sediments. The man, who was probably in his late thirties and had suffered from a dental abscess, was seated with legs bent under his body, and head and shoulders forced downwards, in order to fit his body into the small grave pit. He had been daubed with red ochre, and beside him were the remains of a small fire probably indicating a ritual. Along with scraps of pearl-shell and a tektite (fused silica from a meteor impact shower), was a most impressive necklace—a single row of 178 pierced Tasmanian Devil's teeth taken from perhaps more than 100 animals, each tooth pierced for stringing. This burial dates to about 6800 years BP (Before Present), and since then the Tasmanian Devil has become extinct on mainland Australia. The man had been dead at least a week before he was buried—perhaps the task of digging into the brick-hard calcareous sand of the lunette was too arduous for his companions. He was large, and as his knees and head stuck out prominently from the hole, they cut a niche at the bottom of the grave to accommodate his feet which were in the way, and his knees were then bent inwards. Finally, to compress his body into the hole (perhaps in exasperation), he was pushed down with considerable force, sufficient to dislocate his neck and shoulders. The grave pit was then filled with red sand collected nearby.

The 'Bunyan burial', recently discovered north of Cooma, is of a similar age. This grave contains a double inhumation—an adolescent male and an elderly woman—with the upper skeleton parts washed away by floodwater. One of the woman's teeth has a distinct groove, probably from drawing plant fibres between her teeth to make string; she also had dental caries—the oldest known example of this tooth decay in Australia. The grave goods found with the human remains include bone points and spatulas, marsupial jaws probably used as engraving tools, pieces of ochre, and a necklace of 327 pierced wallaby and kangaroo teeth.

Perhaps the most significant cultural evidence excavated in an Australian burial came from Lake Mungo in western New South Wales. A female cremation burial was identified in 1969, providing the world's oldest known cremation rite, some 26,000 years old. Other ancient cremations are known now from this area. A few hundred metres distant, but some thousands of years older, a male was buried in an extended position, and had been covered in red ochre. As ochre does not occur near Mungo, a quantity of this pigment must have been transported there, providing a clue to the existence at that remote period of communication between regions. Significantly, both these people were unquestionably modern *Homo sapiens*.

The cremation burial of a young woman occurred on Lake Mungo's shore over 20,000 years ago, the world's oldest known cremation. Pleistocene. The eroded remains had been disturbed by sheep. (D. J. Mulvaney)

Dating the past 3

Archaeologists frequently are asked of their finds: 'how old are they?' Several scientific laboratory techniques available today may provide satisfying answers in 'years ago', although most seemingly precise dates must be treated with caution. We discuss some of these dating techniques later in this chapter.

Before about 1950, however, such 'absolute' dates were unavailable, so archaeologists relied upon *relative* 'cultural' sequences in stratified excavated deposits. Just as geologists apply stratigraphic principles to the succession of fossils within layers of rock, so archaeologists used distinctive stone and bone artefact types found within particular excavated layers to infer the succession of human occupation of the site. This produced a relative chronology, in which the contents of lower layers were older than those in overlying layers, and characteristic artefacts became identified as cultural markers.

The traditional models of cultural change are derived from European archaeology, where prehistoric 'cultures' were identified by characteristic artefact types such as stone and bone tools and pottery. The various schemes of Australian prehistoric cultural change have been based largely on stone technology, which is only a small part of Aboriginal material culture but the most durable indicator. There is now better understanding of other material remains, including the remarkable chronological, pictorial and cognitive record provided by rock art, so that stone artefacts play a less significant role in current interpretations of prehistoric chronology.

TINDALE'S CHRONOLOGICAL SEQUENCE

The cultural deposit in Norman B. Tindale's excavation at Devon Downs in 1929 was stratified through nearly six metres and contained rich faunal remains and implements of stone and bone. Radiocarbon dates obtained many years later demonstrated occupation spanning the last 5000 years. Tindale devised a three-stage cultural sequence for Devon Downs, and postulated that each stage represented the arrival of a different ethnic type, and that their intermixing resulted in the range of physical differences evident among the Aboriginal people. His cultural sequence began with the 'Pirrian', which was named after a type of stone spear point found in South Australia. Tindale assumed that this culture had spread across most of the continent. Next came the 'Mudukian', which was named after a type of bone point. Tindale's third and final culture was the 'Murundian', which he believed continued until it was documented by European settlers and which typified Aboriginal culture along the Murray River. On an open river flat near Devon Downs, Hale and Tindale excavated a second cultural deposit at Tartanga, containing implements and human bones. Although the excavators had no proof of any stratigraphic continuity with Devon Downs, they argued that Tartanga was older, and identified a 'Tartangan Culture' from its small artefact assemblage. Tindale later radiocarbon dated Tartanga to about 6000 years BP.

In 1931 Tindale showed that heavy chopper-like stone implements found on Kangaroo Island and on the opposite mainland were different from the ones from Devon Downs, and he inferred that they were of late Pleistocene age. He termed this culture 'Kartan'. We later discuss Tindale's Kartan artefacts in the context of Holocene stone technology, since it is now known that this is where they belong chronologically.

By the 1940s, therefore, South Australian prehistory was interpreted in terms of a five-stage cultural sequence extending back into the Pleistocene. In 1938, Tindale joined J. B. Birdsell on the fieldwork that was to lead to Birdsell's formulation of a theory about Australian racial origins—the migration into Australia of 'Oceanic Negritos' (represented by Tasmanians), and later 'Murrayans' and 'Carpentarians'. Tindale incorporated Birdsell's racial sequence into his cultural synthesis and thereafter postulated that the Kartan and Tartangan people were close relatives of Tasmanians, and that Murrayans were responsible for the succeeding cultures. In later

The 1963 excavations at Fromm's Landing, Murray River, South Australia, a few kilometres from Devon Downs. The deposit covers 5000 years, and the stratified occupation layers contained a rich collection of fauna taken for food. The break in the stratification to the left of the ranging pole was due to flood erosion about 3000 years ago, constituting a flood level higher than any recorded flood. (D. J. Mulvaney)

publications, Tindale employed his five archaeological cultures to correlate artefacts, both ancient and recent prehistoric, from every Australian state and even from overseas. In the face of virulent criticism of his interpretations by Frederick D. McCarthy, he even excavated Noola rockshelter west of Sydney (in the heart of McCarthy's culture region of eastern New South Wales), and claimed a replication of his own South Australian sequence.

The 'cultures' of Frederick D. McCarthy

In 1948, Fred McCarthy published his analysis of a rockshelter at Lapstone Creek, near Sydney. It was the occasion for a synthesis of the prehistory of eastern New South Wales, and inaugurated a new set of archaeological cultures. At that time McCarthy envisaged two cultural phases in New South Wales prehistory, both of which, he postulated, possessed traits distinct from Tindale's South Australian sequence. The earlier culture he named 'Bondaian', after a type of spear barb called bondi point because the implement type was first identified from a site on Bondi Beach. The succeeding culture he termed 'Eloueran' after a distinctive type of adze flake. Subsequent excavations by McCarthy in the picturesque Capertee Valley on the western scarp of the Blue Mountains resulted in the addition of an earlier, third cultural phase, the 'Capertian', defined by implements of simple form, including flakes with finely dentated cutting edges. After his participation in an expedition to Arnhem Land in 1948 McCarthy concluded that elements of most of the South Australian and New South Wales cultures also occurred in the north, along with certain local developments to which he ascribed the labels 'Milingimbian', 'Oenpellian' and 'Kimberleyian' Cultures.

In his earlier work, McCarthy was prone to correlate far-flung examples of prehistoric artefacts, just as Tindale had done, but he proved to be more flexible in framing his cultural phases and in his use of terminology. As his ideas evolved, McCarthy proposed the concept of an 'Eastern Regional Sequence' to embrace his earlier three-stage cultural phases, and the 'Tula Inland Regional Sequence', which included much of Tindale's scheme. There are modern variations of McCarthy's sequence, both in the terminology used and the relative chronology of phases.

In his 1961 review paper, *The Stone Age of Australia*, Mulvaney devoted much of his text to criticism of Tindale's scheme, which he regarded as 'more ingenious than convincing'. While there was merit in a regional approach, Mulvaney argued that the advisability of defining a cultural phase on the basis of a few implement types was questionable—the Pirrian and Mudukian were defined initially by single items, while the Murundian was defined from historical data and not from excavated objects at the Devon Downs 'type site'; at Tartanga, distinctive tools were conspicuous by their absence. While Tindale correctly emphasised the dynamic nature of Aboriginal society, he failed to allow sufficiently for regional diversity and technological adaptation. Tindale was following contemporary thinking in archaeology by invoking migration and racial inroads as the stimulus to cultural change: 'folk' bearing battle-axes or beakers are familiar travellers across the pages of European prehistory books of that time. Greater stress is placed today upon diffusion of ideas or artefacts, rather than mass migration of people, while it is realised that local adaptations and innovations tend to create regional differences in material culture.

While McCarthy's scheme, since modified, is still used in regional studies of the southeast coast, the notion of archaeological 'cultures' (defined by the presence of particular types of stone tools) and their correlation with ethnic groups has passed out of favour. However, Tindale held out till the last, arguing strongly for his cultures and admonishing Mulvaney for disregarding the 'great priority' of his cultural development scheme, in that way claiming the rule of primacy in nomenclature similar to that in biology. He overlooked the individuality and inventiveness of human culture.

MULVANEY'S CONCEPTUAL SCHEME

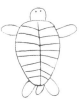

In 1969 Mulvaney introduced in the first edition of this book the concept of an initial Adaptive and emergent Inventive Phases for the Holocene period in Australia, thereby abandoning earlier concepts of archaeological cultures and their associated nomenclature. The Inventive Phase was marked by the widespread adoption of various distinctive small stone tool types during the last few thousand years. In 1965, after his analysis of stone tools from the site of Kenniff Cave in central Queensland, Mulvaney suggested that this phase marked the introduction of another technological innovation—the practice of hafting and helving pieces of stone in multi-component (or composite) tools, whereby the stone was given greater leverage, thrust or cutting power through the use of a grip or handle. Many of the small, well-shaped implements of the Inventive Phase could have proved functional and efficient only by such means. Mulvaney felt that the evidence of culture in Australia during the Pleistocene era was too slight to coin even the labels 'Archaic', or 'Formative'; his concern was to emphasise that Aboriginal society was dynamic and that major technological changes swept rapidly across the continent in postglacial times.

Mulvaney's division of Holocene prehistory into Non-Hafting (or Pre-Hafting) and Hafting Phases was criticised for a number of reasons. There are degrees of hafting, ranging from simple hand-grips to complex handles and fastening devices, which render it difficult to define the term. Simple, unworked stone flakes were demonstrably hafted in historical times, yet most of these tools would escape recognition in the prehistoric record. There were edge-ground hatchets—presumably hafted—excavated from a site in Kakadu National Park and dated to some 20,000 years ago, long before the period which Mulvaney designated as relevant. Finally, hafted tools of Pleistocene age were discovered at other sites. It was obvious that the scheme was too simplistic, but its successor in the 1970s, a somewhat more durable model, fared little better in the long run.

THE TWO TRADITIONS PERCEIVED

At the time Mulvaney was writing the first edition of *The prehistory of Australia* and offering a model of cultural development, dramatic archaeological discoveries were being made in various parts of the continent. Immediately a new framework was built to encompass the new finds—the Core Tool and Scraper Tradition, postulated to be Pleistocene and early Holocene in age, and the Australian Small Tool Tradition, which succeeded it in recent millennia. This two-stage model of technological development was implicit in Mulvaney's description of the Kenniff Cave artefacts.

The first phase was codified by Harry Allen and Rhys Jones on the basis of their collection of inferred Pleistocene-age artefacts on the wind-eroded surface of the Walls of China dune at Lake Mungo. At this 'type site', Allen and Jones noted that stone flakes and cores were large and core tools were numerous. They distinguished four main tool types: blocky, horsehoof-shaped cores, steep-edged scrapers, flat scrapers, and multi-concave scrapers. Essentially, there were three requirements for identifying a Core Tool and Scraper Tradition assemblage: a high incidence of steeply chipped edges on core tools (presumed to have served as heavy woodworking tools); flakes that were thick or large (presumed to be hand-held rather than fixed on handles); and an absence of any of the carefully trimmed new tool types. It was later proposed by Jones that the tradition was pan-continental, and typified the early artefacts found in archaeological sites such as Seelands rockshelter near Grafton, Burrill Lake rockshelter near Ulladulla, Clogg's Cave in the foothills of the Victorian Alps, and Tindale's Kartan sites in coastal South Australia, which at that time were inferred to be Pleistocene. However, one of the difficulties in substantiating this pan-Australian tradition was the small number of stone artefacts in the older archaeological deposits and, particularly, the lack of tool types that were specific to the Pleistocene.

The second technological phase, Australian Small Tool Tradition, came into general use following its proposal by the American archaeologist Richard Gould in 1969. It was defined by the appearance in the Mid to Late Holocene of a suite of new stone tool types characterised by standardised design and specialised functions, such as spear barbs and points, knife blades, wood gravers, and hafted adzes. The occurrence of these new tools was variously attributed to human migrations or the diffusion of technological concepts from overseas, or due to local technological invention.

Both these concepts of the stone tool tradition were immediately accepted by Australian archaeologists, with some relief, for the scheme filled the conceptual void which existed following the critiques of Mulvaney's cultural succession scheme. Mulvaney accepted the concept as 'useful', observing light-heartedly that the inclusion of 'Australian' conveyed a fine sense of prehistoric nationalism.

However, uncertainty about the characterisation of the Pleistocene assemblage was raised in 1973 by Kamminga and Allen in their report on the archaeology of the Kakadu region. The character of their Pleistocene stone assemblages did not possess the essential attributes. It became apparent that other early stone assemblages, including that of Kenniff Cave, were not like the Walls of China collection. There were few large and abruptly chipped flake tools, and high percentages of core tools were lacking. Instead, some demonstrably recent prehistoric sites had a predominance of large stone tools (including core tools). In the following years, Kamminga's experiments on the use of stone tools raised further issues of concern.

One of the important markers of the Core Tool and Scraper Tradition was the horsehoof core, which is a general category of high-domed, roughly discoid-shaped cores, usually half a kilogram or more in weight, which somewhat resembles a horse's hoof when turned upside-down. The term was first used by Tindale, who probably borrowed from late nineteenth-century British archaeology, where it was designated a waste core from stone toolmaking. In Australia, the horsehoof was always regarded as a tool, and was illustrated with its flat striking platform facing down rather than its normal orientation. Prehistorians suggested that it could be a pounder for smashing bones and shellfish, but later settled on hand-held wood chopping and adzing tools. From his experiments, Kamminga concluded that, as British antiquarians had originally judged for

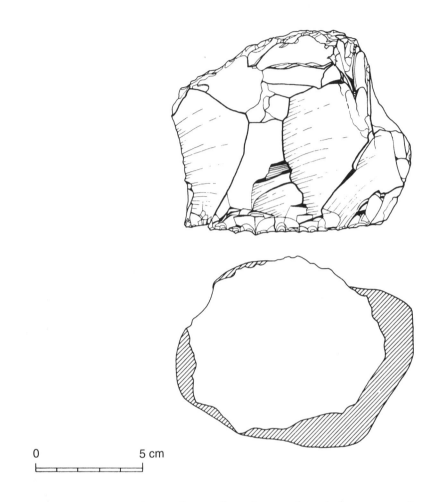

Horsehoof core. Top: side view showing the undercut striking platform. Bottom: the striking platform, with area of abrasion from incidental use as a scraping tool. (G. Happ)

European ones, most horsehoof cores probably were discarded cobble and block cores, and not tools. Many archaeologists now commonly illustrate horsehoof cores oriented with the flat striking platform facing upwards, signalling its interpretation as a core rather than tool. Some archaeologists, however, remain unconvinced. A more general implication was that other types of cores also were being wrongly identified as tools, and possibly even some artefacts identified as large steep-edged scrapers were cores. The core tool component of the tradition was clearly problematic. Two decades on, Allen concluded that the notion of an Australian Core Tool and Scraper Tradition conflicted with the evidence.

For the concept of a Small Tool Tradition the most fundamental problem was that it could not be shown that the new tool types comprised a cohesive historical 'tradition'. This concept of an archaeological tradition had been borrowed from American archaeology, with its Arctic Small Tool Tradition. This set of tool types had come to northern Alaska from Siberia about 2000 years ago, and arguably it was the material expression of an ethnic group. In Australia, however, the tool types do not appear in the archaeological record as a set, or even at the same time, and their distributions are individual; for instance an adze type called elouera is found mainly along a stretch of the eastern seaboard, and the Kimberley point in the continent's northwest. Some new types have distributions of millions of square kilometres, while others are very localised in occurrences. The concept of a tradition is not useful in these circumstances.

There is still no unanimity among archaeologists about how to describe the development of Australian stone technology, and the time is ripe for a new formulation. Innovative approaches to the study of stone technology have been developed by a number of researchers, so a fresh model seems likely. Meantime, in the absence of an agreed alternative, the 'Australian Small Tool Tradition' has survived as a convenient label for assemblages containing the new tool types. We prefer to use the term 'phase' until the nature of the changes is better understood, and we frame our account of stone technology in the context of Pleistocene and Holocene times, though the boundary between them marks no fundamental cultural change in Australia. Implicit in all these models is the concept of a relative time sequence.

RADIOCARBON DATING

Radiocarbon dating was applied during the early 1950s, just as archaeology developed in Australia, so it provided the basic chronological structure for Australian prehistory. One of the three kinds of carbon atoms (or isotopes of carbon) has eight neutrons in its nucleus—this carbon isotope is radioactive because its nucleus is slightly unstable and it is called carbon-14 (written as ^{14}C) or radiocarbon. It is created by cosmic radiation reacting with the upper part of the Earth's atmosphere and transforming nitrogen into [14]C. The total amount of ^{14}C produced in the Earth's atmosphere each year is very small (only about 7.5 kilograms), but it is rapidly oxidised and, as an infinitesimally small proportion of carbon dioxide (CO_2), is circulated throughout the earth's atmosphere. There is continual exchange of carbon dioxide between the atmosphere and water bodies, mostly by wind and wave action. Living plants absorb carbon dioxide from the atmosphere and convert it to sugars and starches by the process of photosynthesis. In fact, all living things incorporate ^{14}C by absorbing carbon compounds from the atmosphere or water, or by consuming other plant and animal life. When life-forms stop growing, their ^{14}C atoms continue to decay spontaneously at a rate of 50 per cent every 5730 years. Because after 37,000 years less than one per cent of the original ^{14}C remains, contamination of samples places an eventual limit on the method.

The most common organic or other carbonaceous material dated in Australian archaeology is charcoal; next most common is shell; less common are bone, resin, wood, beeswax, carbonate encrustation, and small plant fibres incorporated in paint applied to rock art. Most dates are obtained by radiometric ^{14}C dating. With this technique the amount of residual ^{14}C in a material is measured by converting the carbon fraction of the sample into carbon dioxide gas (called 'gas counting'), or into liquid benzene ('liquid scintillation'), and counting the number of radioactive decays that occur over the next few days. The newer and more direct method is called accelerator mass spectrometry (or 'AMS dating'). Carbon atoms in the sample are ionised and accelerated by a charge of at least two million volts. The ions are collected and sorted by a series of magnets and detectors which separate the different carbon isotopes and count them. AMS dating is a great boon for archaeologists because it has the advantage of requiring only a few milligrams of carbon, and most laboratories now provide dates with a high level of precision (in the order of plus or minus 50 years). However, limitations of sample purity and contamination apply to both radiometric and AMS methods; they can be particularly serious for the small samples datable by AMS.

AMS dating has made it possible to obtain dates for Australian rock art. Over time microlayers of silica—and sometimes sulphate and oxalate salts, quartz, charcoal and clay particles—form an opaque coating or 'crust' over rock paintings. An Australian specialist, Alan Watchman, has recently designed a new procedure in which a krypton laser is used in an oxygen atmosphere to oxidise fine organic matter and to decompose oxalate minerals in individual micro laminations in the coatings. The liberated gas is then converted into graphite, which is dated by the AMS method. The oldest date Watchman has determined for rock art is about 25,000 years for a site in Cape York Peninsula. The new method raises the possibility of identifying and dating paintings of different styles across the continent.

INTERPRETING RADIOCARBON AGES

Radiocarbon ages are reported in years before AD 1950, and they have the letters 'BP' (Before Present) following them. Dates are reported with an uncertainty range of one standard deviation, for example 2500±100 BP. For this date there are only two chances in three that the age actually falls within the range 2400–2600 BP, and nineteen in twenty that it falls within two standard deviations, or 2300–2700 BP. Radiocarbon ages are not precise dates, such as AD 1770, but are approximate estimates.

The presentation of radiocarbon dates in this book, as in most other literature on Australian prehistory, is derived from the initial calculation of radiocarbon age, which is based on the assumption that there have been no variations over time in atmospheric concentration of ^{14}C. For some decades it has been known that significant variations did occur in the production and distribution of ^{14}C. The concentration of carbon dioxide in the atmosphere has also varied, so that a 'calibration curve' must be used to convert radiocarbon years to real years (and an associated 'uncertainty'). Radiocarbon dating of a continuous series of tree rings of known calendar age provides a curve for the last 11,880 years. Between the beginning of the tree-ring series and 22,000 years ago, corals dated by radiocarbon and uranium/thorium provide an outline for calibration, but they are less direct and less reliable. The curve against which the age range of the radiocarbon date is plotted is not smooth but irregular; therefore only varying levels of probability are achieved after calibration, and certain periods are not well resolved.

It is important to be aware that the difference in uncalibrated radiocarbon dates and actual elapsed time may be large. In general, most uncalibrated ages are younger than the real ages of the materials sampled. For instance, radiocarbon determinations for early Holocene samples are up to 1500 years younger than their true ages, and the radiocarbon date 17,000 years BP for the peak of the Last Glacial

Maximum converts to about 19,000–20,000 calibrated years BP. Part of the reason dates are too young is that the standard half-life of 5568 years used by dating laboratories is known to be about three per cent too small. We do not refer to calibrated radiocarbon dates in this book, even though they relate more to traditional calendar reckoning. The main reason is that the oldest Australian dates are well beyond the upper limit of the calibration curve which estimates the calendar-year equivalent of a ^{14}C determination.

An ever-present problem for reliable dating is contamination of samples by older or younger carbon, such as occurs when bones and shells are buried in sediment affected by carbonate-charged groundwater, or when humic acids have been absorbed from the surrounding sediment. Another problem is that often archaeologists collect charcoal for dating without knowing its specific origin or process of incorporation into the sediment. Much charcoal in excavated cultural sediments derives from bushfires rather than from cooking or other domestic activity. Displacement of charcoal fragments in a soil, by burrowing insects, earthworms and larger animals, is an ever-present concern; moreover, the age estimate dates the growth of the tree, rather than the date when it was used for firewood. Sometimes the radiocarbon dates on which prehistories are based are more problematic than archaeologists care to admit, particularly as cooking fires may have been scooped down into earlier levels, or the process of human occupation may tread objects down, or scuff them up to more recent levels. The cost of a standard radiocarbon date is a few hundred dollars and an AMS date is more than twice as expensive, so usually only a few determinations are sought for an individual excavation. Commonly only one or two dates are determined for a salvage excavation, and up to four or five in other situations, while a few major sites have more than ten radiocarbon dates.

TRAPPED ELECTRON DATING TECHNIQUES

This group of techniques includes electron spin resonance dating (ESR) and luminescence methods. These techniques rely on quantifying trapped electron charges, which slowly increase over time. They begin at a 'zeroing' event in the past when the sample gave no reading. This zeroing is the event dated. It could be, for example, the formation of calcite (ESR), the baking of a lump of clay in a cooking fire (thermoluminescence or TL), or exposure of sediment grains to sunlight (optical dating) and the subsequent electron accumulation due to the absorption of environmental ionising radiation, and this is accounted for in determining the age of the sample. Of great relevance to Australian archaeology is that, unlike radiocarbon dating, these techniques are not limited to the past 40,000 years.

Archaeologist Bruno David (left) and scientist Bert Roberts collecting sediment samples for OSL (optically stimulated luminescence) dating, while plotting their location on section drawings of the Ngarrabullgan trench. A sample from a lower horizon was dated by OSL to 34,000 years; radiocarbon dating produced an age estimate of around 32,500, a remarkably close agreement. (Bruno David)

TL is the older of the luminescence methods, and is particularly useful for dating materials where heating was the zeroing event in the past, such as pottery, bricks, burnt flint tools, baked sediments beneath hearths. TL can also be applied to sediments where the zeroing mechanism was an exposure to sunlight before burial. Sufficient exposure to sunlight must be guaranteed, or TL will overestimate the date due to the 'residual' TL remaining in the sample at the time of burial. Fortunately, this is rarely demonstrated to be a problem in Australia, though it can be important. To get around this difficulty, optical dating was devised. In this method a beam of visible (usually green) light is shone onto quartz grains extracted from a sediment, and an optically stimulated luminescence (OSL) is emitted from light-sensitive defects (electron traps) within the crystal lattice. As the OSL from quartz is erased by only a few seconds of sunlight, this luminescence is effectively free of the problem of residual electrons.

One problem remains, however. Extremely old quartz grains from decomposing rock that has not been exposed to light for millions of years may become mixed with bleached grains in the sediment; alternatively, older grains may be brought up to younger levels through the action of ants, termites or burrowing creatures. To deal with this problem, the aliquot (or small sample) method, which measures the luminescence of only a few quartz grains at a time, has been developed and is currently being refined in Australia. Both TL and OSL determinations of sand from cultural deposits have been used in recent years to support claims for early human occupation of Australia. Recent chronometric comparisons of paired quartz grains and charcoal samples from Ngarrabullgan Cave in north Queensland indicate that the radiocarbon and OSL 'time clocks' are broadly comparable over at least the last 37,000 years. A second optical dating method (IRSL) developed in the late 1980s uses infrared instead of green light to stimulate luminescence from feldspar minerals—undoubtedly this technique will soon find application to Australian archaeology.

It is appropriate to observe that at present, however, these significant techniques are in their trial stages, so undue reliance should not be placed on age estimations. This applies particularly to those which are not based on a stratified sequence with a mutually consistent age range, where the results of one technique cannot be compared with those of another technique from the same layers.

Changing landscapes 4

With an area of 7.5 million square kilometres, Australia is the smallest of the inhabited continents, and has been heavily weathered over the last 400 million years. It is a land of plateau and plain. Unlike other continents, its horizons are unrelieved by young fold mountains (during the Pleistocene, however, the mountains of New Guinea were part of the same landmass as Australia). Nearly two-thirds of Australia is plateau country averaging between 300 and 600 metres in elevation, which includes almost all the arid western portion. In order to understand the various environmental and ecological contexts of prehistoric existence across the continent and indigenous responses and achievements, it is necessary to sketch salient features of the modern landscape.

TOPOGRAPHY

There are three basic physiographical continental divisions—the eastern highlands, the central plains, and the Great Western Shield. The Great Dividing Range—or, more appropriately in terms of physiography, the eastern highlands—curves along the eastern margin of the continent. Where the highlands are broad, which is mainly in the central portion, there are tablelands with low undulating topography and a temperate climate. Overall elevation decreases northwards, and in Torres Strait low peaks form continental islands. Mountainous Tasmania is its southernmost extension. In the southeast of the continent a few granite mountains reach altitudes of between 1500 and 2200 metres—this region is called the Australian Alps and includes the Snowy Mountains, which are mantled by Australia's largest area of seasonal snow, much loved by skiers. The Snowy Mountains region with Australia's highest mountain, Mount Kosciuszko (2228 metres), is a dissected plateau, but one that ascends abruptly from the surrounding tableland.

Although the eastern highlands are not a true mountain range, they still dictate the drainage and water availability of much of the central plains in eastern Australia. Australia's largest and most permanent river system, the Murray and Darling Rivers and their tributaries, has its headwaters in the highlands. These resource-rich watercourses and their wetlands were a focus of Aboriginal settlement. The central plains also contain two of the most congenial and important plains available for prehistoric occupation—the basalt region of western Victoria, one of the world's largest volcanic plains, over 15,000 square kilometres in area, and the extensive Riverine Plain of the Murray and Murrumbidgee Rivers.

The western two-thirds of Australia contains the parched residual tablelands and plateaus that make up the Great Western Shield, an immensely old continental landmass with an altitude of 300 to 600 metres. There are only three mountain ranges of any stature, the MacDonnell and Musgrave Ranges in central Australia, and the Hamersley Range in the Pilbara region of Western Australia. In the forested southwest of the continent the edge of the Shield, the Darling Escarpment forms an escarpment 900 kilometres long and 300 metres high. Large areas of dissected plateau occur in the Kimberley region of the northwest, with its rugged shoreline, and in Arnhem Land.

CLIMATE

Australia is largely a tropical and subtropical continent. Because it has low relief, the atmospheric flow is mostly unobstructed by topography. The exception to this is the eastern highlands; they obstruct southeasterly ocean winds, thereby producing rain on the seaboard rather than further inland. The major climatic influence is the seasonal passage of air pressure systems from west to east across the

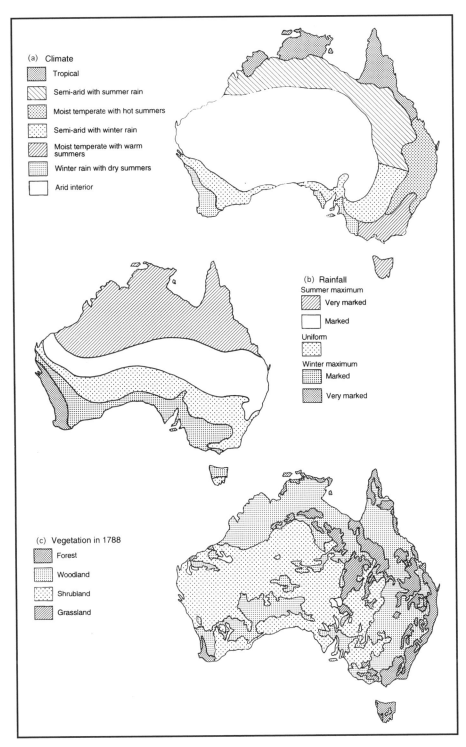

Map 1. *Australia in 1788: (a) Climate; (b) Rainfall; (c) Vegetation. (After Johnson 1992: 58, 70, 71)*

continent. From May to October, low-pressure systems, sometimes thousands of kilometres long, pass across the continent at about latitude 30°S. From November to April, the air masses follow in the same direction on a more southerly path at about latitude 40°S.

Rainfall in winter is associated with southern lows between the high systems. Their associated fronts can penetrate up into eastern Australia in particular, bringing both rain and snow. Middle layer air masses of tropical origin can give rise to widespread rainfall between 25°S and 35°S and also set up 'east coast lows' which bring heavy rainfall to the east coast from 30°S to 40°S. Tropical air masses penetrate southward (towards the pole) in summer between the high pressure systems and interact with southern cold fronts to produce severe thunderstorm rainfalls. A true Australian monsoon rarely penetrates further south than 20°S, but tropical surges intrude on the continent from both east and west to give 'pseudo-monsoons'. Tropical cyclones form in the Coral Sea, Gulf of Carpentaria, Arafura Sea and the Indian Ocean, and may approach and lash the coast with strong winds and flooding rainfalls. Their subsequent rain depressions have been known to cross the continent from both east to west and west to east, producing extreme rainfalls over the arid interior.

The combination of all these influences makes Australian rainfall among the most variable in the world and Australian stream flow even more so. The nature of the air masses moving over the continent is strongly influenced over the last 4000–5000 years by the El Niño–Southern Oscillation (ENSO) cycle of oceanic and atmospheric weather patterns, which enhance the duration of wet and dry periods. The El Niño phase of ENSO currently occurs every three to ten years; it is responsible for cold winters followed by drought, primarily in northern Australia.

The northern third of the continent lies in the tropics and has monsoonal rainfall which peaks in summer, with almost no rain falling in winter. These seasons in the north are known as the 'wet' (hot and humid) and the 'dry' (hot and dry). However, traditional Aboriginal societies perceived five or six seasons in the year, which contrasts with European conventions and indicates the extent of their adaptation to the conditions. Tropical cyclones, sometimes half a dozen a year, lash the northern coastlines during the wet, but tend to lose their force rapidly on land. The extent of the wet in the inland tropics varies from year to year, while the long dry season parches the hinterland and most rivers are intermittent.

While Australia has the largest proportion of arid country of any inhabited continent, much of it is only marginally arid: it lacks the hyper-aridity and barrenness of deserts like the Sahara. This aridity became established on a continent-wide scale over the last two to three million years. Two-thirds of the land mass receives less than 500 millimetres annual rainfall and 55 per cent experiences desert or semi-desert conditions. Currently the areas of lowest rainfall are Lake Eyre and interior Western Australia. Absence of cloud cover means that high temperatures during the day rapidly fall at night. Minimum night-time temperatures are often less than 10°C and can fall below freezing.

The eastern highlands and its coastal plain receive regular precipitation but also are affected by the long-term cyclical effect of El Niño–Southern Oscillation. This moisture is supplied mostly by onshore easterly winds, and occurs more regularly throughout the year than on the rest of the continent. Along the southern continental margin, summers tend to be warm and winters cool or mild (Mediterranean-type climate). Tasmania experiences cold winters and mild, wet summers; however, there are substantial regional climatic differences within the island because of its rugged topography.

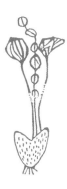

VEGETATION

In 1788 woodland and forest vegetated most of the easternmost third of Australia. The explorer Charles Sturt spoke for all British settlers when he observed that 'he who has never looked on any other than the well-cultured fields of England, can have little idea of a country that nature has covered with an interminable forest'. Even those areas which are designated 'desert' on maps—including the unique parallel sand ridges and inter-dunal corridors of Simpson's Desert, which stretch for hundreds of kilometres in central Australia—supported shrubs and grass vegetation.

To judge from numerous recollections of early British settlers, the introduction of livestock and unsystematic burning had major ecological effects, and these must be taken into consideration when reconstructing the 1788 landscape. Pastoral occupation upset the delicate balance of nature through land clearance, overgrazing, and the introduction of foreign grasses and woody plants. This led to the destruction of grasslands and forest which provided many edible seeds and roots and supported a rich native fauna. Soil erosion and salinity soon followed, and continue to this day to be major factors of land degradation.

Australia has become hackneyed in verse as a land of wattle and gum trees. Indeed these are the two most common genera of woody plants, each having many hundreds of species. They range in size from stunted shrubs to the majestic mountain ash (*Eucalyptus regnans*) and karri (*E. diversicolor*) which are over 60 metres tall. While acacias cover the largest land area, eucalypts adapted to almost all environments. *Casuarina* (sheoak) and fire-sensitive *Callitris* ('pine') were also widespread before the advent of pastoralism.

In the arid and semi-arid zones, there are four major vegetation communities: arid hummock grassland, *Acacia* scrubland, shrub steppe, and arid tussock grassland. The most widespread of these communities is hummock grassland, dominated by grass species collectively called spinifex (*Triodia* and *Plechtrachne* genera) and *Acacia* scrubland, usually dominated by *Acacia aneura* (mulga). Certain species of spinifex grass provided Aborigines with an invaluable natural substance, spinifex resin, used for cementing the components of artefacts, while the heavy timber of mulga was fashioned into many varieties of wooden artefacts. *Acacia* scrubland communities have low shrubs and tussock grasses, so after sufficient rainfall ephemeral herbaceous plants germinate and add profuse ground cover over an endless terrain. Shrub steppe is dominated by scattered saltbush and blue-bush. Except after rain, the ground between the shrubs is commonly devoid of grasses and other plants. Tussock grasslands are dominated by perennial grasses of the genus *Astrebla*, which can be up to a metre in height.

Forest and woodland, including pockets of temperate and tropical rainforest, are found in the eastern highlands and the adjacent coastal corridor, in Tasmania, and in parts of the forested southwest of the continent. Open forest becomes more common west of the eastern highlands. As one moves west, this gives way to grassland and scrubland. Sub-alpine and alpine vegetation is restricted to a relatively small area of higher altitudes of the Australian Alps. There are a number of specialised vegetation communities in coastal environments, some of which were of considerable importance to Aborigines.

'CLEANING THE LAND'

Fire is part of the natural order, and in the hands of Aboriginal hunter-gatherers was an indispensable tool for creative physical and chemical change in the environment. The major cause of bushfires in Australia is ignition of dry vegetation by lightning—estimates for the last few decades range from ten to 97 per cent of all bushfires, depending on the region. Except for areas of tropical and cool temperate rainforest in the east, Australia's vegetation is adjusted to fire and drought. Most notable are the fire-tolerant sclerophyll forests, containing *Melaleuca*, *Casuarina*, and in particular the 'fire-weed' *Eucalyptus*. Typically, Australian vegetation has highly evolved mechanisms of rapid regeneration of fire-devastated areas, two of the important ones being fire-induced germination of seeds and reshooting from underground plant stems insulated from heat and flame.

From the very beginning of European exploration around the coastline and subsequent British colonisation, the Aborigines were seen burning the countryside, at times in a manner that appeared to be wholesale. In the far north in 1623, Carstensz, a Dutch navigator sailing along the coast of west Cape York, recorded that the smoke from Aboriginal burning obscured the sight of land. Far to the southeast, on the Tasmanian coast, a French visitor observed a group of Tasmanians: 'as soon as they landed', he reported, 'they dragged the canoe into the wood and, following their custom, set fire to the shore as they went'. Peron later passed along the same coast, where 'in every direction immense columns of flame and smoke arose, all the opposite sides of the mountains…were…burning for the extent of several leagues'. Similar observations of Aboriginal burning were made as European explorers made their way inland. Ludwig Leichhardt wrote of the Aborigines of central Queensland, they 'light fires all over the place to cook their food but leave them unextinguished', while an exasperated Ernest Giles in 1889 observed, 'The natives were about, burning, burning, ever burning; one would think they lived on fire instead of water'.

When Aboriginal burning ceased in some regions, it was followed by marked changes in the vegetation. In western Victoria, brush grew thickly in areas of former open woodland; even at the beginning of the twentieth century it was possible to gallop a horse near Aboriginal art sites in the Grampian Mountains, where today the brush is almost impassable. In the tropics at Port Essington, the commandant of the settlement noted, within a few years of its foundation, that cattle were becoming lost in the dense brush in what was formerly open woodland. In the northwest of Tasmania, travel corridors through dense forest disappeared and country described by Henry Hellyer as grassy plains in 1827 had been invaded by scrub by 1835.

According to one contemporary of the day, Lieutenant Henry Bunbury, local pastoralists could not burn 'with the same judgement and good effect' as the Aborigines.

ABORIGINAL LANDCARE AND 'FIRESTICK FARMING'

Even if these reports of conflagrations were exaggerated, the firestick was the most powerful Aboriginal tool and was used extensively. Fire from hearth and firebrand did escape when the vegetation was dry and volatile, but most Aboriginal burning was intentional. In tropical northern Australia, controlled burning was a skill requiring sound judgement about fire behaviour, and in Arnhem Land certain productive vine thickets were protected by firebreaks up to a kilometre wide.

The lighting of scrub fires for idle amusement has been documented on occasion, but Aborigines exploited the incendiary potential of fire for a range of different reasons. In northern Australia, Aborigines regularly burned dry vegetation to 'clean up' or 'care for the land'. While this practice was regarded as an obligation to ancestral beings, there were immediate and obvious benefits in the food quest, irrespective of region. Forest, scrub and grassland were torched to keep open travel corridors or pathways and provide more general access to hunting and collecting areas, and to improve visibility. In northwest Tasmania, people burnt forest even while it was raining; these pathways have now been reclaimed by thick forest regrowth. An added benefit of controlled fire in forestland was that there was far less chance of being overtaken by a more intense and unpredictable natural fire. Not least, fire was used to encourage the growth of food plants, such as bracken, cycad, daisy yams and grasses, and for some even to improve their taste.

Norman Tindale in 1959 first raised the probability that the Aborigines created cultural landscapes by producing and maintaining much of Australia's grasslands. Scholars developed Tindale's argument further, demonstrating that the forestland in Tasmania and the southwest of the continent were culturally modified landscapes. Notably, some islands unoccupied by Aborigines when the British arrived had radically different vegetation structure from that of the adjacent mainland. Rhys Jones, who coined the evocative term 'firestick farming', envisaged a massive human impact on Australia's plants and animals, including the possible extinction of the giant marsupials and large-scale reshaping of plant communities. However, Aborigines managed the ecosystem by mosaic fires, which created a patchwork of humanly modified regional landscapes, rather than by large-scale conflagrations. Thus their repercussions upon the continental distribution of plants and animals may have been less.

The concept of 'firestick farming' is now an axiom in Australian archaeology, but the recent challenging contribution to the debate by Tim Flannery changes the emphasis of the Aboriginal role. Before human occupation, he argues, the giant extinct herbivores cropped the vegetation so effectively that the ubiquitous lightning strikes failed to produce destructive conflagrations. As the megafauna became extinct, (attributed by Flannery to human depredation), the vegetation must have grown unrestricted until its excess fuel load resulted in devastating natural fires. It was the Aboriginal firestick proclivity which substituted for the fauna, so maintaining the ecosystem which they had invaded. Flannery's solution, 'that it was this change, not increased fire lighting by Aborigines which holds the answer to the puzzle', is likely to provoke both research and debate.

Flannery's explanation requires long-term Aboriginal activity. Yet those burning regimes observed in historic times may have limited time depths. The ecologist Leslie Head observes that in the monsoonal north the practice of 'cleaning up the country' by frequent low-intensity fires in the early dry season, which mainly clears out grass and undergrowth, is embedded in the present seasonal climate, where natural fires are dependent for ignition on lightning at the end of the dry season. Head observes that the present seasonality in northern Australia was fully developed only in the last 3000 years and she infers that the Aboriginal burning regime in the mid-Holocene may have been different. One of the effects of the ethnographic burning regime is to protect or even encourage the growth of fire-sensitive species, such as *Callitris intratropica* which is now threatened by the advent of intense, lightning-ignited fires. Head infers that the firing regime possibly preserved the pattern of mid-Holocene vegetation.

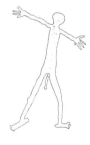

Because of the different climatic and environmental conditions, practices in central and southern Australia were not the same as those in the north. Peter Latz and fellow ecologists at the Arid Zone Research Centre, Alice Springs, have shown that deliberate winter burning of semi-arid grassland and scrubland results in less intense or 'cool' fires, as was the case in the north. This regime creates a complex mosaic of vegetation communities at different stages of fire succession, and the numerous fire-break areas provide refuges for animals, ensuring their range and availability.

In the better-watered regions, Aboriginal burning regimes maintained woodland, scrub grassland and even sedgeland in areas now colonised by dense forest. However, as the palynologist Geoff Hope suggests, the overall effect of burning woodland and open forest may have been to favour eucalypts over some other tree genera rather than to cause wholesale replacement of vegetation communities. The major changes in land use which accompanied British colonisation had a dramatic impact on the vegetation in many regions, the cessation of Aboriginal burning being a factor in these transformations. In the Australian Alps, open forest was invaded by scrub even though the rate of intentional burning increased. In other regions, its reduction had the same effect. As the explorer Major Mitchell perceptively observed in 1848:

> Fire, grass, kangaroos, and human inhabitants, seem all dependent on each other for existence in Australia; for any one of these being wanting, the others could not longer continue. Fire is necessary to burn the grass, and from those open forests, in which we find the large forest-kangaroo: the native applies that fire to the grass at certain seasons, in order that a young green crop may subsequently spring up, and so attract and enable him to kill or take the kangaroo with nets. In summer, the burning of long grass also discloses vermin, bird's nests, &c., on which the females and children, who chiefly burn the grass, feed. But for this simple process, the Australian woods had probably contained a thick jungle of those of New Zealand or America, instead of the open forest in which the white men now find grass for their cattle, to the exclusion of the kangaroo, which is well-known to forsake all those parts of the colony where cattle run. The intrusion therefore of cattle is by itself sufficient to produce the extirpation of the native race, by limiting their means of existence; and this must work such extensive changes in Australia as never entered into contemplation of the local authorities.

PEOPLE AND WATER

Water was a crucial determinant of Aboriginal subsistence and settlement. The forested lands of eastern coastal Australia, Tasmania and the extreme southwest generally have no problem with water supply. In regions where water is scarce or unreliable, Aboriginal tribal territory is larger. In the most arid regions 260 square kilometres was needed to support an individual, whereas in parts of the well-watered eastern zone an average of only 2.5 square kilometres was required.

In a land where evaporation is high (and immense tracts of Australia experience temperatures above 38°C) it is seasonal reliability or variability of rainfall, and not its average, which is the true gauge of the ecological situation. For example, Roebourne on the west coast received 1120 millimetres of rainfall in 1900, but only 3.3 millimetres in 1891; Alice Springs has recorded annual falls ranging from little more than twenty millimetres to over 1000 millimetres. Eventually every part of arid Australia gets some rain, generally at least 200 millimetres a year, but often as little as 100 millimetres. It is not just that rain fails to fall. With a mean annual evaporation exceeding 3200 millimetres, rainwater simply does not stay around for long, and two-thirds of Australia has no runoff to the sea.

There are relatively few permanent rivers in Australia and—except for Tasmania, which has glacial lakes—large freshwater lakes are uncommon. Although maps are dotted with inland lakes, some vast in area, this is deceptive: most are simply dry claypans fed intermittently through poorly defined channels. The largest of these lakes is salt-crusted Lake Eyre, which is also the continent's lowest point (sixteen metres below sea level). Lake Eyre receives an average annual rainfall of only 130 millimetres, while its catchment of 1,300,000 square kilometres receives some water almost every year. When heavy local rain coincides with a monsoonal front in its northern catchment the dual lake basins may fill, but such events tend to occur more than a decade apart.

From the standpoint of Aboriginal occupation, the seasonal dichotomy of wet and dry (or summer and winter) is of prime importance, but not in the core arid zone where water comes directly as rain, though seldom and sporadically. Here there are ephemeral lakes, claypans, rock holes, and springs fed by upwelling waters. The Aborigines knew about groundwater and dug wells to tap it at suitable locations; even dams were constructed on the eastern edge of Simpson Desert. An intimate knowledge and good memory of the water sources was necessary. Should the worst happen, people could survive in otherwise waterless country by extracting moisture from porous mallee roots. Nonetheless, large areas of desert were virtually uninhabited for years until there was sufficient rainfall. Tindale relates that, after general rain in the Western Desert, 'men ventured boldly into areas seen only at such infrequent intervals that they were often in doubt as to whether or not they were trespassing, and they would often flee at the first sign of unidentifiable "smokes" on the horizon or strange tracks'.

Even the rivers which flow from the eastern highlands are more variable in their discharge than the world average. Only a third of the entire Murray–Darling drainage system contributes water to the trunk-stream, the Murray, and even this 2700-kilometre-long river has more than once ceased to flow. The Darling River is Australia's longest, at 3000 kilometres. Yet it has ceased to flow for a period of over two years and a number of periods of over one year in the past 150 years. The minimum annual contribution to the Murray is then zero megalitres, while maximum annual Darling flow has been about 30 million megalitres.

Drought, with its associations of water shortage, searing heat, winds and destructive fires, is possibly the worst natural calamity known to Australians, and weather is certainly their most ubiquitous conversational topic. It also regulated Aboriginal society. Strehlow comprehended its significance for life in arid areas, estimating that, during drought conditions, as much as seven-eighths of the tribal lands in central Australia would be evacuated, while the people retreated to permanent watering-places. The transformation of the red landscapes of central Australia after rain, when a profusion of green grass, wildflowers and innumerable edible plants flourish for a brief season, is remarkable. Strehlow has claimed that it was the challenge of the climatic unpredictability, with its whimsical bounty and famine, which explains the richness of Aboriginal ceremonial and mythological life, the rigidity of their social controls, and their intimate knowledge of and attachment to their land. Human responses to land are more than mere economic determinism, however, as the Aboriginal emphasis on the spiritual bonds of place confirm.

It is difficult to envisage now, after so much of the natural vegetation has been modified during the last 200 years, but pre-European landscapes were sometimes quite different and more congenial to the Aboriginal inhabitants. Some areas were easier to traverse on foot, had more natural water sources and a far greater variety of plant and animal food than could be imagined today. But generalisations are impossible. Australia embraces such major vegetational associations as tropical and temperate rainforest, wet and dry sclerophyll forest, woodlands and grasslands and the extremes of both hot desert and alpine complexes. It is an obvious but necessary observation that Aboriginal economy and technology were adapted to the flora and dependent fauna within each vegetational habitat. It is evident that seasonality was a dominant theme in all but the desert areas. This implies the exploitation of a range of habitats, so that, generally, tribal groups claimed access to resources in a belt at right angles to ecological zones. For example, in the southeast, groups had access to the sea-coast and mountains; in the riverine plains, a section of the river for summer concentration, and a swath of plain for cool-weather exploitation.

Carrying capacity

In a nomadic hunting society, it is the leanest season which is the true gauge of the capacity of a country to sustain a population. So it was also that many early explorers were misled while traversing territory during the wet season or after abnormal rains. Their accurate, yet misleading, reports tempted pastoralists to graze their herds or flocks in areas totally unsuited to intensive grazing. Nature soon depopulated the region of stock, down to its actual carrying capacity. It may be suggested likewise that the Aboriginal population in 1788 had achieved ecological equilibrium. Perhaps the first human arrivals in Australia multiplied rapidly and reached an optimum population level millennia before colonial times. But ecological relationships are dynamic; resources for sustaining human life varied over time, sometimes considerably, and carrying capacities also must have varied greatly. From the time of first British settlement alien diseases devastated Aboriginal societies over much of the continent, and the historical record of both Aboriginal society and landscape reflect significantly altered circumstances to those of preceding centuries.

Norman Tindale correctly emphasised the role of human experience when he wryly commented that Dreaming ancestral beings created and protected natural resources from over-exploitation by developing systems of territorial taboo, enforcing dietary restrictions on social groups and age grades. Such creation beliefs and roles embodied empirical wisdom which ensured survival, and also endowed territories with an organic relationship between places and their owners. This bond between landscape and people was grasped by a perceptive policeman in the Alice Springs district in 1900. Ernest Cowle concluded that 'I believe that every water hole, Spring, Plain, Big Tree, Big Rock, Gutters and every peculiar or striking feature in the Country not even leaving out Sandhills...is connected with some tradition and that if one had the right blacks at that place, they could account for its presence there'.

5

People, language and society

Taking '1788' as a symbol for British occupation, but remembering that first contacts varied regionally for over a century, and that diseases and valued exchange goods travelled faster than the colonial frontier, it is appropriate to consider Aboriginal Australia in what is termed 'the ethnographic present'. With the knowledge of this '1788' data, it may be used with care to probe back in time, using it to reconstruct potential prehistoric demography, linguistic complexity, social organisation, the food quest and technology.

POPULATION SIZE

Unfortunately few early colonists bothered to record population estimates. Most British settlers lacked genuine interest in Aboriginal society or concern for its well-being, and consequently demographic and ethnographic information was lost by default. In order to estimate Aboriginal demography during British colonisation, reliance is necessary on historic observations, ethnographic data, and some archaeology.

The scythe of death

While colonial law provided notional protection from white depredation, away from larger settlements it was often ignored, and even invoked to justify brutal killings by settlers or mounted police. It is likely that upwards of 20,000 Aborigines met violent deaths. Despite this horrific record, the introduction of alien diseases produced the most immediate and major destruction of Aboriginal societies, particularly in populous southeastern Australia. With the spread of pastoralism, the traditional food resources available to survivors were diminished or otherwise alienated. These factors, and the concomitant social dislocation and psychological impact, exacerbated the trend. To offer a single example, the decline in the Aboriginal population in the Lake Eyre region was estimated to be 50 per cent with each succeeding generation; of an original Aboriginal population of about 1830 people, representing six small tribes in early colonial times, the number was only 500 in 1900, and 30 in 1939.

The scourge of smallpox was probably first described in China in 1122 BC, and since then epidemics have swept regions of the world until the virus was recently eradicated. It was a devastating disease even for human populations with some resistance (one epidemic in Britain killed one-twelfth of the population), and it could entirely decimate immunologically susceptible populations. There were two major smallpox epidemics during early colonial times. The first was experienced around Sydney in 1789. How and from where the disease arrived in Australia is unknown—there were no manifestations of smallpox among the British soldiers and convicts themselves, so perhaps Indonesian trepangers introduced it in the tropics. The disease possibly reduced the local Aboriginal population by half. After exploring Broken Bay, a rugged inlet just north of Sydney, the judge-advocate John Collins recorded 'the pox has not confined its effects to Port Jackson, for our path was in many places covered with skeletons'. The Cadigal band, which inhabited the territory immediately around the British settlement, was particularly hard hit—of its estimated 30 to 50 people, only three survived. Wherever its starting-point, this first epidemic may have spread widely across southeastern Australia, because a few years after the disease struck at Sydney, pock-marked Aborigines were seen in the Hunter Valley, at Jervis Bay, and even at Westernport Bay, near the future city of Melbourne.

The second smallpox epidemic was recognised in 1829 and possibly continued spreading for another two years. It probably swept northwards, being observed at Port Macquarie on the central New South Wales coast and possibly reaching into southern Queensland via river corridors. If identification was correct, it also was carried

inland, where it was seen at Bathurst, and southwards to the mouth of the Murray River.

The impact of smallpox may have proved severe on riverine-dwelling people along the Murray–Darling because of their higher population density and their more sedentary lifestyle, which facilitated easier transmission of infections. Venereal diseases and tuberculosis also spread among Aboriginal populations from the first years of British settlement (or even earlier with the seasonal arrival of Macassans), and at times outpaced the expansion of colonial frontiers. For over a century gonorrhoea and syphilis were major causes of infertility, reduction in live births, and premature death. Some accounts of the ravages of venereal disease are heart-rending—whole families were sometimes infected and thereby condemned. No doubt these new diseases were passed from one tribe to another at large ceremonial gatherings.

Population estimates

Social anthropologist Radcliffe-Brown estimated in the 1930 *Australian yearbook* that the 1788 Aboriginal population numbered some 300,000 people. Earlier yearbooks officially stated half that figure, but Radcliffe-Brown's reasoned calculations were not questioned by later anthropologists. If his figure is approximately correct, then the Aboriginal population of Australia declined by 90 per cent in less than a century; but probably the impact of foreign contacts was even more severe than this.

In 1983 the economic historian Noel Butlin offered a revised estimate of at least a million people in the southeast. Certainly previous figures that contributed to the total estimate are unreliable, which is to be expected given the poor quality of basic information. Harry Lourandos has shown from a detailed scrutiny of the journals of G. A. Robinson that the population of the Western District of Victoria in 1841 could have been nearly 8000, double Radcliffe-Brown's earlier estimate for this region. Similarly, Stephen Webb's studies of bone pathologies exhibited by human remains suggest that, along the central east coast and the Murray River, there were larger populations than previously suspected.

While Butlin marshalled an impressive array of evidence for his population estimate, it was highly speculative and one we judge to be probably too high. As Keryn Kefous has explained, the problem is that Butlin used maximum figures for the human carrying capacity of different environmental zones. The actual population density for hunter-gatherers is normally much lower than the theoretical optimum. Also Butlin was overconfident about the availability of particular food staples over large regions, and he did not take into account the crucial factor of available drinking water from year to year. Except in the most favoured regions, long-term carrying capacity can only be reasonably calculated over a sufficient number of years to include normal periodic intervals of resource stress typical of many habitats.

Over most of Australia, the population density was low and people were spread thinly. Favourable environments permitted more concentrated occupation, notably in the northern, eastern and southwestern parts of the continent and along the central and lower Murray River. Queensland perhaps supported up to one-third of the entire population, particularly in coastal regions, while the arid third of the continent, which received fewer than 250 millimetres average annual rainfall, supported only a few thousand inhabitants. The anthropologist Ronald Berndt estimated that only 18,000 people inhabited 650,000 square kilometres of the arid interior from the Great Australian Bight northwards to the Tropic of Capricorn. In some fertile coastal or riverine regions, however, population densities possibly were higher than one person to every eight square kilometres. There are few reliable clues concerning Tasmania's population, but it is estimated at about 3000–5000, a figure corroborated by an exhaustive analysis of the data by Rhys Jones. Colin Pardoe has disputed this and argues for a much higher figure on the basis of genetic evidence. While we detect a tendency among some colleagues to accept higher figures than Radcliffe-Brown's but to dispute Butlin's estimate, our best estimate for the Aboriginal population size in 1788 is some hundreds of thousands, perhaps at most three-quarters of a million.

ABORIGINAL LANGUAGES

The patchy record of Australian languages has been cobbled together from a variety of sources, including word lists compiled by explorers, settlers, government officials, pioneer ethnographers and missionaries, beginning with the journal of Captain Cook. Professional linguistic studies of Australian languages as a coherent academic discipline began only three decades ago. Subsequently, there has been a concerted collaboration between linguists and Aboriginal speakers to salvage the remaining knowledge of the many almost extinct languages. Only a few thousand people today are speakers of the 30 or so extant Aboriginal languages as their first tongue. Most Aborigines living in cities and rural areas speak varieties of English, or Kriol, which is a creole spoken in northern Australia. The creole of the Torres Strait Islanders is called Broken.

Many languages and dialects are known from only a few basic words or scraps of grammar. Least is known about the eight to twelve languages of Tasmania, all of which are now extinct. The best estimate of languages spoken in 1788 is about 250. The number recognised depends upon the definition of dialects, but overall this estimate is for distinct languages, not dialects.

With so many discrete languages and upwards of 700 dialects, it is obvious that only a few languages, such as Warlpiri, northwest of Alice Springs, had thousands of speakers and others only a few hundred. Because marriage partners were commonly exchanged between language groups, most Aborigines were bilingual, and many were multilingual (called regional multilingualism). Some Aboriginal languages were spoken only by members of a single tribe, but there was enormous variation in linguistic discreteness throughout the continent. At times, six or more geographically adjacent tribes spoke dialects of the same language, such as the tribes inhabiting the Western Desert, an area of over a million square kilometres. Sometimes these contiguous dialects were like links in a chain, where the people of each tribe easily understood the dialects of their neighbours because they shared most of their general vocabulary, but they barely understood the dialects of tribes much further along the chain. The Dyirbal language of northeast Queensland, studied for many years by the linguist R. M. W. Dixon, is a chain of ten dialects with only 50 per cent shared vocabulary at its ends, but at least 85 per cent shared between adjacent links. There are intriguing linguistic nuances in this example because correspondence between grammar and verbs is higher at the ends of the chain.

There are several common attributes of Aboriginal languages. First, they have fairly complex consonant systems. For example, English has only three places where the passage of air can be closed off—the lips (as in *b* and *p*), the tip of the tongue against the gum ridge (*d* and *t*), and the back of the tongue against the soft palate (*g* and *k*). Many Australian languages have six such places, as many as any languages in the world. They also use blade of tongue against the teeth, blade of tongue against hard palate, and tip of tongue turned back onto the roof of the mouth (a retroflex sound similar to that of languages in India). Australian languages often have six corresponding nasal sounds (where English just has *m* and *n*). Another notable feature is that they have two rhotics or *r*-sounds, one like that in general Australian English, and also a trill as in Scottish English. Sometimes there can be as many as four *l*-sounds. The sibilants or fricatives *s* and *sh* are universally absent in Australian languages. There are two semi-vowels, *y* and *w*. Most of the languages have only three vowels—*i*, *a* and *u*—but a few have four or more.

Second, words show case, tense and mood by the addition of meaningful segments, which make for very long words. Nouns and verbs have markers on them that indicate who does what to whom, when it is done, and how. New words are derived by adding other meaningful segments. Third, the hunting and gathering lifestyle of Aborigines gives their languages a semantic homogeneity. There is a vocabulary of about 50 words, including *bu* meaning 'hit', which is common to Aboriginal languages. Many languages distinguish classes of nouns, which have classifiers marking them as, for instance, edible flesh or vegetable, male or female (the female noun class in Djirbalngan includes women, fire and dangerous things).

Classification

Despite the existence of a former land connection between Australia and New Guinea and a fairly close biological relationship between Melanesians and Aborigines, no linguist currently argues for any demonstrable common inheritance of vocabularies or other link between their respective languages. It seems that the duration of cultural and geographic separation has been too long for any retention of common language. The one small area of overlap between these two language families is the Meriam Mir language of eastern Torres Strait. It has some borrowed Australian elements, but is most closely related to the language spoken around the Fly River estuary in Papua. Most linguists believe that the Kalaw Kawaw Ya languages or dialects of the western chain of islands belong to the Australian family because the pronouns, which are hard to borrow, fit the Australian mould better than they do Papuan. Both languages have extensive borrowings from each other, and a few Papuan words are found even in Aboriginal languages of northern Cape York Peninsula. The only other evidence of non-Aboriginal language in Australia prior to British rule is the 100 or so Austronesian words (mostly nouns) in Macassan pidgin which was spoken along the coast of Arnhem Land in historic times.

Some 40 years ago the linguist Kenneth Hale recognised that, over most of Australia, languages were similar to each other in the structure of words and the way words relate to each other in a sentence (word order is very free compared with English). To this widespread grouping, which comprises 85 per cent of Australian languages, he gave the name Pama-Nyungan (pronounced 'pahma-nyoongan') from the words *pama* and *nyunga*, respectively meaning 'person' in a Cape York language and 'one' in the southwest. Geographically, this grouping extends across Australia from the east to the west coast and from coastal Victoria to the central and western islands of Torres Strait. The almost 190 Pama-Nyungan languages suffix their verbs and nouns to show grammatical relations, and they form a coherent grouping. The remaining 'Non-Pama-Nyungan' languages share a number of features with Pama-Nyungan, but they form a broad group of languages found only in the Top End and Kimberley region and along the southern coast of the Gulf of Carpentaria. Non-Pama-Nyungan comprises 60 languages in about nine language families. Tiwi, spoken on Bathurst and Melville Islands, is the most aberrant of Non-Pama-Nyungan, which is probably due to cultural isolation. Non-Pama-Nyungan languages express grammatical relations by prefixing a verb with elements that were formerly separate pronouns to indicate the subject and object of a sentence.

Origins and development

Pama-Nyungan is a typological clustering of about twenty internally homogenous language groups. A proto-Pama-Nyungan cannot be demonstrated because apparently there are no innovations different from proto-Australian (abbreviated as 'pAu'). However, G. N. O'Grady postulated that about 4000 to 4500 years would have been needed for the observed degree of overall diversity to develop. Although some linguists support O'Grady's estimate, others suspect a much greater antiquity. Patrick McConvell has inferred from his reconstruction of language subgroups and evidence of loanwords that Pama-Nyungan began to expand about 6000 years ago from a homeland near the Gulf of Carpentaria, where the greatest linguistic diversity in the family occurs. McConvell postulates that, over a period of about 3000 years, this expansion extinguished diverse language groups in nearly all inhabited regions of Australia, and that speakers colonised previously unoccupied territories. His argument is based on a family tree model of language development criticised by

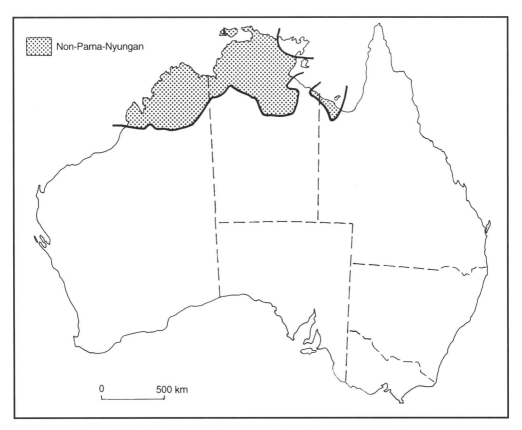

Non-Pama-Nyungan

0   500 km

Map 2. *Distribution of Non-Pama-Nyungan languages in Australia. (R. M. W. Dixon)*

Dixon, and he postulates widespread migrations of people, initially in response to rising seas. Neither of these tenets we find plausible in the Australian situation, and we do not believe in widespread evacuations of people when the seas rose. Those regions that lost much territory quickly were probably least inhabited.

How is the existence of Non-Pama-Nyungan explained? Dixon believes that Non-Pama-Nyungan languages split off from proto-Australian by a process of 'grammatical innovation'—for instance, by making pronominal prefixes to verbs out of free pronouns. From time to time, the notion is resurrected that ancestral Non-Pama-Nyungan was spoken by immigrants who arrived between 3000 to 5000 years ago, bringing with them dingoes and new types of stone implements. McConvell proposes that Aboriginal refugees from the grasslands of northern Sahul were forced to retreat into northern Australia by rising seas at the end of the Pleistocene. We see no substance in any of these speculations and prefer Dixon's explanation of indigenous stable interaction and development.

Dixon believes that the general homogeneity of Australian languages is the result of language development over a long time, to an extent not seen on other continents, and linguistic diffusion which accompanies the exchange of women in marriage and other cultural and social networking between multilingual tribes. This diffusion was facilitated by the general underlying similarity of languages, which meant that it was easier for the transfer of words and grammatical forms from one group to another. This process of diffusion, Dixon argues, did not involve direct replacement of one language by another but a complex interaction between languages during a long period of equilibrium. He postulates at least 8000 years, which is about the time that Australia and New Guinea have been separated. Dixon speculates that language development may have taken even tens of thousands of years. Possibly the Australian language family is the world's oldest and offers a useful model of Pleistocene language development in other continents.

Proto-Australian language

Although most linguists believe in a single proto-Australian (or ancestral) language, there is no indication of what preceded it. To consider two extreme possibilities, proto-Australian could have been spoken by the first people to settle the continent; alternatively, it could have emerged only some thousands of years ago and spread throughout the continent, extinguishing all the other languages of the time. With the latter possibility one would expect traces of pre-existing languages, but there are none, which suggests that proto-Australian is ancient.

There have been substantial changes in Australian languages, even during the last few millennia. Vocabulary changes rapidly as words become antiquated and drop out of use, other words are borrowed from neighbouring languages or are created. Language replacement is accelerated by death taboos which proscribe the use of words that sound like the name of the deceased person.

Lexicostatistics, the rate at which basic vocabulary changes over time, is now discredited as a way of revealing the ancestral relationships between languages, while the family tree model is not thought to be appropriate or useful in the Australian situation. Wholesale diffusion between languages over many thousands of years has obscured ancestral relationships and it is difficult to know whether there has been more divergence than convergence. In other words, there is no family tree, but rather a matting of interwoven vines!

While it has proved impossible to reconstruct the intervening linguistic stages, Dixon and his colleagues have had considerable success in describing some aspects of ancestral proto-Australian language. They have shown that the sound system was remarkably like modern Aboriginal—there were four or five contrasting stops and nasals, two *r* sounds, one or two *l* sounds, and the semi-vowels *y* and *w*. Probably there was contrasting vowel length (*a* as opposed to *aa*) which now occurs only in a few scattered Aboriginal languages. Other essential elements still found in the modern languages include: structurally complex words as well as simple ones; probably a set of nominal classifiers to mark nouns as belonging to different classes (for example, male/female, meat/vegetable); suffixes on nouns and adjectives to show subject/object or possessive relations; only a few dozen simple verbs which are used to make numerous compound verbs. Almost all grammar and some words of modern Aboriginal languages can be shown to derive from the common ancestral proto-Australian.

For archaeologists, historical linguistics provides little information about Aboriginal origins or the timing of first settlement. It does, however, reveal intriguing details about social and cultural change in prehistoric times, such as the contacts between different language groups and the spread of kinship systems. It seems likely that any better understanding of Australia's early linguistic prehistory will have to come from analytical methods yet to be developed. The complex interweaving of Australian languages is difficult to decipher but the overall impression is one of hunter-gatherer societies evolving in isolation over a very long time.

SOCIAL ORGANISATION

In '1788', Europeans accustomed to Native Americans termed the assumed major social divisions within Aboriginal society 'tribes'. The number of tribes has been placed as high as 900, although around 500 is the conventional figure. Today, this social category is better defined as a dialect or language group. These were not territorial entities and their members rarely, if ever, assembled.

Because Australian societies subsisted as hunters, collectors and fishers, they had to adapt flexibly to conditions; they were enriched by pervading spiritual content, moral bonding, and obligations which ensured social order and welfare. A person's social identity was defined by age, gender and kinship ties and an abiding sense of place. While hierarchies of social categories were common to everyone, such order was imbued with flexibility by membership in a number of social categories.

Residential groups comprised relatives, though individuals acknowledged as 'kin' were not always related. The most commonly recognised residential group was the 'band', which varied in size from ten to 50 people. The tract of land, or 'range', exploited by a band in normal times varied greatly in size, from about 15 to 25,000 square kilometres depending on the nature of the country. In some regions society was divided into more inclusive social categories, such as moiety (two categories), section and semi-moiety (four categories), and subsection or 'skins' (eight categories). These related to organisation of ritual, ownership of land and, to some extent, the regulation of marriage. Governance of Aboriginal social life was organised through religion. Authority was based on age, gender and religious status. Although there were no tribal chiefs or ruling councils, it is becoming recognised that in some regions, especially southeastern Australia, certain individuals exerted personal influence. Their status resembles that of 'big men' in Papua New Guinea.

Social structures of hunter-gatherer societies are exceptionally difficult to reconstruct from archaeological remains. However, rock art and burial practices convey information about social perception and relationships. A general theme that has emerged from a number of Australian archaeological studies of stone tool assemblages, rock art and burials is the apparent transformation of social networks from territorially open ones during the Late Pleistocene and Early Holocene to more regional ones in recent millennia. Possible changes in the nature of intergroup relations and other aspects of social organisation are at the centre of the 'intensification debate' which attempts to explain the changes evident in Australia's archaeological record for the last few thousand years. Historical linguistics also offers much promise. The linguist Patrick McConvell has reconstructed section and subsection systems of social organisation from his interpretations of standard language-borrowings. He suggests that sections originated in southwest Australia and diffused north to the Kimberley region between 1000 and 2000 years ago, and that subsections existed for perhaps 1000 years. During the 1960s a campaign commenced to record surviving Aboriginal languages, but the emphasis has now shifted to their analysis and historical development, so significant insights into the role of language in past societies are likely.

THE DREAMING

There was an intimate link between Aborigines and their land. Topographical features, plants and animals invariably were manifestations of ancestral beings from the Dreaming. During this creation era the Aborigines were given 'the law' which sanctioned social order. Special localities retain life essence and spiritual power from creation events. Progressive revelation of the Dreaming record is secret to initiates, to the elders, or to one sex. Women participated in religious life throughout the continent and in the desert regions they maintain their own distinct secret ceremonies. No single person, or even language group, could know more than a small number of all the Aboriginal creation stories.

During the present agitation supporting Aboriginal claims to land title, opponents attach little importance to a place and its related Dreaming stories. This is a denial of the reality of Aboriginal spiritual life, which archaeologists cannot ignore since painted and engraved rocks are emblazoned with hints of ancient beliefs. It is relevant to listen to Alice Springs residents a century ago, Ernest Cowle, quoted at the end of the previous chapter, and Frank Gillen, the postmaster. In 1897 Gillen wrote 'there is not a remarkable natural feature in the country without a special tradition—tradition—Why it is the very breath of their nostrils—that is it was—before the Whiteman came…and trampled tradition…out of them'.

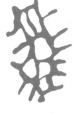

While there are extensive oral and historical records relating to Dreaming places, there is little archaeology, partly because many such sites are too sacred to excavate. Excavations approved by Aboriginal communities in central Australia have demonstrated antiquity of some hundreds of years for encampments at a ceremonial locality on a major Dreaming track. Excavation at Ngarrabullgan Cave (Mount Mulligan) in north Queensland established that the site was visited at times from about 37,000 years BP to around 900 years BP. Its modern status as a sacred and dangerous Dreaming place not suitable for habitation evidently implies that this tradition is no older than a millennium. Historically documented Dreaming stories are also implicit in prehistoric rock art of regions such as the Kimberley Plateau, Kakadu and the Sydney Basin, and a prehistory of the Dreaming may be possible.

CULTURE AREAS

Throughout the continent there are major differences in language, social customs, mythology, artistic styles and technology, and there have been numerous attempts to map complexes of Aboriginal culture traits. The most convincing of these is by Nicolas Peterson, who observed that major culture areas correspond with major drainage basins. His explanation for this correlation is that the topography and environments of drainage basins tend to be internally uniform, while their margins are relatively poor in plant, animal and water resources. Consequently there exists more social interaction between groups living within the basin, and much less between groups living on either side of the marginal zones. There is archaeological evidence for regional continuity of various kinds of culture traits evident in rock art and stone tool assemblages for considerable periods, sometimes thousands of years. However, these are very few compared with those documented for the historical record. Consequently the nature of prehistoric culture complexes is poorly understood, but forms a theme of contemporary investigation.

Subsistence and reciprocity

6

Early colonists judged hunter-gatherer societies so wrongly that they applied the doctrine of *terra nullius*, presuming that Aborgines neither modified the landscape nor 'mixed their labour with the soil' in any way. What a few unheeded anthropologists and other thoughtful observers claimed is evident today—Aboriginal subsistence activities were not random, but premeditated, traditional diet was balanced, and social bonding ensured an individual's identification with a clan's estate.

MOBILITY AND SEASONALITY

Essentially Aboriginal hunter-gatherers were self-sufficient and mobile. In some well-endowed regions, such as the Murray River corridor and certain coastal and estuarine localities, base camps were semi-permanent. In regions not so well endowed, camps were moved more frequently and over great distances. William Thomas, who lived with the Aborigines around Melbourne at the beginning of British settlement, recorded that camp was shifted after about three days. In the Western Desert an American archaeologist, R. A. Gould, accompanied two families through three summer months, during which time they moved camp nine times over a territory of nearly 3000 square kilometres.

When localised or seasonally abundant food or water supplies were available, or when ceremonial obligations demanded, bands aggregated, whereas in leaner times they scattered. In almost every habitat there is evidence that this clustering and dispersal typified the pulsations in the Aboriginal life-pattern in all but exceptionally provident areas. There are examples, particularly from the southeast, which indicate that planned exploitation of seasonal abundance enabled assemblies of several hundred people. On the Murray River, wild fowl and freshwater crayfish in springtime, or netted fish in summer, supported such numbers; in the high plains of the Australian Alps, swarms of nutritious bogong moths attracted Aborigines from all directions. Some other recorded congregations resulted from fortuitous unpredictable bounties, such as a stranded whale. However, other assemblies which must have been adjusted to well-founded environmental knowledge were less transient and are of considerable archaeological interest. Such were ceremonial gatherings in arid areas following good rains, when plant foods abounded. At Goyder's Lagoon, northeast of Lake Eyre, 500 people assembled after floods on the Diamantina River. Even larger numbers are estimated to have gathered every third year for the feasts of the bunya pine nuts (*Araucaria bidwelli*) northwest of Brisbane. In the deserts of the west, it was grass and sedge seeds and the bush potato (*Ipomoea costata*) which supported the gatherings; in Arnhem Land and north Queensland, it was cycad kernels, laboriously pounded and detoxified.

Aboriginal women and children mainly gathered vegetable food, caught birds and small animals, gathered shellfish, and fished. Women and children also participated in communal hunts, and in some instances women hunted large animals, such as seals, on their own. Depending on the area, men spent much of their time hunting the larger animals and birds, and fishing.

ANIMAL FOOD

Subject to local clan or ritual taboos, all Australian animals were eaten. Ten marsupial species weigh between ten and 100 kilograms, and dozens of others—some large marine mammals, crocodiles in the north, small reptiles everywhere, and the large flightless emu and other birds—provided food resources. The larger macropodid species such as red kangaroo were hunted individually, but often with little return. Small marsupials and reptiles provided most protein in the diet throughout much of Australia. Not only was small prey more common, but it was easier to catch; men, women and children all hunted it. Fire was often indispensable in communal hunting of small game: the anthropologist R. M. Berndt describes wallabies coming out of the fired grass 'as thick as rabbits', dispatched with clubs, and piled in heaps ready for collection. Possum provide an important food source in forestlands. Because they sleep in tree holes or nests in dense foliage during the day, they are easy to capture. Many other small marsupial prey once available—bilbi, bandicoots, pademelons, betongs, potoroos, rat-kangaroos—are now extinct or rare because of European pastoralism and introduced predators.

Fish were caught where available (except in Tasmania) with the aid of regionally varied technology, such as canoes, weirs, traps, nets, special fish-spears, and hook and line. Betty Meehan's study of shell-fish gathering among the Anbarra people of Arnhem Land has provided possibly the best account in the world about shellfish in a hunter-gatherer economy, where molluscs were a staple, always available when other food sources were restricted.

Saltwater turtles and dugong were hunted in tropical waters. The dugong, a close relative of the manatee, sometimes gathered in herds of several hundred animals, and a single kill provided an Aboriginal group with about 100 to 150 kilograms of meat and a large amount of fat (the meat is said to taste like beef), although before steel harpoons it was harvested less often. In southern waters, colonies of southern fur seals flourished and these were particularly important in prehistoric Tasmania.

Birds were taken by a variety of means and sometimes provided a substantial part of the meat in the diet. Along the Murray River large numbers of ducks were captured with bulrush-fibre nets up to 55 metres long, while along the southeast coast and Tasmania, muttonbirds (*Puffinus tenuirostris*) and their eggs and chicks were a plentiful seasonal staple. In the Lake Eyre region, during good seasons the chicks of vast flocks of nesting pelicans were culled in a process that Richard Kimber calls 'harvest hunting'. When the young pelicans began to fatten, the Aborigines built a pen on the lake shore, near to their camp, and herded a large number of juvenile pelicans inside. For weeks they would consume the inmates while the mother pelicans continued to feed their captive young. When the last pelican in the pen was eaten, the cycle began again. The ever-alert emu took considerable ingenuity to catch, and in some desert regions various hunting strategies were employed. A brush fence was erected around a water source so that the emu had to follow a track where a hunter waited; a waterhole was drugged with intoxicating *Duboisia* foliage; and a bunch of feathers was dangled on the end of a long pole to excite the bird's curiosity.

The insect realm was not neglected. In central Australia witchetty grubs (*Xylentes* species, grey cossid moth larvae) were a nutritious and much relished food; moths were harvested when seasonally abundant, such as bogong moths in the Australian Alps. Other important insect foods included termites and honey ants. Honey from the stingless *Trigona* bees also provided a bonus in routine foraging, and in some regions, including Arnhem Land, honey gathering was an important seasonal activity. Another desirable insect secretion with comparable nutritional value was lerp, which occurs in southeastern Australia. Lerp, which is made into a sweet energy-drink, is a sugary deposit found on leaves of some eucalypts, similar in appearance to fairy-floss. Peter Beveridge, an early settler near Swan Hill on the Murray River, noted that a man could easily collect more than twenty kilograms in a day when it was in season.

Plant food

Only now are non-Aboriginal Australians becoming aware of the vast variety of nutritious and tasty Aboriginal food plants. Not all types of 'bush tucker' are unfamiliar, however, since some are closely related to major commercial cultivars. These include grass seeds ground into flour, yams, a desert species of sweet potato (*Ipomoea costata*), small yellow or green bush tomatoes (*Solanum* species), mushrooms, macadamia nuts from the Queensland rainforest and the fruit-snack lilly-pilly (*Acmena smithii*).

Bulbs and tubers

Edible bulbs and tubers—equivalent to potatoes, carrots, and radishes in the modern diet—were widespread in Australia and available seasonally or all year round. In tropical Australia, roots and tubers were staples of the wet season, in particular, yams (*Dioscorea* species), and in Cape York wild arrowroot (*Tacca* species). In parts of the southeast, daisy yam (*Microseris lanceolata*) was a staple. This small

Arnhem Land woman preparing waterlily-seed cakes, an important food in the dry season. (Photo by Donald Thomson; reproduced with permission of Mrs D. M. Thomson)

perennial plant with a yellow flower is similar to a dandelion, with a tuberous root the size and shape of a radish. In north central Victoria a settler stated that there were millions of daisy yams across the plain. In some regions the daily tally was eight kilograms per woman. Near Echuca on the Murray River, a woman could collect enough in an hour to feed her family for the day. Daisy yams are now rare because of grazing by sheep and cattle and the absence of Aboriginal fire management.

Often neglected in accounts of important Aboriginal plant foods in forestlands are tubers and bulbs of orchids and lilies, which are better known for their flowers than their food value. Usually these tubers are small, but they may form dense clusters and sometimes are the size of a small potato. Equally valuable regionally are the radish-shaped bulbous tubers of water ribbons (*Triglochin procera*) and roots (rhizomes) of Cumbungi (*Typha* species) which were a staple starchy food along the Murray–Darling river system and in southwestern Australia.

Starch extraction

A number of different kinds of starchy plant foods (carbohydrate sources) needed laborious processing before they became edible. Starch flour was extracted from the fibrous roots of ferns widely distributed in regions of higher rainfall. The most important ferns in eastern Australia were *Blechnum indicum* and *Pteridium esculentum*, the starch tasting much like potato. Other plants that had to be leached in water first were some yam species that had an acrid taste, such as *Alocasia brisbanensis*, *Dioscorea bulbifera* (round or 'cheeky' yam); mangrove seeds, which contain tannin; and, most important of all, cycads.

The cycad family is a primitive group of plants, of which there are two important genera in Australia, *Macrozamia* along the eastern and southwestern coasts, and *Cycas* in the north of the continent. These plants have large cones burgeoning with long hard-shelled nuts, containing starchy kernels between two and four centimetres long. Cycads were exploited throughout their area of distribution and were a staple in the north Queensland rainforests where alternative plant foods were limited. Aged seeds lying on the ground for some months may be eaten raw or cooked without ill-effect. However, fresh kernels, which are about 30 per cent starch, contain toxic and carcinogenic compounds. Numerous variations to process kernels by removing the water-soluble toxin were adopted, but commonly they were sliced or crushed, placed in a bag in running water and leached for up to a week, then ground into a paste, wrapped in paperbark and baked into cycad bread or 'cake'. Queenslander A. Meston observed that 'the flour had exactly the smell and eating properties of arrowroot'. Archaeological evidence for processing of cycad over 13,000 years ago has been found by Moya Smith at Cheetup rockshelter, in a granite dome in Cape le Grand National Park, east of Esperance, Western Australia. Smith uncovered the remains of a macrozamia drying pit of a kind described by George Grey in 1841, indicating a long antiquity for this method of preparation. Other evidence for cycad consumption dates to within the last 4500 years in Queensland.

Seeds

The large-scale collecting of seeds occurs predominantly in the arid and semi-arid zones. In the Lake Eyre region at least twenty varieties of seeds were preferred, while in the more marginal Little Sandy Desert seeds comprised nearly half of plant food species harvested by the Mardu people. Of the 70 plant food species known to them, 42 were seeds harvested in late winter and spring, including those of grasses, sedges, succulents, chenopod herbs, acacias, eucalypts, and small shrubs.

As a rule, wherever cereal grasses were abundant they provided a staple food. Along the Darling River grass seeds were the equivalent staple to bulbs and tubers further east. Among the most important cereals were the seeds of the *Panicum* genus (in particular the wild millet, *Panicum decompositum*) and a sedge (*Fimbristylis oxystachya*). Widely exploited in Australia and an important food source in arid regions are the oily dark seeds of the succulents *Portulaca oleracea, P. intraterranea* and *P. filifolia*, called 'munyeroo', pigweed or purslane. Better known to Europeans however is 'nardoo', the whitish spores of a small clover-like fern (*Marsilia* species), which are extracted from their spore cases by pounding. All of these seeds and spores were ground into flour and made into a cake or damper, so grindstones are an essential component, providing an archaeological indicator to seed food exploitation.

THE FARMING DEBATE

Jack Golson proposed that there was a shift from forest foraging to farming in New Guinea earlier than 9000 years ago, at the time when

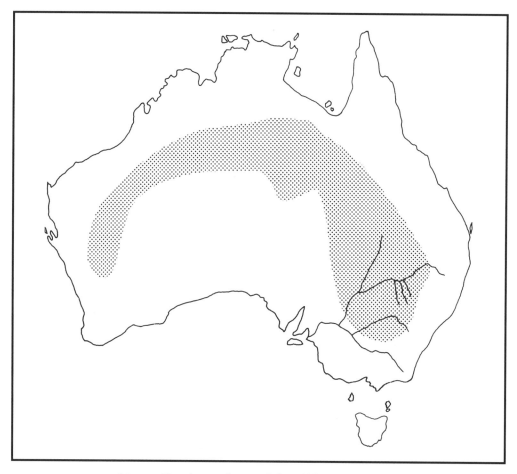

Map 3. *The Aboriginal 'grain belt': edible seed plants grew within the arid and semi-arid zones. (After Tindale 1974: Fig. 31)*

it was still joined to Australia. The evidence comes from excavations at Kuk Agricultural Research Station near Mount Hagen, where Golson traced the course of a long channel in swamp sediments and interpreted it as an ancient drainage ditch. Golson argues that increased sedimentation in the swamp at this level may have been caused by forest clearance around the swamp. Unfortunately, no direct evidence, such as domesticated plant remains, has been found. The ethnobotanist Douglas Yen argued that some of the world's major cultivars, such as sugar cane, the Australimusa group of bananas, and species of taro and yams, are indigenous to New Guinea. The question remains, however, whether these were farmed in New Guinea before the definite appearance of gardening in the tropical forests by about 6000 years BP.

Many different suggestions have been offered to explain why Aborigines did not develop horticulture or farming, or adopt it from their northern neighbours. This question presupposes Western concepts of progress and the moral virtues of industry. It also assumes a profound difference between hunter-gatherers and farmers which is not the case. Some farming peoples in developing countries rely on hunting, gathering and fishing in addition to tending food crops and livestock. Aborigines manipulated the habitat of favoured food resources in ways that ensured their availability and abundance. For instance, in many parts of Australia the extensive turning of soil to collect edible roots and tubers incidentally encouraged the growth of the following year's 'crop'. Even irrigation was practised in one desert region, where runoff channels were blocked to flood expanses of plain where edible grass seeds could be gathered when the country dried out. Most importantly, plant communities were set to the torch, so that the range and amount of potential food resources—grazing marsupials, bracken, yams, wild tomatoes, cycad and many other plants with edible seeds— would increase, either because the removal of long grass facilitated fresh shoots to appear or because the ash enriched the soil. In some regions, including southwestern Australia, north Queensland and Groote Eylandt, the tops of edible tubers were replanted; the planting of seeds is also recorded.

Some Aboriginal groups, like many farming people worldwide, had a relatively high population density, settled lifestyle and high dependence on particular plant staples, and they experienced periodic shortages of food. In general, though, hunting, fishing and collecting wild food provided far greater variety than what was eaten by most pre-Industrial Age farming peoples of the world. Also, with higher mobility and access to emergency foods through their social network, most Aboriginal groups were not subjected to the catastrophic effects of famine in bad seasons. European Australians failed to draw the moral of the testimony for this balanced cultural ecology: one generation of cattlemen sufficed to convert the Birdsville Track region in South Australia into desert, although it had sustained Aboriginal economy for countless generations. Several members of the Burke and Wills expedition died of malnutrition in a region which supported hundreds of Aborigines. Whose values are progressive, therefore, in such environments?

MATERIAL CULTURE

Although much vital information about Aboriginal material culture has been lost since 1788, there remains a remarkably diverse body of documentary accounts, preserved artefacts, and the testimony of rock art. These illuminate arts, crafts, and economic and ceremonial aspects of traditional society. Here we feature aspects that relate most to archaeological issues.

In response to cultural and environmental factors Aboriginal material culture varied considerably from one part of the continent to the other, and even along different stretches of coastline. For instance, while sophisticated outrigger canoes were constructed along the north Queensland coast, there were virtually no watercraft at all along Australia's southwestern and southern coast as far east as the mouth of the Murray River.

A wide range of natural materials was exploited for making artefacts: stone, plant parts and compounds, shell, animal tissue such as skin, fur, teeth, bone, blood, sinew, fat, and even dung—used as a tinder in fire-making and mixed with resin to make a tough adhesive. Bark was especially useful for a wide range of purposes, including canoes, cord, huts, shelters and hunting blinds. Because of its pliability and softness, the paperbark tree (*Melaleuca*) proved invaluable for shelters, water containers and blankets. Shelters were often made from a few bark sheets, but there were more complex house or hut constructions designed for large hearth groups and semi-sedentary occupation. Post-hole features in sediments, circular depressions from pit houses in earth and shell mounds and, in at least two regions, low stone walls may be all that remain of prehistoric residential constructions.

Travelling light

An economy in material equipment was characteristic of every habitat. Even when conditions permitted fairly sedentary habits, ceremonial and other social demands, or the attractions of some locally available food, provided the stimulus for movement. Domestic possessions therefore were generally few and utilitarian. With the notable exception of watercraft and grinding and pounding tools, artefacts needed to be lightweight, preferably multi-purpose and no more numerous or bulky than what could be carried on a day's walk. Simplicity of technology is exemplified by the people of the

Western Desert. During their planned nomadism, the women carried the 'household' equipment—a wooden digging stick, wood or bark container, and in cool weather, a firestick. The men travelled light, with spears and spearthrower (woomera). This spearthrower served many purposes other than to cast the spear further and more accurately. On its handle end was a stone flake, used for cutting and for making and maintaining other artefacts; placed on its side, the spearthrower was used as a friction stick for making fire; it was used as a parrying stick, and as a scoop for digging out lizards or clearing the ground for a camp site, as a clapstick for music, and, if decorated, as a 'map'. Finally, the broad, curved central portion served as a receptacle for food and small articles, and on ceremonial occasions as a palette for mixing ochres, or for holding blood. Tindale reported that in some areas of this desert the game was so limited that a small throwing club, pointed at one end so it could be used as a digging stick, was a man's sole hunting weapon, which he used to fell lizards and hare wallabies.

Hunting weapons

Within the three major classes of lance, hand-thrown and woomera-cast spears, there was a wide range of local designs. Some spears have barbs that are cut directly into the wood of the shaft. Many other varieties are tipped or barbed with sharp points made from stone, wood, bone or stingray spine. The spearthrower was widespread but not used in Tasmania, some parts of eastern Australia, or in Dampierland. Also widespread was that European icon of Aboriginal culture, the boomerang, varieties of which were designed for hunting birds, large mammals and even fish, or for fighting and sport. Even so, no boomerangs were known in Tasmania, south western Australia, and Cape York Peninsula. Clubs and throwing sticks complete the general Australian inventory of personal hunting gear.

Skin cloaks

Over much of Australia people wore very little clothing, the most widespread items of apparel being pubic fringes of various kinds and belts or bands made of plant fibre or spun fur. Nakedness is very much part of the popular image of traditional Aboriginal existence. However, over much of the southeastern third of the continent,

Tasmania and the forestlands of southwestern Australia, people wore cloaks and capes made of animal pelts and, in some areas, of seaweed, grass or flattened reeds. The most impressive skin cloaks consisted of possum skins sewn together with fibre string or sinew. During wet weather they were worn with the fur on the inside. To a lesser extent, wallaby and kangaroo pelts were used for cloaks, though in Tasmania and southwest Australia they were used exclusively. Today few skin cloaks are preserved in museum collections. One of these is a possum-skin cloak from Victoria, which measures 2.3 by 1.7 metres, made from 81 pelts. Methods of preparing the pelts varied regionally. In Victoria they were stretched on a sheet of bark, using small wooden pegs, and set to dry near a small fire. Ashes were rubbed on the inside of the pelt to absorb the fat as the skin slowly dried. To make the skin pliable, its inner surface was scraped to clean off membrane, and then lightly scored with a mussel shell, bone point or stone

Aborigines at Coranderrk, Victoria, c. 1879, wearing possum-skin cloaks. The cloaks are worn here with the fur on the inside for protection against rain and the skins are scored in a cross-hatched pattern to aid flexibility. Although these cloaks were ubiquitous over southeastern Australia, few have survived. (Photo Fred Kruger; F. B. Smith collection)

flake. These incisions formed simple but artistic geometric patterns. Fresh animal fat was applied to make the skin surface waterproof, and it was fastened at the breast with a bone or wood pin or toggle.

The antiquity of skin cloaks in Australia is unknown, and skin-working tools from archaeological sites are rarely identified, though archaeologists continue to search for direct evidence. However, Late Pleistocene people subsisted in very cold windy regions of the continent, and simply to survive the worst weather they must have had some kind of body insulation, presumably including animal pelts and sewn skins. The best evidence may come from the caves in the dense rainforest of southwestern Tasmania (see Chapter 19).

Bone and stone implements

Bone artefacts survive in alkaline deposits, even dating from Pleistocene times. While many uses for bone tools are recorded historically, such as spear prongs, awls and toggles, it is difficult to interpret many of the specimens recovered archaeologically. Marsupial lower jaws and incisor teeth used as cutting, piercing or scraping tools were widespread on the mainland. Most of the teeth on museum specimens are broken or worn from use and it is possible to identify archaeological ones from such traces, including an example from Kakadu National Park that has been dated to 6000 years BP.

The most common artefactual remains are stone artefacts, some of which show considerable skill in their fashioning. Every person in a group would have used stone tools for various tasks, though there was a general division of labour and certain tools were used in the context of male and female tasks. Multi-component tools and weapons, incorporating one or more pieces of stone held firmly in place with adhesive or other binding materials, were widespread; they included knives, hatchets, woodworking tools, and spears barbed with sharp pieces of stone. These artefacts are discussed in Chapter 14. One of the most commonly described in the historical records of the last 200 years is the Aboriginal stone hatchet, which has a considerable antiquity in Australia.

Stone hatchets

With some exceptions, stone tools described as 'axes' in Australian ethnographic accounts and in archaeological reports are hatchets, which were held in one hand during use rather than in two, as steel axes are. The average weight of stone hatchet heads is about half a kilogram. Very tough stone was needed for hatchet heads because the impact stress on its cutting edge is relatively high. The ideal stone is medium to fine-grained basalt or dolerite which has been recrystallised by the intense heat of magma intruding into the bedrock layer already formed. Where suitable stone was unavailable, hatchet heads had to be brought in from other regions, usually by inter-group exchange; sometimes the cost was high. Hatchet heads were shaped by first flaking a piece of stone roughly into shape, and over much of northern and eastern Australia pecking the surface with a hammer. The finished stone 'preform' was then ground on exposed sandstone or quartzite bedrock, usually at a watercourse, or on a portable stone slab, a task that could take an hour or less. Fully ground hatchet heads are seldom found in Australia, and grinding was usually restricted to around the tool's cutting edge. A wrap-around handle of split plant stem or branch about 30 centimetres long was bent tightly around the head and the joint secured with resin or beeswax and tightly lashed. In the nineteenth century, stone hatchets were used throughout much of Australia, the notable exceptions being the southwest (where the unique kodj hammer-hatchet served as its functional equivalent), the Nullarbor Plain and Tasmania. The hatchet was the ideal multi-purpose tool, especially in forests and woodland habitats. Both men and women used stone hatchets for everyday tasks such as extracting honey, insects and small game from trees and fallen logs, and cutting bark sheets and small branches to make shelters and canoes. The butt of

Greenstone hatchet from the Ebenezer Aboriginal Mission in northwest Victoria. Such tools were commonly used to cut toe-holds in tree trunks in the search for possums or honey. (I. McBryde and Museum of Victoria)

the hatchet head served as a hammer and pounder and, laid on its side, the tool served as a convenient, general-purpose anvil.

RECIPROCITY AND CULTURAL DIFFUSION

When Old World prehistorians could not explain the purpose of a site or artefact, the time-honoured formula was formerly to pronounce it 'ritual' or 'ceremonial' and delve no further. However, in Australia such invocations commonly possess meaning for understanding diffusion of ideas across the continent. Throughout Australia, cutting across tribal and linguistic boundaries, there was an interchange of goods along a complex network of mythologically sanctioned pathways and routes; this network belies the notion that Aboriginal society was parochial and static. Earlier anthropologists observed these processes in action, but regarded them mainly as formal, though incipient, business transactions. As early as 1861, A. W. Howitt noted that objects were 'bartered' over great distances along Cooper Creek, and he saw shields made from wood not growing in the region. He also knew of intrinsically valuable personal possessions being exchanged or given as presents. Towards the end of the century, Walter Roth referred to 'local markets' operating in Queensland.

A truer appreciation of the social nature of such activities was first achieved by W. E. H. Stanner. Stanner witnessed *merbok* inter-tribal exchange of gifts in the Daly River area during the early 1930s. His sympathetic account of the implications of these formalised yet restrained transactions constitutes a landmark in Australian economic anthropology, and Stanner expressed its theme succinctly: 'It is the *gift* rather than what is given that matters.' Donald Thomson later observed comparable events in northeastern Arnhem Land, when he studied the 'ceremonial exchange cycle', involving the reciprocal exchange of goods over distances of 500 kilometres. His opinion that the economic importance of the act was incidental to the Aborigines involved is crucial to the notion of ceremonial exchanges. 'It is the preparation for a visit to relatives within the ceremonial exchange cycle to discharge his obligations, the journey, the ritual, the formalities to be observed on arriving at camp, the niceties of behaviour and etiquette, rather than...the goods themselves, that he values.' Most recently Robert Paton has observed the same social behaviour in exchange of stone blades for spears at Newcastle Waters in the Northern Territory.

Nevertheless, there was economic and material gain in formal exchanges, as is evident from an account by James Dawson of a gathering of peoples in western Victoria:

> At the periodical great meetings trading is carried on by the exchange of articles peculiar to distant parts of the country. A favourite place of meeting for the purpose of barter is a hill called Noorat, near Terang. In that locality the forest kangaroos are plentiful, and the skins of the young ones found there are considered superior to all others for making rugs. The Aborigines from the Geelong district bring the best stones for making axes, and a kind of wattle gum celebrated for its adhesiveness. This Geelong gum is so useful in fixing the handles of stone axes and the splinters of flint in spears, and for cementing the joints of bark buckets, that it is carried in large lumps all over the Western District. Greenstone for axes is obtained also from a quarry on Spring Creek, near Goodwood; and sandstone for grinding them is got from the salt creek near Lake Boloke. Obsidian or volcanic glass, for scraping and polishing weapons, is found near Dunkeld. The Wimmera country supplies the maleen saplings, found in the mallee scrub, for making spears. The Cape Otway forest supplies the wood for the bundit spears and the grass-tree stalks for forming the butt piece of the light spear, and for producing fire; also a red clay, found on the sea coast, which is used as a paint, being first burned and mixed with water and lain on with a brush formed of the cone of the banksia while in flower by cutting off its long stamens and pestils. Marine shells…and freshwater mussel shells, are also the articles of exchange.

Regardless of the availability of equally suitable raw materials elsewhere, if an ancestral being was credited with inventing a certain process at a particular place, the local Aborigines concentrated on exploiting the raw material there for purposes of ceremonial exchange. Not all inter-tribal pathways were exchange routes, and the information compiled on those that were is undoubtedly only part of the true picture. Fortunately, details of ceremonial exchange systems were noted in northwestern Queensland and the Cooper Creek–Lake Eyre region by observers of the quality of Howitt and Roth, within the first generation of culture contact. It has been possible to reconstruct the routes taken by various commodities desired by other communities: flint, chert, quartz and a whole range of other rock types, pigments for painting, materials for cordage and basketry, spear wood, feathers, and shells for adornment or making knives, drugs, and artefacts of every kind.

Theoretically, a tribesman at Lake Eyre might possess artefacts which originated in widely different regions, and might pass on to the shores of the Southern Ocean artefacts from the Indian or Pacific Oceans. Provided that the identifications are correct, a ceremonial dance or corroboree (the *Molonga*) was 'exchanged' over 1700 kilometres from northwest Queensland to the Great Australian Bight between 1893 and 1918. Speed of passage is another relevant lesson Australian ethnography offers the prehistorian of trade and exchange. Even a few years within this situation is instantaneous in archaeological time. Such far-flung traditional ceremonial routes, sanctioned by Dreaming events, were termed songlines by Bruce Chatwin.

It is probable that inter-personal contact covered a wider territory in the inland waterways and their surrounding plains than in regions where topography and vegetation imposed greater barriers. While the ceremonial gift-giving ensured that objects travelled great distances, personal movement was more restricted. Tindale describes how, among the tribes of the lower Murray River, a personal trading partner in another tribe was sought for newborn male children; often the two partners never met, the packages being passed along the river hand to hand for over 300 kilometres. Edward Curr explained the world view of one group of Aborigines in southeastern Australia as comprehending a plain with a radius of hundreds of kilometres, with their own territory at its centre.

Because of the prestige attached to an introduced item, there could be significant ramifications for the receiving group. D. S. Davidson witnessed the impact of such innovations upon the Wardaman of the Willaroo area, Northern Territory, in 1930. Although some 800 kilometres east of the Kimberleys, the focus of pressure-flaked, bifacial spear-point production, the Wardaman were adopting these projectile points in preference to their own more sturdy ones. Assuming the validity of Davidson's observations, it is interesting that these objects had outdistanced the knowledge of pressure-flaking techniques; although the technological expertise had not diffused, the idea had done so. At the time of his visit, local stone-knappers were attempting to produce crudely-made imitations from stone which was poorly suited to the technique. Meantime, the Kimberley originals which excited such admiration were liable to break easily, so that the

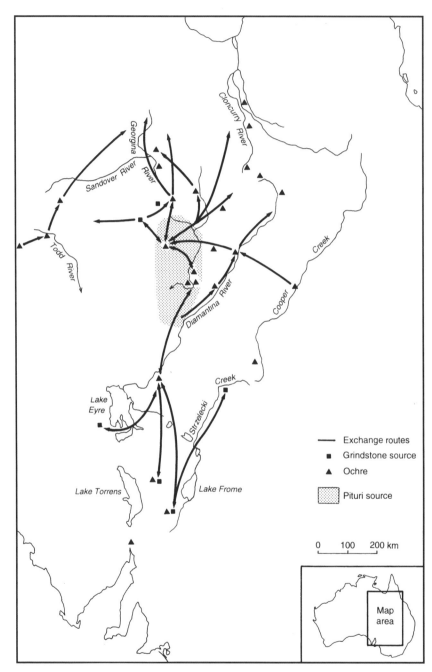

Map 4. *The exchange of pituri, red ochre and grinding slabs in Queensland and South Australia via Dreaming pathways between ceremonial centres. Note the distances that goods travelled; ritual songs and dances were also exchanged along these routes.*

adoption of these new, aesthetically satisfying and prestigious points really disadvantaged the hunters who used them.

Perhaps the most striking example of diffusion of artefacts is that of shell pendants, which served a largely decorative function in their homelands, but which were prized and sacred objects in rituals over 1600 kilometres away. Baler shell (*Melo diadema*) is found in the coastal waters of the Gulf of Carpentaria. The shell was chipped and ground to form an oval ornament up to twelve centimetres long, and was suspended on a string through a perforation. From the gulf, shells became incorporated in the exchange system and specimens were noted or collected far into South Australia, where they were worn by men as pendants to signify status. Kim Akerman has reported baler shells circulating far into Western Australia from the centre, although another exchange cycle commenced on the Western Australian coast with local baler shells. Pearl-shell ornaments of comparable appearance, either plain or incised, were produced in numbers on the Kimberley coast of northwestern Australia. Their distribution must reflect similar exchange patterns, passing by hand through at least eight tribes and travelling a distance of up to 1700 kilometres.

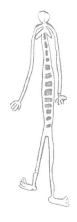

PITURI—THE AUSTRALIAN DRUG TRADE

One of the most prominent items of exchange in central Australia was pituri, the cured young leaves of the *Duboisia hopwoodii* shrub. This two-metre-high plant grows most abundantly in the Channel Country north of Lake Eyre, between the Finke and Mulligan Rivers. Pituri is an addictive psychoactive drug that contains a higher concentration of nicotine than occurs in commercial cigarette tobacco. A brownish-grey quid was prepared from the leaves mixed with an alkali ash from an *Acacia* wood. The addition of this ash to the quid causes a chemical reaction when moistened with saliva, which makes the nicotine even more potent. The Channel Country pituri harvested for trade was the most suitable because of its relatively lower concentration of a highly toxic alkaloid, d-nor-nicotine. An overdose of d-nor-nicotine can prove deadly, perhaps equivalent to a heroin overdose. Care has to be taken even in curing the leaves in heated earth to avoid being affected by fumes. Male tribal elders passed round quids during social and ceremonial occasions. Its other uses were to dampen hunger pains and fatigue, for instance during long-distance travel.

The gathering and curing of *Duboisia* leaves was a trade secret closely guarded from outsiders, including from the first British explorers and settlers in the region. The tribes surrounding Lake Eyre, and in particular the Dieri, controlled the pituri market in central Australia. To collect the *Duboisia* leaves, Dieri men from Cooper Creek journeyed 450 kilometres northwest along Dreaming pathways that crossed Sturt's Stony Desert and the Diamantina River to reach the braided channels of the Georgina and Mulligan Rivers. This expedition occurred yearly during the winter months when conditions were more suitable for long-distance travel. Such was the demand that the Dieri's pituri stockpile was depleted within four months of the expedition's return.

A lagoon base camp in Dieri territory was one of the 'great pituri markets', where George Aiston, a local mounted policeman, saw 'traders loaded up to capacity with pituri and weapons which they had picked up on the way down'. On their arrival 'a time of great activity ensued; trading was kept up until everyone was satisfied and left for home, but as parties were arriving all through the months of the cool weather, the market was open all the time'.

Walter Roth remarked that the 'export' of pituri was the primary reason for the enormous volume of trade and exchange in central Australia and reported that Aboriginal men he met in northwestern Queensland would offer any of their possessions, including their women, to replenish their supply. Pituri and other goods such as grindstones, boomerangs and sanctified ochre from Dreaming quarries, circulated from their particular sources to the rivers flowing into the Gulf of Carpentaria and south to the Flinders Ranges, over an area of more than half a million square kilometres. A hooked boomerang seen in the Western Australian desert, some 1300 kilometres away from its region of manufacture, testifies to the westward extent of this network. The prehistory of the pituri drug trade is unknown, though it may have been a catalyst for diffusion of ideas and material culture over large areas.

The Dieri had other 'essentials' to offer in trade. Every year they mounted other expeditions to travel 300 to 500 kilometres southwards to ochre and grindstone quarries in the Flinders Ranges. For the small woven bags of the highly prized ochre from Pukardu Hill, the Dieri visitors traded feathers, manganese pigment and an assortment of artefacts. For the long trip home, the bags were bundled into loads of up to 30 kilograms and carried on the head. Pukardu ochre continued to change hands far to the north of Lake Eyre, where it was used in important inter-tribal ceremonies.

MOUNT WILLIAM GREENSTONE QUARRY

Mount William, near Lancefield in central Victoria, is one of six major greenstone quarries in a formation aligned north to south through central Victoria. This igneous rock, a diorite formed 500 million years ago and subsequently recrystallised and toughened by geological heat, was typically dark green in colour because of its chlorite content. Because the stone was both easy to grind and tough, it was favoured for making stone hatchet heads. While some of the greenstone sources, such as the quarries in the Howqua Valley in the Victorian Alps, supplied only the local region, the greenstone ridge at Mount William had special significance. Quarrying at Mount William ceased in the 1830s, shortly after British settlers moved into the region. In 1855 when the quarry site was first described by the naturalist, William Von Blandowski, it was marked by an accumulation of flaking debris in an area of more than 40 hectares. The scene resembled an abandoned goldfield. Possibly some of the greenstone had been broken by fire to reduce the size of larger rocks, and there was evidence of digging and levering with poles. In a survey of the site Isabel McBryde recorded more than 250 circular or oval quarry pits, and a number of shafts descending into bedrock. Surrounding these quarry features was an extensive surface layer of flaking debris from roughing out the hatchet head shape. Other concentrations of flaking debris, including low mounds up to twenty metres in diameter, occur down-slope from the greenstone outcrops. While flaking debris is still evident for at least a kilometre along the slope, most of the area Blandowski saw is now hidden by soil and pasture grasses.

According to the ethnologist A. W. Howitt, the last custodian of the quarry was Billibellary, an elder of one of the five clans of the Woiworung tribe. Billibellary had inherited his position and he had the right to mine the valuable stone and distribute it to his kin. Others from related clans had less right of access. Normally, the first exchange of Mount William greenstone for other artefacts and raw materials occurred near the quarry. Most of these were subsequently exchanged at formal inter-tribal gatherings much further afield, such as at Mount Noorat near Lake Keilambete. The sanctified stone was also taken from Mount William by armed parties, or by stealth. No

Mount William diabase quarry c. 1900. There is a quarry pit in the left foreground; stone debris stretches to the crest of the hill and beyond. Hatchets from this quarry were exchanged across the Riverina and into South Australia. (D. J. Mulvaney collection)

doubt the exchange value of the greenstone increased according to the social relationship between the parties and the distance from the quarry. In the 1830s three pieces of greenstone fetched a possum-skin rug, a hatchet head and a number of bamboo spears. Necklaces and belts were also items of exchange in these transactions.

The prehistory of the Mount William quarry was investigated by Isabel McBryde who, in collaboration with rock specialists R. A. Binns and Alan Watchman, had previously sourced prehistoric hatchet heads found in northern New South Wales. McBryde was able to identify 230 hatchet heads in collections from southeastern Australia that had come from Mount William. Sixty per cent of these had been found at least 100 kilometres from the quarry, and half from

300 to 800 kilometres away. The distribution extended northwards across the Murray River and up the Darling River as far as Broken Hill, and across western Victoria into South Australia to the mouth of the Murray River. Only a few specimens were found in Gippsland in eastern Victoria.

The geographical pattern of the finds reflected the dynamics of tribal relationships and mythological beliefs. The distribution of Mount William greenstone corresponds with the territories of tribes that were in alliance, or at least friendly contact, with each other in the early nineteenth century, in particular those of central and north-western Victoria, and to a lesser extent more distant tribes in the border region of Victoria and South Australia. The main concentration of the greenstone hatchets is within the territory of the Kulin group of tribes; they are sparse in the territories of enemy tribes in eastern Victoria. Thus the political and social alliances prevailing in early historic times appear to have been in place for at least as long as Mount William served as a major source of greenstone for long-distance trade and exchange. Determining exactly how long may prove a difficult task, and requires archaeological probing at Mount William and sourcing and dating of prehistoric hatchets excavated at other sites in southeast Australia.

CULTURAL CHALLENGE AND RESPONSE

Europeans once thought of Aboriginal society as changeless. The extent and ramifications of ceremonial and economic exchange prove how wrong were these dogmas. Evidence accumulates, for example, for the rapid growth of pearl-shell trade around the northwest. The most challenging evidence comes from dingo-less Tasmania. Rhys Jones has documented a different kind of innovation there, the intro-duction of dogs by British colonists. Within a few years, the Aborigines changed their hunting techniques and, seeking the companionship of the new animal, incorporated it into their cultural milieu. The implicit social, psychological and material adjustments were profound and, in an archaeological sense, immediate. Significantly, no other European domesticated species was adopted, as Jones suggests, probably because they possessed no such affinity for a hunting society. This combination of cultural selectivity and almost instantaneous acceptance into the lifestyle and mythology of a people is surely relevant to understanding the nature of diffusion of objects and ideas within Aboriginal Australia. For example, two centuries of contact with Indonesian fishermen sufficed to incorporate aspects of their culture into the ceremonial life and art of Arnhem Land. Dreaming times need not invoke a remote chronology.

Seafarers to Sahul 7

The Pleistocene epoch, which conventionally is dated from two million to 10,000 years ago, featured nineteen climatic cycles, known as glacials and interglacials. The last glacial phase began about 120,000 years ago. According to the Milankovitch Theory, cyclical variations in the Earth's orbit reduce sunlight reaching the Earth's surface in summer, allowing extensive icecaps to form on the northern hemisphere continents and at the poles. A less popular alternative theory is that periodic volcanic eruptions produced massive dust-clouds, blocking sunlight and causing lowering of mean world temperature. Whatever the cause, the icecaps expanded and held so much of the world's water that sea levels were lowered by 100 metres or more. During a large scale glacial–interglacial cycle there were many small fluctuations in sea level responding to changes in the world's ice-volumes. Sea level approximated to the present level 100,000 and 83,000 years ago, while around 60,000 years ago it was 30 metres below present level. The last of the worldwide cold phases, and one of the most intense, began at 36,000–25,000 years BP, ending between 15,000 and 12,000 years BP. With the continued warming of world climate from the peak of this last cold period, the sea level rose until it reached 'stillstand' at about its present level at 6000 years BP. The enormous areas of emerged ocean bed which formed the super-continent of Australia and New Guinea is called Sahul, while the extension of southeast Asia which included Indonesia is Sundaland.

SUNDALAND ORIGINS

For most of the last 100,000 years Sundaland extended as far south-east as the eastern tip of Bali, or possibly even to Sumbawa Island, and northeast to encompass Palawan which is separated only by a narrow strait from the other islands of the Philippines. This continental shelf comprised four million square kilometres of land, about half of which is now shallow seabed beneath the Java and South China Seas. At times of lowest sea levels there were three great rivers winding across low undulating land, and two enormous inland lakes, one northwest of Java and the other in the Gulf of Siam. The climate of Sundaland was similar to that of mainland Southeast Asia today, with little change in the equatorial zone and distinct wet and dry seasons in the monsoonal zone, although probably with decreased rainfall. The vast plains of the Sunda Shelf extending to the coast-line were very warm. The diverse Late Pleistocene animal life of Sundaland has been reconstructed mostly from the fossil remains in the Padang Highlands of Sumatra and from Niah Cave in Sarawak. Much of this Asian fauna still inhabits parts of Southeast Asia, but often only as relic populations, and some species are extinct. The larger mammals included elephant, hippopotamus, Javan rhinoceros, giant pangolin, wild cattle, mountain goat, pigs, antelope and deer, leopard, tiger, sun bear, orang-outang and species of monkeys. Many of these species had larger body size than today, probably because the ambient temperature was lower. Strandloopers (seashore foragers) of the reef-girt coastal fringe of Sundaland in their flimsy watercraft were poised on the edge of the known world, to embark on the next leg of their expansion across the globe—the deep-sea islands of South-east Asia.

ISLAND STEPPING-STONES

Between the two great continental lands of Sundaland and Sahul lies the island world of Wallacea, a geographical domain named after the nineteenth-century naturalist, Alfred Russell Wallace. These islands, now the peaks of undersea ridges, are fragments of continental crust and buckled seabed squeezed between the two colliding tectonic plates of Asia and the northwards drifting Australian continent. Wallacea has been subjected to processes of downfaulting, tectonic uplift, rotation, and in the Pleistocene, volcanism—there were at least 500 areas of volcanoes, many of which are active today.

Wallacea is a transition zone between the plant and animal life of Asia and Australia. Sulawesi has an ancient endemic fauna, and the only mammals it has in common with Sundaland are three species of bats. The only large mammals endemic to the main islands of Wallacea were *Stegodon*, extinct species of elephant. Some *Stegodon* species were similar in size to modern Asian elephants, but there was also a dwarf species which may have survived until people arrived. Stegodons were excellent swimmers, and like modern Asian elephants may have swum with a porpoise-like lunge and their trunks protruding from the water like a snorkel. This century, elephants have been observed swimming distances up to sixteen kilometres, drawn by the scent of plant foods on the ocean breeze.

Recent excavations at Mata Menge site on Flores Island have produced challenging evidence, which may establish the presence there of toolmakers during Early Pleistocene times, that is, hundreds of thousands of years ago. As sea crossings probably were always necessary to reach Flores, this would mean that *Homo erectus* used watercraft and possessed greater cognitive abilities than hitherto credited. Sahul only represented a further ocean voyage. Before accepting this crucial evidence, however, we must await further research. The enterprising international team working there includes Australian archaeologist Michael Morwood, and a major multidisciplinary campaign is essential to test the evidence.

CHANGING SEA LEVELS

The Pleistocene was a period of globally fluctuating sea levels. At the beginning of the last glacial cycle, about 120,000 years ago, the sea level was probably slightly higher than it is now; it fell gradually to an extremely low stand during the Last Glacial Maximum about 18,000 years BP, long after humans reached Sahul. For the period in between, the sea level fluctuated several times; on average, it was about 65 metres below the present level.

Archaeologists have attempted to infer from the Pleistocene sea level curve a likely time of first arrival, assuming that shorter sea crossings would be more successful. However, several factors have not been considered: for example, the influence of sea-currents on time involved, or the quality of watercraft.

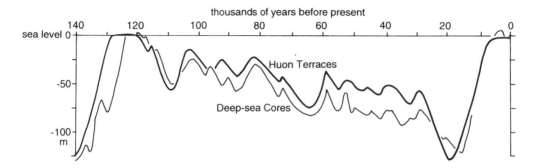

Two commonly used sea-level curves for the last glacial cycle, one constructed from dated raised coral terraces at Huon Peninsula in New Guinea and the other from oxygen isotope determinations from deep-sea cores. The isotope-based curve has lower peaks than the coral terrace one but the two are generally similar. (After Chappell 1993: Fig. 2)

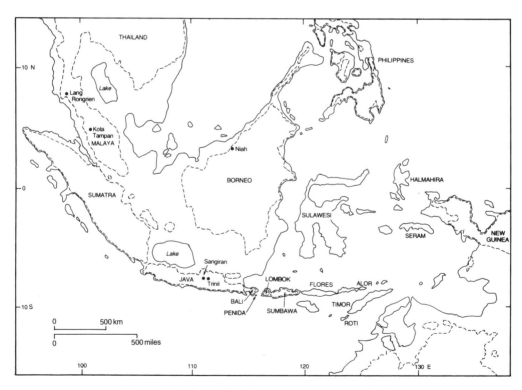

Map 5. The islands of Southeast Asia when the sea level was 65 metres lower than it is today (the average stand before the Late Glacial Maximum).

Alternatively, the biogeographer John Chappell proposes that crossings from the islands of Wallacea to Sahul occurred when sea level was rising or high, rather than low. His presupposition is that coastal and marine food resources in the islands were most abundant during periods of 'aquatic' coastal environments, when there were more coastal shallows and estuaries around the islands. Chappell argues that northwest monsoon winds were stronger during these periods and these winds could have propelled watercraft towards Sahul's coastline.

WATERCRAFT

Though risky, most seafaring in Wallacea was not on the 'high seas', nor in cold waters, as in higher latitudes. The colonisation of Sahul probably required watercraft more advanced than a floating tree trunk or log, at least a simple raft initially. Analogies are drawn from recent hunter-gatherer watercraft, especially Australian ones. Birdsell claimed that the original craft must have been more seaworthy than Aboriginal bark canoes and rafts of the nineteenth century. In northern Australian waters rafts and bark canoes travelled up to 27 kilometres, and there is a record of a 32-kilometre journey in a sewn bark canoe. However, these voyages were in shallow seas where the tide does much of the work, and may not be appropriate examples for the journey from Wallacea to Sahul. Birdsell, and more recently Alan Thorne, raised the possibility that lengths of giant bamboo were lashed together to form a sizeable raft. Bamboo is an ideal material for floats and rafts because its airtight nodes provide exceptional buoyancy. Bamboo craft cannot become waterlogged as did Aboriginal rafts. Also Rhys Jones envisaged palm trunks for rafts, though these are heavier. As there is no physical evidence of early prehistoric watercraft it cannot be presumed that one particular kind was used for sea voyaging. All that can be established is that people did cross distances greater than swimming range and that watercraft must have been required.

ROUTES TO SAHUL

Migration probably followed the shortest sea crossings between the innumerable islands between Sundaland and Sahul. Most Indonesian islands were mountainous and closely spaced together, so many were *intervisible*. The islands tend to have little coastal plain, so a lower sea level would not have reduced significantly the distances between them.

Birdsell's routes to Sahul

Joe Birdsell was the first scholar to review the various island routes from Asia to Sahul, first in 1947 and updated 30 years later. Birdsell simply measured the distances between islands in an easterly direction and connected those closest and most visible to each other, an approach based on the 'shortest distance' principle. Birdsell proposed two alternative routes: a northern one via the large island of Sulawesi to northernmost Sahul (now New Guinea), and a southern one from the southwest tip of the Asian mainland along the islands of the Lesser Sundas to Timor, and finally to the northwest coast of Sahul either direct or via the South Moluccan Islands. Birdsell and other scholars, such as the economic historian Noel Butlin, have favoured the southern route. However, we doubt that coastal hunter-gatherers with simple watercraft would have found the northern alternative too difficult, considering that high land is intervisible along the entire route, that at least for part of the year people would have the benefit of monsoonal rain showers, and that there were prevailing winds drawing flotsam to Sahul.

The northern route

Passage through the northern islands required more and wider crossings, but no direct-line distances between islands were as great as the final crossing on the southern Timor–Sahul route. The tentacled island of Sulawesi, with its foundation of volcanic magma, comprises essentially four mountainous peninsulas, a landmass of about 180,000 square kilometres and, significantly for coastally adapted people, no less than 6000 kilometres of coastline. The first landing in Sulawesi could have occurred anywhere along its long western coastline; the shortest direct-line distance was about 60 kilometres, where two promontories on either coastline face each other. Proceeding eastwards, people had to cross two relatively narrow deep-sea straits, and a further one of about 45 kilometres to reach Sula and ultimately other north Moluccas islands. Sahul was visible from Halmahira and

Gebe, and smoke from bushfires would have signalled the existence of dry land across even greater distances.

The southern route

Birdsell's southern route commences on Bali or Lombok. In the Lombok Strait there is a small island, Nusa Penida, only a few hundred metres from Bali. Some zoologists have argued that this narrow passage may be a scour channel of recent origin and that during the Pleistocene Nusa Penida was a peninsula of Bali. Others have suggested that Lombok Strait did not exist. Even if a strait then existed, people standing on a Bali beach or Nusa Penida could clearly see Lombok's nearly four-kilometre-high Gunung Rinjani volcanic massif. From Nusa Penida there is another crossing of a channel about twenty kilometres wide. Even if this is considered too hazardous, there is every chance that the strong and unpredictable current swept many near-shore watercraft suddenly and irretrievably into the strait. We suspect that Lombok Strait did not long hold up the human colonisation of the Lesser Sunda Islands. Lombok is separated from Sumbawa today by the fifteen-kilometre-wide Strait of Alas which has a maximum depth of about 130 metres. This passage was narrower during the Late Pleistocene. Once they had crossed it, people could have walked to Flores and possibly even as far as the island of Alor, which was about 50 kilometres northwest of Timor, a sea distance much greater than people so far had encountered on this route.

Timor at the time of its human colonisation may have harboured the last of the Stegodons, which weighed as much as four to five tonnes and no doubt provided a welcome source of meat for newly arrived seafarers. On Timor the animal food included species of giant rats weighing up to a kilogram, a giant tortoise, and cassowaries; all the remaining mammals and birds were smaller—mainly bats and a few small marsupials derived ultimately from nearby Sahul.

The distance from Timor to Sahul is the longest on any route through Wallacea, requiring a journey well beyond the sight of land. Separating these two landmasses is the deep oceanic Timor Trough, which is 80 kilometres wide and nearly two kilometres deep. This abyss shelves steeply off the Timor coast. Prevailing sea conditions were more moderate because the Timor Sea was then an oceanic cul-de-sac, blocked from the Pacific Ocean current by the dry land surface of modern-day Torres Strait. Before the onset of the Last Glacial Maximum and at least as far back as 60,000 years ago there

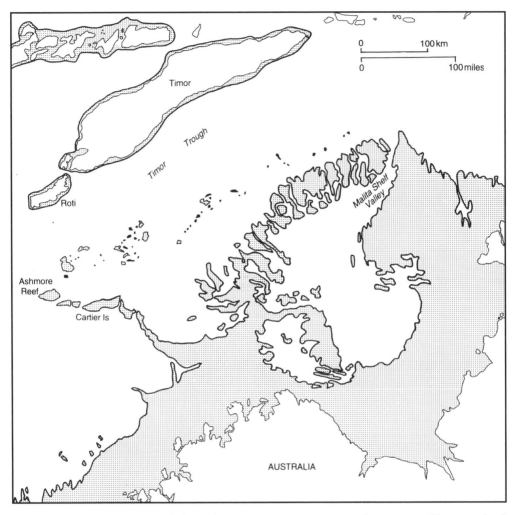

Map 6. *Sahul's northwestern coast opposite Timor during times of lower sea level.*
(Reconstruction based on present-day seabed topography.)

existed an archipelago about 100 kilometres southeast of Timor, comprising more than 60 small, mostly flat-topped, continental islands, now submerged as the Sahul Banks. This island chain stretched along the edge of the Sahul shelf for 750 kilometres and on its southern end abruptly turned landwards as a succession of long narrow islands. Today only a few small areas of the archipelago, such as Cartier Island, remain above water. Even though the near-shore tidal range probably was less than it is today, it may have been sufficient to propel small craft to the Sahul mainland, while a longitudinal current along Sahul's coast may have pulled craft southwards. If sea level then was ten metres lower than it averaged during the Late Pleistocene, not far across the horizon from the continental islands, voyagers would have been swept to the Sahul Rise, a low-lying, fan-like formation of skeletal limestone, intricately incised by narrow tidal channels, which enclosed a bay 240 kilometres wide.

ADVENTURERS OR CASTAWAYS?

Some scholars have argued that the colonisation of Wallacea and Sahul was the outcome of purposeful sea exploration, and they have speculated why people were compelled to go. One explanation has been that the submergence of inhabited mainland and island fringes caused population pressure and resource scarcity. Alternatively, it is fundamental in the human spirit to explore and risk life in quest. The prerequisites were watercraft sufficiently seaworthy to stay afloat for a few hours or days. Tasmanian Aborigines sometimes died in dangerous crossings to offshore islands, testimony to the high level of risk tolerated by Aboriginal seafarers.

For most crossings, people knew that there was land ahead, and could judge the possibilities and risks of the journey. There were also distances of 50–100 kilometres where the mariners could not have seen land in any direction. Seafarers in Wallacea did not need the navigation skills of the Polynesians, because they had to deal only with short distances of tens of kilometres, not thousands, in an island-studded sea bounded in large part by continental landmasses. Would people on the islands nearer to Sahul have understood that there was further land ahead? Noel Butlin considered this issue for the crossing from Timor and concluded that they would have deduced this. Pointing the way were flocks of birds from freshwater habitats—ducks, magpie geese, herons and ibises commuting seasonally to Sahul from the northern hemisphere. If this was not sufficient, the dull glow and kilometre-high smoke plumes of bushfires may have been visible from islands more than 100 kilometres distant.

Rather than being funnelled initially along a narrow route, people on sea-going canoes or rafts may have swept through Wallacea on a broad front, with a capacity to colonise many of the islands within only a few generations. That scholars may be underestimating the early technological capacity for sea voyaging is suggested by new archaeological finds. A rockshelter in a raised coral terrace at Kilu on Buka Island in the northern Solomon Islands, excavated by Stephen Wickler, contains occupation debris dating to about 28,000 years BP. To reach Buka the shortest voyage was 180 kilometres from New Ireland, off northeast Sahul. This date suggests that people may have arrived on the Sahul coast instantaneously in archaeological terms, on an equally broad front, and in relatively large numbers. Once the larger islands closest to Sahul's northwest coast were reached (from north to south, Halmahira, Seram, Kepulauan Kai, Kepulauan Tanimbar, and Timor and Roti), then even waterlogged or swamped craft and their human passengers may have drifted into the shallow waters of the Sahul shelf. Assuming a tidal range comparable to that of today, once there, the craft would have been carried towards the shore by the fast-flowing tide.

Sahul: A Pleistocene continent

8

Sahul, the land upon which the first Aboriginal colonists set foot, was subject to the same climatic and environmental forces which controlled Sundaland. As explained in Chapter 7, around 100,000 and 83,000 years ago ocean levels approximated the present depth. At 60,000 years ago sea level was 30 metres lower. We adopt a conservative approach and focus on the last 50,000 years, which relates to the commonly postulated time span for human presence in Australia. Claims for an earlier landfall are discussed in Chapter 9 but, as hard evidence is lacking, this chapter is concerned with Sahul during the period when it is certain that the continent had been colonised.

From 45,000 years BP to the beginning of the Late Pleistocene 36,000 years BP, moderate temperatures and high rainfalls reactivated ancestral watercourses and filled the lakes on the inland plains of southeastern Sahul. During this time the present-day Arafura Sea was an extensive plain. The Gulf of Carpentaria also was exposed as plains and gently undulating terrain, within which was one of the world's largest lakes, Lake Carpentaria. When full, the surface area of Lake Carpentaria was 70,000 square kilometres, fed by the ancestral rivers of the Northern Territory, western Queensland, and New Guinea's Fly River. The Fly's contribution maintained the lake's water as fresh until the river was diverted by geological uplift to the Gulf of Papua at about 8000 years BP. Paradoxically, from before 30,000 to about 23,000 years BP many inland lakes, including Lakes Eyre and Frome in South Australia, had high water levels. Although rainfall was lower than before, so was air temperature, which therefore reduced the evaporation rate of surface water.

Current archaeological evidence indicates that it was during this period or earlier that people colonised the continent. A testimony to human adaptability is the evidence of people at high altitude in the Papuan highlands by 26,000 years BP and in the gorges of southwest Tasmania, within sight of glaciated peaks. At the other climatic extreme is the abundant evidence of human presence in the Australian deserts before the Last Glacial Maximum. However, widespread settlement of the arid zone remains to be demonstrated as no trace of early human presence has been found in the sandy deserts or at the isolated mound springs in South Australia.

SAHUL DURING THE LAST GLACIAL MAXIMUM

During the period 25,000 to 12,000 years BP very dry and intensely hot or cold conditions prevailed over much of Sahul. That it was windier is indicated by extensive dune-building. This climatic regime peaked 21,000–15,000 years BP, during a period called the Last Glacial Maximum, or LGM. Three decades of geomorphological and palaeoecological research in Australia and New Guinea have provided a reconstruction that is generally reliable.

Small areas within the New Guinea highlands, Snowy Mountains and Tasmania were glaciated during the LGM. Lakes in western New South Wales became seasonally dry and then finally, permanently dry. Vast quantities of dust and salt were carried by the prevailing winds to settle as a red silty clay layer (called 'parna') across the Murray River Basin to the western slopes of the Great Dividing Range. These dust storms in southeastern Australia, presumably unpleasant for human inhabitants, continued unabated for 9000 years.

During the LGM sea level stood 130 metres below present level, so that the Australian continent was one-third larger than now. It encompassed New Guinea, the Aru Islands, other continental islands such as Tasmania and Kangaroo Island, and all intervening seabed including the Gulf of Carpentaria, the Arafura Sea, the Great Barrier Reef, and Bass Strait—a landmass archaeologists call Sahul. Much of the continental shelf that is now ocean floor comprised low-lying

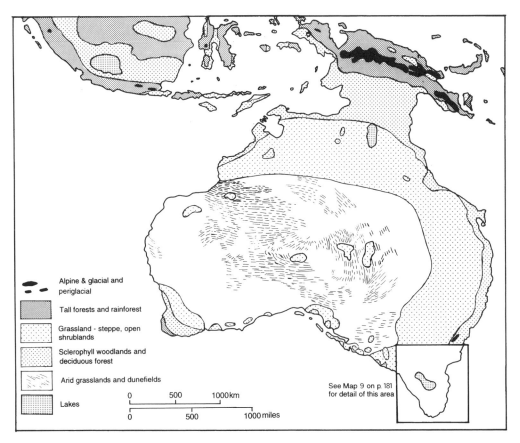

Map 7. *Vegetation of Sahul during the Late Glacial Maximum c. 18,000 BP. This general reconstruction is based on pollen records, fossil fauna and present-day plant distributions. (Reconstruction by Geoff Hope, with contributions for the Tasmanian Peninsula by Paul Augustinus and Beth Gott)*

plains. Some would have been a continuation of the dunefields, but others included resource-rich coastal lakes and lagoons, and rugged hills, plateaus, canyons and river valleys.

To indicate the likely LGM shoreline, it is common practice to use a 200-metre depth contour (isobath) instead of a more accurate 130-metre one. Systematic seabed mapping has not delineated this isobath around all of former Sahul—the priorities of the Australian Navy and mineral exploration companies are not those of geomorphologists and archaeologists. However the continental shelf descends abruptly at about 100 metres below present sea level and the horizontal distance between lower bathometric contours (seabed depth) is relatively small.

The temperature of the ocean around the coast of Sahul at the LGM was 2–4°C below that of today, and the mean monthly temperature on land was probably about 6–10°C lower (in the Snowy Mountains about 10°C lower and in Tasmania 8°C lower). The exposure of the continental shelf as dry land diminished the warm shallow seas north of Australia, reducing evaporation from the ocean and northwest monsoonal effects. Cooling of the oceans further decreased evaporation, and consequently throughout the continent precipitation was less.

Dune whorls dated to this period suggest a strong semi-permanent high pressure system over central Australia. The lack of a warm sea in the Gulf of Carpentaria and the enlarged land surface of Sahul reduced the onshore movement of tropical cyclones and rain depressions. Inland aridity was so intense that lakes as far south as Tasmania dried up, forests retreated, and some tree species became extinct. Over central and southern Sahul severe cold, drought, and strong winds discouraged tree growth, though some species common today must have survived in sheltered or better-watered refuges.

Northern Sahul

Along the length of eastern Queensland there was a coastal plain up to 200 kilometres wide, which for a distance of 2000 kilometres on its seaward margin was girt by a segmented limestone ridge—the relic of earlier Great Barrier Reefs. In cross-section, this ridge rose to as much as 50 metres above sea level on its western side; it dropped in height seawards, to end as a sea cliff on the edge of the continental shelf. Canyons and passes one to two kilometres wide cut in to the ridge, and along its northern part the coastal cliff was pockmarked with sea caves. Nine thousand years elapsed before the sea again islanded the limestone massifs and eventually submerged them.

The spine of Australia's eastern highlands extended on dry land as far north as Papua. Along its least elevated part, present-day Torres Strait was marked only by hills; a few low, granite peaks are now islands. Further north, in the New Guinea highlands, the altitude of the snowline was 1000 metres lower than it is today, and some areas had permanent snow. The altitudinal boundaries of the major vegetation zones were lower by 750 metres compared with those of today.

Much of New Guinea has always been heavily forested, though grasslands were more expansive during the LGM, covering an area of nearly 60,000 square kilometres.

Immediately to the west of present-day Cape York Peninsula was Lake Carpentaria, a vast inland water body, which was periodically saline. The vegetation of the low-lying plain that now forms the Gulf of Carpentaria seabed was largely grassland and sedgeland, with numerous swamps. In Sahul's far northwest extensive plains, now the bed of the Arafura Sea, skirted the rugged escarpments of the Kimberley Plateau.

Southeastern Sahul

Eighteen thousand years ago land was continuous along the length of Sahul's eastern highlands from New Guinea to the southern tip of Tasmania. While the eastern seaboard remained well watered, much of the southeastern interior experienced cold, arid conditions similar to those of modern Patagonia. The eastern highlands from the Queensland border to Tasmania was a region largely of cold steppe and scattered sub-alpine woodland. The climate of the Australian Alps was cold, windy and dry year-round. The tree line, which approximated the mean temperature of 10°C in January (the warmest month), was then much lower, implying lower summer temperatures, and the permanent snow line was 700 metres below its present-day altitude. In the Snowy Mountains the alpine zone was desert, with sparse *Plantago* herbfields. While snow cover above 1600 metres was probably less than a quarter of today's, the highest peaks above 1900 metres were glaciated.

The surrounding tablelands were also cold and windy. On the western side of the highlands the slopes were vegetated by grassland with spring herbs; lower altitudes had forest and box woodland. Rivers flowing from these tablelands traversed the vast western plains and fed inland lake systems, such as the Willandra Lakes where human settlement is known to span more than 30,000 years.

The riverine plains featured active meandering sandy streams, perhaps like the Finke today, with little in the way of fringing forest. In the few millennia before the LGM, the Cadell Fault, between Deniliquin in New South Wales and Echuca on the Victorian side of the Murray River, moved to create a ten-metre scarp which obstructed the Murray and Goulburn Rivers. A huge triangular-shaped lake or swamp (now called Lake Cadell), 80 kilometres long, formed behind this natural dam and then shrank into a group of smaller lakes similar to the Willandra Lakes to the northwest. Eight millennia after the LGM, great forests of river red gum colonised the Barmah region in the southern part of former Lake Cadell.

The Bassian region

The Bassian region during the Last Glacial Maximum was the land comprising Tasmania and Bass Strait. On the eastern margin of this peninsula was the Bassian Rise, the last dry land connecting Tasmania and Victoria. During the LGM the highest point on this rise was only 75 metres above sea level. On the western side of the Bassian Plain was a smaller rise of 55 metres. Between the two rises was Lake Bass, 110 by 260 kilometres, and up to sixteen metres deep. Lake Bass was brackish and occasionally saline, depending on whether its outflow was blocked by dunes, and it was virtually bereft of fish or other animals.

The vegetation of the Bassian Plain was sub-alpine grassland and heathland, with scattered pockets of eucalypt trees in sheltered refuges; it probably looked much like the modern grasslands of Tasmania's Central Plateau. 'Silver frost', which accompanied summer storms, may have eliminated any chance of trees thriving outside their refuges. In spring the grasslands were ablaze with daisies, possibly including the edible daisy yam. The Bassian region was cold and windy, and had reduced precipitation. Icecaps and glaciers exited in the Tasmanian highlands and, though small, were more extensive than those in the Snowy Mountains. Rain forest was preserved only in refuges near the west coast, and other kinds of forest and woodlands in low-lying hilly areas (such as present-day Bass Strait islands). Scrublands and herbfields occurred in the west and northwest of present-day Tasmania.

Central and southwestern Sahul

For the whole length of the southern and western coasts of Sahul, dry land extended 100–200 kilometres seawards from the present coastline. Along the Nullarbor coast, the sea retreated 160 kilometres, considerably extending the arid plain. The Bunda and Baxter Cliffs which form the coastline today were then an escarpment far inland. The extensive lowlands joining Australia with New Guinea regions blocked the generation of the warm Leeuwin Current from the

Indonesian region, and this probably resulted in a colder ocean along the Western Australian coast.

During winter, air masses from the Southern Ocean moved across Australia's interior, intensifying cold conditions. Clear skies would have driven night-time temperatures even lower, and coldness must have taxed the endurance and ingenuity of the Aboriginal inhabitants. Added to cold and windy conditions were severe and frequent droughts and, if these were not sufficiently discouraging, sand storms. Sand dunes and sand sheets accumulated in earlier hyper-arid periods were partially remobilised. An immense parallel-dune system curves around the heart of the continent and towards its periphery, reaching right to the northwest coast. The dunefields of the Simpson and Strzelecki Deserts expanded, as did others towards the Gulf of Carpentaria and across the Murray Basin to the Big Desert and Little Desert in western Victoria (map 7).

THE TERMINAL PLEISTOCENE

After the LGM world temperatures increased, the northern hemisphere icecaps began to shrink and as a response the level of the sea rose. A surge came at 15,000 years BP, when the North American ice sheets melted, but ice sheets in Antarctica began their retreat at 12,000 years BP. The Sahul land area shrank, and the present coastline began to form about 6000 years BP. In New Guinea, from 14,500 years BP, montane forests ascended 800 metres, while glaciers and surrounding alpine and sub-alpine environments in the highlands retreated. The tree line was not closed forest, as it is today, but shrub-rich grassland, and adjustments in the composition of high-altitude forests continued into the Holocene, only to reach stability about 4000 years ago, long after New Guinea became an island.

In Australia, temperature increased by 5–6°C. In the interior there was sufficient rain to sustain vegetation, and dune building decreased. However, over much of the continent, runoff was not sufficient to recharge water bodies diminished by earlier aridity. Freshwater lakes became saline, and prevailing winds picked up sand and dust from their dry beds and deposited it on a fringing dune (called lunette). By 15,000 years ago the Willandra Lakes in western New South Wales were completely dry, as human societies had to respond not only to the invasion of the sea but also to the reduction or loss of bodies of fresh water.

Progressively, dunefields across the continent stabilised and forest replaced former shrubby grassland. In the Australian Alps snow gums and other plants that had survived in sheltered areas of the sub-alpine zone expanded to form the snow gum woodland and forest which exists today. Here the last permanent ice melted by 9200 years ago. From 11,700 years BP many eucalypt forest plants migrated inland and to higher altitudes, replacing extensive grasslands.

When humans arrived on Sahul's shores and dispersed across the continent, they faced a continual series of environmental challenges that persisted throughout the Pleistocene. The adaptability and endurance in colonising Sahul is one of humankind's inspiring epics. It is to the relationship between the environment and early Aboriginal society that we now turn.

IMPACT OF THE SEA LEVEL RISES ON ABORIGINAL SOCIETIES

Many environmental scientists envisage that, for long periods, the rate of sea level rise was limited to ten to 30 centimetres per century (one to three millimetres a year). From 17,000 to 12,000 years BP there was a slow rise from a stand of 105 metres below present. In a major surge beginning at 13,000 years BP, sea level rose 25 metres in a millennium (2.5 metres per century and 25 millimetres a year), and then slowed for the following 2000 years. At 10,000 years BP, parts of the Antarctic ice sheet fragmented to form massive ice floes, which melted as they drifted north, so that sea level surged again, rising fifteen metres. By 9000 years BP sea level stood around ten metres below the present level which was reached at about 6000 years BP. Additionally, enormous releases of water from lakes contained in the lobes of the northern hemisphere ice shields, particularly in North America, may have caused instantaneous sea-level rises of perhaps a metre or so.

Consequences of the loss of land were far-reaching. Vast territories, innumerable camping places, stone quarries, burial grounds, and sacred features, were submerged; the creation of continental islands isolated populations. In most situations the inundation of land was barely perceptible within a human lifespan, and individuals were not displaced from their band or tribal territory. But where coastal terrain was flat, marine transgression during periods of rapid rise would have been noticeable, and even a cause for concern for coastal inhabitants. On the flat Great Australian Bight and Arafura Shelf between 13,000 to 11,000 years ago, the rate of marine transgression reached one metre a week (110 kilometres in 2000 years). Every high tide would have exceeded the previous one, resulting in transient shorelines and ecological communities, and an intertidal zone many kilometres wide. Regions larger than modern tribal territories would have disappeared. Clearly Aboriginal culture was sufficiently flexible to adjust to the demographic effects of marine transgression. Nonetheless, adjustment would have required strenuous efforts, perhaps involving a consolatory philosophy. Even if there were not major migrations, social integration of individuals or tribes who lost territory must have occurred.

Were these dramatic reshapings of territories all forgotten in tribal lore? It is pertinent that there are identified and registered underwater sacred sites off the Arnhem Land coast. R. M. W. Dixon has documented an Aboriginal story which recounts Dreaming events during a period when Hinchinbrook Island was part of the mainland. Recently Dixon has recorded a further tradition that the Queensland coast was formerly further out to sea. There are oral accounts of sea invasions to explain the formation of the Torres Strait Islands, Kangaroo Island, the Montgomery Islands off the northwest coast, and the islands near Perth. The last story, recorded in the 1830s by a British settler, G. F. Moore, is particularly intriguing:

> The natives have a tradition that Rottnest, Carnac and Garden Island once formed part of the mainland, and that the intervening ground was thickly covered with trees; which took fire in some unaccountable way, and burned with such intensity that the ground split asunder with a great noise, and the sea rushed in between, cutting off these islands from the mainland.

These Dreaming accounts are attractive to prehistorians, but it must be cautioned that they are the product of oral transmissions from elders in one generation to younger people in the next. Is it likely, then, that they are factual records of environmental changes that occurred hundreds of generations in the past? Although we suspect not, other prehistorians may give them credibility.

EXTINCTION OF THE MEGAFAUNA

Most marsupial species inhabiting Sahul in the Late Pleistocene survived into modern times. Those that did not include most of the largest species. These extinctions occurred as a mosaic of individual events in different parts of the continent over many thousands of years, continuing until recent prehistoric times. Late Pleistocene marsupial extinctions included two families (*Thylacaoleontidae* and *Diprotodontidae*), at least twenty genera, and numerous species. Also destined for extinction were large monotremes; the giant constrictor *Wonambi naracoortensis*; a huge flesh-eating lizard, *Megalania prisca*, which may have survived until after humans arrived; and several flightless birds, including the mihirung (*Genyornis newtoni*), named after the mythical giant emu of Victorian tradition, though it is not a species of emu, which weighed up to 100 kilograms.

About 40 major fossil deposits show that megafauna were widespread in Sahul. While they did not penetrate deep into the arid zone, many species were adapted to arid conditions. Some palaeozoologists have postulated that the macropodids (large, hopping marsupials) were ruminant-like in their digestion and recycled their urine so that they accommodated seasonal stress better. The exemplar of the semi-arid adapted megafauna was *Diprotodon optatum*, a browser inhabiting the inland region of eastern Australia. This lumbering beast was the size and weight of a rhinoceros, three metres long and standing two metres high. A little smaller in size, but just as impressive, was *Zygomaturus trilobus*, an inhabitant of the forested areas of southeastern and southwestern Australia. *Zygomaturus* had large nailed forefeet and a nasal horn or pad, both evolutionary adaptations for digging roots and tubers. Similar in size was *Palorchestes azael*, a quadrupedal animal the size of a bull, with a short trunk, long mobile tongue, sturdy paws armed with long claws, and powerful forelimbs for grasping and tearing off leaves and bark. This lumbering giant of forest and woodland was widespread in eastern coastal Australia, including Tasmania.

The many extinct macropodids ranged in size from the wallaby-sized rat kangaroo of southeastern Australia, *Propleopus oscillans*, an omnivore of forest and grassland, to the three-metre-tall *Procoptodon goliah*, a grazer that looked much like a kangaroo but was short-faced and had longer arms. Others included the short-faced browsing kangaroo, *Simosthenurus occidentalis*, which weighed about 200 kilograms, and closely related species of the *Sthenurus* genus. There were also megafaunal species of tree kangaroos and close relatives of the swamp wallaby. The largest of the wombat family was *Phascolonus gigas*, at two to three times the size of modern wombats. Monotremes were represented not only by the three contemporary species but by giant,

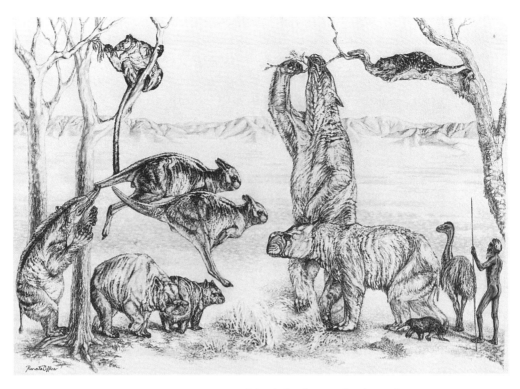

Extinct species of marsupial megafauna, right to left: Thylacoleo carnifex *(in tree),* Genyornis newtoni *(next to man),* Zaglossus, Diprotodon optatum *(side view, upright),* Procoptodon goliah *(hopping),* Zygomaturus trilobus, Phascolonus gigas, Dendrolagus *(tree-kangaroo). (Drawing by Renatta Officer)*

worm-eating echidnas (*Zaglossus* species), whose range included the cold steppe of southeastern Australia and the southwest forests.

During the Late Pleistocene nearly all marsupials had a larger body mass than their modern descendants. Many researchers believe that certain of the large species did not become extinct at all, but simply became smaller because of a strong selective force for smaller body size as modern climatic conditions approached. Such a trend is particularly notable among the grazing kangaroos. The most dramatic size decrease, of about 30 per cent, occurred with the red kangaroo (*Megaleia rufus* became *Macropus rufus*) and eastern grey kangaroo (*Macropus titan* became *M. giganteus*). The ancestral euro (*Macropus altus*) was 20 per cent bulkier than its modern descendant

M. robustus, and the Tasmanian devil (*Sarcophilus harrissii*), which may have become extinct on the mainland only within the last few hundred years, is 17 per cent smaller than its Pleistocene progenitor.

Co-existence of people and megafauna

It is generally accepted today that humans and many species of megafauna co-existed in Australia for at least 10,000 years and possibly considerably longer. In general, megafauna began to disappear before the LGM, perhaps first in the semi-arid zone, and subsequently around the peak of the LGM from the better-watered parts of the continent. According to the ecologist David Horton and archaeologist Richard Wright who excavated at Tambar Springs, some megafauna species, such as *Diprotodon*, may have survived in refuge areas such as the Liverpool Plains of central New South Wales until as recently as 6000 years BP, but this requires firm proof. Other than this broad statement, the dating of extinctions remains highly problematic, and highly contentious, because there is no agreement on two crucial factors: when people first arrived on the continent and when individual species disappeared. Assertions that Aboriginal myths reflect ancient 'race memories' of particular extinct animals are speculative and we give them little credibility. While there is a good case for Tasmanian tigers in Kakadu and Pilbara rock art, impressionistic identification of other extinct fauna in rock art is risky.

Causes of extinctions

There are different explanations for why so many animal species, especially the larger ones, became extinct in Australia within the last 50,000 years. The main arguments concern environmental changes of natural or Aboriginal origin, and over-hunting by Aborigines. However, no single cause is sufficient to explain the disappearance of a large and diverse range of animals adapted to such a wide range of habitats. Least evident is the part humans may have played in the process.

A proponent of natural ecological changes is the ecologist A. R. Main, who argued that a major factor was the decrease in precipitation during the millennia leading up to the Last Glacial Maximum. Main points out that the reduction in surface water would have disadvantaged the large-bodied species that could not evolve to smaller size without compromising their adaptation to low-nutrient

Painting of a Tasmanian tiger (thylacine) and her pup, Kakadu National Park. Bones from this extinct marsupial date from about 3000 years ago. (Paul Taçon)

plant diets within their particular ecological niches. An extreme view of the human intervention explanation is the 'blitzkrieg hypothesis', formulated in the mid-1960s by the American scholar Paul Martin to explain animal extinctions in North America. This argument is that the larger animal species were eliminated by 'overkill' shortly after people first arrived on the continent. Other, less extreme, positions are that small-scale but continuous hunting of megafauna, or large-scale 'firestick farming' which changed the habitat, had cumulative long-term effects that threw megafauna species into an irreversible decline. There also are multi-causal explanations that combine human intervention with climate change, offering a scenario of sustained hunting of species that were ecologically stressed by the onset of the LGM and already on the path to extinction.

Tim Flannery has revived 'blitzkrieg' as the best solution, after arguing against climatic change as the crucial factor. He admits that failure to locate kill-sites, where the beasts were killed and butchered, offers a problem, for the animals inhabited many diverse regions, but if their demise was rapid before 35,000 years ago, the preservation of such sites is less likely. He notes that the heavier, lumbering beasts succumbed, while the fastest kangaroos and wallabies survived, together with burrowing wombats. This suggests that the hunters were responsible, just as they have been factors in the extinction of large animals overseas. Climate change does not select against slow-moving species, Flannery observes.

With the demonstrated antiquity of human colonisation of Sahul pushing beyond the 40,000-year barrier, which is probably earlier than many of the extinctions, the 'blitzkrieg hypothesis' has lost attraction to most scholars, excepting Flannery. Most recently, archaeologist Stephanie Garling has challenged the hypothesis, which she describes as an androcentric hero tale of 'man the mighty predator', promoting a popular image of male hunting bands decimating herds of mega-faunal grazers in the interior grasslands and stalking giant browsers in woodland and forest. Garling challenges Martin's characterisation of megafauna as slow and stupid and naive about human predators. Judging by the behaviour of contemporary native Australian animals, it seems likely that many species of megafauna were not easy prey, and some may have been capable of killing human hunters.

Archaeological evidence for hunting megafauna

Despite both Flannery's provocative book and the discovery of many sites with megafaunal bones, there is not one megafauna kill-site, nor in fact any unquestionable evidence of humans having hunted any of the extinct megafauna species. Generally, archaeologists believe that this is a limitation of the archaeological record rather than a true indication of Pleistocene subsistence. Kill-sites are rare anywhere in the world, so it is not surprising that none has been identified in New Guinea and Australia. Even if such sites exist, as we believe they must, there is the problem of how to identify them. The stone technology of Pleistocene Sahul does not have the equivalents of the Clovis and Folsom points found at mammoth and bison kill-sites in North America. The marks of butchering tools are difficult to demonstrate and, except for a recent claim of possible cut marks from a stone knife, other marks on megafauna bone are from the teeth of predators and scavengers, such as the marsupial lion. Even evidence of burnt bone found with stone artefacts is not sufficient in itself to assume a human association.

Stone artefacts and megafauna bones have been found stratified together in a number of caves in Australia and New Guinea and in the beds of springs, such as Trinkey, Lime Springs and Tambar Springs on the Liverpool Plains in New South Wales. In the absence of direct evidence these associations may only mean that humans and megafauna frequented the same places at different times. More often the bones or the artefacts are intrusive in the critical level and their association is spurious.

An example of a megafauna bone bed around a spring is at Lancefield, 60 kilometres northwest of Melbourne, which was excavated by David Horton and Richard Wright. This bone accumulation, dated to 26,000 years BP, is incredibly dense and represents as many as 10,000 animals. Most of the bones were of *Macropus titan*, the ancestral eastern grey kangaroo, and the remainder species of *Sthenurus*, *Protemnodon*, *Diprotodon*, *Genyornis*, and the modern emu (*Dromaius novaehollandiae*). Horton and Wright surmised that most of the bones were of animals that died during a severe drought. Tooth marks on some bones were probably from *Thylacoleo*, which may have preyed on the weakened animals, or in other ways contributed to the bone accumulation. Although Horton and Wright also found some stone artefacts in the same stratigraphic level as the bone bed, they caution that these may be a chance association. Recent research suggests that the bones may have been washed into the accumulation from elsewhere, and therefore may be much older.

A megafauna bone deposit with stone artefacts at Cuddie Springs in semi-arid northwestern New South Wales may provide a stronger association between stone artefacts and megafauna bones than other known sites. However, even here there is a need to confirm the stratigraphic integrity of the artefacts. The lowest sedimentary unit at Cuddie Springs has bones of *Genyornis*, *Diprotodon*, *Macropus titan* and *Sthenurus* and a few scattered artefacts, dated to 29,000–34,000 years BP. At that time Cuddie Springs was an isolated waterhole in the arid zone. The overlying unit has the bones of *Diprotodon* and other megafauna and a much higher concentration of artefacts, when the site was an ephemeral lake. While most of the artefacts are discards from on-site stone-toolmaking, some are flake tools and fragments of grindstones bearing evidence of use. It is reported that some tools have worn cutting edges and preserved blood residues suggestive of butchering use. However, this and other evidence for possible association of people and megafauna is suggestive only. One concern is that the grindstone fragments from the bone levels are surprisingly old, and would be more at home in a collection dating from the last 3000 years. This site offers intriguing hints that archaeologists are close to demonstrating interaction of people and megafauna, yet we await the residue analysis and firm stratigraphic proof of the age of grindstones.

Speculations about megafauna hunting

David Horton has speculated that large parties of big-game hunters may have inhabited the continent before the extinction of megafauna. If megafauna were hunted on a large scale and their meat preserved, potentially it could have supported a large human population. His argument is speculative and relies heavily on the estimated food values of a kill—some animals could have provided enough meat to feed 25 to 50 people. *Diprotodon* weighed a tonne, *Palorchestes* nearly three-quarters of a tonne, *Simosthenurus occidentalis*, 200 kilograms, while the giant wombat, *Phascolonus gigas*, was up to eight times heavier than living wombats. For a culinary change, there was the giant long-beaked echidna, a 30-kilogram meat delicacy, giant anaconda steak and, if the species still survived at the time people first arrived, the drumsticks and 1.5-kilogram eggs of *Genyornis*. We note that marsupial megafauna have relatively thin skull bone for their size, so it is possible that kills were made regularly by solitary hunters. Perhaps the strategy, practised by Bushmen in Namibia, was to wound the animal and track it until it became exhausted.

Stephanie Garling offers an alternative hypothesis: that human subsistence was broad-based and that hunting strategies targeted game smaller than megafauna species. There are fewer than twenty archaeological sites for which the animal remains have been studied in detail, and it has proven difficult to distinguish the animal bone remains left by people from naturally occurring ones. However, the people who visited the caves in southwestern Tasmania during the LGM hunted primarily Bennett's wallaby and wombat, while the bones from Devil's Lair, a cave in the Naturaliste region south of Perth, suggest that people tended to hunt modern macropods. Garling envisages that megafauna were dispatched opportunistically, when mired in natural traps such as bogs or when disadvantaged in other ways before being encountered by people.

While direct evidence is lacking, we assume that pursuit of at least the smaller megafauna was well within the capacity of Pleistocene hunters, given that people hunted animals as large as red kangaroo, crocodile, emu, seal and sea lion with equipment of very simple design, such as clubs and a range of spears including thrusting javelins. Communal hunting strategies, trapping techniques and the use of fire are widely recorded as hunting aids since '1788' in different parts of Australia, but inferences from the archaeological record remain tenuous.

That megafauna was prey to hunters requires archaeological evidence such as a stone spearhead embedded in a bone, or a butchery site. Stratigraphic associations of megafauna bones and artefacts may indicate nothing more than visitation by megafauna and people at different times, even millennia apart. Even finds of megafaunal bone or teeth fashioned into ornaments or implements may only reflect scavenging bones of animals that had died naturally. Until direct archaeological evidence is at hand, any speculations concerning prehistoric menus belong more appropriately to a nostalgic Dreaming.

9 The initial colonisation

The first human inhabitants of Sahul probably stepped ashore some-where along the northwestern coast. Archaeology cannot provide a precise answer about the timing of first settlement because much of this region remains to be explored and test-excavated, and also there is a margin of error or uncertainty in chronometric age determinations. During the foundation era of first colonisation, the human population was probably very small and may not have left sufficient traces to be 'archaeologically visible'. It is possible, therefore, that people arrived more than a thousand years earlier than the dates determined for the oldest archaeological traces of human occupation of sites.

The environment may have been familiar to the first people. In the far north, along the coast of the New Guinea region, the low-lands were covered with tropical rain forest similar to that of islands to the west. To the immediate south, the vegetation was monsoonal eucalypt woodland, providing a familiar vista to people from Timor or Roti. An important difference, however, was Sahul's abundant and diverse marsupial fauna. The home islands of the first people only had a small variety of mammals derived originally from Sundaland, and scarcely any that had come from Sahul. If humans arrived in Australia before 40,000 years ago, probably only two or three marsupial and reptile predators could have been a threat to them or competed for large game.

When people first explored the southern margin of the continent, they may have encountered the five-metre-long giant anaconda, *Wonambi naracoortensis*, which weighed up to 100 kilograms. Like its distant cousin in South America, it probably lay submerged in still waters with nostrils just above the waterline. No doubt *Wonambi* was capable of squeezing to death any wallabies and smaller prey that ventured to the water's edge at night. The marsupial 'lion', *Thylacoleo carnifex*, inhabiting the forested and rocky regions of southern and eastern Australia, was the largest marsupial carnivore, about the size of a leopard. *Thylacoleo* had massive cutting teeth which were like scissor blades, and incisors that are equivalent to pincer-like canines. It was arboreal, and had powerful limbs and large claws on its forepaws for climbing and grasping. Possibly *Thylacoleo* pounced on its prey from a low limb and dragged the carcass back up the tree. Whatever its hunting strategy may have been, it appears to have consumed only certain parts of its prey, such as the internal organs, leaving the remainder of the carcass for scavengers. In any case, it remains to be established whether this fauna co-existed with humans, or whether these species were extinct by then.

MODELS OF COLONISATION

It is unlikely that the first people in Sahul either denied their natural human instinct to explore or assumed that the region of their landfall was the best of all possible worlds. Even if they had penetrated inland, there was less constraint in following the coastline, for the sea had borne them from their coastal homeland to Sahul's shores, and for survival of a people pre-adapted as hunter-gatherers of the coast and sea it offered their best chance of survival in a strange land.

This premise of dependence on the resources of the sea and littoral zone is the basis of the 'coastal colonisation hypothesis' proposed by Sandra Bowdler in the late 1970s. Bowdler postulated that the first colonists subsisted primarily on fish, shellfish and small terrestrial animals, and that they had little interest in hunting large land animals. She argued that human settlement was confined to the Sahul coastline for many thousands of years, and that only later did people expand along river corridors to exploit the rich aquatic resources of inland water bodies. It was only at the end of the Pleistocene, she believed, when the sea invaded low-lying territory, that some populations were compelled to subsist without marine or aquatic resources.

As the number of early known prehistoric sites increases, their distribution has broadened to include non-coastal habitats, and there is no comfortable fit between Bowdler's model and these contemporary archaeological findings. Critics have pointed out that Bowdler perceived a coastal economy to be that of highly specialised strandloopers of the littoral zone, not the more generalised exploitation typical of many Aboriginal groups living along the Australian coast in the nineteenth century. Because many food staples were seasonal, both along the coast and inland, people moved around for at least part of the year. Bowdler's concept of Pleistocene coastal adaptation implies that people were so specialised that they were unable to adapt to conditions away from the coast. This suggests that people were uninventive, unadaptive and lacked curiosity. The continent was empty of other people and, while some coasts were richly endowed with food resources, others were almost bereft of them. Inland there were vast expanses of tropical and temperate forestlands and woodlands, and grasslands inhabited by grazing marsupials. That the population of Sahul would be tied to a marine-aquatic subsistence for thousands of years is a denial of the human spirit.

An alternative scenario to that of Bowdler is offered by David Horton, who envisages progressive colonisation of Sahul's environmental zones—the better-watered regions first and the arid core last. Woodlands were prime country because they supported a greater diversity of animal species. Horton proposes that during the Last Glacial Maximum, when the arid zone became less hospitable, its human inhabitants retreated to well-watered coastal regions. He envisages that colonisation was effected by generalised hunting and gathering reliable abundant staples. Woodlands were prime habitats for hunters, supporting a great diversity of animal species, including now-extinct megafauna.

'Fast-trackers'

The only certainty about the early phase of colonisation is that at least most of Sahul was explored and occupied well before 30,000 years ago. A number of prehistorians, ourselves included, believe that Sahul may have been colonised very rapidly, and that physical and most environmental barriers were insignificant in stemming the flow of humanity across the continent. Possibly the only factor limiting this territorial expansion was the rate of human reproduction. This model of colonisation is called the 'fast-tracker hypothesis'.

Joe Birdsell was the first proponent of fast-tracker colonisation, and in an influential paper published in 1957 he proposed that it required only a few centuries to spread across the Sahul. Birdsell estimated that the descendants of an original group of 25 colonists would have numbered almost 300,000 in the space of 2204 years. While this particular calculation was based on outmoded assumptions about carrying capacities of different environmental zones, it provides some idea of how swift the process of geographic spread and population increase may have been.

In support of the fast-tracker hypothesis, archaeologists David Rindos and Esme Webb surmised that only basic hunter-gatherer adaptations were the prerequisite for continent-wide settlement, and that colonisation of the different habitats required only adaptation by degree. There are two elements to their persuasive argument. The first is that colonisation of a new habitat, including the desert core, requires neither profound cultural innovation, nor optimum extraction of resources, nor even a large population; and second, that the greater the degree of local adaptation to one kind of environment, the slower the process of colonising different habitats. They argue that more nomadic and dispersed people are more likely to cross environmental boundaries and outpace a highly adapted, territorially focused group, such as specialised littoral-dwelling people.

Although we consider the fast-tracker hypothesis the more reasonable of the two, it remains exactly that—a hypothesis. The archaeologist David Frankel cautions that the spread of early dates for human occupation provides no scope at this stage for demonstrating either rapid or slow colonisation—the chronology simply is not sufficiently fine-grained to tell.

SEARCH FOR THE OLDEST SITES; IDENTIFYING STONE TOOLS

Before any claim for the earliest human artefacts gains general acceptance in the profession, two fundamental requirements must be met: that objects dated are in fact artefacts; and that, if the artefacts themselves do not provide the material for a chronometric date, they are the same age as the dated material, usually surrounding sediments or hearths.

The criteria for distinguishing stone artefacts from naturally broken pieces of stone have developed over the last century. In most circumstances they allow reliable identification of stone flaking, which involves a swift, low-angled blow to a stone core. Much of the stone chosen for making flaked tools is homogenous and isotropic (the mechanical properties are the same in all directions). A hard siliceous stone called chert, and its variety flint, offers some of the best flaking opportunities. If a pebble or lump of stone (a *core*) is struck with a rounded piece of tough stone (a *hammer*), the flakes produced have a distinctive conchoidal (shell-like) form and markings. In particular, the contouring of the flake surface and the presence of concentric undulations is similar to that on a bivalve shell. Conchoidal flaking happens in nature, but only in particular circumstances, as when cobbles of hard isotropic stone are tumbled violently against other tough rocks during a flash flood. Natural flaking virtually never happens at places where humans made or discarded stone artefacts; and almost never creates a pattern of breakages that can be confused with human design. The context of the finds is also important, because only particular kinds of rock were used to make flaked stone tools, and the presence of any flakes of these rocks away from their natural place indicates that they are cultural relics. Some stone types are so distinctive and so commonly used by Aborigines that the archaeologist does not even need to examine a stone flake closely to know that it is an artefact.

Less certainty prevails in identifying a stone artefact when a piece of flaked stone has been used without any removal of finer flakes to shape it or resharpen its edge. This further chipping is called retouch or secondary trimming. There also may be difficulties if the stone is coarse-grained, or is quartz which tends to fragment when struck. Eroding quartz outcrops and quartz pebbles are widespread in Australia and provided much of the stone for tools, but most often quartz does not exhibit readily apparent conchoidal markings. One of the difficulties in assessing claims for the oldest stone artefacts is that most specimens are of quartz. Some artefactual quartz, however, is readily recognisable because it is the product of 'bipolar flaking'. This is when a piece of stone, often a small pebble, is positioned on a stable stone surface with the fingers and smashed into fragments with a stone hammer.

The ground surface is scuffed and trodden down by people inhabiting an encampment, particularly when it consists of loose sediment, such as on a sand dune or sandy rockshelter. People may scoop out a comfortable sleeping hollow or dig into the ground, for various reasons—to make an earth oven, cache valuables, or prepare a grave. Should disturbance of this kind occur, artefacts may end up below the bottom of the original cultural horizon. Artefacts that appear to be old may also be 'lag deposit'; this occurs when a surface is stripped by erosion, leaving behind the heavier objects from different depths, including artefacts, which are later covered by new sediment. A major disturbance of seemingly straightforward archaeological deposits is bioturbation—reworking of sediment mainly by ants, termites and earthworms. The problem can be complex, because both artefacts and pieces of charcoal, commonly used for radiocarbon dating, may have shifted from their original positions.

Some disturbances are well marked in a site's stratigraphy and pose no problem of interpretation, but this is not often the case. Many of Australia's most significant stratified archaeological sites have only a shallow archaeological deposit. Often this consists of a topmost layer of dust or soil a few centimetres deep; over sand or clay with no distinct layering; and lowermost, disintegrating bedrock or rubble. Sometimes, a site has well-defined, different-coloured layers, suggesting distinct depositional events, but such strata may form naturally as a result of groundwater percolation and fluctuations in the water table. Identifying the products of a single toolmaking event, by finding which artefacts can be refitted ('conjoined'), shows that sometimes artefacts produced at the same time have been spread to different levels without the slightest indication of disturbance in the stratigraphy.

DISCOVERY AND DATING OF PLEISTOCENE SITES

In 1960 the oldest dated relics in Australia were less than 9000 years in age. Norman Tindale claimed a much older age for his 'Kartan Culture' artefacts from Kangaroo Island, and Alexander Gallus for Koonalda Cave on the Nullarbor Plain and for a river bank terrace site at Keilor on the northern outskirts of Melbourne. These, however, remained unproved and it was generally believed at the time that Australia had remained uninhabited until the Holocene era.

Mulvaney's announcement in 1962 of a Late Pleistocene age for Kenniff Cave in central Queensland provided the crucial evidence from a stratified and dated archaeological sequence for Pleistocene settlement in Australia. Mulvaney noted a distinct change in stone technology at a level dating to about 4000 years ago. Radiocarbon dating revealed that the lowest particles of charcoal in the cultural deposit dated to 16,000 radiocarbon years. The Pleistocene barrier in Australian prehistory was raised.

The development of radiocarbon dating in the 1950s had been a boon to Australian archaeology. It coincided with the beginning of professional excavations of deep stratified sites—a strategy adopted by archaeologists at the Australian National and Sydney Universities. Within four years of the dating of Kenniff Cave, there were similar radiocarbon dates for Koonalda Cave, Burrill Lake on the New South Wales coast, and three rockshelters in Kakadu National Park, demonstrating occupation older than 20,000 years. Sites of comparable antiquity were also found in Papua New Guinea, highlighting the need to frame prehistory in the context of Pleistocene Sahul as well as the modern continent of Australia.

The 1970s brought still earlier dates for human occupation on the shore of Lake Mungo in western New South Wales, and at Devil's Lair, a cave in southwest Australia. These findings established firmly a prehistory of more than 30,000 years, and the possibility of at least 40,000 years. By 1980 over twenty Pleistocene-age sites had been identified. Today there are more than 150—over half are rockshelters and caves, and many of the others are cultural horizons in sand dunes.

Some of the best evidence for Australia's human past is buried in crescent-shaped sand and clay dunes, termed lunettes, bordering the shorelines of dry lakes in the southwest, and in southeastern Australia, mostly in the western Riverine Plain. Today, these lakes are normally totally dry, but in the past their water levels fluctuated between empty and full. When the lake floor is dry, it is scoured by wind erosion so that sand and clay particles are blown to the far edge of the lake, where they accumulate to form a fringing dune. These lunette beaches provided excellent camping places—shade trees, soft, sandy ground, and fresh water and food from lake and hinterland immediately at hand. Prehistoric sites are continuously exposed in these dunes as a result of farming-induced soil erosion, and in some sedimentary horizons carbonate-charged water percolating through the matrix has preserved bone and shell. The lunettes are a layered time capsule containing the bones of extinct fauna, human burials, and evidence of everyday life in distant prehistoric times possibly for as long as humans have been in Australia.

The Late Pleistocene antiquity of sites that have stood the test of time, such as Devil's Lair and those in the Lake Mungo region, has been reinforced by comparable ages of many others scattered throughout the continent—for instance, three limestone caves in the rainforest wilderness of southeastern Tasmania, a rockshelter at Mandu Mandu Creek, Northwest Cape, Western Australia; further north along the coast are Koolan Shelter 2 on a rocky island of the Buccaneer Archipelago, and the small rockshelter of Sandy Creek 1 near Cooktown on the northeast coast.

The predictions of 40,000 years or more have a firmer foundation than they did in the early 1970s. Within two decades archaeologists had added 30,000 years to Australia's prehistory, indicating that human colonisation of Sahul preceded that of the Americas. In Old World terms the antiquity demonstrated for human settlement of Sahul equates with the Upper Palaeolithic or perhaps the earlier Mousterian in Europe, when modern humans were expanding westwards and supplanting the indigenous Neanderthals. Sahul is emerging as fundamental in reconstructing the prehistory of modern humans.

UNCERTAIN LEADS

The first major dispute about the evidence for Pleistocene antiquity concerned Koonalda Cave. An investigation by Richard Wright corroborated the claim by Gallus, and Koonalda's place in the history of Australian archaeology is assured on the credential of its antiquity alone. However, Wright demonstrated that most of the supposed flint artefacts were pieces naturally fractured by the growth of gypsum crystals in small cracks within the stone. Other flints were quarry waste and not tools of European Palaeolithic style, as Gallus had asserted. Gallus had also claimed great antiquity for stone artefacts from a site on the Maribyrnong River near Keilor. As early as 1961, Mulvaney expressed caution in accepting his claim. Despite a number of investigations over the last three decades, there remain a number of unresolved issues over its dating. The geomorphologist Jim Bowler has inferred an age of at least 26,000–36,000 years, and possibly 45,000 years on stratigraphic grounds. However, as before, there is a fundamental problem over the artefactual status of much of the stone and bone items. The best that can be said is that some of the stone artefacts are at least 30,000 years old.

In the 1980s another site, Upper Swan River, was hailed as a dramatic advance in the dating of human settlement of Australia.

This site, which was initially exposed during commercial excavation of clay, is on the Swan River floodplain a few kilometres from Perth. A large-scale excavation by Robert Pearce uncovered flaking debris of quartz, quartzite and chert, some of which fitted together, indicating that there had been little vertical movement of artefacts in the sediment. Radiocarbon determinations from wood and resin samples stratified above the cultural horizon provided dates of 32,000 to 38,000 years BP. Since then, however, there have been questions about the artefacts and radiocarbon dates which have never been resolved. Since the artefacts were not reported in detail, nor further excavation undertaken to address the issues raised, the site remains enigmatic.

A few years after the claim for Upper Swan, a date was reported of 40,000–50,000 years BP for stone artefacts found in a gravel quarry at Cranebrook Terrace on the Nepean River, western Sydney. There is no dispute about the dates, which are radiocarbon determinations on preserved wood and thermoluminescence dates of sand. However, the stone items are simple flakes found in a cobble stream bed and there are serious doubts about their identification as artefacts. With the discovery of more promising sites the debate about the antiquity of human settlement has moved on and Cranebrook Terrace is no longer an issue of debate.

BEYOND 40,000 YEARS?

In the small community of Australian archaeologists, there is now more disagreement and deeper division over the issue of earliest human settlement than there was a decade ago. Claims based on archaeological evidence range from about 40,000 to over 100,000 years ago. It is prudent at this stage to await refinements in dating techniques, and to insist that any inferences concerning human presence must be substantiated by producing artefacts or other evidence of occupancy in firm stratigraphic context. As we have said, during the era of first colonisation the human population was probably very small and may not have left sufficient traces to be identifiable by archaeological fieldwork. Also, the very earliest sites must have been inundated by the last sea level rise, so these 'first' sites are unlikely to be discovered.

Kakadu settlers?

Kakadu National Park in western Arnhem Land, the largest park in the world's tropical region, is a treasure trove of hunter-gatherer archaeology. In 1948 archaeologists F. D. McCarthy and Frank Setzler visited the Alligator Rivers, now within the park, as members of a *National Geographic* scientific expedition to Arnhem Land, at that time a relatively remote region. While engaged on graduate fieldwork nearly twenty years later Carmel White (now Schrire) discovered near the East Alligator River some of Australia's oldest sites. She unearthed ground-stone hatchet heads older than any others known in the world. Within a few years large uranium deposits were discovered close to the most prospective archaeological areas and the Alligator Rivers region was suddenly a focus of national attention, and of scientific studies sponsored by the Australian government and mining companies. Environmental and archaeological assessments were commissioned, and the findings provided the case for declaration of the park and its subsequent World Heritage listing. Included among the sites excavated by Harry Allen and Jo Kamminga during the archaeological survey were the rockshelters of Malakunanja and Nauwalabila, both of which had deep cultural deposits, and radiocarbon dates of around 18,000–20,000 years BP for the deepest particles of charcoal. Since stone artefacts occurred below these dated levels, even older occupation was a possibility.

Foremost among the searchers for the earliest human occupation sites in Australia is the peripatetic archaeologist Rhys Jones, who as early as 1979 had predicted 50,000 years for initial human settlement. Jones' conviction about the great time depth of Australian prehistory drew him to these two highly prospective rockshelters during two field trips a decade apart. In 1990 Jones and his collaborators, Mike Smith and the luminescence-dating specialist Bert Roberts, announced that Malakunanja had been first occupied by humans some 50,000–60,000 years ago. At the time this claim was widely publicised by the media and had enormous public impact. It was soon followed by a similar claim for Nauwalabila, which Jones had re-excavated a decade earlier.

Nauwalabila

Halfway along the western escarpment of Deaf Adder Gorge, a valley of spectacular scenery and a storehouse of Aboriginal rock art and archaeological sites, is Djuwarr Lagoon, an idyllic and obviously important Aboriginal camping place in earlier times. The surrounding rockshelters are adorned with art in the X-ray style, and nearby there is a cliff-side quarry for stone spearheads. Nauwalabila rockshelter, formed by the tilt of a half-buried slab of cliff fall, is a kilometre from the lagoon. The Nauwalabila deposit comprises 2.5 metres of sand overlying decayed sandstone rubble. In the first excavation Kamminga obtained radiocarbon dates from levels above the rubble. In the enlarged trench Jones dug, he was able to penetrate the decaying rock at the base of the deposit. He claimed that artefacts were found in all levels and into the basal rubble. Using the optically stimulated luminescence (OSL) technique Jones and Roberts dated the sands sequentially at five depths where artefacts were present, estimating a maximum age of 53,000–59,000 years for the cultural deposit. Unfortunately, the artefacts from the rubble have not been described or illustrated, nor properly assessed by other archaeologists, which leaves open the question of whether occupation is really earlier than the radiocarbon dates indicate.

Malakunanja

Malakunanja rockshelter is an inclined cliff face in a rocky plateau outlier 65 kilometres northwest of Nauwalabila, near Magela Creek, a tributary of the East Alligator River. Faded rock paintings of rifles, a buggy wheel and a man dressed in Western clothing testify to recent Aboriginal camps, possibly early this century when the Aboriginal community was involved in commercial buffalo hunting. A test pit excavated by Kamminga in 1973 uncovered a buried shell midden 50 centimetres thick, which had accumulated from about 6300 to 3600 years BP when nearby Magela Creek was the upper arm of a coastal estuary. Beneath the midden was a layer of coarse yellow sand about 4.5 metres deep, accumulated from the slow weathering of the sandstone plateau. Within this sand layer were stone artefacts, including three grindstones, to a depth of about two metres below ground surface. A radiocarbon date of about 18,000 years BP was determined from fine charcoal particles above the lowest stone artefacts. In the subsequent excavation by Jones, the lowest stone artefacts were recovered at the same depth as previously, but this time samples of sand down to a depth of about 4.5 metres were taken by Roberts for thermoluminescence dating (TL). The deepest sample dated to over 100,000 years, and the one from just above the lowest artefact-bearing

The arrow in this picture indicates Malakunanja rockshelter at the foot of an outlier from the sandstone escarpment, Kakadu National Park, close to Jabiluka uranium mine. TL dates suggest possible occupation at least 50,000 years ago, but the question of dating is unresolved. (D. J. Mulvaney)

level was 45,000 years, with an uncertainty of 9000 years around that age. Assuming a constant rate of sediment build-up, Jones and his colleagues estimated that the lowest artefacts, at nearly three metres depth, were about 50,000 years old.

Over the years, the claim for Malakunanja's great antiquity has been challenged by a number of archaeologists. One concern has been the large 'uncertainty' in the crucial TL age determination, which provides an age range of 41,000–63,000 years, a considerable antiquity nonetheless. Another problem, potentially more serious, is that the lowermost artefacts may have moved downward in the sand layer, not an uncommon occurrence in a beach-like sand body, and they may even have come from the occupation period marked by the shell midden. Jones and his colleagues have fiercely defended their

TL dates, arguing that they are in stratigraphic sequence and are consistent with the radiocarbon dates for the upper levels. They also argue that the flakes in the lowest levels were found lying flat, rather than at angles as one would expect if they had settled downwards. Also some of the artefacts overlaid a feature they identified as a small pit. Almost a decade after Malakunanja's re-excavation, there is still no detailed excavation report to corroborate the momentous claim made about the site. Unless the site is excavated yet again, there may be no clarification of its antiquity. Determining the extent of any downward movement of artefacts through processes of bioturbation may be difficult since, in simple terms, the deposit is a 6000-year-old midden, overlying a sand body showing no stratification. As with some of the earlier claims for very old sites, rather than being fully assessed, and either corroborated or dismissed, the Kakadu claims have been sidelined by the rapid pace of new discoveries and the inevitable shift in media attention.

JINMIUM

The most recent claim, that for Jinmium rockshelter near the Keep River, Northern Territory, was the biggest 'media splash' in the history of Australian archaeology and headline news around the world. The joint research team from the Australian Museum and Wollongong University, archaeologist Richard Fullagar, ecologist Lesley Head and luminescence dating specialist David Price, claimed at least 116,000 years for the earliest human occupation at Jinmium. Media hype inflated this figure to a possible 170,000 years, the proposed age of the lowest dated sediment below the artefact levels. With great drama the headline in the *Sydney Morning Herald* announced 'Unveiled: outback Stonehenge that will rewrite our history', and feature stories were bylined 'Unearthed. Australia's *lost* civilisation' and 'a find that is about to rewrite the prehistory of Australia and change the world view of how civilisation developed'. This was followed quickly by a call for caution in the editorial of the national newspaper, *The Australian*. Essentially, what the Jinmium team had done was date by the thermoluminescence technique the sediment around the lowest artefacts, comprising only a few small quartzite flakes.

The general response of archaeologists and dating specialists to the claim that Australian prehistory was more than twice as old as the previous 30 years of fieldwork had shown was profound scepticism. Evidently an administrative hitch resulted in the media being briefed prematurely about the Jinmium claim. It was another three months before the site report was published in the journal *Antiquity*, so professional colleagues did not have the opportunity to properly assess the evidence at an early stage. It also was premature for another reason. There was a possibility that quartz grains from decomposing rock may have been included in the TL samples, and therefore Bert Roberts, another TL specialist, was cross-checking the TL samples with a variant of OSL, called the 'aliquot method'. This method is designed to identify grains that have not been properly bleached and it uses only about ten quartz grains rather than the usual average of 4000. The results of this study were at least a year away.

The first refutation of Jinmium came only a few months after the initial public announcement. By examining the data published in the *Antiquity* article, the luminescence specialist at the Australian National University, Nigel Spooner, was able to show that the TL samples had not been completely zeroed by exposure to sunlight, and the dates were probably overestimated by a factor of ten. Confirmation of Spooner's results is now available with the publication of OSL and radiocarbon determinations showing that the level originally dated to 50,000 years is only about 3000 years old and the entire occupation probably falls within the Holocene period.

SEEKING SOLID FOUNDATIONS

The 'Jinmium affair' demonstrated the need for caution in accepting claims for very early sites, not only by the media and the public but also by professional archaeologists. The temptation to grasp the Holy Grail of Australian archaeology is great. Perhaps there will always be claims for yet older sites, paralleling the American experience, in which new claims are regularly made and just as regularly dismissed. Seeking firmer foundations for the beginning of Australian prehistory, we turn to two sites which have considerable promise: Ngarrabullgan Cave, 100 kilometres west of Cairns in north Queensland, and Carpenter's Gap rockshelter in Windjana Gorge National Park in the central Kimberley region.

Ngarrabullgan Cave is situated on the top of Mount Mulligan, an eighteen-kilometre-long mesa surrounded by dry sclerophyll woodland. In Aboriginal lore the mesa was the home of a wandering evil spirit. A small excavation in the cave by Bruno David in 1993 revealed an undisturbed cultural deposit only 36 centimetres thick, yet finely layered with a total of 27 distinct strata. These strata, dated both by radiocarbon and OSL methods, record numerous episodes of low-intensity human occupation, beginning with a single thin stratum older than 37,000 years BP. The cave was occupied sporadically until about 32,500 years BP, and then apparently abandoned until the mid-Holocene. Carpenter's Gap rockshelter, excavated by Sue O'Connor, is a large elevated shelter in tropical semi-arid country on the other side of the continent. The shelter has a panoramic view over a plain and the King Leopold Range. Nearby are permanent rock pools, well stocked with fish and freshwater crocodiles. An AMS radiocarbon date from above the lowest cultural level provided a date of 39,700±1000 years BP. A study of paired radiocarbon and luminescence samples is currently being undertaken to confirm the site's antiquity. The importance of these two sites is not only the evidence of very early human occupation but the permanent dryness of their deposits which has preserved organic remains. This is especially the case at Carpenter's Gap shelter, where fragile plant remains, such as saltbush seeds, fragments of bark and wood shavings, have been recovered. Such excellent preservation and fine stratigraphy makes it more likely that the radiocarbon determinations are reliable, and also permits far more scope in reconstructing human activities in the sites than would normally be the case.

Ngarrabullgan Cave and Carpenter's Gap point to the likelihood that people first set foot on an Australian shore around 40,000 years BP or earlier. However, all radiocarbon determinations around 40,000 years BP require scrutiny because they are close to the effective dating limit of the technique. Organic matter 50,000 years old has practically no radioactivity left to measure; a microscopic amount of younger carbon atoms from a contaminant, such as compounds from decomposing organic matter, will give it a renewed charge of radioactivity which will make the age determination thousands of years less than it should be. It is sometimes impossible for dating technicians to know when such contamination has happened. Cross-dating of luminescence and radiocarbon samples from Ngarrabullgan demonstrates that corroboration of very old radiocarbon determinations is possible for individual sites, but it may be that a number of other archaeological sites around Australia with radiocarbon dates of more than 30,000 years BP are much older and future dating may assist. Despite this concern we are not yet confident in the claims that people arrived at least 50,000–60,000 years ago which are commonly publicised by the media. More objective evidence is the prerequisite.

It is essential to establish a true chronology if the questions of Aboriginal origins and reconstruction of the early occupation of the continent are to be achieved. Progress must depend upon the continued close collaboration of archaeologists, earth scientists and chronometric dating specialists, but it is an issue of considerable national interest and would benefit from a national funding effort. Meantime, research in Flores and adjacent eastern Indonesian islands is indicating the possibility that they were reached by a sea voyage so early that *Homo erectus* or another hominid species may have been involved. Detailed publication of stratigraphy, artefacts and chronology from a major excavation are necessary to solve these issues. An early landfall in Australia or New Guinea may be discovered, but it remains hypothetical today.

FIRE TRAILS FROM THE PAST?

Another consideration which interests some prehistorians is the inferences to be drawn from charcoal. As the human population spread across Sahul they took with them fire, and the potential to create cultural landscapes by constant burning. Since the 1980s it has been pollen analysts who have reconstructed past vegetation patterns and fire histories, and who initially claimed to have the evidence for the earliest human presence in Australia. These histories are interpreted primarily from identification of preserved pollen grains extracted from sediments from the beds of lakes or swamps. A 'pollen diagram' is constructed, based on frequencies of different pollen grains and fine charcoal particles. Chronometric ages determined from sediment samples fix the local record into the wider climatic and environmental record.

Three pollen records figure prominently in these claims, and media reports about them have contributed to the widely held assumption that people must have come to Australia before 50,000 years ago. The first claim was made in the early 1980s by the ANU palynologists Gurdip Singh and E. A. Geissler for Lake George, near Canberra. The pollen in their cores indicated cycles in vegetation, from open herbaceous vegetation during glacials to *Casuarina* woodland and forest during interglacials, over a period of hundreds of thousands of years. A vegetation shift to eucalypt-dominated forest along with a dramatic increase in charcoal particles occurred in sediments believed to have been deposited around 125,000 years ago. Singh and Geissler argued that phenomenon may indicate human intervention in the fire regime. Richard Wright, a Sydney University archaeologist, has since shown that the vegetation change they identified probably occurred about 60,000 years ago, which is still beyond the known archaeological record. Currently, the only certainty about the record of fire in the Lake George cores is that there was a marked increase during the Holocene and the change from fire-sensitive species to eucalypt dominance possibly was coincidental.

Lynch's Crater in the rain forest of eastern Cape York has a sedimentary record spanning the last 190,000 years. The pollen analyst Peter Kershaw has identified a dramatic changeover from fire-sensitive *Araucaria* pine and vine forest to open sclerophyll containing a large proportion of eucalypts at about 38,000 years BP. This pollen change is accompanied by a dramatic increase in charcoal particles. Kershaw's date is comparable to ones from the early archaeological sites discussed above. In 1994, Kershaw reported a similar pattern in pollen and charcoal from seabed cores drilled 80 kilometres from the coast of north Queensland, on the outer edge of the continental shelf. Kershaw dates this event to about 100,000–140,000 years ago, which is considerably earlier than at Lynch's Crater. This dramatic claim has not stood unchallenged. Archaeologist Peter White has examined the pollen diagram and argues that a similar influx of charcoal not attributed to human presence also occurred more than a million years ago, and that the later concentration of charcoal is not part of a trend and is likely to be a chance occurrence due to variation in hydrology.

There can be no single signature of prehistoric Aboriginal burning because different vegetation communities require different burning strategies. Currently, there is no consensus among pollen analysts and ecologists that a dramatic, sustained increase in charcoal particles in a water-borne sediment indicates a human firing regime rather than natural causes. Claims for human activities 60,000 or over 100,000 years ago based on pollen and fire records are not sufficiently convincing to project Australian prehistory well beyond the time depth demonstrated by the more reliable archaeological findings.

The original Australians 10

For decades Aboriginal Australians attracted scientific interest because it was believed that their physiology, social system and material culture were unchanged relics of the primeval human stock. So it was assumed that their brains were childlike and their society mirrored 'primitive' humanity before agricultural people 'progressed'. This was nonsense. Yet it must be stated that Aboriginal people—past and present—hold potential clues to many issues common to all races and significant for Aboriginal self-knowledge of their origins and cultural development. Australian Aborigines have survived in relative geographical isolation for an incredibly long time, thus escaping the inroads of conquering peoples, racial admixture and accompanying diseases until 1788.

Both living Aboriginal people and their ancestors carry vital genetic, medical and nutritional clues to understanding their origins, dispersal and adaptation to varied habitats. Analysis of mortuary practices and grave goods provides insight into past intellectual life, virtually knowledge of Dreaming times.

Regrettably, the unethical treatment of Aboriginal people, living or deceased, by evolutionary minded scientists in earlier decades has now reaped the whirlwind. Many indigenous people oppose much current research into blood group genetics, DNA testing, or the systematic excavation and recording of ancient burials and their grave goods. However, future Aboriginal scientists are themselves likely to investigate these vital aspects of the place of indigenous people and their ancestors in the human family.

HUMAN ORIGINS

There are two general hypotheses about human evolution, commonly labelled the 'multi-regional evolution' and the 'Out-of-Africa' hypotheses. The first posits that *Homo erectus* populations in Africa, Asia and Europe evolved in isolation in their own directions, with only some gene flow between them, and that they are the basis for today's major racial populations. Implicit in 'multi-regionalism', implying long regional continuity lasting a million years or more, is the assumption that *Homo erectus* and *Homo sapiens* are the one species. The alternative 'Out-of-Africa' hypothesis, formulated by the Harvard palaeoanthropologist William Howells, is argued by various molecular biologists, archaeologists and human biologists. Their contention is that *Homo erectus* and *Homo sapiens* originated in Africa and successively colonised Europe and Asia with very little or no interbreeding between them. It is assumed that anatomically modern humans overwhelmed *Homo erectus*, Neanderthal Man and any other hominids living at that time, but their ascendancy in Eurasia is poorly dated. Modern humans may have first appeared as long as 240,000 years ago in Africa, but perhaps only colonised the Southeast Asian mainland just prior to their further conquest of Sahul.

The Out-of-Africa hypothesis has attracted the popular press with its so-called evolutionary molecular clock. This 'clock' measures evolutionary time from the constant but slow rate of mutations in human mtDNA (strands of DNA in mitochondria, which are small energy-generator organelles found within larger cells). MtDNA is passed on only in the female line. The molecular biologist Rebecca Cann and her colleagues inferred from DNA sampling of living populations around the world that the original ancestors lived in Africa about 200,000 years ago and that descendant populations emerged at different times to form major geographic lineages or races. Critics of the 'clock theory' have shown that certain mathematical procedures underpinning the theory are wrong, and they argue that mtDNA is under strong selection and therefore does not necessarily change at a constant rate. The latest proponent of the evolutionary clock, David

Penny, uses a different statistical procedure, which he calls the 'Great Deluge Method'. This provides more parsimonious phylogenetic lineages, which support an Out-of-Africa model. An important finding is that at least fifteen different mitochondrial lineages are evident in the Australian Aboriginal population. The closest relatives of some of these mtDNA lineages are African, Indian, Chinese, and European which, as with shape of the crania, may mean nothing more than that there was a common pool of mtDNA since leaving the African homeland and that this extra-homeland pool was diverse, while still being a subset of the original gene pool. In the current situation, it is best to await further research. Some multi-regionalists argue that the Out-of-Africa theory would be disproved if the DNA evidence can be dismissed, but DNA evidence is not crucial to the theory.

Even though *Homo sapiens* has the widest geographic range of any species of large terrestrial mammal, the shape of the human skull is remarkably homogeneous. For regional populations of *Homo erectus* to have evolved into today's populations of *Homo sapiens* would require very substantial gene flow between groups vastly distant from each other, in Asia, Europe and Africa over one to two million years, a proposal that is difficult to imagine. Colin Groves departs from the general Out-of-Africa model, in questioning whether *Homo erectus* is directly ancestral to modern humans. He defines an ancestral Afro-European hominid lineage, *Homo heidelbergensis*, and regards the Asian *Homo erectus* fossils as another lineage or species. Others have also criticised the traditional formulation of recent hominid evolution. Interpretation of hominid fossils is not straightforward—it is sometimes described as a 'moveable feast'. A solution must await future refinements in genetics research and systematic excavation to increase the sample of pre-*Homo sapiens*.

AFFINITIES OF THE FIRST AUSTRALIANS

The Aboriginal population today exceeds 200,000 people. At least 50,000 trace their ancestry entirely from Aboriginal forebears of pre-colonial times; most others have Irish, English, Scottish and less often Chinese, Indonesian, or Beluchi ('Afghan'), as well as indigenous, ancestors. In general physical appearance Aboriginal Australians are distinct from other major human lineages, such as sub-Saharan Africans, Mongoloids of East Asia, and Caucasoids of southwest Asia and Europe. In scientific terminology Aborigines (including

Tasmanians) are Australoid, and are part of the Australo–Melanesian lineage when grouped with Melanesians. The indigenous people of New Guinea, Vanuatu, the Solomon Islands, New Caledonia, and to a lesser extent Fiji and certain islands in eastern Indonesia, share close ancestry with Australian Aborigines. There may also be a close relationship between Australo–Melanesians, and with the Negritos of Southeast Asia who are commonly regarded as descendants of the original inhabitants before incursions by Mongoloids from the north. When Australia and New Guinea were separated between 8500 and 8000 years BP, the human populations of these lands went their separate ways both biologically and culturally. Despite the thousands of years of genetic isolation, on the basis of skull measurements Aborigines and Melanesians are invariably positioned closest to each other on the world ethnic map.

While studies of blood group genetics provide some evidence for a common genetic relationship between Aborigines and Melanesians, they offer no clues about affinities with other populations before near modern times. In humans there are at least nine principal blood group systems, which are identified by distinctive antigen molecules on the surface of the red blood cells. Among Aborigines of fully indigenous ancestry, the subgroup A_2 antigen is absent and B rare in the ABO blood group system, and the S antigen in the MNSs blood group system is virtually absent, though it is very high in Melanesia. Where present in the contemporary Aboriginal population the S antigen indicates a degree of European ancestry, as does the Rh negative combination (cde) in the Rhesus blood group system. The absence of the Mongoloid marker gene D1[a] in the Diego blood group system distinguishes Aborigines from East Asians generally.

ABORIGINAL PHYSICAL FEATURES

Humankind's major lineages are defined in terms of observable differences in physical traits such as skin, eye and hair colour, and the shape of the eyelids, nose, lips, and skull. Conventional wisdom is that such traits are often environmental adaptations, but there is little evidence to support this belief. Recent statistical studies have shown that the shape of the Australo–Melanesian cranium (the skull without its jawbone) is closest to black Africans living south of the Sahara Desert and next closest to Caucasoids. However, similarity in cranial shape does not necessarily mean close biological relationship.

The most comprehensive study of physical variation among Australian Aborigines is by the American biologist Joe Birdsell, who published his monumental synthesis of genetic data in 1993. Birdsell's synthesis is the outcome of more than 40 years of personal research and the addition of data from the research expeditions undertaken before World War II by teams from the University of Adelaide. Other more specific studies are mostly concerned with bone anatomy and blood genetics. Birdsell has shown that there is continuous, graded variation (clines) over distance in the frequency and degree of development of individual physical traits. Birdsell's results support several earlier studies, which found north to south clines extending down the east and west coasts, while others extended across the continent. Interestingly, a few traits, such as skin colour and degree of body hair, appear to correlate with environment, but most cluster geographically with abrupt changes in variation. There are detectable genetic constellations from which different regional populations may be plotted, such as the Tasmanians, Bentinck Islanders and Murray River peoples.

Mean Aboriginal stature ranges between 154 and 175 centimetres according to region (an average of 164 centimetres), with the tallest people found in the Kimberley region. The typical linear body form and relatively long limbs are physical adaptations to a hot, dry climate.

Eye (actually iris) colour varies from light to dark brown. Dark brown skin colour is common, and is darkened further by the sun. There is a strongly clinal pattern in the colour of skin exposed to sunlight, with darker skin in northern Australia, particularly along the north coast and in the northwest of the continent, and lightest in the southeast, and in the south generally.

Hair colour is black to dark brown, but lighter shades also occur. There is a genetic mutation for blondness in children of the Western Desert with its centre in the southern part. In this region, children's hair colour is ash blond to tawny; it darkens with age, mostly after puberty. The same mutation occurs also among the Gayardilt of Bentinck Island in the Gulf of Carpentaria. The gene involved is not the same as one responsible for blondness in Europeans—in three of the desert tribes the frequency of the mutation approaches 100 per cent.

Pre-colonial Aborigines had moderate to pronounced beard and body hair. Hairiness was more pronounced for men of southeastern Australia, especially on the coast and in the Murray River corridor. In Cape York Peninsula and the southwest of the continent, beard growth was scant. In general, abundant body hair and beard growth were closely linked with tendency to baldness, and these attributes are increasingly apparent from west to east across southern Australia. Head hair varies from straight to very curly, with straight to wavy most common—in Western Australia low wave is typical, whereas people in the north Queensland rain forest had strongly curly hair, and in Tasmania it was tightly coiled.

Cranial anatomy

The part of the human skeleton that provides the most information for tracing evolution and genetic relationships is the skull, and in particular the cranium. There are often considerable differences between the male and female skull, which are greater than for other major populations of the world (such differences are termed sexual dimorphism). Typically, Aboriginal crania are long and narrow, and arched along the top (called vault gabling). A distinctive feature is relatively thick bone forming the cranium wall. With Aboriginal male crania the supra-orbital region—the brow ridges, the glabella, which is the area of bone just above the nose, and the lateral trigones at the outer ends of the brow ridges—is more prominent than for any other people. The glabella region may protrude outwards as much five millimetres. This feature is most common in the people of northern Australia, in particular those of the Kimberley region and the Top End. There is also a tendency for mid-facial prognathism (forward jutting of the facial bone between the nasal aperture and the upper front teeth). The bridge of the nose between the eye sockets is depressed and wide, and the upper jaw is large: in fact, the Aborigines in general have the largest jaw and teeth of any people in the world. There is a north–south gradient for tooth size, increasing from Cape York to the Murray River; however, desert Aborigines have the smallest teeth. Tooth wear in adults is distinctively hunter-gatherer in nature, with heavy, flat wear on the crowns caused by fine quartz particles which adhere to food. There is little tooth decay, but dental abscesses and osteoarthritis of the jaw are not uncommon pathologies.

AFTER DARWIN

In the nineteenth century, following Charles Darwin's revelations about evolution of species, there emerged a strong scientific interest in Australian Aboriginal anatomy based on the incorrect assumption that Aborigines were primitive relics of the dawn of human time. In 1863 the apostle of Darwinism, Thomas Huxley, writing in *The antiquity of man* by geologist Charles Lyell, compared Australian skulls with those of a recently discovered Neanderthal. Even as late as 1907 the anatomist W. Ramsay Smith informed his audience at the Australasian Association for the Advancement of Science that 'Australian Aborigines have furnished the largest number of ape-like characters. The more one investigates the truer does this statement prove to be.' These judgements were not easily replaced by reason. Even Baldwin Spencer, in his time the world authority on Australian Aborigines, instructed those who visited his museum in Melbourne that Aborigines 'may be regarded as a relic of the early childhood of mankind left stranded...in a low condition of savagery'.

Until recently, diversity in the world's human population was explained by intercontinental race migrations and ethnic blending, usually involving two or three basic stocks. As early as 1870, when Thomas Huxley published his racial systematisation, most evolutionists regarded mainland Aborigines as one racial type and Tasmanians as another, the survivors of the supposed original, more primitive inhabitants. Griffith Taylor in his book *Environment, race and migration*, published in 1937, envisaged waves of Aboriginal colonists sweeping before them a 'Negrito' race. While by the turn of the century Alfred Howitt had realised that Tasmanians were actually Aborigines, profoundly isolated for thousands of years by a sea barrier, the two-wave migration theory had followers until well after World War II. For instance, the South African anatomist E. A. Hooton declared that Aborigines were predominantly 'archaic Caucasian' with an admixture of Melanesian and Tasmanian Negrito. The ethnic migration scheme recently had support from Birdsell and Alan Thorne, a leading Australian palaeoanthropologist from the Australian National University. Birdsell relied largely on evidence of external physical features of living Aborigines, and Thorne on finds of prehistoric human bone.

BIRDSELL'S THREE WAVES OF PEOPLE

Joe Birdsell undertook biological studies in Australia from 1938. To explain the large variation in Aboriginal physical traits he observed, Birdsell formulated a hypothesis of 'tri-hybrid' racial composition, a genetic intermixing of three separate Late Pleistocene migrations into

Australia. Birdsell proposed his hypothesis in 1949, providing some evidence in 1967 and his full account of the data only in 1993. He postulates that the first wave was of short, slightly-built people with dark skin and woolly hair, called Negrito, which in Spanish means 'little Negro'. Many archaeologists believe that Negritos inhabited Southeast Asia before the arrival of Mongoloid people from the north, and that they survive today as relic populations on the Andaman Islands and as Negrito–Mongoloid mixed groups in Malaysia and the Philippines. Birdsell's model postulates the Negrito arrival in Australia some time before 30,000 years ago, and interprets some of the burials at Lake Mungo as their remains. His Australian Negritos survived only as relic populations in two refuges—his twelve tribes of 'Barrineans' in the tropical rain forests of the Atherton and Herberton Tablelands in northeast Queensland, and the Tasmanians, saved from the full onslaught of later invasions by the rise of the sea, but like the Barrineans, to a degree genetically intermixed with later invaders.

Birdsell's second wave of migrants, the Murrayians, was linked to the Ainu of Japan. Ainu have light skin, abundant body hair, an incidence of male baldness (uncommon among Mongoloids), and a Caucasoid-like body build; hence they have been regarded in the past as a relic population of archaic Caucasoids. According to Birdsell, the Murrayians conquered the Australian Negrito tribes and settled along the Murray River. His third wave of immigrants was the Carpentarians, or archaic Australoids, whose Asian descendants are relic populations in south India and Sri Lanka. Birdsell postulated that, from an initial population of possibly only a few hundred people, the Carpentarians expanded into a population of 100,000 or more inhabiting northern Australia, in particular around the Gulf of Carpentaria, the arid zone, and the forestlands of southwestern Australia. These people he describes as tall and linear in build, with sparse body hair and no propensity for baldness. Birdsell's scheme had the support of Norman Tindale, who linked it to the changes in stone tools in his excavation at Noola Rockshelter in the Blue Mountains west of Sydney.

Critics claim that the physical variations Birdsell relied on are not fundamental, but may be explained easily by other processes of genetic change. There is less agreement that different Negrito groups in Southeast Asia are the remnants of a single indigenous population predating the Mongoloid hegemony. In the 1970s Sydney anatomists N. W. G. Macintosh and Stan Larnach made detailed craniometric measurements of eastern Australian crania, including some from the Cairns rain forest people. They could not distinguish the rainforest people from other Aborigines, and nor has linguistic evidence for their separate origin ever been found. Subsequent researches by Thorne and others, in a range of biological fields, provided little evidence to support Birdsell's theories, which are in any case irrelevant to present-day issues in recent human evolution.

The various hypotheses about Aboriginal ancestry continue to lack firm data. Apart from Torres Strait languages, no ancestral links with languages overseas have been demonstrated; 50 years of blood genetic research has failed to provide any clue to Aboriginal origins; and there is no convincing evidence for historical relationships between early Asian and Australian stone technology. Only biological attributes, particularly those of bones, provide a little evidence. It is unfortunate that general authors still recount the tri-hybrid racial theory despite the evidence to the contrary.

'THE MARK OF ANCIENT JAVA'

The notion that Australian Aborigines were a 'stationary remnant of primitive humanity'—a living fossil—prevailed in the scientific literature well into the 1930s. In such an intellectual environment it was inevitable that Aborigines should be linked with early hominid finds from Indonesia and China. In the 1930s, abundant fossils of *Homo erectus* were unearthed at Peking Man Cave close to Beijing. Chinese scholars carried out the excavations, but the American anatomist attached to the Beijing Medical College, Franz Weidenreich, formally described the fossil bone and artefacts. Weidenreich saw common features between the skull of Peking Man (*Homo erectus pekinensis*) and modern Chinese, and a similar development from Javanese *Homo erectus* fossils to modern Aborigines and Melanesians. His scheme subsequently has been carried forward by some palaeoanthropologists as part of the 'multi-regional evolution hypothesis'.

Before Alan Thorne excavated the now famous site of Kow Swamp, and before the Willandra Lakes (Mungo) finds, Australia's early human record was based mainly on four fossils. In 1886 a stockman found the first of these, a crushed cranium of a teenage boy, in a dry creek bed near Warwick, southeastern Queensland. The 'Talgai cranium' was never reconstructed from its fragments, nor properly dated. Its supposed primitiveness is unclear to most present-day palaeoanthropologists. The next find, hailed as a breakthrough in the search for the first Australians, was a broken cranium recovered in 1925 by irrigation canal diggers very close to Kow Swamp near the Murray River. The 'Cohuna cranium' was a male whose features suggested to contemporary scholars a 'primitive' countenance, but in the 1960s the anatomists Macintosh and Larnach showed that the bones fit within the range of variation of recent prehistoric Aboriginal crania. In the history of Australian palaeoanthropology it only foreshadows the discovery of other Pleistocene burials from the same lunette dune fringing Kow Swamp. Fifteen years after the discovery of the Cohuna cranium, another well-preserved but incomplete male cranium was found by quarry-men in a terrace of the Maribyrnong River near Keilor, outside Melbourne. The original report attributed the cranium to a small, slightly-built Negrito presumed to be ancestral to the Tasmanians, but it is in fact that of a tall, large-boned man, of terminal Pleistocene age at the earliest. The last of the early discoveries, made in the 1960s, was a male cranium from Tumbridge Station, west of Mossgiel, New South Wales. The 'Mossgiel cranium' is now dated to only about 6000 years old.

By the mid-1960s the impression gained from this small assemblage was that they were ancient and 'primitive' in appearance. N. W. G. Macintosh originally followed Weidenrich's theory about the continuation of *Homo erectus* traits in Australian Aboriginal crania and, in collaboration with Stan Larnach, he compiled a list of eighteen 'archaic' features which he believed stamped the Aborigines with the 'mark of ancient Java'. Only a few years later however, in the light of his further studies, Macintosh changed his mind and it was Alan Thorne who would become the champion of the regional continuity theory.

KOW SWAMP

In 1967, when Thorne was reviewing the Museum of Victoria's collections of human bones, he noticed some heavily-mineralised fragments of skeleton, lying unregistered in a box at the back of a cupboard. Thorne noted that some pieces of skull bone showed features similar to those of the Cohuna cranium. Methodical detective work fastened upon a label inscribed 'Bendigo Police' which led Thorne to the findspot near the small town of Leichville in northern Victoria. Significantly, the bones had been uncovered by canal

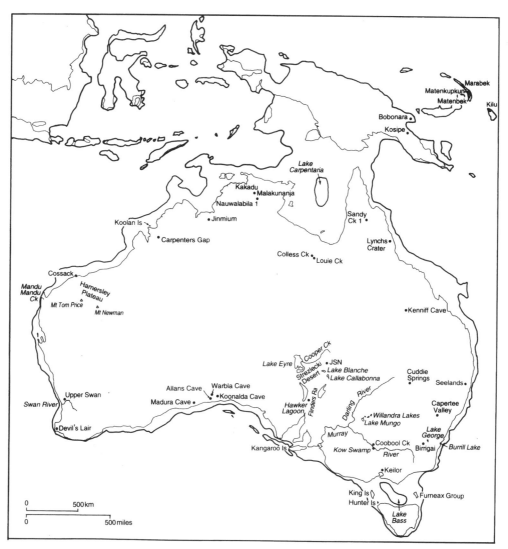

Map 8. *Archaeological sites in Pleistocene Australia.*

diggers near an irrigation reservoir called Kow Swamp, less than ten kilometres from the Cohuna cranium find made in the same dune (or lunette).

From 1968 Thorne excavated at Kow Swamp for several years. The lake had held fresh water from 13,000 years ago, when the level was highest, to 9000 years ago. During this time, and periodically

157

until 2000 years ago, prevailing southwesterly winds formed a lunette dune. In this four-metre-high dune, and in the silty lake bed, Thorne uncovered the fragmentary remains of more than 40 people. With one exception, they had been buried in shallow graves, extended on their left side or with their knees drawn up towards the chin. Most of the burials were fragmentary and thickly encrusted with carbonate from upwelling groundwater. Burials that were not in the carbonate-rich zone were poorly preserved, and of the most ancient crania, barely two were complete—KS 1 and KS 5. The older series of four Kow Swamp burials is dated to between 13,000 and 9500 years ago (terminal Pleistocene to Early Holocene). In 1990 the Museum of Victoria unconditionally returned the entire collection to the Echuca Aboriginal community and presently its fate remains obscure.

THORNE'S 'ROBUST TYPE'

Reconstruction of the most ancient skulls (KS 1, 5, 9 and 14), revealed that the Kow Swamp people were characterised by a large, long, thick-walled cranium, rugged facial bones, a strongly sloping, flat forehead, and low-set rectangular eye sockets. Notably also, the jaw and neck muscle attachment on the cranium were strongly marked. Thorne concluded that the Kow Swamp skull had an 'archaic' countenance, and that it provided the link between *Homo erectus* fossils of Java and modern Australian Aborigines. Thorne also identified as indicators of a 'robust' ancestral people the earlier finds made at Cohuna, Talgai and Mossgiel. Since then he has added the Cossack skull from Western Australia, and human remains from Lakes Tandou, Nitchie and Garnpung in western New South Wales. In a 1989 study of a salvage collection made at the Willandra Lakes, Steve Webb identified three more.

Like Macintosh and Larnach, Thorne compiled a list of features which he argued were a distinctive regional set characterising the Australian robust type and Asian *Homo erectus* fossils, and in particular, a fossil cranium called 'Sangiran 17' from the Solo River in central Java. Although the Solo River terraces have been a rich hunting ground for hominid fossils, their age is uncertain. Conventional age estimates range from 300,000 to over a million years. Recent electron spin resonance dates of 27,000 to 53,000 years for animal teeth found in the fossil beds are unconvincing, but if they are correct they indicate that *Homo erectus* survived in Southeast Asia

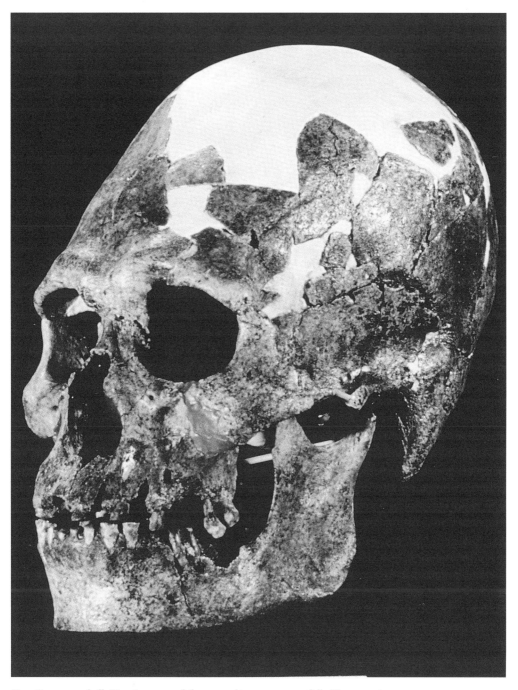

Kow Swamp 5 skull. Despite unusual features, this person was fully Homo sapiens.
(A. G. Thorne)

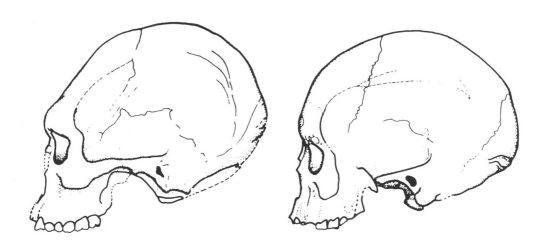

Thorne's robust and gracile types of crania. (Colin Groves)

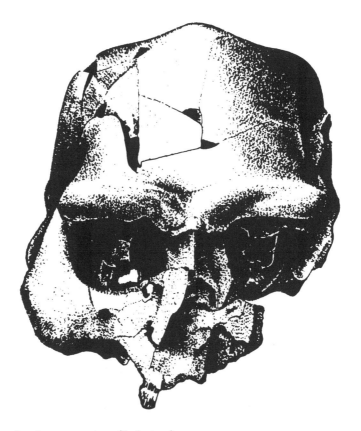

Sangiran 17 cranium. (S. Sartono)

longer than anywhere else in the world and may have co-existed with modern humans for a very long time. This result is so unexpected that further stratigraphic research and chronometric dating are necessary before this claim may be accepted.

LAKE MUNGO LADY

In 1968 the geomorphologist Jim Bowler identified a sandy-carbonate block containing fragmented bone, eroding from Pleistocene-age sands of the Lake Mungo lunette. Bowler first thought that the concretion was of food remains, but after careful excavation it was identified as the remains of a fire and grave pit, containing the burnt and smashed bones of a young woman, no more than nineteen years of age. Not much more than a quarter of the skeleton remained, but Thorne deduced that the body had been cremated on the beach, and afterwards the bones were smashed and scooped into a conical-shaped pit about twenty centimetres deep. The leg bones and even the bones of the feet had been extensively smashed. The fire had not cremated the whole body and the woman's spine had barely been touched by the flames. Thorne meticulously reconstructed the fragments of cranium to find that large areas were missing—of the face, only parts of the teeth and lower jaw remained—which made it difficult to compare the find with other fossil crania.

Near the Mungo 1 burial there were fifteen patches of black deposit roughly circular or oval in shape, which are the remains of shallow hearths and earth ovens up to a metre wide. These features contained finely fragmented charcoal, burnt and broken animal and fish bones, fragments of emu egg, mussel shells, and sometimes stone artefacts. Radiocarbon dates from these cultural features range up to 32,000 years, and Bowler now suspects that the true ages may be even greater. The normally accepted date for the Mungo 1 bones is 24,710±1270 years BP. Though the burial is not as old as often reported in the scientific literature and the popular press, it is the oldest known human cremation and, along with Mungo 3, one of the oldest sets of human remains so far recovered in Australia.

Thorne's reconstruction revealed that the woman was short and light-boned. She was so lightly built that the muscle markings on the bones, including the skull, were barely perceptible. Her skull was oval in shape, thin-walled, her forehead was rounded, and her brow ridges and teeth were small. Thorne reported that, while each non-metric trait was within the range of modern Aborigines, the skull was ultra-gracile, that is, ultra-modern and ultra-feminine in appearance—a surprising result in view of the younger Kow Swamp finds.

In 1992, at a formal ceremony on the Lake Mungo lunette, the Mungo 1 remains were returned to the custody of local Aboriginal groups, where they are securely stored in a temporary keeping-place.

THE 'TWO WAVE' HYPOTHESIS

In 1974 Thorne altered his evolutionary scheme for Australia, arguing that Aborigines were a hybrid of two physically different colonising peoples who arrived during the Pleistocene era—the first wave of colonisers, a robust type from Java directly descended from Javan *Homo erectus*; and the second wave of New Australians, the delicately-built Lake Mungo type, which had spread into Southeast Asia from southern China. This gracile type Thorne believes is ultimately descended from a north Asian *Homo erectus*, exemplified by the Peking Man fossils. In support of this hypothesis, he drew parallels between the features of his single gracile specimen at Lake Mungo and fossil finds in Asia, in particular, the discoveries at Liujiang in China, Wadjak in Java, Niah Cave in Sarawak and Tabon Cave in Palawan (all of which have problems of dating but probably all of Pleistocene age). Although the gracile Mungo 1 type is more than 12,000 years older than the robust Kow Swamp type, Thorne predicted that older robust specimens inevitably would be found and that the Kow Swamp burials were of a relic Murray River corridor population, retaining more of the original population's physical features.

LAKE MUNGO 3

A few years after his momentous discovery of the Lake Mungo cremation, Jim Bowler located a second human burial half a kilometre to the east, recently exposed by heavy rainfall. These remains were called Lake Mungo 3. The position of the shallow grave beneath the dune's upper Mungo Unit suggested an age of 28,000–32,000 years BP. Within this grave the body had been laid out with hands clasped together and knees slightly flexed; ochre daubed generously on the body had stained the sand of the grave-fill a pink colour. Steve Webb, who examined the bones for evidence of disease, identified chronic osteoarthritis in the right elbow, which probably caused considerable suffering during the person's last few years of life.

The cranium is not rugged like those of Kow Swamp, but it is large and thick-walled. Thorne believes that the individual is a male aged about 50 years, and argues that it is a good example of his Early Australian gracile type, but his determination of sex was recently challenged by Peter Brown. Interestingly, Webb has also noted an unusual form of wear on the teeth, which may have been caused by stripping plant fibre for cord and netting—not unexpected for people who fished the lake, but perhaps more likely a women's activity.

King Island skeleton

In the late 1980s the archaeologist Robin Sim and a member of the Tasmanian Aboriginal Centre were excavating an ancient sea cave in a coastal cliff on the southwest of King Island in Bass Strait. Unexpectedly, they uncovered a human burial, which had to be reburied immediately after field recording to fulfil a condition of the excavation permit. The disposition of the bones suggested that the body had been exposed for some time before burial. A radiocarbon date of 14,000 years BP was obtained from small pieces of charcoal from the grave-fill, but this could be older than the burial itself. Measurements taken in the field indicate that the cranium and teeth fit comfortably within the range exhibited by Aborigines of southeast Australia during recent prehistoric times. Thorne's inclusion of this individual in his gracile type rests fundamentally on it being a Pleistocene period, adult male. However, Peter Brown has recently argued that the individual could be female. Thorne and Sim strongly deny this possibility, and the significance of the King Island skeleton remains controversial.

Two races or the two sexes?

Webb's recent examination of a variety of fossil bone from the Willandra Lakes lent some support for Thorne's division of gracile and robust. However, in separate re-analyses of Webb's data, Groves and Pardoe conclude that the robust and the gracile dichotomy in the sample of fossil bone is simply sexual dimorphism—the robust skeletons are males and gracile ones females (or else juveniles) within a regional population that has the normal range of physical variation. Even with modern Australian Aborigines there is considerable sexual dimorphism in the size and ruggedness of bone structure. The broader implications for Thorne's theory of two ethnic groups are obvious, and no doubt this issue will become the focus of intensive research. Thorne may prove to be correct, but Peter Brown has stated his position forcefully: 'there were indeed two human populations present in the Pleistocene of Australia, one of them more robust than the other, but these are called men and women.'

THE ROBUST TYPE FROM SUNDALAND?

The concept that Aborigines descended directly from *Homo erectus* in Southeast Asia is challenged by Groves, and by Marta Lahr at Cambridge University. Nearly all the anatomical traits used to support the regional continuity theory are disputed. One of these is the outward projection of the facial bone below the nasal passage, which was identified by Thorne and an American palaeoanthropologist, Milford Wolpoff, from their reconstruction of the Sangiran 17. A later reconstruction by a Japanese scientist, Hitoshi Baba, eliminates this trait. Another postulated attribute is thick cranial vault wall: Steve Webb has shown that the cranial wall of ancient Australians is only superficially similar to that of East Asian *Homo erectus*. The inner and outer layers of human cranial vault are formed by compact bone; sandwiched between these layers is spongy, cancellous bone called diploë. While all three layers contribute about equally to bone thickness in the Javan *Homo erectus* fossils the diploë is considerably thicker than the tables of compact bone on Willandra Lakes individuals, and the trait may have survived in some parts of Australia into the Holocene era. Webb also observes that the internal structure of the brow ridge area in ancient Australian crania is different from Javan *Homo erectus*, which implies a separate evolution.

Groves argues that nothing in Thorne's common trait list is exclusively Asian or Australian. He proposes that genetic isolation of different groups occurred when people colonised Eurasia and that every human population retains some traits that date from the time the species first spread into Eurasia. Such archaic features, Groves postulates, include forehead flatness, large teeth and brow ridge, smooth contouring of the bone surface from inside the nasal passage to the upper front teeth, a long cranium (which was universal in human populations until only a few thousand years ago), and possibly thick skull bone. That most of these features are retained by Aborigines may be a consequence of more profound genetic isolation in Australia than elsewhere. Following another line entirely, Richard Wright challenges the very notion that the traits of the Kow Swamp people are archaic or 'primitive' at all. He argues that in Australia a large bone and muscle structure was needed to support large teeth because of the abrasive dust and grit particles adhering to much of the food consumed.

Questions about the 'robust' sample

One of Thorne's robust individuals from the Willandra Lakes is a piece of bone called WLH 50. This is an isolated, undated and highly enigmatic surface find of heavily silicified top portion of a skull and fragments of post-cranial bones, encountered on the shore of Lake Garnpung in 1980 by archaeologists Jeannette Hope and Michael Macintyre. The piece of skull was heavily mineralised by opaline silica and salts suggesting great age. Thorne suspects that WLH 50 is more than 50,000 years old, and argues that until it is better understood it should be regarded as fossil hominid rather than modern human. The specimen is not yet formally described, but Thorne reports that its measurements are similar to those of *Homo erectus* skulls from Ngandong, central Java, implying that it is intermediate between these ancient Indonesian fossils and modern Australian Aborigines, and similar to the original colonists of Australia. The most distinguishing features of WLH 50 are its extremely flat frontal bone and the thickness of its vault wall (nearly a maximum of twenty millimetres, whereas modern Aborigines have a range of thirteen to sixteen millimetres). Webb has examined the specimen and suggests that at least some of the distinctive features may be the result of disease that affected the diploë bone tissue through which the blood flows, such as congenital anaemia. Colin Groves dismisses WLH 50 as evidence for regional continuity, and argues that the fossil is more similar to a 120,000-year-old human fossil in the Omo Basin in Africa than it is to *Homo erectus*. Given that it is undated, WLH 50 may figure too prominently in current debates about Aboriginal origins.

Critics also question whether some other of Thorne's robust specimens constitute good evidence. For instance, Howells argues that it is the Lake Nitchie specimen's large size which gives it a robust appearance. Some other human remains are not very ancient. The

Mossgiel skeleton is only about 6000 years old, while a date of 15,000 years BP for the Tandou skull is not from that bone but from a nearby midden. Finally, the Cossack skull was found in a Mid-Holocene coastal dune and therefore may be from a recent prehistoric burial.

The issue of forehead flattening

When the Kow Swamp discoveries were published in the journal *Nature* in 1972, there appeared in the same issue an editorial essay written by Don Brothwell of the Institute of Archaeology, London. This article caused a stir in Canberra because Brothwell questioned Thorne's argument that the sloping forehead demonstrated a link with *Homo erectus*. Brothwell judged that the slope on the reconstructed crania was too extreme for it to be natural, concluding instead that it must have been the result of artificial deformation, observed among certain other populations. Thorne countered that flattening of the back of the cranium, indicative of head binding, was absent on the Kow Swamp individuals. At the same time Larnach and Macintosh reported their observation that the flattening noted on the Cohuna cranium was dissimilar to that of *Homo erectus*. The issue remained controversial until 1981, when Peter Brown described forehead flattening on crania from Coobool Creek.

In 1980 Peter Brown, then a graduate student at the Australian National University, examined the remains of 126 individuals collected in 1950 from an Aboriginal cemetery in a sand dune at Coobool Crossing, on a tributary of the Murray River. Despite seven years of research, Brown was unable to locate the cemetery or establish with certainty the antiquity of the human remains. He postulated, however, that they are probably the same age as the oldest finds made by Thorne at Kow Swamp.

Brown studied 33 complete crania and a further nine which he reconstructed from fragments. The skulls were well preserved, but most of the post-cranial bones had not been collected by the fossickers. He noticed forehead flattening on some of the crania and, with his much larger sample (Thorne had only two specimens), Brown was able to demonstrate artificial cranial deformation—displacement on the back of the cranium as well as the front, and thickening of the spongy bone layer (or diploë) inside the vault wall. Brown showed that the flat frontal bone on crania from Coobool Creek and Kow Swamp, and the single Cohuna specimen, were the result of artificial deformation. Further, he claimed that the deformation resulted not from binding the head, as practised in the nearby Melanesian islands, but from regular pressing of the newborn's head by the mother, probably during the first twelve months after birth, a technique of head moulding observed in the last century in Cape York Peninsula. It should be noted, however, that Thorne's detailed analysis of his finds is awaited, so further evidence may become available on this vexed issue.

HOLOCENE GRACILISATION

Evidence accumulated since the late 1980s suggests a process of physical gracilisation from before 13,000 to less than 6000 years BP, at least in the Murray River corridor where it is evident in the Kow Swamp and Coobool Creek individuals. Brown characterises these Pleistocene Australians as follows. In overall stature both men and women were tall. There was considerable variation in head shape, but all were long-headed and males had distinctively thick cranial bone, although measurement and description are complicated by prehistoric artificial cranial deformation. The face was long and broad, with wide nasal apertures and wide, flattened nasal bones. The lateral trigones at the outside ends of the brow ridges made the skull look wide above the eye sockets, and this is a distinctive feature of the Coobool Creek crania. The cheekbones were rugged, the skull bone between the teeth and opening for the nasal passages projecting forward, and the jaw and teeth large.

Brown has demonstrated that the essential change in physical form in Australia from Pleistocene to Holocene is a shift in stature and body size—people became smaller and tended to be less robust in appearance (there is not always consistent correlation between stature and skeletal robusticity). Brown also found that the difference in the size of the teeth of men and women became less.

There is retention of some Pleistocene features, such as guttering of the nasal opening of the skull, the rounded lower border of the eye sockets, the marked narrowing of the skull behind the temple, and considerable breadth of the lower back part of the skull. The changes in the skull are concentrated on the face, upper palate, lower jaw and teeth, which all became smaller, and there is less outward projection of the face between the lower margin of the nasal aperture and the upper teeth. This gracilisation of the skull is linked to reduction in the musculature of the head and neck. There were other physical changes in Murray River populations unrelated to cranial gracilisation, such as further depression of the upper part of the nose and more prominence of the glabella, two features noted by Brown in his samples of Holocene riverine people.

Around 10,000 years BP, average male stature at Coobool Creek was 174 centimetres, which along the Murray River reduced to 166 centimetres by 2000 years BP. Two examples suggest that Pleistocene Aborigines were taller: Nacurrie 1 dated to about 11,500 years BP, a male with an estimated stature of 177–180 centimetres, and Lake Nitchie Man, who stood about 182 centimetres tall (both over six feet). Meanwhile females decreased from a Pleistocene average of 165 centimetres to the modern average of 157 centimetres. Both male and female stature decrease by five per cent, equivalent to a mass decrease of 17–20 per cent, from 68 to 57 kilograms for males and 56 to 44 kilograms for females. Along with such change in body size, basal metabolic rate also must have decreased significantly.

What is the driving force causing the human inhabitants of Australia to become smaller over thousands of years, and to evolve a more gracile skull? Brown links the trend in Australia to a global adaptation to climatic change during the Early Holocene. Pardoe suggested size decrease was a response to a deteriorating riverine environment, which caused increased population pressure, famine and disease. Webb had demonstrated previously that population pressure in this region indeed was a stress factor. More recently Pardoe commented that it might be a response to the extinction of megafauna and consequent dietary changes, but such a hypothesis lacks archaeological evidence. The commonly held explanation for gracilisation of the skull elsewhere in the world is that selection pressure on the teeth relaxed because of a radical change in diet and food preparation when intensive farming appeared. This hypothesis would seem less important in Australia, and significantly Brown has found that teeth decreased in size proportionally less than the skull.

POPULATING A CONTINENT

There is very little direct evidence for human colonisation of islands in Wallacea. The best so far is an early date of about 30,000 years BP at Leang Burung 2 cave in southwest Sulawesi, but it is possible that first settlement of even the furthest islands was considerably earlier. Perhaps these islands acted as an evolutionary filter by the process of 'founder effect'. This occurs when a small breeding population arrives in new territory, such as an uninhabited island. The genetic variation represented by this group is only a very small sample of the total pool of the parent population and it is susceptible to random drift in gene frequencies. Genetic changes may also result from environmental selection, as Charles Darwin showed, especially on islands. Some of the shorter crossings to the islands of Wallacea are swimmable by humans, and a hominid as intelligent as *Homo erectus* may have been among the few terrestrial mammals capable of making longer sea-crossings. Recent excavations on Flores may have shown that hominid toolmakers had crossed to islands near Sahul hundreds of thousands of years ago, but their physical appearance is unknown. Detailed evidence from the crucial site is awaited before conclusions are possible.

No prehistorian envisages fleets of hunter-gatherers setting off from Southeast Asian islands to colonise Sahul. Instead we postulate that a very small but extended founder population arrived on Sahul's northwestern shore as a trickle of individuals and small groups, possibly as few as 50–100 people in all, over a span of many years. After a few millennia of population expansion within the continent, new arrivals probably contributed little to the population's existing genetic makeup. For example, Pardoe suggests that 50 people arriving 5000 years later might contribute only 0.01 per cent to the total gene pool.

If passage across Wallacea was incremental over many thousands of years and involved small breeding populations, the first Australians may have diverged genetically from the ancestral population in Sundaland. The oldest well-dated human remains in Australia are those from Lake Mungo. No other remains are reliably dated to earlier than 15,000 years BP and it is only after this time that evidence of physical form is much more abundant. Allowing a conservative estimate of 25 years per generation, at least 400 generations lived in Australia from a hypothetical first landing 40,000 years ago until the time of Mungo Lady.

It is reasonable to question some of the interpretations based on the few individuals representing the 625 generations between 40,000 and 15,000 years BP. What can be said is that the Australian countenance in skull form dates from the Late Pleistocene and that the oldest known human remains are probably of people directly ancestral to modern Aborigines. Regional differences in physical form are seen not only in living people but also in the prehistoric skeletal record. One notable example is the lean, long-limbed, desert-adapted morphology of the Willandra Lakes people which is evident from about 24,000 years or more BP.

The factors responsible for most genetic difference are founder effect (when an initially small population colonises a new territory), local environmental adaptation and variation in the rates of gene flows between populations. Relying on limited data, Birdsell estimated that traditionally only one-fifth of the population in an average tribe was responsible for new births and that only about twelve per cent of marriages were inter-tribal (assuming constant reciprocal exchange of women between six neighbouring groups). Birdsell's estimates translate to a low rate of gene flow across tribal boundaries—about 0.06 per cent per generation. However, over the millennia such genetic links between sociolinguistic groups have resulted in genetic gradients across regions, and across the continent as a whole. The rate of gene flow is highest between adjacent populations which possess common cultural and environmental attributes.

Rising seas at the end of the Pleistocene separated Sahul's Australo-Melanesian population into three primary areas—New Guinea, the mainland of Australia and Tasmania. The profound isolation of the Tasmanians for at least the last 8000 years is evident from their distinctive physical features, such as tightly curled head hair and the pentagonal-shape and bulging sides (called 'parietal bossing') of the typical Tasmanian crania. In a landmark study of non-metric cranial traits, Pardoe has shown that despite these obvious physical differences, a close biological kinship is still evident between Tasmanians and the Victorian Aborigines who inhabited the opposite mainland. The Aboriginal inhabitants of the Keppel Islands off the Queensland coast also exhibit genetic differences attributed to isolation. While human crania from the Keppel Islands are unquestionably Aboriginal in character they are also unusually smooth and rounded, which distinguish them from those of the mainland. Similarly, people of the interior deserts, particularly the Western Desert Aborigines, exhibit several unique genetic patterns which R. L. Kirk has argued result from both genetic drift and natural selection in a harsh environment. The frequency of the N gene in the MNSs blood group system reaches its highest world value in this region, and a long period of isolation is implied.

For longer than any other population of *Homo sapiens*, the ancestors of the Aborigines inhabiting Sahul, and later Australia, were genetically cocooned from the rest of humanity in Eurasia. This is reflected in part by the devastation caused by alien viruses and bacteria since 1788. Both living people and the physical remains of the earlier inhabitants over tens of millennia provide vital evidence for inferring Aboriginal origins and regional interrelationships within the continent.

11 Pleistocene settlement

When the first edition of this book was written, only eight sites had proved Pleistocene human occupation, mostly in southeastern Australia. In contrast to that almost blank map, today the map is dotted with sites covering some 40,000 years, with indications of an even older human presence. This chapter surveys these continent-wide discoveries.

There is archaeological evidence that by 25,000 to 30,000 years BP, and even earlier in some regions, people had colonised most habitats in Sahul, such as the well-watered and arid coasts, tropical rain forests, cold steppe and shrub grasslands, and the peripheral desert country. Firm evidence for early colonisation of the desert core is, however, still lacking. Certain regions have received far better archaeological scrutiny than others. There are various reasons for this, often to do with logistics and convenience, and now more commonly because of environmental impact studies. Densely populated parts of Australia have received greatest archaeological coverage, because this is where most development occurs and travel is easy. Other regions, such as Kakadu National Park, have a rich Pleistocene-age heritage, and here reconnaissance is ongoing. There was very little archaeological field-work in arid Australia before the 1980s. In this region archaeologists tend to focus attention on the more prospective areas around permanent water sources. Widespread stripping of sediments in the deserts by wind during the Last Glacial Maximum (LGM) probably destroyed many existing open-air camp sites, and most discoveries are made in caves and rockshelters, possibly not commonly occupied by desert people.

PLEISTOCENE COASTS AND ISLANDS

At the average sea level of about 60 metres below the present level before the LGM there existed islands a short distance off the northeast New Guinea coast, one of which has since been reduced to its uplands, now the d'Entrecasteaux Islands. Further north lay the large oceanic islands of New Britain and New Ireland, slightly larger than they are at present. A cluster of small islands lay off the northwest Sahul coast, where only Browse Island, Scott Reef and Rowley Shoals remain to mark their former existence. A few small rocky islands were dotted along Sahul's southwest coast, and emanating from a peninsula (present-day Kangaroo Island) south of modern Adelaide there was a string of narrow islands, the first of which was more than 300 kilometres long. Small continental islands were scattered along Sahul's eastern coast and, off the southern extremity of the Tasmanian Peninsula, in the frigid Southern Ocean stood a few windswept rocky peaks.

There has been no attempt to plot the disposition of Sahul's continental islands during the LGM, but the margin of the continental shelf descends more steeply between 100 and 200 metres below the present level, so there were far fewer islands and islets than before or after this epoch, while the present Great Barrier Reef was only a narrow coral fringe on the shelf's edge. Tropical waters around northern Sahul may have been as much as 4°C cooler than at present, with decreased monsoon rainfall and cyclonic activity. In general, southern waters were 2°C cooler, although a warm ocean current probably flowed along the coast of New South Wales, which was 40 to 50 kilometres east of its present position. This warm current implies wetter conditions for the forested southeast coast. Bass Strait did not then exist.

Sahul's northern coast and nearby deep-sea islands

One of the oldest dated sites in coastal northern Australia is Koolan Island Shelter 2, excavated by Sue O'Connor on a rocky island of the

Buccaneer Archipelago, within easy reach of the west Kimberley mainland. The bottom cultural layer of this site may be older than 29,000 years BP. Comparable evidence for early human presence also has been found further south, in a small limestone shelter at Mandu Mandu Creek, North-West Cape. At this unimposing site the archaeologist Kate Morse uncovered the remains of Australia's earliest seafood meals of shellfish, fish and crab, which date to about 32,000 years BP.

Recent excavations at Matenkupkun and Matenbek cave on New Ireland have corroborated a prediction in 1973 by W. W. Howells that sea voyaging across the Bismarck Sea to New Guinea's nearer oceanic islands commenced tens of thousands of years ago. These two spacious caverns are in a fifteen-metre-high limestone terrace just behind the present-day shoreline. Matenkupkun for the most part is well lit and dry, providing a comfortable living area. During World War II Japanese soldiers dug away the top part of the cultural deposit while fortifying the cave, but they left untouched a dense midden layer nearly 1.5 metres deep, which was probed in the 1980s by archaeologist Chris Gosden. The basal date for this midden is 21,000–32,000 years BP. Matenbek cave, which has a midden of similar composition, has a basal date of 18,000–20,000 years BP. Small fragments of glassy obsidian occur in the lower levels and derive from lava formations 350 kilometres to the west. While the precious stone may have travelled overland for most of the distance, it would have required crossing at least the 30-kilometre-wide Saint George Channel. Although numbers of obsidian flakes in the early levels of the sites are small, they may indicate deliberate voyages between islands; if so, there must have been the capacity for deliberate voyaging to Sahul's northeast coast.

New Guinea highlands

Before widespread forest clearance in the New Guinea highlands, the region abounded with birds, giant rats, small marsupials and arboreal animals such as tree-kangaroos, cuscus, ringtail possum and fruit bats. The highlands, environmentally isolated by the expanse of seasonally dry territory to the south, had its own indigenous species of forest-dwelling marsupial and monotreme megafauna which co-existed with humans until possibly as recently as 14,000 years BP. The extinct fauna that once inhabited the mid-montane forests included at least two species of *Protemnodon*, a diprotodontid, a small *Zygomaturus,* and an oversized tree-kangaroo weighing up to twenty kilograms. The upper montane forests were probably poorer in potential food resources, where several species of pandanus would have provided a staple of edible kernels in a region otherwise poor in starch foods.

Human presence in the highlands during the Pleistocene was demonstrated in the 1970s by archaeologists Peter White and Mary-Jane Mountain. Several sites have now been excavated, but they provide only limited information about human subsistence and there is no coherent Pleistocene prehistory for the region. Although New Guinea's wet tropical lowlands also must have been inhabited at the time, there is only a tentative date of 40,000 years for waisted axe-like tools eroding from a volcanic ash layer near Bobongara on the Huon Peninsula. The key highlands sites are Kosipe, at almost 2000 metres above sea level, and Nombe rockshelter at 1720 metres. People periodically visited Kosipe between 26,000 and 15,000 years BP, possibly to collect kernels from pandanus growing around a nearby swamp. Pollen cores from the swamp show increased deposition of charcoal particles around 30,000 years BP, which has been interpreted as evidence of human firing of the landscape, possibly to increase the yield of pandanus kernels.

AUSTRALIAN FORESTLANDS AND WOODLANDS

There has been considerable archaeological fieldwork in regions that were forested during the Late Pleistocene. One of the first sites identified was a large rockshelter at Burrill Lake on the southern New South Wales coast, which was first occupied during the LGM around 20,000 years BP. Two other sites inland from the south coast have been excavated more recently by P. G. Boot, Bob's Cave and the open-air riverbank site of Bulee Brook 2, both of which have terminal Pleistocene ages. Similar ages have been determined at two further sites near Sydney. One is Shaw's Creek on the western edge of the city near the Blue Mountains escarpment; the other is Loggers shelter, on Mangrove Creek, north of Sydney, which is now submerged in a reservoir. Human occupation in these sites appears to have been ephemeral, suggesting a low population density in the region at the end of the Pleistocene. In contrast, there is a rich concentration of stone artefacts in a sand dune at Moffats Swamp near Newcastle, which is also of terminal Pleistocene age. Much of the eastern coast is fringed by Pleistocene sand bodies which are threatened by sand-mining for heavy minerals. Many of these vast accumulations of sand are time capsules containing all the stone artefacts discarded or lost on them since people first traversed this part of the continent. Such sandy, wooded areas are often adjacent both to the sea and fresh water, so their potential for archaeology is great. Even when mining enterprises replant the mined areas, they can replace neither the evidence of human occupation nor the stratigraphy, a reality overlooked by industry.

Proceeding northwards along the coast, only a single early site has been found near the outskirts of Brisbane. Many of the more ancient sites in the woodlands of north Queensland are better known for their rock art than for the potential of their cultural deposits. The list of Pleistocene sites in this region is growing rapidly as a result of intensive archaeological surveys since the 1980s. The first discovery was Early Man Rockshelter, which was occupied before the LGM. The most recent is Ngarrabullgan Cave (Mount Mulligan) which was probably first visited by people before 37,000 years BP.

The southwest

The temperate, forested southwest of the continent is increasingly prospective. Since 1973 the most outstanding Pleistocene site is Devil's Lair, a limestone cave five kilometres from the sea in the Naturaliste Region south of Perth. At this site Charles Dortch and Duncan Merrilees of the Western Australian Museum directed eight excavation seasons over as many years. Their work was so meticulous that 95 per cent of the cave's deposit remains intact. While Western Australia has produced exciting discoveries of Pleistocene occupation within recent years, when Devil's Lair was first dated it was unique evidence for early settlement in the southwest.

Human occupation of Devil's Lair began around 31,000 years BP, probably when the entrance had widened sufficiently to admit people. The abundant animal bone remains preserved by the cave's alkaline deposit provide the region's key environmental record. These reveal a much richer mammal fauna in Pleistocene times than that of today, including animals of both wet and dry habitat. During this period forests, woodlands and heaths surrounded the cave. A proportion of the animal bones was left by scavengers such as the Tasmanian devil which denned in the cave (hence the name Devil's Lair). Between

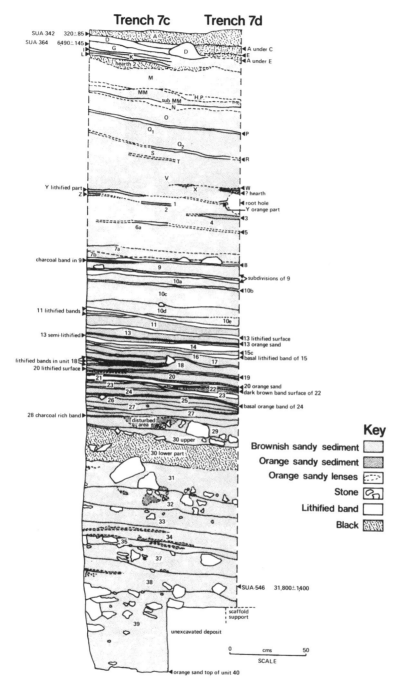

Stratigraphic section of a trench at Devil's Lair with dates through 30,000 years, proof that the southwest was occupied by that time. Radiocarbon dates were produced by the University of Sydney laboratory; SUA signifies the sample reference number followed by the age estimate. (C. E. Dortch)

12,000 and 6500 years ago the entrance was obstructed by rubble and a sheet of flowstone up to 30 centimetres thick sealed in the entire six-metre-deep deposit (of which the upper 4.5 metres is archaeological). The cavern finally reopened 300 years ago, when collapse of the roof at the back of the cave created a new entrance. The deposit's distinctive lenses of sandy sediment and lightly cemented layers, separated by layers of flowstone, constitute a superb sequence of over 100 layers and sub-layers, which are dated by a series of 30 radiocarbon determinations—more than for any other archaeological site in Australia.

Excavations in the caves of the Naturaliste Region during the 1990s have added to the previously isolated record from Devil's Lair. At Tunnel Cave, Joe Dortch excavated a sequence of hearths and occupation layers dating from 22,000 to 8000 years BP, which parallel those at Devil's Lair. Most of the artefacts in the excavation are from a series of hearths dated to 17,000–16,000 years BP, and a cluster around 12,750 years BP. The latter occupation corresponds to a thin but archaeologically rich occupation floor lying between two sheets of flowstone (calcium carbonate) at Devil's Lair.

As with open-air sites of Pleistocene age in the southwest, the stone artefacts at Tunnel Cave and Devil's Lair are mostly small pieces of quartz and pieces of fossiliferous chert obtained from outcrops on parts of the coastal plain that were inundated by rise in sea level ending in the Mid-Holocene. Although the excavations at Devil's Lair provided some of Australia's earliest bone implements and ornaments, the artefact density is surprisingly low, and human visits, made over a period of twenty millennia, were probably infrequent and of short duration. Tunnel Cave provides a similar picture of human visitation. Analyses of abundant animal remains in both caves suggest that the visitors practised a land-based economy in which the larger marsupials were preferred prey. At both sites, emu eggshell fragments are associated with artefacts and hearths, indicating that people sometimes visited these sites at a time of year when they could collect emu eggs, probably during late winter or spring.

Several Pleistocene open sites have been located in the southwest, ranging in age from 29,000 years BP at Helena Valley near Perth to 18,000 years BP at Quininup Brook in the far southwest and 10,000 years BP at Mimim Cove on the Swan River. While these ages are probably broadly correct, those for excavations at some other sites such as Upper Swan, Arumvale and Ellenbrook are questionable.

COLD STEPPE AND MOORLANDS OF SOUTHEAST SAHUL

A zone of cold steppe grassland, with shrubs and stands of eucalypts in protected locations, and tundra-like herbfields, stretched from the tablelands of northern New South Wales, across most of the southeastern highlands, west as far as Adelaide, and south through most of Victoria and across the Bassian Plain to the southern tip of Tasmania. Similar steppe is found today in frost hollows in the Central Plateau of Tasmania and in the Monaro region around Cooma. Cold and dry windy conditions prevailed. Conditions were particularly harsh in the Australian Alps and Tasmanian highlands, where the highest mountain peaks were glaciated and periglacial conditions extended down to at least 1000 metres above sea level. Tasmania had several glaciers with ice mantle over about 1000 square kilometres. The pollen record reveals that the alpine zone was a cold desert with sparse herb-fields—an exceedingly harsh environment with limited food resources for humans. There is no archaeological evidence to indicate that people visited the alpine regions of southeastern Sahul during the Pleistocene, but they may have done so when weather conditions allowed. The lack of 'archaeological visibility' of people may have much to do with low-level seasonal visitation or occupation of regions with unstable and rapidly eroding land surfaces.

Because the structure of the vegetation has changed so much, there are problems in reconstructing the plant foods of the cold steppe lands and herb-fields. The pollen records for the steppe indicate abundant perennial herbs, some of which may have provided bulb and tuber staples; sheltered groves of trees and bushes would have contributed fruits. The relative poverty of artefacts in Pleistocene levels of sites suggests that the general region was sparsely settled, especially at higher altitude, and little visited. Although the New England region has been reconnoitred intensively, there is no archaeological evidence of early settlement. In the Blue Mountains, a heavily dissected plateau west of Sydney, there are only a few sites with Pleistocene artefacts: Lyrebird Dell rockshelter and Walls Cave near Blackheath, and low-altitude rockshelters in the Capertee Valley. The scarcity of stone artefacts suggests occasional, brief visits only. That the cold steppe was sparsely populated during the LGM is also suggested by Birrigai rockshelter in the Australian Capital Territory, which is at an altitude of 730 metres in the northern foothills of the Australian Alps, and by cave sites on the Bassian Plain.

People visited Cave Bay Cave on Hunter Island about 2000 years before the LGM, when the island was a low ridge on the western side of the Bassian Plain, probably within the region of cold steppe. Testimony to repeated, sporadic visits are thin deposits of ash containing pieces of smashed quartz and fragmented marsupial bones, probably the remains of meals. The sea was then about 40 kilometres distant, but people could have exploited the coastal fringe as well as the steppe hinterland. Evidently, people ceased visiting the cave during the LGM, when the climate became colder and the coastline migrated further away.

A sea cave on King Island, recently excavated by Robin Sim, provided similar evidence of ephemeral Pleistocene human visitation. Sim also excavated a cave and rockshelter on islands of the Furneaux Group, formerly wooded terrain on the eastern edge of the Bassian steppe, where she unearthed fossil and scallop shell artefacts and quartz crystal implements, the bones of grey kangaroo and burnt eggshells of an extinct emu. Low-level intensity of occupation was relatively consistent throughout.

There are perhaps 40 sites in Tasmania known to contain Late Pleistocene cultural deposit; eight have been excavated and provide basal occupation dates ranging between about 21,000 and 35,000 years BP. If the sea-level curve based on oxygen isotope is broadly correct, then Tasmania was a peninsula of Sahul from before 50,000 years until 12,000 years ago, and the earliest human occupation in Tasmanian sites may signify the arrival of people in southeastern Sahul.

SOUTHWEST TASMANIA

Southwest Tasmania is like Kakadu and the Willandra Lakes in that it is a focus for intensive archaeological field investigation of Pleistocene-age habitation sites, all these regions qualifying for the World Heritage List. The rugged terrain, and the cold, damp forests of southern beech and Huon pine with their closely spaced under-storey of tree ferns, pose considerable difficulties for archaeological survey. However, the rewards are great since the rock formations of quartzite and limestone have innumerable caves and rockshelters hidden within dense rain forest. Cultural deposits often have been sealed by 'moonmilk', a calcium carbonate flowstone thought to have formed during the last millennia of the Pleistocene. During the Last

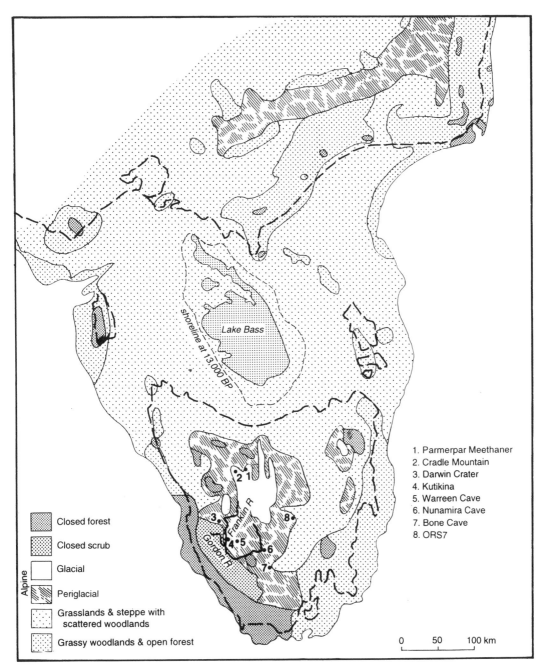

Map 9. Tasmanian Peninsula during the Late Glacial Maximum. (Reconstruction by Paul Augustinus, Geoff Hope and Beth Gott. The glacial and periglacial limits are based on Davies, 1987, and Kiernan, 1990, with revision by P. Augustinus)

Lake Bass

shoreline at 13,000 BP

Franklin R
Gordon R

1. Parmerpar Meethaner
2. Cradle Mountain
3. Darwin Crater
4. Kutikina
5. Warreen Cave
6. Nunamira Cave
7. Bone Cave
8. ORS7

Closed forest

Closed scrub

Glacial

Periglacial

Grasslands & steppe with scattered woodlands

Grassy woodlands & open forest

Alpine

0   50   100 km

Glacial Maximum the southwest region was predominantly grassy moorland, with shrubs and stunted trees in protected gullies and gorges. Human occupation of the caverns and rockshelters appears to have ended at about 13,500 years BP, when dense forest and scrub colonised much of the region, but possibly people continued to penetrate the region and their camp sites are still to be discovered.

THE DISCOVERY OF KUTIKINA CAVE

In 1976 a handful of stone artefacts gathered from the floor of Beginners Luck cave on the margin of the southwest forest provided evidence for human presence in this region during the last glaciation. Part of the floor consisting of cemented limestone fragments was excavated with great difficulty and, while only a handful of stone artefacts was recovered, the basal date of the cultural horizon was Pleistocene. The Sydney University Speleological Society had discovered dozens of other caves in limestone cliffs along the Gordon and Franklin Rivers in 1977. Kevin Kiernan, a geomorphologist at the University of Tasmania, noted stone artefacts and bone fragments eroding from the floor of a cave later named Kutikina. Kiernan returned to Kutikina with archaeologists Don Ranson and Rhys Jones, who excavated about half a cubic metre of sediment—very little, but enormously productive in terms of artefacts and animal food remains. The cultural deposit spanned the period from 20,000 to about 15,000 years BP, which was surprising for this was a period of great climatic stress. This southeastern tip of Sahul was the most southern part of the inhabited world during the Pleistocene, and only 1000 kilometres north of the sea ice surrounding the Antarctic continent.

During the LGM, Kutikina was situated about 100 kilometres from the west coast. Probably there was a mixture of vegetation communities near the site: scrubland on ridges, patches of grassland in the valleys and relic rain forest in more sheltered locations. At higher altitude was alpine moorland and at the head of the Franklin was a twelve-kilometre-long glacier feeding meltwater into the river.

Kutikina cave today is hidden by dense rain forest, although only a few metres from the river. It comprises a large entrance chamber eighteen metres long, and 200 metres of passages with numerous openings to the surface above. The floor of the chamber is sealed by calcium carbonate flowstone covered with stalagmites. Below this stone cap is more than a metre of sediments. The bottom deposit comprises alluvial

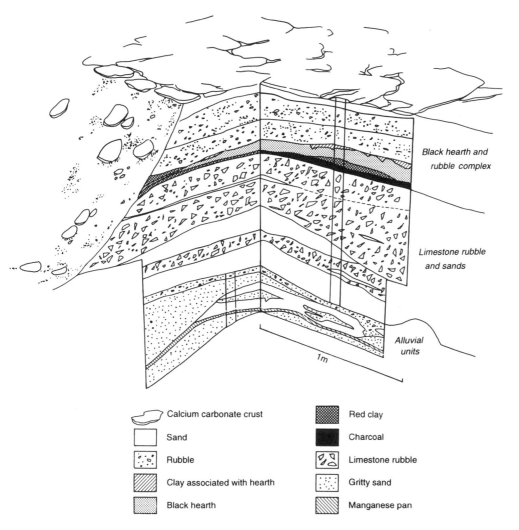

Black hearth and
rubble complex

Limestone rubble
and sands

Alluvial
units

1m

Calcium carbonate crust		Red clay	
Sand		Charcoal	
Rubble		Limestone rubble	
Clay associated with hearth		Gritty sand	
Black hearth		Manganese pan	

Stratigraphy of Kutikina cave established occupation between about 20,000 and 15,000 years BP. Thick calcium carbonate seals the deposit, indicating the wet, humid conditions which accompanied the forest's return. (Adapted from Kiernan et al. 1983)

gravels covered with thick lenses of fine sand. Overlying this are lime-stone fragments ice-shattered from the wall and roof of the cave. The upper deposit contains the cultural horizon, comprising clay lenses baked red by ancient campfires. Like Devil's Lair the deposit was a sealed time capsule, but one much richer in artefacts and food remains. In less than a cubic metre of deposit there were about 37,000 stone artefacts (largely from glacial outwash pebbles found in the river), some sharp-tipped bone points, and 35 kilograms of bone fragments, nearly all from Bennett's wallaby. Identifiable tools include notched and roughly denticulated flakes, small core fragments with abruptly retouched edges and, in upper levels, 160 small thumbnail-like scrapers and a few flakes of glassy impactite from a meteorite crater 26 kilometres northwest of Kutikina.

Darwin Crater

Artefacts of impactite (Darwin glass) have been found in small numbers in Pleistocene cave deposits over much of the southwest. These are sourced to a meteorite strike at the Andrew River, a tributary of the Franklin, which occurred some 700,000 years ago. The impact site is called the Darwin Crater, which was originally a kilometre wide and 200 metres deep but is now filled with clay and peat, and camouflaged by dense tea-tree scrub. Siliceous bedrock was melted by the impact and ejected as a shower of molten silica drops, mostly within a two-kilometre-wide splash zone on the western side of the crater. Around the rim of the crater, a team led by Rhys Jones and Jim Allen found pieces of impactite up to four centimetres long. Although only small tools could be made from the glass, it provided finer cutting edges than any type of stone, and during the Pleistocene was transported distances of up to 100 kilometres within the southwest. Kutikina and the 'Darwin glass' played a crucial role in the battle to prevent the Franklin valley from being flooded.

Fight for the Franklin

In the early 1980s the Tasmanian Hydro-Electric Commission planned to dam the Gordon River below its confluence with the Franklin River, which would have flooded the valley and its limestone caves. When the development was opposed by environmental groups, a heated public debate ensued. A newly elected federal Labor government intervened on the side of the environmentalists and, because the region was a World Heritage area, used its Foreign Affairs powers to prevent the dam. During those highly charged times there were further archaeological expeditions to the region, and Pleistocene cave sites were located in rapid succession along the lower Franklin and Gordon Rivers and

Nunamira Cave, southwest Tasmania, during excavation in 1988. This limestone region today lies concealed within the temperate rainforest, but when occupied the country was scrubby moorland. (Richard Cosgrove)

their tributaries. The Southern Forests Archaeological Project, based at La Trobe University, has extended reconnaissance to a number of other river valleys in southwest Tasmania where there are rugged gorges containing innumerable caves and rockshelters.

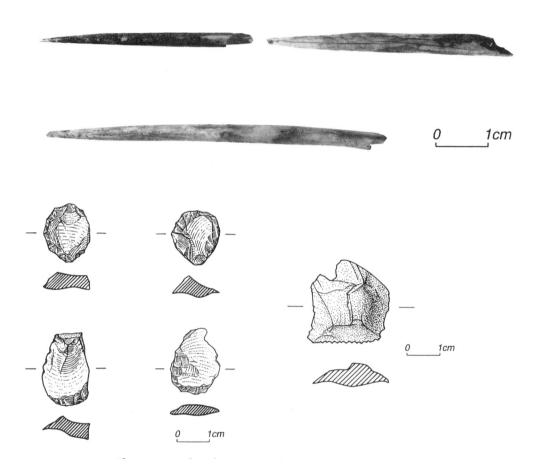

Pleistocene artefacts from Bone and Nunamira Caves: bone points (top), thumbnail scrapers (left), dentated flake tool (right). (Richard Cosgrove; drawn by Wei Ming)

The Southern Forests Project

Eleven kilometres east of Kutikina is Warreen Cave in the Maxwell River valley, a site first test-excavated by Don Ranson in 1986 and later by Jim Allen during the La Trobe University project. This is the oldest known site in the southwest, and provided a sequence of dates from about 35,000 to 16,000 years BP. Allen unearthed more than 20,000 stone artefacts, predominantly small quartz flakes, and about

140,000 fragments of animal bone, mostly of Bennett's wallaby, but also wombat, Tasmanian devil and in the older layers, eastern quoll.

Two other important sites are Bone Cave, at the headwaters of the Weld River, a small cavern sheltered from the prevailing wind, which was excavated by Allen; and Nunamira Cave on the Florentine River, excavated by Richard Cosgrove. Both sites were visited by people from about 30,000 years BP. Small test excavations uncovered bone points, thumbnail scrapers, and large amounts of bone fragments of Bennett's wallaby. Many of the stone artefacts were struck from quartzite river pebbles collected near the caves, but there were also other stone types which had come from sources further away, including impactite from Darwin Crater.

Subsistence in southwest Tasmania

The presence of notched scrapers implies smoothing spear shafts or sharpening wooden spear tips. The ubiquitous thumbnail scrapers, commonly made of quartz, chert or fine-grained silcrete, are particularly intriguing. Richard Fullagar has studied a number from Kutikina for traces of use-wear, and deduces that they had been hafted and used for woodworking or skinning. Tom Loy and Rhys Jones, however, identify their retouch as backing to facilitate a secure finger grip, and conclude that they were used as general-purpose cutting tools. Their small size and standardised design suggests to us that they were functionally specialised and may have served as blades on a multi-component tool or weapon. If so, then this is significant, since the Tasmanians did not possess multi-component tools by the time the British colonised the island. Ian McNiven has speculated that their increased use was a technological solution to the need for higher mobility when environmental conditions became more difficult during the LGM.

Spatulate and sharp-ended bone points made from wallaby were found at several caves, and archaeologists Cathy Webb and Jim Allen have suggested that they may have served as spear points, toggles for cloaks, or awls for making furskin cloaks or other items of clothing. Essentially, the functions of these ancient bone points are not known with any certainty.

Only part of the inhabitants' diet is evident from the cave deposits, because plant remains are not preserved. Even if the range of plant foods was limited, potential staples such as tubers and bulbs may have been plentiful, especially in the summer months. The large quantities of bone fragments in all excavations are predominantly from Bennett's wallaby, a sedentary grazer of grasslands and herb-fields which congregates in forest margins. Jones hypothesises that the visitors to the caves were specialised hunters who did not have a large plant component in their diet. Cosgrove and other archaeologists noted that the wallaby bones had been smashed to expose the marrow, which contains fatty acids that help convert meat protein to energy. When wallaby flesh is consumed regularly, it increases blood flow and thus helps to keep the body warm in a cold environment. However, Cosgrove cautions that, although the cave deposits have dense concentrations of cultural material, this may represent visits separated by hundreds or even thousands of years, rather than from regular seasonal camping.

The only evidence indicating the time of year people visited the caves is the presence of emu eggshell fragments, suggesting occupation in late winter or early spring. In the western side of the southwest forest, locally obtained milky quartz was used almost exclusively by the people visiting caves, while Darwin glass has a restricted distribution. In the eastern side, most of the flaked stone was of locally gathered quartzite pebbles and chert. Generally, in the southwest small amounts of stone were carried from more distant sources. This evidence is not sufficient to reconstruct the regular movement of people on the landscape, whether seasonal or otherwise. It is certainly possible that the visitors to the caves travelled long distances across the open terrain of the Bassian region and that they regularly spent part of the year on the coast, collecting shellfish from rocky platforms, harvesting sea birds, chicks and eggs from rookeries, and perhaps hunting big game like elephant seals and southern fur seals. Possibly they also hunted ponderous sea lions, which currently breed on Macquarie Island near Antarctica but which also bred in Australian waters until recent millennia. However, Porch and Allen question whether the west coast was exploited during the Late Pleistocene.

BEYOND SOUTHWEST TASMANIA

Cosgrove has excavated two sites in regions adjoining the southwest which provide a broader picture of the human occupation of Pleistocene Tasmania. The first is Parmerpar Meethaner rockshelter, in the Forth River valley, just below Cradle Mountain in central north

Tasmania. The shelter has a sequence of occupation from about 34,000 to the last few hundred years BP, and along with Warreen Cave it is currently the oldest archaeological site in Tasmania. During the LGM the vegetation around Parmerpar Meethaner was similar to that of the southwest valleys—sub-alpine moorland with stunted shrubs and trees along watercourses. Glaciers existed on Cradle Mountain Plateau only three kilometres distant. In the assemblage of Pleistocene animal remains, Cosgrove identified possums, potoroo, pademelon and wombat, and in the artefacts, small end and thumbnail scrapers of quartz, and flakes of chert that probably came from sources in northwestern Tasmania.

Cosgrove's second site is a sandstone rockshelter called ORS 7, located on the Shannon River near the eastern edge of the Central Plateau. During the Late Pleistocene this area was one of mixed grassland and woodland. Human occupation at ORS 7 began at about 30,000 years BP and continued into the Holocene. The bone remains indicate a wider range of food animals, though there is less evidence of hunting than at sites in the moorlands of the southwest. Flaked stone in the site is all from local sources. The lack of evidence for long-distance transport of Darwin glass, and a notable absence of thumbnail scrapers, reflects differences between east and west which are yet to be understood. Cosgrove suggests that the southeast was cold and drought-prone, and food resources scattered and less predictable than in the southwest.

In less than twenty years, Tasmanian research has produced vital evidence for human exploitation of resources under glacial conditions. The chronology exactly parallels that of western Europe during the Upper Palaeolithic, and Rhys Jones has sketched some of the parallels. The Tasmanian discoveries certainly possess international significance for later Pleistocene human colonisation.

12 Conquest of the deserts

Most of the arid zone, almost two-thirds of the continent, has been desert for many millions of years. However, before the Last Glacial Maximum (LGM) part of its periphery was better watered because of cooler temperatures and lower evaporation rates, and regions such as the Willandra Lakes and the Victorian Mallee alternated between arid and semi-arid. With the onset of the LGM, monsoons in northern Australia weakened, and precipitation in the arid zone decreased overall by 30–50 per cent. Much of the continent became hyper-arid, with more frequent and probably longer-lasting droughts. Because it was windier, the dunefields again became mobile.

In 1976 the geomorphologist Jim Bowler proposed a model of arid-zone colonisation. Bowler envisaged human settlement before 30,000 years BP, followed by the forced abandonment of the least habitable deserts during the LGM and recolonisation of these regions at the end of the Pleistocene when climatic conditions had improved. Bowler's model has been tested by archaeological fieldwork in different parts of the arid zone since the 1980s, and still stands today, embodied in the various schemes of arid zone prehistory.

Some archaeologists specialising on the arid zone, such as Mike Smith, who excavated in central Australia, and Scott Cane, whose field areas have been the Nullarbor Plain and Western Desert, argue for settlement of even the most forbidding deserts in central and Western Australia before the LGM. However, Peter Veth, who surveyed a region of dry, salt-crusted lakes in the north of the Western Desert, argues instead that the sandy deserts remained empty of people until the Mid-Holocene, when the necessary technology and survival strategies emerged to cope with such marginal habitats. Most archaeologists who have excavated sites in the arid zone believe that the onset of hyperaridity during the LGM caused a general contraction of human settlement, and that perhaps only rare exploratory visits were made to the most arid deserts. General settlement models tend to be supported by evidence from particular desert regions.

Ron Lampert and Phil Hughes, who surveyed desert regions around Lake Eyre, conclude that this part of the arid zone was first inhabited before 22,000 years BP. They postulate that during the LGM settlement contracted to better-watered country in the south, such as the North Flinders Ranges on the margin of the arid zone. Here they found stone artefacts scattered over 50 hectares of deeply eroded lunette at a small ephemeral lake called Hawker Lagoon. In the dune they identified three artefact-rich strata, the lowest dating to 15,000 years BP. Lampert and Hughes hypothesise that after the LGM people made occasional forays deep into the desert from refuges such as this, and that progressive recolonisation of the desert began in the Early Holocene when food and water again became relatively plentiful.

Peter Hiscock has discerned similar contraction of settlement during the LGM more than 1000 kilometres to the north, at Lawn Hill Station, northwest Queensland. Before 18,000 years BP the region was semi-arid, as it is today, and the distribution of water sources facilitated long-distance travel. Hiscock's excavations in caves within the gorges of Colless and Lewie Creeks have shown that the inhabitants exploited the resources of all the major landforms in the region—plain, plateau top and plateau gorges. Hiscock argues that during the LGM human settlement contracted to gorges which had more permanent water and that only occasional excursions were made across the plateau for hunting and for collecting toolmaking stone. Hiscock envisages that, during this period, small populations were tethered to oases such as those at Lawn Hill, throughout the arid zone. Mike Smith follows a similar line of argument in his model of 'desert refuges'. Smith postulates progressive depopulation of the lowlands of the arid zone during the LGM and contraction to highland 'refuges' such as the Pilbara uplands and the MacDonnell Ranges.

While the arguments for abandonment of much of the arid zone during the LGM are persuasive, Scott Cane has played devil's advocate, proposing that the increased aridity may not have proved so catastrophic for desert people, even in the northern part of the arid zone which relies on monsoonal rains. In some of the most marginal deserts, such as the Great Sandy Desert, rockholes would still have held precious water, and in terms of human needs perhaps not significantly less than they do today, especially if evaporation was less. Cane speculates that the soaks of the Great Victoria Desert may still have been reliable, and notes evidence of human presence at sites on the southern margin of the Nullarbor Plain even when environmental conditions were at their worst. What may appear to urbanised archaeologists as seemingly impossible living environments, Cane argues, 'cease to become so if one knows the moods of the country'. Cane may be correct to challenge this conventional interpretation of the archaeological evidence. Often the sequences of radiocarbon dates from sites in the arid zone are insufficient to identify periods of abandonment with any certainty. Similarly, relative densities of stone artefacts in different levels of a site, often used as the measure of occupation intensity, may reflect nothing more than visits centuries or even millennia apart, especially when archaeological deposits are thin. Therefore, in many instances it is even difficult to show that settlement of a region was continuous rather than punctuated.

There is now no question that people inhabited the margins of the arid zone well before the LGM and during this period of greatest aridity. However, despite claims to the contrary, there still is no firm evidence of human settlement of Australia's desert core before the Early Holocene. Because we have faith in human curiosity and endurance, and because some years must have witnessed more congenial conditions, we suspect that in time such evidence will be recovered. We turn to some of the regional prehistories of desert periphery and core which assist broader reconstructions of Pleistocene arid zone prehistory.

DISCOVERIES AT THE WILLANDRA LAKES

In the late 1960s the geomorphologist Jim Bowler was reconstructing the evolution and hydrology of the Willandra Lakes, about 100 kilometres northeast of Mildura, on the Murray River (Map 10). These former lakes are located in the semi-arid zone, on the eastern

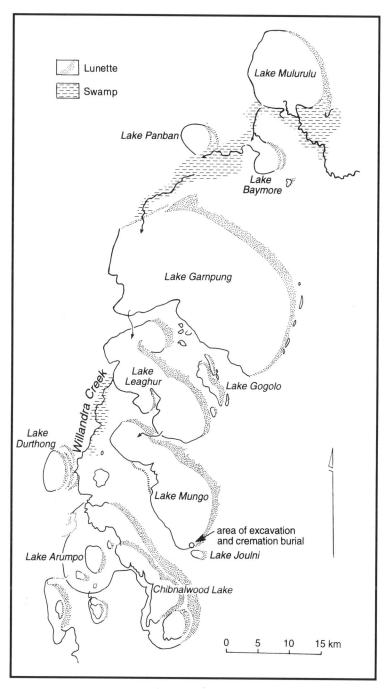

Map 10. The Willandra Lakes system, formed as branch of the Lachlan River, at a lake full stage around 30,000 years ago. (After P. Clark)

fringe of the continental dunefield. Rainfall is low and unreliable, evaporation extremely high. The landscape is one of bluebush and bladder saltbush on the hard dry lake beds, and mallee woodland on the surrounding sand plains. The dry lakes form a chain of thirteen basins, ranging in size from six to 400 square kilometres. From north to south, five major basins make up the present system—Lakes Mulurulu, Garnpung, Leaghur, Mungo, and Arumpo. During the LGM they lay about 150 kilometres within the arid zone's shifting boundary.

In the early 1960s these lake beds had not even been identified as such, and it was Bowler who named them. Bowler inferred that various exposures of artefacts, shells and hearths eroding from the fringing lunettes were very ancient. He urged archaeologists, including Mulvaney, to visit the region, particularly Lake Mungo, where he had found a hearth containing bones later identified as a cremation burial (see Chapter 2). Since then, the Willandra Lakes have been the focus of more extensive interdisciplinary research than any other part of Australia (with the possible exception of Kakadu National Park), and the region's expanding Pleistocene horizons have served to place Australia firmly on the stage of global prehistory. The area now has World Heritage listing because of these geomorphological and archaeological discoveries.

During cooler times in the Late Pleistocene one ancient branch stream of the Lachlan River, Willandra Billabong Creek, which is now dry, then replenished the shallow lakes. Fifty thousand years ago the lakes retained 1000 square kilometres of fresh water up to ten metres deep, and high lake levels prevailed for the following 15,000 years. Major drying began at about 30,000 years ago, successively northwards to Lake Mulurulu, and the continental dunefield expanded southwards through the region. By 15,000 years BP all lakes, except those highest in the catchment, were completely dry, a condition which has prevailed until the present with only ephemeral water during occasional rains. The end of significant human settlement at the lakes is marked by the accumulation of an extensive shell midden, Garnpung 1, dating to around 15,000 years BP, which originally may have contained up to 100 cubic metres of shells. After this time there are no identified traces of Aboriginal occupation until 5000 years BP.

The Willandra Lakes have produced many more dates for human occupation prior to the LGM than any other part of Australia. The kinds of sites which occur on or near the lunettes are human burials, small middens (often simply shell lenses), hearths and earth ovens, lithic scatters and stone quarries. There are twelve major constellations of Aboriginal camping and burial localities in the lunettes and along the 200 kilometres of shorelines. Almost 350 sites are now formally recorded, and no less than one-third of these are certain to be older than 10,000 years. Sites older than about 30,000 years occur mostly on the Arumpo, Garnpung and Mungo lunettes.

Typically, hearths are small areas of charcoal-blackened earth, sometimes surrounded by a scatter of stone artefacts. In the carbonate-rich sediments small oven pits ('earth ovens') with burnt fish and animal bones have been found. These comprise cooking stones or lumps of baked clay resting on a thin band of ash and charcoal in shallow depressions. Because stone is rare, intentionally-fired clay heat retainers substituted as cooking stones. Their frequent survival has provided opportunities for luminescence dating in tandem with radio-carbon assay. About one-third of the dated hearths and ground ovens in the lunettes belong to the period of high-water level before 30,000 years ago. Assessing the palaeomagnetism of oven stones, physicist Mike Barbetti demonstrated a near-reversal of the Earth's magnetic field around 30,000 years BP, which he named the 'Mungo Excursion'.

STRATIGRAPHY OF LAKE MUNGO LUNETTE

There is no better example of the effect of environmental change on lunette stratigraphy than the high dune at Lake Mungo, which is the most intensively studied of any in Australia. The stratigraphy in relation to dating of human burials is discussed below.

Massive erosion has dissected the calcareous skeleton of Lake Mungo's lunette and exposed its archaeological wealth along several kilometres. This newly mobilised dune, nearly 30 kilometres long and dazzlingly white in the intense sunlight, was named by local pastoralists the Walls of China after the Chinese labourers who worked on nearby Gol Gol Station in the last century. The southern end of the lunette is especially productive in relics, because there the layers are thinner and erosion has stripped the surface, exposing the sequence of deposition.

Bowler's research demonstrated that the lunette comprises four major stratigraphic units laid down during the Pleistocene. The oldest unit is a red-orange soil developed on clayey sands, called the Pre-Mungo unit, which is not normally exposed by modern-day erosion. During the time of its formation, beginning more than 70,000 years ago, the lake level fluctuated between full and empty, and

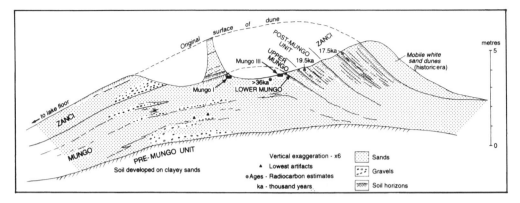

Stratigraphic cross-section of the southern end of the Lake Mungo lunette. (Jim Bowler)

unfortunately for archaeologists its top part was eroded away during periods of high water level. Immediately above the Pre-Mungo is the Mungo unit (divided into upper and lower horizons) comprising a sediment of sands and clay particles blown from the lake bed. In places the upper unit has been cut and re-formed by small waves during a high lake level. The Mungo unit sands signify fluctuating but often full lake conditions from about 40,000 years BP to about 25,000 years BP. At the end of this period the lake was generally shallow and saline, though its water level fluctuated frequently. In the lee of the dune the Mungo unit is overlain by the Post-Mungo unit, which is not yet formally named, and over all the earlier strata is the Zanci unit, deposited during the cold dry climate of the LGM. Zanci sediments were formed from saline muds and clays which were swept up from the drying lake bed by the prevailing southwesterly winds. At about 15,000 years BP the lake dried for the last time and lunette-building ceased and the Pleistocene layers were covered by soil and drift sand.

THE LAKE MUNGO EXCAVATION

In 1973 Mulvaney directed an Australian National University team who excavated a trench in an uneroded part of the Lake Mungo lunette, not far from the place where Australia's oldest known human cremation was discovered. One of the advantages of digging a sand dune site such as this is that virtually every stone object, bird gizzard stones excepted, is an artefact or other item transported by humans (a manuport).

Before carefully excavating a trench by hand, an enormous amount of overlying sand was shifted by bulldozer. When Mulvaney completed the work, this trench, stepped along its sides to avoid collapse, was nine metres long and up to five metres deep. The lower part of the Zanci unit sediment was found to be culturally sterile, which represents abandonment when the region was waterless. Below this, evidence of human occupation extended throughout the 1.75 metre-deep sediments of the Mungo unit. Near the top of the unit Mulvaney encountered a solitary hearth, later dated to about 31,000 years BP. Stone flakes and small pieces of red ochre were found in the half-metre of sand below the level of the hearth. Also, in a strand-line of shelly beach sand in the lower part of the unit there were a few water-rolled stone flakes. These artefacts are undated but must be very ancient. Bowler predicts that the strand-line may be dated to about 40,000 years BP.

LIFE AT LAKE MUNGO

Fresh water, aquatic foods and the shady wooded lunette slopes of the Willandra Lakes provided ideal conditions for encampment. The human bones eroding from sand show few signs of malnutrition, and bone fractures sustained in a fight or accident have healed quickly. Generally, the picture is of well-fed, healthy people who had a varied high-protein diet, probably provided by a wide range of food resources.

Deposits of freshwater mussel shell, typically thin and sometimes better described as shell lenses, are commonly encountered eroding from the lunettes. Lake Arumpo and Lake Leaghur, in particular, have extensive shell lenses dating from 24,000 years BP. The oldest known is about 26,000 years BP, but there may be earlier ones. Historically, freshwater shellfish were collected in summer in the waterways of the Murray–Darling river system. The Pleistocene shell deposits also contain the bones of Murray cod and golden perch, and remains of crayfish which must have been caught in the shallows of lakes and streams. The fish may have been a major attraction of the lakes and possibly large numbers were caught with nets. However, there is no abrasive wear on teeth from human burials to suggest that

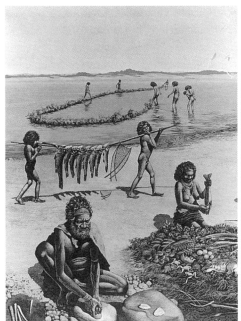

Life at Lake Mungo about 30,000 years BP. *This reconstruction is based upon archaeological finds and inferences drawn from them, but telescopes data across thousands of years into one day. (G. Caselli)*

large quantities of fibre were processed for net making, as was the case along the central Murray River during the Holocene. A superb bone point sharpened at both ends found on the Mungo lunette may have been a prong from a fish-spear similar to ones known historically. Almost certainly the find is more than 17,000 years old. Presumably waterbirds were caught, possibly seasonally and in large numbers, but if so their fragile bones have perished long ago. Fragments of emu eggshell in middens at Lake Mungo suggests encampment during late winter to spring. The marsupials represented by bones in hearths, earth ovens and middens are mostly small to medium-sized species, such as bettong, hare-wallaby, rat-kangaroo, bandicoot, native cat and wombat and the now extinct Tasmanian tiger. All but the last of these animals were still common in the region a hundred years ago. The preferred habitat of most of the species was the woodland fringe around the water bodies, but some others are from a more arid habitat, indicating wider-ranging hunting and foraging. Historically, bettong and hare-wallaby were hunted with the aid of fire, which may also have been the practice during the Pleistocene.

The stone tools were of simple design made from flakes and it is thought that they were 'scrapers', used primarily for making wood and bark artefacts. These tools were of silcrete which outcrops along low ridges on the shores of Lakes Chibnalwood, Leaghur and Mungo, where there are concentrations of toolmaking debris, including blocky cores a kilogram in weight.

Despite the wealth of archaeological sites, the nature of settlement and subsistence is poorly understood. Possibly people in the Pleistocene congregated at the lakes during summer and dispersed into the drier country during the winter months, in the manner of the local Barindji people of the Darling River. However, extreme environmental changes have occurred since the Pleistocene lakes were brimming with water, and continuity of lifestyle cannot be assumed. Notably, the shell middens tend to be small and scattered, which has led Harvey Johnson, the regional archaeologist in the Willandra Lakes World Heritage Area, to ask whether the aquatic food resources have been overemphasised at the expense of terrestrial animals, especially the small macropods and reptiles. However, many of the small marsupial bones in the archaeological sites may not have resulted from human activity, and the answer may lie with other kinds of evidence.

MENINDEE LAKES

Clearer evidence for arid-zone subsistence than that generated by three decades of archaeological studies on the Willandra Lakes should be provided by the investigations by Jane Balme and Jeannette Hope at the Menindee Lakes, further west, and deeper into the desert. These are ancient overflow lakes along the anabranch channels of the lower Darling River that were main watercourses during the Late Pleistocene, before the present course of the Darling was established. After the Willandra Lakes began to evaporate around 15,000 years BP, the Menindee Lakes still held fresh water and remained a source of aquatic food.

In all, 32 Pleistocene sites have been identified, all except one in the Lake Tandou lunette. The oldest dated to 27,000–22,000 years BP. Most are small concentrations of mussel shells over an area of about two square metres surrounded by more fragmented shell, but some also contain artefacts and the remains of crustaceans and small mammals. Such sites probably represent minor short-term camps, or 'dinnertime camps'. Three of the more notable sites are Casuarina Ridge North, which has a concentration of the bones of hundreds of golden perch; Yabbie Kill site, comprising almost exclusively the remains of dozens of yabbies; and Major Swale, where the well-preserved remains of over 250 golden perch and hundreds of crayfish may be the bounty of a single foraging trip. Jane Balme postulates that the range of aquatic foods and the technology used for their procurement may have remained unchanged during the whole of recorded Menindee Lakes prehistory. Although the inference has been drawn that large social groups may have existed during the Pleistocene, no obvious base camps have been found, despite intensive searching. The character of archaeological sites is similar to those at the Willandra Lakes.

LAKE EYRE REGION

The main phase of Lake Eyre's much larger predecessor, Lake Dieri, ended about 100,000 years ago. There were subsequent lacustrine phases of shorter duration until about 60,000 years ago, but after that time Lake Eyre was probably much the same as it is today (during the Early Holocene Lake Eyre did receive more water but it was saline and only a few metres deep). Lake Eyre is presently nearly 10,000 square kilometres in area. While the water-borne sediments in the tributary palaeo-channel that drain into the lake are fossiliferous with the bones of vertebrates, including megafauna, all may predate the arrival of people in Australia.

Stretching for several hundred kilometres along the edge of the Great Artesian Basin, from the northern end of the Flinders Ranges to Lake Eyre and northwest to Oodnadatta, are series of mound springs fed by upwelling subterranean water. The springs are marked by rounded cones or domes of sediment less than a metre to 25 metres high, which are usually well vegetated. The current rates of water discharge range from a bare trickle to a substantial flow, but at some springs the water is strongly saline or alkaline and at none is it particularly fresh-tasting. Ron Lampert and P. J. Hughes have examined a number of mound springs between Lake Callabonna and Oodnadatta, which served as major permanent water sources in largely waterless desert. They found at least one large lithic scatter at each mound spring, but only at two was there even a suggestion of human occupation older than the last few thousand years.

To the northeast of Lake Eyre lies an extensive dunefield, the Strzelecki Desert, where there are innumerable small claypans and shallow lake beds between longitudinal dunes. Exploration of the dunefield for oil and gas has paved the way for archaeological reconnaissance, revealing widespread Holocene-age occupation. Impressive rockshelters and caves, or large open-air base camps, are not always the sources of crucial evidence of human presence in the arid zone. The most modest of archaeological sites, isolated hearths without associated stone artefacts provide the clues. The earliest evidence of human occupation in the Strzelecki Desert is the site of JSN (named after a nearby seismic line) discovered by geomorphologist Robert Wasson in 1979. The JSN locality is a large claypan, nearly half a kilometre long, in the middle of the Strzelecki dunefield about 60 kilometres north of Lake Blanche. Around the margin of this claypan and in the dune sands are lithic scatters and hearths. Substantially they are Mid to Late Holocene in age, but the cultural feature found by Wasson was a small circular hearth containing fragments of mussel shells, charcoal and burnt clay, and dated to about 13,500 years BP. Eucalypts and acacias probably grew in stands around the area at the time, as they do today. Since this rare discovery was made, two hearths five kilometres apart and dating to about 12,000 years BP have been found in dunes near the lower Cooper Creek. These few hearths and some possibly associated stone artefacts may imply nothing more than brief encampments during long-distance travel or rare opportunistic foraging during the closing millennia of the Pleistocene.

THE NULLARBOR PLAIN

This hyper-arid limestone plain has always been a marginal habitat for humans. During the LGM the Bunda and Baxter scarps, which define the present-day coastline of the Great Australian Bight, were 160 kilometres inland and the plain was thousands of square kilometres larger. The resources of the ocean were then far more accessible. Nonetheless, the human population must have been small and highly transient, and may have relied on food resources such as large macropods when they were most accessible and abundant. In the nineteenth century the Aborigines of the Nullarbor foraged in the open woodland along the coastline, and around waterholes on the

Nullarbor's northern periphery. Except after widespread heavy rainfall, they avoided the rest of the plain.

Koonalda Cave

The most famous of the plain's archaeological sites is Koonalda Cave, described by one archaeologist as an 'awesome Gothic chamber'. Initial archaeological discoveries at the cave in the 1950s were followed by further excavations here and at others near the coast. Only in later decades have sites further inland been investigated, as part of an assessment for World Heritage listing.

As a semi-permanent source of water in a large expanse of featureless country, Koonalda Cave may have been an important stop along an ancient route from the coast to the present-day settlement of Cook on the northern edge of the Nullarbor. Australian prehistorians are indebted to the persistence of the first excavator, Alexander Gallus. The demonstration of Koonalda's antiquity was sensational news at a time when no other site showed that humans occupied this inhospitable region so early. In 1967 Richard Wright excavated a trench in the cave floor. Radiocarbon dating of hearths indicates at least occasional visits from 22,000 to 13,000–15,000 years BP. During this period the coastline was far to the south and Koonalda lay deep within a profoundly arid, featureless plain. During these visits people must have clambered down 60 metres of cliff face and sloping floor and walked more than 250 metres into the darkness of the cave to gouge out flint nodules from its walls. The cave is also notable for finger-markings on its walls that are believed to date from visits 20,000 years ago.

Since the 1960s at least 60 archaeological sites on the Nullarbor have been investigated, mostly caves below ground level within 50 kilometres of the coast. Although some caves such as Koonalda, Warbla and Abracurrie are very large, most are relatively small. In local Aboriginal lore the chambers below the plain were fearsome places. The caves on the eastern side of the Nullarbor were believed to be inhabited by Ganba, a Dreaming snake whose breathing is said to be responsible for the roaring sounds emanating from narrow subterranean vents. On the western side the caves are said to be inhabited by Mamu, or evil spirits, and the large caves are 'devil's camps'. Although animal bones, including extinct megafauna, are preserved in the cave sediments, there is no evidence that they resulted from human hunting.

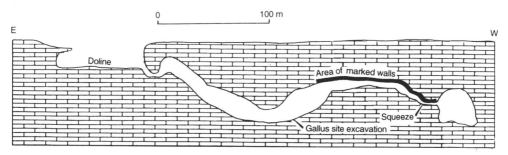

Schematic section of Koonalda Cave, showing location of excavation and area of ancient wall markings within total darkness. The cavern beyond the 'squeeze' contains further markings over a narrow ledge above deep water.

Allen's Cave

One of the more important excavated sites is Allen's Cave, located west of Koonalda in wooded country near the present-day coast. Like Koonalda, it is a doline, created by the roof collapse of a subterranean cavern. Over time, wind and water-borne sediments have buried the rubble from the roof, infiltrating the overhanging edges of the doline and its underground channels. It is a well-appointed cave, offering protection from the intense heat of summer and the chilling winds of winter, with natural air-conditioning provided by an underground chute. The area around the cave is generally waterless, despite the proximity of the coast, and it would have been even more arid during much of the Pleistocene.

A sounding was dug through the five-metre-deep sediments in 1970 and subsequently by Scott Cane and Rhys Jones nearly two decades later. The oldest radiocarbon date for the cultural sediments is around 20,000 years BP for a hearth containing burnt bone. Cane and Jones propose that thermoluminescence determination of 40,000 years dates the earliest human occupation, though the identification of lowermost stone fragments as artefacts is problematic. If their claims are corroborated, then Allen's Cave has the oldest known evidence for settlement of the arid zone.

Not surprisingly, the evidence of human visitation on the Pleistocene Nullarbor is sparse, and particularly so for sediments laid down during the LGM. One of the notable finds at Allen's Cave was a fragment of abalone shell dated to about 16,000 years BP, which must have been brought from the distant coast. At that time the site was situated in a treeless expanse of saltbush scrubland typical of the true Nullarbor, and equally arid: further inland it was possibly too water-less even for transit. However, silcrete flakes were discarded in the cave from about 10,000 years BP when wetter conditions commenced, indicating that people were probably travelling between the coast and the stone sources on the northern margin of the plain, perhaps for the first time.

PILBARA REGION

The Pilbara region in northwest Western Australia has always been arid. On its western margin is Mandu Mandu rockshelter, with its date of about 32,000 years BP for human occupation. The highest part of the Pilbara is the Hamersley Plateau, a seemingly inhospitable habitat for humans, with very hot summers, unreliable rainfall, and few rockholes; all the watercourses are intermittent. Aboriginal heritage and environmental impact assessments have resulted in more than 50 archaeological surveys on the Hamersley Plateau. These surveys demonstrated that the region is rich in archaeological sites—over 900 are recorded, including occupation and innumerable engraved art sites, human burials and stone arrangements. There is a continuous background scatter of stone artefacts throughout the plateau; at a lithic scatter near Mount Tom Price the artefacts comprised fifteen different types of stone. More than twenty rockshelters have been test-excavated, but perhaps several thousand rockshelters and caves with occupation deposits remain undiscovered. The most notable are Mount Newman rockshelters P 0107 and P 2055, which were formed near hilltops by weathering of softer rock just beneath the hard caprock. The first shelter has basal occupation deposit dating to about 21,000 years BP. The second contains 33 fine layers of water-borne sediment, with occupation deposit dating from 26,000–27,000 years BP, after which there are few artefacts until about 6000 years BP, when evidence of human activity at the site again becomes stronger. The small numbers of stone artefacts recovered from sediments spanning many thousands of years suggests only intermittent human presence.

CENTRAL AUSTRALIA

The only site in central Australia claimed to have Pleistocene occu-pation is Puritjarra rockshelter (literally, 'shade area') in an escarpment in the Cleland Hills, 75 kilometres west of the MacDonnell Ranges. This capacious shelter is well shaded by mid-morning and offers protection from the prevailing winds. Murantji rockhole, the only permanent water source in the Cleland Hills, is only 30 minutes' walk distant, while small rockholes closer by hold water after occasional showers.

Puritjarra provided the excavator, Mike Smith, with an ideal habitation site for establishing the antiquity of human settlement in the arid core. Regular occupation of the shelter ceased only in the 1930s, when Aborigines settled at Hermannsburg Mission. The shelter has a compact stratigraphy. The upper layer of loose gritty brown sand, 40 centimetres deep, contains hearths; beneath it lies a red clayey sand layer, 60 centimetres deep, containing scattered small particles of charcoal, overlying consolidated rubble. The rate at which the sediment accumulated, almost all of it from the slow weathering of the shelter, is considerably lower than at other central Australian sites which Smith excavated. The reason is that windblown dust has been trapped at the shelter's entrance and accumulated as a low mound. The lowermost artefacts were found in the middle of layer two at a depth of about a metre. The radiocarbon date for this level was 22,000 years BP, and Smith postulated that from this time until 6500 years BP, when layer one began to accumulate, the shelter had seen sporadic visits by humans. Smith calculated that only an average of three artefacts per millennium had been discarded during this period of more than 15,000 years.

The unusually low sedimentation rate may be important to the interpretation of the finds. Only about 40 centimetres of deposit separates the layer with Mid to Late Holocene artefacts from the one with the lowermost Pleistocene artefacts. The small Pleistocene assemblage includes a few items of microblade technology that only first appeared in central Australia at about 4000 years BP. Thus the earliest date for human occupation at Puritjarra may be problematic because of possible ancient disturbance of the cultural sediment.

Puritjarra is important, also, as one of the few archaeological sites where microscopic phytolith analysis has been applied. Doreen Bowdery identified these microfossils of plant biogenic silica which formed within the plant structure. Each species produces distinctive shapes and as they survive under almost any conditions, their potential for regional floral and environmental reconstruction is great. Her collaboration in this project established that during the Pleistocene, vegetation consisted mainly of trees and shrubs, whereas from about

7000 years BP a great increase in grasses occurred, indicating a climatic regime of summer rains. The subsequent appearance of grindstone technology at Puritjarra suggests that grass seeds were harvested, providing a new food resource.

ARID LANDS AND PEOPLE

It is evident from research across Australia's vast arid core that its outer margins were inhabited, at least periodically, from before 30,000 years BP. Even the Nullarbor was penetrated, to judge from the evidence of Allen's Cave. Depopulation of much of the arid core is indicated during the LGM, although foraging expeditions probably occurred opportunistically from semi-arid bases, such as the North Flinders Ranges. The puzzle is that evidence for early occupation is so elusive. Smith's continuing investigations at Puritjarra may shed more light on the issue.

Pleistocene artefacts 13

The vast bulk of surviving prehistoric material culture comprises stone artefacts, for the simple reason that stone is the least destructible of the natural materials used by Aborigines. There are probably billions of stone artefacts buried in the ground, not only at prehistoric habitation sites such as rockshelters, where they become concentrated because the habitation area is confined, but almost everywhere across the landscape. Aboriginal pathways and areas where people regularly visited are often marked by a 'background count' of artefactual stone fragments, and for one reason or another this count may be so high that archaeologists experience difficulty distinguishing it from evidence for prehistoric camp sites.

While stone artefacts provide invaluable evidence for human presence and activities in a particular area, they represent only a small portion of past material culture or technology. Prehistoric artefacts made of other perishable materials rarely survive for archaeologists. The organic materials which are most likely to last are bone and shell, but usually only in alkaline contexts such as occur in limestone caves, lime-rich sediments, and shell middens. Important but unexpected discoveries are made sometimes of organic materials: well-preserved wooden implements 10,000 years old were unearthed from the peat of Wyrie Swamp in southeastern Australia. There are also less direct sources of evidence about former artefacts, such as the black stain in the fill of a grave near the Murray River, which is all that remains of a large wooden bowl, and the distinctive tooth wear noted on a skull from the same area, which indicates that the individual had habitually stripped large quantities of rushes, probably to make fibre string for fishing nets.

CULTURAL BAGGAGE

Australian Aboriginal material culture has its ultimate origins in the first colonists' artefact repertoire, part of their so-called 'cultural baggage'. Possibly their technology resembled that of historical Aboriginal coastal societies, but there is a vast time gulf separating them which has not been bridged by relevant archaeological findings. Archaeologists draw upon more general ethnographic analogy for some guidance. Deeply embedded in hunter-gatherer lifestyle is the sexual division of labour, common to all human societies, not only hunter-gatherers. Thus there would have been specific men's and women's tools and weapons, though there is no universal allocation of particular items; for instance, in the Torres Strait Islands women used fishing spears, whereas along the coastline of Australia this is usually an item of men's equipment.

The first Australians probably had watercraft or other technology for hunting and collecting coastal and marine resources. Presumably also they knew how to make fire. Their cultural inventory must have included the two most important items of hunter-gatherer equipment: the spear, a man's weapon; and the digging stick, used by women for food-gathering tasks and occasionally for fighting. The digging stick is a length of straight hard dense wood about 0.5 metre to two metres long, with a point or blade at one or both ends. This was the most essential item of hunter-gatherer technology for procuring food. The most basic design of hand-cast spear, used by men for hunting and fighting, was a single piece of straight wood with a sharpened tip. Spears designed for fishing tend to be multi-pronged. Another weapon common throughout Australia is the throwing stick. A wood or bark dish or plant-fibre bag was essential for carrying food collectables. The paper-like bark of *Melaleuca* (paperbark) was particularly suitable for this purpose without much effort, but in central Australia very large elongated wooden bowls with fine parallel incisions were made. As well as basic hunter-gatherer material culture, the first people must have brought a detailed knowledge of useful plants and animals found both in their former homeland and their new abode in northern Sahul.

ANCESTRAL TECHNOLOGY

Archaeologists have always sought to link Southeast Asian stone technology with that of Australia, in our view without obvious success. Following Hallam L. Movius' classic study of the East Asian Stone Age in the 1940s, it has been customary to assume that Southeast Asia was a separate 'cultural' province in Eurasia, with stone technology distinguished by conservatism and 'monotonous and unimaginative' pebble choppers and flake tools. G. G. Pope argues that the common alternative to stone for cutting tools in Southeast Asia was bamboo, and that this is why the stone assemblage lacks style.

There are only a few Late Pleistocene artefact collections from excavated sites in Southeast Asia dating to before or around the presumed time of Sahul settlement. If Australian stone technology has its origin in a Sundaland tradition, one characterised by Peter Bellwood as general pebble and flake industries, it will be exceedingly difficult to demonstrate this, because there is little that is distinctive about them. Core tools displaying a degree of regularity are reported for northern Vietnam. While these artefacts are suitably early, their identification as tools may not be accurate. It is only with the appearance of flaked pebble tools called 'Hoabinhian' (named after a Vietnamese province), that well-designed stone tools appear. The Hoabinhian is spread across southernmost China, mainland Southeast Asia, and the northern end of Sumatra. The implement most commonly recognised in the stone tool kit is a pebble adze, flaked on one face, and with natural pebble cortex on the opposite face. Hatchet heads of ground stone are also sometimes found, and the Malaysian archaeologist Adi Taha has recognised a third implement: a thin, oval-shaped piece of stone flaked on both faces. For decades after its first discovery in the 1920s the Hoabinhian was thought to be Late Pleistocene in age, but the radiocarbon dates for the earliest sites cluster around 10,000 years BP, millennia after humans settled Sahul. The earlier Southeast Asian industries, as far as they are known, represent minimal investment of time into flaking stone into tools with basic methods. No functions have been demonstrated for the tools.

Only two archaeological sites in Malaysia are known to be older than about 30,000 years. One of these is the gravel bed of an ancient river on the margin of a former lake in Kota Tampan oil palm plan-tation in the Malay Peninsula. In this locality were found hammer stones, cores, and thousands of flakes, all of quartzite, indicating a former 'workshop' where pebbles and cobbles were flaked to make stone tools. Overlying this deposit is a layer of volcanic ash at least 1.5 metres thick. Its mineral composition identifies it as being from the last eruption of Mount Toba in northern Sumatra, which occurred about 74,000 years ago. This eruption, which ejected 3000 cubic kilo-metres of pyroclastic matter, creating a volcanic caldera 100 kilometres long, was one of the most cataclysmic on earth in the last few mil-lion years and it is thought to have brought about pronounced global cooling. The Kota Tampan assemblage conveys little impression of design other than that imposed by the commonality of pebble shape and size. The second Malaysian site is the Great Cave at Niah in Sarawak, where the oldest cultural levels possibly date from 42,000 to 38,000 years BP, and associated artefacts comprise only a handful of formless hammer-struck stone flakes.

Because of its particular antiquity, the most relevant mainland Southeast Asian site is Lang Rongrien, a rockshelter high in a lime-stone tor in south Thailand, which has a radiocarbon date of about 37,000 years BP for a level above the lowest artefacts. However, these artefacts comprise only flakes with chipped edges, called 'scrapers' by archaeologists, and pebble artefacts of no particular distinction. In island Southeast Asia there are no known sites older than around 30,000 years BP which have been attributed to modern humanity.

Unless there is greater sophistication of early Southeast Asian stone industries than is apparent now, the most advanced technological inheritance colonists could have brought was basic stone flaking. Given that they were coastal dwellers, no doubt using organic materials such as bamboo, bone and shell, they may have come with little knowledge about stone toolmaking. The basic methods of flaking stone are so ancient and require so little input of knowledge that no direct cultural relationship could be demonstrated.

EARLY CULTURAL CLUES IN SAHUL

Whenever the first migrants stepped ashore in Sahul there is reason to believe that local adaptations and innovations were vital elements in their new world. As colonisation of Sahul progressed, the basic elements of the foundation hunter-gatherer material culture evidently continued through the Pleistocene even into the present era. Yet innovation and diversification occurred as new environmental zones were settled—the tropical rain forests of northeast Queensland, the temperate woodlands and grasslands, the intensely cold sub-alpine region of the New Guinea highlands and southern Tasmania, and the hot arid interior of the continent. There is no evidence that any aspect of material culture was influenced directly or otherwise by transformations occurring overseas until recent times. All earlier innovations may have had their origin within the continent.

THE AESTHETIC DIMENSION

Ideological insight is provided by further challenging finds. Excavations of Pleistocene cultural deposits have revealed pieces of red, orange and purple ochre, and even glittering ochre. A pink stain in the sand fill of a 30,000-year-old grave at Lake Mungo suggests body painting. Rock art at many sites is also demonstrated (see Chapter 20).

The finds of Pleistocene-age ornaments, though few in number, are indications of a range that may have been as diverse as that observed ethnographically and to be found in museum collections. What is not preserved are the more perishable organic components, such as reed segments, plant-fibre string and bindings, resin, wax, gum, fur, skin and feathers. In the lowest layer of Mandu Mandu rockshelter, dating to about 32,000 years BP, Kate Morse excavated the remains of 22 small cone-shell beads with their spires pierced and body whorls removed—possibly the remains of the oldest known necklace or headband in the world. At Devil's Lair, in layers dating to the terminal Pleistocene and the Last Glacial Maximum, Dortch discovered three beads made of segmented macropod fibula. With Pleistocene rock art distributed from Arnhem Land to Tasmania and burials dating across some 30,000 years, it may be assumed that the invisible baggage of the first colonists had aesthetic and spiritual dimensions, rendering details of their original stone technology irrelevant in human terms.

WOODEN ARTEFACTS

As yet, there is no direct evidence of Pleistocene wooden artefacts in Australia, other than the stone tools used to manufacture and maintain them, but this evidence is abundant. The ubiquitous finds of woodworking tools in archaeological deposits spanning the known antiquity of human settlement of Sahul indicate the importance of wooden artefacts throughout prehistory, and stone spokeshaves with neat concave cutting edges indicate the maintenance of wooden spears. Tantalising evidence of the diversity of earlier wooden artefacts was discovered in 1974 at Wyrie Swamp, near Millicent, South Australia. Preserved in the peat were 25 wooden artefacts dated by radiocarbon to 10,000 years ago. These fragile remains, some only fragments of artefacts, included returning boomerangs; one-piece spears with simple sharp points or with barbs cut into the solid wood; and digging sticks of various lengths but most short, and possibly for collecting the starchy rhizomes of swamp plants. The boomerangs are the oldest known wooden specimens in the world.

BONE TOOLS

Some of Australia's earliest known bone implements, sharp-tipped and spatulate-ended bone points, have been excavated from limestone caves in southernmost Australia, at Devil's Lair in the southwest, Clogg's Cave in the foothills of the Victorian Alps, Cave Bay Cave on Hunter Island in Bass Strait, and caves in the southwest forests of Tasmania. Invariably these are made from macropodid long bones, but one example, from Cave Bay Cave, is a foot bone of a swan with a polish that appears to be use-wear. These finds are sufficient to demonstrate that bone tools were widespread in Late Pleistocene Sahul. Bone-working techniques included grinding and perforation. The functions of Pleistocene bone implements are not known with any confidence and are the subject of much inference by prehistorians, who have interpreted the polish observed on some of them, which is not specific to a particular use, or drawn parallels with the ethnographic record. Some could be spear points, others awls for making skin garments, or pins for securing cloaks, items which may have been essential for survival in the frigid windswept regions of Sahul. In particular, the spatulate-ended bone tools found at Bone Cave in southwest Tasmania are believed to be for flensing and making furskin garments, such as wallaby-skin cloaks. During the Pleistocene tools of animal teeth seem likely though none have been recognised in excavated deposits.

STONE MATERIALS USED FOR TOOLS

In Sahul dozens of different varieties of stone were used for cutting, scraping, pounding and chopping implements. They can be allocated to two broad groups based on their mechanical properties—those which are hard and brittle, suitable for flaked tools; and those that have soft constituent minerals but are tough, and therefore easier to shape by grinding and able to resist heavy impact without breaking. Sandstone which is neither hard compared to the first group, nor tough, was used for grindstones.

One of the commonest types of stone used for flake tools is quartz which is available over much of Australia; in some regions it is almost the only flakable stone to be found. Quartz can occur as large crystals, but it was not usually these attractive crystals which were available, but veins in host rocks of various kinds. Because of its hardness quartz is common as pebbles in watercourses, from which much of it was gathered for toolmaking. The stone is composed of extremely small hexagonal crystals of silicon oxide, which give it a glossy texture. When pure it is translucent, but minute traces of minerals may add colour, and most quartz has microscopic vacuoles filled with gas or liquid which give it a milky appearance. Because of its tendency to have abundant internal flaws, quartz ranges in flaking quality from very poor to manageable, and it tends to shatter into small pieces when struck with a stone hammer. Its great advantage is that these small pieces are often sharp-edged, and often this was all that was required for a small cutting task.

Another important stone type which found widespread use in Australia is a hard siliceous stone called silcrete, which is rare in the rest of the world except for South Africa. Silcrete is most often grey in colour, but red, brown, yellow, and even green occur in artefact collections and some may have been specifically selected for aesthetic or symbolic reasons. Silcrete formed as sedimentary layers over vast, poorly drained regions of Australia more than twenty million years ago, and is the solidification product of hot, silica-rich solution derived from layers of sandstone that have completely weathered away. Silcrete is found from coast to coast, outcropping from layers usually one to two metres thick or as water-worn stones. Remnants of former expanses of silcrete are the capstone of buttes, mesas and ridges which are so much a part of the landscape in arid Australia. Whenever these remnants are eroded, for up to thousands of square kilometres the plains are covered in flaking quality 'gibber' gravel, such as Sturt's

Stony Desert. Silcrete matrix is fine crystalline quartz and sometimes some non-crystalline (amorphous) silica. Within this are scattered quartz grains or clasts. Under low magnification, silcrete is often easily identifiable by the sheared quartz grains reflecting brightly in a sea of finely textured coloured matter. Flakes have reasonably sharp, durable edges, and it was used for all kinds of tasks including heavy-duty woodworking.

A third stone type, which commonly occurs in Pleistocene stone assemblages, is chert, which is also known as flint in its nodular form in a limestone layer. Flint is the main stone type used in the highlands of New Guinea, and further south it erodes from Jurassic and Cretaceous limestone, mainly along the southern fringe of the continent. Chert or flint is hard siliceous stone composed of microscopic interlocking grains or crystals, mostly quartz, but also chalcedony and other minerals. The stone may be so fine-grained as to appear almost translucent, but small amounts of accessory minerals give it many different colours.

Finally, there is a group of less common siliceous stones which are notable on a regional scale. One is the lava glass, obsidian, which was traded long distances by sea from two islands off the northeast Sahul coast. There is also an outcrop in southeastern Cape York Peninsula, but there its use was local. Flakes of obsidian have edges that are sharper and finer than a surgical steel scalpel. In southern Australia, an extraterrestrial shower of molten silica provided arid-zone dwellers with a bonus of glass, albeit only small pieces (tektites), and in Tasmania glass was formed by the impact of a meteor (Darwin glass). Chalcedony was used wherever convenient sources were found as its properties are similar to those of chert. Finally, hard quartzite, with its granular texture and less-keen edge, was also put to service. Though probably not preferred for most tasks, it was a basic material in some areas.

FLAKING METHODS

During the Pleistocene, basic flaking techniques were practised, and one tool type, the hatchet head, was finished by grinding it on an abrasive stone. A common flaking technique was bipolar flaking, which dates back at least two million years elsewhere in the world. We have discussed bipolar flaking in Chapter 9 in relation to identifying Australia's earliest stone artefacts. It is an efficient way of

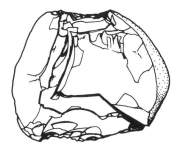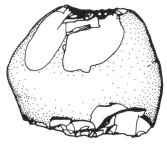

Bipolar core, retaining some pebble cortex. (Drawn by G. Happ)

producing small, sharp fragments from a very small core and is done by holding a piece of stone, commonly a small quartz pebble, on a hard surface and smashing it with a hammerstone. After a few blows the core sustains distinctive battering damage which is easily recognised, especially when slightly magnified. Sharp fragments with battering are detached, along with a special type of flake called a 'compression flake'. The discarded bipolar cores tend to be roughly rectangular or wedge-shaped.

A range of different core shapes result when a core is relatively large and compressive force is not important in the fracturing process. The particular outcome depends in part on the stone type and the original size and shape of the core. One distinctive variety is the block core. This includes a type called horsehoof core which has a characteristic undercut striking platform. In an upside-down position it resembles a horse's hoof, hence the name. This core type is derived from a split cobble or a blocky piece of stone, usually silcrete or an igneous rock that has one or more naturally flat surfaces. These faces served as striking platforms for flake detachment. When one flat surface became exhausted by repeated detachments, increasingly including failed ones, the core was rotated and another flat surface struck with the hammer, until it also was spent. As flakes were struck progressively around the periphery of the cobble or block, the core became wider towards its base. This happens because flakes sometimes stop short in a hinge or step-like break, and therefore stone is removed from the upper part of the core in greater volume than from its lower part.

Water-worn pebbles selected from gravels along watercourses and sea coasts were convenient sources of flakable stone, because their shapes were convenient for hammerstones and pounders, and with minimal flaking could be turned into hand-choppers and hatchet heads; depending on local geology, gravel beds provided a choice of stone types useful for a wide range of tasks, and the quality of the stone had already been tested by the forces of nature for its mechanical strength and durability.

TOOL TYPES

Possibly from the beginning of human settlement of Sahul, some stone tools were fixed onto wooden handles, either directly or with aid of cement of some kind. For some tool types this innovation is easy to infer because of the tool's design features, but for most flake implements there is little way of determining the former presence or absence of hafting. In general, most Pleistocene-age flake implements may have been held directly in the hand.

The majority of stone items in any excavated assemblage consists of flaking detritus from toolmaking. When stone tools are of basic design, much of the character of an assemblage is determined by the stone types used and the natural shaping of pieces selected as cores. Archaeologists make a classificatory distinction between flake and core tools, but at times this has served to confuse rather than to clarify the characterisation of assemblages. The most serious limitation has been the lack of understanding about the functions of stone tool, or even the essentials of accurately discriminating between the tools and elements of discarded flaking debris from their production. Some disagreements have involved stone cores thought to have been used as hand-held choppers and hand-adzes, but which do not have the telltale evidence of such usages in the form of use-worn or neatly resharpened cutting edges. Conversely, many simple flake tools are not identified as such because they have no chipping on their edges (called 'retouch' by archaeologists).

The tool component of early stone assemblages is largely composed of flake tools though there are also ones finished by grinding and possibly by hammer-tapping. Ubiquitous, but not normally found in high numbers in stone assemblages are hammers of tough stone, often pebbles, and anvil stones of no particular distinction—usually their only distinguishing feature is the damage from use. As we explained in Chapter 3, we consider that the concept of the Core Tool and Scraper Tradition no longer serves any useful purpose in labelling Pleistocene assemblages.

FLAKE SCRAPERS

Many Pleistocene flaked stone implements have retouch along at least one edge. Sometimes this was done to shape the primary flake so that it suited a particular purpose, but more often it was done to rejuvenate a dulled or fracture-damaged cutting edge. Occasionally, a flake is given a saw-like edge. This general group of retouched items is often included in a classificatory 'grab-bag' called flake scrapers, a label inherited from nineteenth-century European antiquarianism. Despite the obvious meaning of the term, probably in many cases these implements were neither intended nor used for scraping wood or any other material, and sometimes the retouch is misunderstood. For instance, refer to the illustration of a Pleistocene 'end scraper' excavated from Burrill Lake rockshelter. This specimen's convex retouched end is not a utilised cutting or scraping edge. The unretouched side of the implement is use-chipped, and was probably a cutting edge. The retouched end probably was convenient to hold in the hand—this implement was perhaps a knife.

Scrapers come in a wide variety of shapes, and certain formal categories are recognised on the basis of overall size, the plan-shape, and the angle of retouched edges. There is sometimes a high degree of subjectivity in allocating scrapers to one category or the other, and we offer here only a basic typology. Flakes with straight retouched edges are called, fittingly enough, 'straight-edged scrapers' and it is presumed on the basis of analogy with recent Aboriginal stone tools that many of them were used to scrape or shave wood. There is evidence from Kangaroo Island of small hafted rectangular wood scrapers around 11,000 years BP, and possibly 1000 years earlier at Devil's Lair.

Another scraper category comprises concave and notched varieties. Notches were made by a single hammer blow on the side of a flake which leaves a deep, semicircular indentation. Concave scrapers are flakes that have similarly inward curving cutting edge, but are finely retouched along this edge. Many concave scrapers must be notched scrapers that have been resharpened. Extrapolating from observations of their use in Australia's dry interior, it can be inferred that in general notched and concave scrapers served as hand-held spokeshaves for manufacturing and maintaining cylindrical or pointed wooden artefacts, such as spear tips and digging sticks.

There is also a mixed group of flake scrapers exhibiting a convex

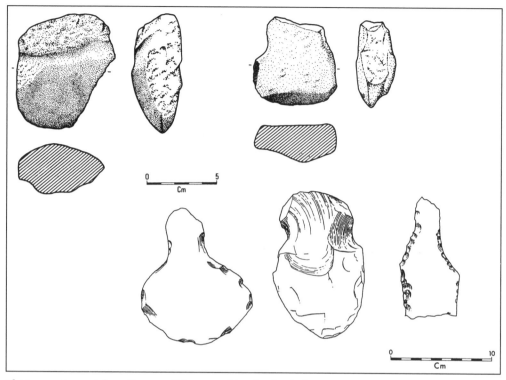

Pleistocene stone artefacts. Top row: Edge-ground hatchet heads dating to 18,000–20,000 years BP, excavated from Nawamoyn rockshelter in Kakadu National Park. Bottom row: Unground, tanged and waisted implements from Kosipe, New Guinea. (Drawn by W. Mumford)

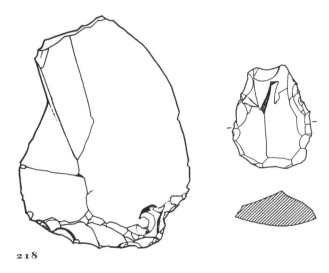

Far left: 'End scraper' from the lower level of Burrill Lake rockshelter. Microscopic study reveals use-wear on the tool's right-hand edge and not the retouched end. This tool probably served as a knife with a handle or grip, length 4.8 centimetres. (Drawn by G. Happ)

Near left: A scraper 3.5 centimetres long excavated from Seton cave on Kangaroo Island and dated to 11,000 years BP; it was probably mounted on a handle. (Ron Lampert) edge shaped by retouch. A 'nosed' type is sometimes recognised, but of current interest is the small 'thumbnail scraper' which is similar in shape to a person's thumbnail and tending towards that size. These implements first occur in archaeological sites before the onset of the Last Glacial Maximum. The functions of thumbnail scrapers and other convex flake implements are poorly understood.

WAISTED 'AXES'

An assortment of large, waisted or stemmed stone tools has been found in New Guinea and Australia. None of those in the south are dated and they may be post-Pleistocene in age. Many more have been found in New Guinea, and well-preserved ones at four sites—Kosipe, Yuku and Nombe in the highlands, and Bobongara on the coast of the Huon Peninsula—confirm their presence in the Pleistocene tool-kit. They are made of a variety of coarse-grained stone types and their general design suggests use as hafted axe or hatchet heads in the main, and some as pounders. This group is not coherent in terms of shape and size, and the single attribute of waisting for the fitting of a handle is not sufficient to infer that the finds relate to each other culturally.

The oldest are claimed to have been found at Bobongara, where dozens were collected eroding from a layer of volcanic ash, provisionally dated by thermoluminescence to about 40,000 years BP. These specimens are flattish cobbles of tough, fine-grained igneous rock, roughly flaked on one face and notched or 'waisted' for the fitting of a handle. The wear on some suggested that the handle may have been a piece of split rattan. A large-area excavation was undertaken by Peter White at Kosipe, which is on a ridge projecting into a swamp near Mount Albert Edward. Waisted axes and a few other stone artefacts were found stratified within a series of volcanic ash layers laid down by eruptions of nearby Mount Lamington. These axes, some shaped by grinding the surfaces as well as flaking, had been left behind or lost during visits between 26,000 and 15,000 years BP. White postulated that they had been used in seasonal collecting of the seeds of pandanus, which grows abundantly in the swamp. The discoverers of the Bobongara specimens offer a similar identification, but they add collecting of other staple plant foods and general bush clearance to suggestions of use.

EDGE-GROUND HATCHETS

One of the most surprising finds in Australia at the time of their discovery was a collection of fifteen hatchet heads of ground stone dating between 18,000 and 23,000 years BP. These were excavated by Carmel Schrire from Malangangerr and Nawamoyn rockshelters near the East Alligator River in Kakadu National Park. All have been bifacially flaked and their cutting edges shaped by grinding on an abrasive stone such as sandstone. Two are grooved along their sides for the fitting of a short bent-wood handle. Another is indented or waisted, and still another tanged. These varied features assisted attachment of handles. Their technological similarities with Papua New Guinea specimens may prove relevant. This find was sensational in

Nawamoyn shelter, formed by a huge mass of sandstone which fell from the eroding Arnhem Land escarpment. It was here in 1965 that edge-ground and grooved hatchets of dolerite or hornfels were excavated, dating before 18,000 years BP. (D. J. Mulvaney)

archaeological circles at the time of its discovery in the 1960s. It was believed previously that grinding stone into axe heads and wood-working tools was a marker for Neolithic farming societies, as it was for Europe. A few years later, hatchet heads dating back 30,000 years were found in Japan.

In terms of the rock types, general size and shape, manufacturing method and likely type of handle, the Kakadu hatchet heads are essentially no different from many nineteenth-century ethnographic examples collected from around Australia. Since Schrire's discovery there have been more such finds in northern Australia, indicating a much longer antiquity for this implement type and more widespread distribution. For instance, a small quartzite example, squarish in shape, with waisting and a pecked groove for securing a handle, was recovered from a layer of rubble probably older than 30,000 years BP in Sandy Creek 1 rockshelter in north Queensland. Also, small flakes chipped off ground stone tools have been found in at least three other Pleistocene sites, namely Widgingarri 1 and Miriwun rockshelters in northwestern Australia and Ngarradj rockshelter in Kakadu National Park. Since no hatchet heads older than 4500 years BP have been found in southern Australia it is presumed that they were distributed only across northern Australia and New Guinea before then, and some prehistorians suggest the reason was basically environmental. We remain perplexed as to why over tens of thousands of years such a useful, multi-purpose implement of such simple design was never invented or adopted by people exploiting the forestlands of south-eastern Sahul.

GRINDSTONES

In the main, grinding and pounding stones excavated from Pleistocene deposits in Australia appear to be 'expedient', in that they are minimally altered and are not noticeably specialised. It is inferred that they were used for as broad a range of activities as observed ethnographically in Australia, which includes pounding meat, cracking nuts, and grinding plant food and pigment. Evidence for widespread processing of grass seeds is lacking. However, at Cuddie Springs, an ephemeral lake near Brewarrina, New South Wales, Judith Furby has found stone artefacts, including grindstone fragments, in apparent association with bones of extinct megafauna. These sediments have dates of up to 30,000 years BP. The grindstone fragments are polished by wear identical to that seen on grass-seed millstones. Their importance in the food quest is apparent from the distance that had to be travelled to obtain the stone, most of which came from a spectacular sandstone quarry at Mount Druid, a walking distance of 100 kilometres. If the artefacts at Cuddie Springs are really as old as the bones, the site is destined to be one of the most significant for reconstructing the lifeways of Pleistocene Australians. However, secure archaeological evidence for grass-seed grinding dates to the Holocene period.

Holocene stone tool innovations 14

Archaeologists have devoted considerable field and laboratory time to attempting to determine the date of the initial colonisation of Australia. It is this issue that attracts media attention, to the neglect of the later millennia of Aboriginal occupation. During the Holocene period, particularly the last 3000 or more years before British colonisation, many innovations took place, which are particularly evident in stone technology.

CLIMATE AND ENVIRONMENT

The Early Holocene commenced around 12,000 years BP with moderate warming and increased rainfall approaching modern conditions. Tropical monsoons intensified and possibly between 10,000 and 3000 years ago summer rainfall over much of Australia exceeded modern conditions, so lake levels rose. Sea level also continued to rise, but at a more rapid rate of ten to fifteen metres per thousand years. By 6000±250 years BP the sea had risen to about its present level. Some geomorphologists assert that at 4500–3000 years BP the sea level fluctuated about a metre or more above its modern level, but today the evidence for this is neither consistent nor widely accepted.

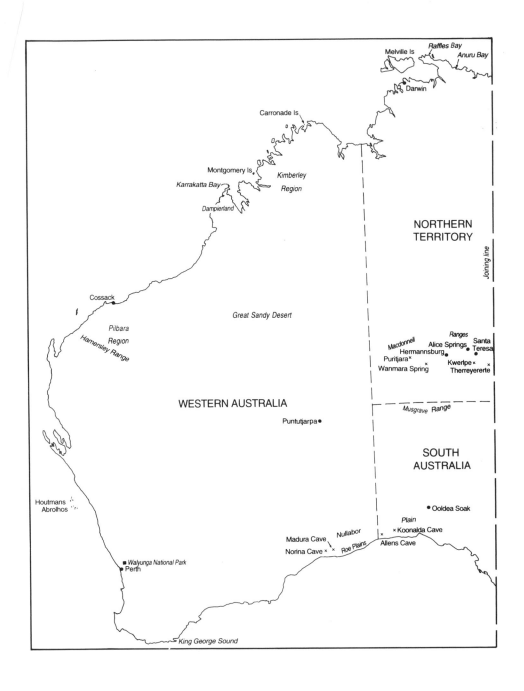

Map 11. Places of archaeological significance mentioned in the text.

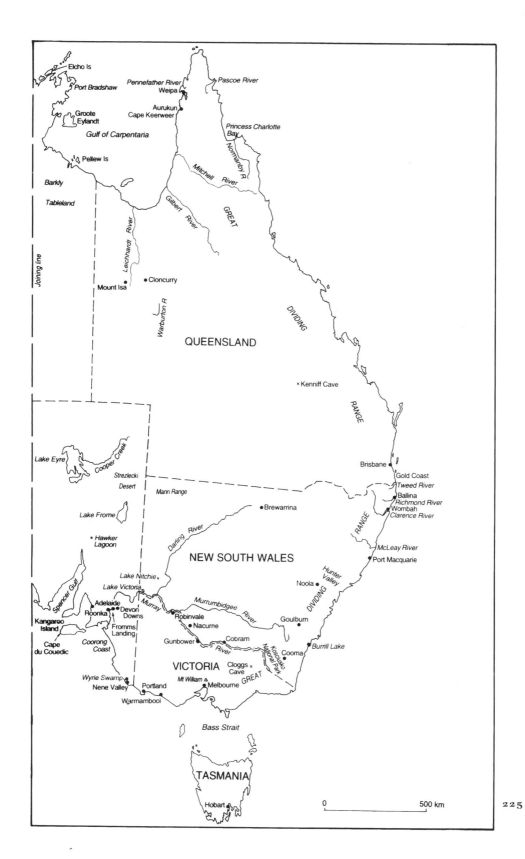

225

A warm climatic phase, called the Holocene Warm Maximum, began at about 8700 years BP and lasted at least until the sea level stillstand at about 6000 years BP; some scientists argue that this phase ended at about 4500 years BP. The evidence for a long period of warm moist climate, most apparent towards the end of the phase, has been gleaned from pollen records, the build-up of alluvial fans, and dating of driftwood in stream-channel sediments. Throughout mainland Australia mean annual temperatures were 0.5°C to 3°C higher than present. The consequence for the Australian Alps was dramatic, with the alpine zone reduced to about one-fifth of today's area. In effect, snow cover almost disappeared. However, in Tasmania, which lies at more southerly latitudes and is surrounded by the Southern Ocean, the temperature range was similar to that of today, though there was more precipitation. Annual rainfall in Australia was greater then than it had been for tens of thousands of years, or would be subsequently, increasing by 20 to 50 per cent; in the better-watered regions of the continent the lakes were brimming, and in the arid interior conditions at the very least were slightly wetter.

Beginning about 4000 years BP, there was some renewed but minor activity in the growth of longitudinal dunes in the arid zone, and this has been attributed to windier conditions which abated about 1000 years BP. Between about 4000 and 2000 years BP the arid zone became slightly drier than today, and presumably there were more droughts. During this time climatic conditions over the rest of Australia were similar to today, though Tasmania, which often missed out on periods of more congenial weather, became cooler by about 3°C.

These significant environmental changes, particularly the general climatic amelioration, set the context for complex regional cultural and technological developments which are an increasing focus of archaeological research. In the history of archaeological interest, it was the variety in stone tool technology and typology which first attracted attention.

EARLY HOLOCENE STONE INDUSTRIES OF SOUTHEASTERN AUSTRALIA

Two distinct regional variants of early Holocene stone technology have been identified in southeastern Australia—the Gambieran flint industry, and the diverse Kangaroo Island industry. The chronologies of these are not fully known because only a few chronometric dates are available.

Gambieran flint industry

Gambieran artefacts are found along the coast between Portland in Victoria and Robe in South Australia. The industry was first described in 1940 by F. D. McCarthy, but it was Norman Tindale who provided the name, after the Mount Gambier volcanic caldera, which experienced its last episode of volcanism only 4500 years ago. Nodules of flint are abundant in this region of limestone, especially along the coast in backshore ridges and cobble beaches. Flint was also gouged from the walls of caves. There was no stratigraphic context for any of the early finds, but they were known to be old because they were found eroding from *terra rossa* soil of consolidated dune, adjacent to more recently formed sand dunes in which they were absent. Because the flake tools were patinated and stained red by their long period of burial, a Pleistocene age was postulated. It was only when wood and stone artefacts were excavated in the 1970s from the peat of Wyrie Swamp that an early Holocene age for Gambieran artefacts was established, and subsequently corroborated by David Frankel in his excavation at nearby Koongine cave.

Gambieran implements include flake-scrapers, with convex, concave or straight cutting edges. Taking into account the size and superb flakability of the local flint, Gambieran tools are not comparable to Pleistocene ones. However, a particular tool of standardised design, called a 'Gambieran discoid', is suggestive of later, Mid-Holocene stone technology. This tool is a large flake steeply retouched into a discoid or semi-discoid shape and varies considerably in size; its function is unknown.

The Kartan

In 1931 the discovery of stone artefacts at Murray Lagoon on Kangaroo Island was reported by Norman Tindale and B. G. Maegraith. Tindale later gave the name 'Kartan industry' to these artefacts. The assemblage comprises pebble choppers flaked on one side only (originally called 'Sumatraliths' after similar pebble tools in Southeast Asia); horsehoof cores; steeply retouched flakes, some domed (called 'karta'); hammer-anvils probably used for pounding hard seeds; and

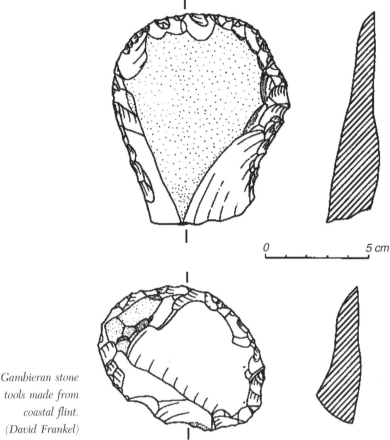

0 _____ 5 cm

Gambieran stone tools made from coastal flint. (David Frankel)

pounders indented with a waist to fit a handle. Most of these artefacts are made from quartzite and are large.

Kartan-like artefacts also occur on the Fleurieu Peninsula on the
opposite mainland. After five decades of searching Kangaroo Island
and the peninsula, local Adelaide collectors located more than 100
Kartan lithic scatters. Tindale enthusiastically identified Kartan in far-
flung corners of Australia—at Port Augusta, the Flinders Ranges,
Tasmania, Calligillup in the extreme southwest, and at Roebourne in
the northwest, which he claimed on the basis of a single flake. He
made the sweeping claim that the Kartan derived from Southeast
Asian pebble industries and was brought to Australia during the Late
Pleistocene. He identified these first colonists as Negritos, who must

have been overcome on the mainland by later immigrants. Not surprisingly, Tindale's postulated distribution was challenged by both McCarthy and Mulvaney.

In the 1970s Ron Lampert carried out an intensive field survey of Kangaroo Island, including the excavation of Seton Cave inland from the island's south coast. The deepest layer revealed human occupation from about 16,000 years BP. At that time of lower sea level Seton Cave lay in an upland stretching from the Pleistocene coast, about 30 kilometres northwest of the former mouth of the Murray River. This region was then drier, and vegetated with grassland, heath and open woodland. The earliest stone assemblage comprised flakes of flint obtained from sources up to 50 kilometres distant. Apart from occasional visits, the site was then unoccupied until about 11,000 years BP, with final abandonment at about 4300 years BP. Significantly, there was no trace of the Kartan industry in the cave, and Lampert presumed that it must have predated this period of occupation. He therefore backed Tindale's hypothesis that the Kartan was Australia's first stone technology and Southeast Asian in origin. Lampert postulated two stone assemblages on Kangaroo Island—the Kartan, which he saw as a regional variant of the Core Tool and Scraper Tradition, and its successor, which he designated the Kangaroo Island Small Tool Industry.

The proposition of a Pleistocene Kartan has had some currency among prehistorians, but was never accepted wholeheartedly. Mulvaney, in his 1961 review of Australian prehistory, warned against constructing a Kartan Culture with no stratigraphic context. Until the field survey and excavations in the mid-1980s by Neale Draper, not a single Kartan site on Kangaroo Island or the Fleurieu Peninsula had been dated. The Kartan has shared the fate of the Gambieran, and is shown to be Holocene in age.

Draper demonstrated that there is no real cultural succession on Kangaroo Island, but that the two stone industries were a response to the local availability of flakable stone—quartzite for one and quartz and chert for the other, with further dissimilarity caused by the different activities carried on at coastal and inland sites. Chert was scarce on Kangaroo Island and there is little of it in the assemblages. As for quartz, even though Adelaide collectors had reported its presence in Kartan lithic scatters decades ago, it was neglected because the focus of their attention was solely on the large quartzite artefacts, the emblems of antiquity and the presumed evidence for the Southeast Asian connection.

Draper found that unifacially flaked cobbles were left at sites all over the island. Some of these were made at inland cobble beds but probably most originated on the coast where there are abundant cobbles. At Cape Du Couedic on the southwest coast Draper excavated a spacious rockshelter situated at the top of a precipitous limestone cliff. The cultural deposit spans a period of only 2000 years, from about 7550 to 5500 BP. Notable finds were two unifacially flaked pebble tools, typical markers of Tindale's Kartan Phase, one associated with the bones of a sea lion and the other found in a fireplace. Draper suggests that the tools had been used to butcher sea lion and possibly also served as cores for small flake implements. There was also a large amount of flaking debris from making choppers, and a few flakes struck from their blunted cutting edges. Examples of a second type of typical Kartan tool type, the hammer-anvil, were also uncovered, and numerous smashed quartz artefacts similar in character to the stone assemblage at Seton cave.

Draper observed during his fieldwork that large quartzite block cores (horsehoof cores and at least some of the karta type) occurred in sites at inland lagoons and streams. This stone comes from local quartzite formations within the plateau region of the island. Flakes are under-represented in early collections from these sites, which was interpreted to indicate that the quartzite cores were tools rather than waste products from stone flaking. No doubt some stone cores were used as tools, but virtually all the sites visited by Adelaide collectors had been ploughed, and pastoralists are known to discard larger stones along fence lines. It is probable that there was 'collector bias' in favour of the largest stone artefacts.

MID-HOLOCENE CHANGES IN STONE TECHNOLOGY

From the earliest days of archaeological excavation, researchers identified a range of stone artefact types that were later known to be of Holocene age. Many of these implements were small and carefully retouched. The Kenniff Cave excavations in the early 1960s provided firm evidence that these types belonged to the last few thousand years. Elements of the new technology, called the Australian Small Tool Phase, are apparent in the Early Holocene in southeastern Australia, but from about 5000–6000 years ago new implement types become widespread. There is no evidence that they have a single place of origin, and they appear in the archaeological record at different times.

Some of the new types are fully prehistoric in that they were no longer made by the time the British arrived, while others continued into historical times. The new types appear in both flaked and ground stone technology. Many are stone elements of multi-component tools and weapons, such as knives and daggers, some with elegantly decorated handles, neatly trimmed spear points and barbs, special-purpose gravers and drills, and woodworking adzes, flaked and edge-ground chisels, and millstones. The new flaking techniques and implement types did not reach Tasmania, which had been completely isolated from technological developments on the mainland. Tasmanian stone technology has its own separate development and individual characteristics. Notably, when Europeans arrived the Tasmanian tool-kit had neither edge-ground nor hafted stone tools.

To existing stone technology was added not only implement types but new, innovative flaking techniques and production strategies, requiring more training in stone toolmaking than before, with a corresponding increase in skill and craftsmanship. Blade-making techniques appeared, which required sometimes considerable preparation of the core and suitable stone material to facilitate the production of long narrow flakes. To produce regularly shaped stone blades requires initial flaking of a core to give it at least two long flake scars that have an intersection forming a long straight ridge down the core's side. When cores have a number of these longitudinal ridges, they tend to be prismatic in shape. A long thin, straight-sided flake, much like a penknife-blade in shape, is produced by striking the top of the core at a point just behind one of these longitudinal ridges. This is mechanically predestined because the fracture must follow the alignment and geometry of the ridge. In cross-section the blade-like flakes are triangular or quadrangular, depending on the number of longitudinal ridges along the outside, or dorsal, surface. Very small stone blades, called bladelets or microblades, are the earliest artefact types to appear, and are distributed across the southern part of the continent. These bladelets were detached from cores usually less than five centimetres long. While microblades sometimes were used without further modification, the end products usually were microliths, small bladelets abruptly trimmed to a standard design, which were probably spear barbs. It was only within the last 2000 years that stone blades of a much larger size, called macroblades, began to be made. Macroblades are found in northern and central Australia, where they were used as knife and fighting pick blades and as spear points.

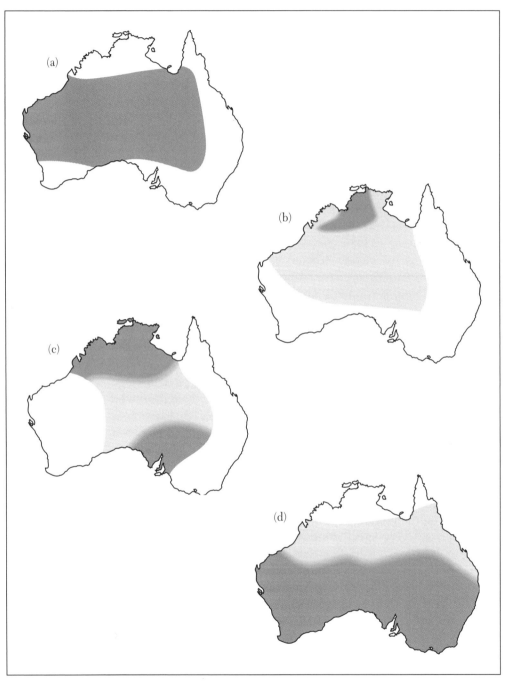

Map 12. *Distributions of stone tool types (dark shading indicates main concentrations): (a) tulas; (b) macroblades (dark shading indicates area of archaeological finds); (c) unifacial and bifacial points; (d) microliths. (Rebecca Parkes)*

While the application of pressure in shaping a tool or to resharpen its cutting edge is apparent in the Pleistocene, it reached a new level of sophistication in the production of delicately retouched spear points. The adoption of finely shaped spear points and spear barbs also heralded a dramatic increase in controlled heating of siliceous stone such as silcrete and chert. This process reduced the fracture toughness of the stone and permitted finer workmanship. With heat treatment the stone core was buried in sand under a small fire and baked for about eight hours at a temperature of at least 300°C. In altering the mineral composition and structure of the stone, it also reduced its fracture toughness, which made possible the creation of longer flakes with finer cutting edges. In iron-rich siliceous stone there were also colour changes from grey or yellow to red, purple or pink, which may have had aesthetic appeal or symbolic meaning.

CHRONOLOGY OF NEW TYPES

Spear points fashioned by finely executed pressure flaking heralded the beginning of the Australian Small Tool Phase. As outlined above, the best estimate for the first appearance of these points is 6000–5000 years BP, which is the age range for specimens excavated from Nauwalabila rockshelter in Kakadu National Park. The first appearances of the other implement types are spread over the succeeding millennia, and some even appear to be less than 1000 years. One of the difficulties in reliably establishing the first appearance of a new implement type is that the specimens buried deep in an archaeological deposit are not necessarily in their original stratigraphic context even though there is no evidence of disturbance in the sediments. A classic example of this has been demonstrated by Norma Richardson, who studied the stone artefacts from Kenniff Cave, excavated many years before by Mulvaney. Richardson used a procedure called 'conjoin analysis', in which flakes are fitted onto the cores from which they had been struck. She found that, despite the exact chronology that had been argued for the new implement types, their true ages could be anywhere between 5000 and 2500 years BP.

While there are claims of 6000 years BP for microblade technology and delicately retouched microliths, their more certain first common occurrence in different regions dates to about 4000 years BP. In the 1000 years that followed, microlithic technology diffused across southern Australia. It became well established in southwestern

Australia, and particularly so in southeastern Australia where microliths and flaking debris from microblade production occur extensively in the uppermost sediments of Aboriginal camping localities. Although microliths are found primarily in southern Australia, there also have been discoveries of small numbers in some northern localities.

MICROLITHS

Microliths are small implements made from regular blades struck from a small core and from other kinds of flakes including pieces from bipolar cores. Some prehistorians have preferred to call these implements 'backed blades', though not all are made from blade-like flakes. Distinctive features are a generally triangular cross-section, penknife-blade or various geometric shapes, and abruptly-angled retouch which has shaped both the flake into its standard design and provided the implement with a thick, blunt back. The retouch was done by pressing a small stone hammer or retoucher onto the flake's edge while it rested firmly on a wooden base. Microliths range in length from just under a centimetre to five centimetres, with most about two to three centimetres long. Some are so tiny that low magnification is needed to identify them with certainty. Rock types from which microliths are made include silcrete, chert, chalcedony, good quality quartz, and certain kinds of fine-grained volcanic stone.

There are about six basic microlith types in Australia—the 'bondi point'-type, which was first found in the dunes of Bondi Beach at the end of the nineteenth century, and a range of geometric shapes, mostly triangular, trapezoidal, and segment or half-moon shapes. The major distribution of the bondi point is along the southeast coast, but specimens have been found as far north as the Keppel Islands. A crescentic variation of the segment occurs in a small part of coastal Victoria and there are isolated occurrences of microliths obliquely angled at their distal end in New South Wales and Western Australia. Geometric microliths are commonly found inland and across to the Western Australian coast. There have been a few isolated finds of microliths in lithic scatters in the Northern Territory and northwestern Queensland. Since these appear to be made from locally available stone, there is no reason to assume that they were traded from the south where microliths are common. The antiquity of these

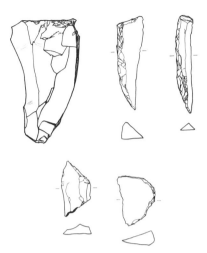

Microblade core, 5.5 centimetres long (top left), bondi points (top right) and two geometric microliths (bottom). (Drawing by G. Happ)

northernmost finds is not known, but they may be of recent prehistoric age.

At Fromm's Landing, Mulvaney obtained the first reliable dates for microliths in stratigraphic context. This radiocarbon determination of about 4000–5000 years BP still serves as a fair approximation marker within a cluster of early dates from different excavation around the country. There are some earlier dates in mainland Australia, for instance, 6000 years BP at the Northcliffe silcrete quarry in the continent's southwest and at Bushranger's Cave near Brisbane on the east coast. However, it is possible that some implements at these sites have settled downward in the sediments. The best set of dates is around 4000 years BP, when they first appear in the Pilbara region of Western Australia, and along the eastern seaboard as far north as Cape York Peninsula. They did not appear in the forestlands of the southwest until about 3000 years BP. Microliths disappear at many archaeological sites between about 1000 and 2000 years BP, but in some areas on the east coast they continue until a few hundred years ago. It is possible that microliths were still being made along the Darling River and other areas when British colonists arrived.

In the past there has been speculation about microlith function, and uses as periwinkle-pickers and body scarification knives were even suggested. None of these, however, offered an explanation of why such vast numbers have been found. For instance, at Arcoona west of Lake Torrens some 20,000 microliths were collected and are now in the South Australian Museum.

It is widely thought that microliths were probably barbs on hunting and fighting spears, a function suggested originally by Mulvaney in 1960. Transversely broken microliths are common finds at sites on the eastern seaboard, representing failures during their production or discarded pieces during spear repairs. Hafted microliths have never been found, but there are examples from rockshelters in the New England and Pilbara regions that have traces of hafting resin on them.

THUMBNAIL SCRAPERS

Very small thumbnail scrapers were also made from flakes struck from microblade cores, normally associated with bondi points or other microliths, but always in small numbers. They are much more regular in shape than pre-microlithic thumbnail scrapers, and it is unlikely they were used to scrape wood or other material since no woodworking use-wear has been detected on them, and none have been resharpened to an exhausted 'slug' form. We add to the speculation about their function with the suggestion that they may be components of a spear armature ensemble.

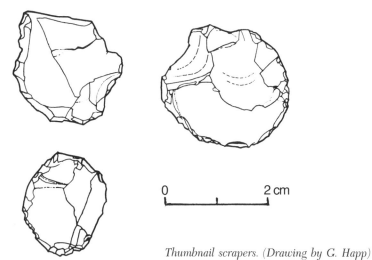

0   2 cm

Thumbnail scrapers. (Drawing by G. Happ)

Plate I *Hawk trap, Victoria River Downs. A brush roof hid the hunter. (Darrell Lewis)*

Plate II *Hatchet grinding grooves on a sandstone rock in Kangaroo Valley, New South Wales. (D. J. Mulvaney)*

Plate III *Necklace of kangaroo teeth, marsupial jaws and hammerstones found with the Cooma burials.*
(New South Wales National Parks and Wildlife Service, S. Cohen)

Plate IV *Aboriginal plant foods. Clockwise from top left: vanilla lily* (Arthropodium *sp.) from the Australian alps—such tubers are widespread (B. Gott); rhizome of* Typha domingensis *(Cumbungi), a staple food in southeastern and Western Australia (B. Gott); lerp on a* Eucalyptus behriana *(bull mallee) leaf, a sugary casing spun by minute insects (B. Gott);* Macrozamia communis *cycad, a carbohydrate staple along the east coast of Australia—it requires leaching to remove toxicity (D. J. Mulvaney).*

Plate V *Central Australian women's equipment. Left to right: pitchi (or coolamon), a carrying vessel made of lightweight wood; pad of hair and feathers, placed on the head for carrying a pitchi; set of flat-faced grindstones; digging stick; and millstone and muller for wet-seed grinding. (M. A. Smith)*

Plate VI *Jinmium rockshelter, Keep River area, Northern Territory, site of disputed claims of great antiquity for human occupation. (Ken Mulvaney)*

Plate VII *Aerial view of Lake Mungo lunette after rain, looking north over area of archaeological discoveries; the lake bed is on the left.* (D. J. Mulvaney)

Plate VIII *Excavation through the Lake Mungo lunette, 1973. The dark horizon is the Mungo unit and the date of a hearth just below this floor level was around 32,000 years* BP. (D. J. Mulvaney)

Plate IX *Cape du Couedic rockshelter, Kangaroo Island, a mid-Holocene occupation site. This coastal shelter was visited for about 2000 years, around the time the sea reached its present level. The deposit contains the bones of locally extinct sea lions and both 'Kartan' and small flake tools.* (Neale Draper)

Plate X *Awabakal people exploiting the sea coast in about 1820, probably at Red Head, near Newcastle. (Painting by Joseph Lycett; courtesy National Library of Australia)*

Plate XI *Left: The main panel at Yankee Hat rockshelter, Australian Capital Territory. Right: Panel of stick figures at Mount Grenfell, New South Wales. (G. L. Walsh)*

Plate XII (left) *Quinkan figures in the Laura rock art province, Queensland. (G. L. Walsh)*

Plate XIII (below) *Arnhem Land art, the Taçon–Chippindale scheme. Clockwise from top left: large naturalistic kangaroos; Dynamic Figure Style hunter spearing an emu, with the dashes symbolising the flight of the spear (and perhaps the spirit or life essence of the bird); Yam figure holding the tail of a Yam Style rainbow serpent; Kangaroo in X-ray Style. (G. L. Walsh)*

Plate XIV *Long panel of anthropomorphic figures, Victoria River District, Northern Territory. (G. L. Walsh)*

Plate XV *Anuru Bay Macassan trepanging site, Arnhem Land. The tall tree is a tamarind; fourteen lines of stones which supported trepang boiling cauldrons are located at the right, and the mangroves provided fuel. (D. J. Mulvaney)*

Plate XVI *Kimberley Wandjina art being renewed by a traditional artist in 1966. (Western Australian Museum)*

FLAKED STONE POINTS

Varieties of finely flaked spear points appear in the archaeological record at about 5000–6000 years BP and begin to disappear after about 2500 years ago. In the north and centre they are succeeded by a new type of long stone blade, which spread over the last 1500 to 1000 years. In the Kimberley region a new type of bifacially pressure-flaked spear point with a serrated edge also appears, but it may be a recent innovation. The manufacture of such attractive artefacts flourished following the availability of European glass and porcelain.

UNIFACE AND BIFACE FLAKED POINTS

These flaked points are commonly made of quartzite or silcrete. Although they range between one and eight centimetres in length, most are small; in Arnhem Land their length is between three and five centimetres. As a general group, uniface and biface points are distributed from the north to the south coast across the central third of Australia. Within this region there are discrete southern and northern varieties of uniface points. Biface points occur only in the north and some appear to be reshaped uniface points. If found overseas, many of these stone points would probably be identified as arrow heads, but there is no evidence that the Australian Aborigines ever possessed the bow. Undoubtedly they were spearheads.

The southern uniface points (formerly called pirri point) are symmetrical and leaf-shaped. One side of the point bears extensive flaking, usually by pressure. The butt end is commonly thinned by flaking from both sides. The flake scars, which run inwards from the sides of the implement, meet in the centre, giving it a low triangular cross-section. Some roughly shaped specimens in the far south are of poor-quality stone. Considerable variation occurs locally among the northern uniface and biface points, where they occur together in archaeological deposits, with uniface ones usually in the majority. Many have been made by percussion flaking with a small hammer, but others have the extra finish of delicate pressure-flaking. The bulb of force is usually left untouched on northern uniface points. At Ingaladdi rockshelter in the Northern Territory, stone points appear only about 3000 years ago, and their template is a standardised flake of lancet shape. While such a flake preform has not been demonstrated for other sites it is probably more widespread. A local attribute

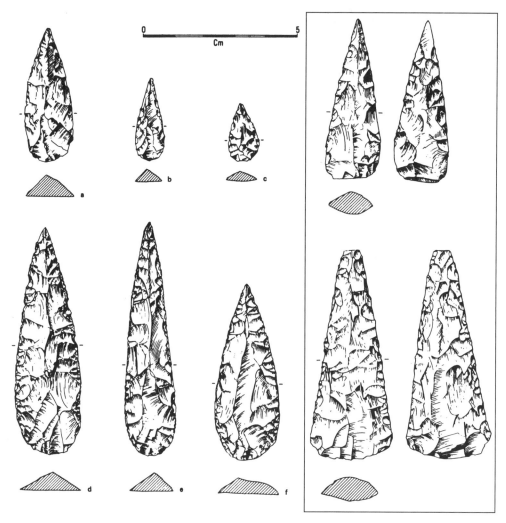

Left: Unifacially flaked points; right: bifacially flaked points. (Drawings by W. Mumford)

of some of the Ingaladdi points is fine serration of their edges by pressure indentation.

KIMBERLEY POINT

Many prehistorians judge the bifacially flaked Kimberley point to be Australia's most aesthetically appealing type of stone implement. They are made from fine-grained siliceous stone suitable for pressure-flaking or heat-treated to improve their flaking quality. Those made of stone range in length from two to ten centimetres. Those made of bottle or plate glass and made during the last hundred years (many by Aboriginal inmates of Broome Prison as curios for sale to visitors), may be as much as twenty centimetres long. After a flake-blank is selected, it is shaped into a preform by flaking with a small hammerstone and then pressing off smaller flakes by applying pressure with a short pointed shaft of dense wood. The final stages carefully thin the preform by more delicate pressure-flaking with a pointed bone and complete it with fine serration or dentation along its edges. There may be two regional varieties, distinguished by the fineness of the pressure-flaking and serration, but this has yet to be demonstrated by detailed typological study.

On the Kimberley Plateau and in the semi-arid country to the west, Kimberley points were hafted on a spear used for hunting euros and other large game. Ethnographers have observed that they are much more fragile than other types of stone points, and that there was a high breakage rate. The tribes of the eastern Kimberley region acknowledged the limitations of their own product: they imported mulga-tipped hunting spears from the south because their performance was superior. But the incidence of breakages may be overplayed because the smaller specimens, which are most common, are less fragile. Kimberley point manufacture required more skill than that needed for making any other stone tool type in Australia. The missionary J. R. B. Love remarked that 'spearhead making is the most constant employment of the men'—it was a tribal craft.

Kimberley points were admired by people living as much as 1400 kilometres southeast of the Kimberley region. The demand for them in the desert arose not only from their aesthetic qualities but also from their mythological significance, which they had acquired since leaving the Kimberley Plateau. Those carried to central Australia and the Western Desert became knives, and they were given a resin and wood handle, decorated with lines and dots. These knives were male prestige items; they were used strictly for such ceremonial activities as circumcision operations, some even after their edges became blunt.

Tindale observed many decades ago that Kimberley points appear to be a very recent addition to the Aboriginal tool-kit. They have been found only rarely in archaeological deposits, such as at Sleisbeck rockshelter in the southern part of Kakadu National Park, and then only in the topmost level. We assume that the Kimberley point could

Tool-kit for making Kimberley points: eighteen spear points, some unfinished, in a paperbark parcel tied with human hair; bone and wood pressure-flaking tools; two large finished points, the right-hand one made of glass. (Museum of Victoria)

only have developed out of a pre-existing tradition of pressure-flaking, and if this is the case, then either it has a greater antiquity than demonstrated, or the earlier biface points continued to be made in the northwest until very recent prehistoric times.

MACROBLADES

Macroblades are large, more or less prismatic, pointed stone flakes, with one or more ridges aligned along the length of the flake. Usually they are of quartzite and silcrete, or of chert in regions where cores of suitable size are available. The size range is about five to more than 30 centimetres. Sometimes they are retouched on the butt or along their lateral margins.

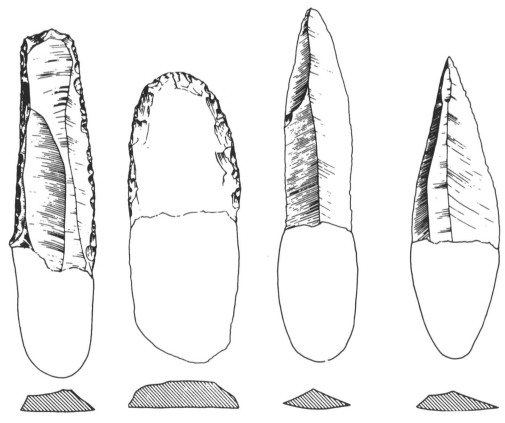

Macroblades with resin grips (called 'leilira') collected in central Australia a century ago. (Drawing by W. Mumford)

Baldwin Spencer observed the production of macroblades in central Australia and noted that for every acceptable blade a score of similar ones was discarded; on one afternoon at Camooweal in north-western Queensland, Walter Roth watched four old men strike off a total of 300 flakes before one was considered suitable for hafting. However, the stone cores at some macroblade quarries are prismatic, but at other quarries they are less formalised. Hafted macroblades in museum collections are not always as symmetrical and regular in size as might be expected from ethnographic accounts.

Macroblades served a number of different purposes: primarily they were the points of spears for fighting and for hunting large macropods, and also the blades of knives and fighting-picks. The more specialised functions included ritual body scarification, and surgical circumcision and sub-incision. One variety was retouched on its end and used as an eating utensil. In central Australia the all-purpose macroblade knife, called 'leilira', had a resin hand-grip, or a resin-hafted wooden handle. The knives carried by the men were usually long, pointed flakes. In Wongkangurru country around Lake Eyre, macroblade duelling knives had a curve to their end for ripping the skin of an opponent during ritualised combat. Women's macroblade knives were trimmed to have a rounded distal end.

One type of retouched macroblade is known archaeologically from the Kakadu region and further south around Katherine, where it has been found in rockshelters. They are retouched into rectilinear or squarish shapes, and often have a squared, concave or obliquely angled distal end; one specimen we examined was even pointed on one side of the end. The function of these rectilinear retouched blades is not known, but one specimen in the Australian Museum has hafting resin on its butt. These peculiar implements are not documented ethnographically, though they are at least recent prehistoric, and they are unique in the Aboriginal stone tool-kit. We speculate that they may have served as special-purpose spearheads or knives, but the quartzite from which they are made provides little scope for testing the hypothesis by a use-wear studies.

Harry Allen has studied macroblades in detail and traces their origin to the east Kimberley and Victoria River regions. Diffusion outwards from this point of origin occurred only during the last 1000 to 1500 years. In Kakadu, which is not far distant, macroblades appeared only in the last 1000 years, and in central Australia they are probably even more recent arrivals; by the twentieth century they had spread halfway down the Western Australian coast and, inland, to the northern edge of the Nullarbor Plain.

Large workshop-quarries for macroblades are found throughout their area of distribution, from coastal Arnhem Land to the arid interior. Stone blades were traded widely from mythologically sanctioned quarries, the most famous being Ngilipitji, 45 kilometres inland from Blue Mud Bay in eastern Arnhem Land, which was first recorded by Donald Thomson. Ngilipitji blades were carefully wrapped in paperbark tied with string to protect their edges during their journeys to other parts of Arnhem Land. Robert Paton has observed that the social and ritual functions of exchange were an end in themselves and the utilitarian value of the stone was relatively insignificant.

Flaking spearheads at Ngilipitji quarry, eastern Arnhem Land, 1935. Note the display of quartzite spearheads, trade-bundles and hammerstones. (Photo Donald Thomson; reproduced with the permission of Mrs D. M. Thomson and Museum of Victoria)

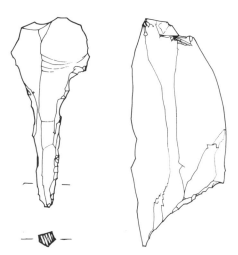

Left: drill, central Queensland; right: obliquely retouched blade, Boulia region, western Queensland. (Drawings by G. Happ)

Blade technology in western Queensland

Evident from a few collections made at lithic scatters in the Boulia district of western Queensland is a flourishing blade technology with its own distinct regional character. These collections, now in the Queensland Museum, are largely unstudied. They contain implements of fine cherts and silcretes, and types include large points with oblique trimming and drills made from small prismatic blades. The drills were possibly used in making wooden artefacts and may have been hand-held. These collections are undated but may originate within the last few centuries, some perhaps dating to the early historic era, though there are no ethnographic observations documenting this centre of technological innovation.

Juan knife

The Juan knife is a long flake with abrupt retouch forming a stout back. Nineteenth-century specimens have a skin or resin hand grip. Although the knife's geographical distribution is poorly documented in historical records, it is known ethnographically from western, central and coastal Queensland. There are only a few examples in

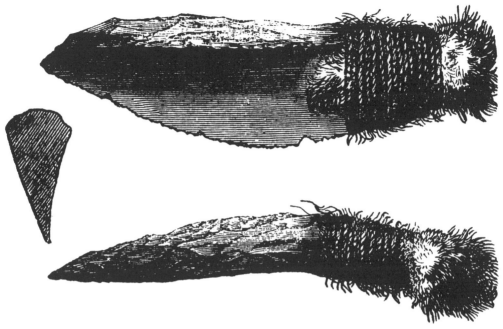

Juan knife, Queensland, length 11.4 centimetres. (John Evans, Ancient Stone Implements, 1897:293)

museum collections. A single archaeological specimen was found on Great Keppel Island off the Queensland coast. As it is of silcrete, which does not occur on the island, it must have come from the mainland. Only two or three Juan knives have turned up in archaeological excavations, and one from Kenniff Cave is less than 600 years old.

HAFTED WOODWORKING SCRAPERS

A generalised type of flake scraper of similar character to some Pleistocene ones, but not evidently linked to this earlier appearance, was widespread within the continent during the Mid and Late Holocene, and is known ethnographically from the arid zone. These implements have been called 'burren adzes', and also are known by several other names (we count five), none of which is particularly appropriate nor used consistently by archaeologists. The ethnographic specimens,

245

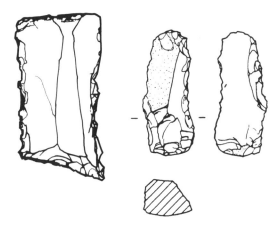

Left: rectangular macroblade, Sleisbeck, length 6.7 centimetres; right: wood scraper, formerly hafted, length 4.6 centimetres. (Drawings by G. Happ)

which were primarily used to chisel and scrape wood, are flakes of chert, chalcedony or fine-grained silcrete, fixed with resin or gum cement onto the end of a wooden handle or spearthrower. One long side of the flake is presented as the cutting edge and has use-wear from wood scraping, and on its upper face resharpening retouch scars. Typically they are progressively retouched until the remnant slug form is replaced with a fresh flake. Archaeological examples, which are usually about three to four centimetres long, fit within the range of ethnographic examples. Their distinguishing attributes are their smallness, generally rectangular shape, retouched cutting edge (sometimes opposing cutting edges when they have been reversed in the cement) and use-wear from woodworking. A few from Cape York Peninsula have traces of hafting resin still preserved on their surfaces. Occasionally they have backing retouch. Worn-out wood scrapers have abruptly stepped retouch along their cutting edge, and under magnification these edges have a rounded cross-section and smoothing polished from the effects of dust and grit during the tool's use.

The small scrapers are found archaeologically over most of Australia, particularly the inland region, from Cape York Peninsula, where they first appear only about 2000 years ago, to the lower

Murray River, and across the arid zone to the forestland of south-west Western Australia. It is possible that the catalyst for their spread throughout the interior was their value as a component of lightweight maintenance and hunting equipment.

Warlpiri man from Yuendumu using a tula adze mounted on a wooden handle, with characteristic two-handed grip. This arid-zone tool almost certainly was a regional invention. (Robert Edwards)

247

TULA ADZE

The most commonly encountered new-fashion tool-type in arid Australia is the tula adze, which has an earliest radiocarbon date of 2700–3600 years BP at the central Australian site of Kwerlpe, and continued to be made until replaced by steel in the twentieth century. Ethnographically, the tula was mounted on two types of artefacts. One is a robust adze handle, somewhat similar in appearance to a short throwing club. This handle was grasped with both hands and drawn towards the operator to adze, shave and incise wood. Tulas were also mounted on the handle end of a lightweight multipurpose spearthrower, particularly in regions where long distances between water sources had to be traversed. The size range for tulas is large (1.5 to six centimetres in width). Those on spearthrowers were smaller, functioning not as adzes but as light-duty wood scrapers, mostly for making and maintaining spears, and for butchering tasks. Occasionally a tula was provided with a simple resin grip and served as a knife.

The fundamental elements of this design are the convex contour of the tool's underside surface and the convexity of the cutting edge

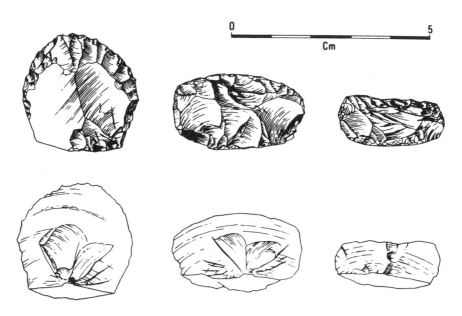

Tula adze flakes, in various degrees of wear. (Drawing by W. Mumford)

in plan-view. These features are derived from the surface curvature of the conchoidal flake from which the tool is flaked. The part of the flake around this bulb was removed by careful flaking. The convex face provided by the bulb of force acted to distribute the stress of adzing impact progressively and uniformly along the cutting edge as it cut into the wood, and minimised the bending stresses in the resin haft during use. The stone types used are silcrete, chert and chalcedony, and strong regional preferences are evident—chert was favoured in central Australia and southwest Queensland, while in the Lake Eyre region the most common stone was fine-quality silcrete. The tula's cutting edge required continual resharpening, which resulted eventually in a steep undercut edge, the same as for the hafted flake scraper. This progressive modification resulted in decreasing size to a slug form. Not surprisingly, most tulas found in archaeological sites are discarded slugs.

Archaeologists have claimed that the tula is a local invention of unique design. It is ideal for working intractable timbers of Australia's arid region, and in particular acacias such as mulga and gidgee. The tool's design is simple but sophisticated: this relatively small, lightweight flake tool could be employed to adze dense wood more effectively, and with more flexibility and precision than a heavy stone chopper, which no doubt it supplanted. The ability of the tula to operate efficiently, even when it was reduced to a narrow slug by resharpening, depended upon the quality of the resin used to fix it on the handle. The best quality was porcupine grass (*Triodia* species), and the best of these, *Triodia pungens* which emits an aroma when softened by heat. The distribution of *Triodia* is within that of tulas and the two are inextricably tied—without the resin there would be no tula, and in regions where *Triodia* did not grow it had to be obtained by trade. We believe that the case for the tula being an innovation of the Australian arid zone is very strong.

PIRRI GRAVER

The pirri graver is the most recently identified ethnographic stone tool of the arid zone and was formally described only in 1985. Prior to this time, all but one specimen in museum collections had been misidentified as tulas or other woodworking tools and, in one instance, as a hafted microlith. This wood graver is made from the curved distal end of a flake of chert, chalcedony or fine silcrete. Often

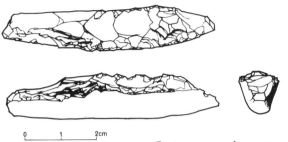

Pirri gravers and a pirri graver slug.
(Drawings by G. Happ)

a flake was chosen which has a hinged end, where the fracture that formed the flake has curved back up. All of the flake except for this curved part was eliminated by flaking, which left a heavily retouched top face on the tool. The cutting edge of the graver is at the end, or sometimes on both ends if the tool has been reversed in its resin haft. The largest examples are eight centimetres long, but most are considerably shorter than this, and because of resharpening, which progressively shortens the tool, it has a discard slug, similar to the tula. Pirri gravers have a range of curvatures and cutting edge widths which match the grooves regularly cut into different kinds of wooden artefacts; for instance, broad, shallow grooves are found on light-wood shields and coolamons, medium-sized grooves on boomerangs, and narrow grooves on spear shafts. We envisage that men kept graduated sets of pirri gravers for applying the finishing touches to the different wooden artefacts.

All the ethnographic and archaeological specimens have been found within the distribution of tula adzes, so this tool type may have been as widespread and equally dependent upon *Triodia* resin. Most hafted examples are from the Aboriginal tribes living around Lake Eyre, but a number of surface archaeological finds extend the distribution to the channel country of western Queensland, which was linked to the Lake Eyre region by a long-distance exchange network. Other unequivocal finds are from semi-arid country further north and in northwestern Australia. Most archaeologists are still unfamiliar with the tool type and it will be many years before its patchy distribution is clarified. The stone artefacts commonly associated with pirri gravers in lithic scatters include tulas and elements of microblade technology, indicating a recent prehistoric context. To date, only one specimen has been identified in an

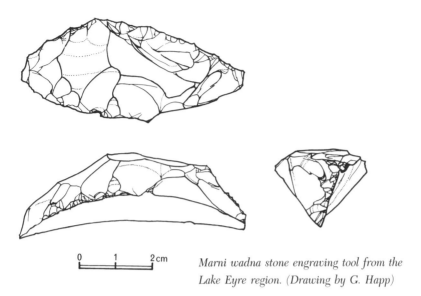

0   1   2 cm

Marni wadna stone engraving tool from the Lake Eyre region. (Drawing by G. Happ)

archaeological excavation, from the topmost layer at Intirtekwerle rockshelter in central Australia.

MARNI WADNA

This ethnographic stone tool type was first described in the 1920s by mounted policeman George Aiston, who was stationed near Lake Eyre. Like the pirri graver, the marni wadna is a specialised hafted wood graver of the arid zone for making grooves of V-shaped cross-section on a range of wooden artefacts, including women's digging bowls. It is closely linked with the pirri graver and the tula, in its probable antiquity, uses, mode of hafting, transformation of shape to a slug form during use-life, and probably also origins and geographical distribution. All three have designs which are apparently unique in stone technology.

The marni wadna is superficially similar in shape to the elouera found along the eastern seaboard in that it is shaped like an orange segment. In size these tools range up to about nine centimetres. The shape is achieved by striking off a right-angled corner of a core. The ends of this triangular-sectioned flake are then chipped with a small hammerstone, partly by bipolar flaking, to create a thick semicircular back, intended as the top of the graver. Like the pirri graver, the

251

cutting edge is an end of the segment-shaped tool. Progressively as the edge is resharpened, the tool becomes shorter on one side than the other, and more asymmetrical, until it is discarded as useless.

Eleven archaeological specimens, all from lithic scatters, and two mounted ethnographic specimens have been identified. The distribution of these is the Lake Eyre region and the Barkly Tableland to the north, the territory of the Wambaya tribe which participated in the central Australian exchange network. Although the marni wadna may have a wide distribution in Australia's arid zone, it is so specialised that it may be archaeologically rare.

ELOUERA

The elouera is one of the most recent additions to the Aboriginal stone tool-kit and may have appeared only about 1600 years ago. In archaeological sites they are found either in association with, or above, microlith-rich levels. Possibly they were still in use in 1788, but if so there is no surviving description. The implement resembles an orange segment in shape, with a somewhat triangular cross-section, and blunting retouch forming a thick back. The underside of the tool is the inner fracture face of the flake selected as the tool blank, and it is flat or moderately convex. Most specimens are between three and four centimetres wide, although exceptionally large ones three times this size have been found in lithic scatters in the Hunter Valley, New South Wales. The stone types favoured for making eloueras are silcrete, chalcedony, and a fine-grained silicified tuff (formed from volcanic ash). Eloueras have been found on the central and southern coastline of New South Wales (from Port Macquarie in the north to Murramarang in the south) and inland from Sydney at least as far as the sandstone gorges incised into the western edge of the Great Dividing Range.

Most eloueras display a distinctive smoothing wear on their cutting edge, prompting much speculation about their use. Suggestions have included skinning and butchering knives, wood scrapers and even body scarifiers. While the surface abrasion is similar to wear sometimes seen on hafted stone adzes, few eloueras have been resharpened by edge-retouch which is necessary to maintain normal flake adzes. Also, the pronounced edge blunting on eloueras is notably different, and sometimes the stone from which they are made of poor quality. These can only indicate that maintaining sharpness was not

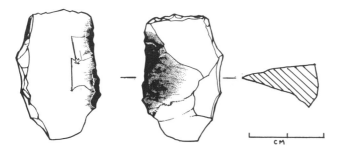

Elouera with use-polish (indicated by stippling). (Drawing by G. Happ)

important for the tool's efficiency. We believe that the elouera may have been fixed on the end of a wooden handle, or perhaps even a digging stick, and used to obtain or process food plants that had woody or strongly fibrous tissue. Candidates are cumbungi (*Typha*) and bracken fern. General ethnographic analogy indicates that such a tool would have been used primarily by women. Replicative experiments using hafted eloueras and identification of any microscopic plant residues preserved on cutting edges of archaeological specimens are necessary to clinch an identification of their function.

GROUND-STONE TOOLS

In the Early Holocene ground stone tools continue in northern Australia, but are only represented from Cape York Peninsula and Kakadu by a few complete specimens of hatchet heads and some flakes struck off ground tools. In ethnographic contexts the possum-hunting and honey-collecting implement, the ground-edge hatchet, continued in tropical Australia. Ground stone technology first appears in southeastern Australia at least 4300 years BP, and by the nineteenth century there is considerable variation in hatchet head styles, and the addition of some smaller implement types, such as chisels and what may be a knife. None has ever been found in Tasmania, suggesting diffusion from the north after the sea cut Tasmania off from the mainland.

There is considerable size and shape variation in the design of hatchet heads. This is because the stone materials suitable for hatchet heads are obtained as large pieces up to cobble size, and they are amenable to the full range of shaping methods, flaking, pecking and grinding, which allow precise three-dimensional modelling. The plan-shape of hatchet heads is often rectangular, but there are marked regional variations in the size, shape and the degree of finish, both archaeologically and in collections of nineteenth-century specimens. One common variety of hatchet head is made from a water-worn pebble, minimally flaked to rough out the cutting edge, and ground a little on this flaked area, which often is only on one side. At the preferred gravel beds along the Shoalhaven River, and the Snowy River near Jindabyne in New South Wales, flattish pebbles were selected and flaked on the spot.

Among the most interesting variants are large pecked and grooved hatchets in southeastern Australia. Victorian specimens are known with one or two encircling grooves and one or more median or diag-onal grooves which extend round the butt to join the encircling grooves. Although these were certainly designed to facilitate the firm attachment of a handle, there are no historical records of specimens so hafted, and the type is truly prehistoric. Another unusual feature of these tools is their large size and weight (some weigh more than two kilograms). There are other distinctive and elegant types, includ-ing a cylindrical one and a pecked oval type made from dolerite outcrops around Cloncurry and Mount Isa in Queensland. These were keenly sought by the Aborigines living around Lake Eyre, who exchanged pituri for them.

In southeastern Australia fine-grained whetstones for resharpening hatchets and edge-ground adzes were added to the tool-kit; while the specimens appear to be recent, none have yet been properly dated. Also evident in southeastern Australia are small edge-ground pebble adzes or chisels, some over ten centimetres in length. A few of these have abrasion on their butt ends from hammer usage, which may be from flaking microblade cores. Similar implements are known ethno-graphically in the Kimberley region. A distinctive edge-ground knife, named bulga knife by Frederick McCarthy, occurs along the central New South Wales coast and inland as far as Goulburn. It is ovoid or rectangular in plan and has a straight cutting edge formed by grind-ing both sides, similar to most hatchets. The only dated specimen, about 600 years old, is from an excavation west of Sydney.

Distributed in the semi-arid country from Adelaide to north of the Flinders Ranges is the peculiar reniform scraper, a kidney-shaped implement made from thin, tabular pieces of siltstone, shale or phyllite, chipped to shape and then ground smooth around its periphery and on its cutting edge. Herbert Basedow, the distinguished

Adelaide physician and ethnologist, was instructed by an Aboriginal elder in their use to scrape furskins for cloaks. A use-wear study by Kamminga is consistent with this function. Except for a single fragment excavated at Roonka cemetery on the lower Murray River, all the known examples are surface finds, and most are broken pieces. They appear to be a Holocene tool-type, and may date only to recent prehistoric and early historic times.

GRINDSTONES

At the time of British colonisation the inventory of Aboriginal grindstones included at least five different types, each of which was specialised to varying degrees for processing particular plant products. Preference for different designs to suit specific grinding tasks is evident, but no comprehensive study exists. The sample of excavated grindstones is very small compared to numerous specimens found on

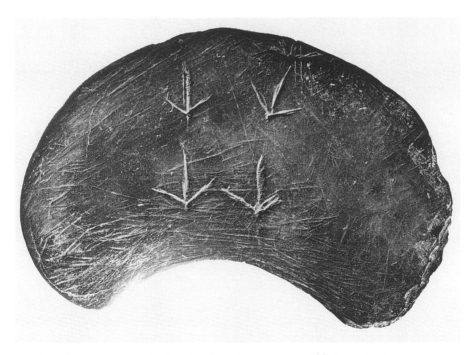

Reniform slate scraper from Findon; length 11.8 centimetres, width 6.3 centimetres. (South Australian Museum)

the surface, mostly of Late Holocene age, which cram the storage shelves of Australian museums.

The grinding of 'soft' grass seeds may have an antiquity similar to that of the harder seeds, and there are finds suggesting a continuation of dry grinding from the Pleistocene and through the Holocene. Millstones for wet grinding do not appear in full force until 3000 to 4000 years ago at the earliest, and more definitely within the last 2000 years. By historic times wet milling was practised throughout much of the arid zone and along the rivers flowing west from the Great Dividing Range. The specialised millstones and mullers for wet milling are the heaviest of all grinding stones and are easily distinguished. They are large, hammer-pecked sandstone slabs with one or more narrow grooves about ten centimetres wide worn into the surface. The mullers (or top-stones), are round or oval in plan-shape when they are first used but become more elongated and finally triangular or crescent-shaped as they wear. At least one side develops a convex facet. Such large artefacts are often numerous at old camp sites. For example, at Wanmara Spring near the MacDonnell Ranges in central Australia, Mike Smith counted up to 400 mullers scattered over an Aboriginal camp site, along with less-numerous pestles and mortars used for crushing hard seeds.

Although stone tools or stone components of multi-component tools comprised only a small part of prehistoric tool-kits, they are of considerable diagnostic value to those seeking to reconstruct ancient technology and subsistence patterns. In the first place they survive more readily than other materials, while the considerable regional and temporal variations in artefact fashions over the past five millennia or so testify to the dynamic nature of Aboriginal society.

Theories and models: Explaining change $\quad$ 15

The technological innovations of the last few millennia and their social and economic implications promoted numerous theories to explain them. This chapter examines some of these competing explanations.

FOREIGN ORIGINS OF NEW STONE TECHNOLOGY?

For many decades it was difficult for most scholars to believe that microliths and advanced pressure-flaking techniques originated within the continent. They invoked their origins in Indonesia or mainland Southeast Asia and even searched for them. One exception was a self-taught authority on stone tools, a retired East India Company merchant, Herbert Noone, who visited Australia in the 1940s and contributed to McCarthy's 1946 stone tool typology memoir.

We see no reason to infer that any of the innovations in stone technology derive from overseas—whether from castaway fisherfolk, waves of conquering immigrants, or Torres Strait traders. New Guinea is excluded as a possible source on the grounds of artefact typology alone. A single Melanesian-style polished stone axe was found in the last century on Whitsunday Island, but it is unique in Australia and may have been a trade item ultimately passed down from New

Guinea. As for the Torres Strait Islands and both mainlands opposite, most tools were made of shell, bone and other organic materials rather than stone, and flaked stone artefacts from archaeological excavations are nondescript in appearance. Microblade technology first appeared in mainland Southeast Asia at about 8000 years BP, probably from southern China, and ultimately was brought to the Philippines and Indonesia. In Java, Sulawesi and certain other islands there are various types of microliths and points that are superficially comparable to Australian ones. While earlier scholars took the similarities as evidence of a historical link, we find no persuasive evidence linking the Australian and Southeast Asian stone technologies at any time in the past. Australian microliths and retouched points are distinctively Antipodean in style. From a geographic plot of radiocarbon dates for Australian microliths Robert Pearce inferred a probable origin in southeastern Australia and their spread northwards over the following thousand years, which is the wrong point of origin and direction of diffusion if microliths had come from overseas.

Despite the considerable evidence to the contrary, some archaeologists still argue that the new implement types are a single cultural package from overseas, even speculating that the dingo and the practice of plant detoxification in food processing were also part of this package. The evidence is lacking. Detoxification of cycads dates from the Early Holocene or before, while the adhesive properties of *Triodia* resin (spinifex) throughout the arid regions offer one logical explanation for the adoption and regional adaptations of composite tool technology. As for the dingo, it was a late migrant.

THE DINGO

The dingo (*Canis familiaris*) is a feral dog, directly descended from the early domestic dog of Southeast Asia. Its ultimate ancestry is from the Indian wolf (*Canis lupus pallipes*). The close resemblances between the dingo and living indigenous domestic dogs in Southeast Asia indicate that both varieties have remained relatively pure-bred since their separation and that they still form a single early breed of dog.

Most commonly the dingo has a ginger coat, with white paws, chest and tail tip. It is thought that the various other colourations seen today are the outcome of admixture with European dogs. The dingo breeds once a year; it is usually solitary although in some regions it hunts in pairs or in packs to run down large animals. It

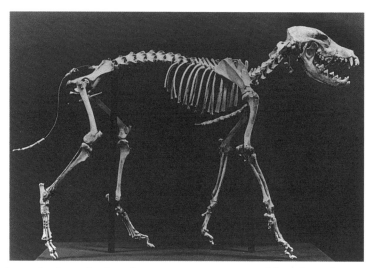

Skeleton of a dingo dated to about 3000 years BP, excavated by John Mulvaney at Fromm's Landing.

can bark when seriously alarmed but does not do so in normal circumstances (a propensity for barking was selected in developing the modern breeds of domestic dogs). In some parts of Australia, especially the dry interior, semi-domesticated dingoes, which support themselves by foraging around camps, were used by Aborigines in hunting, for instance, to find and run down emus, kangaroos and wallabies, and corner bandicoots and possums. They were also camp scavengers, and served as guard dogs and companions useful for keeping warm during cold nights. In southeastern Australia the dingo was not commonly a camp dog, perhaps as N. B. Tindale has suggested, because it could not be trusted to leave alone valuable furskin cloaks. Although the dingo was credited with keeping malevolent spirits away from camp and integrated in Dreaming mythology, it was never portrayed as a heroic creation being.

Australian dingoes were first observed by the crew of a passing vessel in the Torres Strait Islands in 1792 and, until this century, it was assumed that the dog had arrived with the ancestors of the Aborigines. However, this did not explain why dingoes never reached Tasmania, which was separated from the mainland when rising seas created Bass Strait about 12,000 years ago. The oldest reliable radiocarbon date for the bones of a dingo in Australia is 3450±95 years BP, from Madura Cave on the Nullarbor Plain. Two other radiocarbon dates are slightly younger than the Nullarbor find—about 3200 years BP from a canine tooth from a midden at Wombah in northern New South Wales and 3000 years BP for an almost complete skeleton of a male dingo Mulvaney excavated at Fromm's Landing.

The arrival of the dingo in northern Australia by 3500–4000 years BP fits reasonably well with the evidence for dogs in Borneo by about 4500 years BP, and on Tikopia and the Solomon Islands by 2750 years BP. There is little doubt that dogs were first taken to the islands of Southeast Asia and Melanesia by Asian seafarers spreading progressively eastwards in their sturdy outrigger canoes. The introduction of the dingo into northern Australia could have occurred during exploratory landings on the Australian coastline or through seafaring misadventure. A leading authority on the dingo, L. K. Corbett, speculates that these Asian dogs not only served in hunting, and guarding and as companions, but also as a food delicacy. Dingo was not usually eaten in Australia, but is still much relished in parts of Southeast Asia and New Guinea and might have survived its shipment as live meat.

While the earliest evidence of dog in New Guinea is less than 1000 years old in the highlands, and no more than 2000 years BP on the south coast, it is likely that much older remains will be found. The New Guinea wild dog, also kept by villagers for hunting and companionship, is smaller than the dingo but in other respects very similar. It is therefore possible that the dingo first arrived in mainland Australia, and more specifically northern Cape York Peninsula, from coastal Papuan villages via the Torres Strait Islands.

Considering that it took the introduced red fox only 70 years to cross Australia, the dingo's expansion across the continent from its point of arrival similarly may have taken only a few decades. It has long been assumed that it was responsible for the disappearance of the meat-eating Tasmanian tiger (thylacine) and Tasmanian devil from mainland Australia. These two marsupials survived into modern times only in Tasmania. David Horton has argued that if the dingo had contributed to their continental demise the process had been attritional and ended perhaps less than 1000 years ago. However, archaeological evidence for the latest appearance of both the tiger and devil on the mainland coincides with the early dingo remains around 3000 years ago. Engravings of thylacines occur on rock surfaces in the Pilbara or as paintings in Kakadu National Park. For various reasons these images are assumed to be ancient.

CULTURAL DIFFUSION

Another hoary theory is that new concepts, not only stone tools and dogs, came through contact with people to the north of Australia. Grafton Eliot Smith, the expatriate Australian anatomist and influential theorist of cultural diffusion, argued that elements of Aboriginal material culture had been derived from abroad. Debate continues about the extent of foreign influence on Aboriginal culture. From time to time, over many thousands of years monsoon winds must have swept small watercraft from Southeast Asia and Melanesia onto the north Australian coast, probably with minimal cultural impact on Aboriginal societies. For some 250 years Indonesians (Macassans) have visited Arnhem Land to collect trepang and, although direct influence on local cultures is demonstrable, there is no definite evidence of more widespread consequences. For a far longer period there existed sustained transfer of culture across Torres Strait, between coastal people in southern Papua and the Aborigines of Cape York (see Chapters 18 and 21). At about 8500–8000 years BP the remaining isthmus between New Guinea and northeast Australia was breached by channels initially as little as 200 metres wide, which later merged to form the nascent Torres Strait. Even before the creation of Torres Strait, the regional culture of forest dwellers in New Guinea must have differed from that of their southern neighbours who inhabited drier woodland and grassland environments. However, when rising sea cut the isthmus between New Guinea and Australia accelerated development of two very distinct cultural domains followed. Long-distance trading expeditions in Torres Strait, which facilitated two-way cultural diffusion between Papua and Australia's northeast, may have begun millennia ago, but the evidence for island occupation is limited to the last few hundred years. Enduring cultural influences on New Guinea transmitted by Asian seafarers began during the expansion of Austronesian-speaking people expansion eastwards across the Pacific thousands of years ago. Some of these acquired cultural traits may have been taken across Torres Strait and ultimately incorporated into Australian culture.

TRADERS OF TORRES STRAIT

Virtually no direct cultural link existed between Australia and New Guinea in early historic times. All social contact and exchanges from

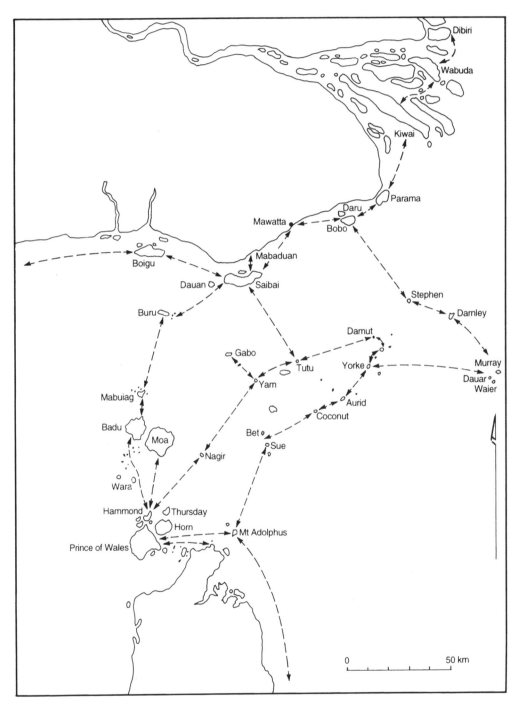

Map 13. *Historical trade routes in Torres Strait. (After Moore 1979)*

either landmass was with and via the Torres Strait Islanders. The Papuan coast of Torres Strait is flood-prone, and in the nineteenth century it sustained only a few scattered communities of ferocious Kiwai head-hunters. The Kiwai were not dedicated seafarers, and had no interest in directly trading with people on the Queensland coast, let alone settling there. However, in historic times some Torres Strait Island groups sailed canoes as far south as the Pascoe River on the east coast and the Pennefather River on the west coast of Cape York Peninsula, a distance of 140 kilometres from its tip. Cultural influence on the material culture is most obvious along the coast of Queensland at least as far as the Keppel Islands, but it may have been more penetrating than this.

The material culture of Torres Strait Islanders had a distinct coastal Papuan character. Probably the most important introductions were those of marine technology, in particular the outrigger canoe. The double-outrigger was used down the west coast of Cape York to Aurukun, and on the east coast as far as Princess Charlotte Bay, and occasionally further south; in the nineteenth century single outriggers were in use along the coast south of Princess Charlotte Bay and in the Whitsunday Islands. Other than the second-hand canoes traded by the Islanders they were local variations and diverged in construction and design features from the Papuan prototype. Melanesian-style fish-hooks diffused along the coast to the Tropic of Capricorn and their first appearance is in a midden on North Keppel Island at about 800–900 years ago. Shell fish-hook lures used along the southeast Australian coast are most probably an independent Australian innovation of comparable antiquity.

The American ethnologist and diffusion theorist D. S. Davidson in the 1930s studied the distribution of Aboriginal cultural traits, and proposed considerable cultural influence on northern Australia, at least in the material domain. His list of foreign introductions included three kinds of knotless netting—simple loop, loop-and-twist, and the most complicated type of knotless netting in Australia, the 'figure-eight' or 'hourglass' technique, which in the nineteenth century was spreading southward from Cape York Peninsula. Davidson speculated that the basic loop-and-twist technique may have derived ultimately from Southeast Asia in recent millennia, with its elaboration in New Guinea, and diffusion across most of Australia. Other items include string figures, two techniques of coiled basketry and the pineapple-headed club. While the distribution patterns provide strong circumstantial evidence of diffusion, direct archaeological corroboration for these inferred borrowings proves elusive. However, the introduction of outrigger canoes and fishing gear enabled a more efficient, intensive and daring exploitation of marine resources than was possible with traditional technology. Dugong and turtles, for example, may have been easier to catch. Whether this resulted in a greater population density remains conjectural.

In addition to its sea lane for diffusion of Papuan culture, Torres Strait acted also as a filter: only certain items and ideas were passed on to Australia and only some were integrated. The use of the bow and arrow must have been understood by some Aborigines who traded with the Islanders, yet they did not adopt the weapon. It was rather the Islanders who desired Aboriginal spears and spearthrowers. Neither was Papuan-style horticulture adopted, even though it was practised in a tenuous way by the Kaurareg of Prince of Wales Island, who planted small plots of sugarcane and yams when the turtle-hunting season proved disappointing.

CULTURAL ADAPTATION EXPLAINED

Recent research on technology, use-wear and tool design have clari-fied understanding of the new stone implements which served as cutting or piercing components of tools and weapons such as knives, adzes, chisels and spears. All were designed for repeated long-term use and, for some, resharpening by retouch to maintain cutting efficiency. The design attributes to maximise the number of resharpenings are particularly notable for the tula adze and gravers of arid Australia which were used until little remained of the original implement. Blades, which are essentially thin, narrow elongated flakes, are of simple design but provide a maximum length of straight sharp cutting edge proportional to the flake's mass, so they make ideal knife blades and spearheads. In general, the expenditure of time and effort in producing the new types was much greater than for tools showing little design, or so-called 'expedient tools'. In particular, fashioning blade implements, Kimberley points and the like required standardised flaking operations and selection of better-quality stone or its improve-ment by heat treatment. If suitable stone was not locally or freely available, the investment in acquiring it was sometimes considerable.

Stone flaking is easily learned, and there is nothing particularly complex about fashioning the new types of implements. Indeed, stan-dardised flake tools were being made during the Pleistocene, and implements like those of the Australian Small Tool Phase could easily have been made much earlier than they were, which poses the obvious question: why were they not? That they reflect or are linked to fundamental changes in culture and human subsistence is assumed by many archaeologists, who offer a number of alternative explanations. The issue cannot be resolved until more is known about the uses and efficiency of stone tool types. For example, there are still differences of opinion about microlith functions. Although we are convinced that they were spear armatures, others suggest that they were used in the hand for cutting, or cemented onto a short stick to form a long knife edge, similar to a taap.

Explanations posed on terms of environmental change, increased efficiency in food procurement, and adaptive advantage have proved popular. Kamminga made microscopic studies of new implement types and believes that the new woodworking tool-kit of the arid zone was demonstrably an adaptation to desert conditions, depending upon the excellent adhesive properties of *Triodia* resin. Speculations about the adoption of finely shaped spear armatures have included their use in spearthrowers, and the cost-effective maintenance of barbed spears for hunting large animals. Neither is supported by evidence of experimental spear use. Mike Morwood noted correlations between the appearance of spear armatures and changes in faunal remains in southeast Queensland sites, but suspects a shift in hunting strategy from individual pursuit of large game to communal hunting of small game, which has implications for more general changes in subsistence behaviour and culture. Explanations such as these tend to be viable only on the regional scale.

RISK-MINIMISATION

Peter Hiscock recently developed an elaborate model, in which microliths, stone points and tulas were elements of a portable tool-kit used by highly mobile groups of people in exploring new territories between about 6000 and 3000 years bp. These groups needed to reduce short-term risks because they were only partially familiar with these territories. Their adaptive strategy included standardising implements, which would make them more reliable and easier to maintain; conserving stone by using specialised flaking procedures for making microblades; and extending the use-life of implements so as to reduce the effort needed to provide replacements. Hiscock adds the corollaries that rapid environmental change caused by the final stage of the rise in sea level may have increased the need for minimising risk in some areas, and that most of the implements became redundant after adaptive pressure lessened during the Late Holocene. Continued use of the implements until late prehistoric and early historic times is attributed to their social or symbolic values. Interestingly, risk minimisation and the need for increasing mobility have also been suggested by Ian McNiven in explaining the use of thumbnail implements in southwest Tasmania during the Last Glacial Maximum.

Many of the assumptions built into the risk-minimisation model are suspect. For instance, we question the premise that microliths were multifunctional, or that stone microliths and spear points were particularly efficient or risk-minimising compared with the alternatives. The notion that blade flaking is an economical way of using stone, proposed earlier to explain Upper Palaeolithic blade technology in Europe, has been challenged for Australia, where considerable wastage in preparatory heat treatment and microlith manufacture is evident. The most obviously adaptive tool, the tula, was never abandoned. Like several other implement types, such as macroblades, Kimberley points, gravers and Juan knives, they continued in use into colonial times.

Hiscock believes that, beginning about 6000 years BP, people recolonised virtually uninhabited territories. This is questionable. Such territories, mostly in the arid zone and the eastern highlands, could hardly have been so devoid of people with detailed resource experience that there was no transfer of knowledge between local inhabitants and incoming people. Our discussion of Patrick McConvell's theory on language migration and Peter Veth's model of arid zone colonisation are relevant here (see Chapter 5). The assumption that it would have taken hunter-gatherers thousands of years to become familiar with a region's resources recalls Sandra Bowdler's 'coastal colonisation hypothesis', in which coastal-adapted populations were incapable of inhabiting the interior of Pleistocene Sahul. Both hypotheses ignore the ability of hunter-gatherers to master new environments with simple technology. They draw upon principles of animal biology, overlooking the reality of human inventiveness and adaptability in overcoming obstacles.

Spear armatures as status symbols?

The social aspects of stone implements were highlighted in 1971 by the anthropologist Nicolas Peterson. The prestige factor in possessing well-crafted implements, often highly symmetrical and aesthetically attractive, cannot be discounted in explaining the appearance and spread of fashions in prehistory. Kimberley points and macroblades were exchanged along ceremonial trackways, and so might become fashionable. Peterson proposed that spear points and barbs made of wood or bone may have been more efficient than their stone equivalents. A notable example concerns finely retouched Kimberley points, which are time-consuming to make, but fragile. There seems no explanation other than status and fashion, also, to explain why the Warlpiri people in central Australia used spears with macroblade heads while their neighbours, the Arrernte, used spears with barbs cut into the wooden shaft. A notable feature of microlith distribution is that it encompasses a range of environments, from alpine to sandy desert, and across innumerable tribal boundaries. It is difficult to understand how environmental factors could have played a significant role either in their diffusion over a large expanse of the continent or in their abandonment.

As the following section illustrates, the appearance of Small Tool Phase implement types in different parts of Australia is cited as evidence of social and economic 'intensification', particularly increased productivity and efficiency, which we reject as the total explanation. The role of the new types in the social realm has barely been explored, largely because evidence is difficult to glean from the archaeological record. While chronological links with increased regionalisation of art styles have been suggested, these remain appealing but tentative ideas. We believe that a number of different factors are probably responsible for the appearance of new implement types and for their particular distributions in Australia, not least technological and social ones. A single all-encompassing explanation for their origin eludes existing archaeological data.

THE 'INTENSIFICATION DEBATE'

Since the 1980s Australian archaeology has been characterised by a continuing debate about whether social and economic complexity ('intensification') occurred during the last few thousand years. The concept has been used variously by geographers, anthropologists and archaeologists to explain changes from low levels of production and productivity, such as commonly found among hunting and gathering societies, to more intensive economies. Complex

Artificial channel dug by Aboriginal eel fishers at Toolondo, western Victoria, part of 3.75 kilometres of drainage channels connecting swamps, so as to optimise eel movement and trapping potential. Excavation proved the drain between swamps to be 2.5 metres wide and one metre deep. (D. J. Mulvaney)

hunter-gatherers manage environments to increase the yield of food; they are involved in trade and exchange of goods; they tend to be semi-sedentary; they have high population density with village-style settlements, and social ranking of individuals. The concept was first promoted in Australia by Harry Lourandos, who sought to explain apparent changes in archaeological sites and intensities of land use and evidence for semi-sedentism in southwest Victoria during recent prehistoric times. Notable within this region were extensive networks of channels joining lakes and swamps, designed to harvest large quantities of annually migrating eels. Lourandos interpreted these channels and traps, which required communal effort, as evidence for intensification of production and a more sedentary lifestyle. Added support for this interpretation came independently from research by Peter Coutts and Elizabeth Williams, who identified extensive mound systems as residential bases, associated at times with eel or fish traps.

Lourandos argued that socio-economic factors were the driving forces of Australian prehistoric cultural change and that the recent trajectory was towards increased cultural complexity. It was a provocative view in the context of the time. Professional archaeology had been spearheaded for two decades by Cambridge-trained archaeologists who supported the theme of 'man and environment' and interpreted change in terms of environmental adaptation. The role of prehistoric social systems and social mechanisms was relatively neglected, and ethnographic situations reported by early observers were projected back into prehistory. No one denied that social changes occurred, and some were acknowledged, but Lourandos offered an all-encompassing explanation for diverse changes in the archaeological record, beginning at about 5000 years BP and increasing sharply within the last 2000 years.

Archaeological evidence

As fieldwork increased archaeologists working in different regions of the continent reported increases in the number of habitation sites and greater evidence of human activity at individual sites, covering the last few thousand years. These changes were interpreted to signify more frequent visits, larger groups of people, or more sustained periods of encampment, which were thought to be the consequences of increased population density and sedentism and/or of changes in the ways people organised themselves and used the land. Greater social and economic complexity also is inferred from the appearance of new types of sites, such as cemeteries and channel complexes for trapping eels, the adoption of new stone technology, and increasing regionalisation of rock art styles in northern Australia over the last 3000 years. The theory is that exchange networks along Dreaming tracks, which were presumed to be newly developed, reflected changed interaction between territorial groups and in their social organisation.

Social and economic intensification are seen to be causally interlinked. Increased manipulation or control of the environment, combined with improvements in extracting food resources, led to increased population density and to the formation of new territorial and alliance systems between different groups. It is argued that the new implement types of the Small Tool Phase were technological innovations that contributed to increased productivity. Intensified economic production and larger, more densely settled populations possibly resulted in increased exploitation of marginal habitats or settlement of new territories, such as sandy deserts in the arid zone, semi-arid Mallee country in northwest Victoria, the montane regions of the Great Dividing Range and some islands off Australia's east coast.

Archaeological testing

Almost two decades after Lourandos first championed the concept of socio-economic intensification, no general consensus exists about its viability. The 'intensification debate' as it is now known, has its supporters and critics, with others uncommitted. Some critics take issue with the theoretical underpinnings of the concept; others question the archaeological evidence. In his insightful book *Continent of hunter-gatherers*, Lourandos has drawn together the strands of the debate in favour of his explanation.

The argument for intensification presumes that before about 5000 years BP Aboriginal groups had larger territories, lower levels of sedentism, less social ranking, and lower-scale investment in food procurement. However, it is important to remember that archaeological survey procedures favour younger sites, which also are likely to contain better-preserved materials. For example, the variety and quantity of faunal remains usually decrease with increasing age. It becomes problematic to infer the nature of earlier social and economic systems from archaeological evidence which normally becomes sparser with age.

Without adopting an explanation of extreme environmental determinism in the shaping societies and subsistence, it is evident that settlement patterns and fluctuations in population density must be linked with environmental circumstances. While there was always a degree of flexibility in environmental adaptation, people living in the most marginal habitats were more constrained in their options, and their survival depended on risk-minimising strategies to survive. The question is *which* strategies did a people adopt, and why?

Natural population increase is seen as a cause of social and economic changes by many archaeologists who believe that major changes have occurred in Aboriginal society during the last 5000 years or so. Interestingly, Lourandos and his followers argue that the archaeology really only implies that there were changes in culture and society, in what people did, rather than in population sizes. They do not see population growth as ultimately causing these socio-cultural changes, although population increases were probably involved. The fundamental issue concerns the relative importance and interplay of these different factors—population, culture and environment. Once sea level reached near stability some 6000 years ago ('still-stand'), the coastal zone began to mature. In northern Australia large areas of coastal plain were added through natural beach formation and by rivers depositing their loads of suspended sediments. This continuing seawards movement of the shore is termed progradation. These new coastal plains with mangroves and extensive freshwater wetlands, contained rich food resources, best exemplified by the Alligator Rivers region of Arnhem Land and by the territory of the Wik people of eastern Cape York Peninsula. Richly endowed estuaries and wetlands also formed and matured along the southeast coastline of Australia. Most of the shell middens on the New South Wales and southeast Queensland coast date to this period, and increased human activity within the last 3000 years is evident in the intensively studied regions around Moreton Bay and Sydney. Darrell Lewis and Paul Taçon have independently inferred from the increased regional variation of rock art that natural increase in food resources resulted in greater population density and a tighter packing of clan territories in the Kakadu region. Environmentally driven population increase is also cited by John Beaton for the accumulation of large shell mounds between 2000 and 500 years BP in Princess Charlotte Bay, northern Queensland. The slight seawards fall of the Murray River meant that the rising sea level raised river level far upstream, so rock-shelters at Devon Downs and Fromm's Landing were intensively occupied from about 5000 years ago. Environmental changes along the narrow Murray River corridor, which traverses semi-arid country, probably played a major role in the emergence of complex societies, encouraging sedentism, strong corporate identity and cemeteries.

Expansion of human settlement within the last few thousand years into regions that have few traces of prior human presence is another currently debated issue. Mike Rowland has explained the settlement of islands along the Queensland coast, where all open-air midden sites date within the last 2000 years, as a consequence of reef development and cultural diffusion of new technology from New Guinea. Interestingly, there is a similar expansion of settlement along the western and southern coasts of Tasmania, which could not have any connection with mainland events. The more widespread occupation of the arid zone, with its extended routes for ceremonial exchange of prestigious and economically valuable goods may be explained as another instance of socio-economic intensification, competing with explanations of environmental adaptation and technological innovation.

Artefact discard rates

The criteria used in estimating relative site use and intensity of human activity, and in particular the rate at which artefacts are discarded within a site over time, are debated issues. Alternative explanations for these phenomena include changes in settlement pattern and in stone technology. The adoption of microlithic technology and unifacial and bifacial point manufacture must have been responsible for dramatic increases in artefact discard rates, especially if flaked stone was much less important beforehand, or if stone-barbed spears were a new weapon. Just at one excavation at Curracurrang rockshelter in the Royal National Park south of Sydney, thousands of microliths were recovered, along with a much larger amount of microblade flaking debris. This applies not only to microliths but to uniface and biface spearheads as well. We have estimated that more than 200 pieces of flaking debris are the result of flaking a single Kimberley point. Flaking debris from making spear armatures at some sites is enormous. We agree with Bruno David, a supporter of intensification, that to be significant indicators, artefact discard rates should be correlated with other changes such as in ochre, charcoal, bone and shell, and with changes in the numbers of occupation sites in an area.

A challenging concept

Intensification as a pan-Australian phenomenon may prove difficult to demonstrate, but the concept has provoked heated debate and influenced research directions. There exists compelling supporting evidence in some regions, at least, as the evidence marshalled by Lourandos suggests. Recent research in southeast Cape York by Bruno David indicates that environmental conditions were optimal before an unprecedented increase in cultural deposits at rockshelter sites from about 5400 years BP. David also excavated sites in the Victoria River District, Northern Territory, and identified similar changes occurring there around 1400–900 years ago, inferring that northern Australia may have experienced a population explosion.

The 'intensification debate' challenged perceptions of causation and change in Australian prehistory and broadened research directions. Archaeologists are indebted to Lourandos for introducing theoretical concepts and explanations across a broad traverse of Australian prehistory.

People of 16
the coast

The rise in global sea level which commenced during the Pleistocene continued at a more rapid rate during the Early and Mid-Holocene, until it reached its present level at about 6000 years BP, forming a coastline more than 40,000 kilometres long. Where the land surface was low-lying, it was rapidly submerged; for example, at 8000 years BP the sea invaded the Arafura Plain of northwestern Australia at the rate of 25 to 45 metres annually. Some areas of the continental shelf were so low-lying and had such a low gradient that during periods of accelerated sea-level rise the shoreline migrated inland at the phenomenal rate of a metre a day. Along precipitous stretches of the coast, such as the 300-kilometre-long Banda Scarp in the Great Australian Bight, there was general stability of the coastline very early, but along the rest of the coast land surface continued to be lost to the sea, with consequences in terms of both coastal ecology and Aboriginal subsistence.

COASTAL PROGRADATION

It was only after the sea level stabilised in the Mid-Holocene that the environmental and topographic evolution of most of Australia's present coastal fringe commenced. Along much coastal land centuries of continual erosion of the foreshore followed, sometimes for 2000 years. Once the nearshore seabed had been reshaped, the coastline began to build outwards (or prograde) by processes of onshore and estuarine sedimentation. Broad progradation plains were formed, especially at the mouths of large rivers on the northern coast, and the entrances of drowned river valleys were sealed by sand spits, behind which formed salt marshes, swamps and lakes.

On a continental scale the extent of coastal progradation is less noticeable, but on a local or regional scale up to thousands of square kilometres of land were added, including new or expanded habitats that offered an enhanced range of resources for Aborigines. Coastal progradation was far more extensive in northern Australia than in the south. Most of the Gulf of Carpentaria coast is recent progradation for distances inland of five to 30 kilometres and there are now extensive deltas and alluvial flats on the Mitchell, Normanby, Leichhardt and Gilbert Rivers, much of which are flooded during the wet season.

INCREASE IN COASTAL EXPLOITATION?

Human exploitation of the coast continued during the period of sea-level rise, but because nearly all coastal sites belonging to this period were flooded by the sea, or are deeply buried by coastal sedimentation, little is known about the nature of settlement and subsistence. Only a few Early Holocene-age shell middens have been excavated, and these are from different parts of the continent; for instance, at Koolan Shelter 2 on a rocky island in the Buccaneer Archipelago in west Kimberley, at Swan Lake near Portland, Victoria, in the Nene Valley in coastal South Australia, and at Rocky Cape in northwest Tasmania.

Many Australian prehistorians believe that humans increased their exploitation of the coastal fringe after the sea level stabilised, and particularly within the last 2000–3000 years. The evidence for this is the increasing number and size of habitation sites during the last few millennia, though this may be due in part to better preservation and 'archaeological visibility' of more recent shell midden sites. Harry Lourandos has postulated that socio-economic factors are responsible for increased settlement and exploitation, while other prehistorians have opted for technological advances, or a shift to exploiting marginal littoral resources in response to increased population pressure. In some regions, such as in Kakadu and southeast Queensland, the timing of such increases corresponds with significant ecological changes along the coastal fringe—the coastal zone was maturing, and in the process those areas became more productive and invited increased subsistence activities.

Nature of coastal settlement

The nature of settlement in coastal lands (within 50 kilometres of the sea) was strongly influenced by the range and abundance of coastal and hinterland resources, the prevailing sea and weather conditions, and coastal topography. The most productive coastal ecotones were islands and coral reefs, tidal estuaries and rivers, and wetlands. Base camps were often positioned around the margins of coastal wetlands, and at sites between southwest Victoria and southeast Queensland they commonly contain stone choppers or pounders used in processing bracken rhizomes from freshwater wetlands.

Along coasts where marine and littoral resources were accessible and abundant, human population density was commonly three to four times greater than it was immediately inland. Donald Thomson may have witnessed the extreme in near-sedentary lifestyle in eastern Cape York, where he lived for five months with people who fished and hunted dugong. During his stay the camp was moved six times but the distance never exceeded about 300 metres each time. All these camping localities had an abundance of food resources. At the other extreme, along some arid coasts people sought little sustenance from the sea and population density was exceedingly low. The settlement pattern was equally varied, ranging from near-sedentism near the littoral zone, to seasonal settlements, or visits throughout the year. The following section examines coastal occupation by selecting a number of regions for which contrasting economic or important archaeological evidence exists.

Kakadu National Park

The coastal floodplain of Kakadu is inundated for six to eight months each year, for up to two metres depth in the wet season. In the past two millennia people camped on mound sites located on the floodplains, and along the rocky outliers near the margin of the wetlands, including rockshelters used as base camps thousands of years before. Seasonality is pronounced, and dominated the lives of Kakadu's inhabitants during recent prehistoric times at least. Although people exploited the lowlands between the Arnhem Land plateau and the coast, when the floodwaters subsided during the dry season they also exploited all the region's major environmental zones, including the mangrove-fringed coast, woodlands, rainforest patches, rivers and freshwater lagoons.

Most of the present-day wetlands evolved recently, associated with a shift in human settlement and lifestyle. At about 8000 years BP the sea invaded the valleys of the Alligator Rivers, and from this time to the present the coastal plain has continuously prograded, redistributing the sediment carried from the plateau country by the rivers as coastal fringe. There was rapid infilling of the Alligator Rivers estuary, and until 3000 years ago there were thousands of hectares of broad tidal flats surrounding the inlets, colonised by mangrove forest, in places almost to the plateau escarpment. This 'big mangrove swamp' phase was succeeded for a period of over 1000 years by a landscape of unvegetated salt flats and grasslands with mangrove forest mostly along meanders in the rivers and the coastal littoral zone. Kakadu's freshwater wetlands and lagoons, the tranquil scenery commonly depicted in the park's tourist literature, are only 3000 years old. The first to form were the lagoons on the upper reaches of waterways. About 1800 years ago, when continued siltation allowed grasses to colonise the floodplain, the tidal channels became insulated by natural levee banks, broad low ridges of fine alluvium. These levees ponded torrential wet-season rainfall, as river discharge from the plateau country created hundreds of square kilometres of freshwater wetlands, which by 1300 years ago had expanded to their present extent.

The oldest shell middens

The oldest middens, accumulated between about 7000 and 3000 years BP, are found in rockshelters within the rocky sandstone outliers facing the lowlands near the wet-season shoreline. Excavated middens include the now famous sites of Narradj Warde Djobkeng, Malakunanja, Nawamoyn, Malangangerr, Paribari, and a rockshelter on Argaluk Hill overlooking Oenpelli settlement, usually interpreted as base camps. The shellfish are of many different mangrove and mud-flat species, with preference for those easily collected in quantity at low tide. Also present are the claws of small crabs, suggesting foraging along the landward margin of mangrove forests; and the bones of long-necked turtle and brackish and freshwater fish species, indicating visits to tidal channels and freshwater swamps. Undoubtedly, wet-sieving would recover the remains of plant food in these estuarine midden deposits, but so far, only Paribari rockshelter has revealed such dietary information. Six plant foods were recorded, all of which still form part of traditional Aboriginal regional diet. Artefacts found in the middens include small bone points, presumably fishing spear prongs, and spatulate-ended bone points, grinding and pounding stones, hatchet heads, and shells used for cutting and scraping.

Freshwater-wetlands base camps

Inevitably changes in shellfish ecology meant shifts in the location of base camps, and some rockshelters were abandoned. From about 3000 years BP, shell middens composed of mangrove and mudflat species accumulated on the floodplains. Changes in species composition over time reflect the natural contraction of the mangrove forest to the edges of rivers and coast.

During the last 1500 years many base camps were positioned on wooded fringes of freshwater lagoons and on river bank levees in the freshwater swampland, particularly along the South Alligator River. Although these sites were not inhabited permanently, the changing seasonal ecology of the wetlands allowed some groups to live all year within this zone by making short trips between sites. Rhys Jones proposes that the creation of these wetlands provided an ecosystem that was far richer in resources, able to support a substantially denser population and possibly a more sedentary lifestyle. There are clues to such changes in the rock art, discussed in Chapter 20. Vast flocks of magpie geese were attracted to the freshwater wetlands, providing meat, eggs and feathers, and there were other waterfowl, fish, turtles, freshwater crocodiles, mussels and the abundant and much-relished file snakes. Chinese water-chestnuts (corms of the spike rush, *Eleocharus dulcis*) grew abundantly in the swamps, and digging them from the mud was a major chore of the women and children.

Most of the wetlands base camps were scavenged for artefacts by visitors in the decade prior to the creation of Kakadu National Park, and considerable damage was caused also by water buffaloes which resulted in widespread erosion. One wetlands site is over half a kilometre in length and 150 metres wide, and estimated to contain some 1.5 million stone artefacts. Common large artefacts are grinding slabs and upper grinders, and mortars and pestles, indicating heavy dependence on plant foods such as waterlily seeds. There are two kinds of pestles, a round or oval-shaped one, and an unusual cylindrical stone with one or both ends worn down by abrasion. This elongated pestle may have been used with a type of grindstone with a hemispheroid grinding hollow. Some of the pestles are of attractively coloured schist. The plant food processed with the pestles is not known, but Jones and Meehan have suggested that it was spike-rush corms. Other manuports (natural stones carried to the site) and artefacts include cooking stones, pieces of stony red ochre, edge-ground hatchet heads (sometimes in surprising abundance), small flake chisels worn to narrow slugs by repeated resharpening, occasional small retouched spear points, and large prismatic blades made from white quartzite.

In 1845 the explorer Ludwig Leichhardt camped at one of the wetland base camps adjacent to the South Alligator River. Jones and Meehan suspect that this was Ki'na, a lagoon site they excavated in 1981. They believe that the site was occupied in the late dry season when red waterlilies in the lagoon were ready to harvest. Leichhardt recorded that the people in the vicinity of his camp were engaged mostly in fishing and digging edible roots. He also remarked that the men carried bundles of short, lightweight spears, used for hunting the migratory magpie geese which congregated in vast flocks in the wetlands. Occupation of Ki'na spanned only the last 300 years. Today the site is marked by scatters of stone artefacts, fragments of shell, and a low mound, possibly accumulated from thousands of pieces of termite nest carried to the camp for use as heat retainers in earth ovens.

CHANGES IN STONE TECHNOLOGY

Rockshelter sites located in the valleys incised into the plateau reveal changes through time in the choice of stone artefacts. Those artefacts prior to about 6000 years BP are mostly of milky quartz, quartz crystal and some chert, all of which are locally available. Changes in the popularity of stone materials, such as an increase in chert, to some extent reflect the advent of new implement types and the pressure-flaking technique. The cherts were commonly used for making finely flaked spear points and small chisels which make their appearance at about 4000 years BP. The advent of the new technology, including the last addition, a long prismatic spear point, was accompanied by a sudden increase in different coloured quartzites from sources in Kakadu. One excavation produced maroon chert, supplanting red and white mottled chert, probably indicating that stone was brought from the south.

One of the intriguing puzzles of Kakadu archaeology is the function of an unusual flake implement displaying a bright use-polish along its cutting edge. Many specimens have blunting retouch along their back margin and are similar in appearance to orange-segment-shaped eloueras of the central New South Wales coast. The Kakadu implement is found in large numbers at prehistoric base camps at the lowland freshwater lagoons, and to lesser extent in rockshelters on the edge of the wetlands. In 1948 a well-preserved use-polished flake mounted in a handle was found in a rock crevice during excavation of a rockshelter near Oenpelli. This tool resembles a mini-hatchet; its association with freshwater lagoons in the dry season is strong, and has focused speculation about the tool's function. Over the years postulated uses have included harvesting rice and cutting reeds or bamboo for spear shafts. However, experimental work by Kim Akerman of the Northern Territory Museum shows that most probably the tool was used by women to trim and flatten spike-rush stems for mats and body apparel. In the early twentieth century pandanus leaves became the preferred material for making mats and baskets, probably because of missionary influence.

Anbangbang 1 rockshelter

Evidence of settlement around freshwater lagoons in the drier woodland of Kakadu's coastal plain comes from Anbangbang 1, a site excavated by Jones in 1981. This site is a commodious shelter formed by collapse of a cliff face at Nourlangie Rock, a popular tourist destination. The shelter was first occupied more than 6000 years BP, only becoming a regular camping place when Anbangbang lagoon and the freshwater wetlands were fully evolved 800 to 1200 years ago. The well-preserved plant remains retrieved from the 'wetland phase' top layer indicate visits throughout the year. Together with mussel shells, fish bones, turtle and other food remains, they indicate hunting and gathering in the different ecotones within short

The 'mini-hatchet' found in a rockshelter near Oenpelli in 1948. The rough quartzite flake protruding from the resin has a bright use-polish; length 34 centimetres. (Australian Museum)

walking distance of the site. Bone bipoints, some with traces of resin cement on their surfaces, may have been fish-spear prongs. Pieces of wooden spear barbs, and even wood shavings and string made from bark fibre and fur attest to comprehensive resource exploitation.

AURUKUN AND WEIPA SHELL MOUNDS

Immense shell mounds are found in the estuarine tributaries of Archer and Albatross Bays on the coast of western Cape York Peninsula. Similar large shell mounds exist on Milingimbi Island and the adjacent Arnhem Land coast. There are an estimated 500 mounds around the township of Weipa, the smallest less than a metre thick, the largest towering thirteen metres above the surrounding coastal plain. The ethnographer W. E. Roth visited Albatross Bay in the late nineteenth century and saw huts and fireplaces on top of some mounds. He suggested that the steep climb was worthwhile, for there was escape from the ravages of mosquitoes and sandflies. Roger Cribb has noted that shelly deposits encouraged the growth of shade trees, and he argues that this was the reason people returned year after year. The trees also would have provided dry places during the wet season.

The Weipa mounds contain about nine billion shells, weighing a total of nearly 200,000 tonnes. The bulk of the shells are common cockle (*Anadara granosa*) and there are small quantities of mud clams, oysters and other mangrove species. The oldest mounds are found along former shorelines hundreds of metres from the prograding shore. They began to form at about 2500 years BP, possibly 500–1500 years after *Anadara* colonies became established in mudflats. A cluster in the radiocarbon dates points to a period of accelerated mound-building at 700–2500 years BP. The most recent mounds date to within the last few hundred years and are located in present-day mangrove swamps fringing the estuaries.

The identification of the mounds as Aboriginal was questioned about 1960 when large deposits of bauxite were discovered in the region. In response to this, the archaeologist Richard Wright excavated Kwamter shell mound on the Embley River in 1963. Wright found small amounts of animal bones and stone and bone artefacts, and concentrations of charcoal and ash, all of which are common in shell middens. Among the artefacts were small bone points which had probably been used in fishing gear, such as spear prongs, fish-hooks and harpoon barbs. Most of the Kwamter mound was built up over a hundred years, around 1000 years BP. While further fieldwork by other archaeologists has supported Wright's conclusion of Aboriginal origin, some doubt again was raised a few years ago, which was broadcast widely by the media. Tim Stone argued that the mounds are scrub-fowl nests, and that the birds had scratched up the shells from wave-deposited shelly ridges. In response to this new challenge, a re-study of both mounds and scrub-fowl nests has provided substantial support for Wright's original assessment. The composition of shell mounds differs fundamentally from both the surrounding sediments and the wave-sorted *Anadara*-rich shell banks which, in any case, are not found close to the mounds. There should be no further doubt that these impressive mounds were artificial accumulations, built up during the wet season, which is when shellfish were collected in quantity along Cape York Peninsula.

COASTAL SOUTHEAST QUEENSLAND

The best-understood region archaeologically is around Brisbane and the Gold Coast, as far west as the Great Dividing Range and south to the Border Range and the Tweed River. The coast in this area is dominated by the enormous triangular embayment of Moreton Bay, and the sand islands of North Stradbroke, Moreton and Bribie. To the north, Fraser Island is the largest sand island in the world. Most of the archaeological work has been undertaken from the University of Queensland, concentrating mainly on the coast and estuaries, which are subject to urban development.

Thousands of shell middens have been located on islands and headlands, estuaries, and beach dunes. Nearly all these sites are younger than 2000 years, with only a few more twice this antiquity. Stone tools associated with these sites include microliths made from locally outcropping silcrete and to a lesser extent chert, bracken pounders, grindstones, and hatchet heads. The most common stone type recovered in these coastal sites is quartz.

Prior to the Holocene, Aboriginal occupation of southeast Queensland was probably sparse, and sterile sediments underlie Holocene cultural layers in many rockshelters. Despite intensive surveys, only one site with Pleistocene occupation has been identified—an open-air camp locality in Brisbane containing stratified stone artefacts. The sea-level rise in the first half of the Holocene shaped the region's coastline, including Moreton Bay when the ancient dunefields of

Fraser Island and the mainland were partly submerged or islanded. Six thousand years ago people probably inhabited the forested valleys, collecting yams and cycad kernels from the hinterland and hunting small mammals, while good fishing was available in the estuaries. Although much of the coastal zone was heathland, which was poor in animal and bird life, its wetlands provided starch-rich bracken rhizome ('bungwall'). In the early nineteenth century bracken was a staple plant food, and historical records describe women digging it from the swamps and later pounding it at nearby base camps. A heavy, wedge-shaped stone tool, resembling a blunt-ended chopper, was used to separate the tough fibres in the rhizome before extracting the starch, and these tools are prolific at prehistoric coastal base camps. One bracken pounder excavated by Ian McNiven from a pippi midden on Teewah Beach, north of Noosa Heads, proved to be 4000–5000 years old. While there is no reason to doubt this age, all other dated specimens in the region are younger than 1000 years.

Changes in settlement and subsistence first appear in the region's archaeological record at about 3000–4000 years ago. In particular, during the last 1000 years there was a large increase in the number of archaeological sites along the coast, especially shell middens on the sand islands, including Moreton Island, where most are less than 500 years old. In the hinterland the number of ceremonial bora rings and painted rockshelters increases. Archaeologists have interpreted the complex of changes to indicate increased sedentism, population density and territoriality, and the advent of large, inter-group ceremonial gatherings. From changes in animal bones at habitation sites, Michael Morwood infers a shift from solitary to communal hunting.

Broadbeach cemetery

The emergence of more sedentary lifestyle and increased territoriality also may be inferred from an Aboriginal cemetery at Broadbeach on the Gold Coast, dating to about 1000 years ago. The cemetery was on a sand ridge dug illegally for lawn top-dressing. No government legislation then existed to protect the site, but a rescue excavation by Laila Haglund in the 1960s saved the surviving human remains from destruction. When in use, the cemetery was probably fringed with rain forest; it provided a location convenient to both coast and hinterland resources. The 140 burials discovered probably belonged to a single residential population, while the continuity of burial practices indicated this use for only a short period. The majority of interments

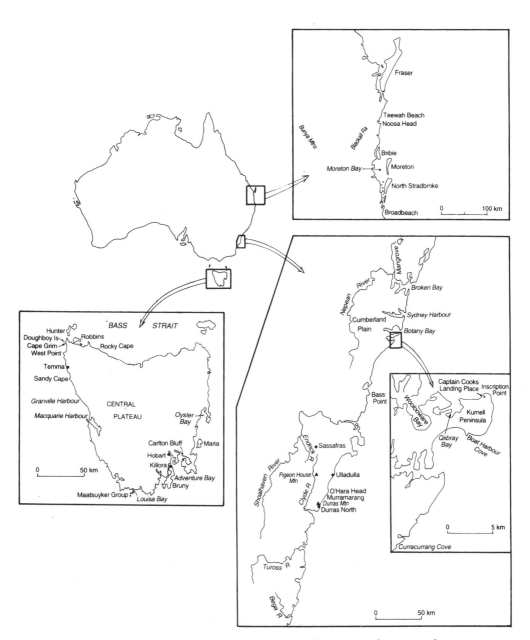

Map 14. Coastal sites in southeast Australia.

were bundle burials, with the bones wrapped in bark or animal skin as a final stage in disposal. In some cases the bodies were laid in a shallow pit, and one grave contained dismembered body parts neatly laid out. Possibly the primary burials represented the defleshing stage that preceded reburial as a bone bundle.

Coastal fishery

Ian Walters proposes that the advent of intensive specialised marine fishing underpinned the new social and economic order. Walters analysed the fish remains from eight sites around Moreton Bay, and identified the commencement about 1000 years ago of year-round inshore fishing, with whiting targeted at particular times of the year. Fish were most abundant between April and July which, along with waterfowl, shellfish, crustacea, turtle and dugong, and bracken fern, provided sufficient food to support a relatively dense coastal population. In 1853 the Reverend Henry Stobart observed that a single dugong was sufficient to feed 30 families. Clearly, there were times of resource glut during the year, and opportunities for social gatherings and feasting. Walters argues that the reason for the abundance of marine food was the silting of Moreton Bay 1000–2000 years ago, which was accompanied by the spread of mangrove forest and seagrass beds, and the creation of large areas of shallow, turbid water which sustained inshore fish populations.

The 'feast food' of the hinterland was bunya pine nuts (*Araucaria bidwelli*). The bunya pines in the Bunya Mountains and Blackall Range northwest of Brisbane fruited every year in January and February. At three-yearly intervals, however, they produced a superabundance. The huge bunya pine cone is up to twenty centimetres long, containing nutritious and tasty seeds up to four centimetres long; these were roasted and ground into flour. The 'bunya nut festivals' brought people from other regions to congregate in ceremonial meetings numbering 1000. Some bunya pines in Bunya Mountains National Park still have toeholds in their rough bark, a testimony to this ceremonial food.

THE SYDNEY REGION

In terms of numbers of prehistoric sites the Sydney Basin is one of the richest archaeological provinces in Australia, comparable with Kakadu National Park. There are many thousands of Aboriginal sites, more than half containing rock art, and in Sydney's sandstone belt at

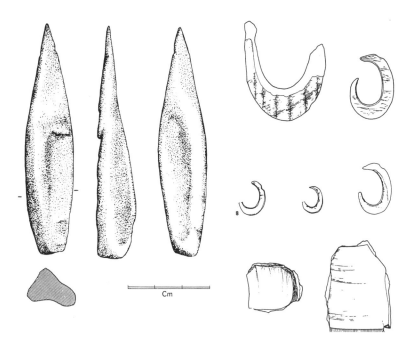

Fish-hook file (left), turban shell blanks (bottom right) and fish-hooks (top right), some with notches to hold the line, from a rockshelter in Wattamolla Cove, Royal National Park, south of Sydney. (J. V. S. Megaw)

least 1500 rockshelters contain cultural deposit. Hundreds of shell middens have been recorded along the coast and in estuaries, with stone quarries, hatchet-grinding localities, wells and ceremonial grounds inland. Little was recorded about the meaning of the rock art found throughout much of the Sydney region (see Chapter 20).

Frederick McCarthy, then a curator at the Australian Museum, was the pioneer of archaeological fieldwork in Sydney's west. His considerable work was built on in the 1960s by Vincent Megaw, who undertook with his archaeology students a major survey and excavations along the southern coast and estuaries of the Royal National Park. Excavated prehistoric sites in the Sydney region are mostly rock-shelters located in bays and estuaries, and typically contain midden deposit. The common stone implements found throughout the region are microliths, mostly of the bondi point variety, eloueras, small thumbnail scrapers, pebble hatchet heads and at coastal sites only, fish-hook files (see Chapter 14).

Prehistoric settlement

The Sydney region comprises a plain of clay and silt, the Cumberland Plain, almost bereft of rockshelters, surrounded by sandstone plateau deeply incised by rivers. The suburbs stretch continuously along the coast for 50 kilometres. This coastline has estuaries and wetlands, small lagoons and swamps barred by Holocene-age sand spits, and headlands with wave-eroded rock platforms extending into the sea.

During the Mid-Holocene, rising sea invaded the deep gorges and valleys, creating Botany Bay and the magnificent waterways of Sydney Harbour and Broken Bay. Beginning about 5000 years BP, which is about 1000 years after the sea level stabilised, the discard of stone artefacts in rockshelters increased. Most of the coastal rockshelters excavated have occupation evidence only over the last 2500 years BP, which may correspond to the time when the coastal wetlands had fully developed, providing inexhaustible supplies of fish and waterbirds and other foods and materials (most of these wetlands have been transformed into golf courses and suburban sports fields). While rockshelters containing habitation deposit increased markedly from about 1000 years BP, their artefact numbers declined, possibly reflecting either technological change to organic materials or a decline in occupation intensity.

Historical records

When the British first explored around Sydney Cove, they encountered four local tribes: the Eora who inhabited Sydney Harbour, the Kuring-gai to the north, the Tharawal to the south, and the Dharug of the inland plain. The few historical records relate mainly to people inhabiting the coastal fringe, and little is known about the hinterland people. Because Sydney's shores and estuaries are suburbs, many shell middens and rockshelters with cultural deposits are now in residents' yards. The suburbs are bounded in the north and south by large national parks which have thousands of undisturbed rock art and habitation sites. At some midden sites in southern Sydney the topmost levels contain European artefacts, such as old glass, pottery sherds, buttons and the occasional musket ball, which date to the early decades of contact with the British settlement.

Shell middens

The dietary content of Sydney's shell middens evinces local resources—molluscs from estuary and rocky platform; fish caught by spear, fishing line, and possibly by scoop net; and the scavenging of large marine mammals such as stranded whales. The first professional excavation in coastal Sydney was in a well-appointed rockshelter overlooking Curracurrang Cove in the Royal National Park. The Curracurrang shelter provides a long sequence of human occupation, from 7500 years BP until after the arrival of the British. Megaw unearthed bone points, comparable to ones on fishing spears taken by James Cook and Joseph Banks from an Aboriginal encampment at nearby Botany Bay, and small stone files for making shell fish-hooks. The occurrence of seal and whale bones added to the marine emphasis of the technology and dietary evidence. However, the shelter was much richer in microliths than in artefacts of bone or shell. In one layer alone, dating from 2500 to 2000 years BP, Megaw recovered over 1000 microliths and 50,000 small flakes. This is strong evidence for the production and repair of spears for hunting land animals, therefore suggesting a more diversified subsistence base than evident at sites that Megaw subsequently excavated at Kurnell on the southern shore of Botany Bay.

Originally, Kurnell Peninsula had been covered by banksia thickets, cabbage-tree palms, and stands of tall eucalypts such as southern mahogany. Middens of locally extinct mud oysters occur in its bays, and in a dunefield the shifting sands constantly reveal stone artefacts. In 1770, after firing several muskets to ward off Aborigines, Captain Cook landed at a small Aboriginal encampment on the foreshore of Kurnell. A sketch drawn at the time, possibly by Cook himself, faithfully records the landing. This area is now Captain Cook's Landing Place Historic Site, a popular picnic spot, with imposing memorials to Cook and Joseph Banks and an on-site museum where there is a display about the site's Aboriginal past. Along the foreshore, beneath the well-kept lawn, an extensive shell midden up to two metres deep includes the remains of the Aboriginal encampment Cook visited. The food remains at this site indicate exploitation of an adjacent coastal wetland, now covered by shifting sand dunes, as well as the harvest of the sea. An extraordinarily large number of fish-hooks highlights the importance of line fishing during the closing centuries of Aboriginal occupation in Botany Bay.

CUMBERLAND PLAIN

During Mid-Holocene to Late Holocene times, Aboriginal subsistence on the Cumberland Plain (a large part of present-day western Sydney) was different from that of the coastal fringe with its rugged topography, beach fronts and estuaries. Most archaeological work in

Left: Trident fish spear, collected by Captain Cook and Joseph Banks at Kurnell in 1770. Prongs average 60 centimetres in length; the points are made of fish spines and marsupial bones. (J. V. S. Megaw) Right: Enlargement of one of the points of the trident fish-spear.

this well-watered woodland and forest region has been for environmental impact studies, as one would expect for Australia's largest city. It is the most archaeologically reconnoitred area in Australia, and more than 600 prehistoric sites are recorded. Rockshelter sites do not occur here because there are few sandstone outcrops, and the commonly recorded sites are surface scatters and below-ground stone artefacts dating to within the last 3000 years. Certain accumulations of ancient river gravels contain silcrete, fossil wood and silicified volcanic tuff, which were used locally for making flaked stone tools and probably traded to other parts of the Sydney region. Basalt for making hatchet heads was obtained from gravel beds in the Nepean River, where today worn grooves exist on rock platforms at places along the river bank where the flaked pebbles were ground to their final shape.

SOUTH COAST OF NEW SOUTH WALES

The first professional excavations on the south coast were by Ron Lampert in the 1960s. Lampert's classic site was Currarong 1 rockshelter on the Beecroft Peninsula. Currarong had been occupied for the last 3700 years. Its food refuse comprised shellfish from estuary, rocky platform and sandy beach, and the bones of seabirds, fish, and small marsupials, including bandicoot and swamp wallaby, which were probably hunted in the immediate area. Lampert also excavated another midden in a sea cave at Durras North, a deposit spanning the last few hundred years. It revealed a strong focus on the resources of the sea. Hundreds of bone points were uncovered, almost certainly fish spear prongs, many of them fragments of split bone ground to a point at one or both ends.

Lampert's reconstruction of recent prehistoric coastal settlement was of year-round exploitation of estuarine wetlands, with more focus on littoral resources during summer. During the twenty years following Lampert's synthesis, prehistorians tended to favour a model of seasonal transhumance between coast in summer and hinterland in winter. The problem with this is that the historical records suggest considerable Aboriginal presence in the forested hinterland, which has not yet been adequately searched for archaeological sites. Analysis of human bones from south coast burials by Steve Webb has shown that the general level of health during the last few centuries was probably high, but there had been regular seasonal episodes of nutritional stress. Evidence of seasonal 'feast and famine', however, does not necessarily imply transhumance. To a large extent the appeal of the coastal fringe would have depended on prevailing environmental conditions, and these may have been significantly warmer after the sea level reached its present point. Fossil corals from rock platforms along the Illawarra coast are believed to date to around 2900 years BP, implying a sea temperature about 2.5°C higher than it is today, and more comparable to Coffs Harbour 550 kilometres to the north. The few coastal middens on the south coast so far examined, however, have not indicated dietary changes that could be linked to warmer marine conditions and a different range of resources.

Since 1981 Ian Farrington's fieldwork classes from the Australian National University have cumulatively searched 1000 square kilometres of the south coast. There also have been numerous field surveys for environmental impact assessments as the region is experiencing development pressure. The distribution of the prehistoric sites (mostly stone artefact scatters) suggests a concentration of settlement in the larger river valleys, such as the Shoalhaven, Clyde, Tuross, Endrick and Bega, where extensive sites were found on river terraces and flats. One of the largest stone artefact accumulations in stratified riverine sediments is twenty kilometres inland from the coast, at Blue Gum Flat near Pigeon House Mountain. The excavator, Phil Boot of the New South Wales National Parks and Wildlife, has shown that the oldest artefacts at this site date to about 4000 years BP.

Stone artefact scatters also tend to be found on broad ridgelines that were probably travel corridors through the forested hinterland. However, Farrington believes that travel corridors cannot explain all the sites on elevated land because lithic scatters are also found on hill tops, such as Durras Mountain in the Murramarang Range. He suspects that ceremonial activities were probably performed in the vicinity of rock painting sites, of which a number are known in the region. There is no indication of long-distance trade and exchange on the south coast, either historically or from the archaeological record. The flaked stone in sites reflects local availability: silcrete is a commonly used material north of Murramarang, from sources around Ulladulla, while in the south there is a variety of volcanic stone types, and in river valleys the predominant stone is quartz.

Prehistoric camping grounds on coastal headlands

The largest camping localities on the south coast are headlands, such as Bass Point, Murramarang, O'Hara Head and Clear Point, which are spaced apart about every five to ten kilometres. Today these headlands are cleared of the tea-tree, banksia and eucalypts that originally grew there and which sheltered the camps from sun and wind, so these windswept headlands today have lost some of their appeal. On such cliff-tops are sand accumulations within which shell middens and stone artefact scatters occur, sometimes accumulated in layers separated by dune sand. Because they were cleared of vegetation, erosion often uncovered this evidence of occupation. Stone tool collectors eagerly scoured such areas for artefacts. They termed the eroded patches 'blowouts'.

The largest of all the coastal headland sites is on Murramarang Point. Here there was a complex of camping sites within an area of about twelve hectares. Since the turn of the century Murramarang has been a favourite spot for artefact collectors, and today most of the stone implements and discarded flakes and hammerstones exposed in earlier decades have disappeared. At O'Hara Head only five kilometres to the south Farrington's teams have recorded twenty separate sites, and undoubtedly there are many more hidden within the mantle of dune sand. South coast headlands were a focus for Aboriginal settlement because there was greater ecological diversity, contrasting with the beaches and sand dunes between them. For instance, the range of ecosystems within a five-kilometre foraging distance of Murramarang comprise marine, nearshore island (habitat of mutton birds, penguins and seals), rocky platform, sandy beach, freshwater wetland, mangrove-fringed estuary, dry sclerophyll forest, and temperate rainforest in the hinterland range. Besides shellfish, the midden deposits contain bones of fish, seal, whale, land mammals such as possum, and birds. An enormous amount of debris from microlith production occurred at Murramarang, an abundance testifying to the relative importance of land hunting along the coast. Murramarang is also a locality where unfinished pebble hatchet heads have been collected in large numbers and four areas of grinding grooves nearby testify to the local manufacture of hatchets, an indispensable implement for hunting and gathering in the forest.

CHANGES IN TECHNOLOGY

An issue of debate among archaeologists for many years has been why changes occurred in hunting and fishing technology along the central and south New South Wales coasts. When the British arrived in

1788, Aboriginal men were seen fishing with spears up to four metres long; the shaft was made of fitted lengths of *Xanthorrhoea* (grass-tree) flower-stalk and the three or four prongs were small pieces of marsupial long bones ground to a point. First Fleet diarists observed women catching fish, mostly snapper, by angling with a hook and line from canoes. This fish-hook was made from a flat, oval-shaped piece chipped from the wall of the large turban shell, *Ninella torquata*. This preform was abraded until a hole appeared at its centre, and the hole widened with a slender, pointed file of schist or sandstone. The hook was finished by filing it into a distinctive C-shape, from one to three centimetres long, with a notch near its end for attachment of a fibre or hair line. The opalescent lustre of the nacre surface lured fish, so bait was unnecessary (see p. 285).

Shell fish-hooks and stone files have been recovered from coastal shell middens from Newcastle to south of Mallacoota in Victoria. Their antiquity is not known precisely, but they first appeared before 700 years ago and possibly as early as 1100 years BP. Sandra Bowdler argued that with the advent of line-fishing, women had less time for shellfish gathering in the intertidal zone, and they therefore concentrated on mussels which are easily collected on rock platforms. While the adoption of angling may have implied major ramifications for Aboriginal culture over the last 1000 years, research by Richard McKay and Peter White suggests that the increased quantity of mussel shells in some middens was probably due to shellfish ecology rather than a shift in women's subsistence activities.

In the Sydney region, and more generally in southeast Australia, the amount of bipolar flaking of quartz in archaeological deposits begins to increase from about 2000 years BP and intensifies over the last 1000 years. However, the evidence for this trend is uneven as not all sites contain bipolar flaking products. A corresponding trend is that microliths and microblade technology begin to disappear. These changes are seen in coastal rockshelters at Gymea Bay, Currarong and Curracurrang in Sydney, and in sites further south in forest hinterland, such as Sassafras shelter and Bob's Cave. The most commonly accepted explanation is that microblade technology and its end product, microlith spear barbs, were abandoned in preference to lacerating barbs made from sharp quartz fragments. In the Sydney region and in many other parts of southeast Australia, such quartz flakes were arranged in single or double rows along the tips of 'death spears' in early historic times. British settlers also observed the terrible wounds they caused. This change in stone spear barbs may have been accompanied by the

Head of a death spear, with a single row of stone barbs. (C. E. Dortch)

advent of new spear design or different uses for the spear. However, there is very little experimental research on quartz flake and microlith barbs and certainly none on their comparative performance.

SOUTHWESTERN AUSTRALIA

Available evidence from archaeological surveys in the southwest would imply sparse occupation at all times were it not for the testament of the historic records. European explorers and colonists at the Swan River and King George's Sound (Albany) detailed observations of Aboriginal life, documenting the enormous variety of plant and animal foods that the local Nyoongar people obtained from many environments. The best sources for the first decade of British settlement from the 1820s are the journals of Captain Collet Barker and the explorer George Grey, and accounts by the settler G. F. Moore and naval surgeon Scott Nind. Reconstructing Late Holocene subsistence patterns from these records, Sarah Meagher, Sylvia Hallam, June Anderson, and Martin Gibbs have shown that rich estuarine and coastal wetland resources, such as marine fish, wildfowl, reptiles, turtles, freshwater molluscs and crayfish, roots, tubers, and bulrush corms, supported large congregations of people throughout the summer. In winter these groups dispersed and moved into the interior, exploiting roots, tubers, and marsupials. Hallam also has documented the extent of Nyoongar control of the land through use of fire.

Thanks to the persistence of several archaeologists, a few key sites with abundant, well-preserved food remains corresponding to those foods documented in the historical literature have been found, at Devil's Lair, Tunnel Cave, Cheetup rockshelter, Rainbow Cave, Witchcliffe rockshelter, and Katelysia rockshelter. C. E. Dortch argues that limited exploitation of marine shellfish, suggested by numerous small shell scatters in coastal dunes, is perhaps best explained by the viability of alternative subsistence practices, particularly summertime estuarine fishing. Marine fish remains at Katelysia rockshelter, located on the shore of Wilson Inlet, west of Albany, indicate estuarine fishing from at least 2000 years BP. Following an important review of estuarine fish traps by Warwick Dix and Sarah Meagher, Dortch sought stone structures identifiable as tidal weirs on old shorelines and in estuaries and lakes, and succeeded in locating Australia's first known prehistoric underwater sites, at ten metres depth on the floor of Lake Jasper. Quartz and silcrete scatters located in an inundated landscape of tree and grass-tree stumps suggest regular use of a woodland and swamp environment at 4000 years BP, when Lake Jasper was created. A survey of the southern forests by Robert Pearce resulted in 300 sites, indicating low-level but persistent use of this environmental zone. Evidently seasonal movements to exploit some of these historically documented foods were long established by the time of British occupation.

Stone technology

One of the most important Holocene sites in southwestern Australia is Walyunga, 40 kilometres north of the Swan River near Perth. Pearce, who excavated the dune site, identified two phases in a sequence of predominantly quartz artefacts. In the early phase, from 8000 to 4500 years BP, small steep-edged flake scrapers (probably used in woodworking) are common, and persist in smaller numbers in the late phase, which continues after 3200 years BP. Characterising the late phase are small flake scrapers, an implement type of the desert interior, which probably had been used on a handle, and microliths, which appear in various shapes, including from 3000 years BP a squat version of a bondi point.

The kodj and taap

The historic material culture of the southwest includes some important elements that were probably local inventions, such as capes of sewn kangaroo skins, and two multi-component tools found nowhere else in Australia, the kodj hammer-hatchet and the taap toothed-knife. The edge-ground hatchet, so common elsewhere in Australia, has been found only at few isolated surface sites, so it seems probable that hatchets arrived in small numbers by exchange across the desert. The equivalent of the hatchet in the southwest forestlands was a lightweight general-purpose tool called the kodj. This unusual implement has one or two roughly discoidal or semi-discoidal flakes of igneous stone, such as granite, either trimmed or sharp-edged, set in opposite

Taap saw-knife with three quartz teeth (length 44 centimetres). (C. E. Dortch)

sides of a large ball of resin and mounted on the end of a thin, pointed handle. One stone served as a hammer head, the other as a mini-hatchet head. The taap toothed-knife was used for butchering seals and other large animals, comprises a row of two to as many as ten small, irregularly shaped stone chips, usually quartz flakes, secured with resin along a short wooden handle. At least some of the stone teeth were blunted by abruptly angled 'backing' retouch to prepare them for hafting, but they are not technically regarded as microliths. The antiquity of the kodj and taap is not known, because none of their stone parts has yet been identified in archaeological deposits.

Drowning of fossiliferous chert sources

Several hundred artefacts of Eocene fossiliferous chert, a rock known from offshore drill-holes, are exposed in Late Pleistocene and Early Holocene archaeological horizons along the lower west coast and offshore islands. Chert artefacts are also known from excavations at Devil's Lair, Tunnel Cave, Arumvale, Quininup Brook, Dunsborough, and Walyunga. They show petrological variations along a north–south gradient and rapidly decline in number with distance from the west coast. John Glover, a geologist, infers that fossiliferous chert was quarried from outcrops distributed along now-submerged parts of the coastal plain off the lower west coast; thus most chert artefacts predate Mid-Holocene sea-level stabilisation, 6500 years BP. Artefact sequences at Dunsborough and Walyunga show that chert only disappeared from these sites 4500 years BP; either Aborigines recycled ancient chert artefacts, or they visited onshore sources that became inaccessible some time after sea-level stabilisation, perhaps through burial under recent coastal dunes.

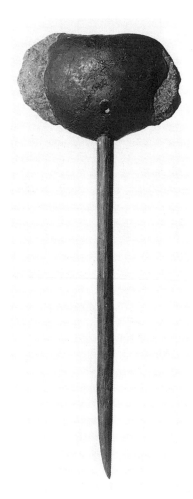

Kodj hatchet from near Bunbury, Western Australia. The granite stone on the left-hand side has some smoothing from use, but neither stone is trimmed by flaking. The length is 23 centimetres. (W. Ambrose and Museum of Victoria)

A Mid-Holocene depopulation?

An argument for Aboriginal responses to putative Mid-Holocene environmental changes was made by William Ferguson, who proposed that a Mid-Holocene expansion of unproductive tall open forest caused a large-scale regional depopulation by 6000 years BP. Moya Smith, a Western Australian Museum archaeologist, refuted Ferguson's evidence for depopulation by demonstrating that many of his sequences show occupation throughout the Holocene. The new environmental reconstruction supports Smith's interpretation. Initially, pollen sequences suggested a Mid-Holocene wet phase, favouring an expansion of tall open forest, while marine fossil beds in the Swan River, dated to 4000–6000 years BP, were believed to demonstrate low freshwater discharge, implying low rainfall. Research by palynologists Jane Newsome and Elizabeth Pickett counters this interpretation. In 1993 they concluded that none of the Holocene pollen sequences show strong evidence for climatic change. Western Australia's long coastal belts are some of the most archaeologically unexplored but potentially informative areas of prehistoric Australia.

Australia's coastline is so extensive and varied in resources and habitation conditions that it is impossible to generalise. However, that some coastal peoples comprised among the continent's densest populations seems evident; but the rapid coastal expansion of modern Australian settlement has ensured the destruction of much of this evidence, particularly on the eastern and southeastern seaboard.

Regional challenges and responses

17

The story of the exploitation of Holocene landscapes is testimony to the adaptability and creative talents of prehistoric groups. While the dense rain forests of southwest Tasmania, some islands, and parts of the arid lands may have been uninhabited except for opportunistic forays when conditions permitted, the continent experienced land use which varied dramatically between regions. This chapter reviews some major regions, commencing with the mountainous southeast.

THE SNOWY MOUNTAINS

The southeast Australian Alps today are recreational 'snow country' with extensive nature parks and ski resorts. In pre-European times they proved equally attractive to the Aborigines, who travelled great distances in summer to participate in ceremonies and spend some months subsisting on the seasonally abundant food resources. The best-known archaeological region of the alps is the Snowy Mountains in New South Wales, which ascend abruptly from the surrounding tableland. Between mountain peaks are broad, shallow, semi-enclosed valleys, called 'high plains'; two major rivers, the Snowy and Thredbo, which have incised deep parallel valleys opening on to the tableland to the north. There is an altitudinal succession of vegetation communities, from montane forest to sub-alpine snowgum, rising to alpine herb-fields. The area of sustained snow cover (snow persisting for 120 days) is about 100 square kilometres.

The first archaeological field projects were undertaken during the 1970s by Josephine Flood and Val Chapman in the Snowy Mountains and their northern approaches. Flood's wide-ranging reconnaissance provided the framework for a regional prehistory set in the wider context of the southeastern highlands. Subsequently, with continued development of recreational facilities in the 1980s, a large number of highly focused site surveys for environmental impact studies contributed further detail. The first archaeological excavations were carried out in the Snowy Mountains only in 1988, revealing an extensive cultural horizon in the uppermost sediment of elevated flats above the Thredbo River, on the southeastern border of Kosciusko National Park. Numerous prehistoric sites have now been examined within the valley of the upper Snowy River, mostly lithic scatters, sometimes with undisturbed archaeological deposit. Along the Snowy River, workshop areas occur where hatchet heads were made from river cobbles. Because most artefacts are simple quartz flakes, they are commonly difficult to identify as artefacts; but also present are hammers, pounders and grindstones made from volcanic stone, and microblade flaking debitage and microliths made of quartz or silcrete. Because most sediments in the mountains derive from granitic bedrock they are acidic, and with the exception of small pieces of charcoal rapid deterioration of organic materials occurs, leaving only stone artefacts as human testimony.

The mountain people

Historical accounts of Aborigines in the alps are scant, but they have intrigued prehistorians and the public alike because they describe the bogong moth festival. In the lean winter months in the Snowy Mountains only small groups of Aborigines foraged, mostly in the lower montane valleys and on the adjacent tableland. The alpine region at this time of year was virtually without food resources and dangerous because of the harsh and unpredictable weather. The forested montane zone with its fast-flowing watercourses continued to provide wombats, which are seasonally easier to catch basking in the sun near their burrows. Possums are also available in winter but overall the numbers of mammals and birds significantly decreased. Edible tubers and rhizomes were available, though some of these are less palatable in winter.

Aboriginal occupation of the mountains changed dramatically during summer. The Ngarigo bands were joined by other bands from surrounding tribes, such as Ngunawal and Jaitmatang, and by the Yuin people who had trekked from the southeast coast. Probably well over a thousand people gathered together at two ceremonial grounds in the Jindabyne and Wollondibby Valleys in the north of the mountains to perform inter-tribal rites. These annual congregations were essential in maintaining strong social, political and religious ties between the tribes, but not all were peaceful, and there was enmity between the Yuin and the inland tribes south of the main range. A colonial settler recalled one fight that occurred near the present Lake Crackenback resort, and the grave of some of those killed in the clash has been located nearby. In normal years these gatherings took place as early as October; by November they had split into small parties on their way to their favoured base camps at higher altitudes.

Routes into the mountains

One of the major ceremonial grounds was identified as 'Kalkite' by colonial settlers, which has been identified with a bora ring near the junction of the Snowy River and Wollondibby Creek near Jindabyne; the ring is now submerged under a reservoir. Possibly this bora ring was for local Ngarigo use, while the corroboree ground was nearer Mount Kalkite on the northern margin of the Jindabyne Valley. In any event, it was from this general area that the Yuin groups traversed the Snowy River valley to a shallow alpine valley called the Snowy Plain. Further ceremonies occurred at a location deep in the main range. The second major area of congregation probably was near the foot of Mount Crackenback, a short walk from the road to Thredbo Village. This area of the Wollondibby Valley is sheltered from strong winds, and formerly it contained a small but resource-rich swamp.

The Thredbo Valley offered a route into the main range and was also the route taken by Aborigines travelling into the mountains from the Mount Crackenback area. Before logging and land clearance for pastures, tall canopy woodland protected these flats from the cold winds that sweep down the valley. Archaeological surveys have located prehistoric camps, while artefacts occur along the length of the valley. Where Kamminga excavated on flats above the river, artefact densities increased to 2000 per cubic metre. Above 1200 metres, however, only small lithic scatters occur, interpreted by Flood as summer camps; those above the winter snow-line are high-summer alpine camps—a site near the saddle of Perisher Gap at 1830 metres is the highest on record.

Bogong moths and the food quest

Written records and oral traditions passed on by early colonists attribute the cause of the summer transhumance into the mountains as due to the arrival of millions of bogong moths, which were considered by the Aborigines to be a great delicacy. It was estimated that several tonnes were collected each summer. The bogong moth is common throughout Australia's temperate zone and even in the subtropics. The species comprises two distinct populations: one is widespread and sedentary; the other migrates via a high-altitude jet stream to the Australian Alps to spend the summer months in a torpid state (called aestivation) in shaded localities, such as under boulders on scree slopes. The harvesting of this insect began as early as October, and in normal years it continued until February or March. Sources imply that moth-harvesting and preparation of cakes from scorched and pounded insects were exclusively a male activity. One oral tradition suggests that camps were made at lower elevations, presumably in sheltered localities, and excursions made to the alpine zone. Important moth aestivating sites occurred on both sides of the upper Thredbo Valley at altitudes above 1400 metres, and there is direct access to major aestivation sites in the main range and in high Perisher Valley. Surviving testimony to these moth-harvesting sites are the place-names, Bogong Creek, a major melt-water tributary of the Thredbo River, and Paddy Rush's Bogong, a granite peak about two kilometres from Thredbo resort.

The Aboriginal predilection for bogong moths must have excited the sense of curiosity of British settlers and its prominence in the recollections probably overstates its contribution to the diet. It has also been argued by some prehistorians that social and political factors were fundamental driving forces for the seasonal movement of Aborigines to the alps. In particular, Sandra Bowdler proposed that moths were a 'communion food' associated with men's ceremonies, and that it was the women's task to collect a staple plant food, the daisy yams (*Microseris lanceolata*), to support the large ceremonial gatherings.

The daisy yam, a perennial herb with a radish-like tuber up to eight centimetres long, was an important staple in many parts of southeastern Australia, especially on the basalt plains of western Victoria where it grew in vast numbers. However, that species probably does not grow at altitudes above about 1200 metres, while the species that is common in the Snowy Mountains has a fibrous root, probably edible but less tasty. While 'feasting' on moths certainly occurred and no doubt some daisy yams were collected, the alps in summer provided a wide range of food resources, in sufficient amounts to sustain a vastly increased population.

Bogong moths were not an entirely secure food resource: parasitic infections or droughts could dramatically reduce numbers before the southward flight, and strong westerly winds during the migration or a sudden cold snap in the alps sometimes decimated populations. Undoubtedly bogong moths provided important nutrition in good years, but Aboriginal subsistence in the alps was more broadly based than this. Setting aside possible cultural preferences, the potential food resources included a wide range of land animals, birds, reptiles, insects, and small crayfish which were numerous in the small lakes and bogs of the alpine zone. There are other predators of the moths, including thousands of sluggish overfed currawongs and ravens, which in turn must have been easy prey for Aboriginal moth-harvesters. From spring, through summer, there was honey from the hives of stingless native bees: the dry sclerophyll forest on lower slopes probably produced the edible sugary exudates called manna from the manna gum, candlebark, and red spotted gum, and the white sugary capsules (called lerp) of tiny sap-sucking insects.

A preliminary assessment of available plant foods may be derived from botanical studies in the Snowy Mountains and from historical literature for adjacent regions. The more important dietary staples were those with edible tubers or starch-rich rhizomes, such as orchids, lilies, water ribbons, and bracken, providing more than half of the potential plant food species in the Snowy Mountains. It is the vegetated part of the alpine zone which has the largest and most concentrated growth of edible tubers, because tuberous plants receive more intense and prolonged sunlight in the alpine zone than they do in forested areas at lower altitudes. One of the consequences of regular burning of the montane forest would have been to encourage the growth of such edible tubers.

Migratory origins?

The earliest evidence for human presence in the Australian Alps dates back only about 4000–5000 years, as is the case for the New England tablelands in northern New South Wales. In the Snowy

Mountains this antiquity is provided by Kamminga's excavations at Crackenback Village. In the southeast highlands generally a trend is discernible towards more intensive occupation of rockshelters from about 3000 years ago, accompanied by an increase in the number of habitation sites. Possibly this is accentuated by archaeologists who find it easier to recognise lithic scatters that contain distinctive stone microblade flaking debris and microliths. The antiquity of bogong moth migration to the alps must be at least a few thousand years, but whether it extended back to the Mid-Holocene warm maximum, with average temperatures about 2–3°C warmer, is unknown. During that period the area of snow cover was reduced to about one-fifth of its present distribution, though cold and windy conditions still prevailed on the mountain summits. Because the alpine zone was smaller, the major aestivating localities may have been more concentrated, while surrounded by a larger area of snowgum forest in which the moths fed. Possibly the moths were then abundant; yet they may have coasted the prevailing winds all the way to the central plateau of Tasmania. It is worth noting that high-altitude sites of the southeast mainland and Tasmania frequently occur on the sunny slopes in sheltered locations, close to water, and adjacent to different vegetational zones. These are issues which future research must probe.

EMERGENCE OF MURRAY RIVER SOCIETIES

The 2950-kilometre-long Murray River originates in the Snowy Mountains and flows westwards, then south to the Southern Ocean. It is fed along its course by many tributaries, three of which are large rivers, including the sometimes majestic Darling River. The Murray carries little water compared to rivers of similar length on other continents, because it flows through poorly watered, semi-arid country that experiences high evaporation. Comparatively modest in water volume it may be, but in terms of prehistoric human subsistence and demography it was Australia's Nile.

Prior to about 14,000 years BP the river channel was relatively straight, wide and shallow, and the water it carried seasonally was cold and swift-flowing: aquatic resources such as shellfish were not abundant, and there was little habitat diversity along the river corridor. The modern Murray River and it resource-rich riverine microenvironments began to develop towards the end of the Pleistocene, when its channel became narrower and more sinuous, and the water

Canoe of a sheet of eucalypt bark, typical of watercraft on still, inland waterways in southeastern Australia. Photographed c. 1879 by Fred Kruger, on the Yarra River at Coranderrk Aboriginal Station, Victoria. The man standing wears his possum skin cloak with the fur outwards, while the other man has his cloak reversed. (F. B. Smith collection)

it carried was warmer and flowed more slowly. Evolving along the central and lower Murray River during the Holocene was a landscape of meandering river channels, and relict billabongs—cut-off river channels forming still-water lagoons—small lakes, swamps and low sand dunes, forming seasonal wetlands in the wider riverine plain.

By the early nineteenth century, the central and lower Murray River and the lower Darling were possibly the most densely populated areas of Aboriginal Australia. The impact of alien diseases which preceded British exploration and settlement was so devastating to these closely packed riverine communities that the number who died is unknown. These communities were semi-sedentary and localised. Although canoes of very shallow draft were fashioned from the bark of river red gum (*Eucalyptus camaldulensis*), which lined the river banks, people usually did not travel long distances up or down the river; nor did they venture far from the riverine corridor, which is about twenty kilometres wide, or as far as people can walk carrying a skin water bag. Along some stretches of the river, such as near its junction with the Darling River, there are no permanent sources of fresh water away from the river for tens of kilometres.

Food resources that sustained such a high population density along much of the Murray River were available at different times for at least nine months of the year, though mostly abundant from spring to early autumn; they were largely restricted to the riverine corridor. These resources included at least 40 types of plant food; and 27 species of animals; six species of large fish; two crustacea, including crayfish up to three kilograms in weight; and shellfish, frogs, birds, reptiles and insects. Some plant foods, such as Eumong seeds (*Acacia*) were collected away from the river. Plant-fibre nets up to 90 metres long and nearly two metres high were used to trap fish, ducks and large game, such as kangaroo and emu. Fish proved a staple resource; such large quantities were caught in brushwood traps that cartloads were sold to British settlers. Some idea of the richness of resources in South Australia's lower Murray River and the intensity of occupation was provided by Mulvaney's two excavations at Fromm's Landing, where deposits rich in charcoal and ash contained bones or teeth of 30 species of native mammals, reptiles, emu eggshell, Murray cod, yabbies, and masses of mussel shells.

Flooding occurred almost annually in spring and regulated life along the river by replenishing the food stocks. Winter was the lean season; when the rains ceased to fall in the catchments, the Murray and Darling Rivers occasionally dried to standing pools of water. At such times there was terrible famine: the water became more saline and fish failed to spawn or migrated upriver, crustacea burrowed into the ground, migratory birds were less numerous, and many of the plant foods of the wetlands unavailable. During the Late Holocene there may have been droughts lasting two years or more every decade, which means a number of serious droughts during a person's lifespan. Research on skeletal pathology of central Murray River populations by Steve Webb has provided evidence for periodic famine and disease. Webb also noted a very high incidence of anaemia, compared to hunter-gatherer groups from elsewhere in Australia and other parts of the world, especially in young children, and postulates that the cause was endemic intestinal parasites.

Cemeteries

The interpretation of human burials to provide insight into ancient ritual practices, health and diet are discussed in Chapters 1 and 10. While this subject arouses much emotion, it is vital cultural and scientific evidence which cannot be ignored: otherwise, ancient societies may never be fully appreciated. The most notable and distinctive prehistoric sites within the Murray River corridor are cemeteries, some modest in size, others comprising thousands of burials, but always in sand dunes. The most notable cemeteries in the annals of Australian archaeology are Kow Swamp, Coobool Creek and Roonka, but many others are being continually exposed by the treading of stock and wind erosion, such as at Lindsay Island, Poon Boon, Robinvale, Lake Wallawalla, Snaggy Bend, Wallpolla, and Swanport near the mouth of the Murray, to list only some. The largest of all, at the southern end of the Lake Victoria lunette, which is estimated to contain 10,000 burials, has been disturbed by the conversion of the lake into an irrigation reservoir.

The only systematically excavated cemetery along the Murray River is at Roonka Flat, within a limestone valley over a kilometre wide, near Blanchetown in South Australia. Here the channel of the Murray River is sinuous, and reed-filled lagoons attractive to waterbirds mark its earlier course; on either side of the gorge is semi-arid country with sand dunes, formerly vegetated with dense mallee scrub. The excavation of Roonka, directed by Graeme Pretty, began in 1968 and continued for a decade. In all, 216 complete and fragmentary burials were uncovered, most poorly preserved, with surviving bones fragmentary and deformed by their long burial. Stratification was complex and difficult to interpret because of ancient reworking of sediments and modern erosion resulting from land clearance for stock grazing. The chronology of the site was determined by the largest number of available different dating methods of any other archaeological site in Australia, including thermoluminescence, palaeomagnetism, uranium fluorimetry (which measures the rate at which traces of uranium are diffused into buried bone by groundwater), and both conventional and AMS radiocarbon dating, producing an unparalleled number of almost 250 age estimates. While there is still some uncertainty about the antiquity of the earliest burials, the range is from at least 7000 years BP until the nineteenth century. At about 4000 years BP there was a substantial increase in the number of burials, but almost

90 per cent belong within the last 2000 years, which is a pattern repeated at other cemeteries as well.

Colin Pardoe, who has studied Murray River cemeteries for over a decade, has argued convincingly that the size and density of Aboriginal communities along the central and lower Murray River must have increased dramatically during the Holocene era, and that this phenomenon is fundamentally a response to the more productive riverine environment of the modern Murray River and the cultural adjustments that were made. His key archaeological evidence for such dramatic transformations of Aboriginal society and culture is the emergence of the cemeteries, and the burials they contain, in particular the genetic relationships derived from studying the crania.

Burials before the cemetery era were often located on high ground near the river, but there are very few demonstrably older than 7000 years BP. Cemeteries first appear along the central Murray River between 10,000 and 13,000 years BP, such as those at Kow Swamp and Coobool Creek. By about 7000 years BP, the practice of demarcating specific localities as burial grounds had spread downriver, ultimately to the mouth of the Murray. At all the cemeteries examined by archaeologists there is evidence of camping—lenses of mussel shells, charcoal or ash, cooking stones—and at least in the nineteenth century one such cemetery dune was used as a base camp when the surrounding area was flooded. However, Pardoe believes that domestic use of the localities mostly preceded their dedication as cemeteries, but because the graves are dug into older sediments these unrelated remains are often found in the same levels.

Genetic isolation of the riverine people

There scarcely can be any greater environmental contrast than the Murray River and its Mallee hinterland west of the river's confluence with the Murrumbidgee River. Red sand dunes vegetated with blue-green saltbush stretch into the distance for hundreds of kilometres; there is less than 250 millimetres of unreliable rainfall annually and only scattered and unreliable food resources, including mammals, emus, reptiles, and some plant foods such as *Acacia* seeds. Significantly, the contrast between these two habitats began to accentuate at about the same time as cemetery burial became common along the Murray River. For many thousands of years prior to this time the groundwater level in the Mallee was high and stream-fed lakes were filled to overflowing, but at about 7000 years BP lake levels began to fall, and by 5000 years BP these lakes were dry or saline.

The contrast between hinterland and riverine habitats is mirrored by the pattern of human demography. J. B. Birdsell estimated that population density along the Murray River was 20 to 40 times greater than in territory commencing only a few kilometres into the Mallee. Pardoe observes that many features of soft tissue and skeleton show marked differences between people of the Murray River and those to the north, which is interpreted as substantial social and genetic isolation of the riverine people from those of the hinterland.

Ethnographic reconstruction indicates that the kinship system of the central Murray River communities was 'exclusive', and relatives were identified only within a few clans which exchanged marriage partners; all other people were outsiders or strangers. Tribal territories were relatively small and boundaries well defined. This 'corporate organisation' was defined by centralised political control more marked than anywhere else, and hereditary transfer of power.

Pardoe's studies of the cemeteries projects the fundamentals of this ethnographic reconstruction of social and political order many thousands of years into the past. One of his most intriguing findings is that there is a cline in cranial traits along the Murray River, which indicates primarily gene flow between adjacent groups along the river corridor—people intermarrying with their neighbours who shared the same culture and mode of subsistence, as distinct from hinterland people. Pardoe's statistical studies of the cemetery burials demonstrated that this pattern had probably operated since the terminal Pleistocene. As the river corridor became increasingly isolated, environmentally and culturally, riverine groups started to differentiate from each other physically, because gene flow between them was restricted to a territorial chain defined by the river corridor, in contrast to the more varied genetic mixing which was occurring in the rest of Australia. As with a dialect chain, the groups farthest away from each other along the river showed the largest differences, and yet they also were becoming more distinct from adjacent non-riverine populations. By the Late Holocene, the differences in the incidence of non-metric attributes of crania along the river exceeded those between crania from such far-flung regions as Cape York Peninsula and Western Australia. Thus, while the Murray River tribes cluster together genetically, they are also the most highly differentiated regional population in Aboriginal Australia.

Cemeteries and society

Further information about prehistoric society and relationships between riverine populations has been gleaned from cultural practices evident from the burials and from the very existence of the cemeteries. A number of crania from Kow Swamp and Coobool Creek, in the region where cemeteries appear to originate, reveal that at about 9000 years BP it was the practice to alter the natural shape of infants' crania by flattening the frontal bone, which would have made them appear distinctively different. Pardoe suggests that this may have reinforced group identity, much like body scarification. Similarly, ritual removal of the central upper incisor tooth of men (called tooth avulsion) becomes evident at about 7000 years BP along the Murray River from Gunbower to Cobram (including Coobool Creek, Nacurrie and Kow Swamp cemeteries), and continues at least until 3500 years BP. The practice is known from other regions of southeastern Australia in the nineteenth century, but the distributions do not link with that along the Murray River.

At Roonka cemetery, some graves had offerings of two valves of a mussel shell placed at the bottom of the grave on either side of the body, a custom not yet detected elsewhere. However, at Robinvale areas of charcoal from small fires were found by Sandra Bowdler and local Aboriginal community members in four of eleven graves they excavated. These fires had been positioned next to the person's head or knees. Charcoal from a double burial in this group provided a date of about 3000 years BP. There is also evidence of fires in grave pits at three other localities along the Murray River, including Roonka, and an example further north, at Lake Nitchie, where the mortuary practice is dated to about 6800 years BP. In the majority of grave pits excavated, no associated grave goods were identified, though Roonka is the notable exception along the Murray, for here numbers of ornaments or necklets have been found with the human remains. Even stone artefacts are rare, probably because there are few sources of flaking stone along the river, and quartz had to be brought from distant sources. Such artefacts are possibly inclusions in the grave-fill and not directly associated with the interment. An indication of the rarity of artefactual stone was provided by the Fromm's Landing excavation, where in two layers 600 quartz pieces weighed only 420 grams.

Pardoe reports that the standard type of burial in the Murray River corridor is supine extended (laid on the back) with arms straight and head orientated west–southwest; but there are also semi-flexed interments, with the body lying on either side, cremations, mainly of younger women, and bundle burials, all of which are Late Holocene in age. Pardoe discerns a common tradition of burial custom along the river in the preferred orientation of burials. The patterns of burial orientation, sex and age structure are similar at Roonka and Wamba Yadu cemeteries, which are more than 500 river-kilometres apart along the lower and central Murray River. At cemeteries further upstream, the pattern is different. Women and children are generally buried more variably and in different directions from men; more children are buried in cemeteries than in individual graves. At Roonka the few children were usually buried with adults and bore traces of either red or white pigment. Finally, as Pardoe has emphasised, the existence of large cemeteries along the river, in use for thousands of years, undoubtedly indicates a strong group identity, and ownership of land by localised, relatively sedentary descent groups. Identifying with place, therefore, is not only a modern phenomenon.

SETTLEMENT OF THE ARID ZONE

By the end of the Pleistocene, Australia's arid zone had become better watered and more hospitable for humans, and for the most part humidity increased during the succeeding few millennia. While there is considerable evidence for human settlement within the periphery of the arid zone during the Pleistocene, widespread occupation of the vast expanse of deserts is not apparent until the Mid-Holocene, with the basal dates for many excavated sites clustering between 7000 and 4500 years BP.

After the end of the Pleistocene, the Menindee and Willandra Lakes in western New South Wales had been encompassed within the shifting boundary of the semi-arid zone. The Menindee Lakes still held water, and during the Early and Mid-Holocene habitation sites became larger and more numerous than before. Many of the shell middens on the lunettes are extensive deposits 20–30 centimetres thick and contain the remains of large numbers of fish and bird species. This is a clear indication of more-permanent base camps and probably larger groups of people inhabiting the region. Further to the east, the Willandra Lakes had dried out by the end of the Pleistocene and were subsequently watered only by local showers. Although conditions in the region by 5000 years BP were even drier than today, there was an increase in the number of hearths and ovens on the margins and beds of the dry lakes. This modest evidence for more intensive settlement parallels that evident at the Menindee Lakes.

To the south, still within the semi-arid zone, the Mallee of north-western Victoria has a record of sparse human presence during the Early Holocene, possibly indicating occasional visits to the region. Permanent occupation of the Raak Plain and Lake Tyrrell near the edge of the Mallee country may have occurred during the wetter Mid-Holocene Warm Phase. Anne Ross, an archaeologist who has intensively surveyed the region, postulates that settlers had come during this period from the Murray River corridor only 60 kilometres away. If increases in stone artefacts are a reliable indicator, the Mallee only experienced a dramatic increase in occupation within the last 2000 years.

Six hundred kilometres to the northwest, at Hawker Lagoon in the North Flinders Ranges, Ron Lampert and Phil Hughes excavated an open-air site eroding from a lunette. Reoccupation of this site in the Holocene began only about 5000 years BP. Lampert and Hughes suggest that the lagoon was much less important earlier in the Holocene because there was more surface water available in the region generally. It is thought that at Hawker Lagoon, and probably throughout Australia's desert core, the period of most intensive human presence began only about 1500–1000 years BP and lasted until the nineteenth century. There is a strong case for cultural rather than environmental changes being responsible for this increase. Archaeologists have concentrated on seeking early occupation sites, but here is a reminder that the later stages of Australian prehistory hold many intriguing issues for future research.

LAKE EYRE REGION

Paradoxically, although the country around Lake Eyre is hyper-arid and drought-prone, the water sources were sufficient to support relatively large groups of people. The reason is that the channels of the Warburton and Cooper Creek, which discharge into Lake Eyre, have major river flows when monsoonal rain falls hundreds of kilometres upstream in Queensland and the Northern Territory. Currently, this is an almost annual event. Waterholes are common along these channels; most are saline or dry during prolonged droughts, but a few are permanent and up to several kilometres long. Other important but remote water sources are mound springs, where water wells to the surface. Areas of Holocene-age camping debris occur at many of these water sources. In the region there are also innumerable small ephemeral lakes and claypans which are occasionally replenished by rain. Although these are essential for exploiting country rarely visited at other times, these sources are short-lived because of the exceptionally high evaporation rate. Across the region the location of lithic scatters and other habitation debris reveals a strong preference for camping on sandy ground. Although Aborigines in historical times preferred the water from the few permanent waterholes, rockholes and soaks, they also visited isolated mound springs. Many of these springs have been investigated by Lampert and Hughes, Stan Florik, Vlad Potezny and others for environmental impact assessments. Lampert was informed by an Adnyamathanha elder that occasionally, in very good seasons, his people trekked from their regular base in the Flinders Ranges to a mound spring near Lake Frome. Despite difficulties of access to many mound springs, there is at least one extensive lithic scatter up to several hundred metres long. Typically, these scatters contain unifacially flaked spear points, geometric microliths, tula adzes and millstones, denoting visits within the last 5000 years.

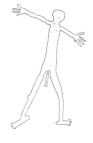

STRZELECKI DESERT

A series of ephemeral, shallow (playa) lakes in the Strzelecki Desert east of Lake Eyre has been investigated by Elizabeth Williams. She found large expanses of shell midden where river channels led into large ephemeral freshwater lakes. These deposits contained stone artefacts, clay heat retainers, and animal and fish remains. Their existence is consistent with ethnographic reports of large Aboriginal communities living semi-permanently in areas with abundant and predictable food resources. Field surveys of both the freshwater and playa lakes indicate that all dated archaeological sites are Mid- to Late-Holocene in age.

The work of Williams and Mike Smith in the vicinity of a Pleistocene site called JSN reveal further details about the region's occupation. A date of 13,500 years BP was obtained by Wasson for JSN, while other hearths nearby date to 14,000–10,000 and 2500 years BP. JSN is located in the midst of a substantial dunefield and there appears to be no reliable water source nearby. Unusually for such a location, the site contains a relatively large number of hearths, and extensive lithic scatters. Despite the Pleistocene dates for the hearths, the types of stone artefacts represented—such as seed grinders, unifacially flaked spear points and microliths—strongly suggests that they are Late Holocene in age. The stone from which the artefacts were made has been sourced to 100 kilometres distant, rather than from the closest localities 40–50 kilometres distant which are near reliable water. Unexpectedly, because the stone is from so far away, the artefacts are not markedly reduced in size by flaking. This patterning can be explained if stone utilisation is considered in terms of re-supply time, rather than merely distance from source. Williams and Smith hypothesise that people used the JSN site as a stop-over point for travel through the Strzelecki dunefield. People would have been aware that stone sources were only a few days' travel away. Probably visits to the site were relatively short, so that the demand for stone was easily met by stock-in-hand. The JSN artefacts contrast with those found on sites adjacent to the freshwater lakes mentioned earlier. Although the lakes are also some distance from stone sources, the artefacts, unlike those at JSN, are heavily reduced and recycled. It is suggested that this patterning is due to a greater population density and degree of residential stability at the lakeside sites which had abundant food and water resources.

NULLARBOR PLAIN

Rainfall on the coast of the Nullarbor Plain did not increase until the sea rose to its present level. The earliest evidence for human occupation at Madura Cave, near the southern end of the 1600-kilometre-long bush turkey Dreaming track, dates to about 8000 years BP. By this time the region around the cave had changed from arid scrubland to coastal woodland. At nearby Norina Cave, on an escarpment overlooking the coastal plain, visitation continued throughout the Holocene. Artefact densities at both these caves increased markedly around 4000 years BP, and it is tempting to assume that increased or more sustained visitation was responsible. Although little is known about the antiquity of routes from the Nullarbor coast to central Australia, considerable potential existed. Flint and silcrete are found in lithic scatters on the northern margin of the plain, possibly marking visits by people who had travelled both from the southern coast and the desert interior.

Ooldea Soak, also known as Yuuldul, situated in sand dunes on the northeast edge of the Nullarbor Plain, is the only permanent and reliable water source in the region. Here rain water is contained below ground surface by an impervious layer of clay. When the explorer Ernest Giles reached the soak in 1875, he declared it 'a fearful place' with only 'a shallow native well in the sandy ground of a small hollow'. The nearest other water source was Pidinga Rockholes, nearly 60 kilometres away. Despite its less than idyllic setting, the soak was a crucial water source for people travelling across the desert during at least the last few thousand years, and an important trade centre. The social worker Daisy Bates recorded that one small group had come to Ooldea from the Mann Ranges, a straight-line distance of 1600 kilometres. Such groups zig-zagged across the countryside for up to two years, seeking out and exploiting food and water resources opportunistically. Stone artefact scatters around Ooldea Soak stretch for several kilometres along wind-deflated dunes and have densities of 200–700 artefacts per square metre. Silcrete is common in lithic scatters and must have been brought from sources in central Australia, such as the Everard Ranges. Formal artefact types are typical of the Small Tool Phase and include heavily worn woodworking adzes and chisels, microliths and small cores, as well as glassy fragments of tektites from meteorite impact 700,000 years ago that showered much of the arid zone with globules of molten sediment.

CENTRAL AUSTRALIA

The prehistory of central Australia derives largely from the research of Mike Smith who excavated a number of archaeological sites there in the mid-1980s. A key site for the arid core is Puritjarra rockshelter in the Cleland Hills. Smith's excavation indicated occasional Holocene visits before 6500 years BP, and more frequent visits afterwards, though only intensively from about 600 years ago. Smith also reported a marked trend towards increased site use and greater numbers of recent prehistoric sites in the better-watered ranges, and at open-air habitation sites south of the MacDonnell Ranges. One of these sites is Intirtekwerle rockshelter (meaning 'stinking rockhole', which refers to a large ephemeral rockhole nearby), in a narrow sandstone escarpment of the James Range. The rockshelter was a favoured camping place because of easy access to different environments. Occupation possibly began some five millennia ago, but only intensified at about 850 years BP, when it offered a tenfold increase in the density of flaked stone artefacts and increases in charcoal from campfires and animal bones.

LITTLE SANDY AND GREAT SANDY DESERTS

Major archaeological fieldwork in the Great Sandy and Little Sandy Deserts in northwestern Australia began only recently. Extensive surveys by Peter Veth east of the Pilbara iron-ore mines located sites dating only to the last 3000–4000 years BP, some of them large lithic scatters at permanent water sources, probably denoting base camps. One of these scatters at Kadaru (well number 24) on the Canning Stock Route, contains more than a million stone artefacts. Other lithic scatters at ephemeral water sources are small. Veth also examined hundreds of rockshelters but found artefacts in only 50 of them, five of which he excavated. While Veth's dating of the artefact-rich sediments has recently been questioned, his finding of increased artefact discard between 1400 and 800 years BP is consistent with the general picture of increased human presence in central Australia around this time.

EXPANDING DESERT DOMAINS

There are different explanations for the apparent population increase and technological changes in the arid zone. Smith postulates that the favourable environmental conditions of the Early to Mid-Holocene resulted in population increase and ultimately in 'demographic packing'. This period was followed at 4000 years BP by lean times lasting 1000 years, when the climate became marginally drier. The reduction of food resources, Smith argues, provided strong incentives to exploit labour-intensive foods, such as grass seeds, and to adopt labour-saving production processes and devices. An alternative scenario is argued by Peter Veth, who proposes that settlement of the arid zone from refuge areas occurred in stages during the Holocene. Veth postulates that lowland desert 'corridors' were recolonised first, and that the sandy deserts were inhabited from 5000 years BP when population density reached a critical point and new, adaptive alliance systems and subsistence technology developed that made possible the conquest of the most marginal desert environments. The safety net needed for this last stage of colonisation, Veth argues, is the extended (or 'inclusive') kinship and long-distance links between groups, characteristic of arid-zone social systems in historical times. Whether such change came about only in recent millennia is debatable, since extended kinship is considered by other scholars to have been a Pleistocene phenomenon, evident from such archaeological evidence as Panaramittee Style rock engraving.

Relevant to Veth's model is linguistic evidence for settlement of the Western Desert, where the population was united by common social organisation, mythology, language and material culture. The linguist Patrick McConvell argued that proto-Western Desert language was brought by a wave of immigrants from the Pilbara region about 2000 years ago. Although the region in which Western Desert language is spoken is vast, it is a marginal environment and its Aboriginal inhabitants were necessarily few in number. We are not convinced that migration into the region was responsible for a single Western Desert language throughout the region, rather than the normal processes of social interaction between small groups sharing a common culture and lifestyle. McConvell correlates his postulated migration with the timing of increased artefact discard at excavated sites and other archaeological phenomena, but the links appear to be tenuous. Evidence for territorial expansion of Western Desert people is also seen in the sharp biological boundary in blood genetics and incidence of the mutation for tawny-coloured hair at the eastern boundary with the Arrernte tribe. If this was indeed the case, the question remains which tribes were on the move?

That the sandy deserts were uninhabited before the Mid-Holocene is questioned by Scott Cane, who sees no reason to believe that desert people were not adequately adapted since Pleistocene times. His reasons are the same as those he advanced for assuming widespread and continuous settlement of the arid zone during the Pleistocene (see Chapter 12). Cane notes that the Nullarbor Plain has a long prehistory without any evidence of a marked technological change. He points out that, to a large extent, the nature of reliable water sources influences the pattern of human settlement in particular deserts, and that long-term survival of a population required basic but different subsistence strategies. For instance, in the Great Sandy Desert in the northwest of the arid zone, rockholes are the most common and reliable water sources. These rockholes are filled by monsoonal rain and are sufficient to sustain people for the rest of the year. People travelled in small groups from one water source to another; although the highly nomadic resident population was small, it was widely spread throughout the region. In the Great Victoria Desert to the south, people congregated in larger groups based at major soaks, whereas further south again, on the Nullarbor Plain, people migrated along the wooded coastal corridor and along the northern edge of the plain, avoiding its treeless and waterless interior except during times of unusually high rainfall. Perhaps the issue of colonisation of the deserts hinges on a demonstration that during the Early Holocene population numbers were very low rather than that there were no inhabitants at all.

TRADE AND EXCHANGE NETWORKS

The trade and exchange networks criss-crossing the arid and semi-arid zones served as the main lines of communication between far-flung tribes. Undoubtedly they facilitated the diffusion of innovations, both technological and conceptual. In Chapter 6 we discussed the Lake Eyre Basin trade and exchange network, which extended from Spencer Gulf on the southern coast to the Gulf of Carpentaria. Along its routes were carried the drug pituri, ochre, artefacts and ceremonies. Specialised production of artefacts for trade may have set the scene for developments in stone and wood technology and their rapid adoption throughout the deserts. In the nineteenth century, craft specialisation in spears, boomerangs, shields and baskets was particularly noted among the Wangkamana of the Mulligan River, who inhabited the best pituri-growing area.

The first archaeological indication of inter-tribal ceremonial gatherings associated with trade and exchange routes has been obtained by Mike Smith who excavated at the Therreyererte ceremonial site in the Rodinga Range, in the Simpson Desert, southeast of Alice Springs. Therreyererte is an extensive open-air camping locality on a sandy alluvial fan close to an important native cat totemic site. This Dreaming trail begins at the head of Spencer Gulf and continues for 2500 kilometres to the north coast. In mythology these creation beings introduced the male initiation rite of sub-incision to the central Australian tribes. Hundreds of people from different tribes congregated at Therreyererte to participate in ceremonies staged after the summer rains, when there was an abundance of food, and water filled the rockholes. During the rest of the year, the locality was of no particular interest to the local clan because the waterholes were dry. The archaeological site is marked by a lithic scatter of over 100 artefacts per square metre, including several hundred grindstones.

Immediately below ground surface is a layer half a metre thick, rich in artefacts. Smith estimates that an abrupt increase in the number of stone artefacts occurred about 500–600 years ago, probably marking the commencement of inter-tribal ceremonies at this locality, possibly coinciding with the origin of Dreaming mythology. A similar pattern of recent prehistoric intensification is reported for the important, but undated, kangaroo ceremonial locality of Keringke, near Santa Teresa settlement. Smith infers that these large ceremonial gatherings were an outcome of earlier, more fundamental cultural changes in arid-zone prehistory.

TECHNOLOGICAL DEVELOPMENTS

During the last 3000 years stone implement types characteristic of the Small Tool Phase appear on sites in the arid zone associated with a greater density of artefacts. They must reflect advances in desert adaptation. The new assemblage includes the triumvirate of tula adze, pirri and marni wadna gravers (see Chapter 14), all sophisticated hafted tools of innovative design. They were lightweight, efficient in use, and had a long working life. The stone of which they are made was conserved by design elements that permitted repeated resharpening of the cutting edges with little reduction of efficiency until they reached slug form, at which point they were replaced. The tula adze must have supplanted large stone choppers and, along with hand-held flake scrapers, these three stone tool types constituted an ideally portable woodworking tool-kit. The gravers were used for finishing a range of wooden artefacts used in the food quest. For instance, the pirri made the fluting on boomerangs of a type that in early historic times diffused in all directions from central Australia. Wind-tunnel experiments have shown that such fluting enhances the flight of a boomerang by reducing drag. The graver was used also to carve the necessary riffles on women's grass-seed winnowing dishes, and for the much broader fluting on their light-wood coolamons. Implications of the emergence of these unique stone implements are as yet unknown, but we are convinced that they are indigenous arid-zone innovations and an integral part of a new material culture adapted to desert conditions. Spinifex occurring throughout much of the arid regions provided craftsmen with an ideal resinous adhesive.

Another hafted woodworking implement common in the arid zone, but which had a wider distribution, is the hafted small flake

scraper. Most often these were hafted onto a spearthrower and used for general cutting and light woodworking. Possibly they signify when spearthrowers (and the corresponding new spear types) arrived in northern and inland Australia, but there is no direct evidence for this. The occurrence of microlith spear barbs and flaked stone spearheads in arid-zone assemblages more clearly denotes changes in spear design, but whether this had to do with improved functional efficiency or simply fashion is yet to be elucidated by experimental studies.

Beginning perhaps as early as 3000–4000 years BP but definitely within the last 2000 years in central Australia, an increase occurred in the harvesting of certain kinds of seeds from herbs and grasses, and the common practice of wet milling. This change is marked by the appearance of paired millstones, which are often found in large numbers at prehistoric base camps: the wet-grinding millstone is a hammer-dressed sandstone slab sometimes over twenty kilograms in weight, with distinctive long, narrow grinding grooves. In the Western Desert these millstones were difficult to obtain, and passed on from mother to daughter.

According to Smith, the seeds of trees, shrubs and succulents must always have been eaten; the large-scale harvesting of grass seeds marked a shift in emphasis, but to what effect? Smith postulates that population pressure forced females to rely on previously marginal or emergency food resources. Grass seeds are abundant and have a long 'shelf-life', but bread and seed cakes were not the preferred food. Gathering the seeds, winnowing and milling were arduous and time-consuming (it may take two to four hours to grind a kilogram of flour). Also, the grindstones had to be obtained, sometimes from sources hundreds of kilometres away. New millstones were not always easy to acquire, especially in the Western Desert. Tindale describes a woman's song about the laziness of her husband who would not journey to get her new ones. She laments that her top stone is worn so thin that her fingers are abraded and bleeding as she grinds the grain for his bread. From an economic perspective, seeds are costly in energy expenditure.

Whether or not climatic change is involved, it is possible, as Veth argued, that a grass-seed economy facilitated the settlement of the most marginal desert regions during the last 3000 years. As a reliable food resource, grass seed could sustain large groups for a short time and facilitated inter-tribal gatherings during favourable times. It proved an important dietary staple not only in marginal regions but across a larger expanse of grass-seed country, a prehistoric grain belt, which extended in a crescent across Australia's semi-arid and arid zones (see Map 3). According to Tindale, if the grain harvest was poor for more than two years, it was necessary to virtually evacuate tribal territories. Extended kinship networks therefore were a pre-requisite for survival to enable people to move to kin territories with better yields or alternative resources. The reconstruction and dating of the interplay of environmental, economic and social factors that propelled occupation of the arid zone will prove both rewarding research and a true test of archaeological method.

18 Island settlement

There are hundreds of offshore islands and islets around Australia, and in northern waters extensive reefs and small cays, which have emerged only in the last few millennia. As sea level rose during the Holocene, existing islands were submerged, while new ones were created from elevated parts of the receding coastline. These progressively diminished in area as the sea continued to rise to its present level, transforming large islands into archipelagos or clusters of islands and islets. Access was easy at first by walking across tidal flats and swimming deeper narrows. Islands were permanently occupied or visited until they became too small to sustain a human population or too difficult to reach from the mainland. Peter Veth demonstrated such abandonment of the Montebello Islands off the Pilbara coast, as Robin Sim did for Flinders Island in Bass Strait.

Occupation of the largest islands along the southern coast continued after their formation 10,000–12,000 years BP—Tasmania, Kangaroo Island and, in Bass Strait, King Island and 'greater' Furneaux Island, although it is not known whether these people had watercraft. All of these isolated populations, except the Tasmanians, either abandoned their island homelands or were isolated and became extinct thousands of years ago. In the north, Aboriginal bands probably continued to inhabit Bathurst and Melville Islands, which are accessible by crossings of less than ten kilometres between islets, and Groote Eylandt off the east Arnhem Land coast. These became islands between 6,000–7000 years BP; considering their size,

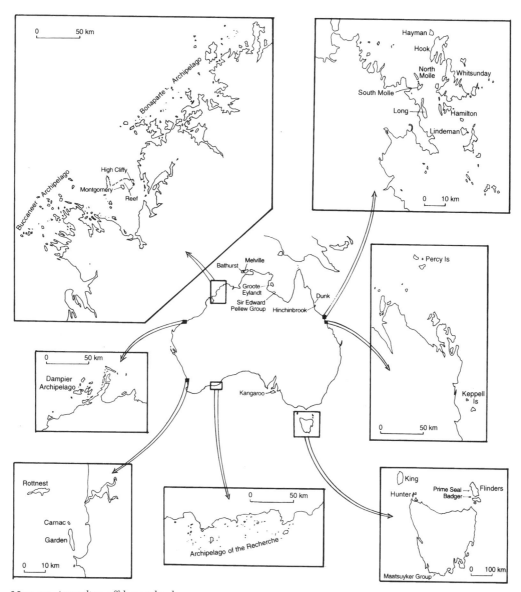

Map 15. *Australian offshore islands.*

accessibility and resources, these lands probably continued to be permanently inhabited. The cultural isolation of the Tiwi people of Bathurst and Melville Islands is evident thereafter in their distinctive culture and language.

Aboriginal groups were able to live more or less permanently on some small offshore islands. Certainly this was so for the Wellesley Group in the Gulf of Carpentaria, North Keppel Island, and possibly for the Whitsundays off the east coast of Queensland, and for the Montgomery Group off the Kimberley coast. The land area of these islands was relatively unimportant because of marine productivity, especially from tidal shallows and coral reefs. Many other islands with abundant food resources, at least seasonally, are scattered around Australia's coastline, and archaeological sites on a number reveal human visitation for thousands of years.

Sea-going Watercraft

Warm northern Australian waters, with their large tidal ranges, saw the greatest diversity of watercraft, ranging from simple floating logs to sophisticated sailing vessels. One basic craft was a rectangular or V-shaped raft made of logs lashed or pegged together with rattan or cord. Along the Queensland coast bark canoes up to three metres long could carry half a dozen people and their gear. These canoes were made from one to three bark sheets, narrowed and sealed at their ends. In some places, longitudinal strips of bark were sewn together for the hull, and gunwales and horizontal stretchers added to give it structural support. There is one account of a 32-kilometre voyage in a sewn bark canoe between the mainland and the Sir Edward Pellew Islands in the Gulf of Carpentaria.

The Torres Strait Islanders had dugout canoes with outriggers and sail, which was an elaborated Papuan design. The outrigger log-hull canoe was known from Torres Strait down the Queensland coast to the Whitsunday Islands, and the design had probably diffused in recent prehistoric times from the Papuan coast via the islands of Torres Strait. Strong, stable and safe craft such as these outriggers provided greater scope for marine hunting and fishing, and increased ability to exploit offshore islands. The basic dugout canoe was also introduced to the Arnhem Land coast by Macassans, who used them for gathering trepang, but these canoes were first made locally only in the early twentieth century, when steel hatchets had replaced stone ones.

Coastal waters of southern Australia are colder and rougher than in the north and voyaging in simple craft was difficult and dangerous. In Tasmania a distinctive canoe-shaped float, which may have originated some 3500 years ago, was used for crossings to nearshore

Australian watercraft: (a) Square-ended dugout canoe, capable of carrying six adults (Cairns); (b) Bark canoe with a stretcher, ribs and gunwales of wood (after Roth 1910); (c) Bark canoe with tied ends common on the southeast coast and Port Jackson in 1788; (d) V-shaped log raft made of saplings with their thicker ends forming the rear (Wellesley Islands, Gulf of Carpentaria). (Drawings by Val Lyons)

islands and even to islands twelve kilometres distant. On the Victorian and New South Wales coasts, bark canoes were occasionally used for sea voyages of up to seven kilometres. These were frail craft made from a single sheet of bark compressed and tied at its ends, designed essentially for the quiet waters of estuaries, rivers and lakes.

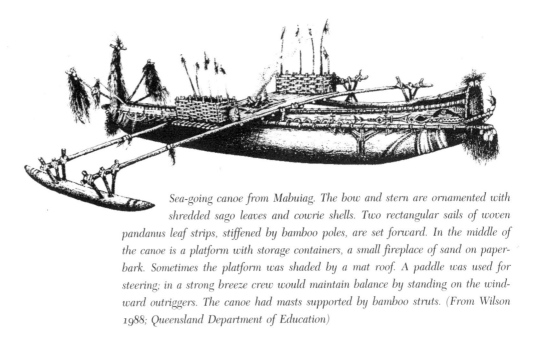

Sea-going canoe from Mabuiag. The bow and stern are ornamented with shredded sago leaves and cowrie shells. Two rectangular sails of woven pandanus leaf strips, stiffened by bamboo poles, are set forward. In the middle of the canoe is a platform with storage containers, a small fireplace of sand on paper-bark. Sometimes the platform was shaded by a mat roof. A paddle was used for steering; in a strong breeze crew would maintain balance by standing on the windward outriggers. The canoe had masts supported by bamboo struts. (From Wilson 1988; Queensland Department of Education)

Tasmanian float canoe, originally sketched by C. A. Lesueur in 1802, near Schouten Island, eastern Tasmania. (From J. Bonnemains et al. 1988, Baudin in Australian Waters, Plate 29)

Exploitation of offshore islands

Few distant islands beyond swimming capability have produced evidence of visitation from the mainland before about 3500 years ago. The exceptions include the Montebello Islands, some of the Kimberley islands, nearshore islands off the east coast and those of northwest Tasmania, discussed later. Most archaeological material found on islands dates from the last 2000 years, but chiefly the last 1000 years.

What are the reasons for this general trend? Some prehistorians link the apparent increase in exploitation and settlement either to social or technological changes on the mainland or to increased population density and pressure on coastal resources. Their claimed dates of island settlement and other changes do not always correlate, and we follow Sue O'Connor's reasoning that regional and local adaptations offer a better explanation than a 'prime mover'. Undoubtedly, local environmental and ecological changes over the last few thousand years, such as the growth of coral reefs, set the scene, or were catalysts, for the exploitation of islands. Innovations in watercraft also are fundamental to the process: the invention of canoe-shaped floats in Tasmania (see Chapter 19) and the consequences of the diffusion of sea-going outriggers in the northeast has been noted by prehistorians; for the Queensland coast, Mike Rowland identifies new designs of fishing gear which may have been Papuan-inspired. Marjorie Sullivan proposes that on the New South Wales coast there was an increase in population density linked with the appearance of line fishing and improvement in watercraft. Beginning about 2000 years ago, offshore fishing increased, and it was inevitable that islands were explored and their food resources harvested; shellfish, seals, and nesting seabirds were major attractions for the mainlanders. However, islands off the Victorian coast were never important for subsistence and there is no demonstrable pattern of regular seasonal visits, although occasional occupation of some sites begins within the last 2000 years. Denise Gaughwin and Richard Fullagar considered that circumstances on the mainland, such as social unrest or times of scarcity, propelled people to exploit the islands, but that they never became marine-oriented in their subsistence strategy.

The northwest coast

In historic times the people of the Kimberley coast and Dampierland used rafts of mangrove wood with paddles, called kalum. This craft comprised a double layer of mangrove poles, nailed together with long wooden pegs, a little over three metres long and tapered at one end. Those of Dampierland could carry four people and their dogs. These were true 'tide-riders' designed for the tidal range of nine to twelve metres, one of the world's largest, which in narrow channels between reefs could generate currents of up to eighteen kilometres an hour. Thus, according to Kim Akerman, an eight-kilometre journey need take only an hour and a half. For the uninitiated these waters were treacherous: the coast and islands are littered with the sunken vessels of later mariners who had insufficient understanding of the tides.

At King Sound and Collier Bay on the Kimberley coast, the Bardi, Djawi, Yaijibayi and coastal Worora made periodic visits to the reefs and islands of the Buccaneer and Bonaparte Archipelagos. These crossing were up to eight kilometres, and by island-hopping reached sixteen kilometres from the mainland. Montgomery Reef is the largest reef complex off the Kimberley coast. At high tide there are only two large sand islands about twenty square kilometres in area, called the Montgomery Islands; across a narrow channel on the landward side are some small sandstone islets. During low tide the reef emerges around the islands and mudflats, providing a resource-rich area of 300 square kilometres. The Montgomery Reef was exploited by the Yaijibayi people, who were probably permanent inhabitants without regular access to the mainland. This community of about 50 people were related to the coastal Worora. There are permanent soaks on the sand islands, which allowed exploitation of the reefs for dugong, turtles, fish, shellfish, crustaceans and seabirds; large yams grew on the sand islands. Sue O'Connor, the archaeologist who investigated the islands, suggests that they were occupied permanently no more than 3000 years.

The largest sandstone pinnacle is High Cliffy Island, one kilometre long and 300 hectares in area, formed by rising sea 8000–9000 years ago. In the dry season it is waterless, has little vegetation and is bereft of mammalian life. O'Connor recorded many circular dry-stone walls up to a metre high, which are the remains of paperbark-roofed huts. A midden twenty metres long in the middle of the island contains shells and the bones of reef fish and turtles. At a depth of 70 centimetres there is evidence of at least a fleeting visit from the mainland at 6700 years BP, but most evidence derived from intensive deposition from 650 years BP until the 1920s, when Aboriginal parents brought their children from a mission settlement to learn hunting and gathering skills. A nearby rockshelter revealed only twenty centimetres depth of cultural deposit with a basal date of about 3000 years BP, containing continuous intense cultural deposition, indicating increased exploitation for the last few thousand years, with possibly the most sustained occupation during the last 1000 years.

THE WELLESLEY GROUP

The Gayardilt and Lardil people permanently inhabited the Wellesley Group in the Gulf of Carpentaria, with their base camps on the largest two islands, Mornington and Bentinck. Around the islands are seagrass beds on which dugong and turtles feed, and after summer monsoonal rains fish were attracted to the seawater's lower salinity. The islanders employed rafts for tide-riding around the islands, but these could not have been particularly seaworthy. Not only were they prone to waterlogging but the lashing tended to fall apart in choppy seas, and for emergencies people carried a supply of spare cord wound around their waists. Oral traditions recount tragic misadventures during crossings. Gayardilt and Lardil languages are most closely related to Gananggalinda on the mainland opposite, but genetically the islanders deviate from the founder population; unlike mainlanders, the Gayardilt have a high frequency of B group blood type and an absence of A group, and have a mutant gene for tawny hair. On cultural and linguistic grounds, J. B. Birdsell proposed that the islands were probably settled only about 1000 years ago, but no archaeological work has yet examined this possibility.

TORRES STRAIT ISLANDS

In the 150 kilometres of sea which separates Papua New Guinea from Cape York Peninsula there are more than 100 islands, as well as innumerable islets and partially exposed sandbanks and cays (see Map 13). The islands have a land area of just over 1000 square kilometres, and this is more than doubled if tidally inundated reefs are taken into account. On the western side of Torres Strait are the 'high' continental islands of volcanic rock, the largest being Prince of Wales, rising to an altitude of nearly 250 metres, and there are eight satellite islands, including Thursday, Horn and Hammond. Between some of these high islands are elongated patch reefs, and channels between the reefs where the tidal currents are strong; these channels no doubt served as tide-riding sea lanes for canoes. The central and eastern islands of the strait are typically small flat coral reefs with a thin cover of sandy soil. To the east is the Great Barrier Reef, which comprises numerous small compact reefs separated by channels up to 35 metres deep. In the far north there are a few sand cays and tiny volcanic islands and islets with fringing reefs, including Murray Island (Mer), an old volcanic crater rim rising to altitude of 230 metres. The shallow sea behind the Barrier Reef is mostly devoid of reefs but there are a few patch reefs, some of which have cays with vegetation, including coconut palms. In shallow waters towards the western islands there is a belt of large platform and patch reefs stretching southwards from the Papuan coast. Adjacent to the Papuan coast are large silt islands, and Daru Island, which has a nucleus of volcanic rock.

History and ethnography

The earliest historical record of contacts between Islanders and Europeans was with Spanish explorers led by Luis Vaez Torres in 1606. From this time there were fleeting visits by passing European vessels until the 1840s, when the British arrived to chart the waters. During the next 30 years Torres Strait was a sea lane for maritime traffic from eastern Australia to colonial ports in East Asia, and a small number of Europeans lived in the islands to develop a pearling industry. In 1871 the London Missionary Society established stations on the main islands, and from then on traditional beliefs were actively discouraged.

Most of the early documentary accounts of Islander culture relate to the western islands. The main source is *Reports of the Cambridge anthropological expedition to Torres Strait*, a six-volume work edited by Alfred Haddon and published between 1901 and 1935. Haddon first visited the islands in 1888 in his capacity as a marine zoologist, and he was so fascinated by Islander culture that he returned a decade later with a scientific team to document the remaining traditional material culture and oral traditions—his team even included a musicologist. The second major source is the journal of O. W. Brierly, the artist on HMS *Rattlesnake* during its surveying expedition to northern Australia and Papua in 1848–50. Brierly had earlier taken part in an expedition to the Snowy Mountains and acquired a keen interest in Aboriginal culture, but it was 1979 before a transcription of his notebooks was published. Besides his own observations during the vessel's stay in the islands, Brierly interviewed a young Scottish woman, Barbara Thompson, the sole survivor of a shipwreck, who had lived with Islanders on Prince of Wales for five years until rescued by the *Rattlesnake*.

Subsistence and trade

Only twenty of the islands have sufficient fresh water for permanent human settlement, but many small islands were visited briefly during sea travel or hunting and fishing. When the islands were annexed, the fourteen Islander groups probably numbered about 3000–4000 people. When the pearling industry was established, many of the South Sea Islanders brought in to man the vessels intermarried with locals, and the descendant population now numbers about 25,000 people, of whom one-third live on the islands.

There was little terrestrial animal life to hunt on the islands and subsistence drew predominantly on the sea. Coral reefs are a larder of fish, turtle, dugong, crustacea and shellfish. Green sea turtles and loggerhead turtles are abundant and are easily caught during mating and egg-laying. Hawksbill turtles are also common and were taken mainly for the carapace. Dugong were more plentiful in the western part of the strait, where Islanders built hunting platforms in the shallow feeding grounds. Where it was viable, cultivation of Papuan food crops was practised, especially in the central and eastern islands; the soils of the southwestern islands close to Australia are poor, and wild plant foods were collected instead. Pigs were probably introduced from Papua to a few islands; thereafter there were feral populations, but these were never numerous. Significantly, pigs were not incorporated into myths, traditions or ceremonial exchange. Had they been brought to the Australian mainland, the Aborigines would have obtained a new large animal resource.

Probably from the beginning of permanent settlement on the islands, trade was necessary for survival. There was little timber useful for making artefacts and none suitable for canoe hulls. By the nineteenth century, a network of routes linked all the inhabited islands and extended to the coasts of Papua and Cape York Peninsula. A regular point of contact on the Australian mainland was Evans Bay at the tip of the peninsula; a more frequented entrepot was Mount Adolphus Island (Morilag) about ten kilometres offshore within the territory of a mainland tribe. Along the inter-island sea lanes were carried raw materials, artefacts and food. From Cape York came red ochre and spears in exchange for food and artefacts. The Islanders traded women to the Papuan villagers, along with pearl-shell harpoons and ornaments, dried fish, turtle, and human heads; they returned with sago, cultivated yams, coconuts, sugar cane and tobacco, and in the material domain, timber posts, hand drums, bows and arrows, cassowary feathers and bird-of-paradise skins, stone club heads and, most importantly, outrigger canoes. Most new canoes were made to special order in Dibiri and Wabuda villages in the Fly River estuary. These were dugout hulls with single outriggers, designed essentially for river travel. First they were taken to Saibai Island off the Papuan coast, where they were fitted with an extra outrigger, two masts and pandanus-mat sails, washboards and a platform. With these additions the canoes were now ocean-going and had the necessities for long voyages. Their average length was about fourteen metres, with the capacity to carry up to a dozen people. Often small fleets were organised and heavily manned for voyages of up to 80 kilometres; some central Islanders even sailed as far as the Pascoe River on the east coast of Cape York Peninsula.

The Torres Strait double-outrigger canoe design may ultimately have been Indonesian, adopted originally by coastal people on the western tip of West Irian and from there diffused eastwards. The sails, however, are of the style seen along the northern coast of New Guinea and its closest oceanic islands, but possibly the canoe was independently developed in Torres Strait and adapted for local conditions and needs.

Archaeological evidence for settlement

There have been three archaeological surveys in the islands beginning in 1970, respectively by David Moore, Ron Vanderwal and Mike Rowland. Late prehistoric and early historic sites include large rock-wall fish traps in the eastern islands, middens, rockshelters, and stone-pile lookouts on headlands. Torres Strait rock art comprises simple outline figures; rockshelters on the high western islands contain paintings of anthropomorphic figures and fishing themes, while the basaltic eastern islands have stylistically distinct engravings on boulders.

Archaeologists have excavated on Murray Island in the northeast and on the western high islands of Prince of Wales, Moa and Nagir, and Pulu Islet off Mabuiag. In all, five sites have been dated, but none is older than 700–800 years. On the whole, the results of excavations suggest increased human activity during the centuries before European arrival. It is assumed by many archaeologists that traces of earlier island settlement have yet to be discovered, and a general agreement of possibly 4000 years for voyaging and sustained island settlement within the strait. The circumstantial evidence for this length of time is mostly biogeographical in nature.

Antiquity of human occupation

For at least 80,000 to 120,000 years before Torres Strait formed, the land surface in this region had been low-lying plain, with rolling hills vegetated by savanna and open woodland—an unremarkable and monotonous landscape where there was no reason to locate base camps on the few rocky areas that would later become islands. By about 17,000 years BP the region was a wide isthmus, narrowing over succeeding millennia until the land bridge was breached at 8500–8000 years BP. The competing tidal demands of the Indian and Pacific Oceans must have caused very strong currents and surges, and perhaps even daily maelstroms, in the constricted waters of the channels. Although the sea-crossings were short, only the foolhardy would have considered regular ventures in such treacherous conditions and in watercraft far less sophisticated than the outrigger canoes of Torres Strait of the nineteenth century.

Initially, the Prince of Wales Group and other high islands immediately north of it were part of a single large island. As the sea continued to rise, this island shrank to form two smaller islands separated by shallow sea. Finally, in the last millennium of sea-level rise, it transformed into clusters of islands and rocky pinnacles. David Moore postulated that small groups of people may have lived on the southwestern islands during this period but that year-round subsistence was doubtful. In historic times, the Kaurareg of the Prince of Wales Islands traded for food from other Islanders and from Cape York Aborigines, especially during times of scarcity. In particular the Kulkalaig of Nagir Island provided them with cultivated plant food, sago and dried turtle meat. The shortage of fresh water on most islands of the Prince of Wales Group was sometimes acute, and wells were carefully maintained. Moore reports that the Kaurareg had problems even obtaining drinking water at their base camp at Port

Lihouon, facing the Australian mainland, where excavation revealed occupation during the last few hundred years. It is difficult to argue that a population could have been sustained before the development of an extensive and regular trade network.

The extensive coral reefs, small cays and sand islands, so characteristic of modern Torres Strait, developed only about 5000–4000 years BP. In the east, Bramble Cay, Darnley Island and the Murray Islands were isolated motes in the sea, without fringing coral reefs, so permanent human settlement of the islands before reef development was unlikely. Most of the Papuan coast was then tens of kilometres further north. Progradation of this coast and the formation of the present nearshore silt islands resulted from sediments discharged from the Fly River, which currently carries an annual sediment load of about 100 million tonnes. It is most likely that sustained occupation of the islands occurred no earlier than about 4000 years BP, facilitated largely by marine technology of Papuan derivation. The thrust of the archaeological evidence which indicates only recent prehistoric occupation and its intensification during the last few centuries cannot be ignored, and the long-distance trade network, ultimately linking New Guinea and Australia, may not be much older than this.

The Islanders

While the Islanders at European contact were not politically united, they shared material culture, customs and beliefs. Some aspects of this may be traced to Papua, such as head-hunting and its tools, arts and crafts, cultivated crops and shell-bladed hoe, probably the result both of Papuan trade contacts and the baggage of migration.

In general, the Torres Strait Islanders resemble Papuans rather than Australian Aborigines in physical features. However, there are north-to-south clines for general build, shape of nose and skin colour, which reflect geographic proximity to either mainland and the strength of kinship ties and trading relationships. Stephens, Darnley and the Murray Group Islands in the northeast were almost certainly colonised by horticultural fisher-people from the Fly River estuary. The inhabitants of the silt islands along the Papuan coast also are essentially Papuan in appearance and culture. However, a degree of Australian Aboriginal genetic inheritance in the western and central islands, as far north as Saibai, is evident from family ties as well as physical features. As one would expect, Aboriginal ethnic origins and cultural affiliations are most apparent in the southwest islands, which are geographically closest to Cape York. But genetic intermixing was continual and varied according to many circumstances. Intermarriage occurred between Kaurareg and mainland tribes, and captured Aboriginal women were taken back to the islands; visitors to Prince of Wales Island in 1849 were the Gudang from Cape York, the Badulaig from Badu Island, who sojourned for nearly three months, and the entire population of Nagir Island, who stayed nearly two months catching turtles.

Of all the Islander communities, the Kaurareg of Prince of Wales Island had the strongest links with the Australian mainland, mostly with the Gudang and Unduyamo of northeast Cape York Peninsula, with whom they sometimes stayed for periods during the dry season. Although the Kaurareg social system was Islander and essentially dissimilar to that of the nearby mainlanders, they hunted and collected the same range of seasonal food resources and prepared them in the same manner; they used spear and throwing stick rather than bow and arrow; their totemic system was Australian, and their mortuary customs were very similar to those of the Gudang. An Australian relationship embodied in the mythological saga of *Kwoiam* involved the southwestern islands. The totemic figure *Kwoiam*, 'of wild throat and half-wild heart', was the first to make shell eye emblems, which were important trade items in the strait. *Kwoiam* had crossed from the Australian mainland to Prince of Wales Island and to Mabuiag Island in mid-strait. Subsequently, stories relate, after slaying his mother he went on a head-hunting rampage as far as the Papuan coast. The fundamental division in language corresponds only in part with the physical data—while Papuan languages are spoken in the eastern islands, Aboriginal languages are spoken in the west, including even the ethnically Papuan people of Saibai, Boigu and Dauan.

ISLANDS OF THE CENTRAL QUEENSLAND COAST

More than 600 continental and reef islands are scattered along Australia's eastern seaboard north of the Tropic of Capricorn. Although most are tiny, they are more numerous than on any coastline of equal length elsewhere in the world. Archaeological findings reveal that people have been visiting the islands for about 5000 years, with an increase in exploitation only within the last 2000 years. One archaeologist specialising on this coast, Mike Rowland, has argued that permanent or semi-permanent settlement occurred on a number of the islands, including Hinchinbrook, Dunk, the Whitsundays and the Keppels. A community of possibly more than 100 people lived on Whitsunday Island. Archaeological findings reveal that inhabitants exploited at least eight of the other 130 islands in the Cumberland and Northumberland Group, targeting particular resources, such as turtles around Long Island and stone on South Molle, which was used for flake tools and hatchets.

The prehistory of the Whitsunday Islands is based on Bryce Barker's excavation of a rockshelter at Nara Inlet, Hook Island. This island is about sixteen kilometres from the mainland, but at the time the shelter was first occupied, prior to 8500 years BP, it was only about two kilometres out to sea. The shelter was seldom occupied until about 2500 years BP, at which time an increased range of marine and other foods is evident from the midden remains, and new items of technology include pieces of ground turtle shell (possibly fish-hook blanks), a dugong harpoon barb, and shell knives.

The most distant inhabited islands off Australia's east coast are the Percy Isles, a group comprising two major, and nine smaller, volcanic islands. The largest, Middle Percy Island, is 85 kilometres from the nearest mainland and could not be seen from it. However, it was possible to island-hop in bark canoes (described by one European settler as 'little cockle shells'), which were paddled even as far as the outer edge of the Great Barrier Reef. The longest single crossing between these islands is 27 kilometres, which testifies to the ability of simple bark canoes in warm ocean. Rowland envisages seasonal visits by a fleet of perhaps fifteen canoes carrying at least 25 people. An excavation by Andrew Border revealed that exploitation, possibly seasonal, of at least one of the islands began about 3000 years ago. The presence of large rock oyster middens on Middle Percy Island points to more intensive human occupation within the last 1000 years.

In the southern part of the Great Barrier Reef, thirteen kilometres from the mainland, are the Keppel Islands, of which two are large—North Keppel and Great Keppel. There is evidence that the people of the Keppel Islands were genetically and culturally distinct, though W. E. Roth records that they commuted to the mainland in bark canoes to visit coastal people who spoke a similar language. While none of the prehistoric middens on South Keppel are older than 800 years, one excavated by Rowland on North Keppel began to accumulate at about 4300 years BP. The similarity of this settlement record with that of the Percy Isles suggests that regional changes, such as the expansion of coral reefs and the introduction of new marine technology, increased access to the islands and the potential of their resources.

BASS STRAIT ISLANDS

The main islands of Bass Strait formed between about 12,000 and 7000 years BP. Two decades of archaeological fieldwork has established that human occupation of most islands ceased shortly afterwards and they remained unoccupied until Europeans arrived. The notable exception is Flinders Island, the largest in the Furneaux Group, which has been intensively surveyed for sites by Robin Sim. At shell midden sites excavated on Prime Seal Island and Badger Island, occupation ceased about 9000 years ago. Sim's findings indicate that the Islanders probably lacked watercraft; as the sea level rose, human settlement was confined to Flinders Island, which has an area of over 1000 square kilometres, where occupation ceased at least 5000 years ago. Sim argues that the lower precipitation in the Mid-Holocene may have caused catastrophic long-term drought and widespread depletion of food resources. Even today, fresh water is in short supply during the summer months.

The scarcity of prehistoric sites on King Island, which is 84 kilometres from the Tasmanian coast, suggests that it was abandoned around the time the land was cut off as an island. There are, however, two small middens dating to about 1000 and 1900 years BP. Sim argues that they are the camps of castaways who were attempting to cross to Hunter Island from the northwest coast of Tasmania, and that the adverse winds, tides and currents probably prevented their return.

THE KANGAROO ISLAND MYSTERY

In the early nineteenth century, when naval landing parties led by Matthew Flinders and Nicolas Baudin landed on the shore of Kangaroo Island, they found it uninhabited. Flinders remarked on the 'extraordinary tameness' of the kangaroos, and his men took advantage of their innocence to stock up with supplies of kangaroo and seal. Here was a puzzle, termed the 'Great Kartan Mystery' in Australian archaeology. Kangaroo Island is Australia's third-largest, after Tasmania and Melville Island. With an area of 4400 square kilometres, an equitable climate, long coastline and abundant plant and animal food, it was capable of supporting hundreds of hunter-gatherers. The potential foods included many of the mainland animal species, some locally adapted, such as a dwarf emu, and fur seal and sea lion colonies (a male sea lion may weigh two tonnes).

At about 9500 years BP the rising sea invaded a valley four kilometres wide through which had flowed a tributary of the Murray River. This was the beginning of Backstairs Passage, today a sea strait 14.5 kilometres wide, which separates Kangaroo Island from the mainland. The Ngarrindjeri of the lower Murray River and Coorong coast have a Dreaming story which some prehistorians speculate may refer to the rise of the sea level and its creation of Kangaroo Island. In this story the ancestral being Ngurunderi chased his two errant wives from the Murray River estuary westwards along the coast. In a desperate effort to escape, the women started to wade across the shallows to Kangaroo Island; Ngurunderi commanded the sea to rise and flood the passage, drowning his wives. The story also describes aspects of island topography not evident from the opposite mainland, where the people called it 'Karta'—the abode of spirits of the dead.

Prehistoric human presence on the island was first demonstrated in 1903 by a find of stone artefacts, and corroborated by other similar discoveries in the following decades. In Chapter 3 we described this stone technology and N. B. Tindale's interpretation of it as the tools left by a relic Negrito people isolated on the island. In the early 1970s Ron Lampert was able to show by excavations that people had continued to inhabit Kangaroo Island long after its formation.

Exactly when the period of human occupation ended is still not known for certain. Lampert found many sites strung along the modern coastline which date to about 6000 years BP. Radiocarbon dates from four sites located in different parts of the island indicate human occupation as recent as 4200–4400 years BP. Lampert conjectures abandonment of the island at about 2500 years BP, which is the date of a major change in bushfire regime around Lashmars Lagoon at the island's eastern end. The density of charcoal particles in the lagoon's muddy sediment reveals a change: from frequent low-level fires, presumed to be lit by humans, to infrequent large fires, presumed to be naturally ignited. Pollen in the sediment indicates that the increase in charcoal was accompanied by change from *Casuarina* to more fire-tolerant *Acacia* and *Eucalypt* forest. While this evidence has been interpreted as the consequence of human abandonment,

Neale Draper, who worked on the island's prehistory during the 1980s, argues that the process of vegetation change was gradual and that this fire record is therefore inconclusive. Draper offers later dates for human presence, several of them from open-air encampments on the shore of a former lagoon at Rocky River, in an area of grassy plain and relict Pleistocene sand dunes. In one dune there are occupation lenses containing implements of flint that had been collected 80 kilometres away. Draper's occupation sequence at Rocky River ranges from 6000 to possibly less than 1000 years BP. It remains possible, therefore, that Aborigines still inhabited Kangaroo Island until only a few centuries before European arrival.

Extinction or abandonment?

Why did people disappear on Kangaroo Island? The first suggestion, a crucial deficiency of cobalt in the island's soil, was offered by Tindale. However, this explanation was not supported by later health research. The notion of a small, inbred population languishing in isolation for thousands of years, finally to die out, has also appealed to some prehistorians. On the other hand, Lampert has argued that climatic change was the fundamental cause. Relying on estimates of population numbers on the mainland in the historic period, Lampert calculated that only a few hundred people could have exploited the island in the long term, and that environmental deterioration plunged this population below its reproduction survival threshold. While Draper suspects that there was a prehistoric change from permanent settlement to seasonal or occasional visitation, he does not link this to environmental shifts.

One of the major issues in the debate about the fate of the Islanders is whether they, or the people on the adjacent coast, had sea-going watercraft. The northern coast of Kangaroo Island can be seen clearly from the plateau's edge, opposite on the mainland, and vice versa. While Backstairs Passage may be 'millpond smooth' on some occasions, the prevailing wind is unfavourable and the waters were infested with shark. Ordinarily, Backstairs Passage was not swimmable. There is a historical account of an Aboriginal woman swimming from the island to the mainland to escape sealers who had held her captive. Others would not have survived such an attempt. Sadly, despite the remarkable endurance of this woman, she died shortly afterwards from her ordeal. Lampert dismisses any possibility that a still-water bark canoe of Murray River design was sufficiently seaworthy. Historically no watercraft were seen along the southern Australian coast from the mouth of the Murray River westward, so if ever regular visits on rafts or canoes occurred, this technology had been abandoned completely before AD 1800. On Kangaroo Island itself the so-called rivers are actually of creek size, and it is quite conceivable that the former inhabitants did not even possess still-water canoes. That the dingo failed to colonise Kangaroo Island as it did the mainland during the last 3000–4000 years may provide slim evidence that people did not cross back and forth to the mainland. However, until there is a reliable date for the last human presence on the island, there can be no convincing explanation for why the human population vanished.

ISLANDS OF AUSTRALIA'S SOUTHWEST

There is no historical record for any kind of watercraft in the southwest of Australia and no offshore islands were inhabited when Europeans arrived. The many exhaustive surveys by Charlie Dortch on the islands near Fremantle revealed only a few artefacts of fossiliferous chert, mostly on adjacent Garden Island. All these finds must predate the islands' formation. The few artefacts from Rottnest Island, nineteen kilometres offshore, are older than 7000 years BP. Near the town of Esperance, on the Southern Ocean coast, are 75 islands of the Recherche Archipelago, home to many seals and muttonbirds. These waterless islands, visible from the coast, must have been rarely visited, given the lack of watercraft; only an undated stone scatter on Middle Island suggests the briefest of visits.

Since the 1970s research has extended the understanding of offshore settlement. It is interesting to reflect that whatever the technology and prowess of Pleistocene voyagers to Sahul in covering considerable distances, this is not apparent for subsequent times. Evidence accumulates that when sea level rose and created islands around the periphery of Australia, the most distant ones were not visited. Possibly adverse tides, currents and, in the south, cold weather conditions and sea temperatures discouraged voyaging. However, it may also be that in the north the earliest watercraft were more seaworthy than those of later times.

Tasmania 19

Tasmania was sundered from the continent by rising seas about 12,000 years ago, when the isthmus that previously existed was about 65 kilometres wide. In the span of about 1500 years the nascent Bass Strait widened to 60 kilometres, with barely any islet refuge for hapless wanderers from either shore: the strait was just too wide and sea conditions too adverse for sea traffic between the two landmasses. Eventually Bass Strait widened to 150 kilometres, ensuring that the genetic and cultural isolation of the Tasmanian Aborigines was profound.

THE TASMANIAN ABORIGINES

Rhys Jones, the pioneer of Tasmanian archaeology, has estimated that at the time of British colonisation there were 70 to 85 bands in Tasmania, each comprising between 30 and 80 people, and a total population of around 4000–6000. However, Colin Pardoe noted from a study of crania that, for such a population size there is a less than expected degree of genetic drift between Tasmanians and mainland Australian Aborigines. He believes that the population may have been larger, or alternatively a relatively high degree of intermarriage occurred between the island's territorial groups.

Tasmanian society was completely isolated for some 500 generations, longer than any other Aboriginal population in Australia. Although there are reasons to believe that Tasmanian and southeastern

mainland languages were related to each other before the creation of
Bass Strait, all that linguists are able to say about the modern languages is that their sound system is not particularly different. There
must have been some genetic divergence between Victorian and Tasmanian populations during the Late Pleistocene because of continental
clines in gene frequencies, but Pardoe has detected close affinities in
non-metric cranial traits. His study demonstrates genetic relationships
over a period twice as long as any other similar study in the world.
The primary agencies of physical change are genetic drift, which must
prevail in such a small isolated population, and environmental adaptation, especially in terms of body size and shape. A notable Tasmanian
feature is the head hair, which is tightly coiled, in contrast to the wavy
hair of Victorian Aborigines; but it is not known whether this is an
ancient feature or due to genetic change during isolation.

HISTORICAL TASMANIAN CULTURE

The historical record of Tasmanian society and culture began in 1642,
when the Dutchman Abel Tasman landed on the east coast. His men
saw no people but observed widely spaced foot-holds on a tree, and
presumed that they had been made by men 'of unusual height'. The
first brief meeting between Tasmanians and Europeans was with
Nicholas Marion du Fresne, who anchored in Marion Bay in 1772,
near Hobart. In the following year Tobias Furneaux sailed into
Adventure Bay, Bruny Island, but he encountered only abandoned
camps. Captain James Cook sailed into Adventure Bay in 1777 during
his last voyage, and on this occasion friendly contact was made with
about twenty people of the Nuenonne band. Cook presented each
with a string of beads and a commemorative bronze medal, an event
faithfully sketched by the ship's artist. The hunch-backed Tasmanian
in the lower right of the picture (p. 342) 'was not less distinguishable
by his wit and humour', according to William Bligh who accompanied Cook. Probably he is the first indigenous Australian identified
personally in historical records, and he was identified again eleven
years later by Bligh, who had returned to Adventure Bay in the
Bounty. One of Cook's bronze medals was found in 1914 at the northern end of Bruny Island. Later French expeditions, led by Bruny
d'Entrecasteaux and Nicolas Baudin, provide the best early historical
records of the Tasmanian, including some fine drawings.

A succeeding era of contact began in 1803 with the landing of a

Tasmanian Aboriginal residents at Oyster Cove, photographed in 1858 by Bishop Nixon. N. B. Plomley identified the people in the photo as (back) Tippoo Sahib and Patty; (centre) Mary Ann; (sitting, from left) Wafferty, Trugernanner (Truganini), Caroline and Sarah. (J. W. Beattie Album, courtesy of W. L. Crowther Library, State Library of Tasmania)

small British party at Risdon Cove on the Derwent River, where the convict settlement of Hobart Town was founded. Thus began a period of almost unremitting conflict which was to decimate Tasmania's Indigenous population within a few decades in one of the most

Captain Cook (and his officers, including William Bligh) offering gifts to men of the
Nuenonne band on landing at Adventure Bay, Bruny Island, 29 January 1777. Cook
presented each man with a string of beads and a medal. About twenty men were
assembled and the deformed man, right front, was recognised by Bligh upon his
return there in 1788 on HMS Bounty. *(Detail of a sketch by John Webber; Naval*
Historical Library, British Ministry of Defence, London)

appalling chapters in Australia's colonial history. Governor Arthur
declared martial law for the purpose of eliminating Aborigines from
the regions then settled by the British.

To extend the policy of Aboriginal depopulation and land appro-
priation, George Augustus Robinson was commissioned to round up
the more isolated groups for resettlement. Robinson was an extraordinary man, a stonemason by trade and a lay preacher; his motives
were both humanitarian and financial. Robinson succeeded in per-
suading about 100 people to leave their ancestral homelands for exile
on Flinders Island, but more than half of them died within a decade
of their exile. Those who survived were settled at Oyster Cove, near
Hobart, but to no avail—the last of these exiles, Truganini, died in

1876. Descendants of Tasmanian Aboriginal women who lived with sealers and whalers reside today on Bass Strait islands, in Tasmania and in other parts of Australia. Robinson's voluminous field journals, which document his travels and contact with Tasmanian Aborigines from 1829 to 1834, have been meticulously edited by N. J. B. Plomley. While British colonisation had begun a generation before, Robinson's journals are invaluable for interpreting Tasmania's terminal prehistory and its fateful early historical record.

MATERIAL CULTURE

When first encountered by Europeans, the material culture of the Tasmanians appeared so rudimentary that evolutionary theorists used it as a storehouse of fossil facts. Edward Tylor dubbed Tasmanians the 'representatives of Palaeolithic Man', and the naturalist John Lubbock implicitly denied their humanity with his mechanistic aphorism: 'The Van Diemener and the South American are to the antiquary what the possum and sloth are to the geologist.' Tasmanian technology was simple in the extreme. The tool-kit lacked such mainland Australian artefacts as the spearthrower, boomerang, shield, hunting net, trap, any fishing equipment, hatchet, adze, millstone for grinding grass seeds, or any multi-component tool or weapon.

Stone was not ground to fashion tools, although the technique is a 'first-order innovation', evident simply by observing nature. Its omission as an element of technology must have had a cultural basis. In this respect, the Tasmanians were like the Incas of Peru, who made wheeled toys for their children's amusement but never applied the concept to develop wheeled transport. That the Tasmanians did very occasionally grind stone tools is evident from a specimen we have examined in the Tasmanian Museum.

Cords and ropes were only two-ply. To keep the body warm, only a cape made from a single kangaroo or wallaby skin was worn over one shoulder—compared with the magnificent possum-skin cloaks of Victoria, this was a modest garment indeed for a cold climate. A small luxury seen on the southeast coast was an animal-skin cushion. The most notable male weapons were a solid wooden club and a single-piece wooden spear about three metres long. Women used a digging stick and club, and a large, pointed wooden wedge for debarking trees and prising shellfish from rocks. Bags were of skin, kelp or woven rushes. Stone tools apparently consisted of hand-held flakes, cores or pebbles, and although some of these are skilfully shaped and retouched, blade production and pressure-flaking techniques were unknown.

Because of their profound isolation, the Tasmanians missed out on innovations that became widespread across southeastern Australia. Although the canoe-shaped float was a major Tasmanian innovation, there is no other demonstrated evidence for an increase in technological complexity over time. It is even possible, as Jones originally suggested, that some items were discarded from the Tasmanian inventory of material culture within the last few thousand years, such as boomerangs and sewn skin cloaks. However, the issue is a complex one. Simplicity of artefact design does not necessarily mean lack of sophistication, nor inadequate return. To understand the 'functional fit' of artefacts and material culture in the context of Tasmanian subsistence and culture, we must not only make a technical evaluation of performance and efficiency but also appreciate the role of the artefacts in their social and cultural contexts.

The Tasmanian population may have been small, but there is no reason to believe that it was declining before the destruction wrought by British colonisation. Nor is there any indication that the simple technology of the Tasmanians was poorly adapted and deprived them of major resources. Archaeological findings indicate the opposite: that populations were expanding, at least territorially, and they were making choices not to exploit certain food resources that were readily available to them. Religious beliefs and practices are poorly documented, but it is known that the Tasmanians obtained ochre from several sources and used it extensively. The recently relocated quarry site of Toolumbunner in northern Tasmania was visited by Robinson in 1830 when it was in operation. Toolumbunner must have played an important role in ceremonial life, as other ochre quarries did on the mainland.

The introduction of dogs into Tasmania by British colonists offers insight into the technological adaptability of these isolated people. Unlike mainlanders, Tasmanians lacked the companionship of dingoes, but not by choice. As early as 1839, the explorer Sir Thomas Mitchell argued cogently that the Aborigines had reached Tasmania before the formation of Bass Strait, but before dingoes arrived to cross by the same means. Dogs from the British were assimilated into their hunting economy with such rapidity that by 1830 they were as numerous as in mainland Aboriginal camps, and evidently were being incorporated into mythology.

Tasmanian canoe-shaped floats

The most intriguing Tasmanian construction was a canoe-shaped float about four to 4.5 metres long. This watercraft is described variously, and we use the descriptive term 'canoe-shaped float' (see p. 324). This unique craft was first described by Louis Freycinet of the Baudin expedition which visited the southeast in 1802, and later by G. A. Robinson. Buoyancy was provided by short bundles of *Eleocharis* sedge stems, or the bark of stringybark or paperbark trees, which were tied together to form long tapered cylinders. Three rolls of bark, or five of sedge, were bound together by grass-twine lattice and their ends tightly bound to form the upturned bow and stern. The inside breadth was nearly a metre. According to Freycinet, these craft usually carried between two and four adults and their gear, or if necessary up to eight adults and a few children. As in the bark-sheet canoes in mainland southeastern Australia, there was a small clay hearth at one end for cooking, and there was an added luxury of comfortable grass seats. Canoe-shaped floats were used on rivers, in estuaries, and for crossing to offshore islands—except on the north-east coast, where people did not swim and the islands visible from the mainland were regarded as the domain of the dead.

Robinson was told by his Aboriginal informants that canoe-shaped floats were able to handle rough sea conditions because they were difficult to overturn and effectively unsinkable; even so, many people had been lost at sea within living memory. By any standard these craft were frail, and were therefore preferentially used in calm weather. Since they were not paddled, but polled with a spear or pushed through the water by swimmers, they could have made little headway against tidal currents. The dating of island visitation around Tasmania suggests that this craft may have an antiquity spanning the last 2000 years.

SETTLEMENT AND SUBSISTENCE CHANGES

Major changes in Tasmania's archaeological record commence in the Mid-Holocene, particularly an expansion of settlement from about 4000–3000 years BP. This evidence shows colonisation of previously unoccupied or seldom visited regions, such as the south and west coasts, nearshore islands of the northwest, the forested hinterland of the north coast and the Central Highlands. Artefacts of spicular chert (often described as spongolite chert) are witness both to this territorial expansion and the emergence of a regional exchange network. Such changes seem to parallel those occurring around the same time in the southeastern mainland, though there can be no historical link between them. In part, the explanation may lie in environmental changes, but cultural factors are no doubt also involved. Harry Lourandos suggests that regular Aboriginal burning opened up the interior forestland and that territorial expansion was therefore culturally driven. Shifts in the nature of coastal settlement, such as travel to offshore islands, may be linked to the advent of watercraft or the adoption of a new design. One notable change in coastal economy from about 4000 years BP is the addition of abalone and crayfish to the diet along the west and northwest coasts, perhaps linked to the adoption of diving for marine food collection, and also to the use of watercraft.

NORTHWEST TASMANIA

In 1963 Rhys Jones began a series of excavations at the now-famous sites of Rocky Cape and West Point on the northwest coast, providing the first reliable stratigraphic time-depth for the island. These pioneering excavations remain the foundation of Tasmanian prehistory.

Rocky Cape

The evidence for Holocene settlement of northwestern Tasmania prior to 3000 years BP comes largely from two caves about a kilometre apart at Rocky Cape. Between them they provide an almost continuous six-metre sequence of habitation from about 8000 years BP to the nineteenth century. Because the seabed descends steeply on this part of the coast, the present shoreline was formed well before Mid-Holocene sea level stability, enabling a coastal economy to develop early. Rocky Cape South Cave contained an immense, roofed shell midden over two metres thick, well stratified, and rich in stone and bone remains. The accidental discovery in 1967 of an inner cave (actually a cavity), sealed when deposits of midden debris accumulated in front of it, enabled Jones and Harry Lourandos to extend excavations during 1967 into the alcove. It offered a unique experiment in Australian archaeology, because the ground surface was littered with

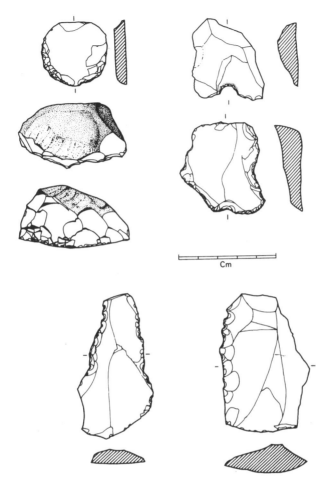

Stone scrapers excavated at Rocky Cape. (Rhys Jones)

shell and bone refuse and discarded stone tools, left by the last occupants of these cramped quarters. To judge from the radiocarbon date for charcoal from the floor, this had occurred about 6500 to 7000 years ago.

The stratified deposit at Rocky Cape North was three metres deep, with the bottom 60 centimetres corresponding to the period of occupation at South Cave. Two major phases of occupation are apparent in the Rocky Cape deposits. The lower two metres in the north cave provided a large faunal assemblage suitable for dietary reconstruction. Well-made points and spatulas of wallaby fibula bone testify to a bone-working tradition during the early period, when stone tools

347

consisted of unifacially flaked pebbles and relatively undifferentiated retouched flakes, mostly of local quartzites. The contrasting upper levels, dating from about 5500 years BP, contained no bone tools and were poorer in faunal remains. They were characterised instead by an abundance of stone artefacts, including small, concave-edged flake implements, disc-like core tools with use-worn cutting edges, and numerous tiny flakelets. Fine-grained spicular chert from west-coast quarries supplemented local sources after about 2500 years BP.

The food remains in the Rocky Cape middens indicate predominantly littoral exploitation of fur and southern elephant seals, fish and shellfish species. Beginning in levels dating to around 3800–3400 years BP, fish bones disappear from the deposit, indicating that this important food source was no longer consumed, an issue discussed below. In an exhaustive analysis of a sample of the fish bones from Rocky Cape, Sarah Colley identified more than 30 species. Fish from rocky reefs predominate, especially wrass and leatherhead, but other species from sandy bays, estuaries and the open sea also occur. Colley and Jones suggest that most fish may have been caught in baited box traps thrown into the sea off the small rocky peninsulas between the coastal cliffs at Rocky Cape. Other identified fish species, such as leatherjacket, mullet, whiting and barracouta, cannot be caught with box traps and may have been taken in tidal traps of cobble walls.

WEST COAST

A narrow corridor of sedgeland existed along the rugged west coast in the early nineteenth century. This was a cultural landscape maintained by frequent Aboriginal burning, probably from the time of first settlement, at least 4000 years BP on the upper and 3000 years BP on the lower stretches of the coast. When this burning ceased, the rainforest reclaimed the corridor. To some extent Aboriginal settlement was concentrated within this coastal fringe, where large semi-sedentary base camps were positioned close to seal colonies, but also near the edge of the rainforest which provided raw materials and certain food items. Jones argued that the most difficult time of year for the inhabitants of these camps was winter, when shellfish, primarily abalone, was the primary source of meat protein, along with the occasional seal or stranded whale. In spring, large numbers of nesting muttonbirds and eggs were also available, though possibly not a preferred food; and seals, especially the southern elephant seal, were increasingly available into the summer months. The significance of forest foods, especially edible plants, to the inhabitants may have been greater than the archaeological and historical records imply. Reports by early explorers, and an escaped convict from the Macquarie Harbour prison settlement, testify to at least occasional Aboriginal excursions inland along the more accessible river valleys. Archaeological evidence for such trips into the densely forested hinterland comes from a Holocene-age riverbank camp site in the southwest. However, bird and animal life is relatively scarce and plant food is limited to a few items, such as tree fern heart and some species of fungi.

West Point middens

Between Cape Grim and Sandy Cape, numerous large shell middens mark the locations of summer base camps. Jones excavated one of the middens in a sand dune on the rocky promontory of West Point, almost 2.5 metres deep, which accumulated between 1800 and 1200 years ago, with only a single major period of abandonment. Jones recovered over 20,000 bones from his excavation, mostly the remains of young elephant seals. Shellfish, mostly abalone, were also collected, but formed a minor part of the diet. No elephant seal colonies existed in the region when the British arrived, so Jones postulates that they had been hunted to extinction, causing the abandonment of the base camp. Cultural links between this site at West Point and those at Rocky Cape were evident from the style of the stone tools and the presence of spicular chert.

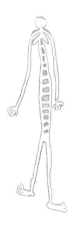

Spicular chert quarries

Artefacts made of a chert containing sponge spicules (called spicular chert) have been identified in a number of prehistoric sites in northwest Tasmania—along more than 400 kilometres of the coast, from Macquarie Harbour on the central west coast to Rocky Cape on the north coast. Such artefacts also are found on Hunter Island, and at sites inland to the northern foothills of the Central Plateau. The earliest spicular chert artefacts are dated to about 2500 years BP but they are more common from 1800 years BP. For many years the source of the chert was not known, but in 1984 a complex of sites, where flat tabular chert blocks and rounded nodules had been dug up, was discovered by foresters about nine kilometres inland from Temma, a small settlement 40 kilometres south of West Point. Other outcrops of the chert have been found at No Man's Creek and Granville

West Point. Intersecting trench excavations into the midden, 1964–65. Besides shell there were enormous quantities of bones of elephant seals, now extinct in the area. (Rhys Jones)

Harbour, and others in the region are probably hidden beneath dense scrub. Excavating at one of the sites near Temma, Richard Cosgrove unearthed a large quantity of chert flaking debris, and pebble hammerstones which must have been brought from the coast. Probably stone-toolmaking occurred at the spicular chert exposures and at nearby camps, and the artefacts carried to nearby coastal base camps, and as trade items further afield.

SOUTHEAST COAST AND HINTERLAND

The southeastern coast is rugged, though estuaries have formed from drowned river valleys and there are a few coastal plains. The oldest habitation site located along this coast is a midden of oyster shells at Carlton Bluff in the extreme southeast. This midden began to accumulate about 7300 years BP, well before the sea level stabilised. Shellfish gathering is more evident after 6000 years BP in the bays and estuaries and on rocky nearshore islands. Large middens reflect local availability of shellfish species—along low-energy coasts they are predominantly of oyster and mussel, and along higher-energy coasts they are warrener and mussel species. Remains of large abalone and cray-fish, favoured seafoods in historical times, are found only in middens less than 1000 years old, which indicates the recent practice of diving into deep water, a woman's task. Although the overall contribution of shellfish to the diet may have been small, the east coast middens tend to contain few animal bones or stone artefacts, suggesting that the sites were camps positioned primarily for gathering shellfish, and may have proved a staple when other food sources were rare.

Individual surveys of the forested hinterland by Harry Lourandos, Steve Brown, and Richard Cosgrove failed to locate evidence of intensive exploitation or increased human presence over time. Rockshelters are common, and those located on valley floors contain cultural deposits, the oldest dating from about 4500 years BP. Numerous lithic scatters, and a number of quarries at outcrops of cherty hornfels, also occur inland. There is increasing evidence that Aborigines regularly burnt the forestlands, probably over thousands of years. Despite the valuable corpus of relevant historical records and a number of archaeological surveys, prehistoric exploitation and settlement of the forested interior are still poorly understood. The settlement pattern envisaged by Brown is of year-round movements between coast and hinterland, with flexible resource exploitation, but the relative importance of these environments for subsistence remains to be determined.

CENTRAL HIGHLANDS

Glaciers in Tasmania's Central Highlands did not completely melt until the Early Holocene. As they retreated, they left thousands of small lakes and ponds scattered within a transformed landscape of grassland and open woodland. Throughout the year conditions are generally cold and wet, with chilling winds and frequent frosts. The archaeology of this region was pioneered in the 1970s by Harry Lourandos. In the early 1980s more detailed surveys were undertaken by Richard Cosgrove and Ian Thomas, and hundreds of sites have been recorded. Most are lithic scatters, but there are also a few rock-shelters and two stone quarries in moraine deposits. The oldest dated levels are younger than 3000 years, but it is believed that, as the glaciers retreated, people moved up the valleys in the summer months from lower-lying regions to hunt macropods and wombats. A number of lithic scatters located in windswept grassland may be evidence for brief hunting trips during high summer. Larger scatters have been found on western slopes protected from the prevailing winds and in the timbered margins of marshes, where the widest range of food resources are available. Protection from the cold wind was a prime consideration. Not surprisingly, habitation sites are rare above an altitude of 1200 metres, which parallels the pattern demonstrated for the Australian Alps.

VISITING ISLANDS

Tasmania's islands and rocky islets were abundant sources of birds and marine life. In particular, the islands were breeding grounds for seals, and for seabirds such as albatross, seagull and muttonbird. The quantity of such potential resources should not be underestimated. In 1798, on the day they discovered Bass Strait, George Bass and Matthew Flinders observed a vast flock of muttonbirds passing overhead for 90 minutes, which Flinders generously estimated to number over 100 million.

Jones has calculated that there was an inverse relationship between the length of a sea journey to an offshore island and the amount of visitation. For islands very close to the coastline an additional variable is its size. Islands two to four kilometres offshore—still a swimmable distance if the watercraft swamped—were visited regularly by whole bands, though only on a seasonal basis for islands smaller than 70 square kilometres. Islands of more than 90 square kilometres, such as Robbins, Maria and Bruny Islands, were the home estates of bands of about 30 to 50 people. Large shell middens on Bruny Island testify to continuous settlement or visitation since its formation by rising sea about 6000 years ago. Sea crossings of five to eight kilometres to islands were made during good weather and on a seasonal basis, but only if the target island was rich in seals or other important food resources. The prospect of serious trouble rose sharply on longer sea crossings of thirteen to fifteen kilometres. Crossings of this length were occasionally chanced, probably only by special hunting parties of people most able to survive the journey. It is unlikely that islands further away than fifteen kilometres were intentionally visited.

Island exploitation

In early historic times the rocky Doughboy islets, within swimming distance of Cape Grim in the extreme northwest of Tasmania, were visited in summer for their reserves of muttonbird, seal, wallaby, shell-fish and crayfish. Nearby Robbins Island was also visited by groups of up to 50 Aborigines. Further out to sea is the 24-kilometre-long Hunter Island, six kilometres off Tasmania's northwest tip. The island's coastline is generally cliffed with a few beaches at the foot of the escarpment, and Pleistocene dunes on the western side. It is uncertain when the low-lying siltstone plateau that forms Hunter Island was first cut off from the mainland, since it is possible that there was a connecting sand spit before about 4500 years BP. Although there is no historical account of Aborigines having visited the island, there are more than 120 shell middens and rockshelters containing deposits from human occupation. Probably most of the middens date to the last 1600 years, and it is suggested by archaeol-ogist Sandra Bowdler that they are the camps of family groups rather than special hunting parties. One of the middens, built up between about 900 and 1000 years BP in a sand dune at Little Duck Bay, contains a large quantity of animal and bird bones, especially seal bones, and circular depressions which are characteristic features of a type of dome-shaped hut seen in the nineteenth century on the Tasmanian west coast. Similar to huts in middens in stormy Tierra del Fuego, these huts were made of turf or bark laid over a frame of tea-tree stems, with the floor sunk into the midden for protection against cold winds. The depressions in the Hunter Island midden therefore may indicate considerable antiquity for this hut design.

The seasonal rhythm of subsistence along Tasmania's cold and rugged southern coast was determined largely by the breeding cycle of seals and seabirds, as it was in the north and west. The prehistory of this part of the coast is based largely on the excavations by Ron Vanderwal at Louisa Bay and on the Maatsuyker Islands. The clos-est of the Maatsuyker Islands was six kilometres out to sea, and crossings were therefore avoided in winter when fierce storms swept in from the Southern Ocean. The earliest evidence for human exploitation on this coast is dated to 2700–3000 years BP. The food remains found in an excavation in Louisa Bay indicate that in winter people collected shellfish, and hunted marsupials, seabirds, and the occasional stray seal. In summer there were visits to the islands to hunt fur seals and harvest a bounty of muttonbird and fairy prion from the rookeries. Direct evidence of voyages for the last 600 years comes from Vanderwal's excavation on one of the islands. However, a subsequent excavation by Gary Dunnett on the mainland opposite revealed the bones of numerous seabirds, which suggests that the crossings may have commenced by at least 2000 years BP.

THE FISH FOOD DEBATE

When Europeans first encountered Tasmanians, they observed that people did not eat scaled fish: it was refused when offered to them by French parties, and William Bligh was bemused by the absence of fish bones in any of the encampments his men examined. Some decades later, Robinson wrote in his journal that people were shocked and dismayed on seeing a fish being roasted on his campfire. It is not certain that scaled fish were taboo everywhere in Tasmania during the colonial era, because traditional culture had been destroyed so quickly, but such an assumption is widely accepted. Not all marine life was proscribed along with scaled fish—sea mammals, shellfish, crustacea, and even stingray were much relished. The taboo on eating fish must have been enshrined in creation mythology, but any record or memory of such tradition is now lost.

Debate over reasons for this dietary restriction was raised early by Rhys Jones, following his excavations at Rocky Cape. Fish were eaten there from its first occupation 8000 years ago, when the sea approached its present position, until about 3500 years BP, when fish bones disappear from the sequence.

No other archaeological deposit in Tasmania dated to the last three millennia has revealed any fish bones and the loss of fish from the diet appears to be an island-wide phenomenon. Jones explained the sudden disappearance of scaled fish from the diet as a religious pro-scription; this food was not an essential part of the diet, but its loss must have resulted in some degree of hardship, especially during winter. He considered the change as a subsistence maladjustment, linked to other inferred losses of material culture.

Harry Allen proposed that fish may not have been nutritionally important because most of the fish represented were low in fat and calorific value. A host of other seafood, such as shellfish, penguins, muttonbirds and seals, provide richer sources of essential fat and oil (for instance, a single seal pup provides more energy value than 150 large fish). Allen argued that there had been a drop in water tem-perature at 3500 years BP; if fish was already a marginal item in the diet, switching the focus to higher-return and more easily procured resources, such as seals or other land mammals, was a predictable adaptive response.

Other archaeologists have argued different versions of this food-replacement theme. Research by Colley and Jones on the fish remains from Rocky Cape indicate that the fishing methods used, such as trapping with baited box trap and tidal trap, are not particularly labour-intensive. Gary Dunnett re-examined shell samples from the site and demonstrated that large abalone became the most common shell around the time fish bones disappear. It seems probable that the two changes are expressions of a general shift in coastal subsistence and technology, possibly beginning in the northwest and not fully established on the east coast for another 2500 years. At Rocky Cape, trapping of fish is discontinued completely and replaced by the women diving for abalone (and presumably crayfish), possibly using watercraft, with the men active in other, perhaps new, pursuits. A further aspect of this shift was reduced dependence on other intertidal shellfish species. No doubt, other aspects of this major economic and social change will be uncovered by excavation, such as possible changes in seasonal movements, in the relative importance of mammalian food resources, and in male food-getting activities.

BONE POINTS

Related to the issue of dietary change is the virtual disappearance of sharp-tipped and spatulate-ended bone points in archaeological sites. Bone points are known from Pleistocene cave sites in the southwest, and at Rocky Cape 37 well-made bone points and spatulas of wallaby fibula occurred in levels dating before 3500 years BP. Only one archaeological specimen belonged to the period of fish avoidance. Their disappearance from the tool-kit is extraordinary, because they are such a low-level innovation, are easy to make, and have such a wide range of uses. Neither are the points of the right design for fish-spear prongs. Bowdler speculates that awl-like bone points found in the coastal middens were needles for making fishing nets, which explains why they disappeared along with fish bones. However Colley, who studied the Rocky Cape fish bones, has found no evidence to indicate that fish were caught by nets. An alternative suggestion offered by Jones is that they were awls for piercing eyelets in sewn skin cloaks and that their disappearance is a consequence of simplification of skin garments.

PROSPECTS FOR ARCHAEOLOGY IN TASMANIA

With startling evidence for Tasmania's Pleistocene colonisation mostly concealed beneath rainforest until the 1980s, together with controversial cultural changes in the Holocene, this long-isolated island raises some of the most challenging problems in the global prehistory of hunter-gatherer societies. During the 1980s the exciting prospects for research in the southwest seemed set to challenge many assumptions and provide data for comparison with the contemporary Upper Palaeolithic occupation and exploitation patterns in Western Europe. The antiquity of settlement, the existence of art, the selective use of food resources and the distribution of Darwin glass from the meteorite impact source are research topics of global relevance. More importantly, on the cultural side they shed light on past society in Tasmania. Were fish and bone points discarded from routine activities mainly because of cultural decisions? Note the creative resilience of a people, under assault from European disease and violence, in adopting dogs into their lives within one generation. At the other temporal extreme, they hunted within sight of glaciers at the bottom of the inhabited world. These were isolated people indeed, but their lives and activities paralleled those of their mainland kin from whom they were separated for hundreds of generations.

It therefore is most unfortunate that archaeological fieldwork is largely suspended in Tasmania due to the rupture in relations between dedicated archaeologists and the Tasmanian Aboriginal Land Council. Archaeologists have done more than discover and publicise the evidence for the antiquity of achievements of all Aboriginal ancestors, Tasmanians included. They have been advocates of land rights and the education of Aboriginal people to undertake their own research. A Land Council spokesperson announced that 'the community has to be convinced that excavation is essential to answer a question that they feel is important', while rejecting concepts of universal heritage or the obligations so imposed. It is unfortunate that the research which served to elevate Tasmania's Aboriginal past to international renown and respect should be dismissed as irrelevant to the interests of contemporary Tasmanians. It is therefore paradoxical and disappointing that archaeologists are seen as the 'enemy'. At present both sides are losers. We can only hope that archaeological fieldwork and analysis can recommence in co-operative partnership, devoid of mutual acrimony and confrontation.

Art on rock 20

European Upper Palaeolithic art has dominated the literature on the origins of artistic expression for over a century, together with the rock art of southern Africa and India in recent decades. That engraved and painted images date from Pleistocene Australia cannot now be disputed, so Australian rock art ranks with the oldest-known images of artistic expression. Some optimists wonder whether Australia possesses the world's oldest art galleries.

It is significant that excavations in every state have recovered ochre pigments in the basal levels of many Pleistocene sites. Obviously pigments were widely transported even around 30,000 years BP, indicating aesthetic appreciation and purpose. Connect this with the practices of cremation and ochred inhumations at Lake Mungo around the same time and it must be inferred that spiritual meaning and abstract thought typified the creative life of societies. It should be no surprise, therefore, that proof of early art forms has been established.

Aboriginal rock art is the pictorial record of Australia's human past—the encrypted beliefs of hundreds of generations of people, the images of their spiritual and earthly world, their material possessions, and their sense of personal and group identity—fragments of prehistory located in place. From the 1930s Fred McCarthy and Charles Mountford were the outstanding recorders for three decades until critical academic interest developed. Research grew rapidly from the 1960s, and today there are numerous researchers in the area. This

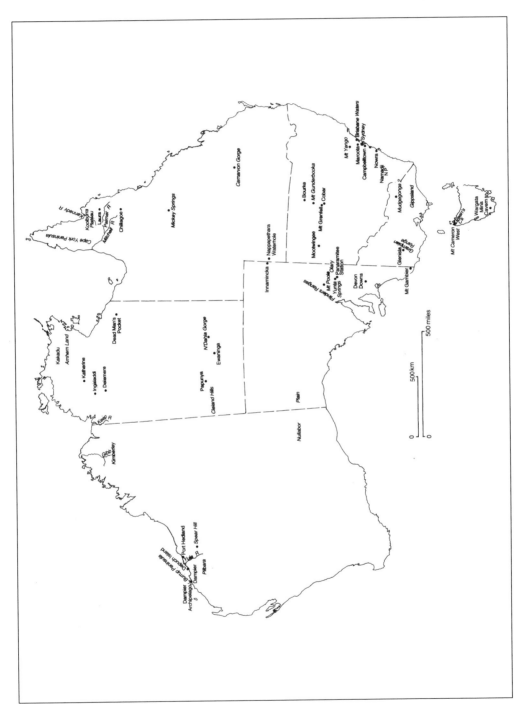

Map 16. *Rock art sites in Australia.*

expanding field embraces students from diverse backgrounds, although archaeologists are prominent and have led the way. Much of the research still concerns the discovery, preservation and accurate recording of the art. Although many thousands of sites are on state registers, only a small fraction is individually recorded or described, while conservation raises great problems.

Regions exhibiting spectacular art are becoming relatively well documented through activities such as graphic recording, archaeological excavations, interpretation using ethnography as a guide, but particularly consultation with Aboriginal clan owners. Other regions, such as the Mount Lofty Ranges only a short distance from Adelaide, are neglected. Sufficient reliable dates and estimates now exist to formulate a general continental chronology and a few regional sequences. Chapters 20–22 describe regional rock art styles and provinces, and traces their antiquity and development, issues which have preoccupied most rock art researchers since the 1970s.

Another exciting direction for research is reconstructing the dynamics of past social and symbolic systems and identifying cultural change, with questions about prehistoric culture boundaries and networks of trade and exchange, perception of social identity, social networking between groups, population density and material culture. Such interpretations are necessarily speculative but they have provided new insights into the world of ancient Australians.

Rock art is no longer studied in isolation but is linked with other aspects of the archaeological record and with reconstructions of past environments. For instance, contemporaneous changes in rock art and stone tool assemblages have been interpreted as indicating transformation of social networking from an open system during the Late Pleistocene and Early Holocene to regional ones during the last few thousand years. Much Australian rock art is the expression of beliefs about the Dreaming and relationship to the land. It is therefore the most valuable type of material evidence for reconstructing the prehistory of Dreaming beliefs and practices and the links to particular sites and country. The recently postulated beginning of Rainbow Serpent imagery in Kakadu rock art 6000 years ago has been presented as evidence of a continuous religious tradition from that time. On the other hand, for the Victoria River District it is argued that the Dreaming was not commonly expressed through rock paintings until about 1400 years ago and that at this time there may have been fundamental changes in the concept of the Dreaming, the way it was communicated, or the ritual practices associated with it.

IMAGE RECOGNITION

A problematic but fundamental issue in rock art studies is 'image recognition'. Early researchers readily identified animal species, but close collaboration with Aboriginal artists establishes that an animal motif, for instance, may assume many meanings. It may represent a food item, a mythical being, or something completely different; some motifs may represent symbols signifying clans or territories. For instance, the stencil of a boomerang may indicate that the locality was within the territory of a particular group. Layers of meaning in rock art are being acknowledged today, together with shifting perspectives from simplistic identification of figures to complex ideology.

In many cases, certain details allow identification of a motif as a species or an artefact, or even identify an individual artist, but this information may not be obvious to an untrained observer. Shapes and detail in rock art are often generalised, making them difficult to identify with precision. Some researchers judiciously use a qualifier symbol (such as !) for certain motif categories to emphasise that they do not necessarily reflect the object intended by the artist. For instance, some pictures of anthropomorphs (meaning human-like) are accurate representations of spirits or Dreaming beings. The pitfalls inherent in discussing the identification of rock art figures led John Clegg to aptly declare that 'most study of prehistoric pictures consists of a tottering structure of unlikely inferences on untestable assumptions on dubious observations'. One of the research trends is to study recurrent patterns rather than to identify meaning in individual motifs.

Superficial historical observations, readily available in the Australian literature, could persuade an archaeologist in search of an explanation, but it is inadvisable to argue from the historic to the remote past. For example, whereas Dreaming creative forces in Arnhem Land emphasised female fertility-mother concepts, mythical clan heroes in the Kimberley were male, and were more directly associated with natural forces—rain, lightning, animal species. Should the ancient art in these regions be validly interpreted in terms of this modern ethnography? How would a scholar interpret the concentric circles and sinuous lines on an ancient rock engraving from central Australia? To the initiated Aborigines of the region, these motifs may be symbolic portrayals of tribal territory, with rockholes, hills and tracks; and may also signify the wanderings and feats of totemic ancestors. However, the sands are always shifting, and even to people of a neighbouring tribe the same motifs may carry signficantly different symbolic meanings, just as artists 100 generations ago may have intended very different symbolism for similar images.

ROCK ART CONSERVATION

The preservation and clarity of rock art is dependent on a combination of environmental factors: the weather, surrounding plant communities, the insects and animals which visit or inhabit the sites, the geological structure and durability of rock surfaces. Some art is preserved beneath a natural hard coating of silica that has built up on the rock surface. However, the art usually deteriorates, sometimes at an alarming rate to judge from the fate of images known to be painted within the past 50 years.

In most areas of Australia, paintings and engravings are intimately tied to contemporary Aboriginal beliefs and rituals of group or self identity, often requiring the periodic rejuvenation of motifs. At ceremonial sites where people paid homage to, and renewed ties with, spirits and ancestors, this was undertaken by men or women who were recognised custodians, or the chosen artists who stood in the right relationship to the places. Post-European cultural dislocation has caused these customs to disappear almost everywhere, and the art deteriorates without rejuvenation. The traditional practice of repainting as a legitimate option in contemporary site management has been accepted within government statutory bodies. As an act of conservation and cultural continuity, repainting is an issue which highlights the sometimes competing heritage values possessed by an Aboriginal site.

We refer to the controversial repainting of art at the Gibb River, aired in the Australian media and in the pages of *Antiquity* in 1992. In a government-funded programme, a group of Aboriginal youths was brought from Derby to repaint eight Wandjina sites in the Kimberley region. Intended by a local Aboriginal corporation as a heritage training programme for the younger generation, some Aboriginal people and archaeologists judged the clumsy repainting to be misguided, or even desecration, while others viewed it as fulfilment of a traditional renewal obligation and an expression of Aboriginal self-determination. One Aboriginal community leader affirmed: 'we must look after the images so that life on earth will continue.'

The controversy surrounding this issue is still alive in the community and will bear on the evolving relationship between Aboriginal people, their rock art heritage, and conservators in the European tradition. Concerned people have asked of this practice—What if a site of some 20,000 years is identified? Should it be repainted by traditional artists? At present, many Aboriginal people consider ancient images to have been there since the Dreaming, so they would not wish to modify them.

TECHNIQUES OF ROCK ART PRODUCTION

Artists made lasting images on rock surfaces following two basic processes—the application of matter such as pigment or beeswax, or the physical removal of the rock surface by pecking or pounding. Pigment was either mixed and applied as a liquid medium to form a paint, or drawn using a dry crayon or charcoal. Painting was executed using either a finger or an impromptu brush such as a chewed twig or a feather. Paint was also blown from the mouth around an object to create a stencilled negative print, sometimes with masterful control that is testimony to practice and experience. What are commonly called engravings involved breaking or abrading the rock surface to expose lighter-coloured unweathered rock. These techniques were not mutually exclusive, and engravings also had pigments applied to them, such as the 'vulva' motifs at Carnarvon Gorge in Queensland and the pecked eyes of creation beings in the Kimberley region.

Pigments for painting and drawing

The ingredients of traditional pigments all came from plants and minerals little modified from their natural form. Sometimes minerals were heated to change their colour or hue. Almost all the red, yellow and brown pigments are derived from iron-rich minerals, like haematite (Fe_2O_3), commonly known as 'red ochre', siderite, a yellow-coloured iron carbonate, and goethite ($HFeO_2$), a yellow to brown mineral which forms naturally as a weathering product from the other iron minerals. An impure version of goethite, the mineral limonite ($FeO[OH].nH_2O$), which has a vitreous lustre, was also used. Haematite was by far the most common pigment, but it also was used for other purposes and formed an important commodity of exchange. The colour ranges from various shades of red to mulberry, and even near-black when it is aged on a rock face. Fragments or nodules of dense rock can be abraded on wetted sandstone to produce a paint; if the source contains clay minerals, it forms a soft substance. Haematite is chemically stable and is durable on rock surfaces because its microscopically platy structure provides strong adherence properties. Impure haematites, such as pieces of laterite, do not preserve as well.

Charcoal, which normally provides black colouring, was ground and mixed as paint or applied from a charred stick. Manganese minerals were also used, as they are often found naturally occurring with minerals for yellow and brown colour, although there is little archaeological evidence for their use.

Like red, white is deeply imbued with symbolism and power in Aboriginal religion. White mostly comes from kaolin-type clays, rich in quartz particles; when flecked with mica, it is iridescent. Some carbonate minerals have been identified, such as huntite, dolomite and calcite, which were ground to powder and mixed with water. All these white paints have poor preservation, because the carbonates may be chemically unstable and form salts; they also have poor adhesion, so they tend to flake off surfaces. Consequently, white pigment usually indicates that motifs are not old. Some white paints, such as the surface wash in the Wandjina style paintings of the Kimberley region, survive only a few decades. The colour blue has only rarely been recorded. Although a natural blue was used in Wandjina period art of the Kimberley region, the only blue paints identified in modern times are Reckitt's Blue (ferrous ferrocyanate), a commercial bleach, and 'ultramarine', a modern commercial paint.

A serious problem that has arisen in understanding older paintings is that some red, yellow and brown pigments are chemically unstable and can change colour over time—yellow or brown limonite pigment changes to red under hot dry conditions if the pigment's goethite converts to haematite. Similarly, yellow siderite minerals alter to shades of red when heated sufficiently. It is small wonder that the oldest known paintings are red, providing a warning to those who interpret ancient art as predominantly red in its original state.

Engravings

Breaking a rock surface by pounding or 'pecking' with a hammer is termed 'rock engraving' by archaeologists, although the method is rougher than this term normally implies. The most popular engraving technique was hammering small holes at intervals to form an outline, then connecting them with a narrow pounded groove (with a width of no more than two centimetres). Intaglio, or the pecking of an area of stone to form a negative impression of the image, was also practised. Less common, except in a few regions, was the abrading of a line. Engravings are found commonly on stone softer than quartzite, such as sandstone, limestone, fine-grained granite and dolerite, and where the sub-surface is much lighter in colour than the weathered 'skin', so that the visual effect is dramatic, even to the extent of white against a black backdrop. Sometimes a rock pavement that was particularly favoured or ritually significant is densely engraved for hundreds of square metres.

Stencils

Stencils are a specialised technique for creating an image of a real object; they are distinct from most other forms of art, which rely on the free-hand interpretation of the artist. The most common stencils are of hands, but they may be of an animal, plant or artefact, or an abstract form. Hand stencils possibly equated with signatures; and those that used haematite pigment may remain for thousands of years. Perhaps it was a 'signed' record of a casual visit or of a ritual event, such as the re-use of a nearby sorcery painting. Paul Taçon reports that among traditionally-oriented people in Kakadu hand or forearm stencils were a person's ceremonial 'signature'. After the death of an important individual, the identifying stencil is infilled with lines representing bones, and clan and other tribal symbols. Transformed into a group symbol, it assumes a moderate degree of ritual potency and power.

At some sites elsewhere in Australia, the stencils are arranged in patterns in association with other designs, suggesting that they were part of a narrative or artistic composition. The most elaborate use of stencil motifs occurs in the sandstone country around the Carnarvon Range in southern Queensland. These stencils were masterfully blown, with remarkable control direct from the mouth, to create imaginative composite designs. One exceptional motif of a ten-metre-long coiled snake is composed of 284 individual diamond-shaped stencils; another at a cave called The Tombs is the complete stencil of a man with arms outstretched.

Finger fluting

One form of 'engraving' found in caves, and which is interpreted by some as a deliberate art form, is the use of fingers to mark a pattern into a soft surface layer of calcite crystals (called moonmilk) or weathered carbonate. These finger markings appear as fluted meandering designs and have been found in caves in the Mount Gambier region, on the Nullarbor Plain, East Gippsland, and in Australia's southwest extremity. With the exception of Tasmania, this distribution corresponds with moonmilk formation in the limestone caves of southern Australia.

The most famous site containing finger markings is Koonalda Cave on the Nullarbor Plain. In total darkness, some 300 metres along an underground cavern and in part reached only by crawling through a narrow passage, there are thousands of meandering finger grooves impressed into soft limestone. Long V-sectioned incised lines also occur. Some markings have been dated by circumstantial evidence. First, rubble has fallen from the roof abutting onto part of the marked area. R. V. S. Wright, who directed one of the excavations at the site, obtained a date of about 20,000 years BP from the remains of a fireplace nearly twenty centimetres beneath the earth floor adjacent to the marked wall and presumably only occupied after the rock fall, although this is disputed. This charcoal is thought to be from a fire lit during the last prehistoric excursion into the darkness of the cave. In another excavation Alexander Gallus retrieved a small slab of limestone with incised markings some two metres below a surface dated to more than 31,000 years BP, though further dating suggests that the age is around 20,000 years in conformity with the stratigraphy.

Robert Bednarik has argued that the finger fluting found in southern Australian caves was a Pleistocene-age rock art tradition, at least as old as 30,000 years. The Koonalda dates are relevant to that claim. At three undated caves with finger fluting near Perth, Bednarik suggests juveniles were responsible. This means that it is most likely to be play, children's 'finger painting', although ceremonial activities for youths are also possible. Fluting may have been done for decoration or identification, perhaps associated with rituals, but it remains enigmatic. However, it is questionable whether finger fluting was a stage in the evolution of art in Australia, or whether it belongs only to that early period.

CLASSIFICATION OF ROCK ART

In the process of describing rock art, archaeologists have used several basic conventional divisions: the difference being abstract or

Finger fluting in Koonalda Cave. Some authorities consider it to be 20,000 years old. (Robert Edwards)

naturalistic images, and between Simple and Complex Figurative styles. Although useful to the archaeologist, it is important to remember that for the artists such concepts were meaningless. Abstract motifs require 'inside' knowledge to enable their levels of meaning to be 'read'. Yet figurative motifs, which resemble recognisable things to non-Aboriginal eyes, may have equally operated as icons with levels of encrypted meaning. To their creators, 'abstract' designs may have been just as 'figurative'. Although alien categories such as 'figurative' and 'abstract' remain part of contemporary analysis, modern research attempts to remodel the way art is qualified, so that intrinsic components become the primary concern.

Along the whole of eastern Australia, rock art may be classed as

Simple Figurative, and consists of painted, stencilled or engraved outlines, or solid forms, with a small degree of embellishment in the far north. Although eastern Australian art is characterised by its figurative component, a substantial proportion is non-figurative or abstract. Complex Figurative art, regarded in Eurocentric terms as more 'sophisticated', is found only in the Kimberley region and Arnhem Land. Complex Figurative Style appears to be a later innovation, added to a range of Simple Figurative and abstract styles. The small sample of art preserved and identified from remote prehistory is abstract and Simple Figurative in form.

PLEISTOCENE ARTISTS

One of the major obstacles to constructing regional and continent-wide sequences of Aboriginal artistic traditions is the difficulty of accurate dating, combined with poor preservation at the majority of early sites due to natural deterioration. The problem was that Australian rock art studies possessed no objective time depth. The fallen engraved slab excavated in an upper layer at Devon Downs in 1929 was the sole stratigraphic date for which some antiquity could be inferred. For the rest, it depended on subjective attribution of depictions of artefacts or animals, extinct or living, or on the degree of weathering of a rock surface, or on studies of superimposition of motifs. None provides absolute chronology and all rely upon fallible human judgement.

Systematic unravelling of stylistic superimposition by Fred McCarthy contributed a relative sequence for some regions, yet it proved rash to correlate over vast distances. Recent field studies, including areas of Kakadu, Cape York Peninsula and the Australian Alps, have met with success, and the new technique of microstratigraphic AMS radiocarbon dating developed by Alan Watchman offers a whole new dimension to the scientific dating of rock art.

Mulvaney was the first to date engravings older than 5000 years by stratigraphic association at Ingaladdi in 1966. But only some shelters and caves with art have floor sediments with datable cultural materials; and only very occasionally has such material been linked directly to the art. Often these other cultural remains only provide an approximate time at which people were first present. The Early Man Shelter on Cape York Peninsula is an exception. Excavations by Andrée Rosenfeld demonstrated that floor surfaces had been engraved before fires were lit over them around 13,000 years BP.

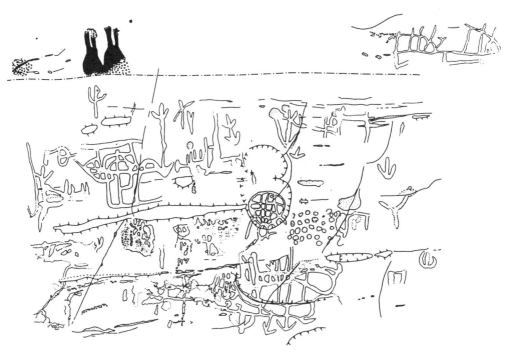

The main engraved panel at Early Man Shelter, near Laura, Cape York, dated to older than 13,000 years BP. The painting of fruit bats (top left), partly obliterated by sedimentation, is at least 1000 years old. The panel is about 2.5 metres by 1.8 metres. (A. Rosenfeld)

Archaeological evidence testifies to a remarkable antiquity for art. Koonalda Cave was claimed as the oldest known art site, but that evidence is inferential. Watchman's pioneering dating of organics and oxalates in finely laminated encrustations on art, however, suggests an antiquity of at least 25,000 years in Cape York. In the southwest of Tasmania, Ballawinne Cave, Keyhole Cavern and Wartata Mina Cavern all have hand stencils thought to date to at least 14,000 years BP, but there is no direct evidence for this. A further date of about 20,000 years BP from pigment at a painted shelter in Dead Man's Pocket in the Northern Territory is disputed. Such dates only represent initial pioneering research, and prospects for future dating seem good. It could be argued, however, that hand stencils may relate to a form of ceremonial identification with a place, and that such ritual motifs are strictly not art forms.

Rock art of temperate Australia 21

Across the southern half of the continent, regions exhibit distinctive artistic styles and motifs, doubtless reflecting different cultural traditions. Yet the art also depended for its survival upon geology and climate. Geological formations that offer extensive flat pavements or smooth vertical surfaces, particularly sandstone, provide optimal opportunities for engraving or painting. Pigments are likely to survive, however, only when protected from the elements. The fact that paintings occur in caves and rockshelters, while engravings are also found across open localities, in part is a consequence of differential survival rather than cultural choice.

PANARAMITEE STYLE

Objective assessment of major regions commenced with the recognition of the Panaramittee Style. This generalised category served for three decades to order an immense corpus of rock art, although it is unlikely to be supported by detailed field surveys and analysis. Panaramitee Style rock engravings are sometimes called 'track and circle' or 'Classic Panaramitee' because animal tracks and seemingly abstract circle motifs predominate. Examples are found over semi-arid country, extending from western New South Wales to eastern South

Australia, and northwards to around Alice Springs. There are dozens of engraved localities: the best-known are in the Olary region, such as the original 'type sites' on Panaramitee Station, and at Mount Poole, Innamincka, and many places in the Flinders Ranges.

Sturts Meadow in New South Wales and N'Dahla Gorge in central Australia have been studied in detail, and in the latter region two further sites, Ewaninga and the Cleland Hills, have received close attention. Rock engravings at Nappapethera Waterhole in southwest Queensland are stylistically similar to Panaramitee and may extend its known distribution.

Herbert Basedow in 1914 was the first to recognise a consistent range of motifs and their regular proportions at the sites in the Flinders Ranges. His description was subsequently elaborated by Charles Mountford and Robert Edwards. These 'classic' sites each have thousands of engravings, most less than ten centimetres long. Animal and bird tracks number nearly half of the motifs at any site, and more than 80 per cent are tracks, circles and lines, hence the label 'track and circle'. Less common are human footprints, groups of dots and figurative motifs such as reptiles; anthropomorphic figures are rare.

Expanses of flat rocky ground near permanent springs and rockholes where people camped provided surfaces for the engravings. Robert Edwards recorded sites at Wharton Hill on Tiverton Station, near Panaramitee. Here, cyprus pines grow along an intermittent creek where piles of cooking stones mark the locations of former camp sites. At the rocky base of the hill there are small hollows that collect rainwater and serve as natural reservoirs even when the creek is dry. Around the hill Edwards counted nearly 3000 engraved motifs; in descending order of frequency, they were kangaroo and emu tracks, circles, human footprints, dots, crescents, lizards and star-shapes.

Regional differences within Panaramitee Style

For many years it was thought that Panaramitee was stylistically uniform across its distribution, until Natalie Franklin statistically examined widely separated sites and found regional variations. The most important regional indicator is that each major locality usually has a special motif of its own, such as the sixteen small engraved 'faces' discovered at Cleland Hills, small figures of people with headdresses at N'Dahla Gorge, and net-like motifs at Panaramitee Station. At N'Dahla Gorge there is not much variation in animal tracks, but a definite tendency towards complex types of non-figurative designs,

A weathered pavement of Panaramitee Style circle and track motifs, Ooraminna, central Australia. (Robert Edwards)

twenty of which are based on the circle. At Mootwingee the pattern is more complex because only about 80 per cent of the motifs are considered to be Panaramitee Style; the rest are Simple Figurative. At the nearby sites in Sturts Meadow there are exposures of mudstone along a creek bed, where fresh engravings are grey-blue which in time discolour to dark grey-brown. Of more than 130,000 motifs, John

Clegg has classified them into more than 50 types of motif, mostly bird and macropod tracks, a small proportion of human tracks, and non-figurative crescents, circles, dots, and other more complex designs. The extraordinary homogeneity in the groups of motifs on different rock exposures suggests either a short passage of time from the first to the last engraving events, or a long continuity of tradition.

A pan-Australian style?

In the 1970s the idea prevailed that the Panaramitee Style could have a continent-wide distribution. This was inferred by Robert Edwards, who examined engraved art sites in arid regions, and observed that linear, circle and track motifs frequently were patinated or heavily weathered. Edwards identified similar motifs in Tasmanian engravings, and questioned whether this non-figurative art form came with the first migrants. The problem with the hypothesis of continent-wide Panaramitee Style is that there are only two basic motifs, tracks and circles, which are ubiquitous across time and space. The key Tasmanian rock art site of Mount Cameron West is now thought to be less than 2000 years old and is no longer considered an example of Panaramitee Style.

Ever since Edwards raised the prospect, researchers have tried to extend the distribution of Panaramitee across the Nullarbor to the extreme southwest of the continent and beyond the eastern highlands to the east coast. So-called 'residual' Panaramitee Style is said to occur at Mount Yengo rockshelter, near Sydney, where track and circle motifs could be 4000–6000 years old (see p. 382). Ancient engravings excavated at the Early Man Shelter near Laura are also linked to Panaramitee. These include areas of pits, and four or five motifs made up of interlocking lines forming shapes like grids, radiating lines and trident-like motifs (possibly bird tracks). But there are also links with the more recent rock art at that shelter: certain fundamental differences contrast with Panaramitee Style, circles being infrequent, and human, macropod and possibly bird tracks absent. Attempts to extend the style beyond the interior may be a case of a bridge too far, and as with most pioneering schemes, future research may establish that the artistic similarities were more apparent than real.

Antiquity

It has been assumed that Panaramitee Style is very old since the claim by Basedow in 1914 of engraved Diprotodon tracks at Yunta Springs, presumably a sure indication of the Pleistocene. More tantalising evidence of great antiquity came in 1929, when Mountford reported an engraved head of a saltwater crocodile at Panaramitee Station, and decades later, the discovery of a marine turtle and saltwater fish. Yunta Springs was revisited by Norman Tindale, who speculated that some engravings of large kangaroo and emu tracks could have been those of extinct giant fauna. None of this evidence is accepted today. The so-called crocodile head makes a particularly interesting story. Crocodiles disappeared from southern Australia millions of years ago, so the lines that make up the motif could mean anything, including overlapping net-like engravings which are a distinctive motif for the locality. An identification was provided to Ronald Berndt by an Aboriginal informant in 1943: part of the lines depict a powerful magical stick, representing the body of a spirit, with each part of the complex motif imbued with mythological meaning.

Geochemical dates for desert varnish on engravings at Karalta, South Australia, of around 40,000 years BP, have been dismissed. For the time being the antiquity of the Panaramitee Style is not known, but it may have persisted until terminal prehistoric times. The common motifs constitute part of contemporary central Australian artistic tradition, which is obvious even for Papunya dot paintings on canvas. One modern interpretation of circles is that they are water-holes, and lines radiating from these circles are the paths taken by ancestral creation beings. Such interpretations of undated art, how-ever, are speculation. It is easy to peck engravings into the rock pavements of Yunta Springs and Mootwingee, which in part have a thin capping of hard, fine-grained sandstone overlying a less-siliceous, softer sandstone. Other than cultural proscription there is no reason why Aborigines should have ceased to engrave there. Needless to say, a number of sites, such as N'Dahla Gorge, Sturts Meadow and many others, have fresh-looking engravings, including diagnostic motifs of the Panaramitee Style—tracks and circles. Evidently Aborigines added to the corpus of engravings from time to time, possibly over thousands of years. Whether their symbolism remained constant is another matter, both through time and from region to region.

SOUTHEASTERN AUSTRALIA

Widely scattered throughout eastern Australia, in areas of suitable rock formations, and especially concentrated in the southeast, is a style of rock art characterised by Simple Figurative motifs. It is defined by simple outlines or stick figures, with solid or linear infills, together with simple geometric designs. Stencilling is also found over most of the southeast of the continent. The art style, particularly the abstract motifs, has parallels in carved tree designs and decoration on wooden artefacts. Paintings and drawings usually are rendered in a single colour, red, black, orange or white being most common. The style extends mainly from the southern Queensland coast throughout New South Wales and Victoria, and as far west as the Mount Lofty Ranges east of Adelaide. This broadly defined distribution pattern crosses numerous environmental and cultural boundaries and provides a general grouping within which smaller regional variations occur.

In the northeastern highlands of New South Wales the figures are painted in outline. Further west, in semi-arid country around Bourke and Cobar, the regional variation of the style is characterised by small and animated motifs (called miniature figures) often arranged to form scenes and lively expressions of group movement. It was through the dedication of Fred McCarthy that the style of central west New South Wales is well documented; his fieldwork remains an important resource, together with a subsequent survey by Ben Gunn.

The miniature figures, usually no more than 30 centimetres high, are painted on the rock with a finger or a twig brush. They depict animals, fish, birds and, importantly, human-like figures and artefacts. Hunting scenes are common and include large communal hunts with spears and net traps. Other scenes depict rows of dancers facing each other. McCarthy interpreted some paintings as hunting magic. Painted rockshelters are found mostly around more reliable rockholes, and they delineate evidence of prehistoric domestic activity. Some of the galleries are extensive: one at Mount Grenfell is 26 metres long. McCarthy's excavations in painted rockshelters at Mount Grenfell and Mount Gunderbook provide an earliest date of only about 2000 years, but paintings remain undated.

SOUTHEASTERN HIGHLANDS

The sites that have been studied most intensively are three shelters at Yankee Hat, Nursery Swamp and Rendezvous Creek in Namadgi National Park, Australian Capital Territory. These contain mostly paintings and some drawings of anthropomorphs, stick figures, animals, and abstract linear designs. Interestingly, there are no stencils, a characteristic shared by other sites on the southern tablelands and far south New South Wales coast. Kelvin Officer, a specialist on the rock art of southeastern New South Wales, has identified two phases of art, including repainting, in the Namadgi sites. The earlier paintings are weathered and are less diverse than the later motifs, suggesting the development of a localised style. The later phase was perhaps associated with permanent occupation of the highlands following climatic amelioration. While no definite chronology is available for the two-phase sequence, occupation from one shelter predates 3700 years, while at another some motifs resemble pack-horses and therefore may be recent.

The art style at the sites in Namadgi National Park is found further south in the southern highlands and in rocky outcrops on the riverine plain further west. Many of these places in the foothills of the Victorian Alps have been recorded by Ben Gunn. Frequently they occur in clusters centred on a shelter with a large gallery of art, a general distribution which corresponds to the ceremonial network associated with the summertime bogong moth festivals in the alps.

The Garden Range 1 and Mudgegonga 2 rockshelters exemplify such ceremonial sites. A test pit revealed that the former had not been occupied. The rock face is plastered with an extravagant array of motifs, 174 in all, many now water-damaged. Unique for its depiction of anthropomorphic 'Euroa men' figures, the shelter is surrounded by three satellite rock art sites. Gunn believes Mudgegonga 2 was probably located on the summer route into the Victorian Alps. There is complex superimposition of at least thirteen art layers grouped into five distinct art phases. A figure of a potoroo is the only painting of that species in Victoria. With its hundreds of motifs, this is the second-richest rock art site in Victoria. Radiocarbon dates of the archaeological deposit suggests intermittent Aboriginal use of the shelter for 3500 years, and the art may correspond with this occupation. Gunn's analysis of the paintings reveals a number of similarities with that of the Grampians Range to the west.

THE GRAMPIANS AND FURTHER WEST

Much of Victoria's rock art lies in the sandstone ridges of the Grampians, in the mid-west of the state. Here there are hand prints and stencils, paintings of small stick figures, and abstract linear motifs such as lines, bars and circles, almost all in red ochre applied with the finger. The motif range is limited and the main theme is the repeated depiction of specific motifs, such as 'lizard man', identified by Gunn, which occur at twenty sites in the Grampians, and rows of short lines or 'tally marks' (at one site, Glenisla, there are at least 1800 of them). The meaning of the art is unknown and it is undated; archaeological deposit in one of the sites is up to 3500 years old. The general style of painting and drawing simple human and animal figures and abstract motifs is also found in the Mount Lofty Ranges just east of Adelaide. The range of stencilled art terminates in the Grampians, with one site containing 70 stencils; none is reported further west. Four hundred kilometres to the north, in the Flinders Ranges and Olary district, the paintings are stylistically different.

SYDNEY REGION

Sydney and the surrounding sedimentary geological basin which forms its hinterland is singular for the abundance of its rock art heritage in an urban region—there are more than 4000 known rock engraving sites in greater Sydney (less than half of them recorded in detail) and more than 3000 rockshelters with pigment art. The ungainly term 'pigment art' refers to pictures made by drawing or stencilling pigments such as ochre or charcoal onto rock surfaces. Colours are from the standard palette, black, white, red and yellow, with the rare appearance of orange. The engravings and drawings mostly consist of lines which enclose space; some outline representations are approximately life-size. There are several whale engravings many metres long. Figures in pigment art are slightly smaller and often have linear infill. If the images are read as depictions of what they seem to resemble, many aspects of Aboriginal secular and spiritual life are portrayed.

This extraordinary art record occurs in the ubiquitous bedrock exposures in the deeply eroded Hawkesbury sandstone formation which gives Sydney its rugged topography and spectacular views. This sandstone weathers into caverns; thousands of rockshelters are scattered along ridges and waterways, while engravings occur on ridge and plateau tops. During a recent field survey in a small area of the heavily dissected plateau just north of the city, 30 new art sites were recorded, indicating that many sites remain undiscovered. They occur as far west as the Blue Mountains, southwards towards Wollongong, north across the estuaries of Broken Bay, and almost as far as the

Hunter River. The relentless growth of Sydney has destroyed vast numbers of engravings. A large fish under the floorboards of a garage is nearly all that remains of a once major complex at Point Piper near central Sydney.

Engravings

Engravings were encountered on the ridges around Sydney Harbour by men of the First Fleet in 1788. It is little wonder that the engravings were noticed so early, for there are still some preserved a stone's-throw from the central business district. Recording of some of these sites began in the nineteenth century, culminating in the production in a monumental descriptive work by the surveyor W. D. Campbell in 1899. More systematic recording was carried forward by Fred McCarthy initially, and then by other Sydney-based researchers, including Lesley Maynard, John Clegg and Jo McDonald.

Hawkesbury sandstone abrades easily. The engraving method was to peck pits into the rock and then join them together by abrading a groove with a more resistant stone, probably with the aid of water. Experiments have demonstrated that engravings can be made at a rate of 1.25 metres of groove per hour, so relatively little effort was required for this art form. Not all engravings were done by single individuals. Clegg has observed distinct asymmetry in the limbs of some figures, suggesting that more than one person was involved in abrading the outline. When first engraved, the colour of the freshly exposed sandstone would have highlighted the outline of the figures on the rock face, but within a few years these grooves discolour to the dull grey or brown of the surrounding rock. The rate of weathering of exposed rock faces is rapid and many engravings are now so faint that they are visible only when the sun is low and casts an oblique light.

Most engravings are Simple Figurative outline motifs or 'silhouettes', approximately life-size, but some are much larger than life. There are also many motifs that are not so obviously figurative, such as circles and isolated lines. These are classified as abstract or non-figurative designs, although such classification may be a Eurocentric lack of traditional perspective. Topographic features in the rock surface occasionally are integrated as an element in the motif, or to frame it. The most common motif is a simple design interpreted to be a human footprint, and sometimes these are arranged in trails. Also in the repertoire are birds, land and marine fauna, and depictions of

Emu with a clutch of eggs and a set of bush turkey tracks at Devil's Rock near Sydney. (Jo McDonald)

artefacts including spears, boomerangs, dillybags, hatchets and fishing lines. Anthropomorphic figures are a major theme among the motifs, especially in the region's south. Engravings of human figures are typically full frontal, mammals and birds in profile, and reptiles from above. Men and women often wear waist belts or necklets, and occasionally what may be a headdress; males especially, tend to have enlarged sexual organs. Some figures are thought to be representations of the Dreaming beings Baiame and Daramulan, who figure in the traditions recorded by Alfred Howitt of many southeast Australian tribes.

A minority of sites contain single motifs; a few motifs comprise the norm, but occasionally there are more than a hundred. Compositions include men hunting a kangaroo, feasting on a stranded whale, or what may be family portraits. Some motifs are easy to identify; others are enigmatic outlines defying interpretation. On the plateau top overlooking Brisbane Water is sited a series of figures that have presented a puzzle since their discovery. To some they appear to be a line of rabbits; to others, dancers at an initiation ceremony, mythical beings, or stylised depictions of koalas or bandicoots. These are interesting alternatives (we prefer the dancers) but it is uncertain whether the figures were all engraved at the same time.

While the majority of motifs may be secular, it is likely also that some scenes depict Dreaming events, such as for instance the rivalry between the emu and the bush turkey, which resulted in the emu becoming flightless and the bush turkey laying few eggs. There is evidence that some engravings were renewed or retouched after their original execution by abrading shallow silhouette grooves or by changing the shape of the outline.

Pigment art

About 90 per cent of the pigment art in rockshelters comprises drawings and stencils; the rest is painting or combinations of painting and drawing. Unfortunately many of the motifs are unidentifiable, among other reasons because of poor preservation. Hand stencils are common, as are drawings of macropods and other terrestrial animals, and human and anthropomorphous figures. Marine animals are predominant in coastal regions, replaced by land animals further inland. Beyond the Sydney Basin, south of Nowra, painting becomes the dominant technique and the range of motif types becomes more restricted and specialised. Human and anthropomorphic figures dominate the figurative assemblage and stencils disappear entirely. Interestingly, Bernard Huchet has found that this corresponds with the boundary between two exchange networks he calls Koori and Yuin.

One of the more impressive drawing and stencil sites near Sydney is a rockshelter at Canoelands, Maroota, northwest of Sydney. The shelter is dry and comfortable, providing a panoramic view over a gorge; it is adjacent to a creek with rock pools, and an area where hatchet heads were ground and sharpened. On the rear wall of this overhang are superimposed drawings, in black, white and yellow, of human and animal figures, and nearly 50 hand stencils and stencilled boomerangs and ornaments. The fauna is a veritable larder—eel and fish, echidna, kangaroo, koala, possum, turtle, emu and eggs. Across the wall stretches a long red line with large spheres at both ends— perhaps a bora ring with a track leading to it. Surveying all is a large striped anthropomorph wearing a waist belt and grasping a boomerang (possibly the creation being Baiame) in black, white, red and yellow pigment.

Regional variation

Recent analysis of the art sites by Jo McDonald has revealed the existence of stylistic clines (graded series) within the Sydney Basin.

Engraved figures at Brisbane Water, north of Sydney, interpreted as either humans, animals or mythical beings, or possibly dancers in a corroboree. (Campbell 1899: Plate 24, Fig. 3)

It also seems likely that the Georges River, a major waterway to Sydney's south, was the boundary between the Sydney Basin rock art style and the art province to the south. There are no emus or mythological beings in the engravings found south of the river; and the proportion of tracks to other motifs is much less; whales are less stylised; and kangaroos are shown with four limbs rather than the usual two, and emus with two limbs rather than only one, which is the usual northern convention. Similarly, the drawings and paintings in rockshelters have different conventions of perspective. Possibly the river was a cultural boundary between northern and southern tribal groups.

Dating

Rock art in the Sydney Basin style continued to be produced until the end of traditional Aboriginal life-style in the region, and the latest rock engravings and drawings provide some glimpses of that period of profound transition. Among the drawings of contact themes are the bulls in Bull Shelter near Campbelltown in Sydney's southwest, and engravings of European sailing ships.

A site that may provide some definitive answers about dating is Mount Yengo rockshelter northwest of Sydney, test-excavated by consultant archaeologist Jo McDonald. This site, possibly a base camp, has the second-largest amount of art in any shelter in the Sydney region, with both engravings and pigment art, totalling more than 500 individual motifs, mostly hand stencils. Buried under the floor

Ancient panel of engraved circle and tracks in Mount Yengo rockshelter, near Sydney (Jo McDonald)

Rock engravings at Mount Cameron West, Tasmania, exposed by excavation in 1968, with a presumed age of less than 2000 years. This art was covered by sand until it partly eroded in the 1920s. (Robert Edwards)

sediment of the shelter is a panel of engraved circles and animal tracks, basic motifs which fit within the range of Sydney Basin style but are more reminiscent of demonstrably ancient rock art across Australia. The sediment accumulated adjacent to the panel is dated by radiocarbon to older than about 2500 years, and McDonald argues cogently for an antiquity of 5000–6000 years for the engraved art. She also contends that the paintings were produced within the last two or possibly three millennia. Radiocarbon dating of pigment art has produced a range of dates from about 2500 years to about 500 years BP.

TASMANIA

One of the most intriguing rock engraving sites in Australia is at Mount Cameron West, on the wet and windy northwest coast of Tasmania. The engravings are only a few metres from the beach, on friable limestone rock faces buried beneath sand-drift and overgrown by vegetation. Similar motifs were described by George Robinson in 1830 on rocks at Green's Creek, a few kilometres south.

The motifs are mostly variations on the circle theme, but there is also a barred geometric design reminiscent of an ancient Egyptian cartouche, and until recent years the site was thought to be part of the pan-Australian Panaramitee Style of Pleistocene age, although there is no dominance of track motifs in Tasmania. An excavation in 1968 by Rhys Jones and Harry Lourandos in a shell midden on part of the site revealed that engravings had been covered about 1500 years ago, which provides a minimum age for the art.

Close to the present Tasmanian coastline there are a few other engraving sites, all small and of unknown antiquity. Rock painting sites are similarly scarce in Tasmania. Significantly, however, they include three caves deep in the southwest forests which have panels of hand stencils and red ochre smears presumably dating to the Pleistocene. Three rockshelters are known with hand stencils in red or yellow, probably not very old (one of these is drowned by a reservoir), and two sites with only a few lines of paint. Even these fragmentary survivals are significant because they testify to aesthetic concerns among a people whom early Europeans claimed lacked any artistic sense. Whether art formed part of the intellectual baggage carried to Tasmania by the original colonists is an issue awaiting solution.

Rock art of tropical Australia 22

The vast areas of sandstone formations in Cape York, Arnhem Land and the Kimberley region are storehouses of prehistoric and European contact art on a scale which has been appreciated only since the 1960s. The Kakadu region has been inscribed on the World Heritage Register partly because of its artistic significance, while it seems likely that future years may witness the inscription of the other two regions. In all three art provinces the surviving heritage may span the period from Pleistocene to historic times.

SOUTHEAST CAPE YORK PENINSULA

In dissected sandstone plateau country west and southwest of Cooktown, particularly in the Laura district, there are hundreds of rockshelters containing painted figurative and non-figurative art, some of it spectacular. Pecked engravings also occur, some of which are ancient. The painted art was first investigated by Percy Trezise, who located prospective rockshelters from the air while a commercial pilot. Trezise originally called the style 'Quinkan', the name of local spirit beings, which also is the name that local elders gave to a distinctive anthropomorphic figure peculiar to the region. The Laura Style, as it is now called, emphasises bold areas of colour, predominantly red, but also white and yellow. Common are human and animal-like figures of simple form and little elaboration of infill detail. Some of these figures are adorned with headdresses, fringed belts or pendants, or have what is thought to be body scarification. Stencils of hands, artefacts and plants are also common. Most of the figures are less than a metre long, but a number are so huge that they dominate the confines of the rockshelter. Despite the apparent jumble of paintings on rock faces, there are recurring associations between some types of motifs, offering a potentially rewarding avenue of research on Laura art.

Noelene Cole, Alan Watchman and Michael Morwood are constructing a scheme of stylistic development of Laura painted art, based on their continuing study of multiple superimpositions of figures. Although hard pieces of pigment with worn facets from rubbing to make paint have been found in all the archaeological excavations, most were discarded less than 1000 years ago, suggesting a dramatic increase in rock painting occurred around Laura.

That the painting style continued into the historical era is readily demonstrated by a number of modern subjects, such as horses, pigs, rifles, and figures identified as native police, presumably painted no earlier than the Palmer River gold rush of 1873. Stencilled spear-throwers occur in the more recent superimpositions, and boomerangs in earlier ones, possibly reflecting a change in hunting technology in the region during the last few centuries. Two AMS radiocarbon date of about 750 years BP were determined for this painting style from a rockshelter called Yam Camp excavated by Morwood. The sample for the date came from fragments of tiny plant fibres, probably from crushed orchid bulb used as a binder, which had been preserved in the paint.

At the site of Laura South, Alan Watchman has dated to about 24,600 years BP fine microlayers of patina covering red pigment. The painting itself is hidden beneath the opaque coating on the rock surface, and identification of the painting's style will have to wait for a further development in rock art detection.

Laura engravings

The latest style of pecked engraving in the Laura region appears to belong to the same tradition as the figurative pigment art. At the Amphitheatre Site an engraving of a dingo tentatively dates the style to the last four millennia.

An earlier non-figurative engraving style, which may have continued into recent prehistoric times, has been dated at the site of Early
Man, one of a cluster of decorated rockshelters fifteen kilometres east
of Laura township. Early Man has a partially buried frieze of linear
designs heavily patinated by age. The designs include cupules (pits),
radiating lines, enigmatic trident-like features, and rectilinear mazes
and grids. The buried portion is older than 13,000 years BP. Similar
non-figurative designs occur on a fragment of sandstone excavated at
Sandy Creek 1 shelter by Morwood, dated to about 14,400 years BP.

Further south, in the upper Flinders River region of north Queensland, similar abstract engravings occur. They are undated but are
patinated and may be very old. Andrée Rosenfeld, who excavated
Early Man, has suggested that there was a distinct north Queensland
style of non-figurative engraving art. At Mickey Springs Site 34 in
the central Queensland highlands, a rockshelter at the only permanent water within an area of dry scrubland, there is a panel of
engravings comprising tracks, circles, arcs and lines. The bottom of
the panel is buried by the earth floor. An excavation by Morwood
uncovered sets of short, vertical lines and a bird track. A small hearth
from just above the lowest ones date to about 10,000 years BP. The
lines above these are about 8000 years BP. Engravings on the wall
above floor level are of paired macropod tracks, bird tracks, circles
and pits. Pieces of engraved rock exfoliated from this panel also lay
in the excavated sediments. The small size of the hearths, and the
paucity of stone artefacts and preserved food remains in these sedimentary levels, suggested to Morwood that the people who pecked
the engravings visited the site in small transient groups. More recent
discoveries add weight to Rosenfeld's proposal.

Koolburra Plateau

The sandstone Koolburra Plateau is only 50 kilometres northwest of
Laura, but between the two art regions flows the Kennedy River,
which may have defined a cultural boundary. The two regions share
basic similarities in the motifs and techniques of painting. One major
difference is that in Koolburra Plateau sites there are many figures
with both human and animal features, whereas in Laura art, and in
Australia generally, such figures are rare.

The common use in Koolburra painting of white pipe-clay, which
tends not to last long, indicates that a large proportion probably belong
to late prehistoric and early historic times. Pieces of ochre, many of

which may have been for rock painting, occur throughout excavated cultural sediments, and show a sharp and sustained increase in the use of paint after about 1800 years BP. At Green Ant rockshelter, a panel of patinated engravings underlies the paintings and, fortunately for archaeology, also extends below the earth floor. Fresh-looking engravings of human hands and feet, turtles and spearthrowers are pecked over non-figurative motifs such as circles, pits, mazes, lines, and bird and animal tracks, similar to the Laura region. The site was first occupied shortly before 8500 years BP, and the older patinated engravings could be as old as this, though all that has been determined is that they were pecked before about 1700 years BP.

KAKADU NATIONAL PARK

Western Arnhem Land is a rock art province of considerable international prominence. Most of the sites discovered are within Kakadu National Park, where the current estimate runs to as many as 7000 sites. In the south the most recent rock art style has affinities with that of central Arnhem Land, while the Alligator Rivers region in the north of the park has links east along the coastal fringe.

The region is abundant with food resources, with many sheltered camping places in overhangs and boulders at the foot of the main escarpment and in rocky residuals on the adjacent coastal plain. The rock is hard siliceous quartzite or sandstone, much of it resistant to weathering, which offered attractive smooth surfaces for artists. In fact, the rock surfaces are so durable that Kakadu has one of the longest records of art in the world; a tradition that survived until the 1960s on rock faces continues today on bark and paper for the market.

Stylistic succession

The identification of styles and their chronological sequence has been recast and refined a number of times since initial study of the art by Charles Mountford, the leader of the American–Australian Scientific Expedition to Arnhem Land in 1948. The debate opened with the important field surveys from the 1960s by Eric Brandl, Robert Edwards and George Chaloupka. They elaborated on Mountford's basic styles of Mimi figures (largely equivalent to today's 'Dynamic Figure Style') and X-ray. These hyperactive human and presumably mythological 'Mimi' constituted Mountford's earlier style, succeeded by the X-ray Style, which until recently was painted by Gunwinggu, Gagudju and Jawoyn people.

The research field of Kakadu art is far more crowded now. Resolving its antiquity and its stylistic changes over the millennia has proved to be a complex task beset by conflicting interpretations. Some researchers have even advocated that one particular style was brought by peoples displaced by rising sea level at the end of the last glacial epoch. Although the environmental factor is relevant, it is unlikely to be the only one. Essentially, there are three alternative schemes, which we name after their proponents.

The first was proposed by Chaloupka during the late 1970s and refined in 1993. His scheme is based upon image identification and overlying motifs correlated with environmental and habitat changes through the past 50,000 years. It has a postulated beginning long before 20,000 years ago, in the Pre-Estuarine Period, characterised by imprints of hands, grass and other objects on the rock surface. Some 20,000 years ago the 'Large Naturalistic Figure Complex' developed, for which there are claimed depictions of extinct animals such as megafauna, thylacine and Tasmanian devil. Then follow stylised and schematised motifs of lively character, the 'Dynamic Figure Style', centred on dynamic humans bearing weapons and headdresses. Later in this period was also the 'Yam Figure Style' in which yams adopt anthropomorphic features, and images of the Rainbow Snake appear. The Estuarine Period Chaloupka dates to 8000 years ago, when motifs of estuarine fish and saltwater crocodile appear. A phase of 'Intellectual Realism' commences about 4000 years later, characterised by a complex of X-ray motifs and by outline figures of beeswax preserved on rock faces. The freshwater phase belonging to the present floodplain deposition followed some fifteen centuries ago, featuring magpie geese and items of recent Aboriginal material culture.

Chaloupka's pioneering scheme achieved much in ordering this vast complex of images, exhibiting its richness and stimulating its conservation. His chronology has attracted criticism, as has his identification of some motifs, but his approach in relating environmental features to human cultural activities is persuasive. Significantly, his scheme was based upon years of fieldwork in partnership with relevant clan leaders.

Darrell Lewis has formulated a contrasting regional sequence based on the identification of artefacts in the paintings, in particular hunting and fighting weapons, and on their association with other motifs in the same style. Lewis orders them into the following chronological sequence:

- *Boomerang period:* Animated human figures dressed in ceremonial gear, with hatchets, stone-headed spears and spears with a single row of barbs carved into the shaft, dating from the height of last glaciation and ending just before the Holocene.
- *Hooked stick and boomerang period:* Human figures, often fighting, with hooked sticks that may be spearthrowers and multi-pronged and multi-barbed spears, dating from the Early Holocene. This period sees regionalisation of art styles, and the appearance of the Rainbow Serpent and other associated mythological motifs.
- *Broad spearthrower period:* Spearthrowers with a more rounded shape became fashionable, and stone spearheads are of the 'leilira' type, the appearance of which Lewis dates to about 5500 years ago in this region. There was much stylistic variation, but well-defined regional styles are not evident.
- *Long spearthrower period:* X-ray art appears when the freshwater wetlands environment is established about 2000 years ago and continues almost to the present.

The third and most recent scheme is proposed by Paul Taçon and Christopher Chippindale, who undertook a laborious study of superimposition and linear relationship of hundreds of motifs at two major sites. These researchers do not argue for continuous painting over thousands of years but for punctuated periods of prolific artistic endeavour, possibly beginning at least 10,000 years ago. Their scheme is as follows:

- *Old phase:* Large naturalistic animals (and no human figures) are followed by a proliferation of Dynamic Figures; this phase may also have hand stencils.
- *Intermediate phase:* Commencing about 6000 years ago (perhaps between 6800 and 5300 years BP) when the sea rose to its present level and estuarine conditions prevailed. This saw the beginning of cultural diversity in Kakadu and regionalism in its rock art. Several styles have been identified. These include simple infilled figures holding boomerangs, hooked sticks and other weapons, sometimes arranged in animated battle scenes. Often these figures are positioned close to drawings of flying foxes. There are also Yam Figures—large anthropomorphs and animal figures with yam-like bodies—painted over or near waterlily bulbs. There is pronounced regionalism in painting of Yam Figure motifs. Sometimes they are associated with a Rainbow Serpent which is a subject that continues into recent Kakadu rock art. Multi-coloured paintings also first

appear in this period. This phase corresponds in part with Chaloupka's 'Simple Figures' (those with boomerangs) and the 'hooked stick and boomerang period' of Lewis.

- *Late phase:* Named the 'Complete Figure Complex', meaning X-ray and associated paintings, this phase is thought to date from about 3000 years ago to the 1960s, but mostly within the last 1000 years. In terms of subject matter the paintings are similar throughout this period, though the earlier paintings tend to contain less detail. There are also plain-infill figures, stick figures (sometimes in complex battle scenes reminiscent of the Dynamic Figure Style), stencils, and hand and artefact prints. A claimed innovation of this period is pressed beeswax design, though radiocarbon dating demonstrates that beeswax figures were made from about 4000 years ago into the twentieth century.

Although there are notable areas of concordance between these three art schemes, debate about the identification of Kakadu art styles and their chronologies will no doubt continue. The styles and motifs are attractive and contain much ethnographic detail. The following section discusses their cultural implications.

The Dynamic Figure Style

The two general styles recognised 50 years ago by Mountford, Dynamic Figure and X-ray, still provide the fundamentals of the contemporary schemes, so we examine Mountford's two styles in more detail. Dynamic Figures are red paintings of humans, anthropomorphs and animals, usually less than 50 centimetres high and often much smaller. 'Sprays' of grass or other plant fibres, done by flicking grass or leaves wetted with red paint onto the rock face, are sometimes found above main panels of Dynamic Figure scenes and are often accompanied by hand prints or stencils. Compositions of Dynamic Figures never fail to impress the viewer. Male figures, usually with headdresses and body ornaments, are engaged in hunting and combat—some scenes show skirmishes with spears being thrown and avoided by dexterous movements, combatants throwing boomerangs and spears, men wounded or killed, and a pervading sense of excitement, and pathos—chasing foes and scenes of comradeship. Taçon and Chippindale question whether these fighting scenes depict or celebrate real events, and suggest that perhaps they are symbolic or metaphorical, perhaps events involving mythological beings. Whatever the case, the concept of fighting and warfare is evident and these possibly represent the world's oldest depictions of combat.

Small lines and dashes, called 'speed marks', are found emanating from the mouths and faces of human figures and animal-headed beings, and also at their feet if they are running, or along the trajectories of spears they have cast. It is widely accepted that, at least in most cases, these marks indicate sound and motion, just as similar lines do in modern comics and cartoons; a few may indicate dust being kicked up, and dashed marks coming from the mouths of figures may be expelling breath or life essence rather than words or singing. The dashed marks around one figure of a woman pierced by many spears suggest blood flowing from her wounds. Whichever of these interpretations is preferred, the convention is an important artistic innovation. Given its probable antiquity, the style must take a prominent place in global art history, for the convention is an innovation in iconography, irrespective of its current role in Western art.

These bellicose little figures express both energy and motion on the walls of rockshelters and on other protected rock surfaces well beyond the borders of Kakadu, across the East Alligator River into contiguous territory of the Arnhem Land Aboriginal Reserve, and southwards into Jawoyn tribal territory nearly as far south as Katherine. Aborigines say that they were painted by the Mimi, tall, thin spirit-people who are so frail that they can only hunt in still weather and who long ago lived in these rockshelters.

No evidence of regional variation in the figures has been determined in terms of colour (they are always red), subject matter, or the manner in which they are painted. Taçon interprets this homogeneity as reflecting an adaptation to the relatively uniform semi-arid environment which prevailed during the terminal Pleistocene, during which large tribal territories and more flexible tribal affiliations are assumed, as there would be no strong desire or need to express strong group identity and land ownership through the signature of rock art.

Some of these red figures are so old that even overlying minerals are bonded permanently onto the rock surface. When found in superimposition with other paintings they underlie the X-ray motifs. Darrell Lewis identified a painting of a Tasmanian devil near Jim Jim Creek, and numerous animal figures are identified as Tasmanian tigers (see p. 125). This evidence does not confirm a Pleistocene antiquity, though all evidence considered together makes it possible that they are thousands of years old. Chaloupka has identified a few paintings he calls 'Post-Dynamic Figures', and these appear to be imitations of Dynamic Figures, but lack animation and true artistry. Perhaps it should not surprise if Aborigines of a later era were as much impressed by these ancient scenes as are visitors to Kakadu today.

X-ray paintings

These images are called 'X-ray' because most of them are naturalistic depictions with three or more internal parts of the body shown, such as backbone, heart, lungs, fat, muscle, digestive tract, nerves and long-bones. They are part of a larger style that also has solid colour, stroke and dash infill, different types of stick figures, stencils, and impressed beeswax motifs. 'X-ray' is a convenient but not entirely apt description of this component of the Complete Figure Complex Style, but we retain it because it is now enshrined in popular vocabulary. The main colours are red, yellow, white and purple, and in recent decades new colours, including pink, black and blue, have been added to the palette. The corpus of subjects is diverse: there are depictions of humans, mythical beings, animals, artefacts and abstract motifs. Depictions of women and procreation are prominent in X-ray painting; an image in Deaf Adder Gorge portrays a pregnant woman, others depict childbirth and breast feeding. Aboriginal elders told Taçon that power was transmitted by the paint, especially when it was applied in a cross-hatching pattern. What is reproduced by the paint is the brightness and iridescence of creation beings. Thus these images had power and, as in other parts of Australia, were repainted. Analyses of the pigments used at different galleries point to the likelihood that large numbers of motifs were painted over a short span of time, perhaps by a single person or a small group of people.

Fish are important in the traditional diet in Kakadu and they are the most common subject in the X-ray paintings. Some of the largest fish paintings are nearly two metres long, and a few have identifiable contents depicted in their stomachs, such as insects or small fish. In these pictures the three dimensions are conflated to two by stylistic conventions, which are similar to wall paintings in ancient Egyptian tombs. The most important part of the fish, its fillets, are depicted lying above the backbone. The external features shown are the fins, head and mouth, gills and whiskers (called barbels); the internal organs are segmented backbone, sometimes with spines, the digestive tract and organs, the choice fillets of flesh, optic nerves to the eyes, and the gill arches.

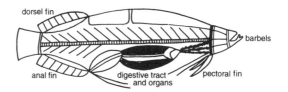

Kullubirr, saratoga *(Scleropages jardini)*

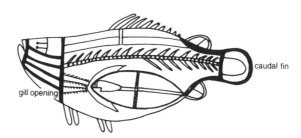

Namangol, silver barramundi *(Lates calcarifer)*

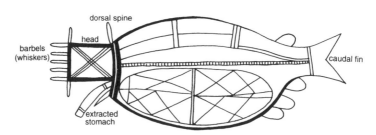

Anmakwari, lesser salmon catfish *(Hexanematichthys leptaspis)*

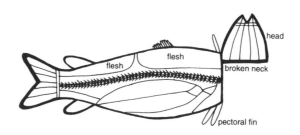

Matjabarr, mullet *(Liza diadema* and *Lisa dussmieri)*

Species of X-ray Style fish, Kakadu National Park. The fish are generalised. (Paul Taçon)

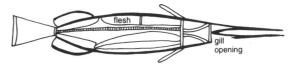

Burrugulung, freshwater long-tom *(Strongylura kreffti)*

From this bounty of anatomical detail at least twelve different fish species can be identified, while some species also are painted with clan designs, such as lozenge or hatching, which gives them a group logo. The bony saratoga is the easiest to identify; but silver barramundi is the most commonly painted, and often the older, larger females are depicted in greatest anatomical detail. Fork-tail catfish are portrayed frequently with a long fat object hanging from the neck, which Aboriginal elders identify as an extruded stomach (said to taste like calamari), usually squeezed out after breaking the neck, in preparing the catfish for cooking. Eel-tail catfish are usually painted small, less than 50 centimetres in length, with a square or rectangular head and numerous whiskers, which is typical of large, fat specimens in life. Other painted species are mullet, freshwater long-tom (which are very distinctive), bream, and the archer fish. Popular with visitors to Ubirr is a painting of an archer fish shooting a jet of water at a spider. Taçon believes that most of the fish paintings depicted catch brought back to camp. Species like the primitive archer fish, mud cod, and ox-eye herring, which are small or unpleasant to taste, are rarely painted.

The roots of X-ray painting lie within earlier rock art, and researchers have noted that internal anatomy is sometimes depicted. Progressively, X-ray designs became more complex, until the final stage where they are elaborate and formalised with developed abstract versions of internal organs. For at least the last 1000 years territorial ranges have been quite small because of the abundance of freshwater food from the wetlands, and these good times are reflected in the pronounced regionalism of the X-ray style, mostly expressed in the choice of colours and subjects. The Jawoyn sub-style, in which red and white bichrome X-ray paintings predominate, was identified by Chaloupka; now the Gagudju, Kundjey'mi and Gunwinggu sub-styles have been added. The final style in the evolution of X-ray paintings on rock walls consists of simple red, white or yellow figures with the same range of subjects but exhibiting only one or two features of internal anatomy, or sometimes none at all.

The artistry of the last Aboriginal to paint large galleries of X-ray, Najombolmi of the Bardmardi clan, can be seen at Nangaluwurr and Anbangbang at Nourlangie Rock. One scene was painted for a film made in the early 1960s by David Attenborough. Najombolmi died in 1964 but other Aborigines painted occasionally even into the 1990s. Such continuity allows the insight which marries the prehistory of Kakadu to the present.

The art of the Kakadu region, possibly stretching from Pleistocene times to the present, is an inspiring treasure-house of painting. In its artistic merit, its sheer volume, and its humane insight into both symbolic and everyday life, depicting interrelationship between culture, technology and environmental change, this corpus is unsurpassed globally. This alone justifies the region's World Heritage listing.

THE PILBARA

The semi-arid region of the Pilbara in northwestern Australia is known for its immense deposits of iron ore and its profoundly ancient eroded rock outcrops, some billions of years old and of particular interest to palaeontologists and earth scientists. It is less well known that the Pilbara is prolific in Aboriginal rock engravings, possibly the most copious in Australia, if not the world.

Dense areas of engravings on dolerite and fine-grained granitic rock, a number of square kilometres in extent, occur on Burrup Peninsula near Dampier, and some engravings are now surrounded, incongruously, by solar salt pondages and other installations. All but one of the rocky islands of the Dampier Archipelago contain large engraving sites (most are found on Angel and Dolphin Islands, where at one site there are more than 4000 engravings). Depuch Island, which lies midway between Dampier and Port Hedland, is also bountiful in rock engravings, as are the limestone pavements around the town of Port Hedland. Inland from this coastal axis are widely dispersed engraving sites, with concentrations most common in the upper catchments of the Yule and Shaw Rivers, and along a stretch of the De Grey River. Throughout the region rockshelters are scarce, so paintings are rare.

Whether on the coast or inland the engravings are commonly located at former base camps and at favoured hunting and fishing localities; the subject matter of the art often reflects these activities. At most engraving sites around Dampier there are ephemeral creeks and seasonally replenished rock pools, such as Skew Valley (which also has shell middens), Gum Tree Valley and Kangaroo Valley. Elsewhere the granitic bedrock retains water just below the surface of the ground in country that appears to be waterless to the inexperienced visitor. Domestic camping activities are evident at the sites, particularly grinding patches on the rock where grass-seed flour was made, which was a woman's task; sometimes the grinding occurs between engravings. While the abundance of anthropomorphic motifs suggest Dreaming themes, it must be assumed that a large proportion was intended for public viewing—the most common motifs in one valley are human figures on vertical rock surfaces, clearly public art and perhaps relating to women. In Skew Valley some small atypical engravings were found in a cleft of a rock into which only children could have squeezed.

Engravings are also found at isolated wells or in areas some distance from water, and this has some bearing on their interpretation. The remains of what are believed to be men's camps are found at small wells on high ground around Dampier, where numerous engraved turtles and their eggs occur on stone slabs. This led the investigator, Michel Lorblanchet, to propose that turtle-increase ceremonies were performed here during the wet season when the wells contained water. The common explicit sexual themes of many engraving compositions in the upper Yule River area suggest ceremonial activities or love magic or, to some viewers, depictions of ritual sex.

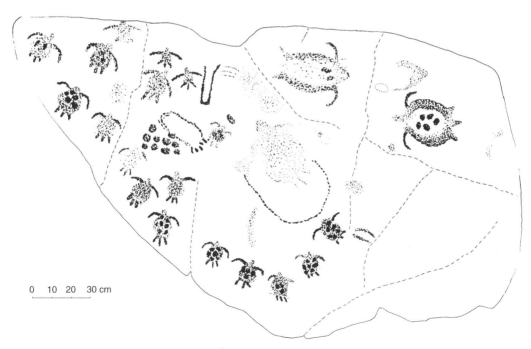

0 10 20 30 cm

A scene of turtles coming ashore to lay their eggs, engraved at Dampier, Western Australia. (M. Lorblanchet)

Within the Pilbara there are significant differences in style and content, and no researcher has proposed that the engravings belong to a single coherent style. However, there is overall unity in the coastal sites, presumably reflecting similarities in environment and culture. The stylistic correspondence between coastal Pilbara and Sydney Basin engravings has been remarked upon since their first description, but they have no historical links, and commonality results from the popularity of certain subjects, especially tracks, sea-life, and some of the anthropomorphs.

Coastal Pilbara engravings are mostly simple outlines, and some intaglio, predominantly naturalistic and Simple Figurative motifs, which range in size from about ten centimetres to 2.5 metres, with a tendency towards natural size. At least 50 motifs are documented; many of these are anthropomorphs, sometimes with greatly exaggerated sexual organs, hands and feet. A unique and imposing figure is of an eagle with wings outstretched and wearing an anthropomorphic headdress. There are many engraved Tasmanian tigers on Burrup rocks. Other subject matter testifies to a preoccupation with the food quest—animal tracks, insects, birds and eggs, land fauna and marine mammals, such as whale and dugong, and other marine creatures, in side view, but often showing both the eyes. All the hunting equipment is displayed, some in intricate detail—for instance, spearthrowers, multi-barbed spears, and varieties of boomerangs for fowling, fishing and close combat. Interestingly, both left- and right-handed returning boomerangs are identified. More abstract designs occur, such as concentric circles and spiral designs, and possible body ornaments and body painting designs. Aboriginal informants identified two buttock prints of a man ornamented with rows of feathers.

In the interior, the theme of sea-life is replaced by land mammals and other subject differences, but their distinguishing attributes are the predominance of the intaglio technique, greater variation in style, and the elaboration of anthropomorphs. These figures vary in size from quite small on boulders, up to five metres on expanses of granite pavement. They are either plain intaglio, or more complex with internal anatomy and other detailing.

A striking example of an inland site is the Spear Hill Complex, about 150 kilometres east of Port Hedland. An area of granite boulders and pavements, some more than a square kilometre in area, exhibit clusters of engravings. The latest designs were probably executed in recent prehistoric times. In one composition dingoes circle and attack macropods. There are the usual bird and animal tracks, but those engravings which are inferred to be be the latest are mostly anthropomorphs, in full or partial intaglio, wearing headdresses with radial, herringbone, loop or ladder-like projections.

One of these anthropomorphic types is called the 'Woodstock Figure', identified as a special motif some decades ago on Woodstock Station. This curvilinear figure has long antennae-like headdresses, forked hands and feet and, frequently, exaggerated sexual organs. Local Aboriginal people claim no traditional knowledge about the figures, and are adamant that they do not play a role in any ritual, though one researcher proposed a kangaroo creation-being identity.

Various lines of evidence indicate that rock engraving ceased when pastoralists occupied the Pilbara. Tindale reports that, during his visit to Port Hedland in the 1950s, he was told by Kariyarra people that the engravings were the work of a former tribe, the Minjbururu or 'stone hatchet-people', who figure in local folk-traditions. However,

Woodstock Figures, including sexual motifs, Pilbara region. (G. L. Walsh)

Tindale observed that the subjects reflected the present-day environment and traditional artefacts. His museum collection contained a boomerang from the region which had animal motifs burnt into its surface identical to those in engravings. The absence of spears with pressure-flaked Kimberley points suggested to him that they may pre-date the first arrival of this trade item from the northeast, but in any event this cannot be long ago. According to Ian Crawford, engravings were still being made on the dolerite boulders of Depuch Island in the early part of the twentieth century.

Claims of great antiquity of some engravings have been based on both superimposition and degree of patination. For the interior H. P. McNickle, proposes a changeover from predominantly outline to intaglio method, whereas Lorblanchet proposes that deep pecking was succeeded by finer shallow pecking of linear and silhouette designs at Dampier. In Lorblanchet's sequence, many geometric patterns and concentric circles are old; bi-lobed motifs (buttock prints) are inter-mediate; and human figures with exaggerated hands and feet are the most recent. Other specialists contest such sequences. The petrologist A. F. Trendall as early as 1964 reported that colour gradations and even method of engraving were conditioned by the depth of original crust on the rock and not their age. The best evidence so far is the radiocarbon dating of four pieces of engraved rock excavated by Lorblanchet from a shell midden in Skew Valley. One with three stick fig-ures in profile is older than 3700 years BP, and a coiled snake engraving is older than 2600 years BP. The midden comprised two shelly layers, with a single shellfish species in each layer. The upper layer species, *Anadara grandosa*, was scattered through-out the areas of engraving. Lorblanchet thus surmised that most engravings date between 4500 and 2200 years BP, although he also makes an ambit claim for much greater antiquity.

20 CM

10 CM

0

Engravings on a fragment of rock pavement exca-vated from shell midden deposit at Dampier, dated to older than 3700 years BP. (M. Lorblanchet)

VICTORIA RIVER DISTRICT

The Victoria River District (VRD) is a region of sandstone country about 100,000 square kilometres mid-way between the Kimberley and western Arnhem Land. Its

eastern boundary is along the headwaters of the Daly River, Northern Territory, while on its west it merges with the Kimberley region.
While exploring the area in 1856, A. C. Gregory encountered two
shelters with paintings which were recorded by the expedition artist.
These shelters were relocated in 1985, by which time some of the
paintings were barely visible. Much pioneering fieldwork was done by
Darrell Lewis, and later by H. P. McNickle and Ben Gunn on behalf
of government agencies, and in the 1990s excavations were undertaken.
Despite this art recording, the VRD remains only partly explored.

The VRD comprises one of the great rock art regions of the world,
exhibiting engraving and a succession of two painting styles. As in
much of Australia generally, stencilling of hands and artefacts is
common throughout the region. According to the archaeologists,
sharp increases in ochre in three excavated art sites about 1400 years
ago may herald new strategies of territorial behaviour and systems of
land management associated with increased rock painting. They further speculate about a possible change in perception of the Dreaming,
the way it relates to land, and how this relationship is expressed in art.

Most of the better-preserved paintings with white colouring are
probably recent because the pigment used deteriorates quickly, while
a range of post-contact motifs occur, including scenes of armed men
on horseback, herds of cattle, sailing vessels, and a red outline figure
of a steer with a small VRD brand in white pigment on its rump.
Humanlike figures and anthropomorphs in two or three colours are
a dominant theme in this phase, with painted figures typically large
and sometimes spectacular. One rockshelter near the Keep River has
the second-largest recorded rock painting in Australia—a snake or
Rainbow Serpent at least 24 metres long and more than a metre wide.
Snake motifs, typically with animal head and ears, are common in
VRD, the adjacent Kimberley region and western Arnhem Land,
indicating a regular depiction of the Dreaming serpent over a large
area of northern Australia. Examples of other large VRD paintings
include a seven-metre saltwater crocodile, a five-metre saw shark, and
numerous larger-than-life macropods and emus.

According to Lewis, some influence from non-figurative desert art
occurs in the south of VRD, but the strongest artistic and mythological relationships are with the Wandjina art style of the Kimberley
region. These links were first identified by D. S. Davidson, an American anthropologist who wrote a number of seminal works during the
1930s concerning the geographical distribution of rock art styles and
artefacts in Australia.

Many sites and paintings are still part of a living tradition of the local Wardaman people. Perhaps the best-known rock painting in the Victoria River District is the Lightning Brothers at Yiwarlarlay 1 rockshelter on Delamere Station. Oral history attributes this painting to Emu Jack, who is said to have painted it near the end of World War II. These figures are of two mythical brothers, the handsome Yagjagbula, and his unattractive older brother Jabirringgi. Paintings resembling the Lightning Brothers are repeated at other sites in the region. The figures are usually standing beside each other with eyes blankly staring out at the viewer. Often they are adorned with rayed headdresses, and some have an engraved penis. Aspects of Dreaming mythology are symbolised in the colours and line work, in their head-dresses and the objects they hold in their hands. The Dreaming story of the two brothers has existed in the region long enough for a number of repaintings, which are an intrinsic part of rituals carried out at the art sites. These motifs, and associated ritual and mythol-ogy, are linked to the spirits of the Dreaming beings that give the land its identity. At Yirwarlarlay, the land of the Lightning Brothers, they are the actual brothers. At Garnawala they are Djangural, elder Dreaming beings who took over the young ones as the Rainbow Ser-pent; at Murning they are hawks, and so forth. In thus marking the local landscape, paintings of this type also express the events of the land—its seasons, plants and animals. Like the Wandjina rock paint-ings, which we describe below, their purpose relates to regulating the seasons and increasing important plant and animal resources. Anthropomorphs in contorted postures have been identified by Wardaman people as sorcery paintings.

Early paintings and engravings

In the west of the VRD region Darrell Lewis identified a probable earlier style of small red figures which are reminiscent of the Dynamic Figures in Kakadu art some 200 kilometres to the northeast. Evident parallels are painting techniques, compositions of human-like figures, the range and association of motifs (headdresses and boomerangs), the detailing of hair on animals, the association with hand and boomerang stencils and prints made by fibre drenched in red ochre paint. Lewis interprets some as so similar to Dynamic Figures that they would not be out of place if found in Kakadu. While their antiq-uity is unknown, they are all red and occur on the most durable sandstone surfaces, protected from exposure to the elements.

Rock engravings in the VRD were produced by a diverse range of techniques—abrading, pounding, pecking, and even scratching lines. Most are lines, grooves and pits; at one remote site there are hundreds of engraved designs on a sheer rock face. Abraded grooves are mostly short, straight lines, but sometimes they are arranged around concentric circles, or composed as stick figures or bird tracks. Ingaladdi rockshelter on Willeroo Station has a large number of these linear marks, and buried rock fragments fallen from the shelter wall have provided a minimum age of about 5000–7000 years, but they could be much older.

KIMBERLEY REGION

There are claims that rock engravings and cup-shaped depressions are the oldest rock markings in Australia, including the recent dramatic claim for 50,000-year-old cupules at the Jinmium site, but this dating is disputed. The earliest paintings in the region are called Bradshaw Figures. The most recent style, called Wandjina art, in which large figures of Dreaming beings are the central theme, continues to the modern era.

Bradshaw Figures

These engaging human figures were named after the pastoralist Joseph Bradshaw who first described them. In local Aboriginal belief, however, they are Jungardoo, invisible spirit people created during the Dreaming by a Wandjina. According to myth, these spirit people taught the people how to pressure-flake stone points. Interestingly, the Bradshaw Figures carry an entirely different spear type, and it is the absence of stone-pointed spears in the paintings that suggests their antiquity. Most of the figures are 10–80 centimetres high, and have been painted with a feather or hair brush in shades of red to purple. Given the inclusion of considerable adornment, it seems probable that the figures are engaged in ceremonies.

There is considerable disagreement over the classification of different types of Bradshaw Figures. We describe the three types proposed by David Welch, though more recently Grahame Walsh has published a more complex chronological scheme. The type Welsh regards as the oldest are in a single colour and more or less naturalistic in form. This type he divides into two varieties—'Tasselled

(a)

(b)

Bradshaw Figures: (a) Tasselled Figures with 'wands', skirts and bracelets; (b) Bent Knee Figures wearing sashes, holding boomerangs (580 x 290 millimetres); (c) Clothes Peg Figures, with multi-barbed spears; (left figure 450 x 160 millimetres). (G. L. Walsh)

(c)

Figures' and 'Bent Knee Figures'. Tasselled Figures are in various shades of red and naturalistic in form. Often they have an abdominal paunch (like a 'beer gut'), long delicate fingers, and arm and leg muscles indicated by fine line work, and adorned with long tapering headdresses, bracelets, waist belts and tassels. Occasionally Tasselled Figures carry boomerangs, but never spears, spearthrowers or fighting picks.

Bent Knee Figures are usually painted in black or mulberry red. Like Tasselled Figures, they have conical headdresses, the difference being the addition of a knob on its end. No figure has tassels hanging from a waist belt, and they wear a different kind of skirt. Their forearms are thick, possibly to indicate bands and bracelets, and commonly their legs are bent at the knee. Fingers are rarely indicated. Bent Knee Figures often hold boomerangs or an object that looks like a fly-whisk. Some also hold a curious triangular object that may represent a dillybag.

The latest style in the Welsh scheme is the Bichrome Style Figure. The bodies of these full-frontal figures are usually segmented, because the gaps between areas of ochre had originally been painted with another pigment, probably white huntite, which has perished. Some figures are naturalistic and animated, others are more schematic and rigid, somewhat like a clothes peg. Bichrome Style Figures are adorned with sashes and tassels, carrying a spearthrower which is occasionally fitted with a multi-barbed spear.

Bradshaw Figures have been linked to Kakadu's Dynamic Figures, and in particular the ones with similar multi-barbed spears. There are other common attributes already referred to in the context of the VRD art—in painting techniques, composition of human figures, range and association of motifs (headdresses and boomerangs), detailing of hair on animals, and association of the figures with hand and boomerang stencils or grass spray-prints. Some archaeologists speculate that the style evolved from a regional painting tradition that was inundated by the post-glacial rise in sea level. The figures have such charm that they have beguiled many commentators into speculation about a foreign origin or inspiration, much the same as for the Wandjina art described below. Welch has speculated about cultural links with New Guinea on the basis of imputed similarities in body ornaments. In 1997 the controversy over Bradshaw art made a considerable 'media splash' with the public debate over Grahame Walsh's conjecture that a 'mystery race' of small, slender people with a remarkably sophisticated culture had immigrated to northern Australia from the rainforests of Indonesia, leaving only the Bradshaw Figures as a testament to their existence. We see no merit in any of these speculations about foreign origins, and invoke parallels in painting style and subject matter, such as the ornaments and weapons, from within the continent, particularly Arnhem Land.

Until the 1990s the antiquity of the Bradshaw Figures was evident only from the depiction of multi-barbed spears, which had disappeared from the Kimberley region before early historic times. It was surmised that Bradshaw art had terminated before the changeover from multi-barbed spears to more complex ones comprising multiple shaft sections and a finely flaked stone point. The first archaeological appearance of these stone points in the region can be no earlier than about 3000 years BP and they may even be considerably younger in age.

Two different chronometric ages of Bradshaw Figures have now been reported. One is a luminescence determination of about 17,500 years from quartz grains in a mud-dauber wasp nest adhering to one of the paintings. If this date is correct, then the Bradshaws are among the oldest depictions of human figures in the world. However, this report coincided with an announcement of considerably younger AMS radiocarbon determinations of the art. Alan Watchman has dated fine organic materials embedded in the paper-thin laminations of paint and accreted minerals on two figures. One described as a 'cane Bradshaw' figure dates to about 3900 years BP, and a tasselled figure to about 1450 years BP. Tentatively, we prefer the radiocarbon over the luminescence dates because the samples relate more directly to the actual paintings, but these techniques applied to rock art are still in their experimental stages, so the dates remain provisional. Even, so we link this art to that of the Dynamic Figures in Kakadu.

Wandjina paintings

Some of the world's most spectacular rock paintings are the numerous painted galleries in central and western Kimberley, south to the Napier Range and east to the Forrest River. There are two dominant motifs at these sites: ancestral creation beings collectively named Wandjina, in the form of anthropomorphs; and themes of animals and plant food. The primary focus of a gallery may be a Wandjina, a crocodile, Rainbow Serpent, frilled-neck lizard, eagle, or dingo. Wandjina figures are usually surrounded by edible animal or vegetable items which relate to increase rituals performed at the galleries. The occurrence of dominant subjects at a site other than Wandjinas is frequent. It seems likely that Wandjina mythology is an addition to an earlier and more widespread mythology about animal creation beings. For example, each clan along the convoluted Rainbow Serpent Dreaming track through the Kimberley region has its own gallery of serpent paintings executed in exactly the same artistic style as Wandjina figures. Whatever the main subject may be, each painting site and each large figure has a name. Some painted figures are enormous. One snake-like anthropomorph belonging to the Early Wandjina phase is over 40 metres long—the longest known rock painting motif in the world.

The first task in painting an expanse of rock face as a backdrop for the Dreaming figures was to spray it with a white paint of powdered huntite. Wandjina figures may be up to five metres long, occurring as solitary figures or in groups. Full-length paintings have conventionally thin arms and legs; others depict only a head. Sometimes they are horizontally positioned to fit them into the limited space of a rock surface. The head is large with eyes and a nose detailed but no mouth on its mask-like face. Wandjina figures wear red headbands, hair belts and armbands. Red painted lines on the body signify the Wandjina's body paint and probably symbolise falling rain.

Wandjina ceremonies concern rain, fertility, and ensuring the abundance of plant and animal species. Yams are part of Wandjina mythology, and large paintings of yams may be placed around the central figures, together with other food items and hand stencils. Wandjina images were dangerous to touch because the spirit beings were capable of killing persons who showed even the slightest disrespect, intended or otherwise. They control the monsoon rains of the wet season, and when angered cause fierce thunderstorms and floods, or strike down with bolts of lightning anyone who displeases them. Wandjinas also have a more agreeable side, sending life spirits or baby spirits and amenable to requests for hunting and fishing success.

Ensuring future rainfall required renewing or touching up particular Wandjina 'self-portraits' or even a complete repaint of a gallery. Just before the monsoon season the repainting was undertaken, secretly and only by male elders who were chosen for their artistic abilities. After repainting, large numbers of men gathered at the site to carry out the necessary ceremonies.

Figures were painted in the western Kimberley in 1920s, but after this time the continuity of traditional practice and ceremonies was broken in most places. By the 1960s only a few aged people still repainted the Wandjinas, and it was declared by the men who went with Ian Crawford to visit the neglected and barely recognisable figures at one site that the Wandjinas 'have gone away'. Repainting or superimposition of one generation of motifs over older ones have accumulated as many as 40 layers at one recorded site, building up the paint to a surprising thickness. Wandjina mythology is still evolving, and along with it the painting style. Careful examination of superimpositions of Wandjina figures reveals that the earlier ones, perhaps of the last century, were elongated compared with the stocky figures of recent years. Eyelashes are a late embellishment.

ART IN PROSPECT

The corpus, variety and quality of much Australian rock art places it at the forefront of ancient art forms, along with that from Western Europe, Southern Africa and India. In numbers of images it is probably unsurpassed. Its importance in the future reconstruction of prehistoric environments, economies and technologies is assured, as researchers undertake detailed examination of sites for superimposition, stylistic change, images represented, statistical analyses, and evidence whereby to date the art. However, above all these factors is the reality that they were products of human intellect and artistry extending back into the Pleistocene. At the other end of the time scale, the images were being painted or engraved into this century. Art galleries of immense longevity, they offer priceless testimony to an Aboriginal intellectual and aesthetic heritage extending back into deep time.

Asian and European newcomers

23

While it is convenient to commence the European history of Australia in 1788, with the permanent British settlement at Sydney, it is a misleading rule-of-thumb to apply to the whole continent, which was progressively colonised by European settlers up to the present century. Settlement in nearby Victoria was delayed until 1834, while in the Northern Territory, after half a century of false starts, European permanency was achieved only in 1869, with the settlement at Darwin, and even then most of the territory was still beyond the reach of colonial administration. Earlier colonies in tropical Australia, and many accounts of early sea contacts or land explorations, stand in the same relation to Australian prehistory as Caesar's *Commentaries* to prehistoric Iron Age Britain. The fitful insights into indigenous societies and personalities which such sources provide are termed protohistory by some European scholars. It may prove less confusing to name this phase in Australia as the early colonial period.

As the British vessel *Investigator* worked to the southwest around Cape Wilberforce in squally, monsoon conditions, frequent tacking was necessary. After 105 days of coasting the Gulf of Carpentaria, Matthew Flinders had concluded his meticulous charting of its waters, on 17 February 1803. A few hours later, six ungainly vessels hove in sight, sheltered within a strait between islands off the Arnhem

Macassan praus off Port Essington, sketched in 1840 by Lieutenant Owen Stanley of HMS Britomart; *note the tripod mast. (Mitchell Library)*

Land coast. Flinders summoned all hands to action stations, to display their puny armament.

Flinders anticipated piracy, but the result was more mundane; the only exchanges were pleasantries and the British flag. These wooden praus, weighing from ten to 25 tonnes, were equipped with bamboo-slatted superstructures, oblong sails of matted palm-leaf and two steering oars. They had sailed out of the southern Sulawesi harbour of Macassar (now Ujung Pandang), two months previously to collect and process trepang. Flinders learned from Pobassoo, the friendly Bugis squadron commander, that 60 praus and over 1000 men were working on the Arnhem Land coast that season. Flinders named an island in Pobassoo's honour, and the place of their meeting, Malay Road.

This was a symbolic moment in Australian history, when Asian and European first met in territorial waters. Although for centuries European and Asian nations had been potential arbiters of the fate of Australia's indigenous population, colonial possession of the continent was deferred until the age of the Industrial Revolution. Seafarers, both accidental and intentional, had skirted the northern and western shores and many had stepped ashore; but Australia presented an uninviting vista to these visitors whatever their race or class. Even the Indonesian trepangers hastened home annually; they left behind them no permanent colony, forts or factories in this alien land they knew as 'Marege'.

In the chronicle of early contacts with the Aborigines, it is interesting to reflect that Flinders represented a new phenomenon in northern waters. Unlike earlier voyagers driven on by the westerly gales in the roaring forties, or sailing out of Asia, he embarked from an Australian base and bore the British flag north and west from Sydney. Neither was he repelled by what he observed of people and nature in tropical Australia, as were so many sailors before him. Perhaps his attitude is to be explained by his acclimatisation on the more inviting eastern seaboard and by the fact that he was not a merchant venturer seeking profitable returns. But Flinders was also a product of that intellectual climate of opinion in the West, the Age of Reason, when the educated elite described and evaluated the natural world in more objective terms. Unlike many of their predecessors, they were concerned to provide factual accounts of peoples and places. Often a tinge of uncritical romanticism led them (but not Flinders) to populate the new lands with improbable 'noble savages', while experience usually taught them that all people were less than perfectly happy and some less noble than others, they *were* people.

Flinders' landscape artist, the talented William Westall, is an interesting example of these intellectual influences. His delineation of the Macassan praus in Malay Road was accurate, while his economical portrait of Pobassoo endowed the man with personality. Indeed, through Westall's eyes and Flinders' pen, Pobassoo emerges as the first individual Asian in Australian history.

This encounter between Europe and Asia in 1803 heralded the imminent reversal of the tide of any cultural diffusion, which throughout Australian prehistory had run from Southeast Asia and, for several millennia, New Guinea. During historic times the impetus for colonising northern Australia came from southern cities.

EUROPEAN 'DISCOVERY'

Schoolchildren are taught that the first discoverers of Australia and its indigenous population were Europeans. They know that the

Spaniard Luis Vaez de Torres almost won this honour in 1606, by sailing through the strait which bears his name; but he hugged the New Guinea coast. By a coincidence Australian shores were charted earlier in the same year, by a Hollander, Willem Jansz, who reached western Cape York Peninsula. However, it is probable that the children are misinformed concerning these priorities, although it is impossible to clinch the argument by citing earlier navigators whose records are of comparable quality to those testifying to the fleeting Jansz episode.

Eurocentric historians of exploration have been inclined to assume that those lands unknown to Europeans existed in some limbo of uncharted and static seas, awaiting redemption by some imaginative navigator. As a corollary and by definition, any island was remote and isolated. Some historians dismiss this matter of priorities as idle speculation; the shape of the first sandal- or boot-print on Australian shores is not their concern. To Andrew Sharp, writing a book *The Discovery of Australia*, Asian evidence for contact was irrelevant to his theme: 'their knowledge made no impact on the world at large or on the history of Australia.' The truth is, however, that visits to prehistoric Australia did have repercussions for the Aborigines living there, and sometimes this alien influence was profound.

TRADE-WIND NAVIGATION

Northern Australia straddles the monsoonal belt, which for several months brings moisture-laden winds of the northwest monsoon from island Southeast Asia. Even today, lost or disabled Indonesian fishing craft are blown ashore in Arnhem Land, while remote beaches are strewn with coconut husks, lengths of bamboo and other intrusive flotsam. George Windsor Earl, a visitor to the islands east of Timor and only 580 kilometres from Australia, observed of their seafaring inhabitants around 1840, that nearly every village mourned the loss of praus blown to the southeast. Writing around 1600, Manuel Godinho De Eredia recorded several examples of Portuguese and native craft and one Chinese junk being blown to the south of various Indonesian islands by the monsoonal winds.

Because of the constancy of these winds, the trepang fleet out of Macassar made its journey of some 2000 kilometres to an Arnhem Land landfall within ten to fifteen days, including a final stretch of about four days without sight of land. Indeed, the problem was to control craft travelling at perhaps five knots at the end of its voyage, so that the prevailing wind did not blow it aground. It is recorded that four praus were wrecked on Melville Island in this fashion during 1847, while in 1890, three of the fleet of thirteen praus were lost. Before the monsoonal season ended, the surviving craft spread out in squadrons and combed the shallow harbours of Arnhem Land and the Gulf of Carpentaria, often reaching the Sir Edward Pellew Group, over 1100 kilometres distant to the southeast.

The Kimberley coast of northwestern Australia and Cape York Peninsula were the other potential areas where culture contact was facilitated by the monsoons. Large fleets of trepanging praus were observed off the Kimberley coast during the nineteenth century. At that time, a large Bugis ('Macassan') population lived on Sumbawa Island, and they were associated with the Australian trepang industry. It is probable, but unproved, that they sailed with the monsoon direct from the Sumba region, an ocean crossing of perhaps 800 kilometres. It is not surprising that the west-coast industry was considered to be more hazardous than work in the northern coastal waters, but the superior quality of the catch provided an incentive for the journey. It is possible that archaeological fieldwork may reveal the contrasting material relics on Kimberley and Arnhem Land trepanging sites, reflecting such different points of departure for the praus. However, archaeological survey indicates that the Kimberley sites are comparable with the more extensive ones in Arnhem Land, as fieldwork by Michael Morwood has established.

It follows that, if the monsoon facilitated the outward journey, the return to island Southeast Asia was equally feasible when the southeast trade winds blew after late May. The knowledge of this fact is one of the tantalising elements of Eredia's tale of Chiaymasiouro, a ruler of southeastern Java in 1600, who voyaged 800 kilometres south (and east?) of Java for twelve days. The fact that he visited a fabulous land is irrelevant here. What is significant is that 'when the southerly monsoon wind sets in, he started back for his own country', and arrived safely there in 1601.

Whether the Australian route was accidentally discovered (as Pobassoo informed Flinders), or whether it happened on many occasions from various islands (as seems probable), the circumstances necessitate that the coast was frequented by many alien visitors. These intriguing archaeological prospects in tropical Australia offer an interesting parallel with Roman imperial history: Roman captains trusted the monsoons to speed them direct across the Indian Ocean to India and back to Egypt. It also raises a new perspective for early Australian history, by changing the emphasis from the conventional problem pondered by earlier historians, who asked how and why Australia was 'discovered' in the seventeenth century, to an assumption that evidence of earlier alien discoveries will be forthcoming. The true discoverers, explorers and colonists of the entire continent were the ancestors of the Aborigines.

THE TREPANG INDUSTRY

Australia's first export industry was based upon the knowledge of the monsoons; the commodity was trepang (the sea-slug, or *bêche-de-mer*), a member of the Class *Holothuroidea* and the animal phylum *Echinodermata*. Soup made from the dried body-wall of certain species was in demand in China both for its culinary and its alleged aphrodisiac properties. At Canton a century ago, 30 varieties were traded and the Australian product was sold as average quality. Controlled by Chinese merchants chiefly resident in Macassar, it was a major industry from Borneo to the Aru Islands and Australia. Around 1820 trepang was said to be the largest Indonesian export to China.

Explorers Flinders and P. P. King investigated the Australian industry in territorial waters and in Timor, and concluded that a single prau might contain 100,000 dried trepang, weighing about five tonnes. On this estimate, therefore, the 60 praus constituting the 1803 fleet caught and processed six million animals. A modern estimate is for a harvest of 300 tonnes of dried flesh. J. Crawfurd, who was Sir Stamford Raffles' assistant in Java between 1808 and 1817, estimated a prau's cargo at only three tonnes, but observed that 'the fishery of the trepang is to China what that of the sardine, tunny, and anchovy is to Europe'.

Captain Collet Barker was commandant of the British outpost at Raffles Bay in 1829. His journal recorded the arrival of 34 praus, but as some sailed past the bay, he was told by prau commanders that the total number was 60 or 70. His head count of the crews totalled 1053, so the total on the coast that year cannot have been fewer than 1500 men.

The industrial process within a shallow bay might occupy from a few days to three weeks. The trepang was either collected by hand, speared or trawled. Small dugout canoes, termed 'lepa-lepa', were carried on the praus for this purpose. (King observed nineteen canoes supplying four praus.) The Aboriginal 'lippa-lippa' canoe is a direct borrowing. Praus were grounded on sandy beaches, an encampment was made ashore, and stone fireplaces were constructed adjacent to mangroves, whose wood was used for boiling the animals; large iron cauldrons were carried for the boiling process. After a preliminary boil, the trepang was gutted and recooked in a tan of mangrove bark which coloured and flavoured the flesh. Subsequently it was dried and decalcified by burial in sand, then smoked in prefabricated bamboo and rattan sheds transported for the purpose. Small wonder that Alfred Russel Wallace described the trepang he saw processed in Aru as 'looking like sausages which have been rolled in mud then thrown up a chimney'.

A Macassan base camp, probably at Port Essington in 1843, sketched by Harden S. Melville; the mountain backdrop was an artistic embellishment. Trepang are boiling in cauldrons; beached praus and demountable smoke-houses for curing trepang are in the background. Note the Aborigines in friendly conversation at the left-hand side of the picture. (The Queen, 8 February 1862)

Macassan sites

The field archaeologist has a relatively simple task to locate Macassan trepanging camps. The requirements are deep water and sandy beaches in situations affording protection from the winds and easy access to supplies of mangrove wood. Defence was a further requirement: these sites are on small islands or promontories, because relations with the Aborigines were often poor. European sources contain numerous references to massacres of prau crews and retaliatory measures by Macassans. The situation must have fluctuated regionally and with time, because these same sources contain evidence for amicable, mutually profitable economic relationships. There are also references to Aborigines travelling as crew on the praus and in the 1860s there was an Aboriginal community marooned in Macassar. This movement of Australian Aborigines to Sulawesi and their subsequent return must have proved a dramatic factor in traditional life and a ready source of stories and new ideas.

Fortunately for archaeologists, the trepangers brought with them the astringent fruit of *Tamarindus indicus* which seeded prolifically in places. Tamarind trees serve as botanical markers for their camps, because their height and rich green foliage contrast with the flat seascape. Upon inspection, the area around tamarind trees is sometimes covered with a scatter of potsherds, bottle glass and stone hearths.

The archaeology of 'Macassan' contact with Arnhem Land was first investigated by Campbell Macknight. His most extensive excavation was on a small promontory in Anuru Bay where the trepang occupation covered several hundred square metres, and the surface produced hundreds of potsherds. There were fourteen embayed stone structures, each one apparently intended to hold about five vats, but it is unlikely that they were all in use simultaneously. Ashy depressions mark the sites of former smoke-houses, because their floors were hollowed out in order to protect the inflammable walls from the smoke fire, while hollows dug behind the stone lines indicate where the cooked trepang was buried to remove concretions, preparatory to smoking. Many explorers describe the restless activity within the encampment. Fortunately, a French artist depicted the scene in Raffles Bay in 1839, during the visit of Dumont d'Urville, while a few years later an artist on HMS *Fly* sketched his impressions. Two Macassan burials excavated at Anuru Bay are material substantiation of the industry's high mortality rate referred to in many sources.

Quantities of imported ceramics are found on trepanging sites. Decorated sherds are uncommon, but plain red ware is ubiquitous. So also is glass from square-faced bottles, including some prunts (the trade mark) with Dutch distillery names. There is no evidence to support an Aboriginal tradition that pottery was manufactured in Australia by trepangers. During the nineteenth century, the praus apparently used some pottery manufactured in the Kai Islands, west of Aru, but the bulk of it probably came from Sulawesi. Unfortunately, there is little to differentiate the undecorated ceramics, and much modern pottery throughout Southeast Asia is comparable in form and size. Most pots were globular; although the size varied, rim form was similar, and generally, the fabric was thin and fragile. Thin sections of several sherds showed that they contain volcanic particles not available in Arnhem Land, but which occur in quantity southeast of Macassar. There is remarkable homogeneity in the ceramic evidence around hundreds of kilometres of coastline, on some 250 sites now recorded. East Asian porcelain fragments, many of them attractive pieces, occur commonly on these sites.

Flinders was informed that Macassans first arrived in Australia around 1780, while other early investigators also adduced relatively recent origins. The first positive written reference dates from 1754. Absolute chronology resulting from archaeological activity may alter the perspective, although present evidence confirms it. The Dutch bottles identified so far are nineteenth-century. Three bronze coins of the Dutch East India Company were found by mission authorities at Elcho Island, on a trepanging site described in use during 1882. Two coins are dated 1790 and the third is 1838. In his excavations on sites on islets adjacent to Groote Eylandt, Macknight recovered a coin similar to the Elcho specimens dated 1780, and a corroded specimen probably dated 1746. Macknight obtained some radiocarbon determinations for three sites, ranging from modern to some 800 years ago. There is some evidence that mangrove wood becomes contaminated and provides erroneous carbon dates. Macknight argued cogently that such an antiquity is at variance with the wide range of historical evidence concerning exploitation of trepang in East Asia. He places the beginning of the traffic around AD 1700, after the Dutch captured Macassar in 1667 and possibly restricted piracy.

cms

(a)

(b)

(c)

Macassan artefacts: (a) a Macassan potsherd; (b) Dutch East India Company (VOC) coin, two centimetres in diameter; (c) a prunt (trademark) from Henkes distillery at Rotterdam. (Campbell Macknight)

Fragment of a Chinese porcelain bowl. (Campbell Macknight)

Macassans and Aborigines

Social anthropologists anticipated greater antiquity than this, however, for racial contact between Macassans and Aborigines. It is now realised that its impact upon coastal Arnhem Land society was profound. In addition to such material contributions as the dugout canoe and sail and metal implements, which probably enabled a more successful exploitation of the environment, the influence was more pervading. Macassarese words were adopted into coastal Aboriginal vocabularies. Local place-names still bear witness to this linguistic borrowing, and in the nineteenth century it resulted in a *lingua franca* around the coast. Socially, the repercussions varied from the wearing of the now-characteristic Arnhem Land Van Dyke beard to the adoption of the Malayan smoking pipe. Artistically, the influence on eastern Arnhem Land bark painting motifs was profound.

Schrire has described briefly an Aboriginal site in Port Bradshaw where archaeological manifestations of culture contact occur in the shape of pearl-shell fish-hooks of a J-shape, similar to Macassan metal

417

hooks. Their impact on the Aboriginal inhabitants was considerable, and not only for the exchange of goods. Macknight examined the introduction of smallpox to the population, which may have proved a serious disease and possibly spread to southern tribes during historic times. As Macassan crewmen cohabited with Aboriginal women, there was considerable genetic transfer. Yolngu people still recognise Indonesian kin. During their stay of about twenty weeks, each prau would have fished and processed at six or eight locations, so the opportunities for cultural interaction were many.

More complex than these factors were the ceremonial and mythological repercussions of Macassan contact, which anthropologists have discerned as vital to Arnhem Land Aboriginal ritual and belief. There is an intriguing episode related by Donald Thomson. During the 1930s he found that a clan on the Glyde River had adopted as its totemic symbol a square-faced bottle: those green liquor bottles so ubiquitous on Macassan sites. Thomson found that a copy of such a bottle had been carved from wood, and that the painted design which covered it represented a complex ritual account, linked directly with trepanging. This, he inferred, was a recognition of the economic and social value of glass (and no doubt its contents). Its relevance here is that a foreign object had been incorporated into Aboriginal mythology and social organisation. But there are many further examples drawn from ceremonial song cycles and rituals which prove the integration of the two cultures, despite their evident antagonism during everyday transactions. It is therefore a matter of considerable theoretical interest to ascertain the duration of this trepanging contact period, in order to evaluate the rate at which non-material traits were assimilated into a culture traditionally termed 'conservative'.

Howard Morphy's insightful book, *Ancestral connections*, demonstrates the rapidity of cultural change. Macassan interaction with the Yolngu people was dynamic and deeply influenced art, ceremonial ritual and song cycles. Anthropologists Thomson and Berndt captured much of the sense of nostalgia for times past and the benefits of the interchange in their record of Aboriginal memories of Macassan contact. Yet by the late 1970s explanations and attributed meanings were transformed and new folk heroes had emerged. In his extensive fieldwork Morphy found that 'song cycles that referred once to Macassan trepangers are now associated with the activities of mythological Europeans, referring, for example, to bulldozers being started rather than to iron being forged'.

These transformations give archaeologists cause to ponder on the chronology of fixing events in prehistory. The first bulldozers in the region probably date from around 1942, when wartime airstrips were constructed around the coast. Less than 40 years sufficed to convert otherwise intrusive Europeans into a positive force, supplanting the Macassan innovators. Those who argue for a long chronology in Macassan trepanging contact because of its influence on indigenous art, myth and ceremonial should recall that a date of even 1740 for the first contact is five times longer than that required for the above transformation, which made an icon of bulldozers rather than praus.

It must be concluded that contact was relatively recent and that the ahistorical world view of the Aborigines rapidly assimilated, elaborated and mythologised the Macassan episode until it was represented by modern Aborigines as a golden age. It was more mundane at the time. The Indonesian trepangers neither penetrated the mangrove fringe nor attempted permanent settlement in Australia before the European occupation.

Memories of the Macassan era witnessed a resurgence in 1988. The Indonesian contribution to the bicentennial of white Australian settlement was the gift of a fully rigged and equipped replica of a 'paduwakang' (prau). The arrival of the *Hati Marege* and its crew from Macassar inspired Aboriginal ceremonial activities in northeastern Arnhem Land in 1988. Some 30 Aboriginal families claimed kinship with people in Sulawesi, and the event has strengthened old ties with the Macassans. The vessel is now exhibited in Darwin's Northern Territory Museum, a reminder that Macassans and Aborigines are related in what to them is a timeless Dreaming.

FABLED VISITORS

We see no persuasive evidence for very early Asian or European voyages to Australia, and discourage readers from seriously considering any claims about the wanderings of Israel's lost tribes, the Phoenicians, or extra-terrestrials. The occasional finds of Roman coins, Polynesian stone adzes and other exotica are certainly items brought back by Australian soldiers and Pacific traders returning from overseas, and by others, if they are not outright hoaxes.

The fleets of Chinese junks commanded by the eunuch Ch'eng Ho between 1405 and 1433 made seven famous voyages, and made the Ming emperors known as far as East Africa and western Indonesia. Some of these vessels explored as far south as Timor; and some may have gone beyond, in whatever circumstance, to north Australian waters, but there is no tangible proof of this. The forest products of Timor were known to Chinese merchants resident in Java at least 100 years before Ch'eng Ho sent his junks there. Writing in 1613 of an earlier episode, Manuel Godinho De Eredia reported that a Chinese junk from Macau, laden with Timorese sandalwood, was blown south of Timor. It reached safe haven on an unknown island, which Eredia believed resembled Timor. It was not Australia, but there may have been other incidents when junks were buffeted by the monsoonal winds to these shores.

After this brief Chinese maritime florescence during the Ming Dynasty, it was Arab traders who, in the fourteenth century, extended their influence into Indonesian islands, as far as the spice islands of the Moluccas, and Aru Island on the Sahul continental shelf. The Arabs were interested in trade, as were the Chinese before them and the Dutch after. Even knowledge of a southern landmass may not have induced them to risk exploration—there was no apparent lucrative trade, neither settlements, nor gold, spices, nor saleable bird plumage.

Manuel Godinho De Eredia's account of early Indonesian voyaging

Before contacts across Torres Strait or the annual voyages of Macassans, the most frequent visitors to Australia may have been islanders from the arc of the Lesser Sundas—the trade winds and misadventure still bring fishermen to Australian shores, and such events are hinted at in colonial records.

The tales of fabulous wealth were tangible enough for Eredia, who was officially sanctioned to explore south of Flores and Timor around 1600, in order to visit the reputed Luca Antara. Forlorn Eredia apparently realised that the outbreak of a local war, which prevented him from sailing, cheated him of fame. Critics might dismiss the case, by treating it as dockside gossip, but Eredia is a persuasive writer. He was part-Macassan, and his examples of wayward voyages are Asian and not European. Likewise his written records are of Asian origin. He referred obliquely to Javanese chronicles and to 'Lontares', perhaps a reference to palm-leaf manuscripts normally associated with Macassar. Such sources he claimed, testified to the extent of ancient commerce between the Indies and the rich southern land. Indeed, he was surprisingly precise with his chronology, if sparing with his documentation. According to 'poems, vulgar songs and histories', contact had been close until 1169, but wars had terminated trade and it was only renewed through an accidental voyage from Luca Antara to Java in 1600. Whether Eredia had access to actual records or to fables is conjectural.

Thousands of years previously ancestral dingoes were carried to Australia, possibly from the nearer Indonesian islands. Should we expect to find, eventually, some archaeological traces of such earlier arrivals? The anthropologists Ronald and Catherine Berndt believed that their interpretation of Aboriginal mythology in Arnhem Land requires a pre-Macassan alien contact phase, which they term Baijini. On the other hand, Macknight believes that these myths largely owe their origin to historic Aboriginal experiences in Macassar, where they went on returning praus, and we agree. Tangible evidence of their memories are the stone arranged 'pictures' near Gove of Indonesian houses and other objects.

THE SECRETIVE PORTUGUESE

The case for Portuguese contact has been argued forcefully in recent years. During the sixteenth century, Portuguese merchant vessels navigated the spice sea-lanes, and as early as 1511 Portugal annexed Timor and the Aru Islands off West Irian; this is very close to Australia. The chronicler Pires in 1515, writing when the riches of the Inca and Aztec Americans became known, and Eredia a century later, testify to an enthusiasm for prospective new commercial worlds and optimism for the prospects over the horizon. To Eredia and his contemporaries the lure was gold, and surely such elaborate misinformation was incentive enough for Europeans who were plundering the wealth of the New World. Eredia in his geographical treatise of 1613 mentions various incidents when vessels had sailed out to sea, southwards from Flores, Timor, Solor, Roti and other islands. Many of them reached fabulous lands abounding with gold which would do credit to Sinbad. But commentators have observed that time, distance and direction sailed could otherwise accord with a northwest Australian location for the land of Luca Antara; and believers have discerned the Kimberley coast labelled as 'Java le Grande' on the sixteenth-century Dieppe maps, but we are not among them.

Perhaps the Aborigines themselves were a further inducement for Portuguese interest in Australia, at least in later times. George Windsor Earl, one of tropical Australia's most inquisitive British colonists, visited Timor around 1840. Elderly Timorese recounted to him that

Melville Island had been a major source of slaves for Portuguese slave-traders (which appears to us at least an exaggeration). P. P. King recounted that in 1818 a Melville Islander spoke two Portuguese words, or so he interprets what the man was saying. Here, possibly, was culture contact of a fundamental kind, which may explain the savage treatment meted out by Melville Islanders to shipwrecked Macassans during historic times.

There is a material footnote to hypotheses about Portuguese voyaging south of Timor. Two brass cannons, one of them stamped with what has been claimed as a Portuguese rose, gun mark and crown, were discovered on Carronade Island in Napier Broome Bay, in 1917, on Australia's Kimberley coast; another was found on a nearby reef two years later. The second one was unfortunately melted down for its brass, but the others are preserved at the Australian Naval Establishment at Garden Island, Sydney. They have been also claimed as possibly early-sixteenth-century pieces, made at Seville, Spain. It is worth noting, however, that Macassan praus sometimes carried arms, acquired from diverse sources and probably with a tendency for the antique. We prefer this as the most probable explanation for these armaments.

There also are highly speculative claims for Portuguese voyaging in Bass Strait which depend upon a reconstruction of maps of Java le Grande dating from around 1540, in which it is claimed the coastline of southeastern Australia is illustrated. Linked to this hypothesis are stone ruins on the southern New South Wales coast, actually dating from the whaling era of the 1840s, interpreted as a fort built by the crew of Cristovao de Mendonca; and the famous 'mahogany' caravel, long lost in the sand dunes west of Warrnambool, which more than likely is the skeletal hulk of an early colonial wreck. Those who doubt our claim should remember that American whalers and sealers skirted the southern coastline from the 1790s, ample time for a wreck to weather and its timbers darken.

DUTCH NAVIGATORS

Unequivocal historical evidence establishes that Europeans first met Indigenous Australians in Torres Strait, encounters that foreshadowed the fatal course of racial contact. By a remarkable coincidence, explorers from Holland and Spain both sailed these waters during 1606. They voyaged in opposite directions, completely unaware of each other.

Whether or not Portuguese speculation concerning golden lands in Australian latitudes attracted their vessels south, the Dutch seafarers who touched there were more pragmatic. Around March 1606, William Jansz navigated his Dutch East India Company yacht along the southern coast of New Guinea. Unfortunately his journal is lost, but surviving fragmentary reports reveal that he stepped ashore on western Cape York Peninsula, probably at the mouth of the Pennefather River. Jansz named this landfall, near modern Weipa, Cape Keerweer (or 'turn-again'), and recorded a skirmish with 'wild, cruel dark barbarians'. During the next half-century Dutch vessels navigated every coastline except the eastern seaboard, which awaited Captain Cook. As Dutch vessels bound for Java sailed a course between 35° and 40° south from the Cape of Good Hope, to maximise the winds, seventeenth-century shipwrecks on Australia's west coast have presented archaeologists with an attractive challenge in underwater archaeology. Vandals ruined the rich prize of the *Tryal* (1622), wrecked off the northwest coast. The *Batavia* (1629), the *Vergulde Draek* (1656), the *Zuytdorp* (1712) and the *Zeewijk* (1726) in Houtmans Abrolhos or on the mainland are known wrecks. The Western Australian Museum has been at the forefront in locating and investigating these relics and the Fremantle Maritime Museum exhibits a world-class range of excavated material.

As ethnologists the Dutch were undistinguished, although Jan Carstenz, the captain of the yacht *Pera*, in 1623, and J. P. Peereboom in 1658, collected and described a number of Aboriginal artefacts. Carstenz sought spices and precious metals and found neither; on his landing he killed three Aborigines and kidnapped two others. In the far south Abel Tasman failed to find more than the smoke of Aboriginal fires in Tasmania, while W. De Vlamingh, who spent six weeks in southwestern Australian waters in 1696–97, only succeeded in sighting Aborigines on two occasions during sixteen exploratory sorties into the hinterland. Lieutenant J. Gonzal was more successful in meeting Aborigines in the Gulf of Carpentaria during 1756, when he slyly plied them with arrack and sugar in order to kidnap two of them.

William Dampier was the first Englishman to arrive on Australia's shore, in the vicinity of Karrakatta Bay on the Kimberley coast in 1688. His landfall was a mangrove-fringed beach and sand dunes bordering paperbark swamps. When this literate buccaneer published his *New voyage round the world*, it became a best-seller of 1697. His negative account of New Holland amounted to fewer than 2500 words, but it was more perceptive and accurate than generally has been allowed. His second voyage along the seemingly waterless Dampierland coast, this time as captain of his own vessel, did nothing to alter his unfavourable first impression.

From the earliest human settlers to the last Indonesian trepanger who visited Australia in 1907, Australian prehistory remained oriented towards island Southeast Asia. Captain Cook and Joseph Banks inadvertently shifted the historic balance, which abortive colonial settlements on the north coast failed to redress. Yet historic Australia's recurrent involvement in the same region from 1824 to the present confirms that history, like prehistory, repeats itself.

Glossary

Aborigines With a capital letter, the term applies to Indigenous Australians throughout time.

AMS Accelerator mass spectrometry, a method of dating by which carbon atoms are ionised and accelerated by a charge of at least two million volts.

archaeological visibility Degree to which past human presence or activity is evident from observable archaeological remains.

archaeology Techniques used to study the human past primarily through its material remains.

artefact An object, usually portable, made or shaped by human hand.

bioturbation Reworking of sediments through the action of ground-dwelling life forms such as ants, termites and earthworms.

bipolar A term used in stone technology that refers to the production of flakes by placing the core on an anvil and striking it with a hammerstone.

Blitzkrieg hypothesis Extinction of giant marsupials by rapid overkill after the arrival of humans.

bondi point A small, delicately fashioned type of stone implement, similar in shape to a pen-knife blade, but with a thick margin opposite the cutting edge. Bondi points are commonly found east of the Great Dividing Range and as far north as Great Keppel Island.

BP Before the present (AD 1950); used in presenting radiocarbon dates.

chert A hard siliceous rock suitable for flaking into tools. Flint is a variety of chert.

conchoidal flake The most common type of flake produced by toolmaking. The fracture surface of a well-formed conchoidal flake has a swelling (called 'bulb of force') similar in shape to the surface of a bivalve shell.

core (or nucleus) A piece of stone, often a cobble or pebble but also quarried stone, from which flakes have been struck for toolmaking.

cranium The skull minus the lower jaw (mandible).

denticulated Serrated or saw-like cutting edge on a stone tool.

Dreaming Aboriginal concept of an era in the past, normally remote, when creation activities took place.

ecology The study of interactions between organisms and their environments.

ethnoarchaeology Study of behaviour in contemporary traditional societies—such as stone toolmaking, animal butchering and disposal of refuse—to resolve archaeological problems.

ethnography Anthropological description of 'traditional' or non-industrial culture and society.

flaking Also termed 'Knapping', the process of making stone tools by detaching flakes from a piece of stone, such as from a core (primary flaking) or from a flake detached from a core (retouching).

geomorphology The description and interpretation of landforms.

glaciation A cold period marked by an increase in polar icecaps and glaciers.

gracile As applied to human bones, meaning slender, slightly built, thin boned; sometimes identified as representing an ethnic type.

Holocene The period since the last retreat of the icecaps at the end of the Pleistocene epoch commencing about 10,400 years BP (equivalent to about 11,000–11,500 calendar years).

human ecology The study of human interactions between each other and the environment.

hunter-gatherer A mode of subsistence entirely dependent on hunting, fishing and gathering.

intensification Increased social and economic complexity.

interglacial A warmer period between glacial periods.

intervisible Able to be seen in both ways, as between two islands.

isobath A line on a map joining places on a seabed of equal depth.

keeping-place A structure where sacred objects or human remains are stored by an Aboriginal community.

knapping Flaking stone tools.

Last Glacial Maximum (LGM) The most intense period of cold during the last glaciation, around 20,000 years BP.

lithics A contemporary term to describe stone artefacts.

lunette A crescent-shaped sand dune, often with clay layers, on the windward side of a lake bed.

macroblade A large, prismatic-shaped pointed stone flake.

mandible Lower jaw.

manuport An object carried to a place by humans, (usually stones with no evidence of artificial shaping).

megafauna In Australia refers to extinct species of large marsupials.

microlith A variety of small, delicately retouched implements of various shapes, such as bondi point, segment, crescent, triangle, trapeze, rectangle and obliquely retouched points. These implements are believed to have served as spear barbs.

midden Aboriginal occupation site consisting chiefly of shells with minor components of other refuse such as ash, stone artefacts and animal bones.

montane forest The lower-altitude forest vegetation on mountains.

optically stimulated luminescence (OSL) dating A method of dating which uses green laser light to empty traps in the crystal lattice of mineral grains such as quartz. The method provides dates of up to a few hundred thousand years in age.

palaeomagnetism Changes in the Earth's magnetic field over time recorded as remnant magnetism in materials such as baked clay from hearths.

palynology The analysis of fossil pollen to assist the reconstruction of past vegetation and climates.

phytolith analysis The microscopic study of plant silica to identify species.

Pleistocene The global Glacial epoch or Ice Age, lasting from about two million to 10,000 years ago (Holocene period) when the Earth's climate entered its present warm phase.

prehistory The period from the first emergence of humans to the time of written records (the historic period), therefore varying around the globe.

pressure-flaking Shaping a stone tool by applying pressure to the edge being flaked.

radiocarbon dating A dating method that measures the decay of the radioactive isotope of carbon-14(^{14}C).

radiometric dating A dating method based on the rate of decay of radioactive isotopes in organic materials.

relative dating A dating method that infers a chronological sequence of artefacts where the actual dates are unknown, as in stratified deposits of cultural sediments.

retouch To shape, sharpen or blunt a stone tool by flaking.

robust As applied to human bones, meaning heavy-boned, with a skull of rugged appearance. Sometimes identified as a representing an ethnic type.

Sahul (also Greater Australia) The former continental landmass formed at low sea levels during the Pleistocene, when present day Australia, New Guinea, the Aru Islands, Tasmania and Australia's other continental islands were joined by land. The name derived from Sahul bank, which is an area of shallows off the northwest coast of Australia, and is probably of Macassan origin.

scarification Scars on the body made during rituals by incisions to indicate clan identity.

scraper A flaked stone tool with a straight, concave or convex working edge shaped or resharpened by retouch.

strandloopers People who subsist on the resources of the coastal zone, in particular the littoral zone.

stratigraphy In geology and archaeology, the record and correlation of natural and cultural sedimentary strata.

Sundaland The landmass at low sea levels comprising mainland Southeast Asia, Palawan Island in the Philippines and the Indonesian islands as far east as Bali and Kalimantan (Borneo). The name derives originally from the Sunda people of west Java.

taphonomy The study of processes in which relics accumulate and preserve after deposition.

tectonic plates Major structural features of the earth's crust (drifting continents).

thermoluminescence (TL) A dating technique in which heat is used to release trapped electrons from certain mineral grains. The electron emission is measured to estimate the time elapsed since the material was last heated.

thin-section analysis A technique of cutting thin sections from a piece of stone or potsherd for microscopic examination of its structure and components.

typology The systematic organisation of artefacts into distinctive types or categories on the basis of shared attributes.

tooth avulsion Ritual removal of front teeth.

Wallacea The geologically unstable zone of Indonesian islands lying between the Sunda and Sahul shelves, which includes some fauna from both the Asian and Australian regions.

Endnotes

1 The past uncovered and its ownership

Profession of archaeology in Australia Frankel and Kamminga 1995.

Field archaeology methods Connah 1983.

Uses and limitations of historical records and ethnographic analogy Frankel 1991: 10; Hayden 1992: 127–29; Murray 1992: 8–12; White and O'Connell 1982: 17–22; *Western Desert people* Brady 1987.

History of archaeology in Australia Bowdler 1993; Davidson 1983; Golson 1993; Griffiths 1996; Horton 1991; Huchet 1991; Jones 1979, 1993; Mulvaney 1981a, 1987, 1989b, 1990, 1993; Mulvaney and Golson 1971; Murray and White 1981; White and O'Connell 1982.

Archaeology, heritage and Aboriginal people Burke *et al.* 1994; Davidson *et al.* 1995; Langford 1983; Lewis and Rose 1985; Moser 1995; K. Mulvaney 1993b; Sullivan 1985; Tasmanian Aboriginal Land Council 1996.

Reburial of human remains Bowdler 1992b; Griffiths 1996; Moser 1995; Mulvaney 1989a, 1991; Pardoe 1988, 1991a, 1992; Webb 1987.

The 'intensification debate' David and Chant 1995: 362–63 (see also Chapter 15).

Gender and Australian prehistory Balme and Beck 1995; Beck and Head 1990; du Cros and Smith 1993; *Identifying gender in the archaeological record* Bowdler 1976; McDonald 1995; Meehan 1982.

2 The diversity of surviving traces

Stone artefacts Cotterell and Kamminga 1992: 125–59.

Shell middens Meehan 1982; Mulvaney 1989b; *Richmond River* Bailey 1977; *Sydney region* Attenbrow 1992.

Earth mounds Balme and Beck 1996; Downey and Frankel 1992; Williams 1987.

Ceremonial grounds Frankel 1982, 1991.

Aboriginal pathways Tindale 1974: 75–77.

Quarries Hiscock and Mitchell 1993; *Grindstone quarry* K. Mulvaney 1997; *Macroblade quarry* Paton 1994; *Ochre quarries* Smith and Fankhauser 1996; (Tasmania) Sagona 1994.

Stone hunting hides Lewis 1986; K. Mulvaney 1993a; Smith 1982.

Scarred and carved trees Bell 1979.

Fish traps *Toolondo eel channels* Lourandos 1983a, 1987; Williams 1987.

Human burials *Historical accounts* Hiatt 1969; *Murray River cemeteries* Pardoe 1995; *Broadbeach cemetery* Haglund 1976; *Lake Nitchie burial* Barker 1975; Brown 1989: 6; Macintosh 1971; *Bunyan burial* Feary 1996; *Palaeopathology and forensic studies* Webb 1995; *Grave goods* Feary 1996; Macintosh 1971; Pretty 1986a: 115; Pardoe 1993b.

3 Dating the past

Cultural sequences *Early schemes* McCarthy 1958; Tindale 1957, 1968, 1987: 58; *Reviews* Mulvaney 1961, 1993.
Core Tool and Scraper Tradition *Original formulation, and elaboration* Bowler *et al.* 1970; Jones 1973.
Australian Small Tool Tradition *Original formulation* Gould 1969a: 235; *Critiques* Allen 1990; Allen and Barton 1989: 109–15; Kamminga 1982: 100–03; 1985: 20–21; Kamminga and Allen 1973: 98; White and O'Connell 1982; *Horsehoof core* Kamminga 1982: 85–91.
Dating methods *Radiocarbon dating* Aitken 1990; J. Allen 1994; Barbetti 1993; Bowman 1990; *Rock art dating* Watchman 1993a, 1993b, 1993c.
Trapped electron dating techniques *Luminescence dating* Aitken 1994; Roberts and Jones 1991, 1994; *Ngarrabullgan Cave dating* David *et al.* 1997.

4 Changing landscapes

Climate Bureau of Meteorology 1989; Fitzpatrick 1979; Fleming 1994a; Johnson 1992; Natmap 1986; Langford-Smith 1983; Zillman 1994.
Vegetation Johnson 1992; Fitzpatrick 1979.
Surface water Fleming 1994a, 1994b; *Western Desert* Tindale 1974: 72.
Aboriginal burning *Review of Aboriginal burning* Allen 1983; Hallam 1975; Pyne 1991; *'Firestick farming'* Jones 1969; Tindale 1959; *Recent assessment of impact of Aboriginal burning* Clark 1983; Dodson *et al.* 1992: 129–30; Head 1994a; Hope 1994; Flannery 1994: 229; Horton 1982; (Central Australia) Bolton and Latz 1978: 290–93; Latz and Griffin 1978; *Prehistory of Aboriginal burning* Head 1994a: 175, 178; *European impact* Banks 1989; Mitchell 1848: 412–13; Wakefield 1970.
Sense of place Mulvaney 1989b; *Cowle* Morton and Mulvaney 1996: 11; Rose 1996.

5 People, language and society

Estimates of population size Butlin 1983, 1989; White and Mulvaney 1987; *Critique of Butlin* Kefous 1988; *Western District of Victoria* Lourandos 1977a; *Population decline in Lake Eyre region* Tindale 1941a; *Evidence from palaeopathology* Webb 1984; *Smallpox and other diseases* Butlin 1983, 1989; Campbell 1983, 1985; Dowling 1992; White and Mulvaney 1987; *Sydney region* Kohen 1987, 1988; *Depredation by European colonists* Reynolds 1987: 53.
Australian languages Blake 1988; Crowley and Dixon 1981; Dixon 1980, in prep; McConvell 1990, 1996; McConvell and Evans 1994; Walsh and Yallop 1993.
Social organisation Horton 1994; Keen 1988; *Prehistory of social structure* Morwood 1979; Pardoe 1995; David and Chant 1995; *Linguistic evidence* McConvell 1996: 138–40.
The Dreaming Horton 1994; Lewis and Rose 1988; *Ngarrabullgan Cave* Fullagar and David 1997; *Gillen* Mulvaney *et al.* 1997: 116.
Culture areas Peterson 1976.

6 Subsistence and reciprocity

Animal foods Tindale 1974: 108; *Hunting nets in western NSW* Berndt 1947: 76; *Shellfish* Meehan 1982; *Emu hunting* Tindale 1974: 106–07; *Insects* Kimber 1983; Tindale 1966, 1974: 145.

Plant foods McConnell and O'Connor 1997; Zola and Gott 1993; *Daisy yam* Gott 1983; *Seed food in the arid and semi-arid zones* Tindale 1974: 94–109; *Cycad food value and toxins* Beck 1992; Beck *et al.* 1988; *Antiquity of cycad use* Beaton 1982; Moya Smith 1982; *Intertribal gatherings in arid zone* Cane 1989; *Possible early plant domestication in New Guinea* Yen 1993; *Kuk site* Hope *et al.* 1983.

Aboriginal 'farming' *Effects of digging for plant food* Tindale 1974: 95–96; *Planting seeds* Watson 1983: 43; *Replanting tubers* Hallam 1975; Tindale 1974: 96.

Material culture *Aboriginal artefacts* Australian Gallery Directors' Council, 1981; Horton 1994; Satterthwait 1990; *Technology* Akerman 1991; Kamminga 1994; *Western Desert material culture* Cane 1989; Gould 1969b; Hamilton 1980; (Throwing club) Tindale 1974: 108; *Furskin cloaks* Bosworth 1988; Kamminga 1982: 37–39; *Hatchets* Dickson 1981; *Wood artefacts* Kamminga 1988; *Boomerangs* Cotterell and Kamminga 1992: 175–80.

Reciprocity and cultural diffusion *Ethnographic accounts* Chatwin 1987; Dawson 1881; Paton 1994; Stanner 1933; Thomson 1949; *Reviews* McCarthy 1939, 1977; Mulvaney 1976; Tindale 1974: 80–88; *Shell pendants* Akerman and Stanton 1994; McBryde 1987; Mulvaney 1976; *Ceremonial dance* Hercus 1980; *Pituri (Historical accounts)* Aiston 1936–37; Roth 1901: 31; (Reviews) McBryde 1986; Watson 1983; *Mount William Quarry* McBryde 1984a, 1984b, 1986; Watchman and Freeman 1978; (Recent review) Paton 1993; *Howqua Valley greenstone quarries* McConnel 1987; *Northern NSW hatchet head quarries* Binns and McBryde 1972.

7 Seafarers to Sahul

Causes of world glaciation Gallup *et al.* 1994; Peltier 1994.

Wallacea *Fauna* Groves 1976; Kitchener *et al.* 1990: 108–12; *Swimming elephants* Johnson 1980; Allen 1991; *Artefacts in Flores* Morwood *et al.* 1997: 32.

Sea levels and colonisation Birdsell 1977; Butlin 1989; Chappell 1993.

Watercraft Birdsell 1977: 134–44; Irwin 1991: 14–17; Jones 1989: 754–55; *Aboriginal watercraft* Jones 1976; Thomas 1905; *Dampierland rafts* Tindale 1974: 147.

Routes to Sahul Birdsell 1977; Butlin 1989, 1993; Bellwood 1993; Irwin 1991; *Visibility of bushfires* Dortch and Muir 1980; *Early human presence in the Solomon Islands* Wickler and Spriggs 1988.

8 Sahul: A Pleistocene continent

Climate and environment of Sahul during the Pleistocene Frakes *et al.* 1987; Galloway 1988, 1989; Hope 1989; Hope *et al.* 1983; Nicholls 1989; Singh and Geissler 1985; Torgersen *et al.* 1988; Wasson and Donnelly 1991; *Tasmania* Davies 1967; Kiernan 1990; *The Cadell Fault* Fleming 1984.

Late Pleistocene sea-level rise around Sahul Blom 1988; Chappell 1993, 1994; Thom and Roy 1985; Torgersen *et al.* 1988; *Topography of the drowned continental shelf* Blom 1988; Bunt 1987; Torgersen *et al.* 1983, 1988.

The Dreaming and coastal submergence Birdsell 1993: 11–12; Dixon 1972, in prep; Moore 1884: 8; Tindale 1974: 242.

Megafauna extinctions *Descriptions of species* Archer and Clayton 1984; Griffiths *et al.* 1991; Rich *et al.* 1985; Ride *et al.* 1989; *Causes* Flannery 1990a, 1994: 206–07; Flannery *et al.* 1983; Horton 1984, 1986; *Environmental factors* Horton 1984, 1986; Main 1978; Ride *et al.* 1989; Hope 1994; Hope *et al.* 1983; *Archaeological contexts of megafauna bones* Garling 1994; *Blitzkrieg hypothesis* Martin 1984;

(Critique) Garling n.d.; *Lancefield* Horton and Wright 1981; Flannery 1994: 203; *Cuddie Springs* Furby 1995; *Megafauna hunting?* Horton 1986; *Hunting of game during the LGM* Balme 1995; (Southwest Tasmania) Cosgrove *et al.* 1989; Cosgrove 1990; Jones 1990: 285–86.

9 The initial colonisation

Extinct fauna Archer and Clayton 1984.

Bowdler's coastal colonisation hypothesis *Original formulation* Bowdler 1977; *Critiques* J. Allen 1989; Boot 1994: 320; Hallam 1987; Horton 1981.

Horton's colonisation model Horton 1981.

Fast-tracker hypothesis Birdsell 1957, Birdsell 1993: 17; J. Allen 1989; Rindos and Webb 1992; *Cautionary note about limitations of archaeological data* Frankel 1993: 29.

Identifying stone artefacts Cotterell and Kamminga 1987, 1992: 125–59.

History of discovery of human antiquity Jones 1979; Mulvaney 1961, 1986; White and O'Connell 1982: 42; *Listing of Pleistocene sites* Smith and Sharp 1993; *Koolan Shelter 2* O'Connor 1989; *Mandu Mandu Creek* Morse 1988, 1993; *Sandy Creek 1* Morwood *et al.* 1994.

Uncertain leads *Keilor* Bowler 1976: 64; Gallus 1983; Mulvaney 1998; *Upper Swan* Pearce and Barbetti 1981; (Critical assessment) Bowdler 1992a: 562–64; *Cranebrook Terrace* Nanson *et al.* 1987.

Kakadu sites *Malakunanja* Kamminga and Allen 1973: 45–52; Roberts *et al.* 1990a, 1990b, 1993, 1994; Allen 1994; *Nauwalabila 1* Kamminga and Allen 1973: 95–98; Jones and Johnson 1985; Roberts *et al.* 1993; Allen 1994; Allen and Holdaway 1995.

Controversy over timing of initial colonisation J. Allen 1989; Allen and Holdaway 1995; Frankel 1993; Roberts *et al.* 1994; *Disputes about dating methods and interpretations* J. Allen 1989; Bowdler 1990, 1991, 1992a; Roberts *et al.* 1990a, 1990b, 1994; *Contamination of radiocarbon dating samples* Aitken 1990; Roberts *et al.* 1990a; Chappell *et al.* 1996; *Cross-dating of Ngarrabullgan Cave sediments* David *et al.* 1997.

Jinmium *Original excavation report* Fullagar *et al.* 1996; *Cautionary responses to the claim* Morwood 1996; Smith 1996; *Critique* Bednarik 1997a; *Revised luminescence dates* Spooner 1998.

Ngarrabullgan Cave David *et al.* 1997; David and Chant 1993: 392–95; Fullagar and David 1997.

Carpenter's Gap O'Connor 1995; McConnell and O'Connor 1997.

Pollen records of fire and vegetation change *Lake George* Singh and Geissler 1985, Singh *et al.* 1981: 582; Clark 1983; Wright 1986; *Lynch's Crater and seabed core ODP 820* Kershaw 1994; (Critical assessment of ODP 820) White 1994; *Critical review of pollen and charcoal evidence* Head 1994b.

10 The original Australians

Multiregional evolution hypothesis *Original formulation* Weidenreich 1943; *Contemporary formulation* Frayer *et al.* 1993; *Critics* Groves and Lahr 1994; Lahr 1994.

Out-of-Africa hypothesis Groves 1989b; *mtDNA* Cann *et al.* 1987.

Homo erectus **in Southeast Asia** Pope 1983.

Aborigines in world biological context Kamminga 1992a; Howells 1976, 1989; *mtDNA* Cann *et al.* 1987; *Close affinity with Melanesians* Howells 1989; Larnach and Macintosh 1970; Pietrusewsky 1990.

Blood genetics Kirk 1983: 127–34; Simmons 1976.

Physical variation Birdsell 1993; Howells 1976; Kirk 1983: 90–94; *Cranial form* Fenner 1939; Larnach and Macintosh 1970; *Tooth wear* Richards 1990; *Tasmanian crania* Macintosh and Barker 1965; Pardoe 1991c.

Early historical description of Aborigines; origin theories Hooton 1947: 607; W. Smith 1907; Gray 1937; *Reviews* Jones 1993: 99–101; Mulvaney 1981b, 1985.

Birdsell's tri-hybrid theory Birdsell 1967, 1993; *Birdsell's critics* Kirk and Thorne 1976: 5; Thorne 1977.

Australian Pleistocene remains in general Brown 1987, 1988, 1989, 1994; Habgood 1986; Macintosh and Larnach 1972; Pardoe 1993c; *Palaeopathology* Brown 1989; Webb 1984, 1989, 1995.

Early finds *Talgai cranium* Brown 1989; Pardoe 1993c; *Keilor cranium* Brown 1989, 1994; Bowler 1976; *Mossgiel* Brown 1989; (Dating) Pardoe 1993c: Table 1.

Kow Swamp Mulvaney 1991; Thorne 1969, 1971; Thorne and Macumber 1972; *Palaeoenvironment* Wasson and Donnelly 1991; *Dating of burials* Pardoe 1993c: 84 & Table 1.

Coobool Creek Brown 1989.

Tandou skull Freedman and Lofgren 1983; Pardoe 1993c: 85 & Table 1.

Cossack skull Freedman and Lofgren 1979; Habgood 1986.

Willandra Lakes and the Lake Mungo human burials Barbetti and Allen 1972; Barbetti and McElhinney 1976; Bowler *et al.* 1970; Bowler and Thorne 1976; Clark 1987; Webb 1989, Pardoe 1993c; Mulvaney *forthcoming*; Mulvaney and Bowler 1980.

King Island burial Sim and Thorne 1990; Sim 1994; Brown 1994; Thorne and Sim 1994.

Australasian regional continuity Weidenreich 1943; Frayer *et al.* 1993; Thorne 1971; *Recantation* Larnach and Macintosh 1974; *Critical reviews* Groves 1989a, 1989b; Groves and Lahr 1994.

Challenges to Thorne's robust type Brown 1987, 1989, 1994; Groves 1989a, 1989b; Pietrusewsky 1990; Wright 1976; *Ngandong dating* Gibbons 1996; Swisher *et al.* 1996.

Sexual dimorphism as explanation for robust and gracile crania Brown 1994; Groves 1990; Pardoe 1991b.

Forehead deformation Brothwell 1975; Brown 1981, 1989.

Holocene physical gracilisation Brown 1987, 1989, 1992, 1994; Pardoe 1993b.

Physical adaptation to desert climate Kirk 1983: 154.

11 Pleistocene settlement

Northern coast and deep-sea islands *Koolan Shelter 2* O'Connor 1989; *Mandu Mandu Creek* Morse 1988, 1993; *Overview of early Melanesian sites* J. Allen 1993; *Matenkupkun and Matenbek* Allen *et al.* 1989; Summerhays and Allen 1993: 147; *Kilu* Wickler and Spriggs 1988; *Huon Terraces* Groube *et al.* 1986; Bowdler 1992: 566–67; *Kosipe* White *et al.* 1970; *Nombe* Flannery *et al.* 1983; Gillieson and Mountain 1983.

Australian forestland and woodlands.

Burrill Lake Lampert 1971; *Bulee Brook and Bob's Cave* Boot 1994: 330–32; *Moffats Swamp* Baker 1993; *Wallen Wallen Creek near Brisbane* Neale and Stock 1986; *North Queensland woodlands* David and Chant 1995.

Southwestern Australia *Open-air sites* Helena Valley: Schwede 1983; Quininup Brook: Ferguson 1981; *Kalgan Hall* Ferguson 1985; *Mimim Cove* Clarke and Dortch 1977; *Devil's Lair* Dortch 1984; (Assessment of site's early dates), Allen and Holdaway 1995: 106; Dortch and Dortch 1996; (Environment and subsistence reconstructed from faunal remains) Balme *et al.* 1978; J. Dortch 1996; *Tunnel Cave* J. Dortch 1996; *Questionable early dates* (Ellenbrook) Bindon and Dortch 1982; (Upper Swan) Bowdler 1992a: 562–64.

Cold steppe and moorlands of southeast Sahul.

Blue Mountains Johnson 1979: 24–38; Stockton 1993; *Australian Alps* Kamminga 1992b, 1995; *Birrigai rockshelter* Flood *et al.* 1987; *Bassian Plain sites* Bowdler 1984; Sim 1994; (Revision of Cave Bay Cave dates) Hope 1978: 498, 508.

Tasmania *Review* J. Allen 1993: 146–48; Cosgrove 1995a, 1995b; Jones 1990: 282–84; *Critique of archaeological interpretations* Thomas 1993; *Kutikina* Jones 1984: 52–56, 1990: 279–84; *Darwin Crater* Cosgrove 1995b: 9; Jones and Allen 1984; *Bone Cave* J. Allen *et al.* 1988; *Nunamira and Warreen Caves* Cosgrove 1995b; *Bone tools* Cosgrove 1990: 71; *Thumbnail scrapers* Cosgrove 1995b: 46–47;

McNiven 1994; Webb and Allen 1990; *Speculation about coastal subsistence* Porch and Allen 1995; Dunnett 1993; *Parmerpar Meethaner* Cosgrove 1995a, 1995b; *ORS7* Cosgrove 1995b: 91.

12 Conquest of the deserts

Settlement models Original model: Bowler 1976: 72–73; Subsequent formulations: Hiscock 1988: 258; Horton 1981: 26; Lampert and Hughes 1987, 1988; Ross *et al.* 1992: 101, 108–09; Veth 1987: 107–09, 1995, 1996; *Critique of Veth's model* Holdaway 1996; Smith 1993; *Critique of LGM depopulation hypothesis* Cane 1995: 48–50.

Colless and Lewie Creeks, Lawn Hill Station Hiscock 1988.

Willandra Lakes *General accounts* Clark 1987, Mulvaney and Bowler 1980; *Lake Mungo excavation in 1973* Mulvaney 1974, *forthcoming*; *Pleistocene subsistence* H. Allen 1983: 51–53, 1990; Johnson 1993; Mulvaney and Bowler 1980; J. Hope *et al.* 1983; *Earliest date* Barbetti and Allen 1972.

Menindee Lakes Balme 1995.

Lake Eyre region *Review* Kinhill Engineers Pty Ltd 1995; *Mound springs* Lampert 1985; McLaren *et al.* 1985: *Strzelecki Desert* Williams 1988; *JSN site* Smith *et al.* 1991; *Hearths near Cooper Creek* Veth *et al.* 1990.

Hawker Lagoon Lampert 1985, Lampert and Hughes 1987, 1988.

Nullarbor Plain *Review* Cane 1992, 1995; *Wilsons Bluff* Cundy 1990b; *Koonalda Cave* Wright 1971; (Radiocarbon dates) Hiscock 1988: 265; *Allen's Cave* Cane 1995.

Pilbara Maynard 1980; Brown 1987: 23–25; Hiscock 1988: 263–64; Smith 1988b: 296–97.

Puritjarra rockshelter, central Australia Smith 1987, 1988b: 99–132; Hiscock 1988: 261–62; *Phytoliths research* Bowdery 1998.

13 Pleistocene artefacts

Aboriginal technology Kamminga 1994.

Food plants common to Southeast Asia and Australia Golson 1971.

Stone technology *Basic tenets* Cotterell and Kamminga 1992: 125–59.

Southeast Asian stone technology *Review* Bellwood 1985: 56–68; *Dating* Bronson and White 1992; *Bamboo as a tool material* Pope 1989; *Hoabinhian industry* Kamminga forthcoming; *Kota Tampan* Chesner *et al.* 1991; Majid 1988–89; *Lang Rongrien rockshelter* Anderson 1997.

Body ornaments Akerman 1995; Dortch 1984; Morse 1993; Vanderwal and Fullagar 1989.

Wyrie Swamp Luebbers 1975.

Bone implements Akerman 1995: 174–77; Bowdler 1984: 123–27; Dortch 1984; Jones 1990: 284; *Spatulate bone tools from Bone Cave* Webb and Allen 1990.

Stone technology of Sahul *Stone types* Cotterell and Kamminga 1992: 127–30; Kamminga 1982: 23–26; (Silcrete) Langford-Smith 1983; *Use-wear* Kamminga 1978, 1982; *Flaking methods* Flenniken and White 1983.

Concave and notched scrapers Kamminga 1978: 345–46.

Thumbnail scrapers *Devil's Lair* Dortch and Merrilees 1973: 106–07; *Seton Cave* Lampert 1981: 155; 158–59; *Tasmania* Cosgrove 1995a.

Denticulated cutting edges on flakes from Miriwun and Devil's Lair Dortch 1977: 121, 1984.

Large waisted tools from New Guinea Bulmer 1977; Huon Terraces, Groube *et al.* 1986; Bowdler 1992a: 566–67; Australian waisted tools: Draper 1991; Lampert 1983.

Hatchet heads *Hatchet design and uses* Dickson 1981; *Kakadu specimens* Jones and Johnson 1985: 216; Schrire 1982; *Sandy Creek 1 specimen* Morwood and Trezise 1989; *Miriwun specimen* Dortch 1977.

Grindstones Smith 1988a, 1989; *Cuddie Springs* Fullagar and Furby 1997.

14 Holocene stone tool innovations

Holocene climate and environment Chappell 1982; Galloway 1988; Hope 1994; Kershaw and Strickland 1989; Wasson and Donnelly 1991; *El Niño–Southern Oscillation* Nicholls 1989; *Holocene Warm Maximum* Chappell 1982; Galloway 1988; Kershaw and Strickland 1989; Wasson and Donnelly 1991.

Gambieran industry *Original description* McCarthy 1940: 30–32; Tindale 1941b: 145; *Review* D. Clark 1979; *Dated Gambieran discoid from Wyrie Swamp* Luebbers 1978; *Koongine Cave assemblage* Bird and Frankel n.d.

Kartan Assemblage *Original formulation* Tindale and Maegraith 1931; Tindale 1968, 1981; *Early critics of the Kartan* McCarthy 1958; Mulvaney 1961; *Most recent support for the Kartan Culture* Lampert 1981: 153–55; Lampert and Hughes 1988; *Draper's fieldwork and stone assemblages* Draper 1991, forthcoming.

Heat treatment of stone Domanski and Webb 1992; *Australian occurrences* Flenniken and White 1983; Hiscock 1993a; McDonald and Rich 1994.

Dating the Small Tool Tradition or Phase Richardson 1992; *Early dates for microliths* Brown 1987; Dortch and Gardner 1976; McBryde 1982; Morwood *et al.* 1994.

Microliths Campbell and Noone 1943; Mulvaney 1961: 292–93; Kamminga 1980; Pearce 1974; *Manufacturing method* Dickson 1973: 12; *Northern Australian finds* K. Mulvaney and Pickering 1989; Pickering 1990; Smith and Cundy 1985; *Claims for origin: India via Indonesia* McCarthy 1977; *Australia* Mulvaney 1961; Noone 1943: 280; Pearce 1974; *Earliest ascription of spear barb use* Mulvaney 1960: 78–81; *Evidence of use* Kamminga 1980; McBryde 1985.

Uniface and biface stone points *Type variation and distributions* H. Allen 1994; Kamminga 1978: 328–38, 1985: 3–8; Smith and Cundy 1985; Jones and Johnson 1985: 206, 208; Kamminga 1985: 3; *Chronology* Hiscock 1993b; *Points at Ingaladdi* Cundy 1990a.

Kimberley point *Ethnographic accounts* Love 1917: 26; Tindale 1974: 82–83, 107; *Review and experimental use* Akerman 1980; *Review* Kamminga 1978: 335–37.

Macroblades Allen 1994; Kamminga 1978: 5–6; *Ethnographic accounts* Spencer and Gillen 1899; Roth 1897; *Dating* Allen 1994; *Ethnoarchaeology* Binford and O'Connell 1984; *Ngilipitji quarry* Jones and White 1988.

Juan knife Kamminga 1982: 102; Tindale 1957: 28; *Archaeological specimens* Mulvaney and Joyce 1965; Horsfall 1982.

Hafted flake scrapers Kamminga 1978: 340–44; *Dates for Cape York Peninsula* Flood and Horsfall 1986; Morwood *et al.* 1994; *Date for Kangaroo Island* Lampert 1981: 142–43.

Tula Kamminga 1978: 347–49, 1985: 20; *Oldest dates* Kamminga 1982: 102, Smith 1988b: 124, 247; *Resin for hafting* Mulvaney 1987: 84.

Pirri graver Kamminga 1985; *Excavated specimen* Smith 1988b: 225–26.

Marni wadna Kamminga 1985: 8; *Ethnographic accounts* Aiston 1928: 152; Horne and Aiston 1924: 78–79.

Elouera Kamminga 1977; Lampert 1971: 49.

Hatchets Dickson 1981; *Northern Australian dates and distribution* Morwood and Trezise 1989.

Reniform skin scrapers Edwards 1963; Kamminga 1971: 113–15.

Millstones *General account* Tindale 1974: 102; *Wanmara Spring* Smith 1988b: 163; Smith 1989.

15 Theories and models: explaining change

Postulated foreign origins McCarthy 1940, 1977; *As a cultural package* Beaton 1982; Bowdler 1981: 108, 110.

Microliths *Earliest microliths in southeast Australia* Pearce 1974; *Postulated function as a knife* Fullagar *et al.* 1994; McBryde 1985.

Dingo *Origins* Corbett 1985; Horton 1994; Thomson *et al.* 1987; *Interaction with Aborigines* Tindale 1974: 109; Hayden 1975; Kolig 1973; *Dates for earliest dingo remains* McBryde 1982; Milham and Thompson 1976; Mulvaney *et al.* 1964; *New Guinea wild dogs* Flannery 1990b; van Deusen 1972.

Culture transfer across Torres Strait Davidson 1933, 1934, 1935; Rowland 1987; Mulvaney 1989b; *Netting techniques* Davidson 1933; *Outrigger canoes* Davidson 1935; Roth 1910; Rowland 1982, 1987; *Melanesian-style axe on Whitsunday Island* Rowland 1986.

Various speculations for adoption of spear armatures *Efficient maintenance of spears* Witter 1988: 40; *Adoption of spearthrower* Luebbers 1978; *Change in hunting practices* Morwood 1987: 347.

Arid-zone tool-kit Kamminga 1985: 20–21; Mulvaney 1987.

Risk-minimisation Hiscock 1994; *Thumbnail scrapers and human mobility in Pleistocene Tasmania* McNiven 1994.

Social factors such as prestige and fashion Peterson 1971: 244; White and O'Connell 1982: 124–25; *Kimberley point* Akerman 1980.

The 'intensification debate' *Lourandos' original formulation and amplifications* Lourandos 1983a, 1983b, 1985; 1997; *Reviews* David and Chant 1995: 362–63; Lourandos and Ross 1994; Ross 1989; White and O'Connell 1982: 102–05; Williams 1987: 318–19; *Exploitation of coastal islands* (Queensland) Rowland 1983; (southeast Australia) Gaughwin and Fullagar 1995: 47–48; Sullivan 1987; *Rock art and new tool types* (Sydney region) McDonald 1991: 80; (central Queensland) Morwood 1980; *Regionalisation of rock art* (Kakadu) Lewis 1988; Taçon 1993; Taçon and Chippindale 1994; *Postulated regional changes rather than pan-Australian* O'Connor *et al.* 1993; *Time lag in development of rich coastal environments* Beaton 1985; *Assessing artefact discard rates* David and Chant 1995: 378–79; *Environmental constraints in the desert* Smith 1988b; *Regional evidence for socio-economic intensification* (northeast Queensland) David and Chant 1995: 424, 426; (Victoria River District) David *et al.* 1994.

16 *People of the coast*

Sea level rise on the Arafura Plain van Andel *et al.* 1967.

Modern coastal topography and environments Bunt 1987; *Coastal progradation* Chappell 1982.

Early Holocene coastal exploitation *West Kimberley coast* O'Connor 1989; *Southwest Victoria* Frankel 1991; *Northwest Tasmania* Jones 1977a, 1977b; *Southwest coast* Dortch 1984.

Coastal diet Hallam 1987; Meehan 1982.

Kakadu *Evolution of the Holocene landscape* Hope *et al.* 1985: 237; (Summaries) H. Allen 1986–87: 4; Allen 1989, 1996; Allen and Barton 1989; Jones 1985; Hiscock and Kershaw 1992: 67–68; *Middens in rockshelters* Allen 1986–7: 5–9, 1996: 198–99; *Ethnobotany* Clarke 1985, 1988; *Anbangbang 1 shelter* Clarke 1985, 1988; Jones 1985: 39–64; *Change in stone technology* Jones and Johnson 1985: 206; Hiscock 1996; *Recent freshwater wetlands sites* Brockwell 1989; Hiscock 1996; Jones 1985: 292; (Ki'na) Meehan *et al.* 1985: 143–44; Hiscock and Kershaw 1992: 68; *Flake tools with use-polish* Kamminga 1977: 208–11, 1982: 93–95; Meehan *et al.* 1985: 143–44; Fujiwara *et al.* 1985: 164.

Aurukun and Weipa shell mounds Bailey *et al.* 1994; Cribb *et al.* 1988; Stone 1993; *Ethnographic account* Roth 1901: 1; *Seasonality* Thomson 1939.

Southeast Queensland *General review* David and Chant 1995: 429–50; *Explaining change in archaeological record* Hall 1982; McNiven 1992; Morwood 1987; Walters 1989, 1992a, 1992b; *Bracken (bungwall) pounders* Kamminga 1981; Gillieson and Hall 1982; McNiven 1991; *Broadbeach cemetery* Haglund 1976.

Sydney region *Historical accounts* Kohen 1988; Kohen and Lampert 1987; McDonald 1990; *Kurnell* Megaw 1968; *Cumberland Plain* Kohen 1987; McDonald 1996.

South coast *Review* Boot 1994; *Early fieldwork* Lampert 1966, 1971; *ANU field projects* Knight 1996; *Bone points* C. Webb 1987; *Fossil corals* Bryant *et al.* 1992: 492.

Shell fish-hooks and stone files *Description* Lampert 1971; *Antiquity* Sullivan 1987: 98; *Debate about fish-hooks and mussel shells* Sullivan 1987; Mackay and White 1987.

Microliths and death spears Kamminga 1981.

Subsistence in southwest Australia *Major historical records* Grey 1841; Moore 1884; Mulvaney and Green 1992; Nind 1831; *Reconstructed subsistence patterns* Anderson 1984; Hallam 1975, 1987; Gibbs 1987; Meagher 1974; *Southern forests survey* Pearce 1982.

Food remains in southwest sites Balme *et al.* 1978, 1980; Dortch 1979, 1984, Dortch *et al.* 1984; J. Dortch 1996; Hallam 1975; Lilley 1993; Smith 1982; *Coastal subsistence* Dortch 1997; Dortch *et al.* 1984; *Lake Jasper underwater site* Dortch 1997; *Fish traps* Dix and Meagher 1976.

Stone technology in the southwest *Walyunga* Pearce 1978; *Kodj and taap* Hayden 1973; Kamminga 1982: 32, 85; *Fossiliferous chert* Dortch 1979, 1991; Dortch and MacArthur 1985; Dortch and Morse 1984; J. Dortch 1996; Ferguson 1981; Glover 1984; *Dunsborough* Ferguson 1980.

Mid-Holocene population decline? *Original formulation* Ferguson 1985: 493–97; *Refutation* Moya Smith 1993; *Postulated environmental change* (Pollen) Churchill 1968; *Swan River* (Sediments) Kendrick 1977; (Review) Newsome and Pickett 1993.

17 Regional challenges and responses

Snowy Mountains *Reviews* Flood 1980; Kamminga 1992b, 1995; *Alpine foods* Gott and Geering 1989; Flood 1980: 92; Kamminga 1995: 163–64.

Late prehistoric settlement in southeastern highlands Bowdler 1977: 205, 234; 1981: 110; Flood *et al.* 1987: 22–23.

New England tablelands Godwin 1990: 378–79.

Murray River *Evidence from cemeteries* Pardoe 1988, 1995; *Roonka* Pretty 1986a, 1986b, 1988; P. Brown 1989; Pardoe 1988; *Dating of cemeteries* Pardoe 1990, 1993a; *Modes of burial* Pardoe 1995; *Ritual fire* Bowdler 1983; *Studies of Murray River human remains* Pardoe 1988, 1990, 1995; Pietrusewsky 1990; *Nutritional stress and disease in prehistoric Murray River populations* Webb 1984; *Tooth avulsion* Campbell 1981; Macintosh 1974: 85; Pardoe 1995.

Arid zone *Holocene technological innovations* Kamminga 1985: 20–21, 1988: 28–29; *Late Holocene settlement of Central Australia* Smith 1988b; *Puritjarra* Smith 1988b: 99–132; *Intirtekwerle rockshelter* Smith 1988b: 202–33.

Willandra Lakes H. Allen 1990.

Victorian Mallee Ross 1981, 1982; Ross *et al.* 1992: 106.

Western Desert culture Berndt and Berndt 1942; *Postulated origin of dialects* McConvell 1990, 1996.

Lake Eyre region Lampert 1985; Williams 1988; *Mound springs* Lampert 1985; Lampert and Hughes 1987; *Strzelecki Desert* Williams 1988; *JSN site* Smith *et al.* 1991.

Nullarbor Plain Cane 1992, 1995; *Ethnography* Brady 1987; *Ooldea Soak* Brockwell *et al.* 1989.

Great and Little Sandy Deserts Veth 1987, 1995, 1996.

Smith's settlement model Smith 1989: 314.

Veth's 'corridor and barrier' model Veth 1995, 1996 (see also Dodson *et al.* 1992); *Postulated migration of Western Desert people* McConvell 1996: 135; *Critiques of Veth's model and evidence* Cane 1995: 47–49; Holdaway 1996; Smith 1993.

Trade and exchange networks *Reviews of regional trade networks* Akerman and Stanton 1994; David and Chant 1995: 506–11; McBryde 1987; Mulvaney 1976; *Historical accounts* Aiston 1937; Horne and Aiston 1924: 31, 130; Hercus 1980; *Craft specialisation* Watson 1983: 45; *Therreyererte ceremonial site* Smith 1988b: 276–92.

Technological developments Kamminga 1985: 20, 1994; Smith 1989; *Fluted boomerang* Davidson 1936; *Winnowing dish* Tindale 1974: 99; *Millstones* Smith 1989; *The Aboriginal grain belt* Tindale 1974: 104, 110–11.

18 Island settlement

Island settlement *Review* Bowdler 1985; *Earliest island visits* Barker 1989, 1991; O'Connor 1992; *Marine technology and island settlement* (Queensland coast) Barker 1989; Beaton 1985; Rowland 1996; (Southeast coast) Gaughwin and Fullagar 1995; Sullivan 1982; *Bathurst and Melville Islands* Tindale 1974: 140; *Bentinck Island raft* Tindale 1977: 267–70; *Queensland canoes* Roth 1910; Baker 1988; Rowland 1987; *Longest recorded journey* Spencer and Gillen 1904: 680–82.

Torres Strait *Pleistocene physiography* Harris *et al.* 1992; *Geomorphology* Jennings 1972; *Early history* Beckett 1972; Moore 1979; *Trade* Moore 1978, 1979; Rowland 1987; *Material culture* Wilson 1988; *Prehistory* Moore 1979; Mulvaney 1989b: 62–65; *Archaeology* Moore 1979: 13–15; Rowland 1985; Vanderwal 1973; *Rock art* Cole and David 1992.

Islands of the northwest coast *Northwest coast rafts* Akerman 1975; Tindale 1974: 147; *Montebello Islands* Veth 1993; *Montgomery Islands* O'Connor 1992, 1993, 1994.

Queensland coast Rowland 1986, 1987, 1996; *Mornington and Bentinck Islands* (Population size) Tindale 1974: 29; (Genetics) Birdsell 1993: 441; *Whitsunday Group* Barker 1989, 1991; *Percy Islands* Rowland 1984; Ulm *et al.* 1995: 24–26; *Keppel Islands* Rowland 1982; Horsfall 1982.

Bass Strait Islands Sim 1994.

Kangaroo Island Lampert 1981; Draper 1991, *forthcoming*; *Abandonment* Jones 1977a: 352, 1979: 448; *Lashmars Lagoon* Clark 1983; Draper *forthcoming*; Lampert 1981: 172–77, 184–85; *Cape Du Couedic* Draper 1991; *Ngurunderi story* Draper 1988: 15, *forthcoming*; *Swimming Backstairs Passage* Bull 1884: 5.

Southwest *Recherche Archipelago* Dortch and Morse 1984; *Rottnest and Garden Islands* Dortch 1991.

19 Tasmania

Early historical accounts Baudin 1974; Jones 1988; Mulvaney 1989b; *Robinson journals* Plomley 1966; Jones 1984: 34–36.

Plant food Gott 1992.

Population numbers Jones 1974, 1984: 39; Pardoe 1986, 1991c.

Material culture Jones 1984: 46–48; *Cultural isolation* Jones 1977b: 203; White and O'Connell 1982: 168–69; *Ochre* Sagona 1994.

Dogs Jones 1970.

Canoe-shaped floats *Historical accounts* Plomley 1966: 119, 379, 554, 971–73; *Performance* Jones 1976: 239–50, 1977a: 322–25, 1979; *Antiquity* Sim 1994.

Territorial expansion Cosgrove 1990: 101–02; Jones 1977a: 352; Lourandos 1988: 280–82.

Northwest and west coasts Lourandos 1983b: 42–44, 1988; *Rocky Cape* Jones 1977a: 342–43, 1978; (Analysis of the fish bones) Colley and Jones 1987; (Shellfish content) Dunnett 1993: 249–52; *West Point* Jones 1966; *Spicular chert quarries* Cosgrove 1990: 45–58, Appendix 2; *Hinterland visitation* Thomas 1993.

Eastern coast and hinterlands Brown 1986, 1991a; Cosgrove 1990: 102–05; Dunnett 1993: 247–49; Gaughwin 1985; Lourandos 1977b; *Exploitation of forestlands* Thomas 1993: 2–4.

Central highlands Cosgrove 1984, 1990: 101–02; Cosgrove *et al.* 1990; Lourandos 1983b: 39–41.

Island settlement Jones 1977a, 1979: 448, Jones 1989: 754–55; Sim 1994; *Maatsuyker Group* Vanderwal and Horton 1984; Dunnett 1992; *Hunter Island* Bowdler 1984; *South coast* Dunnett 1992; Horton 1979; Vanderwal and Horton 1984.

Why the Tasmanians stopped eating fish Allen 1979, Bowdler 1980: 338, 1984; Colley and Jones 1987; Horton 1979; Jones 1977a: 343, 1978: 45, 1979; Vanderwal and Horton 1984: 108–13; Walters 1981; White and O'Connell 1982: 161–62.

Tasmanian bone points Bowdler 1980, 1984; Cosgrove *et al.* 1990: 71; Jones 1990: 283–84, 286–87; Kamminga 1984; Webb and Allen 1990.

20 Art on rock

Australian rock art overview Flood 1997; Layton 1992a; Officer 1992, 1993; Walsh 1988.
Reconstruction of prehistoric social and cultural phenomena David and Chant 1995; Morwood 1979; Taçon and Chippindale 1994; Taçon *et al.* 1996.
Custodianship and repainting Mowaljarlai 1992; K. Mulvaney 1993b; Walsh 1992; Ward 1992.
Pigments Clarke and North 1991; Cole and Watchman 1993; Cook *et al.* 1990.
Finger fluting Bednarik 1987, 1989; Cane 1992; Rosenfeld 1993.
Koonalda Cave Wright 1971; Cane 1995.
Techniques Bahn and Rosenfeld 1991; Maynard 1979.
Stencil art Bahn and Rosenfeld 1991; Moore 1977; Morwood 1979; Walsh 1993; B. Wright 1985.
Oldest dates Loy *et al.* 1990; Nelson 1993; Cosgrove and Jones 1989; McGowan *et al.* 1993; Rosenfeld 1993; Watchman 1992, 1993b.

21 Rock art of temperate Australia

Panaramitee Style Clegg 1987; Dorn 1984; Edwards 1966; Forbes 1983; Franklin 1991; Maynard 1979; McCarthy 1988; Rosenfeld 1991; *Proposed Panaramitee in eastern Australia* McDonald 1991; Morwood 1980; Rosenfeld 1991; *Dating Panaramitee* Nobbs and Dorn 1988; Rosenfeld 1991; Watchman 1992, 1993a; *Postulated depictions of extinct fauna* Mountford 1956; Berndt 1987; Chaloupka 1993; Forbes 1982.
Southeast Australia Caldicott 1991; Gunn 1983, 1984; Officer 1984, 1992, 1993; Walsh 1988; *Sydney Basin* Campbell 1899; McDonald 1990, 1991; Maynard 1976; Officer 1984, 1992; Stanbury and Clegg 1990.
Tasmania Brown 1991b; Cosgrove and Jones 1989.

22 Rock art of tropical Australia

Southeast Cape York Peninsula Cole *et al.* 1994; Cole and David 1992; David and Chant 1995; Watchman and Cole 1993; David 1992; Flood and Horsfall 1986; Huchet 1990, 1993; Morwood 1990; Rosenfeld 1991; Rosenfeld *et al.* 1981; Watchman 1993b; Watchman and Cole 1993; *Koolburra Plateau* David and Chant 1995: 411–16, 446–51; Flood and Horsfall 1986.
Sequences of Kakadu art styles Chaloupka 1977, 1983, 1993; Haskovec 1992; Lewis 1988, 1996; Taçon 1988, 1991, 1993; Taçon and Chippindale 1994; *Kakadu pigments* Clarke and North 1991; *Radiocarbon dating of Kakadu art* Nelson *et al.* 1992.
Pilbara Crawford 1964; Lorblanchet 1992; McNickle 1984, 1985; Tindale 1987; Virili 1977.
Victoria River District (VRD) David *et al.* 1994; Lewis 1984; Lewis and Rose 1988; McNickle 1991; Walsh 1988, 1991.
Kimberley region *Bradshaw Figures* Walsh 1988, 1994; Welch 1990, 1993; (Dating) Lewis 1997; Roberts *et al.* 1997; Walsh *et al.* 1997; Bednarik 1997b; (Foreign origins) Hogarth and Dayton 1997; Walsh 1994; *Wandjina art* Crawford 1968, 1972; Layton 1992b; Vinnicombe 1992; Walsh 1988, 1991.

23 Asian and European newcomers

Pobassoo Flinders 1814, II: 228–34; Perry and Simpson 1962.
Monsoons Cense 1952; Earl 1853: 197, 1882.

Trepang industry Macknight 1976, 1986; Mulvaney 1966, 1987; *Dating* Macknight 1976: 94–95; *Historical accounts* Crawfurd 1820, III: 151, 441, 1856: 440; Flinders 1814, II: 231, 257; King 1827, I: 128–38; Mulvaney and Green 1992; Searcy 1909; Wallace 1872: 431; *Kimberley sites* Crawford 1968; Morwood and Hobbs 1997.

Indonesian ceramics Key 1969.

Macassan influences Berndt and Berndt 1954; Thomson 1949; Mountford 1956; Warner 1937: 453–68; Worsley 1955; Macknight 1972, 1986; Schrire 1972; Macknight and Gray 1970; Morphy 1991: 141, 301.

Eredia Mills 1930: 62–67.

Chinese Fitzgerald 1953; Meilink-Roelofz 1969: 25, 87.

Portuguese Spate 1965; Sharp 1963; McIntyre 1977; Williams and Frost 1988; *Suma Oriental* Pires 1944: 210–14; *Cannons* Uren 1940: 25; *Slavery* Earl 1853: 210; King 1827, I: 113.

Dutch Heeres 1899: 36, 42, 81, 122–27 (extracts from journals cited); Williams and Frost 1988; Mulvaney 1987.

Dampier Gray 1937 (entry for 5 January 1688); Mulvaney 1989b: 18–21.

Wrecks Henderson 1986.

References

Abbreviations

AIAS   Australian Institute of Aboriginal Studies
AIATSIS   Australian Institute of Aboriginal and Torres Strait Islander Studies
ANU   Australian National University
AURA   Australian Rock Art Research Association
RSPacS, ANU Research School of Pacific Studies, Australian National University
CSIRO   Commonwealth Scientific and Industrial Research Organisation

Aiston, G. 1928. Chipped stone tools of the Aboriginal tribes east and north-east of Lake Eyre, South Australia, *Papers and Proceedings of the Royal Society of South Australia*, pp. 123–31.
——1936–37. The Aboriginal narcotic *pitcheri*, *Oceania*, 7:373–74.
Aitken, M. J. 1990. *Science based dating in archaeology*. Longman, London.
——1994. Optical dating: A non-specialist review, *Quaternary Geochronology* (*Quaternary Science Review*) 13:503–08.
Akerman, K. 1975. The double raft or *kalwa* of the west Kimberley, *Mankind*, 10:20–23.
——1979. Heat and lithic technology in the Kimberley, W.A., *Archaeology and Physical Anthropology in Oceania*, 14:144–51.
——1980. Notes on the Kimberley stone-tipped spear focussing on the point hafting mechanism, *Mankind*, 11:486–89.
——1991. *Tools, weapons and utensils*. Aboriginal Australia Culture and Society series. Aboriginal and Torres Strait Islander Commission, Canberra.
——1995. The use of bone, shell, and teeth by Aboriginal Australians. In E. Johnson (ed.), *Ancient peoples and landscapes*. Museum of Texas Tech University, Lubbock, pp. 173–83.
Akerman, K. and J. Stanton 1994. *Riji and jakuli: Kimberley pearl shell in Aboriginal Australia*. N.T. Museum of Arts and Sciences, Monograph Series No. 4, Darwin.
Allen, H. 1979. Left out in the cold: Why the Tasmanians stopped eating fish, *The Artefact*, 4:1–10.
——1983. *Nineteenth century faunal change in western New South Wales and north-western Victoria*. Working Papers in Anthropology, Archaeology, Linguistics and Maori Studies. Department of Anthropology, University of Auckland.

——1986–87. Holocene mangroves and middens in northern Australia and Southeast Asia, *Indo-Pacific Prehistory Association Bulletin*, 7:1–16.

——1989. Late Pleistocene and Holocene settlement patterns and environment, Kakadu, Northern Territory, Australia, *Indo-Pacific Prehistory Association Bulletin*, 9:92–117.

——1990. Environmental history in southwestern New South Wales during the late Pleistocene. In C. Gamble and O. Sofer (eds), *The World at 18 000 BP*, Vol. 2: *Low Latitudes*. Unwin Hyman, London, pp. 296–321.

——1991. Stegodonts and the dating of stone tool assemblages in island S.E. Asia, *Asian Perspectives*, 30:243–66.

——1994. The distribution of large blades (leilira): Evidence for recent changes in Aboriginal ceremonial exchange networks. In P. McConvell and N. Evans (eds), *Archaeology and linguistics: Understanding ancient Australia*. Oxford University Press, Oxford.

——1996. The time of the mangroves: Changes in mid-Holocene estuarine environments and subsistence in Australia and Southeast Asia, *Indo-Pacific Prehistory Association Bulletin*, 15:193–205.

Allen, H. and G. Barton 1989. *Ngarradj Warde Djobkeng. White Cockatoo Dreaming and the Prehistory of Kakadu*. Oceania Monograph No. 37.

Allen, J. 1989. When did humans first colonize Australia? *Search*, 20:149–54.

——1993. Notions of the Pleistocene in Greater Australia. In M. Spriggs, D. E. Yen, W. Ambrose, R. Jones, A. Thorne and A. Andrews (eds), *A community of culture. The people and prehistory of the Pacific*. Department of Prehistory, RSPacS, ANU, Canberra, pp. 139–51.

——1994. Radiocarbon determinations, luminescence dating and Australian archaeology, *Antiquity*, 68:339–43.

Allen, J., R. Cosgrove and S. Brown 1988. New archaeological data from the southern forests region, Tasmania: A preliminary statement, *Australian Archaeology*, 27:75–88.

Allen, J., C. Gosden and J. P. White 1989. Human Pleistocene adaptations in the tropical island Pacific: Recent evidence from New Ireland, a Greater Australian outlier, *Antiquity*, 63:548–61.

Allen, J. and S. Holdaway 1995. The contamination of Pleistocene radiocarbon determinations in Australia, *Antiquity*, 69:101–12.

Anderson, D. D. 1997. Cave archaeology in Southeast Asia, *Geoarchaeology: An International Journal*, 12:607–38.

Anderson, J. 1984. *Between plateau and plain*. Occasional Papers in Prehistory 4. RSPacS, ANU, Canberra.

Archer, M. and G. Clayton (eds) 1984. *Vertebrate zoogeography and evolution in Australasia. (Animals in space and time)*. Hesperian Press, Sydney.

Attenbrow, V. 1992. Shell bed on shell midden, *Australian Archaeology*, 34:3–21.

Australian Gallery Directors' Council, 1981. *Aboriginal Australia*. Australian Gallery Directors' Council, Sydney.

Bahn, P. and A. Rosenfeld (eds) 1991. *Rock art and prehistory. Papers presented to symposium G of the AURA Congress, Darwin 1988*. Oxbow Monograph 10, Oxbow Books, Oxford.

Bailey, G. N. 1975. The role of molluscs in coastal economies: The results of midden analysis in Australia, *Journal of Archaeological Science*, 2:45–62.

——1977. Shell mounds, shell middens and raised beaches in the Cape York Peninsula, *Mankind*, 11:132–43.

Bailey, G. N., J. Chappell and R. Cribb 1994. The origin of Anadara shell mounds at Weipa, north Queensland, Australia, *Archaeology in Oceania*, 29:69–80.

Balme, J. 1980. An analysis of charred bone from Devil's Lair, Western Australia, *Archaeology and Physical Anthropology in Oceania*, 15:81–85.

——1995. 30,000 years of fishery in western New South Wales, *Archaeology in Oceania*, 30:1–21.

Balme, J. and W. Beck (eds) 1995. *Gendered archaeology. The second Australian Women in Archaeology Conference*. ANH Publications, ANU, Canberra.

Balme, J. and W. Beck 1996. Earth mounds in southeastern Australia, *Australian Archaeology*, 42:39–51.

Balme, J., D. Merrilees and J. K. Porter 1978. Late Quaternary mammal remains, spanning about 30 000 years, from excavations in Devil's Lair, Western Australia, *Journal of the Royal Society of Western Australia*, 61:33–65.

Baker, N. 1993. Moffats Swamp dune. Preliminary report on archaeological site salvage. Report to RZM Pty Ltd, January 1993.

Baker, R. M. 1988. Yanyuwa canoe making, *Records of the South Australian Museum*, 22:173–88.

Banks, J. C. G. 1989. A history of forest fire in the Australian alps. In R. Good (ed.), *The scientific significance of the Australian alps*. The Australian Alps National Parks Liaison Committee, Canberra, pp. 265–80.

Barbetti, M. 1993. Radiocarbon dating. In L. E. Cram (ed.), *Carbon element of energy and life*. The Science Foundation for Physics, University of Sydney, Sydney, pp. 229–37.

Barbetti, M. and H. Allen 1972. Prehistoric man at Lake Mungo, Australia, by 32,000 B.P., *Nature*, 240:46–48.

Barbetti, M. and M. W. McElhinny 1976. The Lake Mungo geomagnetic excursion, *Philosophical Trans. Royal Society of London*, 281:515–42.

Barker, B. C. 1989. Nara Inlet 1: A Holocene sequence from the Whitsunday Islands, central Queensland coast, *Queensland Archaeological Research*, 6:53–76.

——1991. Nara Inlet 1: Coastal resource use and the Holocene marine transgression in the Whitsunday Islands, central Queensland, *Archaeology in Oceania*, 26:102–09.

Barker, B. C. W. 1975. Periodontal disease and tooth dislocation in Aboriginal remains from Lake Nitchie (NSW), West Point (Tasmania) and Limestone Creek (Victoria), *Archaeology and Physical Anthropology in Oceania*, 10:185–217.

Baudin, N. 1974. *The journal of Post Captain Nicholas Baudin, Commander-in-Chief of the corvettes Geographe and Naturaliste*. Libraries Board of South Australia, Adelaide.

Beaton, J. M. 1982. Fire and water: Aspects of Australian Aboriginal management of cycads, *Archaeology in Oceania*, 17:51–58.

——1985. Evidence for a coastal occupation time-lag at Princess Charlotte Bay (North Queensland) and implications for coastal colonization and population growth theories for Aboriginal Australia, *Archaeology in Oceania*, 20:1–20.

——1995. The transition on the coastal fringe of Greater Australia, *American Antiquity*, 69:798–806.

Beck, W. 1992. Aboriginal preparation of cycad seeds in Australia, *Economic Botany*, 46:134–47.

Beck, W., R. Fullagar and N. White 1988. Archaeology from ethnography: The Aboriginal use of cycad as an example. In B. Meehan and R. Jones (eds), *Archaeology with ethnography: An Australian perspective*. Department of Prehistory, RSPacS, Canberra, pp. 137–47.

Beck, W. and L. Head 1990. Women in Australian prehistory, *Australian Feminist Studies*, 11:29–48.

Beckett, J. R. 1972. The Torres Strait Islanders. In D. Walker (ed.), *Bridge and barrier: The natural and cultural history of Torres Strait*. Department of Biogeography and Geomorphology, RSPacS, ANU, pp. 307–26.

Bednarik, R. G. 1987–88. The cave art of Western Australia, *The Artefact*, 12:1–16.

——1989. Perspectives of Koongine Cave and scientific archaeology, *Australian Archaeology*, 29:9–16.

——1997a. Jinmium blues, *The Artefact*, 20:79.

——1997b. Kimberley paintings dated, *The Artefact*, 20:84.

Bell, D. 1979. Aboriginal carved trees in New South Wales: A survey report. Part 1. Unpublished report to NSW National Parks and Wildlife Service.

Bellwood, P. 1985. *Prehistory of the Indo-Malaysian Archipelago*. Academic Press, London.

——1993. Crossing the Wallace Line—with style. In M. Spriggs *et al.* (eds), *A community of culture. The people and prehistory of the Pacific*. Occasional Papers in Prehistory 21, Department of Prehistory, RSPacS, ANU, pp. 152–63.

Berndt, R. M. 1947. Wiradjeri magic and clever men, *Oceania*, 17:327–65.

——1987. Panaramitee magic, *Records of the South Australian Museum*, 20:15–28.

Berndt, R. M. and C. H. Berndt 1942. A preliminary report of fieldwork in the Ooldea region, western South Australia, *Oceania*, 12:305–40.

——1954. *Arnhem Land. Its history and its people*. F. W. Cheshire, Melbourne.

Bindon, P. and C. E. Dortch 1982. Dating problems at the Ellenbrook site, *Australian Archaeology*, 14:13–17.

Binford, L. R. and J. O'Connell 1984. An Alyawara day: The stone quarry, *Journal of Anthropological Research*, 40:406–32.

Binns, R. A. and I. M. McBryde 1972. *A petrological analysis of ground-edge artefacts from northern New South Wales*. AIAS, Canberra.

Bird, C. F. M. and D. Frankel *n.d.* Excavations at Koongine Cave: Redefining early Holocene lithic technologies in South Australia. Ms for publication.

Birdsell, J. B. 1957. Some population problems concerning Pleistocene man, *Cold Springs Harbor Symposia on Quantitative Biology*, 22:47–69.

——1967. Preliminary data on the trihybrid origin of the Australian Aborigines, *Archaeology and Physical Anthropology in Oceania*, 2:100–55.

——1977. The recalibration of a paradigm for the first peopling of greater Australia. In J. Allen, J. Golson and R. Jones (eds), *Sunda and Sahul. Prehistoric studies in Southeast Asia, Melanesia and Australia*. Academic Press, London, pp. 113–67.

——1993. *Microevolutionary patterns in Aboriginal Australia. A gradient analysis of clines*. Oxford University Press, Oxford.

Blake, B. 1988. Redefining Pama-Nyungan: The prehistory of Australian languages, *Aboriginal Linguistics*, 1:1–90.

Blom, W. M. 1988. Late Quaternary sediments and sea-levels in Bass Basin, southeastern Australia— A preliminary report, *Search*, 19:94–96.

Bolton, B. L. and P. K. Latz 1978. The western hare-wallaby, *Lagorchestes hirsutus* (Gould) Macropodidae in the Tanami Desert, *Australian Wildlife Research*, 5:285–93.

Bonnemains, J. E. and B. Smith (eds) 1988. *Baudin in Australian waters*. Oxford University Press, Melbourne.

Boot, P. G. 1994. Recent research into the prehistory of the hinterland of the south coast of New South Wales. In M. Sullivan, S. Brockwell and A. Webb (eds), *Archaeology in the north*. North Australia Research Unit (ANU), Darwin, pp. 319–40.

Bosworth, M. 1988. *Australian Lives. A history of clothing, food and domestic technology*. Thomas Nelson, Melbourne.

Bowdery, D. 1998. *Phytolith analysis applied to Pleistocene-Holocene archaeological sites in the Australian arid zone*. BAR (International Series) No. S695, Oxford.

Bowdler, S. 1976. Hook, line and dilly bag: An interpretation of an Australian coastal shell midden, *Mankind*, 10:248–58.

——1977. The coastal colonisation of Australia. In J. Allen, J. Golson and R. Jones (eds), *Sunda and Sahul*. Academic Press, London, pp. 204–46.

——1980. Fish and culture: A Tasmanian polemic, *Mankind*, 12:334–40.

——1981. Hunters in the highlands: Aboriginal adaptation in the eastern Australian uplands, *Archaeology in Oceania*, 16:99–111.

——1983. *An archaeological investigation of a threatened Aboriginal burial site near Robinvale, on the Murray River, Victoria*. Report to the Murray Valley Aboriginal Co-operative.

——1984. *Hunter Hill, Hunter Island. Archaeological investigations of a prehistoric Tasmanian site*. Terra Australis 8. Department of Prehistory, RSPacS, ANU, Canberra.

——1990. Some sort of dates at Malakunanja II: A reply to Roberts *et al.*, *Australian Archaeology*, 31:93.

——1991. Some sort of dates at Malakunanja II: A reply to Roberts *et al.*, *Australian Archaeology*, 32:50–51.

——1992a. *Homo sapiens* in Southeast Asia and the Antipodes: Archaeological versus biological interpretations. In T. Akazawa, K. Aoki and T. Kimura (eds), *The Evolution and Dispersal of Modern Humans in Asia*. Hokusen-sha Publishing Co, Tokyo, pp. 559–89.

——1992b. Unquiet slumbers: The return of the Kow Swamp burials, *Antiquity*, 66:103–06.

——1993. Views of the past in Australian prehistory. In M. Spriggs, D. E. Yen, W. Ambrose, R. Jones, A. Thorne and A. Andrews (eds), *A community of culture. The people and prehistory of the Pacific*. Department of Prehistory, RSPacS, ANU, Canberra, pp. 123–38.

——1995. Offshore islands and maritime explorations in Australian prehistory, *Antiquity*, 69:945–58.

Bowler, J. M. 1976. Recent developments in reconstructing late Quaternary environments in Australia. In R. C. Kirk and A. G. Thorne (eds), *The origins of the Australians*. AIAS, Canberra, pp. 55–75.

Bowler, J. M., R. Jones, H. Allen and A. G. Thorne 1970. Pleistocene human remains from Australia: A living site and human cremation from Lake Mungo, western New South Wales, *World Archaeology*, 2:39–60.

Bowler, J. M. and A. G. Thorne 1976. Human remains from Lake Mungo. Discovery and excavation of Lake Mungo III. In R. L. Kirk and A. G. Thorne (eds), *The origins of the Australians*. AIAS, Canberra, pp. 127–38.

Bowman, S. 1990. *Radiocarbon dating*. British Museum Publications, London.

Brady, M. 1987. Leaving the spinifex: The impact of rations, missions, and the atomic tests on the southern Pitjantjatjara, *Records of the South Australian Museum*, 20:35–45.

Brockwell, C. J. 1989. Archaeological investigations of the Kakadu wetlands, northern Australia. MA thesis, ANU, Canberra.

Brockwell, C. J., T. Gara, S. Colley and S. Cane 1989. The history and archaeology of Ooldea Soak and Mission, *Australian Archaeology*, 28:55–77.

Bronson, B. and J. C. White 1992. Radiocarbon and chronology in Southeast Asia. In R. W. Ehrich (ed.), *Chronologies in Old World archaeology*, Vol. 1. Chicago University Press, Chicago, pp. 491–503.

Brothwell, D. 1975. Possible evidence of a cultural practice affecting head growth in some Late Pleistocene East Asian and Australasian populations, *Journal of Archaeological Science*, 2:75–77.

Brown, Peter 1981. Artificial cranial deformation: A component in the variation in Pleistocene Australian crania, *Archaeology in Oceania*, 16:156–67.

——1987. Pleistocene homogeneity and Holocene size reduction: The Australian human skeletal evidence, *Archaeology in Oceania*, 22:41–71.

——1988. How the earliest Australians arrived, *Australian Natural History*, Supplement 2, pp. 52–57.

——1989. *Coobool Creek. A morphological and metrical analysis of the crania, mandibles and dentition of a prehistoric Australian human population*. Terra Australis 13. Department of Prehistory, RSPacS, ANU, Canberra.

——1992. Post-Pleistocene change in Australian Aboriginal tooth size: Dental reduction or relative expansion? In T. Brown and S. Molnar (eds), *Craniofacial variation in Pacific populations*. Anthropology and Genetics Laboratory, University of Adelaide, Adelaide, pp. 33–51.

——1994. A flawed vision: Sex and robusticity on King Island, *Australian Archaeology*, 38:1–7.

Brown, S. 1986. *Aboriginal archaeological resources in south east Tasmania. An overview of the nature and management of Aboriginal sites*. Occasional Papers 12. National Parks and Wildlife Service, Hobart, Tasmania.

——1987. *Towards a prehistory of the Hamersley Plateau, northwest Australia*. Occasional Papers in Prehistory 6. Department of Prehistory, RSPacS, ANU, Canberra.

——1991a. *Aboriginal archaeological sites in eastern Tasmania. A cultural resource management statement*. Occasional Paper 31, Department of Parks, Wildlife and Heritage, Hobart.

——1991b. Art and Tasmanian prehistory: Evidence for changing cultural traditions in a changing environment. In P. Bahn and A. Rosenfeld (eds), *Rock art and prehistory*. Oxbow Monograph 10, Oxbow Books, Oxford, pp. 96–108.

Bryant, E. A., R. W. Young, D. M. Price and S. A. Short 1992. Evidence for Pleistocene and Holocene raised marine deposits, Sandon Point, New South Wales, *Australian Journal of Earth Sciences*, 39:481–93.

Bull, J. W. 1884. *Early experiences of life in South Australia and an extended colonial history.* E. S. Wigg & Son, Adelaide.

Bulmer, S. 1977. Waisted blades and axes. A functional interpretation of some early stone tools from Papua New Guinea. In R. V. S. Wright (ed.), *Stone tools as cultural markers: Change, evolution and complexity.* AIAS, Canberra, pp. 40–59.

Bunt, J. S. 1987. The Australian marine environment. In G. R. Dyne and D. W. Walton (eds), *Fauna of Australia*, Vol. 1A, *General articles*. Australian Government Publishing Service, Canberra, pp. 17–42.

Bureau of Meteorology 1989. *Climate of Australia.* Australian Government Publishing Service, Canberra.

Burke, H., C. Lovell-Jones and C. Smith 1994. Beyond the looking-glass: Some thoughts on sociopolitics and reflexivity in Australian archaeology, *Australian Archaeology*, 38:13–22.

Butlin, N. G. 1983. *Our original aggression. Aboriginal populations of southeastern Australia 1788–1850.* George Allen and Unwin, Sydney.

——1989. The palaeoeconomic history of Aboriginal migration, *Australian Economic History Review*, 29:3–57.

——1993. *Economics and the Dreamtime: A hypothetical history.* Cambridge University Press, Cambridge.

Caldicott, E. 1991. Aboriginal art sites near Adelaide, South Australia. In C. Pearson and B. K. Swartz (eds), *Rock art and posterity. Conserving, managing and recording rock art.* Occasional AURA Publication 4. AURA, Melbourne, pp. 30–33.

Campbell, A. H. 1981. Tooth avulsion in Victorian Aboriginal skulls, *Archaeology in Oceania*, 16:116–18.

Campbell, J. 1983. Smallpox in Aboriginal Australia, 1829–31, *Historical Studies*, 20:536–56.

——1985. Smallpox in Aboriginal Australia, the early 1930s, *Historical Studies*, 21:336–58.

Campbell, T. D. and H. V. V. Noone 1943. South Australian microlithic stone implements, *Records of the South Australian Museum*, 7:281–306.

Campbell, W. D. 1899. *Aboriginal carvings of Port Jackson and Broken Bay.* Memoirs of the Geological Society of NSW, Ethnological Series, No. 1. Department of Mines and Agriculture, Sydney.

Cane, S. 1989. Australian Aboriginal seed grinding and its archaeological record: A case study from the Western Desert. In D. R. Harris and G. C. Hillman (eds), *Foraging and farming. The evolution of plant exploitation.* Unwin Hyman, London, pp. 99–119.

——1992. *Heritage values of the Nullarbor Plain.* Report to the Department of the Arts, Sport, the Environment and Territories, Australian Government, Canberra.

——1995. Nullarbor antiquity: Archaeological, luminescent and seismic investigations on the Nullarbor Plain. Report to the National Estate Grants Program, Australian Heritage Commission, Canberra.

Cann, R. L., M. Stoneking and A. C. Wilson 1987. Mitochondrial DNA and human evolution, *Nature*, 325:31–36.

Cense, A. A. 1952. Makassaars-Boeginese prauw-vaart op Noord-Australië, *Bijdragen tot de Taal-, Land- en Volkenkunde van Nederlandach-Indie*, 108:248–64.

Chaloupka, G. 1977. Aspects of the chronology and schematisation of two prehistoric sites on the Arnhem Land Plateau. In P. J. Ucko (ed.), *Form in indigenous art. Schematisation in the art of Aboriginal Australia and prehistoric Europe.* AIAS, Canberra, pp. 243–59.

——1983. Kakadu rock art: Its cultural, historic and prehistoric significance. In D. Gillespie (ed.), *The rock art of Kakadu National Park.* Australian National Parks and Wildlife Service, Special Publication 10, Canberra, pp. 3–33.

——1993. *Journey in time.* Reed Books, Sydney.

Chappell, J. 1982. Sea levels and sediments: Some features of the context of coastal archaeological sites in the tropics, *Archaeology in Oceania*, 17:69–78.

——1993. Late Pleistocene coasts and human migrations in the Austral region. In M. Spriggs, D. E. Yen, W. Ambrose, R. Jones, A. Thorne and A. Andrews (eds), *A community of culture. The people and prehistory of the Pacific*. Department of Prehistory, RSPacS, ANU, Canberra, pp. 43–48.

——1994. Upper Quaternary sea levels, coral terraces, oxygen isotopes and deep-sea temperatures, *Journal of Geography* (Beijing), 103:828–40.

Chappell, J., J. Head and J. Magee 1996. Beyond the radiocarbon limit in Australian archaeology and Quaternary research, *Antiquity*, 70:543–52.

Chatwin, B. 1987. *The Songlines*. Jonathon Cape, London.

Chesner, C. A., W. I. Rose, A. D. R. Drake and J. A. Westgate 1991. Eruptive history of Earth's largest Quaternary caldera (Toba, Indonesia) clarified, *Geology*, 19:200–03.

Churchill, D. M. 1968. The distribution and prehistory of *Eucalyptus diversicolor*, *Australian Journal of Botany*, 16:125–51.

Clark, D. J. 1979. The Gambieran stone tool industry. BA honours thesis, La Trobe University, Melbourne.

Clark, P. 1987. *Willandra Lakes World Heritage Area archaeological resource study*. Report to NSW Department of Environment and Planning, and Western Lands Commission of NSW.

Clark, R. L. 1983. Pollen and charcoal evidence for the effects of Aboriginal burning on the vegetation of Australia, *Archaeology in Oceania*, 18:32–37.

Clarke, A. 1985. A preliminary archaeobotanical analysis of the Anbangbang 1 site. In R. Jones (ed.), *Archaeological research in Kakadu National Park*. Australian National Parks and Wildlife Service, Special Publication 13, pp. 77–96.

——1988. Archaeological and ethnobotanical interpretations of plant remains from Kakadu National Park, Northern Territory. In B. Meehan and R. Jones (eds), *Archaeology with ethnography: An Australian perspective*. Department of Prehistory, RSPacS, Canberra, pp. 123–36.

Clarke, J. and C. E. Dortch 1977. A 10,000 radiocarbon date for archaeological finds within a soil of the Spearwood Dune System, Mosman Park, Western Australia, *Search*, 8:36–38.

Clarke, J. and N. North 1991. Pigment composition of post-estuarine rock art in Kakadu National Park. In C. Pearson and B. K. Swartz (eds), *Rock art and posterity. Conserving, managing and recording rock art*. Occasional AURA Publication 4. AURA, Melbourne, pp. 80–87.

Clegg, J. K. 1987. Style and tradition at Sturt's Meadow, *World Archaeology*, 19:236–55.

Cole, N. A. and B. David 1992. 'Curious drawings' at Cape York Peninsula, *Rock Art Research*, 9:3–26.

Cole, N. A. and A. Watchman 1993. Blue paints in prehistory, *Rock Art Research*, 10:58–61.

Cole, N. A., A. Watchman and M. J. Morwood 1994. Chronology of Laura rock art, *Tempus*, 3:147–60.

Colley, S. M. and R. Jones 1987. New fish bone data from Rocky Cape, north west Tasmania, *Archaeology in Oceania*, 22:41–47.

Connah, G. (ed.) 1983. *Australian field archaeology. A guide to techniques*. AIAS, Canberra.

Cook, N., I. Davidson and S. Sutton 1990. Why are so many ancient rock paintings red? *Australian Aboriginal Studies*, 1990/1:30–32.

Corbett, L. K. 1985. Morphological comparisons of Australian and Thai dingoes: A reappraisal of dingo status, distribution and ancestry, *Proceedings of the Ecological Society of Australia*, 13:277–91.

Cosgrove, R. 1984. Aboriginal settlement patterns in the Central Highlands, Tasmania. In S. Sullivan and S. Bowdler (eds), *Site surveys and significance in Australian archaeology*. Department of Prehistory, RSPacS, ANU, Canberra.

——1990. *The archaeological resources of Tasmanian forests: Past Aboriginal land use of forested environments*. Occasional Paper 27. National Parks and Wildlife Service, Hobart, Tasmania.

——1995a. Late Pleistocene behavioural variation and time trends: The case from Tasmania, *Archaeology in Oceania*, 30:83–104.

——1995b. *The illusion of riches. Scale, resolution and explanation in Tasmanian Pleistocene human behaviour*. BAR International Series No. 608. Oxford.

Cosgrove, R., J. Allen and B. Marshall 1990. Palaeo-ecology and Pleistocene human occupation in south central Tasmania, *Antiquity*, 64:59–78.

Cosgrove, R. and R. Jones 1989. Judds Cavern: A subterranean Aboriginal painting site, Southern Australia, *Rock Art Research*, 6:96–104.

Cotterell, B. and J. Kamminga 1987. The formation of flakes, *American Antiquity*, 52:675–708.

——1992. *Mechanics of pre-industrial technology. An introduction to the mechanics of ancient and traditional material culture*. Cambridge University Press, Cambridge.

Crawford, I. M. 1964. *The engravings of Depuch Island*. Western Australian Museum Special Publications, Perth.

——1968. *The art of the Wandjina*. Oxford University Press, Melbourne.

——1972. Function and change in Aboriginal rock art, Western Australia, *World Archaeology*, 3:301–12.

Crawfurd, J. 1820. *The history of the Indian archipelago*, 3 vols. Constable, Edinburgh.

——1856. *A descriptive dictionary of the Indian Islands and the adjacent countries*. London.

Cribb, R., R. Walmbeng, R. Wolmby and C. Taisman 1988. Landscape as cultural artefacts: Shell mounds and plants in Aurukun, Cape York Peninsula, *Australian Aboriginal Studies*, 1986/2:60–73.

Crowley, T. and R. M. W. Dixon 1981. Tasmanian. In R. M. W. Dixon and B. Blake (eds), *Handbook of Australian languages*. Cambridge University Press, Cambridge.

Cundy, B. J. 1990a. An analysis of the Ingaladdi assemblage: A critique of the understanding of lithic technology. PhD thesis, Department of Prehistory and Anthropology, ANU.

——1990b. The stone at the end of the world: Reduction process and organization on the Wilson Bluff flint source. Report to National Heritage Studies P/L, Canberra.

David, B. 1992. Cave paintings of the Mitchell-Palmer Limestone Belt: Preliminary results. In J. McDonald and I. P. Haskovec (eds), *State of the art. Regional rock art studies in Australia and Melanesia*. Occasional AURA Publication 5. AURA, Melbourne, pp. 76–82.

David, B. and D. Chant 1995. Rock art and regionalization in north Queensland prehistory, *Memoirs of the Queensland Museum*, 37:357–528.

David, B., I. McNiven, J. Flood, V. Attenbrow, J. Flood and J. Collins 1994. The Lightning Brothers and White Cockatoos: Dating the antiquity of signifying systems in the Northern Territory, *Antiquity*, 68:241–51.

David, B., R. Roberts, C. Tuniz, R. Jones and J. Head 1997. New optical and radiocarbon dates from Ngarrabullgan Cave, a Pleistocene archaeological site in Australia: Implications for the comparability of time clocks and for the human colonization of Australia, *Antiquity*, 71:183–88.

Davidson, D. S. 1933. Australian netting and basketry techniques, *Polynesian Society Journal*, 42:257–99.

——1934. Australian spear-traits and their derivations, *Polynesian Society Journal*, 43:41–72, 143–62.

——1935. The chronology of Australian watercraft, *Polynesian Society Journal*, 44:1–16, 69–84, 137–52, 193–207.

——1936. Australian throwing sticks, throwing clubs and boomerangs, *American Anthropologist*, 38:76–100.

Davidson, I. 1983. Beating about the bush? Aspects of the history of Australian archaeology, *Australian Archaeology*, 17:136–44.

Davidson, I., C. Lovel-Jones and R. Bancroft 1995. *Archaeologists and Aborigines working together*. University of New England Press, Armidale.

Davies, J. L. 1967. Tasmanian landforms and Quaternary climates. In J. N. Jennings and J. A. Mabbutt (eds), *Landform studies from Australia and New Guinea*. ANU Press, Canberra, pp. 1–25.

Dawson, J. 1881. *The Australian Aborigines*. Robertson, Melbourne.

Dickson, F. P. 1973. Backed blades and points, *Mankind*, 9:7–14.

——1981. *Australian stone hatchets. A study in design and dynamics*. Academic Press, Sydney.

Dix, W. and S. J. Meagher 1976. Fish traps in the south-west of Western Australia, *Records of the Western Australian Museum*, 4:171–87.

Dixon, R. M. W. 1972. *The Dyirbal language of north Queensland*. Cambridge University Press, Cambridge.

——1980. *The languages of Australia*. Cambridge University Press, Cambridge.

——In prep. *Australian languages*, Vol. 1. *Their nature and development*; Vol. 2. *A comprehensive catalogue*. Cambridge University Press, Cambridge.

Dodson, J. R. Fullagar and L. Head 1992. Dynamics of environment and people in the forested crescents of temperate Australia. In J. Dodson (ed.), *The naive lands. Prehistory and environmental change in Australia and the south-west Pacific.* Longman Cheshire, Melbourne, pp. 115–59.

Domanski, M. and J. A. Webb 1992. Effect of heat treatment on siliceous rocks used in prehistoric lithic technology, *Journal of Archaeological Science*, 19:601–14.

Dorn, M. 1984. Rock art in Olary Province, South Australia, *Rock Art Research*, 1:91–111.

Dortch, C. E. 1977. Early and late stone industrial phases in Western Australia. In R. V. S. Wright (ed.), *Stone tools as culture markers, change, evolution and complexity.* AIAS, Canberra, pp. 104–132.

——1979. Devil's Lair, an example of prolonged cave use in Western Australia, *World Archaeology*, 10:258–79.

——1984. *Devil's Lair, a study in prehistory.* Western Australian Museum, Perth.

——1991. Rottnest and Garden Island prehistory and the archaeological potential of the adjacent continental shelf, Western Australia, *Australian Archaeology*, 33:38–43.

——1997. Prehistory down under: Investigations of submerged Aboriginal sites at Lake Jasper, W.A., *Antiquity*, 71:116–23.

Dortch, C. E. and J. Dortch 1996. Review of Devil's Lair artefact classification and radiocarbon chronology, *Australian Archaeology*, 43:28–31.

Dortch, C. E. and G. Gardner 1976. Archaeological investigations in the Northcliffe District, Western Australia, *Records of the Western Australian Museum*, 4:257–93.

Dortch, C. E., G. Kendrick and K. Morse 1984. Aboriginal mollusc exploitation in southwestern Australia, *Archaeology in Oceania*, 19:81–104.

Dortch, C. E. and W. M. McArthur 1985. Apparent association of Bryozoan chert artefacts and quartz geometric microliths at an open-air site, Arumvale, southwestern Western Australia, *Australian Archaeology*, 38:45–46.

Dortch, C. E. and D. Merrilees 1973. Human occupation at Devil's Lair, W.A., during the Pleistocene, *Archaeology and Physical Anthropology in Oceania*, 8:89–115.

Dortch, C. E. and K. Morse 1984. Prehistoric stone artefacts on some offshore islands in Western Australia, *Australian Archaeology*, 19:31–47.

Dortch, C. E. and B. G. Muir 1980. Long-range sightings of bush fires as a possible incentive for Pleistocene voyages to greater Australia, *Western Australian Naturalist*, 14:194–98.

Dortch, J. 1996. Late Pleistocene and recent Aboriginal occupation of Tunnel Cave and Witchcliffe Rock Shelter, south-western Australia, *Australian Aboriginal Studies*, 1996/II:51–60.

Dowling, P. J. 1992. When urban dwellers meet hunter-gatherers: Impact of introduced infectious disease on Aboriginal Australians, *Proceedings of the Australasian Society for Human Biology*, 5:39–46.

Downey, B. and D. Frankel 1992. Radiocarbon and thermoluminescence dating of a central Murray mound, *The Artefact*, 15:31–35.

Draper, N. 1988. Stone tools and cultural landscapes: Investigating the archaeology of Kangaroo Island, *South Australian Geographical Journal*, 88:15–36.

——1991. Cape Du Couedic Rockshelter and the Aboriginal archaeology of Kangaroo Island, South Australia. PhD dissertation, Department of Anthropology, University of New Mexico, Albuquerque.

——*In press.* The history of Aboriginal land use in Kangaroo Island. In A. C. Robinson (ed.), *A biological survey of Kangaroo Island.* Department of Environment and Natural Resources, Adelaide.

du Cros, H. and L. Smith (eds) 1993. *Women in Archaeology. A Feminist Critique.* Department of Prehistory, RSPacS, ANU, Canberra.

Dunnett, G. 1992. Prion Beach Rockshelter: Seabirds and offshore islands in southwest Tasmania, *Australian Archaeology*, 34:22–28.

——1993. Diving for dinner: Some implications from Holocene middens for the role of coasts in the late Pleistocene of Tasmania. In M. A. Smith, M. Spriggs and B. Fankhauser (eds), *Sahul in review.* Department of Prehistory, RSPacS, ANU, Canberra, pp. 247–57.

Earl, G. W. 1853. *The native races of the Indian archipelago.* Builliers, London.

——1882. Handbook for colonists in tropical Australia. Revers, London.

Edwards, R. 1963. Preliminary survey of the Aboriginal reniform slate scrapers of South Australia, *Records of the South Australian Museum*, 14:515–24.

——1966. Comparative study of rock engravings in South and Central Australia, *Proceedings of the Royal Society of South Australia*, 90:33–38.

Feary, S. 1996. An Aboriginal burial with grave goods near Cooma, New South Wales, *Australian Archaeology*, 43:40–42.

Fenner, F. J. 1939. The Australian Aboriginal skull: Its non-metrical morphological characteristics, *Transactions of the Royal Society of South Australia*, 63:248–306.

Ferguson, W. C. 1980. Fossiliferous chert in southwestern Australia after the Holocene transgression: A behavioural hypothesis, *The Artefact*, 5:155–69.

——1981. Archaeological investigations at the Quinnup Brook site complex, Western Australia, *Records of the Western Australian Museum*, 8:609–37.

——1985. A mid-Holocene depopulation of the Australian southwest. PhD thesis, ANU, Canberra.

Fitzgerald, C. P. 1953. The Chinese discovery of Australia? In T. I. Moore (ed.), *Australia writes*. Cheshire, Melbourne.

Fitzpatrick, E. A. 1979. Australia. In *Map of the world distribution of arid regions. Explanatory Note*. UNESCO, Paris, pp. 32–38.

Flannery, T. F. 1990a. Pleistocene faunal loss: Implications for the aftershock for Australia's past and future, *Archaeology in Oceania*, 25:45–76.

——1990b. *Mammals of New Guinea*. Robert Brown & Associates, Carina.

——1994. *The future eaters*. Reed Books, Sydney.

Flannery, T. F., M. J. Mountain and K. Aplin 1983. Quaternary kangaroos (Macropodidae Marsupialia) from Nombe Rock Shelter, Papua New Guinea, with comments on the nature of megafaunal extinction in the New Guinea Highlands, *Proceedings of the Linnean Society of New South Wales*, 107:75–97.

Fleming, P. M. 1984. The ecological well-being of the Murray–Darling Basin. Paper presented at the Australian Institute of Political Science Conference, 'Governing the Murray–Darling Basin', 29 September 1984, Canberra.

——1994a. Water resources. In S. Bambrick (ed.), *Cambridge Encyclopaedia of Australia*. Cambridge University Press, Cambridge, pp. 15–17.

——1994b. The hydroecology of the Australian arid zone. Hydrological impact of desertification, November 1994. Report to WMO, Division of Water Resources, Geneva.

Flenniken, J. J. and J. P. White 1983. Heat treatment of siliceous rocks and its implications for Australian prehistory, *Australian Aboriginal Studies*, 1983/1:43–48.

Flinders, M. 1814. *A voyage to Terra Australis*, 2 vols. Nicol, London.

Flood, J. M. 1980. *The moth-hunters*. AIAS, Canberra.

——1997. *Rock art of the Dreaming: Images of ancient Australia*. Angus and Robertson, Sydney.

Flood, J. M., B. David, J. Magee and B. English 1987. Birrigai: A Pleistocene site in the south-eastern highlands, *Archaeology in Oceania*, 22:9–26.

Flood, J. M. and N. Horsfall 1986. Excavation of Green Ant and Echidna Shelters, Cape York Peninsula, *Queensland Archaeological Research*, 3:4–64.

Forbes, S. 1982. Aboriginal rock engravings at N'Dhala Gorge. B.Litt. thesis, ANU, Canberra.

——1983. Aboriginal rock engravings at N'Dhala Gorge, Northern Territory. In M. Smith (ed.), *Archaeology at ANZAAS 1983*. Department of Anthropology, Western Australian Museum, Perth, pp. 199–213.

Frakes, L. A., B. McGowran and J. M. Bowler 1987. Evolution of Australian environments. In G. R. Dyne and D. W. Walton (eds), *Fauna of Australia*. Vol. 1A. *General articles*. Australian Government Publishing Service, Canberra, pp. 1–16.

Frankel, D. 1982. Earth rings at Sunbury, Victoria, *Archaeology in Oceania*, 17:83–89.

——1991. *Remains to be seen. Archaeological insights into Australian prehistory.* Longman Cheshire, Melbourne.

——1993. Pleistocene chronological structures and explanations: A challenge. In M. A. Smith, M. Spriggs and B. Fankhauser (eds), *Sahul in review.* Department of Prehistory, RSPacS, ANU, Canberra, pp. 24–33.

Frankel, D. and J. Kamminga 1995. *Careers Information. Archaeology.* Graduate Careers Council of Australia Ltd, Parkville, Vic.

Franklin, N. 1991. Rock art and prehistory: Explorations of the Panaramitee style. In P. Bahn and A. Rosenfeld (eds), *Rock art and prehistory.* Oxbow Monograph 10, Oxbow Books, Oxford, pp. 120–35.

Frayer, D. W., M. H. Wolpoff, A. G. Thorne, F. H. Smith and G. G. Pope 1993. Theories of modern human origins: The paleontological test, *American Antiquity,* 95:14–50.

Freedman, L. and M. Lofgren 1979. The Cossack skull and dihybrid origins of the Australian Aborigines, *Nature,* 282:298–300.

——1983. Human skeletal remains from Lake Tandou, New South Wales, *Archaeology in Oceania,* 18:98–103.

Fujiwara, H., R. Jones and S. Brockwell 1985. Plant opals (phytoliths) in Kakadu archaeological sites: A preliminary report. In R. Jones (ed.), *Archaeological research in Kakadu National Park.* Australian National Parks and Wildlife Service, Special Publication 13, pp. 155–64.

Fullagar, R. L. K., J. H. Furby and L. Brass 1994. Use-wear and residue analysis of stone tools from Bulga. In Bulga Lease Authorisation 219 salvage excavations. A report to Saxonvale Coal Pty Ltd, by M. Koettig. Vol. 5, pp. 26–105.

Fullagar, R. L. K., D. M. Price and L. M. Head 1996. Early human occupation of northern Australia: Archaeology and thermoluminescence dating of Jinmium rock-shelter, Northern Territory, *Antiquity,* 70:751–73.

Fullagar, R. L. K. and J. H. Furby 1997. Pleistocene seed-grinding implements from the arid zone, *Antiquity,* 71:300–7.

Furby, J. H. 1995. Megafauna under the microscope: Archaeology and palaeoenvironment at Cuddie Springs. PhD thesis, University of New South Wales.

Galloway, R. W. 1988. The potential impact of climate changes on Australian ski fields. In *Greenhouse: Planning for climate change.* CSIRO and Brill, Melbourne, pp. 428–37.

——1989. Glacial and periglacial features of the Australian Alps. In R. Good (ed.), *The scientific significance of the Australian Alps.* Australian Alps National Parks Liaison Committee, pp. 55–67.

Gallup, C. D., R. L. Edwards and R. G. Johnson 1994. The timing of high sea levels over the past 200,000 years, *Science,* 263:796–800.

Gallus, A. 1983. Excavations at Keilor, Victoria. Report No. 3. Excavations in the 'D' clay, *The Artefact,* 8:11–41.

Garling, S. J. 1994 What *was* the menu at Cuddie Springs? Hemoglobin crystallisation of blood residues on stone tools. BA(Hons) thesis, University of Sydney.

——*n.d.* Myth-making in the late Pleistocene: Are notions of human behaviour in the blitzkrieg model derived from fact or fiction? Ms for publication.

Gaughwin, D. 1985. An archaeological reconnaissance survey of the Tasman Peninsula, February 1984, *Australian Archaeology,* 20:38–57.

Gaughwin, D. and R. Fullagar 1995. Victorian offshore islands in a mainland coastal economy, *Australian Archaeology,* 40:38–50.

Gibbons, A. 1996. *Homo erectus* in Java: A 250,000-year anachronism, *Science,* 274:1841–42.

Gibbs, M. 1987. Aboriginal gatherings in the west coastal region of southwest Western Australia: An ethnohistorical study. BA(Hons) thesis, University of Western Australia.

Gillieson, D. S and J. Hall 1982. Bevelling bungwall bashers. A use-wear study from southeast Queensland, *Australian Archaeology,* 14:43–66.

Gillieson, D. S. and M. J. Mountain 1983. Environmental history of Nombe Rockshelter, Papua New Guinea Highlands, *Archaeology in Oceania*, 18:53–62.

Glover, J. E. 1984. The geological sources of stone for artefacts in the Perth Basin and nearby areas, *Australian Aboriginal Studies*, 1984/II:17–25.

Godwin, L. 1990. Inside information: Settlement and alliance in the late Holocene of northeastern New South Wales. PhD thesis, University of New England, Armidale.

Golson, J. 1971. Australian Aboriginal food plants: Some ecological and culture-historical implications. In D. J. Mulvaney and J. Golson (eds), *Aboriginal man and environment in Australia*. ANU Press, Canberra, pp. 196–232.

——1993. The last days of Pompeii? In M. A. Smith, M. Spriggs and B. Fankhauser (eds), *Sahul in review*. Department of Prehistory, RSPacS, ANU, Canberra, pp. 275–80.

Gott, B. 1983. Murnong—*Microseris scapigera*: A study of a staple food of Victorian Aborigines, *Australian Aboriginal Studies*, 1983/II:2–18.

——1992. Plant resources available to the Tasmanian Aborigines. TASUSE Computer Database. AIATSIS, Canberra.

Gott, B. and K. Geering 1989. Plant food available in Victorian alpine areas contiguous with Kosciusko National Park. In J. Kamminga, R. Paton and I. Macfarlane, *Archaeological investigations in the Thredbo Valley, Snowy Mountains*. Report to Faraba Pty Ltd. ANUTECH, Canberra, Appendix A.

Gould, R. A. 1969a. Puntutjarpa Rockshelter: A reply to Messrs Glover and Lampert, *Archaeology and Physical Anthropology in Oceania*, 4:229–37.

——1969b. Subsistence behaviour among the Western Desert Aborigines of Australia, *Oceania*, 39:253–74.

Gray, A. (ed.) 1937. *William Dampier, A new voyage round the world*. Adam & Charles Black, London.

Grey, G. 1841. *Journals of two expeditions of discovery*. Boone, London.

Griffiths, M., R. T. Wells and D. J. Barrie 1991. Observations on the skulls of fossil and extant echidnas (Monotremata: Tachyglossidae), *Australian Mammalogy*, 14:87–101.

Griffiths, T. 1996. *Hunters and collectors. The antiquarian imagination in Australia*. Cambridge University Press, Cambridge.

Groube, L., J. Chappell, J. Muke and D. Price 1986. A 40 000-year-old human occupation site at Huon Peninsula, Papua New Guinea, *Nature*, 324:453–55.

Groves, C. P. 1976. The origin of the mammalian fauna of Sulawesi (Celebes), *Zeitschrift Sp. für Säugetierkunde*, 41:201–16.

——1989a. A regional approach to the problem of the origin of modern humans in Australia. In P. Mellars and C. S. Stringer (eds), *The Human revolution: Behavioural and biological perspectives in the origins of modern humans*. Edinburgh University Press, Edinburgh, pp. 274–85.

——1989b. *A theory of human and primate evolution*. Clarendon Press, Oxford.

——1990. New look at old remains, *ANU Reporter*, 25 February, p. 9.

Groves, C. P. and M. M Lahr 1994. A bush is not a ladder: Speciation and replacement in human evolution. In L. Freedman, J. N. Jablonsky and N. W. Bruce (eds), *Perspectives in human biology*. Centre for human biology, University of Western Australia, Nedlands, pp. 1–11.

Gunn, R. G. 1983. *Garden Range 1*. Victoria Archaeological Survey, Occasional Report Series 18. Ministry for Planning and Environment, Melbourne.

——1984. The rock art areas of Victoria: An initial comparison, *Aboriginal History*, 8:189–202.

Habgood, P. J. 1986. The origin of the Australians: A multivariate approach, *Archaeology in Oceania*, 21:130–37.

Haglund, L. 1976. *An archaeological analysis of the Broadbeach Aboriginal burial ground*. University of Queensland Press, St Lucia.

Hall, J. 1982. Sitting on the crop of the bay: An historical and archaeological sketch of Aboriginal subsistence and settlement in Moreton Bay, southeast Queensland. In S. Bowdler (ed.), *Coastal archaeology in eastern Australia*. Department of Prehistory, RSPacS, ANU, Canberra, pp. 79–95.

Hallam, S. J. 1975. *Fire and hearth*. AIAS, Canberra.

——1987. Coastal does not equal littoral, *Australian Archaeology*, 27:10–29.

Hamilton, A. 1980. Dual systems: Technology, labour and women's secret rites in the eastern Western Desert of Australia, *Oceania*, 51:4–19.

Harris, P. T., E. K. Baker and A. R. Cole 1992. Late Quaternary sedimentation at the Fly River–Great Barrier Reef Junction (northwestern Australia). In R. H. Richmond (ed.), *Proceedings of the Seventh International Coral Reef Symposium, Guam*, Vol. 2. University of Guam Marine Laboratory, Mangilao, Guam, pp. 1146–56.

Haskovec, I. P. 1992. Mt Gilruth revisited, *Archaeology in Oceania*, 27:75–86.

Hayden, B. 1973. Analysis of a 'Taap' knife, *Archaeology and Physical Anthropology in Oceania*, 8:116–26.

——1975. Dingo. Pets or producers? *Mankind*, 10:11–15.

——1992. *Archaeology. The science of once and future things*. W. H. Freeman and Co, New York.

Head, L. 1994a. Landscape socialised by fire: Post-contact changes in Aboriginal fire use in northern Australia, and implications for prehistory, *Archaeology in Oceania*, 29:172–81.

——1994b. Both ends of the candle? Discerning human impact on the vegetation, *Australian Archaeology*, 39:82–86.

Heeres, J. E. 1899. *The part borne by the Dutch in the discovery of Australia 1660–1765*. Luzac, London.

Henderson, G. 1986. *Maritime archaeology in Australia*. University of Western Australia Press, Nedlands.

Hercus, L. 1980. 'How we danced the Mudlunga': Memories of 1901 and 1902, *Aboriginal History*, 4:5–32.

Hiatt, B. 1969. Cremation in Aboriginal Australia, *Mankind*, 7:104–19.

Hiscock, P. 1988. Prehistoric settlement patterns and artefact manufacture at Lawn Hill, northwest Queensland. PhD thesis, Department of Anthropology and Sociology, University of Queensland.

——1993a. Bondaian technology in the Hunter Valley, New South Wales, *Archaeology in Oceania*, 28:65–76.

——1993b. Interpreting the vertical distribution of stone points within Nauwalabila 1, Arnhem Land, *The Beagle*, 10:173–78.

——1994. Technological responses to risk in the Holocene Australia, *Journal of World Archaeology*, 8:267–92.

——1996. Mobility and technology in the Kakadu coastal wetlands, *Indo-Pacific Prehistory Association Bulletin*, 15:151–57.

Hiscock, P. and P. Kershaw 1994. Palaeoenvironments and prehistory of Australia's tropical Top End. In J. Dodson (ed.), *The naive lands*. Longman Cheshire, Melbourne, pp. 43–75.

Hiscock, P. and S. Mitchell 1993. *Stone artefact quarries and reduction sites in Australia: Towards a type profile*. Technical Publication Series No. 4. Australian Heritage Commission, Canberra.

Hogarth, M. and L. Dayton 1997. By whose hand? *Good Weekend, The Sydney Morning Herald Magazine*, 21 June, pp. 30–35.

Holdaway, S. 1995. Review of 'Islands of the interior. The dynamics of prehistoric adaptations within the arid zone of Australia', *Archaeology in Oceania*, 30:43–45.

Hooton, E. A. 1947. *Up from the apes*. Macmillan, New York.

Hope, G. S. 1978. The late Pleistocene and Holocene vegetation history of Hunter Island, north-west Tasmania, *Australian Journal of Botany*, 26:493–514.

——1989. Climatic implications of timberline changes in Australasia from 30,000 yr BP to present. In T. H. Donnelly and R. J. Wasson (eds), *CLIMANZ 3*. Division of Water Resources, CSIRO, Canberra, pp. 91–99.

——1994. Quaternary vegetation. In R. S. Hill (ed.), *History of the Australian vegetation: Cretaceous to recent*. Cambridge University Press, Cambridge, pp. 368–89.

Hope, G. S., J. Golson and J. Allen 1983. Palaeoecology and prehistory in New Guinea, *Journal of Human Evolution*, 12:37–60.

Hope, G. S., P. J. Hughes and J. Russell-Smith 1985. Geomorphological fieldwork and the evolution of the landscape of Kakadu National Park. In R. Jones (ed.), *Archaeological research in Kakadu National Park*. Australian National Parks and Wildlife Service, Special Publication 13, pp. 229–40.

Hope, J., A. Dare-Edwards and M. McIntire 1983. Middens and megafauna: Stratigraphy and dating of Lake Tandou lunette, western NSW, *Archaeology in Oceania*, 18:54–53.

Horne, G. A. and G. Aiston 1924. *Savage life in Central Australia*. Macmillan, London.

Horsfall, N. 1982. Stone tools from the Keppel Islands, *Australian Archaeology*, 14:72–78.

Horton, D. R. 1979. Tasmanian adaptation, *Mankind*, 12:28–34.

——1981. Water and woodland: The peopling of Australia, *AIAS Newsletter*, N.S. 16:21–27.

——1982. The burning question: Aborigines, fire and Australian ecosystems, *Mankind*, 13:237–51.

——1984. Red kangaroos: Last of the megafauna. In P. S. Martin and R. G. Klein (eds), *Quaternary extinctions: A prehistoric revolution*. University of Arizona Press, Tucson, pp. 639–79.

——1986. Seasons of repose: Environment and culture in the late Pleistocene of Australia. In A. Aspimon (ed.), *Pleistocene perspectives*. Vol. 2. Allen and Unwin, London, pp. 1–14.

——(ed.) 1991. *Recovering the tracks. The story of Australian archaeology*. Aboriginal Studies Press, Canberra.

——(ed.) 1994. *The Encyclopaedia of Aboriginal Australia*. Aboriginal Studies Press, Canberra.

Horton, D. R. and R. V. S. Wright 1981. Cuts on Lancefield bones: Carnivorous Thylacoleo, not humans, the cause, *Archaeology in Oceania*, 16:73–80.

Howells, W. W. 1973. *The Pacific Islanders*. Reed, Wellington.

——1976. Metrical analysis in the problem of Australian origins. In R. L. Kirk and A. G. Thorne (eds), *The origins of the Australians*. AIAS, Canberra, pp. 141–60.

——1989. *Skull shapes and the map. Craniometric analyses on the dispersion of modern Homo*. Peabody Museum of Archaeology and Ethnology, Harvard University, Cambridge, Mass.

Huchet, B. M. J. 1990. The identification of cicatrices depicted on anthropomorphs in the Laura region, north Queensland, *Rock Art Research*, 7:27–43.

——1991. Theories and Australian prehistory: The last three decades, *Australian Archaeology*, 33:44–51.

——1993. A spatial analysis of anthropomorphs at rock art of the Laura area, Australia. In J. Steinbring, A. L. Watchman, P. Faultich and P. S. C. Taçon, *Time and Space*, Occasional AURA Publication 8. AURA, Melbourne, pp. 92–100.

Irwin, G. 1991. Pleistocene voyaging and the settlement of Greater Australia and its nearer oceanic islands. In J. Allen and C. Gosden (eds), *Report of the Lapita Homeland Project*, Occasional Papers in Prehistory 20. Department of Prehistory, RSPacS, ANU, Canberra, pp. 9–19.

Jennings, J. N. 1972. In D. Walker (ed.), *Bridge and barrier: The natural and cultural history of Torres Strait*. Department of Biogeography and Geomorphology, RSPacS, ANU, pp. 29–38.

Johnson, D. L. 1980. Problems in the land vertebrate zoogeography of certain islands and the swimming powers of elephants, *Journal of Biogeography*, 7:383–98.

Johnson, H. 1993. Pleistocene shell middens of the Willandra Lakes. In M. A. Smith, M. Spriggs and B. Fankhauser (eds), *Sahul in review*. Department of Prehistory, RSPacS, ANU, Canberra, pp. 197–203.

Johnson, I. 1979. The getting of data: A case study from the recent industries of Australia. PhD thesis, ANU, Canberra.

Johnson, K. 1992. *The AUSMAP atlas of Australia*. AUSLIG and Cambridge University Press, Canberra.

Jones, R. 1966. A speculative archaeological sequence for north-west Tasmania, *Records of the Queen Victoria Museum*, Launceston, 25:1–12.

——1969. Fire stick farming, *Australian Natural History*, 16:224–28.

——1970. Tasmanian Aborigines and dogs, *Mankind*, 7:256–71.

——1973. Emerging picture of Pleistocene Australians, *Nature*, 246:278–81.

——1974. Tasmanian tribes. In N. B. Tindale (ed.), *Aboriginal tribes of Australia*. University of California, Berkeley, pp. 317–54.

——1976. Tasmania: Aquatic machines and offshore islands. In G. de G. Sieveking, I. H. Longworth and K. E. Wilson (eds), *Problems in economic and social archaeology*. Duckworth, Cambridge, pp. 253–63.

——1977a. Man as an element of a continental fauna: The case of the sundering of the Bassian Bridge. In J. Allen, J. Golson and R. Jones (eds), *Sunda and Sahul*. Academic Press, London, pp. 317–86.

——1977b. The Tasmanian paradox. In R. V. S. Wright (ed.), *Stone tools as cultural markers: Change, evolution and complexity*. AIAS, Canberra, pp. 189–204.

——1978. Why did the Tasmanians stop eating fish? In R. A. Gould (ed.), *Explorations in archaeology*. University of New Mexico Press, Albuquerque, pp. 11–47.

——1979. The fifth continent: Problems concerning the human colonization of Australia, *Annual Review of Anthropology*, 8:445–66.

——1984. Hunters and history: A case study from western Tasmania. In C. Schrire (ed.), *Past and present in hunter gatherer studies*. Academic Press, Orlando, Florida, pp. 27–65.

——(ed.) 1985. *Archaeological research in Kakadu National Park*. Australian National Parks and Wildlife Service, Special Publication 13.

—— 1988. Images of Natural Man. In J. Bonnemains, E. Forsyth and B. Smith (eds), *Baudin in Australian waters*. Oxford University Press, Melbourne, pp. 35–64.

——1989. East of Wallace's Line: Issues and problems in the colonisation of the Australian continent. In P. Mellars and C. Stringer (eds), *The human revolution. Behavioural and biological perspectives on the origins of modern humans*. Edinburgh University Press, Edinburgh, pp. 743–82.

——1990. From Kakadu to Kutikina: The southern continent at 18 000 years ago. In C. Gamble and O. Sofer (eds), *The World at 18 000 BP*, Vol. 2, *Low Latitudes*. Unwin Hyman, London, pp. 265–95.

——1993. A continental reconnaissance: Some observations concerning the discovery of the Pleistocene archaeology of Australia. In M. Spriggs, D. E. Yen, W. Ambrose, R. Jones, A. Thorne and A. Andrews (eds), *A community of culture. The people and prehistory of the Pacific*. Department of Prehistory, RSPacS, ANU, Canberra, pp. 97–122.

Jones, R. and J. Allen 1984. Archaeological investigations in the Andrew River valley, Acheron River valley and at Precipitous Bluff—southwest Tasmania—February 1984, *Australian Archaeology*, 19:86–101.

Jones, R. and I. Johnson 1985. Deaf Adder Gorge: Lindner Site, Nauwalabila 1. In Rhys Jones (ed.), *Archaeological research in Kakadu National Park*. Australian National Parks and Wildlife Service, Special Publication 13, pp. 165–223.

Jones, R. and N. White 1988. Point blank: Stone tool manufacture at the Ngilipitji Quarry, Arnhem Land, 1981. In B. Meehan and R. Jones (eds), *Archaeology with ethnography: An Australian perspective*. Department of Prehistory, RSPacS, Canberra, pp. 51–87.

Kamminga, J. 1971. Microscopic and experimental study of Australian Aboriginal stone tools. BA(Hons) thesis, Department of Anthropology, University of Sydney.

——1977. Functional study of an Australian tool type: The elouera. In R. V. S. Wright (ed.), *Stone tools as cultural markers: Change, evolution and complexity*. AIAS, Canberra, pp. 205–12.

——1978. Journey into the microcosms. A functional analysis of certain classes of prehistoric Australian stone tools. PhD thesis, Department of Anthropology, University of Sydney.

——1980. A functional investigation of Australian microliths, *The Artefact*, 5:1–18.

——1981. The bevelled pounder: An Aboriginal stone tool type from southeast Queensland, *Proceedings of the Royal Society of Queensland*, 92:31–34.

——1982. *Over the Edge. Functional analysis of Australian stone tools*. Occasional Papers in Anthropology 12. Anthropology Museum, University of Queensland.

——1984. A recent prehistoric bone point from Site LR–1. In R. L. Vanderwal and D. R. Horton, *Coastal Southwest Tasmania. The prehistory of Louisa Bay and Maatsuyker Island*, Terra Australis 9. Department of Prehistory RSPacS, ANU, Canberra.

——1985. The pirri graver, *Australian Aboriginal Studies*, 1985/II:2–25.

——1988. Wood artefacts: A checklist of plant species utilised by the Australian Aborigines, *Australian Aboriginal Studies*, 1988/II:26–59.

——1992a. New interpretations of the Upper Cave, Zhoukoudian. In T. Akazawa, K. Aoki and T. Kimura (eds), *The Evolution and Dispersal of Modern Humans in Asia*. Hokusen-sha Publishing Co, Tokyo, pp. 379–400.

——1992b. Aboriginal settlement and prehistory of the Snowy Mountains. In B. Scougall (ed.), *Cultural Heritage of the Australian Alps*. Australian Alps National Parks Liaison Committee, Canberra, pp. 101–24.

——1994. Technology. In D. R. Horton (ed.), *Encyclopedia of Aboriginal Australia*. AIATSIS, Canberra, pp. 1056–60.

——1995. Prehistory of the Snowy Mountains, southeastern Australia. In E. Johnson (ed.), *Ancient peoples and landscapes*, Museum of Texas Tech University, Lubbock, pp. 153–71.

——*forthcoming*. The stone assemblage from Sai Yok 1 and the question of Hoabinhian horticulture in Southeast Asia. In M. Santoni, Ha Van Tan and S. Pookajorn (eds), *Proceedings of The Hoabinhian 60 years after Madeleine Colani Anniversary Conference*, 28 December 1993 to 3 January 1994, Hanoi.

Kamminga, J. and H. R. Allen 1973. *Report on the archaeological survey. The Alligator River Fact-Finding Study*. Government Printer, Darwin.

Keen, I. 1988. Aborigines and Islanders in Australian society. In J. M. Najman and J. S. Western (eds), *A sociology of Australian society*. University of Queensland, St Lucia, pp. 182–212.

Kefous, K. 1988. Butlin's bootstraps: Aboriginal population in the pre-contact Murray–Darling region. In B. Meehan and R. Jones (eds), *Archaeology with ethnography: An Australian perspective*. Department of Prehistory, RSPacS, ANU, Canberra, pp. 225–37.

Kendrick, G. W. 1977. Middle Holocene marine molluscs from near Guilford, Western Australia, and evidence for climatic change, *Journal of the Royal Society of Western Australia*, 59:97–104.

Kershaw, A. P. 1994. Pleistocene vegetation of the humid tropics on northeastern Queensland, *Palaeogeography, Palaeoclimatology, Palaeoecology*, 109:399–412.

Kershaw, A. P. and K. M. Strickland 1989. The Development of Alpine Vegetation on the Australian mainland. In R. Good (ed.), *The Scientific significance of the Australian Alps*, Australian Alps National Parks Liaison Committee, Canberra, pp. 113–26.

Key, C. A. 1969. Archaeological pottery in Arnhem Land, *Archaeology and Physical Anthropology in Oceania*, 4:103–06.

Kiernan, K. 1990. The extent of late Cenozoid glaciation in the central highlands of Tasmania, Australia, *Arctic and Alpine Research*, 22:341–54.

Kiernan, K., R. Jones and D. Ranson 1983. New evidence from Fraser Cave for glacial age man in southwest Tasmania, *Nature*, 301:28–32.

Kimber, R. G. 1983. Black lightning: Aborigines and fire in central Australia and the Western Desert, *Archaeology in Oceania*, 18:38–45.

King, P. P. 1827. *A survey of the intertropical and western coasts of Australia, 1818–1822*, 2 vols. Murray, London.

Kinhill Engineers Pty Ltd 1995. Aboriginal heritage investigations. Supplementary environmental studies. Borefield B Development. Olympic Dam operations. Report to WMC (Olympic Dam Corporation) Pty Ltd.

Kirk, R. L. 1981. *Aboriginal man adapting. The human biology of Australian Aborigines*. Oxford University Press, Melbourne.

Kirk, R. L. and A. G. Thorne (eds) 1976. *The origin of the Australians*. AIAS, Canberra.

Kitchener, D. J., C. L. Boeadi and Maharadatunkamsi 1990. *Wild animals of Lombok Island: Nusa Tenggara, Indonesia: Systematics and natural history*. Records of the Western Australian Museum, Supplement No. 33.

Knight, T. 1996. *The Batemans Bay Forests Archaeological Project. Site distribution analysis*. Department of Archaeology and Anthropology, ANU, Canberra.

Kohen, J. L. 1987. Prehistoric settlement in the Western Cumberland Plain: Resources, environment and technology. PhD thesis, Macquarie University, NSW.

——1988. The Dharug of the western Cumberland Plain: Ethnography and demography. In B. Meehan and R. Jones (eds), *Archaeology with ethnography: An Australian perspective*. Department of Prehistory, RSPacS, Canberra, pp. 238–49.

Kohen, J. L. and R. Lampert 1987. Hunters and fishers in the Sydney region. In D. J. Mulvaney and J. P. White (eds), *Australians: A historical library. Australians to 1788*. Fairfax, Syme and Weldon Associates, Sydney, pp. 342–65.

Kolig, E. 1973. Aboriginal man's best foe?, *Mankind*, 9:122–23.

Lahr, M. M. 1994. The multiregional model of modern human origins, *Journal of Human Evolution*, 26:23–56.

Lampert, R. J. 1966. An excavation at Durras North, New South Wales, *Archaeology and Physical Anthropology in Oceania*, 1:84–118.

——1971. *Burrill Lake and Currarong*. Terra Australis 1. Department of Prehistory, RSPacS, ANU, Canberra.

——1981. *The Great Kartan Mystery*. Terra Australis 5. Department of Prehistory, RSPacS, ANU, Canberra.

——1983. Waisted blades in Australia?, *Records of the Australian Museum*, 35:145–51.

——1985. Archaeological reconnaissance on a field trip to Dalhousie Springs, *Australian Archaeology*, 21:57–62.

Lampert, R. J. and P. J. Hughes 1987. The Flinders Ranges: A Pleistocene outpost in the arid zone?, *Records of the South Australian Museum*, 20:29–34.

——1988. Early human occupation of the Flinders Ranges, *Records of the South Australian Museum*, 22:139–68.

Langford, R. 1983. Our heritage—your playground, *Australian Archaeology*, 16:1–6.

Langford-Smith, T. 1983. New perspectives on the Australian deserts, *Australian Geographer*, 15:269–84.

Larnach, S. L. and N. W. G. Macintosh 1970. *The craniology of the Aborigines of Queensland*. Oceania Monograph 15.

——1974. A comparative study of Solo and Australian Aboriginal crania. In A. P. Elkin and N. W. G. Macintosh (eds), *Grafton Elliot Smith. The man and his works*. Sydney University Press, Sydney, pp. 95–102.

Latz, P. K. and G. F. Griffin 1978. Changes in Aboriginal land management in relation to fire and to food plants in Central Australia. In B. S. Hetzel and H. J. Frith (eds), *The nutrition of Aborigines in relation to the ecosystem of Central Australia*. CSIRO, Melbourne, pp. 77–86.

Layton, R. 1992a. *Australian rock art: A new synthesis*. Cambridge University Press, Cambridge.

——1992b. The role of ethnography in the study of Australian rock art. In M. J. Morwood, D. R. Hobbs and G. Ward (eds), *Rock art and ethnography*. Occasional AURA Publication 5. AURA, Melbourne, pp. 7–10.

Lewis, Darrell 1984. Mimi on Bradshaw, *Australian Aboriginal Studies*, 1984/II:59–61.

——1986. Hawk hunting hides in the Victoria River District, *Australian Aboriginal Studies*, 1986/II:74–78.

——1988. *The rock paintings of Arnhem Land: Social, ecological, and material culture change in the post-glacial period*. British Archaeological Reports, Oxford.

——1996. In defence of Arnhem Land rock art research, *Australian Archaeology*, 43:12–20.

——1997. Bradshaws: The view from Arnhem Land, *Australian Archaeology*, 44:1–16.

Lewis, D. and D. B. Rose 1985. Some ethical issues in archaeology; a methodology of consultation in northern Australia, *Australian Aboriginal Studies*, 1985/1:37–44.

——1988. *The shape of the Dreaming. The cultural significance of Victoria River rock art*. Aboriginal Studies Press, Canberra.

Lilley, I. 1993. Recent research in southwestern Western Australia: A summary of recent findings, *Australian Archaeology*, 36:34–41.

Lorblanchet, M. 1992. The rock engravings of Gum Tree Valley and Skew Valley, Dampier, Western Australia: Chronology and functions of the site. In J. McDonald and I. P. Haskovec (eds), *State of* the art. *Regional rock art studies in Australia and Melanesia.* Occasional AURA Publication 5. AURA, Melbourne, pp. 39–59.

Lourandos, H. 1977a. Aboriginal spatial organisation and population: Southwestern Victoria reconsidered, *Archaeology and Physical Anthropology in Oceania*, 12:202–25.

——1977b. Stone tools, settlement, adaptation: A Tasmanian example. In R. V. S. Wright (ed.), *Stone tools as culture markers, change, evolution and complexity.* AIAS, Canberra, pp. 219–24.

——1983a. Intensification. A Late Pleistocene-Holocene archaeological sequence from southwestern Victoria, *Archaeology in Oceania*, 18:81–94.

——1983b. 10,000 years in the Tasmanian highlands, *Australian Archaeology*, 16:39–47.

——1985. Intensification and Australian prehistory. In T. D. Price and J. Brown (eds), *Prehistoric hunter-gatherers: The emergence of social and cultural complexity.* Academic Press, New York, pp. 385–423.

——1988. Seals, sedentism and change in the Bass Strait. In B. Meehan and R. Jones (eds), *Archaeology with ethnography: An Australian perspective.* Department of Prehistory, RSPacS, Canberra, pp. 277–85.

——1997. *Continent of hunter-gatherers. New perspectives in Australian prehistory.* Cambridge University Press, Cambridge.

Lourandos, H. and A. Ross 1994. The great 'intensification debate': Its history and place in Australian archaeology, *Australian Archaeology*, 39:54–63.

Love, J. R. B. 1917. Notes on the Worora tribe of north-western Australia, *Transactions and Proceedings of the Royal Society of South Australia*, 41:21–28.

Loy, T. H., R. Jones, D. E. Nelson, B. Vogel, J. Southon and R. Cosgrove 1990. Accelerator radiocarbon dating of human blood proteins in pigments from Late Pleistocene art site in Australia, *Antiquity*, 64:110–16.

Luebbers, R. 1975. Ancient boomerangs discovered in South Australia, *Nature*, 253:39.

——1978. Meals and menus: A study of change in prehistoric coastal settlements in South Australia. PhD thesis, Department of Prehistory, RSPacS, ANU, Canberra.

McBryde, I. M. 1982. Coast and estuary. *Archaeological investigations on the north coast of New South Wales at Wombah and Schnapper Point.* AIAS, Canberra.

——1984a. Kulin greenstone quarries: The social contexts of production and distribution for the Mt William site, *World Archaeology*, 16:267–85.

——1984b. Exchange in south-eastern Australia, an ethnohistorical perspective, *Aboriginal history*, 8:132–53.

——1985. Backed blade industries from the Graman rock shelters: Some evidence on function. In V. N. Misra and P. Bellwood (eds), *Recent advances in Indo-Pacific prehistory*, Oxford and IBH Publishing, Bombay, pp. 231–49.

——1986. Artefacts, language and social interaction: A case study from south-eastern Australia. In G. N. Bailey and P. Callow (eds), *Stone Age prehistory.* Cambridge University Press, Cambridge, pp. 77–93.

——1987. Goods from another country: Exchange networks and the people of the Lake Eyre Basin. In D. J. Mulvaney and J. P. White (eds), *Australians: A historical library. Australians to 1788.* Fairfax, Syme and Weldon Associates, Sydney, pp. 253–73, 458–59.

McCarthy, F. D. 1939. 'Trade' in Aboriginal Australia, *Oceania*, 9:405–38, 10:80–104, 171–95.

——1940. Comparison of the prehistory of Australia with that of Indochina, the Malay Peninsula, and the Netherlands East Indies, *Proceedings of the Third Congress of Prehistorians of the Far East*, Singapore, pp. 30–50.

——1958. Cultural succession in south eastern Australia, *Mankind*, 5:177–90.

——1977. The use of stone tools to map patterns of diffusion. In R. V. S. Wright (ed.), *Stone tools as cultural markers: Change, evolution and complexity.* AIAS, Canberra, pp. 251–62.

——1988. Rock art sequences: A matter of clarification, *Rock Art Research*, 5:16–42 (with comments).

McConnel, A. 1987. *Report on the Howqua River greenstone area survey and recording of Howqua quarry 1 and 2.* Occasional Report 9, Victoria Archaeological Survey, Melbourne.

McConnell, K. and S. O'Connor 1997. 40,000 year record of food plants in the southern Kimberley Ranges, *Australian Archaeology*, 45:20–31.

McConvell, P. 1990. The linguistic prehistory of Australia: Opportunities for dialogue with archaeology, *Australian Archaeology*, 31:3–27.

——1996. Backtracking to Babel: The chronology of Pama-Nyungan expansion in Australia, *Archaeology in Oceania*, 31:125–44.

McConvell, P. and N. Evans (eds) 1994. *Archaeology and linguistics: Understanding ancient Australia*. Oxford University Press, Oxford.

McDonald, J. J. 1990. *Sydney Basin heritage study: Engravings and shelter art sites. Stage III*, 2 vols. Unpublished report to the New South Wales National Parks and Wildlife Service, Sydney.

——1991. Archaeology and art in the Sydney region: Context and theory in the analysis of a dual-medium art style. In P. Bahn and A. Rosenfeld (eds), *Rock art and prehistory*. Oxbow Monograph 10, Oxbow Books, Oxford, pp. 78–85.

——1995. Looking for a woman's touch: Indications of gender in shelter sites in the Sydney Basin. In J. Balme and W. Beck (eds), *Gendered archaeology. The second Australian Women in Archaeology Conference*. ANH Publications, ANU, Canberra, pp. 92–96.

——1996. The conservation of landscapes: A strategic approach to cultural heritage management, *Tempus*, 6:113–21.

McDonald, J. J. and E. Rich 1994. The discovery of a heat treatment pit on the Cumberland Plain, Western Sydney, *Australian Archaeology*, 38:46–47.

McLaren, N., D. Wiltshire and R. Lesslie 1985. Biological assessment of South Australian mound springs. Report by Social and Ecological Assessment P/L for the South Australian Department of Environment and Planning.

McGowan, A., B. Shreeve, H. Brolsma and C. Hughes 1993. Photogrammetric recording of Pleistocene cave paintings in southwest Tasmania. In M. A. Smith, M. Spriggs and B. Fankhauser (eds), *Sahul in review*. Department of Prehistory, RSPacS, ANU, Canberra, pp. 224–32.

Macintosh, N. W. G. 1971. Analysis of an Aboriginal skeleton and a pierced tooth necklace from Lake Nitchie, Australia, *Anthropologie* (Brno), 12:49–62.

——1974. Early man and the dog. In A. P. Elkin and N. W. G. Macintosh (eds), *Grafton Elliot Smith. The man and his works*. Sydney University Press, Sydney, pp. 83–94.

Macintosh, N. W. G. and B. Barker 1965. *The osteology of Aboriginal man in Tasmania*. Oceania Monograph 12.

Macintosh, N. W. G. and S. L. Larnach 1972. The persistence of *Homo erectus* traits in Australian Aboriginal crania, *Archaeology and Physical Anthropology in Oceania*, 7:1–7.

McIntyre, K. G. 1977. *The secret discovery of Australia: Portuguese ventures 200 years before Captain Cook*. Souvenir Press, Medindie.

Mackay, R. and J. P. White 1987. Musselling in on the NSW coast, *Australian Archaeology*, 22:107–11.

Macknight, C. C. 1972. Macassans and Aborigines, *Oceania*, 42:281–321.

——1976. *The voyage to Maregé: Macassan trepangers in northern Australia*. Melbourne University Press, Melbourne.

——1986. Macassans and the Aboriginal past, *Archaeology in Oceania*, 21:69–75.

Macknight, C. C. and W. J. Gray 1970. *Aboriginal stone pictures in eastern Arnhem Land*. AIAS, Canberra.

McNickle, H. P. 1984. Variation in style and distribution of rock engravings in the Pilbara region (Western Australia), *Rock Art Research*, 1:5–24.

——1985. An introduction to the Spear Hill Rock Art Complex, northwestern Australia, *Rock Art Research*, 2:48–64.

——1991. A survey of rock art in the Victoria River District, Northern Territory, *Rock Art Research*, 8:36–46.

McNiven, I. J. 1991. Teewah Beach: New evidence for Holocene coastal occupation in southeast Australia, *Australian Archaeology*, 33:14–27.

——1992. Sandblow sites in the Great Sandy Region, coastal southeast Queensland: Implications for models of late Holocene rainforest exploitation and settlement restructuring, *Queensland Archaeological Research*, 9:1–16.

——1994. Technological organization and settlement in southwestern Tasmania after the glacial maximum, *Antiquity*, 68:75–82.

Main, A. R. 1978. Ecophysiology: Towards an understanding of Late Pleistocene marsupial extinction. In D. Walker and J. C. Guppy (eds), *Biology and Quaternary environments*. Australian Academy of Science, Canberra, pp. 169–83.

Majid, Z. (ed.) 1988–89. The Tampanian problem resolved: Archaeological evidence of a Late Pleistocene lithic workshop, *Modern Quaternary Research in Southeast Asia*, 11:71–96.

Martin, P. S. 1984. Prehistoric overkill: The global model. In P. S. Martin and R. G. Klein (eds), *Quaternary extinctions*. University of Arizona Press, Arizona, pp. 354–403.

Maynard, L. 1976. An archaeological approach to the study of Australian rock art. MA thesis, University of Sydney.

——1979. The archaeology of Australian Aboriginal art. In S. M. Mead (ed.), *Exploring the visual art of Oceania*. University of Hawaii Press, Honolulu, pp. 83–110.

——1980. A Pleistocene date from an occupation deposit in the Pilbara region, Western Australia, *Australian Archaeology*, 10:3–8.

Meagher, S. J. 1974. The food resources of the Aborigines of the south-west of Western Australia, *Records of the Western Australian Museum*, 3:3–65.

Meehan, B. 1982. *Shell bed to shell midden*. AIAS, Canberra.

Meehan, B., S. Brockwell, J. Allen and R. Jones 1985. The wetlands sites. In R. Jones (ed.), *Archaeological research in Kakadu National Park*. Australian National Parks and Wildlife Service, Special Publication 13, pp. 117–19.

Meilink-Roelofz, M. A. P. 1969. *Asian trade and European influence in the Indonesian archipelago between 1400 and about 1630*. M. Nijhoff, The Hague.

Megaw, J. V. S. 1968. Trial excavations at Captain Cook's Landing Place Reserve, Kurnell, N.S.W., *AIAS Newsletter*, 2(9):17–20.

Mills, J. V. 1930. Eredia's description of the Malacca, Meridional India and Cathay, *Journal of the Royal Asiatic Society, Malayan Branch*, 8:1–24.

Milham, P. and P. Thompson 1976. Relative antiquity of human occupation and extinct fauna at Madura Cave, south-eastern Western Australia, *Mankind*, 10:175–80.

Mitchell, T. L. 1848. *Journal of an expedition into the interior of tropical Australia*. Longmans, Brown, Green, London.

Moore, D. R. 1977. The hand stencil as symbol. In P. J. Ucko (ed.), *Form in indigenous art. Schematisation in the art of Aboriginal Australia and prehistoric Europe*. AIAS, Canberra, pp. 318–24.

——1978. Cape York Aborigines: Fringe participants in the Torres Strait trading system, *Mankind*, 11:319–25.

——1979. *Islanders and Aborigines at Cape York*. AIAS, Canberra.

Moore, G. F. 1884. *Diary of ten years eventful life of an early settler in Western Australia*. Facsimile edition, 1978, University of Western Australia Press, Perth.

Morphy, H. 1991. *Ancestral connections art and an Aboriginal system of knowledge*. University of Chicago Press, Chicago.

Morse, K. 1988. Mandu Mandu Creek rockshelter: Pleistocene coastal occupation of North West Cape, Western Australia, *Archaeology in Oceania*, 23:81–88.

——1993. Shell beads from Mandu Mandu Creek rock-shelter, Cape Range peninsula, Western Australia, dated before 30,000 b.p., *Antiquity*, 67:877–83.

Morton, S. R. and D. J. Mulvaney (eds) 1996. *Exploring Central Australia. Society, the environment and the 1894 Horne Expedition*. Surrey Beatty, Chipping Norton.

Morwood, M. J. 1979. Art and stone. PhD thesis, ANU, Canberra.

——1980. Time, space and prehistoric art: A principal components analysis, *Archaeology and Physical Anthropology in Oceania*, 15:98–109.

——1987. The archaeology of social complexity, in south-east Queensland, *Proceedings of the Prehistoric Society*, 53:337–50.

——1990. The prehistory of Aboriginal landuse on the upper Flinders River, north Queensland Highlands, *Queensland Archaeological Research*, 7:3–40.

——1996. Jinmium and the dilemmas of dating, *The Australian*, 24 September, p. 13.

Morwood, M. J., F. Aziz, G. D. van den Bergh, P. Y. Sondaar and J. de Vos 1997. Stone artefacts from the 1994 excavation at Mata Menge, west central Flores, Indonesia, *Australian Archaeology*, 44:26–34.

Morwood, M. J. and D. Hobbs 1997. The Asian connection: Preliminary report on Indonesian trepang sites on the Kimberley coast, *Archaeology in Oceania*, 32:197–206.

Morwood, M. J., D. Price and D. Hobbs 1994. Excavations at Sandy Creek 1 and 2, *Tempus*, 3:72–91.

Morwood, M. J. and P. J. Trezise 1989. Edge-ground axes in Pleistocene greater Australia: New evidence from S.E. Cape York Peninsula, *Queensland Archaeological Research*, 6:77–90.

Moser, S. 1995. The Aboriginalization of Australian archaeology. In P. J. Ucko (ed.), *Theory in archaeology: A world perspective*. Routledge, London, pp. 150–77.

Mountford, C. P. (ed.) 1956. *Records of the American-Australian Scientific Expedition to Arnhem Land*, Vol. 1. Melbourne University Press, Melbourne.

Mowaljarlai, D. 1992. Ngarinyin perspective or repainting: Mowaljarlai's statement. In G. K. Ward (ed.), *Retouch: Maintenance and conservation of Aboriginal rock imagery*. Occasional AURA Publication 5. AURA, Melbourne, pp. 8–9.

Mulvaney, D. J. 1960. Archaeological excavations at Fromm's Landing on the lower Murray River, *Proceedings of the Royal Society of Victoria*, 72:53–85.

——1961. The Stone Age of Australia, *Proceedings of the Prehistoric Society*, 27:56–107.

——1966. *Bêche-de-Mer*, Aborigines and Australian history, *Proceedings of the Royal Society of Victoria*, 79:449–57.

——1974. Summary report on first Mungo Project season, 17 August–1 September 1973, *AIAS Newsletter*, N.S. 1:21–22.

——1976. The chain of connection: The material evidence. In N. Peterson (ed.), *Tribes and boundaries in Australia*. AIAS, Canberra, pp. 72–94.

——1981a. Patron and client: The web of intellectual kinship in Australian anthropology. In N. Reingold and M. Rothenberg (eds), *Scientific colonialism. A cross-cultural comparison*. Smithsonian Institution Press, Washington DC, pp. 55–77.

——1981b. Gum leaves on the golden bough: Australia's Palaeolithic survivals discovered. In J. D. Evans, B. Cunliffe and C. Renfrew (eds), *Antiquity and man. Essays in honour of Glyn Daniel*. Thames and Hudson, London, pp. 52–64.

——1985. The Darwinian perspective. In I. Donaldson and T. Donaldson (eds), *Seeing the first Australians*. Allen & Unwin, Sydney, pp. 68–75.

——1986. A sense of making history: Australian Aboriginal Studies 1961–1986, *Australian Aboriginal Studies*, 1986/II:48–56.

——1987. The end of the beginning: 6000 years ago to 1788. In D. J. Mulvaney and J. P. White (eds), *Australians to 1788*, Chapter 14. Fairfax, Syme and Weldon Associates, Sydney, pp. 75–114.

——1989a. Reflections on the Murray Black Collection, *Australian Natural History*, 23:66–77.

——1989b. *Encounters in place. Outsiders and Aboriginal Australians 1606–1985*. University of Queensland Press, St Lucia.

——1990. Reflections on prehistory of Cambridge and beyond, *The Cambridge Review*, 111:115–19.

——1991. Past regained, future lost: The Kow Swamp Pleistocene burials, *Antiquity*, 65:12–21.

——1993. Sequi-centenary to bicentenary: Reflections on a museologist, *Records of the Australian Museum*, Suppl. 17:17–24.

——1998. Dr Gallus and Australian archaeology, *The Artefact*, 21, *forthcoming*.

——*forthcoming*. Home thoughts from abroad: Willandra Lakes and the historical and intellectual context of 1969. Special edition of *Archaeology in Oceania* on Willandra Lakes.

Mulvaney, D. J. and J. M. Bowler 1980. Lake Mungo and the Willandra Lakes. In *The heritage of Australia. The illustrated Register of the National Estate*. Macmillan, Melbourne.

Mulvaney, D. J. and J. Golson (eds) 1971. *Aboriginal man and environment in Australia*. ANU Press, Canberra.

Mulvaney, D. J. and N. Green 1992. *Commandant of solitude. The journals of Captain Collet Barker 1829–31*. Melbourne University Press, Melbourne.

Mulvaney, D. J. and E. B. Joyce 1965. Archaeological and geomorphological investigations on Mt. Moffatt Station, Queensland, *Proceedings of the Prehistoric Society*, 31:147–212.

Mulvaney, D. J., G. H. Lawton and C. R. Twidale 1964. Archaeological excavation of rock shelter No. 6, Fromm's Landing, *Proceedings of the Royal Society of Victoria*, 77:479–94.

Mulvaney, D. J., H. Morphy and A. Petch 1997. *'My dear Spencer'. The letters of F. J. Gillen to Baldwin Spencer*. Hyland House, South Melbourne.

Mulvaney, K. 1993a. Hunting with hides, *Records of the South Australian Museum*, 26/2:111–20.

——1993b. Which way you look. Rock art, a dilemma for contemporary custodians, *Rock Art Research*, 10:107–13.

——1997. More than a chip off the old block. A prehistoric sandstone quarry. MA thesis, University of the Northern Territory, Darwin.

Mulvaney, K. and M. Pickering 1989. An ethnographic and archaeological survey of selected archaeological sites on Robinson River Pastoral Lease. Report to the Northern Land Council, Darwin.

Murray, T. 1992. Aboriginal (pre)history and Australian archaeology: The discourse of Australian prehistoric archaeology. In B. Attwood and J. Arnold (eds), *Power, knowledge and Aborigines*. La Trobe University Press, Bundoora, Vic., pp. 1–19.

Murray, T. and J. Allen 1995. The forced repatriation of cultural properties to Tasmania, *Antiquity*, 69:871–73.

Murray, T. and J. P. White 1981. Cambridge in the bush? Archaeology in Australia and New Guinea, *World Archaeology*, 13:255–63.

Nanson, G. C., R. W. Young and E. D. Stockton 1987. Chronology and palaeoenvironment of the Cranebrook Terrace (near Sydney) containing artefacts more than 40,000 years old, *Archaeology in Oceania*, 22:72–78.

Natmap 1986. *Climate*, Vol. 4 of *Atlas of Australian resources*. Series III. Natmap, Canberra.

Neale, R. and E. Stock 1986. Pleistocene occupation in the south-east Queensland coastal region, *Nature*, 323:618–21.

Nelson, E. 1993. Second thoughts on a rock-art date, *Antiquity*, 67:893–95.

Nelson, E., C. Chippindale, G. Chaloupka and J. Southon 1992. AMS dating: Possibilities and some results. Paper presented at the Second AURA Congress, Cairns, 31 August 1992.

Newsome, J. and E. Pickett 1993. Palynology and palaeoclimatic implications of two Holocene sequences from southwestern Australia, *Palaeogeography, Palaeoclimatology, Palaeoecology*, 101:245–61.

Nicholls, N. 1989. How old is ENSO? In T. H. Donnelly and R. J. Wasson (eds), *CLIMANZ 3*. Division of Water Resources, CSIRO, Canberra, pp. 42–61.

Nobbs, M. F. and R. I. Dorn 1988. Age determinations for rock varnish formation within petroglyphs, *Rock Art Research*, 5:108–46.

Noone, H. V. V. 1943. Some Aboriginal implements of Western Australia, *Records of the South Australian Museum*, 7:271–80.

O'Connor, S. 1989. New radiocarbon dates from Koolan Island, West Kimberley, WA, *Australian Archaeology*, 28:92–104.

——1992. The timing and nature of prehistoric island use in northern Australia, *Archaeology in Oceania*, 27:49–60.

——1993. Saltwater people of the southwest Kimberley coast. In G. Burenhult (ed.), *People of the Stone Age. Hunter-gatherers and early farmers*. Harper, San Francisco, pp. 226–27.

——1994. A 6700 BP date for island use in the West Kimberley, Western Australia, new evidence from High Cliffy Island, *Australian Archaeology*, 39:102–7.

——1995. Prehistoric occupation in the Kimberley Region, W.A., *Australian Archaeology*, 40:58–59.

O'Connor, S., P. Veth and N. Hubbard 1993. Changing interpretations of postglacial human subsistence and demography in Sahul. In M. A. Smith, M. Spriggs and B. Fankhauser (eds), *Sahul in review*. Department of Prehistory, RSPacS, ANU, Canberra, pp. 95–105.

Officer, K. 1984. From Tuggerah to Dharawal: Variation and function within a regional art style. BA(Hons) thesis, Department of Prehistory and Anthropology, ANU, Canberra.

——1992. The edge of the sandstone: Style boundaries and islands in south-eastern New South Wales. In J. McDonald and I. P. Haskovec (eds), *State of the art. Regional rock art studies in Australia and Melanesia*. Occasional AURA Publication 5. AURA, Melbourne, pp. 6–14.

——1993. Style and graphics: An archaeological model for the analysis of rock art. PhD thesis, Department of Archaeology and Anthropology, ANU, Canberra.

Pardoe, C. 1986. Population genetics and population size in prehistoric Tasmania, *Australian Archaeology*, 22:1–6.

——1988. The cemetery as symbol. The distribution of prehistoric Aboriginal burial grounds in south-eastern Australia, *Archaeology in Oceania*, 23:1–16.

——1990. The demographic basis of human evolution in southeastern Australia. In B. Meehan and N. White (eds), *Hunter-gatherer demography: Past and present*. Oceania Monograph No. 31, pp. 59–70.

——1991a. Farewell to the Murray Black Australian Aboriginal Skeletal Collection, *World Archaeological Bulletin*, 5:119–21.

——1991b. Competing paradigms and ancient human remains: The state of the discipline, *Archaeology in Oceania*, 26:79–85.

——1991c. Isolation and evolution in Tasmania, *Current Anthropology*, 32:1–21.

——1992. Arches of radii, corridors of power: Reflections on current archaeological practice. In B. Attwood and J. Arnold (eds), *Power, knowledge and Aborigines*. La Trobe University Press, Bundoora, Vic., pp. 132–40.

——1993a. Wamba Yadu Cemetery. A later Holocene archaeology of the central Murray River, *Archaeology in Oceania*, 28:77–84.

——1993b. Ecology of River Murray peoples in the mid Holocene. Paper presented at the Australasian Society for Human Biology, Adelaide, 1993.

——1993c. The Pleistocene is still with us: Analytical constraints and possibilities for the study of ancient human remains in archaeology. In M. A. Smith, M. Spriggs and B. Fankhauser (eds), *Sahul in review*. Department of Prehistory, RSPacS, ANU, Canberra, pp. 81–94.

——1995. Riverine, biological and cultural evolution in southeastern Australia, *Antiquity*, 69:696–713.

Paton, R. 1993. Trading places. A history of the Mt William Aboriginal stone quarry. Unpublished report to the Department of Aboriginal Affairs, Victoria. Robert Paton Archaeological Studies Pty Ltd, Canberra.

——1994. Speaking through stones, a study from northern Australia, *World Archaeology*, 26:172–84.

Pearce, R. H. 1974. Spatial and temporal distribution of Australian backed blades, *Mankind*, 9:300–09.

——1978. Changes in artefact assemblages during the last 8000 years at Walyunga, Western Australia, *Journal of the Royal Society of Western Australia*, 61:1–10.

——1982. Archaeological sites in jarrah forest, southwest Australia, *Australian Archaeology*, 14:18–24.

Pearce, R. H. and M. Barbetti, 1981. A 38,000-year old archaeological site at Upper Swan, Western Australia, *Archaeology in Oceania*, 16:173–78.

Peltier, W. R. 1994. Ice Age paleotopography, *Science*, 265:195–201.

Perry, T. M. and D. H. Simpson 1962. *The drawings of William Westall*. London.

Peterson, N. 1971. Open sites and the ethnographic approach to the archaeology of hunter-gatherers. In D. J. Mulvaney and J. Golson (eds), *Aboriginal man and environment in Australia*. ANU Press, Canberra, pp. 239–48.

——1976. The natural and cultural areas of Australia. In N. Peterson (ed.), *Tribes and boundaries in Australia*. AIAS, Canberra, pp. 50–71.

Pickering, M. 1990. Backed blades from the McArthur River, Borroloola, Northern Territory, *Australian Archaeology*, 31:83–85.

Pietrusewsky, M. 1990. Craniofacial variation in Australasian and Pacific populations, *American Journal of Physical Anthropology*, 82:319–40.

Pires, T. 1944. *The Suma Oriental of Tome Pires*. Hakluyt Society.

Plomley, N. J. B. (ed.) 1966. *Friendly mission: The Tasmanian journals and papers of George Augustus Robinson 1829–1834*. Tasmanian Historical Research Association, Hobart.

Pope, G. G. 1983. Evidence on the age of the Asian hominidae, *Proceedings of the National Academy of Science* (USA), 80:4988–92.

——1989. Bamboo and human evolution, *Natural History*, 10 (Oct.):49–57.

Porch, N. and J. Allen 1995. Tasmania: Archaeological and palaeoecological perspectives, *Antiquity*, 69: 714–32.

Pretty, G. L. 1986a. Australian history at Roonka, *Journal of the Historical Society of South Australia*, 14:107–22.

——1986b. The prehistory of South Australia. In E. Richards (ed.), *The Flinders history of South Australia. Social history*. Wakefield Press, Adelaide, pp. 33–62.

——1988. Radiometric chronology and significance of the fossil hominid sequence from Roonka, South Australia. In J. R. Prescott (ed.), *Early man in the southern hemisphere*. Department of Physics and Mathematical Physics, University of Adelaide.

Pyne, S. J. 1991. *Burning bush: A fire history of Australia*. Henry Holt and Co, New York.

Reynolds, H. 1987. *Frontier*. Allen & Unwin, Sydney.

Rich, P. V., G. F. van Tets and F. Knight 1985. *Kadimakara: Extinct vertebrates of Australia*. Pioneer Design Studio, Lilydale, Vic.

Richards, L. C. 1990. Tooth wear and temporomandibular joint change in the Australian Aboriginal population, *American Journal of Physical Anthropology*, 82:377–84.

Richardson, N. 1992. Conjoin sets and stratigraphic integrity in a sandstone rockshelter, Kenniff Cave, Queensland, *Antiquity*, 66:408–18.

Ride, W. L. D., G. Taylor, P. H. Walker and A. C. Davis 1989. Zoological history of the Australian Alps. The mammal fossil-bearing deposits of the Monaro. In R. Good (ed.), *The scientific significance of the Australian alps*, Australian Alps National Parks Liaison Committee, pp. 79–110.

Rindos, D. and E. Webb 1992. Modelling the initial human colonisation of Australia: Perfect adaptation, cultural variability, and cultural change, *Proceedings of the Australasian Society for Human Biology*, 5:441–54.

Roberts, R. G. and R. Jones 1991. The test of time: Physical dating methods in archaeology, *Australian Natural History*, 23:858–65.

Roberts, R. G., R. Jones and M. A. Smith 1990a. Thermoluminescence dating of a 50,000-year-old human occupation site in northern Australia, *Nature*, 345:153–56.

——1990b. Early dates at Malakunanja II, *Australian Archaeology*, 31:94–97.

——1993. Optical dating at Deaf Adder Gorge, Northern Territory, indicating human occupation between 53,000 and 60,000 years ago, *Australian Archaeology*, 37:58–59.

——1994. Beyond the radiocarbon barrier in Australian prehistory, *Antiquity*, 68:611–16.

Roberts, R. G., G. L. Walsh, and others 1997. Luminescence dating of rock art and past environments using mud-wasp nests in Northern Australia, *Nature*, 345(6271):696–99.

Rose, D. B. 1996. *Nourishing terrains: Australian Aboriginal views of landscape and wilderness*. Australian Heritage Commission, Canberra.

Rosenfeld, A. 1991. Panaramitee: Dead or alive? In P. Bahn and A. Rosenfeld (eds), *Rock art and prehistory*. Oxbow Monograph 10, Oxbow Books, Oxford, pp. 136–44.

——1993. A review of the evidence for the emergence of rock art in Australia. In M. A. Smith, M. Spriggs and B. Fankhauser (eds), *Sahul in review*. Department of Prehistory, RSPacS, ANU, Canberra, pp. 71–80.

Rosenfeld, A., D. Horton and J. Winter 1981. *Early Man in north Queensland*. Terra Australis 6. Department of Prehistory, RSPacS, ANU, Canberra.

Ross, A. 1981. Holocene environments and prehistoric site patterning in the Victorian Mallee, *Archaeology in Oceania*, 16:145–55.

——1982. Absence of evidence: Reply to Keryn Kefous, *Archaeology in Oceania*, 17:99–101.

Ross, A., T. Donnelly and R. Wasson 1992. The peopling of the arid zone: Human-environment interactions. In J. Dodson (ed.), *The naive lands. Prehistory and environmental change in Australia and the south-west Pacific*. Longman Cheshire, Melbourne, pp. 76–114.

Roth, W. E. 1897. *Ethnological studies among the north-west-central Queensland Aborigines*. Government Printer, Brisbane.

——1901. *Food; its search, capture and preparation*. North Queensland Ethnography Bulletin 3, Brisbane.

——1910. North Queensland Ethnography Bulletin 14. Transport and trade, *Records of the Australian Museum*, 8:1–19.

Rowland, M. J. 1982. Further radiocarbon dates from the Keppel Islands, *Australian Archaeology*, 15:43–48.

——1983. Aborigines and environment in Holocene Australia, *Australian Aboriginal Studies*, 1983/II:62–77.

——1984. A long way in a bark canoe: Aboriginal occupation of the Percy Islands, *Australian Archaeology*, 18:17–31.

——1985. Archaeological investigations on Moa and Naghi Islands, western Torres Strait, *Australian Archaeology*, 21:119–32.

——1986. The Whitsunday Islands: Initial historical and archaeological observations and implications for future work, *Queensland Archaeological Research*, 3:72–87.

——1987. The distribution of Aboriginal watercraft on the east coast of Queensland: Implications for culture contact, *Australian Aboriginal Studies*, 1987/II:38–45.

——1996. Prehistoric archaeology of the Great Barrier Reef Province—retrospect and prospect, *Tempus*, 4.

Sagona, H. (ed.) 1994. *Bruising the earth*. Melbourne University Press, Melbourne.

Satterthwait, L. 1990. *Hunting and Gathering*. Aboriginal Australia Culture and Society series. Aboriginal and Torres Strait Islander Commission, Canberra.

Schrire, C. 1972. Ethnoarchaeological models and subsistence behaviour in Arnhem Land. In D. Clarke (ed.), *Models in archaeology*. Methuen, London, pp. 653–70.

——1982. *The Alligator Rivers. Prehistory and ecology in western Arnhem Land*. Terra Australis 7. Department of Prehistory, RSPacS, ANU, Canberra.

Schwede, M. 1983 Supertrench—phase 2: A report on excavation results. In M. Smith (ed.), *Archaeology at ANZAAS 1983*. Western Australian Museum, Perth, pp. 53–62.

Searcy, A. 1909. *In Australian tropics*. George Robertson, London.

Sharp, A. 1963. *The discovery of Australia*. Clarendon Press, Oxford.

Sim, R. 1994. Prehistoric human occupation in the King and Furneaux Island regions, Bass Strait. In M. Sullivan, S. Brockwell and A. Webb (eds), *Archaeology in the north*. North Australia Research Unit (ANU), Darwin, pp. 358–73.

Sim, R. and A. G. Thorne 1990. Pleistocene human remains from King Island, southeastern Australia, *Australian Archaeology*, 31:44–51.

Simmons, R. T. 1976. The biological origin of Australian Aborigines. In R. L. Kirk and A. G. Thorne (eds), *The origins of the Australians*. AIAS, Canberra, pp. 307–19.

Singh, G. and E. A. Geissler 1985. Late Cainozoic history of vegetation, fire, lake levels and climate, at Lake George, New South Wales, Australia, *Philosophical Transactions of the Royal Society of London*, Series B 311:379–447.

Singh, G., A. P. Kershaw and R. Clark 1981. Quaternary vegetation and fire history in Australia. In A. M. Gill, R. H. Groves and I. R. Noble (eds), *Fire and the Australian biota*. Australian Academy of Science, Canberra, pp. 23–54.

Smith, C. 1996. Why caution is the best technique, *The Australian*, 24 September, p. 13.

Smith, M. A. 1982. Stone hunting hides in the Olary region, S.A., *The Artefact*, 7:19–27.

——1987. Pleistocene occupation in arid central Australia, *Nature*, 328:710–11.

——1988a. Central Australian seed grinding implements and Pleistocene grindstones. In B. Meehan and R. Jones (eds), *Archaeology with ethnography: An Australian perspective*. Department of Prehistory, RSPacS, Canberra, pp. 94–108.

——1988b. The pattern and timing of prehistoric settlement of Central Australia. PhD thesis, University of New England, Armidale.

——1989. Seed gathering in inland Australia: Current evidence from seed-grinders on the antiquity of the ethnohistorical pattern of exploitation. In D. R. Harris and G. C. Hillman (eds), *Foraging and farming. The evolution of plant exploitation*. Unwin Hyman, London, pp. 305–17.

——1993. Biogeography, human ecology and prehistory in the sandridge deserts, *Archaeology in Oceania*, 37:35–50.

Smith, M. A. and B. Cundy 1985. Distribution maps for backed blades and flaked stone points in the Northern Territory, *Australian Aboriginal Studies*, 1985/II:32–37.

Smith, M. A. and B. Fankhauser 1996. An archaeological perspective on the geochemistry of the Australian red ochre deposits: Prospects for fingerprinting major sources. Unpublished report to AIATSIS, Canberra.

Smith, M. A. and N. D. Sharp 1993. Pleistocene sites in Australia, New Guinea and island Melanesia: Geographical and temporal structure of the archaeological record. In M. A. Smith, M. Spriggs and B. Fankhauser (eds), *Sahul in review*. Department of Prehistory, RSPacS, ANU, Canberra, pp. 37–59.

Smith, M. A., E. Williams and R. J. Wasson 1991. The archaeology of the JSN Site: Some implications for the dynamics of human occupation in the Strzelecki Desert during the Late Pleistocene, *Records of the South Australian Museum*, 25:175–92.

Smith, Moya 1982. Late Pleistocene zamia exploitation in southern Western Australia, *Archaeology in Oceania*, 17:109–16.

——1993. Recherche à l'Esperance: A prehistory of the Esperance region of south-western Australia. PhD thesis, University of Western Australia.

Smith, W. R. 1907. The role of the Australian Aboriginal in recent anthropological research, *Australasian Association for the Advancement of Science*, 11:558–76.

Spate, O. H. K. 1965. *Let me enjoy: Essays, partly geographical*. ANU Press, Canberra.

Spencer, W. B. and F. J. Gillen 1899. *The native tribes of central Australia*. Macmillan, London.

——1904. *The northern tribes of central Australia*. Macmillan, London.

Spooner, N. 1998. Human occupation at Jinmium, northern Australia, 116,000 years ago or much less?, *Antiquity*, 72:173–77.

Stanbury, P. and J. Clegg 1990. *A field guide to Aboriginal rock engravings with special reference to those around Sydney*. Sydney University Press, Sydney.

Stanner, W. E. H. 1933. Ceremonial economics of the Mulluk Mulluk and Madngella tribes of the Daly River, *Oceania*, 4:156–75.

Stockton, E. (ed.) 1993. Blue Mountains Dreaming: The Aboriginal heritage. Three Sisters Productions, Winmallee, NSW.

Stone, T. 1993. Birds, boffins and blunders, *Australian Geographic*, 29:25–26.

Sullivan, M. E. 1982. Exploitation of offshore islands along the New South Wales coastline, *Australian Archaeology*, 15:8–19.

——1987. The recent prehistoric exploitation of edible mussels in Aboriginal middens in southern New South Wales, *Archaeology in Oceania*, 22:97–106.

Sullivan, S. 1985. The custodianship of Aboriginal sites in southeastern Australia. In I. M. McBryde (ed.), *Who owns the past*. Oxford University Press, Oxford, pp. 139–56.

Summerhays, G. and J. Allen 1993. The transport of Mopir obsidian to Late Pleistocene New Ireland, *Archaeology in Oceania*, 28:144–48.

Swisher, C. C. III, W. J. Rink, S. C. Antón, H. P. Schwarcz, G. H. Curtis, A. Suprijo and Wadiasmoro 1996. Latest *Homo erectus* of Java: Potential contemporaneity with *Homo sapiens* in Southeast Asia, *Science*, 274:1870–73.

Taçon, P. S. C. 1988. Identifying fish species in the recent rock paintings of western Arnhem Land, *Rock Art Research*, 5:3–15.

——1991. The power of stone: Symbolic aspects of stone use and tool development in western Arnhem Land, Australia, *Antiquity*, 65:192–207.

——1993. Regionalism in the recent rock art of western Arnhem Land, Northern Territory, *Archaeology in Oceania*, 28:112–20.

Taçon, P. S. C. and S. Brockwell 1995. Arnhem Land prehistory in landscape, stone and paint, *Antiquity*, 69:676–95.

Taçon, P. S. C. and C. Chippindale 1994. Australia's ancient warriors: Changing depictions of fighting in the rock art of Arnhem Land, N.T., *Cambridge Archaeological Journal*, 4:211–48.

Taçon, P. S. C., M. Wilson and C. Chippindale 1996. Birth of the Rainbow Serpent in Arnhem Land rock art and oral history, *Archaeology in Oceania*, 31:103–24.

Tasmanian Aboriginal Land Council 1996. Will you take the next step?, *Tempus*, 6:293–99.

Thom, B. G. and P. S. Roy 1985. Relative sea levels and coastal sedimentation in Southeast Australia in the Holocene, *Journal of Sedimentary Petrology*, 55:257–64.

Thomas, I. 1993. Late Pleistocene environments and Aboriginal settlement patterns in Tasmania, *Australian Archaeology*, 36:1–11.

Thomas, N. W. 1905. Australian canoes and rafts, *Journal of the Anthropological Institute*, 35:56–79.

Thomson, D. F. 1939. The seasonal factor in human culture, *Proceedings of the Prehistoric Society*, 5:209–21.

——1949. *Economic structure and the ceremonial exchange cycle in Arnhem Land*. Macmillan, Melbourne.

Thomson, J. M., J. L. Long and D. R. Horton 1987. Human exploitation of and introductions to the Australian fauna. In G. R. Dyne and D. W. Walton (eds), *Fauna of Australia*, Vol. 1A, *General articles*. Australian Government Publishing Service, Canberra, pp. 1227–49.

Thorne, A. G. 1969. Preliminary comments on the Kow Swamp skeleton, *AIAS Newsletter*, 2(10):6–7.

——1971. Mungo and Kow Swamp: Morphological variation in Pleistocene Australians, *Mankind*, 8:85–89.

——1977. Separation or reconciliation? Biological clues to the development of Australian society. In J. Allen, J. Golson and R. Jones (eds), *Sunda and Sahul*. Academic Press, London, pp. 187–204.

Thorne, A. G. and P. G. Macumber 1972. Discoveries of Late Pleistocene man at Kow Swamp, Australia, *Nature*, 238:316–19.

Thorne, A. G. and R. Sim 1994. The gracile male skeleton from Late Pleistocene King Island, Australia, *Australian Archaeology*, 38:8–10.

Tindale, N. B. 1941a. Survey of the half-caste problem in South Australia, *Proceedings of the Royal Geographical Society of Australia, S.A. Branch, 1940–41*, 66–161.

——1941b. The antiquity of Man in Australia, *Australian Journal of Science*, 3:144–47.

——1957. Cultural succession in south-eastern Australia from the Late Pleistocene to the present, *Records of the South Australian Museum*, 13:1–49.

——1959. Ecology of primitive Aboriginal man in Australia. *Biogeography and Ecology in Australia*. Monographiae Biologicae 8. W. Junk, The Hague, pp. 36–51.

——1966. Insects as food for the Australian Aborigines, *Australian Natural History*, 15:179–83.

——1968. Nomenclature of archaeological cultures in Australia, *Records of the South Australian Museum*, 15:615–40.

——1974. *Aboriginal tribes of Australia*. University of California Press, Berkeley.

——1977. Further report on the Kaiadilt people of Bentinck Island, Gulf of Carpentaria, Queensland. In J. Allen, J. Golson and R. Jones (eds), *Sunda and Sahul*. Academic Press, London, pp. 247–73.

——1981. Prehistory of the Aborigines: Some interesting considerations. In A. Keast (ed.), *Ecological biogeography of Australia*. W. Junk, The Hague, pp. 1761–97.

——1987. Kariara views on some rock engravings at Port Hedland, Western Australia, *Records of the South Australian Museum*, 21:43–59.

Tindale, N. B. and B. G. Maegraith 1931. Traces of an extinct Aboriginal population on Kangaroo Island, *Records of the South Australian Museum*, 5:275–89.

Torgersen, T., M. F. Hutchinson, D. E. Serle and H. A. Nix 1983. General bathometry of the Gulf of Carpentaria and the Quaternary physiography of Lake Carpentaria, *Palaeogeography, Palaeoclimatology, Palaeoecology*, 41:207–25.

Torgersen, T., J. Luly, P. De Dekker, M. R. Rose, D. E. Serle, A. R. Chivas and W. J. Ullman 1988. Late Quaternary environments of the Carpentaria Basin, Australia, *Palaeogeography, Palaeoclimatology, Palaeoecology*, 67:245–61.

Ulm, S., B. Barker, A. Border, J. Hall, I. Lilly, I. McNiven, R. Neal and M. Rowland 1995. Pre-European coastal settlement and the use of the sea: A view from Queensland, *Australian Archaeology*, 41:24–26.

Uren, M. 1940. *Sailormen's ghosts; the Abrolhos Islands in three hundred years of romance, history and adventure*. Robertson & Mullins, Melbourne.

van Andel, T. H. and J. J. Veevers 1967. *Morphology and sediments of the Timor Sea*. Bulletin 83. Bureau of Mineral Resources, Geology and Geophysics, Department of National Development, Canberra.

van Deusen, H. M. 1972. Mammals. In P. Ryan (ed.), *Encyclopaedia of Papua New Guinea*, Vol. 2. Melbourne University Press, Melbourne, pp. 688–94.

Vanderwal, R. L. 1973. The Torres Strait: Protohistory and beyond. *Occasional Papers in Anthropology*, 2:157–94. Anthropology Museum, University of Queensland, St Lucia.

Vanderwal, R. L. and R. Fullagar 1989. Engraved Diprotodon tooth from the Spring Creek locality, Victoria, *Archaeology in Oceania*, 24:13–16.

Vanderwal, R. L. and D. R. Horton 1984. *Coastal southwest Tasmania. The prehistory of Louisa Bay and Maatsuyker Island*. Terra Australis 9. Department of Prehistory, RSPacS, ANU, Canberra.

Veth, P. M. 1987. Martujarra prehistory: Variation in arid zone adaptation, *Australian Archaeology*, 25:102–11.

——1993. The Aboriginal occupation of the Montebello Islands, north-west Australia, *Australian Aboriginal Studies*, 2:39–50.

——1995. Marginal returns and fringe benefits: Characterising the prehistory of the lowland deserts of Australia (A reply to Smith), *Australian Archaeology*, 40:32–38.

——1996. *Islands in the interior: The dynamics of prehistoric adaptations within the arid zone of Australia*. International Monographs in Prehistory, Archaeological Series 3, Ann Arbor.

Veth, P. M., G. Hamm and R. J. Lampert 1990. The archaeological significance of the lower Cooper Creek, *Records of the South Australian Museum*, 24:43–66.

Vinnicombe, P. 1992. Kimberley ideology and the maintenance of sites. In G. K. Ward (ed.), *Retouch: Maintenance and conservation of Aboriginal rock imagery*. Occasional AURA Publication 5. AURA, Melbourne, pp. 10–11.

Virili, F. L. 1977. Aboriginal sites and rock art in the Dampier Archipelago, Western Australia: A preliminary report. In P. J. Ucko (ed.), *Form in indigenous art. Schematisation in the art of Aboriginal Australia and prehistoric Europe*. AIAS, Canberra, pp. 439–51.

Wakefield, N. A. 1970. Bushfire frequency and vegetational change in south-eastern Australian forests, *Victorian Naturalist*, 87:152–58.

Wallace, A. R. [1868]. *The Malay archipelago*, 4th edn London. (Repr. Gloucester, Mass. 1962.)

Walsh, G. L. 1988. *Australia's greatest rock art*. E. J. Brill-Robert Brown & Assoc., Bathurst.

——1991. Rock painting sizes in the Kimberley and Victoria River District, *Rock Art Research*, 8:131–32.

——1992. Rock art retouch: Can a claim of Aboriginal descent establish curation rights over humanity's cultural heritage? In M. J. Morwood and D. R. Hobbs (eds), *Rock art and ethnography*. Occasional AURA Publication 5. AURA, Melbourne, pp. 47–59.

——1993. Composite stencil art: Elemental or specialised?, *Australian Aboriginal Studies*, 1993/II:33–44.

——1994. *Bradshaws. Ancient rock art of north-west Australia*. Carouge, Geneva.

Walsh, G. L., M. J. Morwood and C. Tuniz 1997. AMS radiocarbon age estimates for early rock paintings in the Kimberley, N.W. Australia: Preliminary results, *Rock Art Research*, 14:18–25.

Walsh, M. and C. Yallop (eds) 1993. *Language and culture in Aboriginal Australia*. Aboriginal Studies Press, Canberra.

Walters, I. N. 1981. Why the Tasmanians stopped eating fish: A theoretical consideration, *The Artefact*, 6:71–77.

——1989. Intensified fishery production at Moreton Bay, southeast Queensland, in the Late Holocene, *Antiquity*, 63:215–24.

——1992a. Seasonality of fishing in south-east Queensland, *Queensland Archaeological Research*, 9:29–34.

——1992b. Antiquity of marine fishing in south-east Queensland, *Queensland Archaeological Research*, 9:35–37.

Ward, G. K. (ed.) 1992. *Retouch: Maintenance and conservation of Aboriginal rock imagery*. Occasional AURA Publication 5. AURA, Melbourne.

Warner, W. L. 1937. *A black civilization*. New York; rev. edn (1958).

Wasson, R. J. and T. H. Donnelly 1991. *Palaeoclimatic reconstructions for the last 30,000 years in Australia: A contribution to prediction of future climate*. Technical Memorandum 91/3. CSIRO, Institute of Natural Resources and Environment, Division of Water Resources, Canberra.

Watchman, A. 1992. [Letter to the editor], *Australian Archaeology*, 35:69.

——1993a. Perspectives and potentials for absolute dating prehistoric rock paintings, *Antiquity*, 67:58–65.

——1993b. Evidence of a 25,000-year-old pictograph in northern Australia, *Geoarchaeology*, 6:465–73.

——1993c. The use of laser technology in rock art dating, *The Artefact*, 16:39–45.

Watchman, A. and N. Cole 1993. Accelerator radiocarbon dating of plant-fibre binders in rock paintings from northeastern Australia, *Antiquity*, 67:355–58.

Watchman, A. L. and R. S. Freeman 1978. Trace element analysis of Aboriginal greenstone artefacts, *Proceedings of the Royal Society of Victoria*, 90:271–81.

Watson, P. 1983. *This precious foliage*. Oceania Monograph, University of Sydney, Sydney.

Webb, C. 1987. Use-wear on bone tools. An experimental program and three case-studies from south-east Australia. BA(Hons) thesis, La Trobe University, Bundoora, Vic.

Webb, C. and J. Allen 1990. Bone tools from the Pleistocene deposits of Bone Cave and M86/2, Southwest Tasmania, *Archaeology in Oceania*, 25:75–78.

Webb, S. G. 1984. Intensification, population and social change in southeastern Australia: The skeletal evidence, *Aboriginal History*, 8:154–72.

——1987. Reburying Australian skeletons, *Antiquity*, 61:292–96.

——1989. *The Willandra Lakes hominids*. Department of Prehistory, RSPacS, ANU, Canberra.

——1995. *Palaeopathology of Aboriginal Australians*. Cambridge University Press, Cambridge.

Weidenreich, F. 1943. *The skull of Sinanthropus pekinensis; a comparative study of a primitive hominid skull*. Palaeontological Sinica, (N.S.) D, No. 10.

Welch, D. 1990. The bichrome art period in the Kimberley, Australia, *Rock Art Research*, 7:110–23.

——1993. Early 'naturalistic' human figures in the Kimberley, Australia, *Rock Art Research*, 10:24–37.

White, J. P. 1994. Site 820 and the evidence for early occupation in Australia, *Quaternary Australasia*, 12/2:21–23.

White, J. P., K. A. W. Crook and B. P. Buxton 1970. Kosipe: A Late Pleistocene site in the Papuan Highlands, *Proceedings of the Prehistoric Society*, 36:152–70.

White, J. P. and D. J. Mulvaney 1987. How many people? In D. J. Mulvaney and J. P. White (eds), *Australians: A historical library. Australians to 1788.* Fairfax, Syme and Weldon Associates, Sydney, pp. 115–17.

White, J. P. and J. F. O'Connell 1982. *Sunda and Sahul. A prehistory of Australia, New Guinea and Sahul.* Academic Press, Sydney.

Wickler, S. and M. Spriggs 1988. Pleistocene human occupation of the Solomon Islands, Melanesia, *Antiquity,* 72:703–6.

Williams, E. 1987. Complex hunter-gatherers: A view from Australia, *Antiquity,* 61:310–21.

——1988. The archaeology of the Cooper Basin: Report on fieldwork, *Records of the South Australian Museum,* 22:53–62.

Williams, G. and A. Frost 1988. *Terra Australis to Australia.* Oxford University Press, Oxford.

Wilson, L. 1988. *Thathilgaw emeret Lu. A handbook of traditional Torres Strait Islands material culture.* Queensland Department of Education, Brisbane.

Witter, D. C. 1990. Regions and resources. PhD thesis, Department of Prehistory, ANU, Canberra.

Worsley, P. M. 1955. Early Asian contacts with Australia, *Past and Present,* 1–11.

Wright, B. 1985. The significance of hand motif variations in the stencilled art of the Australian Aborigines, *Rock Art Research,* 2:3–91.

Wright, R. V. S. (ed.), 1971. *Archaeology of the Gallus site, Koonalda Cave.* AIAS, Canberra.

——1976. Evolutionary process and semantics: Australian prehistoric tooth size as a local adjustment. In R. C. Kirk and A. G. Thorne (eds), *The origins of the Australians.* AIAS, Canberra, pp. 265–74.

——1986. How old is zone F at Lake George?, *Archaeology in Oceania,* 21:138–39.

Yen, D. E. 1993. The origins of subsistence agriculture in Oceania and the potentials for future tropical food crops, *Economic Botany,* 47:3–14.

Zillman, J. W. 1994. Climate. In S. Bambrick (ed.), *Cambridge Encyclopaedia of Australia.* Cambridge University Press, Cambridge, pp. 9–12.

Zola, N. and B. Gott 1993. *Koori plants Koori people. Traditional Aboriginal food, fibre and healing plants of Victoria.* Koori Heritage Trust, Melbourne.

Index